PUBLICATIONS OF THE OSGOODE SOCIETY

The Osgoode Society was formed in 1979 to encourage research and writing in the history of Canadian law. Its efforts to stimulate legal history in Canada include the sponsorship of a fellowship, research support programs, and work in the field of oral history. The Society will publish volumes which contribute to legal-historical scholarship in Canada, including studies of the courts, the judiciary, and the legal profession, biographies, collections of documents, studies in criminology and penology, great trials, and work in the social and economic history of the law.

This volume, containing nine essays, is the second of two designed to illustrate the wide possibilities for research and writing in Canadian legal history. Topics covered include: the role of the civil courts in Upper Canada; legal education; political corruption; nineteenth-century Canadian rape law; the Toronto Police Court; the Kamloops outlaws and commissions of assize in nineteenth-century British Columbia; private rights and public purposes in Ontario waterways; the origins of workers' compensation in Ontario; and the evolution of Ontario courts. In combination, these two volumes of essays reflect the wide-ranging scope of legal history as an intellectual discipline and will encourage others to pursue important avenues of inquiry on all aspects of our legal past.

To Brendan O'Brien, QC
first President of The Osgoode Society
(1979–   )

Essays
in the History of
Canadian Law

Edited by

DAVID H. FLAHERTY

VOLUME II

Published for The Osgoode Society by
University of Toronto Press
Toronto Buffalo London

©The Osgoode Society 1983
Printed in Canada

ISBN 0-8020-3391-1

Canadian Cataloguing in Publication Data

Essays in the history of Canadian law
  Includes bibliographical references and index.
  ISBN 0-8020-3382-2 (v. 1). – ISBN 0-8020-3391-1 (v. 2)
  1. Law – Canada – History –
  Addresses, essays, lectures. I. Flaherty, David H.
  II. Osgoode Society
  KE394.Z85E87   349.71   C81-095131-2

Contents

Foreword

THE OSGOODE SOCIETY

The purpose of the Osgoode Society is to encourage research and writing in the history of Canadian law. The Society, which was incorporated in 1979 and is registered as a charity, was founded at the initiative of the Honourable R. Roy McMurtry, Attorney General of Ontario, and officials of The Law Society of Upper Canada. Its efforts to stimulate legal history in Canada include the sponsorship of a fellowship and an annual lectureship, research support programs, and work in the field of oral history. The Society will publish (at the rate of about one a year) volumes which contribute to legal-historical scholarship in Canada and which are of interest to the Society's members. Included will be studies of the courts, the judiciary, the legal profession, biographies, collections of documents, studies in criminology and penology, great trials, and work in the social and economic history of the law.

Current directors of The Osgoode Society are John D. Bowlby, Archie G. Campbell, Jane Banfield Haynes, John D. Honsberger, Kenneth Jarvis, Allen M. Linden, R. Roy McMurtry, Brendan O'Brien, and Peter Oliver. The Annual Report and information about membership may be obtained by writing The Osgoode Society, Osgoode Hall, 130 Queen Street West, Toronto, Ontario, Canada, M5H 2N6. Members receive the annual volumes published by the Society.

Essays in the History of Canadian Law, Volume II, edited by David H. Flaherty, is the Society's most recent publication. The Society's intention in commissioning two volumes of essays at this early point in its publishing program was to encourage as many scholars as possible to become actively involved in legal-historical research and writing. It was our conviction that legal history in Canada was much in need of the kind of stimulation which a substantial two-volume project of this nature might help to provide; and also that students both of history and of law urgently required a body of work dealing with a variety of legal themes and subject-matters. The essays, we believed, would serve to introduce readers to some of the most significant concerns and issues in the field and would, as we suggested in Volume I, provide an important building block on which a significant tradition of legal history might grow and flourish in Canada. The reception accorded to Volume I by reviewers and by our members encourages us to believe that these objectives are indeed being achieved.

The success of an enterprise of this nature depends on the contribution of many people. In this case, the authors represented in Volume II have worked diligently to achieve a high level of research and analysis and to present their findings in a stimulating fashion which would hold the attention both of the specialist and of the general reader. Volume II opens up wide new areas of Canadian legal history, touches upon numerous current academic interests, and, we believe, offers sufficient scope and variety to satisfy the most demanding of readers.

The Society is greatly indebted to David H. Flaherty, who undertook the onerous task of organizing and editing these two volumes. From the outset, Professor Flaherty was determined that each contribution embody the highest standards of research, writing, and analysis; and to achieve these goals he worked tirelessly and with great skill. He also kept firmly in mind the Society's objective, which he shared, of encouraging new enterprises and working generally to stimulate Canadian legal history as a field. Not least important, he recognized that the nature of our membership, composed principally of members of the legal profession, demanded that the essays achieve a level of readability and general interest that is not present in much current published scholarship.

Professor Flaherty and his contributors have, we believe, carried out their mandate admirably. Many aspects of our legal past, once obscure, have been illuminated. Legal history in Canada, in part because of the substantial contribution of these volumes, is on the way to becoming a respected and respectable field of studies.

Brendan O'Brien
President

Peter Oliver
Editor-in-Chief

Preface

This volume of essays is the second of two designed to illustrate the wide possibilities for research and writing in Canadian legal history. The first was published in December 1981, approximately at the time that this second collection was submitted to the University of Toronto Press for consideration. Thus this volume is intimately connected to the first and in every way a continuation of it. In fact, a number of essays published in this volume were initially intended for publication in the first. The degree of continuity also explains why, as editor, I have not prepared another introduction. In combination, the two volumes are intended to make a joint statement, which we hope will encourage our successors in writing Canadian legal history and stimulate them to improve upon these beginnings.

The rate of publication in legal history tempted me to provide a bibliography as a supplement to my introduction to the first volume. However, the pace of publication is so rapid that even a supplementary bibliography would be outdated before this volume appeared. Thus I would like to suggest several ways in which readers can keep up with new books and articles in English, American, and Canadian legal history. I would recommend the book review section in *The American Journal of Legal History*, and the entries under 'Legal History' in the *Index to Legal Periodicals* and the *Index to Canadian Legal Periodical Literature*. There are also regular bibliographies of articles in legal history in *The Journal of American History* ('Legal and Constitutional') and *The Canadian Historical Review*.

Perhaps it is worth sharing with readers some of my own disappointments with these two volumes, since they at least in part suggest areas requiring study. Despite my interest in geographical representation, I have not managed to publish an essay on the legal history of the Atlantic provinces. I also have been struck by the significance of the legal history of Lower Canada and the province of Quebec during the nineteenth century, yet I have failed to find an acceptable essay in French or English covering any aspect of the subject. I also regret the fact that these two volumes hardly address the important subject of Canadian constitutional history, although the momentous events of 1981 with respect to the constitution did deprive me of the services of several prospective authors, who were distracted by the opportunity to participate in the making of history. Readers will also note the surprising fact that there is very little in these two volumes about the history of the legal profession. This list of omissions does serve as a reminder that no one can complain that the field of Canadian legal history lacks opportunities for significant research.

I hope I will be forgiven for saying an additional word about an issue that continues to surface in the writing of Canadian legal history, but about which I had privately vowed never to write again. I refer to the continuing criticism by historians of lawyers writing legal history. The repeated assertion is that the latter too frequently ignore historical context. The attempted counterclaim by some lawyers is that they are writing as lawyers and not as historians. I hold no brief for 'lawyers' legal history' of the traditional type, which is fast disappearing, and I begin from the belief that legal history is a form of historical enterprise and not an extension of contemporary law as such. Yet I do insist on tolerance of one another and an increased awareness of respective strengths and weaknesses. Too few of us have had the advantages of thorough training in both law and history. Historians trained as such may feel uncomfortable in the analysis of legal materials, while lawyers sometimes lack the understanding of context that comes from continued immersion in a particular historical era. A process of mutual education and self-education is inevitably at work. Hurling brickbats from behind the battlements of one discipline or another will produce sound and fury but not enlightenment and intellectual advances. It is encouraging to note that such overt antagonisms have largely disappeared from the writing of American legal history, in part because the protagonists wore each other out (or died), and in part because historians and lawyers, and sociologists, gradually became more adept in using the various tools needed to write good legal history. I like to think that the contributors to these two volumes have gone a long way to overcome any limitations for writing legal history of the various disciplines in which they were originally trained.

In the preparation of this second volume, I have again appreciated the wise guidance and generous financial support of the Executive Committee of The Osgoode Society. I remain, as well, greatly indebted to the authors of the individual contributions in Volume II and to the scholars who acted as referees for specific articles, especially my colleague Professor Robert D. Gidney. I have continued to benefit from the talents of Professor Peter N. Oliver of York University, the Editor-in-Chief of The Osgoode Society, who commented effectively on each of the essays. In my view one of the great benefits of this enterprise has been the creation of a network of individuals working on the legal history of Canada and interacting with one another. I want to thank again all of the people with whom I have worked on this project during the past three years.

A variety of persons at the University of Western Ontario have offered generous and important assistance to my editorial activities. Mary Stokes contributed to the initial shaping of Volume 2. More recently, Jean H. Dalgleish has assisted me with the index and the detailed editing of the various articles. Frances Kyle has greatly eased the burden of telephones, correspondence, and mailing associated with the preparation of this volume. The reference librarians of the D.B. Weldon Library and the Law Library, especially Marianne Welch, have been unfailingly helpful. My thanks to all of the above individuals.

David H. Flaherty
London, Ontario
15 November 1982

Contributors

CONSTANCE B. BACKHOUSE is Assistant Professor of Law at the University of Western Ontario. A member of the Ontario Bar, she received a Master of Law degree from Harvard Law School in 1979. In addition to her contribution on the history of custody law in Volume 1, she is at work on a major study of women's legal history in nineteenth-century Canada.

G. BLAINE BAKER is Assistant Professor of Law in the Faculty of Law at McGill University. He received his first law degree from the University of Western Ontario and subsequently obtained a Master of Law degree from the Columbia Law School.

MARGARET A. BANKS is Law Librarian and Associate Professor of Law at the University of Western Ontario. In addition to her contribution to Volume 1 of a bibliography of statutes and related publications for Ontario, she is the author of two books and numerous articles relating to history, law, and parliamentary procedure.

JAMIE BENIDICKSON is a graduate of the Faculty of Law of the University of Toronto. He is currently doing graduate work at the Harvard Law School.

PAUL CRAVEN is Associate Professor in the Division of Social Science at York University. In addition to his contribution to Volume 1 on the history of master and servant law, he is the author of 'An Impartial Umpire': Industrial Relations and the Canadian State, 1900–1911 (Toronto 1980).

HAMAR FOSTER is an Associate Professor in the Faculty of Law at the University of Victoria. A member of the Law Society of British Columbia with a degree in law from the University of British Columbia, he also has a Master of Arts degree in History from the University of Sussex in England.

R.C.B. RISK is a Professor in the Faculty of Law at the University of Toronto. He has written extensively on Canadian legal history, including a contribution to Volume 1 on law and the economy in mid-nineteenth-century Ontario.

PAUL ROMNEY is currently a Postdoctoral Research Fellow with the Department of History, University of Toronto. He is investigating the social and ideological roots of the Upper Canadian reform movement.

WILLIAM N.T. WYLIE completed his doctoral dissertation in Canadian legal history at Queen's University. Formerly a lecturer at the University of Alberta, he is currently an historian for the National Historic Parks and Sites Branch of Parks Canada in Ottawa.

Essays in the History of Canadian Law

1

Instruments of Commerce and Authority: The Civil Courts in Upper Canada 1789–1812

WILLIAM N.T. WYLIE

Historians of Upper Canada have tended to portray the law as a closed system. According to William Renwick Riddell, the courts developed in response to the input of judges, lawyers, and politicians, all apparently acting without social interests. The present essay seeks to reverse this tendency. It will argue that the early civil courts were largely shaped by the leading merchants and administrators of the province. While the two groups differed on how the courts should be constituted, they agreed on the value of British justice as a powerful unifying force in Upper Canadian society. As one provincial observer remarked, 'the pure and impartial administration of justice is, perhaps, the firmest bond to secure the cheerful submission of a people, and to engage their affections to Government.'[1] In trying to establish a judicial system which would appear objective, the merchants and administrators faced the problem of moulding public perceptions as well as judicial practice. The two groups were never completely successful because of factors relating to procedure, the nature of legal business, and court personnel. While the following analysis will consider the province as a whole, special attention will be paid to the Midland District, which encompassed the region along the north shore of Lake Ontario between Kingston and the Bay of Quinte in the eastern part of the province.

Two centres of power appeared in Upper Canada before 1812. After the arrival of the Loyalists and retired British soldiers at the end of the American Revolution, a loose alliance of merchants dominated the early communities near Kingston, Niagara, and Detroit. The leaders of this alliance owed their influence chiefly to their commercial ties with local British garrisons and mercantile houses in Montreal and Quebec. After the establishment of Upper Canada in 1791, the power of the merchants was challenged by the formation of a provincial administration, located first at Newark (Niagara) and then at York. The officials in charge depended for their positions on the patronage of the Colonial Office of the British government.[2]

Although the merchants and administrators shared basic goals, they disagreed on how to reach them. Fearful of disorder, they were preoccupied with consolidating their personal positions and avoiding the revolutionary contamination that had beset the United States and France. They stressed the need for stability and the maintenance of the British monarchical connection. Differences emerged, however, on the efficacy of importing British institutions. While the administrators were favourable, the merchants drew on their longer experience in North America to stress the difficulty of adapting such institutions to colonial conditions.

The two élites were in accord on the important role of the state. They were aware of the difficulty of encouraging conservative values in a population which was predominantly American at a time when the institutions traditionally associated with this task, such as churches and schools, were weak or non-existent in most areas. To deal with this void, the two groups sought to develop the apparatus of the state, which at this time filled two major purposes. It facilitated the accumulation of wealth by the élites through land and trade policies. More importantly, by manipulating the institutions of the state, the élites hoped to promote the legitimacy of the existing social structure.[3]

The apparatus of government available for these purposes was relatively limited. During the period covered by this essay the province was divided into districts. In each region the major institutions dealing with legislative or administrative functions consisted of the magistrates meeting in Quarter Sessions and a few officials administering the militia. At the central level after 1791 the government consisted of a small executive and a legislature which met for only a short time each year.[4]

In this situation attention turned towards the courts. Because they dealt with questions of general public concern, the criminal courts were the traditional centre of legal attention. While they remedied offences against public security and order, the civil courts handled only the private grievances of particular individuals. In spite of this fact, provincial leaders in Upper Canada displayed relatively little concern about criminal activity, probably because its incidence was quite low.[5] Instead they concentrated on the settlement of private commercial disputes, which were the staple of the civil courts. The function of the latter was mainly legitimation. Courts facilitated the acquisition of wealth by protecting the property rights of the élites. Far more useful, however, was their ability to minimize social conflict by directing it within the narrow confines prescribed by law. The success of this process depended on public acceptance of the law. For this purpose provincial leaders drew on the powerful mythology of the common law as embodying the basic rights of Englishmen to private property and to freedom from arbitrary authority.[6]

The élites faced a series of difficulties in adapting the English common law to Upper Canadian conditions. Since most settlers were frontier farmers, they possessed little detailed knowledge of legal procedures; yet the common law comprised a labyrinth of rules and procedures established over a period of centuries, some of which were now antiquated and ineffective. This situation suggested the need to import legal experts, but a shortage of funds stood in the way. Limited resources also meant the new settlements had difficulty in paying for the construction of court facilities or for the services of judges and lawyers. Moreover, the British government was reluctant to expend substantial funds in a remote corner of empire.[7] Geography exacerbated the situation. Establishing a unified and convenient judicial system proved expensive in a society composed of a string of isolated communities.

Two embryonic court systems emerged to deal with these problems prior to 1812. While the Loyalist communities were governed from Quebec prior to 1791, provincial officials established a court structure similar to that in use elsewhere in the colony. This system featured regional Courts of Common Pleas, informal procedures, and supervision by lay judges, the most influential of whom were merchants. These judges tried to simplify the technicalities of the common law to meet colonial conditions. After the creation of Upper Canada, the administrators of the province modified judicial procedures to bring them much closer to English traditions. The new system centralized power in the Court of King's Bench and in the hands of professional judges, who insisted on the formal procedures of the common law. The rest of this essay will analyse the origins and evolution of these two systems of justice in more detail.

THE GENESIS OF THE COURTS OF COMMON PLEAS

The development of the first court system was linked to the rise of the provincial merchants. During the American Revolution these traders gathered near Kingston, Niagara, and Detroit to supply local British garrisons and to participate in the shipment of furs between the Great Lakes and the major centres of Quebec. Following the end of hostilities, an influx of Loyalist settlement began. By 1794 when the Courts of Common Pleas were abolished, there were perhaps 4500 inhabitants in the Midland District and 12,000 in the province as a whole. The regional merchants exerted economic influence by controlling access to credit and markets. Because the pioneers were short of cash, they bought imports on credit pending their first agricultural production. When their produce was ready for market, it was sold by the merchants to nearby military posts.[8]

With the assistance of a few prominent settlers, regional merchants made the first demands for the extension of courts and other government institutions. The goals of the merchants were twofold. Local governments and courts would pass and enforce regulations facilitating further development. The traders also sought appointments for themselves and their friends, since these would constitute official recognition of their prominence.[9] In seeking the extension of government, however, prominent Upper Canadians found themselves caught between two warring factions in the province of Quebec: the English-speaking merchants, who had settled in the colony since the British conquest, and the French party, consisting of French-speaking seigneurs and English-speaking officials sympathetic to their cause. Their struggle for hegemony led to political deadlock and to review of the colonial constitution in Britain. In the meantime, after considerable delay, provincial officials introduced in the Loyalist communities an amended version of the court structure already present in the rest of Quebec.[10]

In 1788 the area west of Montreal was divided into four regions, known in later years as the Eastern, Midland, Home, and Western districts. The government of Quebec established Courts of Quarter Sessions and of Common Pleas in each. Because of their general responsibility for local government as well as criminal affairs, the Quarter Sessions received more attention, but the Common Pleas were also highly visible. Three judges were appointed to the Common Pleas in each district. One official was to preside over a summary court for claims of £10 or less, while at least two were to supervise the superior court.[11]

Designed originally for French Canadian society, the Common Pleas none the less suited conditions in Upper Canada in several ways. Because the ordinances of Quebec established courts of unlimited jurisdiction in each district, the problem of travel among the settlements on the frontier was reduced. Because these ordinances attempted to facilitate personal participation by litigants in their own actions, the difficulty posed by a lack of trained lawyers was eased. Finally, the government of Quebec made an important distinction between the existing society of the province and the new communities by permitting English rules of law in the latter, except concerning land title since seigneurial tenure was still in force.[12] This constituted a concession to the Anglo-American background of the Loyalists.

In spite of these advantages, the courts' success depended on the behaviour of the judges. Because they had to be content with the income from fees, only laymen were attracted to these positions. The exception was the Western District, where more legal business was expected and a salaried professional was appointed. Since judges were virtually independent because of their distance from the Court of Appeal at Quebec, the potential for abuse was great. Yet the situation in Midland suggests that the pitfalls were largely avoided because of the character of the judges. The most influential was Richard Cartwright, originally from a mercantile family in Albany County, New York, who had become involved in the provisioning of British bases on the St Lawrence River as early as 1778. By the late 1780s, together with his business associates, Robert Hamilton of Niagara and John Askin of Detroit, Cartwright had achieved a commanding position in the economy of the Loyalist settlements. By dominating both the Courts of Quarter Sessions and Common Pleas, he sought the achievement of his twin goals of commercial development and preservation of the monarchical system.[13]

In dealing with the procedures of the civil courts, Cartwright combined a competent understanding of the law with a desire for innovation. While not deep, his knowledge was adequate to deal with the issues of a pioneer society. He was versed not only in the arguments of Sir William Blackstone but also the more recent decisions of Chief Justice William Mansfield. Yet he was deeply suspicious of the complexities of the law, believing they encouraged subterfuge at the expense of justice. In this respect he reflected mercantile attitudes in his native New York and to some extent on both sides of the Atlantic, which viewed the law chiefly as a vehicle for the enrichment of lawyers. Determined to make procedures more effective, he attempted to shape and simplify practice to fit the needs of suitors.[14]

While Cartwright aimed to make the law more credible, he was only partly successful, mainly because he identified the interests of the district too closely with those of its leading citizens. His treatment of the court hearing claims of £10 or less is an example. In many respects its procedure was exemplary. It met weekly, handled disputes speedily and informally, and kept costs low – usually less than £1. Cartwright and his colleagues tailored judgments to the state of society. Thus awards were sometimes in the form of produce rather than cash, which was in short supply on the frontier. In spite of these steps, however, the judges failed to take advantage of the provision permitting circuits around the district and met almost exclusively at Kingston. This practice effectively placed the machinery of justice out of reach of most rural settlers and reflected the limited horizons of the prominent residents of Kingston. Concerned mainly with larger claims emanating from the district capital, the judges focused more energy on the superior Court of Common Pleas, which held four terms each year in Kingston.[15]

Both in its business and in its personnel the superior court was closely identified with Kingston's leading merchants, who were usually the persons initiating suits. Such actions underlined their financial influence throughout the district and especially the declining influence of retired Loyalist officers who had been unable to establish themselves financially in the countryside. The same prominent Kingstonians served as plaintiffs, witnesses, and jurors and even as counsel or agents for suitors, since in the absence of complex procedures and qualified counsel, the criterion for furnishing assistance was ease of attendance rather than legal expertise.[16] The judges sought to expedite the affairs of these persons both in relation to specific remedies and general procedure.

SPECIFIC REMEDIES IN THE COMMON PLEAS

Deciding the law in particular disputes required judges to exercise discretion in drawing on the appropriate common law precedents. The task was made easier in the superior court by the simplicity of most actions. Cases usually involved the regulation of promissory notes, drafts, or commercial accounts. The conditional bond, common in England and America, did not appear in Upper Canada until later. Involving the creation of a new obligation if a former one was not settled within a specified time, this form of agreement must have seemed unnecessarily complex in the absence of local lawyers and given the limited size of most debts.[17]

Judges enforced the regulations concerning commercial obligations developed in England and colonial America. Negotiability of the note and draft was particularly important in the new communities. Like most obligations, these claims could be transferred to a third party, but the purchaser had the added assurance that some of the defences usually available against the original obligation could not be made against him. This procedure facilitated the use of commercial paper as a medium of exchange in a colony short of both paper money and coinage.[18]

Concerning monetary obligations, the judges modified English rules of evidence slightly to suit colonial conditions. Before launching a suit on a note in England, it was necessary to make a formal protest of non-payment with a notary. While this regulation was also contained in Quebec legislation, it was ignored in Midland, where there were few notaries prior to 1800.[19] It was also made easier to enforce commercial accounts. In England the testimony of a third party was necessary to the transaction. This individual, who was usually a clerk, was crucial because it was felt that the account itself could too easily be doctored by the plaintiff, and the rules of evidence forbade the testimony of the parties themselves. The fact that few traders on the frontier could afford clerks seems to have been the consideration which led the Midland judges to permit the introduction of the account in evidence. Some supporting proof was still required, such as the evidence of witnesses, the assertions of the plaintiff himself until 1792, or the presentation of additional written evidence when other means seemed lacking.[20]

In dealing with particular disputes, judges dispensed with many of the technicalities that surrounded the common law. The substance of the law in England was contained in forms of action which had originated in medieval times and been developed by judicial decisions in succeeding centuries. These forms of action contained unfamiliar words, fictional allegations, and overlapping remedies which were significant barriers to understanding for the uninitiated.[21] Even by the eighteenth century key phrases were still couched in Law Latin, which hid the meaning of some legal terms. Judges in Midland used terms laymen could understand. References to actions of *assumpsit* or *trover*, for instance, were dropped in favour of identifying complaints clearly as 'in debt,' 'breach of agreement,' or 'detaining personal property.'[22]

Fictional allegations had developed because of the way the common law evolved. Since the law had been determined by royal judges in particular decisions, its substance was expressed not in general propositions but in the wordings of established writs and pleadings. Standardized patterns of allegations and responses defined the kinds of claims which courts were willing to hear. Changes had to be accommodated as much as possible within the existing forms, with the result that some wordings were retained long after their original meaning had disappeared. In Midland the judges ignored fictional allegations not essential to the substance of the law.[23]

Overlapping forms of action had also emerged for some wrongs. The medieval actions of debt and detinue, for instance, had been supplemented by the modern variants of trespass on the case, such as *indebitatus assumpsit* and *trover*, which were better suited to the practices of a commercial world. The potentially competing forms had developed around different conceptions of liability and had never been integrated, in part for fear of disturbing the certainty attendant on centuries of precedents. The practice in Midland was to ignore outmoded forms which might confuse the suitor. The appropriate variant of trespass on the case was adopted without insisting on the precise wording necessary to distinguish it from alternative forms of action. Thus monetary obligations were enforced by using standards derived from *indebitatus assumpsit* rather than debt, though claims were described informally as 'in debt.'[24]

GENERAL PROCEDURE IN THE COMMON PLEAS

In guiding a typical case through the superior court, judges drew on regulations established in provincial ordinances. Intended to meet the needs of Quebec, these rules allowed a relatively simple and informal procedure in keeping with the spirit of the law in New France and some colonial American jurisdictions. The provisions evoked a much earlier period in the common law when parties appeared personally in court and before procedure became standardized in written exchanges. Supplemented by several imperial regulations regarding the colonies, the provincial statutes encouraged a practice strikingly different from that in English courts of law.[25]

The procedure for beginning a suit in Midland was relatively simple and effective. Provincial legislation provided for a writ of summons which could be served on any member of the defendant's family. If the defendant failed to appear after service, the plaintiff could present his claim and ask for judgment. If evasion was feared, the plaintiff could obtain writs permitting arrest of the defendant or seizure of his property, but these were virtually unused in Midland, apparently because evasion was not viewed as a serious problem. This was in contrast to the complex situation in England, where the usual means of proceeding was by writs developed to permit arrest (for instance, *capias ad respondendum*), which were commonly utilized merely to summon the defendant; the wording of arrest was then purely fictional. If the defendant could not be located, the process of distress or outlawry became necessary, both of which were dilatory, expensive, and often ineffective.[26]

According to the ordinances of Quebec, parties in the Common Pleas were permitted to plead orally as well as in writing, facilitating the involvement of suitors who might be illiterate or unfamiliar with legal forms. If the defendant contested the case, he could raise questions of fact or law. There was only one example of the latter in the short life of the court in Midland: issues of law were unlikely to arise given the straightforward nature of most claims. The length of pleadings was limited by statute to three stages: the plaintiff's declaration, the answer, and one rejoinder. This eliminated the possibility of protracted exchanges associated in England with special pleading. In such a plea the defendant based his case on the assertion of a single point, either denying a crucial fact in the plaintiff's claim which would put the parties at issue, or confessing his opponent's assertions while introducing new information. If the plaintiff in turn acknowledged these facts but introduced new data of his own, a long series of pleadings might develop in which the skill of the pleader frequently became more decisive than the merits of the case. Recognizing these abuses, the judges of the English courts of law had limited but not abolished the use of special pleading.[27]

Several features of trials initially permitted fuller presentation of evidence than was possible in England. In accordance with the laws of Quebec, the parties were permitted to testify on their own behalf, a practice which was not possible in England at this time for fear the testimony would be biased. This advantage was abolished in 1792 by the Upper Canadian reception statute, which formally introduced the English law in civil matters. The statute, however, did not affect the operation of another provision which continued in force until 1812. This was based on British legislation of 1732 concerning the colonies. Intended as a concession to English creditors with colonial debts, this act permitted the recording of depositions in England when individuals could not appear in the colonial courts. This provision was extended by Quebec legislation to include witnesses who were ill or about to leave the province and was further widened by practice in the Midland Common Pleas to cover any witness who was unable to appear personally in court.[28]

Provisions regarding juries were also advantageous. In Quebec, juries were optional at the behest of the parties. Under these conditions many suitors in Midland chose to save time and expense by avoiding juries, which were requested in slightly less than fifty per cent of the possible opportunities. After 1792 juries became compulsory for questions of fact in keeping with the English tradition. Yet delay was still minimized by the regional structure of the Common Pleas. In England, circuits were necessary between sittings of the central courts in order to permit the convening of juries made up of persons from the area in which the dispute had originated. Such assizes were held two or three times a year, and a delay occurred after the verdict before formal entry of judgment in the central court at the beginning of the next term. In the provincial Common Pleas, because the courts usually sat in the district where the dispute took place, juries could be assembled during each of the four terms and judgment entered while the court was still sitting.[29]

Judges followed English precedents in hearing motions for a new trial or arrest of judgment. To forestall unnecessary delays, such motions were usually refused unless substantial procedural irregularities had occurred. Judges were concerned with the appearance of justice. Thus in *Betton* v *Connor* (1792), in which a battery clearly took place but the jury acquitted apparently because the injury was so slight, the court decided on a new trial. One judge, Hector MacLean, cited Blackstone on the importance of judicial credibility:

Next to doing, the great object in the administration of public justice should be to give public satisfaction. If the verdict be liable to many objections and doubts in the opinion of bystanders, no party would go away satisfied unless he had a prospect of reviewing it, such doubts would with him be decisive: he would arraign the determination as manifestly unjust: and abhor a tribunal which he imagined had done him an injury without a possibility of redress.[30]

The least effective aspect of procedure was probably the provision for appeal after judgment. In claims of more than £10, suitors could appeal to a committee of the provincial executive at Quebec before 1792 and at Newark in 1793. Only one case was appealed from the Midland Common Pleas.[31] Parties were reluctant to travel long distances to argue cases before committees composed mainly of members with no specialized legal knowledge.

The means for enforcing judgments were also more appropriate to the needs of the colony. As in England, the most common form of execution was seizure and sale of the defendant's goods, but if this was insufficient, it was also possible in the Common Pleas to act against a person's land, which was not possible in England. Several English writs permitted seizure of income from land, but real property itself was too important in the mother country as the cornerstone of a social and economic order based on land ownership. In the colonies, on the other hand, there was a shortage of wealth other than the land itself and often little revenue in the form of rents and land profits. Recognizing the difficulties of British creditors in enforcing claims in the colonies, the British statute of 1732 allowed seizure and sale of land in the colonies for debt. This process was used in Midland in approximately twenty-five per cent of the cases where the proceeds of the sale of moveable property did not meet the amount of the judgments. By these various means all but a handful of judgments seem eventually to have been satisfied.[32]

In spite of their efforts to create a procedure in the interests of all, judges could not avoid the charge that they were acting primarily on behalf of the district's leading residents. They exhibited a myopia over court costs similar to that shown in relation to the summary court. By enforcing schedules established in the ordinances, they were able to keep expenses in most suits to £5 or less. This was well within the means of major merchants, but the district was largely populated by recently arrived refugees with little wealth. The income of farmers, small shop-keepers, and artisans fluctuated with the seasons and the success of the latest harvest. Once again because of their personal circumstances, judges failed to appreciate the problems of the poor and to adjust their charges accordingly.[33]

By the 1790s the future of the Common Pleas was precarious. In many respects judges had been successful in establishing a procedure which was speedy and intelligible to the population and provided a fair opportunity for hearing the arguments of both sides. But regardless of the procedure in any one district, there was a lack of central co-ordination to ensure consistency of practice in Upper Canada as a whole. As the society expanded, the legal needs of the colony began to outstrip the capacities of the lay judges. While these factors were outside the control of particular judges, the major difficulty was not. The credibility of the courts had been damaged by their close association with leading residents, particularly the merchants of the Laurentian trading system. While judges in Midland struggled to be objective in individual cases, they had introduced measures consciously designed to facilitate the development of commerce. Alleging public resentment against the courts on these grounds, provincial administrators sought to introduce a much different judicial system.[34]

THE REFORMS OF 1792–4

After 1791 the preconceptions of the small group of immigrant British officials in charge of the new provincial government were crucial in shaping a different judicial structure. The new system showed the influence of John Graves Simcoe, the first Lieutenant Governor. The chief architect, however, was probably William Osgoode, an English barrister, who served as the first Chief Justice of Upper Canada from 1792 to 1794 and then as Chief Justice of Lower Canada until 1802.[35] In their provisions for regional courts of inferior jurisdiction, the two men seem to have drawn on American examples, but the main thrust of their thinking was clearly English.[36] They were determined to impose a centralized court system based solidly on the common law and supervised by professional judges rather than laymen. In doing so, they sought to maximize their personal power, restrict that of the regional merchants whom they distrusted, and ensure the continuation of British control in the interior of the North American continent.

This ambition was part of a larger vision which stressed the conservative aspects of eighteenth-century British Whig thought. Like the merchants, the administrators of Upper Canada emphasized respect for order and authority. Unlike the merchants, provincial officials favoured adopting traditional English institutions to achieve these goals. They proposed an established church to inculcate the value of deference. They supported an agrarian social order in which the possession of large tracts of land would be not only the basis of wealth but also the means of indicating high social rank: in short, administrators sought to create a landed gentry which they would dominate. Until these features could become established, however, the major conservative influence came from state institutions, which were highly centralized and stressed appointive rather than elective positions.[37]

These conservative predilections were encouraged partly by personal inclination and partly by political considerations. With backgrounds in the military and legal professions, administrators tended to revere tradition and suspect progress. They also believed that a more authoritarian attitude to the colonies was developing in Britain. For proof they pointed to the Constitutional Act creating the provinces of Upper and Lower Canada, which seemed to provide for a state church and a colonial aristocracy in the upper province. Regardless of actual opinion in Britain, provincial officials had considerable opportunity to act on their beliefs. During the years prior to 1812, home officials considered British North America to be of little importance and were constantly embroiled in British and European affairs.[38]

The beginnings of a new court system for Upper Canada can be traced to the reorganization of small claims courts in 1792. Some amendment would have been necessary in that year to exempt the summary Common

Pleas from the statute requiring juries to try all matters of fact. Instead, provincial officials took the opportunity to create courts more accessible to the population. Replacing the summary Courts of Common Pleas for claims of £2 and under, the Courts of Requests differed from their predecessors in terms of the officials presiding and the geographical structure. Justices of the Peace rather than judges of the Common Pleas were to be in charge. Because such magistrates resided throughout the province, it was possible to establish courts at various points along the frontier. Justices of the Peace acting in the Quarter Sessions of each district were given the power to split their region into divisions, each of which would contain a court of small claims presided over by at least two magistrates. The new structure had the virtue of flexibility. There was no limit on the number of divisions which could be created or on the authority of the Quarter Sessions to change the boundaries to suit evolving patterns of settlement.[39]

Following this beginning, the rest of the civil court system was reformed in 1794 when the superior Courts of Common Pleas were abolished. Acting on the wishes of Simcoe and Osgoode, provincial legislators created District Courts in each region, but reserved the major power for the new superior Court of King's Bench at the capital. The District Courts could deal only with monetary obligations of £15 and under. The judges of these courts were appointed by the provincial executive and they might be local Justices of the Peace or other individuals whom the administration deemed worthy. These judges had to be content with the income from fees. However, for the three judges of the King's Bench appointed by the British Colonial Office, salaries sufficient to attract British barristers were provided. As in the English superior courts, judges of the court at York held four sittings each year to consider questions of law and also travelled on circuit to each district at least once every year to hold trials of fact. Thus the administrators took effective contol of the judicial system out of the hands of the regional merchants and placed it in the custody of salaried professionals, most of whom were British.[40]

The 1794 legislation also introduced the written procedures of the common law into both the District Courts and the Court of King's Bench. Standardized forms of action and pleadings were associated in England with development of the landed social order, which provincial officials now hoped to emulate. Because of their predictability, these procedures were said to ensure justice. Apologists such as Sir William Blackstone portrayed the common law as a complex system based on general maxims interpreted by the judges in the interests of all. A corollary of this argument was that reform invited chaos: because the law consisted of a series of closely interconnected procedures, change in any one part might endanger the whole in ways not foreseeable in advance. At this level the philosophy of the law acted as a powerful statement in favour of a conservative social order generally.[41]

Finally, the provisions of 1794 made possible the beginnings of a legal profession. In view of the shortage of trained personnel, provincial officials believed that the profession should be developed slowly and in stages. Legislation creating the Law Society of Upper Canada did not appear until 1797, but the proposals of 1794 allowed the Lieutenant Governor to appoint sixteen practitioners. By giving these persons a virtual monopoly over legal practice, the legislators hoped they would be encouraged to make a lifetime career of the law. A legal profession would not only deal with the technicalities and complexities of the law, but would also serve a social purpose by providing the nucleus of a loyal leadership at the local level. This idea was made explicit in the statute establishing the Law Society, whose purpose in part was 'to support and maintain the constitution of the province.'[42]

The 1794 proposals received little criticism in the province except from Richard Cartwright and his merchant colleague, Robert Hamilton of Niagara, both of whom were members of the Legislative Council. They argued that it might be possible to retain some of the simplified proceedings and regional structure of the existing courts while introducing a greater measure of centralized and professional supervision. The key would be the appointment of salaried judges to oversee the Common Pleas. The cost of supporting these judges in four districts, who might meet periodically to consider questions of law, would not be much greater than that projected for the three judges of the King's Bench. In spite of these objections, the official proposals passed through the provincial Assembly with ease, probably owing in part to the dissatisfaction felt with the existing courts. Swift passage was also typical of early legislation. During the régime of Simcoe, Loyalists showed substantial deference to the leadership of British officials making up the first provincial administration. Since most people had little knowledge of the judiciary, they tended to accept the opinions of the law officers of the crown, the most influential of whom was Chief Justice Osgoode.[43]

THE INFERIOR COURTS 1794–1812

After 1794 the majority of civil cases in the colony probably appeared in the courts of limited jurisdiction. Yet because of the paucity of information, only a brief analysis is possible of the workings of these courts prior to 1812.[44] Courts of Requests and District Courts existed in each district. Prospective suitors found the former more convenient than the latter by virtue of geographical location, frequency of meetings, and the nature of procedure. While Courts of Requests met at a number of locations, the District Court usually met only at the regional capital.[45] Sessions of the Requests could be held every two weeks, though they depended on the volume of business. Proceedings were informal; commissioners were not required to base decisions strictly on the precedents of the common law. Like the Court of King's Bench, the District Court held four terms per year. Procedure consisted of written submissions based on the English forms of action.[46]

Fragmentary evidence suggests that proceedings in the Courts of Requests were similar to those in the earlier summary Courts of Common Pleas. The usual cause of action was a promissory note or account. Cases were begun by having a summons left with some adult at the defendant's abode by a person who received a small fee for his service. If the defendant did not appear promptly, the plaintiff obtained judgment. If the claim was contested, oral arguments and hearings were usually conducted in a day. Costs were kept low, in the vicinity of £1 or less.[47]

Because of their geographical convenience, Courts of Requests may have been utilized more frequently than their predecessors. A suitor in the Johnstown District brought eight successive cases to the local court, each for the maximum of £2. This almost certainly represents the division of a larger claim into smaller amounts in order to exploit the greater convenience of the Requests over the District Court. The problem seems to have been one of establishing enough divisions to meet the needs of suitors. In Midland each court served several townships, and some suitors thus had to travel a considerable distance in order to be heard. The stumbling block to the creation of more divisions was the chronic shortage of Justices of the Peace willing to perform duties for which they were grossly underpaid.[48]

The possibility of arbitrary behaviour by judges weakened the reputation of the Courts of Requests. The provision for summary procedure allowed judges to rule according to their estimate of the equity of the situation. The personnel of the courts were prominent local individuals who were likely to be acquainted with some of the suitors and personally interested in some of the disputes. Prior to 1812, allegations appeared of 'trader magistrates' who used their positions to enforce unfair commercial claims for themselves or their friends.[49]

The potential for misbehaviour was greater because of the difficulty of disciplining recalcitrant magistrates. In an unusual step legislators made no provision for appeals, perhaps believing the expenditure in time and money was not justified by the size of the claims. The only means of proceeding against misbehaviour was by dismissing the magistrates or by bringing criminal charges against them. Examples of either were rare. Provincial officials hesitated to remove local officials because of the difficulty of finding replacements. Prosecutions usually depended on the filing of complaints by private citizens, who might be afraid of antagonizing prominent magistrates. Based on the evidence in government and private papers, instances of misbehaviour seem to have been few. Yet the possibility of conflict of interest probably weakened the credibility of the Courts of Requests and their judges.[50]

While Courts of Requests dealt only with claims of £2 or less, the District Courts handled monetary obligations of up to £15 prior to 1797 and £40 afterwards. Thus these courts were capable of handling most disputes which would have appeared previously in the superior Courts of Common Pleas. In spite of some differences the strengths and weaknesses of the new District Courts and the old Common Pleas were remarkably similar. The means of beginning a suit in both courts was a writ of summons which constituted notice to the defendant to appear or have the plaintiff move judgment against him. Because of the regionalized structure, pleadings and motions could be filed in the district without the need for communication or travel to the capital. It was also possible to assemble a jury of local people at the end of each term instead of waiting for a superior court judge to conduct a circuit once or twice a year. Thus both courts offered benefits of quick and relatively inexpensive procedure.[51]

The most significant difference facing the suitor in the District Courts after 1794 was the necessity of making written rather than oral pleadings. Given his lack of experience, a suitor might have been intimidated by the prospect of having to follow a formalized sequence of allegations and responses. This difficulty, however, was eased by the relative simplicity of most claims, which required actions of debt or the appropriate form of trespass on the case, usually *indebitatus assumpsit*. At worst, a suitor might be faced with the inconvenience of seeking a lawyer's advice.[52]

Like the Common Pleas, the District Courts after 1794 were usually supervised by laymen. They tended to be the only persons willing to serve when remuneration was limited to the fees paid by suitors. Were these judges capable of handling the legal questions coming before them? Samuel Sherwood, a lawyer from the Johnstown District east of Midland, advanced a biting attack as part of a general criticism of the court system. Speaking in 1808, he argued that cases of sufficient complexity to merit the attention of professional judges were being brought to the District Courts because of the inconvenience attendant on going to York. When judges of the District Courts erred, suitors were not utilizing their right to refer questions to the Court of King's Bench because the extra time and expense seemed prohibitive.[53] In fact, the proficiency of the judges of the District Courts was probably rarely tested, since most cases were uncomplicated matters based on monetary obligations.[54] None the less, judges' abilities probably fluctuated dramatically. Greater consistency would await more provincial funds to expend on salaried judges and development of an experienced legal profession in the province from which to staff the positions.

THE KING'S BENCH: AN OVERVIEW 1794–1812

After 1794 the King's Bench was the centre of judicial power. While the inferior courts dealt with disputes between small property holders, the King's Bench handled the major claims of the leading merchants against smaller regional traders.[55] Legal business in this court was slightly more complex than before 1794, because of changes in commercial practices resulting from the development of the economy. By 1812 the volume of trade had increased dramatically. Provincial merchants were not only supplying the local garrisons but exporting grain, potash, and timber to Lower Canada.[56] The system required larger extensions of credit and thus greater concern with the security of investments. Merchants moved closer to international practices in adopting bonds and mortgages to secure their claims. These instruments provided the insurance of being sealed agreements and of stipulating a penalty which would become due if the original claim was not met. In the King's Bench the new agreements resulted in the appearance of English actions such as debt on an obligation, covenant, and ejectment relating to real property, in addition to the forms of *assumpsit* appropriate in the enforcement of notes and drafts.[57]

There is some evidence that these more complicated procedures resulted in minor inconsistencies in form, but none that they prejudiced the outcome of individual cases. Since most lawyers were Upper Canadians with limited legal experience, the opportunity for confusion was substantial. Fragmentary records indicate that the profession was guilty of errors in practice, but that judges were willing to tolerate these in order to make the system work. Thus actions in the Docket Books were sometimes described as claims of debt on promises, which seems to confuse the terminology of debt and *assumpsit*. A particular oddity was the recording of one judgment as involving an action of trespass on the case for debt on a bond: at common law, sealed instruments could not be enforced by trespass on the case.[58] The shortage of evidence does not enable a clear explanation of these inconsistencies, but the absence of objections, even from former critics such as Richard Cartwright, suggests that they did not seriously interfere with the process of justice.

While the King's Bench was more successful than its critics anticipated, it did become a centre of controversy. This was partly because of the failings of several aspects of its procedure and partly because, as a highly visible branch of the state, it elicited much partisan comment. Three strains of thought were visible in the debates concerning the King's Bench. Leading merchants and the administrators were opposed prior to 1808 on the question of reform of English procedures and more generally on the desirability of commercial development. Afterwards they tended to unite against those persons with more serious criticisms of the legal and social order. These positions were defined in relation to a series of specific procedural questions in the court, including the means for beginning a suit, the enforcement of judgments, and the problems of delays and costs.

THE POWER OF ARREST IN THE KING'S BENCH

Disagreement concerning initial procedure hinged on the use of the power of arrest. Although the issue was of limited practical concern, it received attention primarily because it underlined the differing social attitudes of merchants and administrators. The merchants sought to shape the use of arrest to suit the interests of colonial commerce, but they were not unanimous on what this entailed. The desire to ensure greater security against evasive defendants by using arrest was offset somewhat by a continuing concern to avoid the disruption of the commercial community which arrest tended to cause. Since both considerations involved substantial deviation from English procedure, they were resisted until near the end of the period by the provincial bureaucracy, which saw the law as the bulwark of a conservative society, distrusted reform, and generally feared the impact of commercial development on the preservation of social order.

In the act of 1794 initial procedure in the King's Bench was based on a simplified version of English practice. Because they were confusing and ineffective, the procedures of outlawry and distress were not imported into Upper Canada. Instead, practice was based exclusively on the writ of *capias ad respondendum*. Though originally intended to permit arrest, it usually served only as a summons. After 1797 it was replaced in these situations by a simple writ of summons in order to reduce confusion. Used for arrest, the *capias* could be served at any time prior to judgment and provided the plaintiff with more security by placing responsibility on third parties for the defendant's behaviour. After serving the writ, the sheriff became liable for the defendant's appearance and in theory could be sued by the plaintiff in the event of an escape. Instead, the officer protected himself, occasionally by imprisoning the defendant, more frequently by finding persons into whose custody the defendant could be released. These individuals constituted the bail. They were made responsible for the defendant's behaviour at the beginning of a suit by entering into a conditional bond to pay a stipulated sum of money if the defendant did not appear for pleadings. At the time of his appearance, their liability was renewed by having them enter into a recognizance to pay the amount of any judgment if the defendant failed to provide satisfaction.[59]

Though the intention of arrest was to prevent the evasion of obligations, English law failed to distinguish between recalcitrant and well-meaning defendants. In commercial cases arrest could be had by swearing that a definite sum was involved of at least £15 or £10 in the instance of commercial paper, such as promissory notes, drafts, or bills. Only if the amount sought was not based on a clearly defined obligation, but represented the plaintiff's claim for more speculative damages, was it necessary to justify arrest by arguing, for instance, that the defendant was likely to abscond. Thus plaintiffs often could use the process to press a settlement from defendants innocent of any deceitful intent.[60]

In Upper Canada the 1794 legislation restricted the use of arrest. In keeping with the practice established in Quebec prior to 1791, arrest was limited specifically to situations in which evasion was likely, and the plaintiff was required in all cases to swear 'that he verily believed that the defendant was about to leave the Province with an intent to deprive his creditors.'[61] This led to an argument between English judges, such as John Elmsley, and provincial merchants. Born and educated in England, Elmsley became Chief Justice of Upper Canada in 1796 and served as Chief Justice of Lower Canada from 1802 until his death in 1805.[62] Though usually more sympathetic to colonial attitudes than his colleagues, on the issue of arrest he expressed the dominant attitudes of eighteenth-century

England concerning the ascendancy of peers and gentry and the sanctification of landed property as the basis of social order.[63] The rights of property, Elmsley argued, deserved protection even at the expense of individual liberties:

I rely on the uniform practice of England for centuries past, as a proof that nothing short of the power which the Creditor in that country has over the liberty of his Debtor can enforce that punctual and exact observance of Engagements on which so much of the welfare of Social Life depends, and that it is better to connive at the abuse occasionally made of that Power, than to expose ourselves to the ten thousand frauds which the want of it will daily suggest and encourage.[64]

Cartwright and his supporters, on the other hand, represented one point of view in the commercial community. Stressing the interdependence of the commercial world, they asserted that arrest was not usually necessary between merchants, since their continued association required a basis of trust. Moreover, the need to raise bail and the possibility of imprisonment tended to disrupt the flow of trade. Thus the power of arrest should be restricted to situations in which evasion was actually likely to occur. This attitude was becoming increasingly influential within the mercantile community in Britain and the United States. A committee of the House of Commons delivered a report critical of the abuses of arrest in the 1790s. Massachusetts enacted reforms to discourage imprisonment except when it was essential to enforce settlements.[65]

In spite of these developments, commentators in Upper Canada expressed increasing concern after 1794 about the danger of evasion. The proximity of the American border created anxiety for merchants. This had not seemed so relevant during the 1780s, since the Loyalists were political refugees who could not safely return to their homes. But with the passage of time, some began renewing ties with old acquaintances as 'the spirit of party and political Rancour began to cool.'[66] More importantly, with the influx of later settlers from the United States who came primarily in search of economic advancement, the original refugees made up a much smaller proportion of the general population. The older settlers became concerned about how the more recent arrivals might react to financial setbacks. Since their personal investment in the province was relatively small, they might prefer to escape across the border rather than face their commercial obligations. The apprehension was summed up in the House of Assembly by Allan MacLean, a prominent Midland barrister, who noted that there was no parallel in England to the present situation in which a defendant near Detroit, Niagara, Kingston, and 'everywhere below on the St. Lawrence ... might walk out of the country at noonday in defiance of his creditors.'[67] As trade expanded and the major merchants became more concerned to protect investments, their attention turned not only to bonds and mortgages but also to the power of arrest on judicial process.

Between 1794 and 1812 merchants and their allies introduced a series of reforms to facilitate the use of arrest, the most controversial of which represented significant deviations from English procedure to suit provincial conditions. An attempt was made to lower the minimum claim necessary to justify arrest. The act of 1794 made no mention of a particular sum, but in keeping with practice in England and Quebec, the King's Bench required a claim of at least £10. In 1808 Allan MacLean and other politicians familiar with local conditions argued that this was inappropriate in an economy in which most people were farmers with a limited income. The scarcity of money and of property which could be converted into wealth meant that £10 was a much larger sum in Upper Canada than in England and made it important to protect the interests of plaintiffs in smaller claims.[68]

Provincial politicians also took steps to prevent escape during the delays caused by the need to travel long distances to serve process. The 1794 act recognized that 'because of want of ready communication throughout the province, it may be practicable for fraudulent persons to escape their creditors before process can be obtained from said court to stop them ...'[69] Because of this danger, legislators made an exception to the requirement that all process must issue from the capital at York. While dealing with arrest, the Clerk of the Peace in each district could examine affidavits and authorize process. When district offices were established in 1797 for filing all process prior to judgment, the official presiding, the Deputy Clerk of the Crown, took over these duties.

In 1798 temporary arrests became possible prior to completion of the usual procedure. An act empowered individual Justices of the Peace to authorize holding the defendant for not more than eight days upon receipt of an oath from the plaintiff of apprehended evasion. Did this include the period prior to the beginning of suits? Richard Cartwright thought that it did, but the wording of the measure was not precise.[70] Between 1798 and 1801 the King's Bench took a narrower viewpoint, even though two of its three judges, William Dummer Powell and John Elmsley, were relatively flexible on other issues. Born in Boston and educated in England, Powell was a prominent judicial figure in Upper Canada for more than thirty-five years. Perhaps because of his North

American roots, he was more sensitive to the needs of commerce than most British judges. Although English-born, Elmsley was also sympathetic to the provincial merchants, with whom he was deeply involved in land speculation. On the question of arrest, however, the court followed the position of Henry Allcock, whose views were more typical of judicial opinion prior to 1812. Allcock was an English immigrant who became Puisne Judge in 1798, Chief Justice in 1802, and following in the footsteps of Osgoode and Elmsley, succeeded to the position of Chief Justice of Lower Canada in 1806.[71] He opposed proceeding on the issue of arrest without clearer legislative authority. The court's decision in his favour reflected the conservative mood in government circles after the departure of Simcoe.

When legislation threatened to modify the power of arrest in 1801, Lieutenant Governor Peter Hunter blocked its passage. The bill in question would have explicitly allowed arrest before service of the initial writ. It would also have lowered the monetary claim necessary from £10 to 40s. It passed both houses of the legislature before Hunter withheld royal assent. While there is no explicit evidence regarding this decision, it is possible to hypothesize on the basis of the government's position at this time. As an administrator Hunter exhibited an acquisitive streak, which was expressed mainly in terms of increasing his income from fees on land grants. He was also absent from the province for extended periods because of his role as commander of the forces at Quebec. During this time the government was dominated on questions of law by Judge Allcock, who was more sympathetic than Chief Justice Elmsley to Hunter's policies on land.[72]

According to his writings in 1801, Allcock was suspicious of any legal reforms. He believed that the British government intended to create in the province a society which was aristocratic and English. A hierarchy based on land had been foreseen in the Loyalist grants of the 1780s, which discriminated between officers and soldiers in amounts allotted. After the arrival of Simcoe, British officials made a conscious attempt to establish the leading administrators as the beginnings of an aristocracy by distributing large tracts of property to them. In Allcock's view the English law, particularly concerning land, constituted the bulwark against the merchants and other speculators in the province who were threatening to upset this hierarchy of property. The administrators in turn would be the guardians of English tradition in the colony and the leading supporters of empire.[73]

Allcock was especially suspicious of the speculative activities of the merchants which, in leading to a redistribution of property, endangered the social order. He was contemptuous of commercial transactions which 'have, generally speaking, taken advantage of the indigent circumstances of the parties, and contracted for the purchase of these lands [of the common settlers] for Considerations outrageously inadequate to their Value ...'[74] Such exploitation, he feared, might cause a reaction in which the British connection would be threatened and an opportunity provided for the rampant forces of American republicanism. If his thinking on the arrest bill was consistent with that on other issues, he would have regarded its provisions as an attempt to interfere with the civil liberties of yeomen on behalf of the greed of traders.

With the passage of time, a different attitude emerged in government. After the death of Hunter in 1805 and Allcock's appointment to Lower Canada in 1806, the colonial administration became more eager to co-operate with the major merchants in order to discourage dissension. Francis Gore established the new spirit after succeeding to the post of Lieutenant Governor in 1806, and Isaac Brock continued the trend after replacing Gore in 1811. In this changed atmosphere politicians again introduced the reforms of 1801, and in 1811 they became law.[75]

While plaintiffs frequently used the power of arrest, there is little evidence of evasion during the period. The court records contain few references which could be interpreted as referring to absconding defendants, and the private papers and press of the period are similarly unrevealing. Plaintiffs used arrest, on the other hand, in almost forty per cent of the cases begun in the Home District around the capital. Situated farther from the border than districts such as Midland, the Home District might have expected fewer cases of evasion. The evidence suggests that plaintiffs were swearing to an apprehension of evasion in order to place pressure on defendants and their friends to settle.[76]

ENFORCING JUDGMENTS IN THE KING'S BENCH

Though widely debated, the power of arrest failed to produce as much comment as the procedure for enforcing judgments. Interest focused on the right of seizure and sale of land in execution of judgment, which had sometimes been used in the Common Pleas when other forms of property had been insufficient to satisfy the claim. Aware that this procedure was not permitted at home, some English-trained judges of the King's Bench challenged the custom after 1794. The subsequent controversy revealed the differing philosophies of those stressing the importance of commercial development and those emphasizing the desirability of a fixed hierarchical order based on the ownership of land.

Though not dealt with in the act creating the King's Bench, the question of execution against land soon received attention. In 1799 the court made its initial ruling by a vote of two to one in favour of the right of seizure and sale of land. This division reflected the difference of opinion in the colony. Chief Justice Elmsley and William Dummer Powell were opposed by Henry Allcock.[77] When Elmsley left the province in 1802, the judicial balance swung in favour of the point of view of Allcock, who was against departures from English practice.

The central legal argument concentrated on whether the 1792 act introducing the laws of England was sufficient to replace for Upper Canada the imperial statute of 1732 which had permitted the seizure and sale of lands in execution in the colonies in order to facilitate the claims of English creditors. Allcock argued that the provincial act which introduced the laws of England 'in all matters of controversy, relative to property and civil rights' did supersede the English act. The provincial Assembly had the power to repeal all British statutes except those categories explicitly exempted in the Constitutional Act. Elmsley and Powell were of the opinion that it was not within the power of the legislature to repeal any imperial statute directly relating to the colony.[78]

The issue of seizure and sale of land stimulated a wider debate on social rather than legal questions. Provincial scribes emphasized that whereas in England substantial returns could be realized by seizing the profits of land, in Upper Canada land was still in the first stages of cultivation. Since agricultural production yielded limited income, the plaintiff might have to depend on the seizure and sale of the land itself. In question was the more general role of land in colonial development. Those stressing the importance of commerce regarded land chiefly as a commodity to be traded in pursuit of wealth and power and sought to remove legal barriers to its conveyance.[79]

According to Chief Justice Elmsley, the transfer of land was the key to stimulating industry. Only by achieving a separation of capital and labour would the more intensive agricultural production be encouraged on which the growth of trade depended. Elmsley noted that most settlers had been granted more land than they could work in a lifetime. In the short run the process of transfer would result in the accumulation of this surplus in the hands of a few speculators such as himself and the merchants. As the country became populated, the value of land, which was still very low, would increase, providing a source of wealth to its owners which could be invested in improvements. Simultaneously, a pool of cheap labour would be created by persons unable to afford their own farms who then would be employed in the systematic exploitation of the land. This separation of capital and labour would result in more intensive cultivation than was possible in the present era of 'miserable cottagers who cannot afford to cultivate their land properly, scraping a subsistence from an acre or two ...'[80]

Henry Allcock and the recently arrived Attorney General, Thomas Scott, expressed the opposing point of view. Another British barrister, Scott later served as Chief Justice of the province from 1806 to 1816. Relatively timid on most issues, he rushed to the support of Allcock on the question of land tenure. Together the two men pointed to the need to protect the colony's landed order by preserving the traditional English restrictions on conveyance of land. Their arguments for an aristocracy based on land ownership by the leading servants of the Crown found little support outside the community at York. More sympathy likely existed for their criticism of the commercial system, which they believed was robbing some small property owners of their birthright.[81]

Following the court decision of 1799, the legislature raised the issue of execution against land in 1801. The outcome revealed a divided parliament and an elected house, in particular, almost evenly split over the issue. Elmsley, Cartwright, and their associates introduced in the Legislative Council the bill favouring seizure, but it passed the Assembly only with the tie-breaking vote of the speaker. Sitting as a member of the Assembly, Allcock spoke against the bill and received considerable support from other members apparently concerned to limit the merchants' power.[82]

Because the 1801 bill was not sufficiently explicit, its opponents were able to delay its implementation for most of the rest of the period to 1812. Assuming the right of seizure, the measure sought only to clarify the steps necessary to invoke it. Allcock persuaded Hunter to reserve the bill on the grounds that it aimed 'to confirm by a side wind the Decision of the Court of King's Bench,' which should first have been appealed to the provincial court of appeal and then to the King in Council in England.[83] The act received royal assent in 1803, but a series of judges in the Court of King's Bench refused to issue the appropriate writs. These judges, all of whom were British in background, seem to have been determined to minimize the power of what Judge Robert Thorpe described as the colonial 'shopkeeper aristocracy.'[84] Schooled in the superiority of the common law, they showed a preference for the judge-made law of England, which amounted almost to contempt for colonial legislation. The attitude received its fullest expression in the person of Allcock. In his correspondence with Hunter, he wrote of always trying to picture legal questions as the leading characters of the English bench would see them.[85] There was no opportunity here for shaping interpretation to the needs of a new society. His letters betray a timidity concerning legal interpretation, a slavish devotion to received wisdom, and an idealized conception of the enlightenment of the English bench, which characterize the émigré mentality at its most extreme. In spite of the efforts of the provincial judiciary, however, an appeal was finally made to the King in Council in 1809, which resulted in a decision confirming the right of seizure on much the same grounds as those of the judgment of 1799.[86]

During the course of this dispute, plaintiffs had been prevented from acting against land to enforce judgments. How important was the right? The issue may be placed in perspective by examining the writs of execution in cases involving suitors from Midland. A study of behaviour in the years when action against land was allowed indicates that plaintiffs proceeded against real property in slightly under twenty per cent of judgments. This suggests that the absence of the process constituted a significant problem for only a small proportion of plaintiffs.[87]

MERCHANTS, ADMINISTRATORS, AND THE PROBLEM OF DELAY IN THE KING'S BENCH

The question of procedural delay was much more serious than the issues of execution or arrest. Of potential concern to all plaintiffs, delays shaped the character of legal business coming before the King's Bench, particularly from districts such as Midland which were situated at a considerable distance from the provincial capital. Dilatory process was partly responsible for the paucity of cases proceeding to judgment from areas outside York and for the means chosen in bringing suits to judgment. Slow proceedings stimulated plaintiffs to seek an agreement with defendants, in which the latter might receive concessions in exchange for an immediate confession. The issue of delay once again revealed the differences between merchants and administrators, though ultimately it also underlined their shared interests in preserving the existing social order.

Procedural delay was partly the result of English procedures and partly due to the impact of provincial geography. The common law restricted the progress of a suit to certain times of the year – the terms when the judges sat in court. The practice of conducting business at these intervals dated from an era of oral pleading when it was desirable to give the parties ample time to appear. Proceedings, however, had become standardized and no longer required regular court appearances. Instead, most proceedings involved the filing of papers with a clerk, which presented an opportunity for speed since it could be done in or out of term. Yet the fiction was that the parties were appearing before the judges. At the beginning of a suit the defendant did not have to answer the plaintiff's summons until the onset of a term regardless of when the writ had been served. When a jury verdict was reached at the assizes, formal entry of judgment was delayed until the start of the next term.[88]

Although these rules slowed procedure, the impact of a centralized structure in a fragmented society was even greater. Delays resulted from the need to file process at York and from the procedure for summoning juries. The first was a problem primarily because of the shortage of attorneys. Legislation had authorized the Lieutenant Governor to appoint sixteen lawyers, whose numbers could be augmented only by the licensing of clerks who had spent five years of apprenticeship in a law office, or by the immigration of attorneys from Britain or the other North American colonies. Under these circumstances relatively few persons qualified. After several efforts were made to increase the number of lawyers by empowering the head of government to appoint more and by increasing the number of clerks who might be employed by each attorney, there were perhaps twenty-five persons in active practice by 1812. A bottleneck developed at York, where about twelve individuals were trying to handle King's Bench cases from across the province in addition to local disputes. Two of these persons were the Attorney General and Solicitor General, whose major public responsibilities took time away from their private practice.[89]

In addition to the congestion of business at the capital, long delays resulted from the necessity to try all questions of fact before juries summoned in the district where the dispute took place. Primarily to save expense, judges held only one circuit each year in all regions, except the Home District, where two were held since the cost of travel was not a deterrent.[90] This compared unfavourably with the Common Pleas and even with the situation in England, where there were two, and in some counties three, assizes per year. The problem was more acute because the provincial King's Bench made use of juries in a wider variety of circumstances than the English superior courts. The difference related to the disposition of uncontested claims. If the defendant did not intend to challenge his opponent's claim, he could fail to appear or enter a confession. Traditionally the latter had advantages for both parties. In return for a promise to pay, the defendant usually received more time in which to fulfil his obligation. The plaintiff gained his adversary's co-operation and did not have to submit his claim to further examination by the court. Circumstances in Upper Canada increased these advantages.

The King's Bench based its default procedure on English practice. When an obligation was clearly defined and calculation simply a matter of computing principal and interest, it was referred to the court for taxation after the filing of a motion which constituted notice to the defendant. When the amount of damages was more debatable and it was desirable to give the defendant an opportunity to object to the size of the claim, the presence of a jury was necessary. This process took longer since it involved a writ of inquiry to the sheriff to summon a jury in the region in which the dispute occurred.[91]

More delay occurred in Upper Canada because the judges took special care to ensure that the defendant was notified of the case against him when he failed to make an appearance. This seems to have been an attempt to compensate for the inexperience of people involved in handling the initial writ. The act of 1794 permitted service by any literate person rather than an experienced official, an allowance which widened the margin for error. After the establishment of district offices, the writ was returned to the district clerks rather than to York. Some of them were attorneys who might be interested in the cases passing through their hands. Responding to these considerations, the King's Bench in 1803 required a rule *nisi* to be filed by the plaintiff at York prior to computation by the appropriate court official, the master in all actions involving commercial paper. This provided the defendant with a period of one term in which to object. In 1809 the judges took the process a step further and required a jury in virtually all cases involving notes or bills of exchange. Bonds were an exception, since as they were sealed agreements, there was less chance of successful objections being raised against their contents.[92]

In England juries charged with assessing appropriate damages were selected separately from those at the assizes and were sometimes available more frequently, since they did not require the presence of a judge of the court. In Upper Canada, however, sheriffs were overburdened with other duties with the result that after 1797 they were permitted to make use of the panels of jurors already assembled to try contested cases. For the plaintiff this permission meant that if his opponent failed to appear, the advancement of his case would have to await the yearly assizes.[93]

Because of delays in procedure by default, it became more attractive for plaintiffs to seek an agreement with defendants to confess. This was reflected in the proportion of judgments by default and by confession in Midland. In England, in spite of the potential advantages of agreements, defaults were still relatively common: as Blackstone noted, many defendants did not have the acumen to confess. In Midland, however, judgments by confession outnumbered those by default by a proportion of two to one. Significantly, behaviour concerning bonds, where delay was not a problem, diverged substantially from other cases. The numbers of confessions and defaults were almost equal.[94]

The severity of delays led almost immediately to proposals for reform. Chief Justice Elmsley introduced three innovations in 1797 touching on court jurisdiction, the return of original writs, and the filing of process. More willing to consider change than his colleagues, he may have been influenced by steps towards court decentralization in New York State. The rest of the official community, however, was suspicious of American influences and finally forced the withdrawal of some of Elmsley's proposals. His least controversial measure was an act which enlarged the concurrent jurisdiction of the District Courts to take in more of the business previously in the exclusive purview of the King's Bench. Their authority in monetary agreements was expanded from £15 to £40 and for the first time they were permitted to hear other kinds of actions, provided they did not exceed £15 or deal with title to land, assault and battery, or false imprisonment.[95]

The second reform in 1797 was more controversial since it allowed the return of the initial writ and the beginning of pleadings out of term. By making each Monday a return day and providing for fifteen days between the issuing of a writ and the appearance of the defendant, Elmsley believed a saving of several months could be achieved in many suits without threatening the interests of defendants. He was, however, acting in advance of English practice to modify a tradition sanctified by centuries of use. The statute was repealed one year later and, while no official explanation has come to light, it seems likely that the statute offended the conservative minds at the capital.[96]

The third measure also received criticism but proved more durable. This was the creation of offices in each district to deal with all matters prior to judgment previously within the exclusive control of the office at York. The change had the advantage of reducing the delay, expense, and other inconvenience contingent on employing an agent at York to file all process. The danger was that it threatened uniformity of practice in the province, given the inexperience of the new officials. This was the factor behind the temporary reduction of their duties in 1798 to the handling of first writs and imprisonment after judgment. Elmsley explained that there had been complaints that the clerks were not making adequate notations to permit review of process by the judges on assizes. However, legislation in 1801 again permitted district offices to file all papers prior to judgment provided the clerks were always prepared to forward a copy of all proceedings. The offices had proven too useful to suitors and attorneys outside York to be abandoned.[97]

What was the impact of these offices on the volume of business? Since they facilitated the early stages of suits, particularly the issuing of initial writs and the filing of pleadings, it is probable that the number of suits begun outside the Home District increased, though no records have survived to confirm this assumption. But the district offices did not facilitate the continuation of suits to judgment because they did not deal with the problem of providing for juries or the need ultimately to refer to York. In fact, the process of a typical suit was now divided between the region and the capital, since it was still necessary to file motions requiring the judges' consideration in the central office and to enter judgments there. This process led many suitors to employ two agents, one in the district and one at York, which tended to result in extra expense and difficulties of communication in the course of a suit.[98]

These procedural problems seem to have affected the number of actions begun in Midland which ended in judgments. Between 1795 and 1806, there were only about four judgments per year. This was significantly smaller than the rate in the Home District of eighteen judgments per year. While there were fewer settlers around York, they were more advantageously situated in terms of judicial process.[99]

The pattern of judgments persisted until the onset of dramatic fluctuations in the economy near the end of the period. Between 1807 and 1809 there was increasing prosperity in the province, especially in the eastern half, because of the influence of the timber trade. As British demand for timber grew during the Napoleonic Wars, suppliers between the Bay of Quinte and Cornwall found they could compete with timber from the Ottawa Valley. Demand reached a peak in 1808–9 when Britain's Baltic supply was not available, but a precipitous collapse in both grain and timber markets between 1810 and 1812 was felt especially strongly in the east. The period of boom and bust produced a large number of unpaid obligations in Midland and resulted in a substantial increase in judgments from ten in 1809 to seventy-four in 1811, after which the rate returned to its previous level. This experience contrasted with that in the Home District, where the economic fluctuations were less severe; the number of judgments remained constant between 1809 and 1812 at approximately sixty-four per year.[100]

After creation of the district offices, criticism shifted from the early stages of suits, which had been the concern of Elmsley in 1797, to later steps. Samuel Sherwood advanced the most radical analysis in 1807. As a prominent Loyalist who felt himself unjustly ignored, he intended in part to embarrass the government. As a lawyer from the Johnstown District, he was perhaps jealous of the advantage of York attorneys, but he was also familiar with the inconvenience of the central court and sympathetic to the plight of regional merchants. Few suitors outside the Home District were bringing cases to the King's Bench, he observed, because of the twin problems of the assizes and the constriction of business at the capital. Thus the District Courts were forced to struggle with the bulk of the business without the requisite expertise. His solution, presented in the form of a bill, was to establish a new system of decentralized courts managed by experienced lawyers.[101]

Sherwood's plan was a conscious evocation of the past. Claiming that Cartwright's criticisms of 1794 had proven correct, he proposed four regional Courts of Common Pleas to overcome the problems associated with the District Courts and the King's Bench. Replacing the former, the new tribunals would be superior in having the benefit of professional judges. Though practice would be based on that in the central court in actions above £10, a simplified procedure would be provided to expedite the process of smaller claims. Since the authority of the new courts would extend to £250 in actions of monetary obligations, they could hear most suits previously handled by the King's Bench. This would relieve the pressure at York and speed the conduct of suits in the outlying areas. The King's Bench would continue to have sole jurisdiction in more important disputes and supervise the procedure of the lower courts, chiefly by means of hearing appeals.[102]

While ultimately unsuccessful, Sherwood's bill received widespread support outside York. It was first presented in 1807 and laid over for further consideration until the following year. Personally in favour of it, Richard Cartwright described the willingness of the legislature to consider change: 'That our present System is not well adapted to the

Situation of the Province we all feel ... I believe the Legislature would be very ready to supply the Expense of any Establishment that might be necessary to make our Judicial System more applicable to our Geographical Situation.'[103] The Legislative Assembly passed the bill in 1808, but the measure finally failed after receiving amendments in the Legislative Council which were unacceptable to the lower house.[104]

Sherwood's plan was defeated in part because of practical considerations of finance and personnel. British officials controlled appointments and salaries in the King's Bench. While it is not clear whether the new judges would be paid in the same way or by the provincial government, it was imperative that expense be minimized. In Sherwood's proposal the costs would not be much greater than before. Each Court of Common Pleas would employ one judge receiving £400 yearly. To reduce expenditures, two of the three judgeships of the King's Bench would be abolished at a saving of £750 each. Since the amount of the new salaries might have discouraged English lawyers from applying, there was a provision for appointment of provincial lawyers by the Lieutenant Governor acting under the great seal of the province. This was clearly in the interests of Sherwood and other colonial attorneys who could claim that they were steadily gaining experience. None the less, serious doubts were raised about their abilities in the Legislative Council. Composed mainly of leading landowners and merchants but not of lawyers, the Council amended the Assembly's bill to restore the power of appointment to officials in Britain. The lower house rejected this revision.[105]

Rising political tensions in the province were partly responsible for this deadlock. During the previous decade land policies had provoked substantial discontent. Residents became angry at the practice of conferring huge grants on leading officials and their friends. Between 1799 and 1805 Peter Hunter tried to increase his income and that of his associates by raising the fees on land grants. To maximize his revenues, he had the lists of Loyalist and military claimants entitled to free grants restricted in size. Their claims were delayed while those of paying customers were processed. Landholders were threatened with eviction if they were unable to make prompt payments. These actions seriously damaged the credibility of the executive and resulted in the first organized opposition to the provincial administration.[106]

Popular frustration was expressed mainly through the Assembly, where politicians with personal grievances challenged the executive's power. The struggle focused on the respective financial powers of elected and appointed officials. While land policy and fees were clearly controlled by the Crown, administrators were more vulnerable in other areas. In 1806 when Alexander Grant, the head of government, attempted to pay the expenses of the judges on assizes without legislative appropriations, a confrontation ensued. Since the courts had been established by provincial statute, this was clearly beyond his powers.[107]

In the resulting struggle the government's opponents enlisted an unusual ally, Robert Thorpe, a judge of the King's Bench. A recent immigrant from Britain, Thorpe had a brief but stormy career in Upper Canada, arguing publicly that the colony was in poor hands and privately that he deserved the position of Chief Justice to remedy this. When this appointment went to Attorney General Scott in 1806, Thorpe began to use the assizes to encourage criticism of the government. Since his actions could be construed as a serious challenge to constituted authority, he was dismissed from the provincial bench in 1807 and recalled from the colony by the British government. With his departure the storm centre passed, although a few of his supporters continued the agitation.[108]

This lingering atmosphere of crisis contributed to the demise of the Sherwood bill. Two legacies of the episode were a fear of disorder bordering on paranoia among some officials and a heightened sense of independence on the part of the Assembly. The former led William Firth, the new Attorney General, to the edge of hysteria in criticizing the bill. Like Thorpe, Firth earned the enmity of his superiors and ultimately was replaced in 1811 because of his penchant for political controversy. The Sherwood proposal, he declared, was a step towards the independence of the colony. Compounding his error, he submitted a petition to the Assembly which argued that the legislature had no right to interfere with the court system. In the wake of its recent confrontations over financial powers, the elected body was not likely to tolerate such displays of disrespect. It rejected the petition, which Sherwood described as the most offensive attack ever mounted on the privileges of the house. This resentment probably contributed also to the Assembly's refusal to accept the amendments of the Legislative Council. The lower house was in no mood to consider modifications to its proposals, particularly when they involved the possibility of providing more employment for English lawyers like Firth at the expense of local legal talent.[109]

CONSERVATISM, COSTS, AND THE POLITICS OF
THE KING'S BENCH

After 1808 pressure for reform of the courts waned as a spirit of conservatism began to grow among leading residents. They became concerned with dangers to the colony both internal and external. Since

1800 the character of the population had shifted with the influx of large numbers of American immigrants of doubtful loyalty seeking cheap land. Prominent merchants and administrators feared these Americans might challenge British control and viewed the complaints regarding provincial land policy as the first signs of this tendency. International developments made the situation more critical. After 1807 an armed clash between the United States and Britain seemed imminent as a consequence of tensions resulting from the Napoleonic Wars.[110]

In this situation the major merchants and their supporters made no further demands for improving the efficiency of the King's Bench. While the difficulty of enforcing claims was exasperating, it was not crucial to those with economic power. Dilatory process might have been fatal to the financial interests of plaintiffs who could not withstand the cost of delay. The merchants with influence in politics, however, also had established sources of credit in Lower Canada. Delay or the failure to satisfy a claim were not likely to be decisive to their economic well-being. Moreover, the inefficiency of the King's Bench encouraged prospective plaintiffs to seek out-of-court settlements. In these circumstances major merchants at centres like Kingston and Niagara possessed substantial informal influence through their control of credit and markets. By manipulating these levers, they could usually gain favourable settlements. This may have made them tolerant of resistance to innovation in judicial process throughout the period.[111]

The atmosphere of political crisis led merchants such as Richard Cartwright to co-operate with the administrators at York. The two groups held a common belief in the superiority of monarchical over republican institutions. The merchants also had an economic interest in maintaining the British connection. The development of the economy on which the influence of the merchants depended was the result of the stimulus provided by the existence of the empire. In the 1780s and 1790s the garrisons had provided the first stable market for local agricultural produce at subsidized prices. After 1800, when exports of grain and timber began to move down the St Lawrence, these were largely dependent on the growth of demand in Britain.

In the new atmosphere Cartwright became the author of a pamphlet published in 1810 defending the government against the indictment of John Mills Jackson. An Englishman who had been pursuing land claims in Upper Canada at the time of the Thorpe crisis, Jackson had published a tract critical of the provincial administration. He argued that government in the colony was being operated in the interests of a few friends of the leading officials at the expense of the majority of the population. The court system was a prime example. It was tied too closely to the machinery of power and patronage centred at York. Because the local judiciary held their positions at the pleasure of the central bureaucracy, arbitrary judicial behaviour had been encouraged in favour of the acquaintances of the administration and the people had lost confidence in the fairness of the law. While acknowledging the close ties between judiciary and administration, Cartwright denied any partiality. The merchant who had favoured substantial reform in 1808 now expressed himself generally satisfied with the judicial system.[112]

The Jackson pamphlet was the most comprehensive expression of a political critique developing over the previous decade in which the courts were frequently a target. The most common objection focused on court costs in the King's Bench. Critics argued that the expenses of suitors in this court were unnecessarily high in order to benefit the lawyers and judicial officials closely tied to the administration. In fact the level of costs would have been difficult for many people to afford. The average expense of a suit was approximately £12 or slightly more than twice the sum usually charged in Common Pleas before 1794. Many residents of the province were still in precarious financial circumstances. In the countryside the income of farmers was usually low, and rural traders frequently were dependent on the success of the next year's grain crop in order to meet past obligations. In the towns government officials and others attempting to live as 'gentlemen' were often in debt because of the high cost of imported goods relative to their incomes. Yet the significance of King's Bench costs was relatively small if placed in a wider context. Whereas expenses had doubled, the value of the average dispute had increased fivefold since 1794. In this situation, costs would more often have been an irritant than a real burden, but they provided an excuse for disgruntled politicians to mobilize resentment against the provincial régime.[113]

Critics raised the issue of King's Bench expenses on three occasions prior to 1812, each time for partisan political purposes. Between 1802 and 1804 the central figure was Angus MacDonell, a leading member of the Law Society of Upper Canada. After being dismissed from several positions under the Crown, MacDonell sought to embarrass provincial leaders by calling a series of judicial officials before the legislature to answer questions concerning their remuneration from fees. Subsequently, he was instrumental in having a bill passed which, in shifting control of fees from the Assembly to the judges of the King's Bench, actually facilitated introduction of slightly higher costs. The issue was revived again by Samuel Sherwood in 1808. Like MacDonell, Sherwood was a lawyer irritated by his lack of influence with the government. Determined to court legislative popularity, he proposed that control of expenses in the King's Bench be shifted back to the Assembly, but dropped the matter when his more comprehensive judicial reforms attracted attention. In 1810 Joseph Willcocks introduced a measure returning fees to the levels of 1794. The leader of the legislative opposition after the removal of Thorpe, Willcocks viewed the court system as a centre of privilege for the friends of the executive. By reducing court fees, this measure would be a means for the populace to strike back. His bill became law because of the support of persons upset with government and the desire of provincial officials to minimize confrontation.[114]

Although minor in itself, the question of costs was raised repeatedly before 1812 because it provided an opportunity for criticism of the privileged groups and institutions of the province. It permitted anger to be directed against the administrators, who seemed to be conducting public policy primarily in their own interests rather than those of the people as a whole, particularly concerning land grants. The issue of costs also allowed expression of resentment against the Court of King's Bench for its role in the provincial economy. Though supposedly defending the rights of all, most claims in the court were by major merchants against smaller traders and property owners. Thus the court may have appeared to be enforcing the agreements leading to the aggrandizement of a few and the impoverishment of others. Moreover, in requiring the losing suitors to pay costs, the court was throwing the expense of its procedures on the disadvantaged. This kind of resentment, in fact, may have damaged the image of the courts both before and after the reforms of 1794.

It is arguable that there was a fundamental tension between the procedural and substantive aspects of the common law. On the one hand, the legal system was presented as an institution in the interests of all mainly on the basis of providing due process. Yet in its defence of property rights, it facilitated the concentrations of wealth and power which seemed to serve only a few. The impact of this contradiction admittedly is hard to document. However, it seems likely that frustration was produced which could be turned against the courts, especially since their procedures and structures already seemed biased in other ways.

CONCLUSION

The evolution of the civil courts prior to 1812 was to some extent the product of the impersonal forces of geography, demography, and financial constraints. Because of the distances of the Loyalist communities from established settlement and the shortage of legal specialists, it was not surprising that regional courts supervised by laymen and exhibiting considerable independence should have emerged first. With the passage of time, a more sophisticated system became necessary. After creation of the province of Upper Canada in 1791, the arrival of professional judges and lawyers from Britain provided the opportunity.

The nature of the evolution was also influenced by key individuals. During the life of the Common Pleas the leading merchants sought to abolish the mysteries of the common law in order to establish a procedure understandable to the layman and conducive to commercial development. After 1794, the professional judges embraced these same technicalities as part of a complex system which would ensure justice. Their views and those of most of their bureaucratic colleagues seem to the modern observer to be out of step with the direction of social development in North America. Evoking an earlier period in English history, they sought to establish a stable landed social order in which commerce would play only a limited part. Their views concerning commercial development were ambivalent. While they realized it was necessary to satisfy popular expectations of prosperity, they also feared its effects in promoting social upheaval and the elevation to prominence of people who were not qualified to preserve their cherished conservative beliefs.

In spite of the efforts of both groups, the courts never seemed equally accessible to all. Before 1794, the merchants of Midland had founded a practice which in its simplicity and lack of delay seemed exemplary. Yet they seemed almost oblivious to the needs of the common man, especially on the issues of costs and geographical accessibility. After 1794 the administrators failed to modify the procedures of the King's Bench sufficiently to make it effective. Especially because of delays, the court was used relatively infrequently except by suitors located in the immediate vicinity of the capital.

The credibility of the courts also suffered from the identification of judges with privileged groups. This was partly the result of financial limitations which led before 1794 to the manning of the courts by lay judges and afterwards to a small provincial administration in which judges were expected to play a central political role. After 1794, for instance, the Chief Justice was the second most important figure in the province next to the Lieutenant Governor. This situation was especially damaging after 1794 because of the behaviour of provincial officials such as Hunter and Allcock. Their self-interested actions may be traced to the precarious financial predicament of the administrators generally. While they aspired to the life of the gentry, their incomes were insufficient to cope with the high costs of food, labour, and imported goods. As a result, they were constantly insecure and on the look-out for new means of personal advancement. Ironically, in their attempts to use the state to consolidate their personal positions, some officials seem actually to have weakened the legitimacy of the provincial régime.[115]

While the civil courts had been intended to encourage acceptance of the social order, they had not been entirely successful largely because of events outside their control. It would not do to exaggerate the problem of credibility prior to 1812. Articulate protest, after all, had been limited to a few individuals who were themselves selfishly motivated. None the less, a pattern had been set in motion which would reap bitter fruit in the 1820s and 1830s. Insecure about their personal futures and fearful of instability, leading figures in the province tended to behave in an arbitrary fashion which damaged their personal credibility and tended to reflect on the institutions of government, including the courts.

NOTES

I would like to acknowledge the co-operation of Parks Canada in the preparation of this essay. I am also indebted to Jim Taylor, Gordon Bennett, and Chris Curtis for their helpful criticisms.

1 John Mills Jackson *A View of the Political Situation of the Province of Upper Canada* (London 1809) 10; the historiography of the courts is scanty; on the writings of Riddell, see Hilary Bates Neary 'William Renwick Riddell: A Bio-Bibliographical Study' (Master's thesis, University of Western Ontario 1977) and Neary 'William Renwick Riddell: Judge, Ontario Publicist and Man of Letters' *The Law Society of Upper Canada Gazette* XI 144–74.

2 The best analyses of these élites are: Bruce G. Wilson 'The Enterprises of Robert Hamilton: A Study of Wealth and Influence in Early Upper Canada: 1776–1812' (PH D thesis, University of Toronto 1978) 2–8; Robert J. Burns 'The First Elite of Toronto: An Examination of the Genesis, Consolidation and Duration of Power in an Emerging Colonial Society' (PH D thesis, University of Western Ontario 1974) 6–7, 26–7.

3 Concerning early conservatism, see Terry Cook 'John Beverley Robinson and the Conservative Blueprint for the Upper Canadian Community' in J.K. Johnson, ed. *Historical Essays on Upper Canada* (Toronto 1975) 338–60; Sydney F. Wise 'Upper Canada and the Conservative Tradition' in Edith G. Firth,

ed. *Profiles of a Province* (Toronto 1967) 20–32; Gerald M. Craig *Upper Canada: The Formative Years 1784–1841* (Toronto 1963) 38–40.

4 James H. Aitchison 'The Development of Local Government in Upper Canada, 1780–1850' (PH D thesis, University of Toronto 1953); Margaret A. Banks in David H. Flaherty, ed. *Essays in the History of Canadian Law* 2 vols (Toronto 1981–3) I 358–61

5 On the extent of criminality, see John M. Beattie *Attitudes towards Crime and Punishment in Upper Canada, 1830–1850: A Documentary Study* (Toronto 1977) 1; John D. Blackwell 'Crime in the London District, 1828–1837: A Case Study of the Effect of the 1833 Reform in Upper Canadian Penal Law' *Queen's Law Journal* VI (1981) 528–67.

6 On the stabilizing mythology of the law, see Douglas Hay 'Property, Authority and the Criminal Law' in Douglas Hay et al., eds *Albion's Fatal Tree: Crime and Society in Eighteenth-Century England* (London 1975) 17–63; Daniel J. Boorstin *The Mysterious Science of the Law: An Essay on Blackstone's Commentaries Showing How Blackstone, Employing Eighteenth-Century Ideas of Science, Religion, History, Aesthetics, and Philosophy, Made of the Law at Once a Conservative and a Mysterious Science* 3rd ed. (Gloucester, MA 1973) 6, 27–8, 187–8.

7 Craig *Upper Canada* 39

8 The Reverend John Stuart to the Bishop of Quebec 2 Oct. 1784 in Richard A. Preston, ed. *Kingston before the War of 1812: A Collection of Documents* (Toronto 1959) 346; John McGill to John Graves Simcoe 8 Jan. 1793 in Ernest A. Cruikshank, ed. *The Correspondence of Lieutenant Governor John Graves Simcoe* 5 vols (Toronto 1923–31) I 272–5; Adam Shortt 'Early History of Canadian Banking' *Journal of the Canadian Bankers' Association* IV (1896) 1–19, 129–44, 235–52

9 In Midland these leading citizens were magistrates by 1785; in 1786 they petitioned Quebec for political and legal institutions; Adam Shortt and Arthur G. Doughty, eds *Documents Relating to the Constitutional History of Canada, 1759–1791* (Ottawa 1918) II 642–4.

10 Alfred L. Burt *The Old Province of Quebec* Carleton Library ed., 2 vols (Toronto 1968) II 102–18

11 Hilda M. Neatby *The Administration of Justice under the Quebec Act* (Minneapolis, MN 1937) 284, 298–305. However, only one judge sat in Hesse.

12 29 Geo. III (1789), c. 3 (Que.); in practice, the Common Pleas in Midland ignored the restriction on real property; for a discussion, see William N.T. Wylie 'Arbiters of Commerce, Instruments of Power: A Study of the Civil Courts in the Midland District, Upper Canada, 1789–1812' (PH D thesis, Queen's University 1980) 113–19.

13 Donald C. MacDonald 'The Honourable Richard Cartwright, 1759–1812'

in *Three History Theses* (Toronto 1961) 12–37. For most of the period the other two judges in Midland were Neil and Hector MacLean; though unrelated, both were retired British military officers who had settled at Kingston.

14 See his arguments in the minutes of the Midland Common Pleas printed in William Renwick Riddell, ed. 'Records of the Early Courts of Justice in Upper Canada' *Fourteenth Report of the Bureau of Archives for the Province of Ontario* (Toronto 1918) 190–353; the minutes of the Common Pleas for the Districts of Hesse (Western) and Luneberg (Eastern) are in the same volume; the Reverend Conway E. Cartwright, ed. *Life and Letters of the Late Honourable Richard Cartwright* (Toronto 1876) 10–11; Morton J. Horwitz *The Transformation of American Law, 1780–1860* (Cambridge, MA 1977) 146–7; Robert Robson *The Attorney in Eighteenth-Century England* (Cambridge, Eng. 1959) 82–3, 134–8.

15 Circuits were provided for in 17 Geo. III (1777), c. 2 (Que.); 'Records of the Midland Common Pleas.'

16 Concerning the pattern of suits, see Wylie 'Civil Courts in Midland' 130–40; 'Records of the Midland Common Pleas.'

17 Ibid.

18 J. Milnes Holden *History of Negotiable Instruments in English Law* (London 1955) 56–64, 79–84, 124–32; Lawrence M. Friedman *A History of American Law* (New York 1973) 235–8; Shortt 'Early History of Canadian Banking' 136–7

19 Holden *Negotiable Instruments in English Law* 55; 17 Geo. III (1777), c. 3 (Que.); Russell to Duke of Portland 11 Aug. 1798 in Ernest A. Cruikshank, ed. *The Correspondence of the Honourable Peter Russell* 3 vols (Toronto 1932–6) II 239

20 William Blackstone *Commentaries on the Laws of England*, 4 vols (London 1765–9; facsimile ed., Chicago 1979) III 368–9; 'Records of the Midland Common Pleas'

21 The development of these actions is described at length in Stroud F.C. Milsom *Historical Foundations of the Common Law* 2nd ed. (Toronto 1981) and Cecil H.S. Fifoot *History and Sources of the Common Law: Tort and Contract* (London 1949).

22 'Records of the Midland Common Pleas'

23 Ibid.

24 Milsom *Common Law* 253–82, 300–60; 'Records of the Midland Common Pleas'

25 17 Geo. III (1777), c. 2 (Que.); 25 Geo. III (1785), c. 2 (Que.)

26 'Records of the Midland Common Pleas'; Blackstone *Commentaries* III 270–92; William S. Holdsworth *A History of English Law* 17 vols (London 1903–72) VIII 229–45 and IX 248–56

27 *Simons v MacLean* (1793), 'Records of the Midland Common Pleas' 311; Holdsworth *History of English Law* IX 264–70

28 5 Geo. II (1732), c. 7; 25 Geo. III (1785), c. 2 (Que.); 32 Geo. III (1792), c. 1 (UC); 'Records of the Midland Common Pleas'

29 25 Geo. III (1785), c. 2 (Que.); 32 Geo. III (1792), c. 2 (UC); 'Records of the Midland Common Pleas'

30 Blackstone *Commentaries* III 391, quoted in 'Records of the Midland Common Pleas' 279

31 *Schultz* v *Carsons* (1790), ibid. 281

32 Thomas Edlyne Tomlins *The Law Dictionary* 4th ed. (London 1835) 'Execution'; 5 Geo. II (1732), c. 7; 'Records of the Midland Common Pleas'

33 20 Geo. III (1780), c. 3 (Que.); 'Records of the Midland Common Pleas'

34 Simcoe to Henry Dundas 2 Aug. 1794 in Cruikshank *Correspondence of John Graves Simcoe* III 3

35 William Renwick Riddell 'William Osgoode – First Chief Justice of Upper Canada – 1792–1794' in *Upper Canada Sketches* (Toronto 1922) 101–26

36 While the Court of King's Bench was based on the English royal courts, the Courts of Requests and the District Courts of Upper Canada were remarkably similar to the small claims courts in American states such as New York; Julius Goebel jr and Joseph H. Smith, eds *The Law Practice of Alexander Hamilton* 5 vols (New York 1964–81) I 15–19.

37 Stanley R. Mealing 'The Enthusiasms of John Graves Simcoe' in Johnson, ed. *Essays on Upper Canada* 311–13; Cook 'John Beverley Robinson' 338–60; Wise 'Upper Canada and the Conservative Tradition' 20–32

38 Mealing 'John Graves Simcoe' 313–14; Craig *Upper Canada* 14–15

39 32 Geo. III (1792), c. 6 (UC); James H. Aitchison 'The Courts of Requests in Upper Canada' in Johnson, ed. *Essays on Upper Canada* 88

40 The King's Bench was established by 34 Geo. III (1794), c. 2 (UC), the District Courts by 34 Geo. III (1794), c. 3 (UC); appeals from the central court were possible to a committee of the provincial executive and from there, in actions of special importance, to the King in Council. No provision was made for a Court of Chancery until 1837. The problems precipitated by its absence are discussed in Wylie 'Civil Courts in Midland' 310–20.

41 Boorstin *Mysterious Science of the Law* 6, 27–8, 187–8

42 34 Geo. III (1794), c. 4 (UC); the Law Society was created by 37 Geo. III (1797), c. 13 (UC).

43 Cartwright's speech 16 June 1794 Cartwright *Life and Letters of Richard Cartwright* 67–72; Cartwright to Isaac Todd 1 Oct. 1794 ibid. 56–64; Cartwright and Hamilton's Dissent 23 June 1794 in Cruikshank *Correspondence of John Graves Simcoe* II 271; Simcoe to Henry Dundas 2 Aug. 1794, ibid. III 2–3

44 The only extant records of the Courts of Requests are the Minutes of the Court

in Grenville County, Johnstown District 1798–1802, in the Ontario Archives (hereafter OA) RG22 Series 8 Vol. 2 (hereafter Grenville County Court of Requests); Records of a Court of Requests in the Johnstown District 1798–1813 in OA Solomon Jones Papers (hereafter Jones Papers Court of Requests); concerning the District Courts, evidence is available in the Documents of the Eastern District Court 1797–1826 in OA RG22 Series 4 (hereafter Documents of the Eastern District Court); for the Home District, see the Financial Accounts of Robert Isaac Dey Gray 1801–4 in the Public Archives of Canada (hereafter PAC) RG5 B2 Vols 5–6 (hereafter Dey Gray Accounts); see also the Memorandum of William Dummer Powell on the Johnstown District Court 13 Sept. 1808 PAC RG5 A1 Vol. 8 3361.

45 In 41 Geo. III (1801), c. 6 (UC), an exception was made for the Midland District Court, which was authorized to conduct sittings alternately at Kingston and Adolphustown.

46 32 Geo. III (1792), c. 6 (UC); 34 Geo. III (1794), c. 3 (UC)

47 Grenville County Court of Requests; Jones Papers Court of Requests

48 Ibid.; Minutes of the Midland District Quarter Sessions Oct. 1808 in OA RG22 Series 7; Aitchison 'Local Government in Upper Canada' 33–53

49 Talbot to Sullivan 27 Oct. 1802 quoted in ibid. 60–2; Jackson *Political Situation of Upper Canada* 11

50 32 Geo. III (1792), c. 6 (UC); Aitchison 'Local Government in Upper Canada' 33–53; Grenville County Court of Requests; Jones Papers Court of Requests

51 34 Geo. III (1794), c. 3 (UC); 37 Geo. III (1797), c. 6 (UC)

52 Documents of the Eastern District Court; Dey Gray Accounts

53 Sherwood's arguments in the Assembly were printed in the *York Gazette* 9 Mar. 1808.

54 Documents of the Eastern District Court; Dey Gray Accounts

55 Dockets, OA RG22 Series 3 III-B Vols 46–7 (hereafter Docket Books)

56 Craig *Upper Canada* 43–51; Preston *Kingston before 1812* lxvi-lxxvii; Arthur R.M. Lower *Great Britain's Woodyard: British America and the Timber Trade, 1763– 1867* (Montreal 1973) 45–57; Wilson 'Enterprises of Robert Hamilton' 2–8, 158–9

57 Horwitz *Transformation of American Law* 167–70; John D. Falconbridge *The Law of Mortgages of Real Estate* (Toronto 1919) 6–7, 57–61

58 *Robins* v *Ansley* (1810), Docket Books Vol. 46; a more thorough analysis of this evidence is available in Wylie 'Civil Courts in Midland' 293–6.

59 34 Geo. III (1794), c. 2 (UC); 37 Geo. III (1797), c. 4 (UC); Blackstone *Commentaries* III 287–92

60 Ibid.; concerning the situation at the beginning of the nineteenth century, see

the marginal notes by William Draper Lewis in the 1897 edition of the *Commentaries* published in Philadelphia.

61 34 Geo. III (1794), c. 2 (UC); because this wording was regarded as too restrictive, it was changed in 1798 so that the plaintiff need only attest to an apprehension of evasion; 38 Geo. III (1798), c. 6 (UC).

62 William Renwick Riddell *The Legal Profession in Upper Canada in Its Early Periods* (Toronto 1916) 49, 180; David B. Read *The Lives of the Judges of Upper Canada and Ontario* (Toronto 1888) 43, 52

63 Hay 'Property, Authority and the Criminal Law' 18–19; Boorstin *Mysterious Science of the Law* 167–86

64 Elmsley to D.W. Smith 21 June 1798 in the Smith Papers, Toronto Public Library

65 Cartwright Memorandum concerning the Parliamentary Transactions of 28 May–9 July 1801 (hereafter Cartwright Memorandum 1801) Cartwright Papers Letterbook II Queen's University Archives (hereafter Cartwright Letterbooks); 'Veritas' *Upper Canada Gazette* 6 Apr. 1798; 'Clio' *Kingston Gazette* 13 Nov. 1810; Holdsworth *History of English Law* VIII 229–45; William E. Nelson *Americanization of the Common Law: The Impact of Legal Change on Massachusetts Society, 1760–1830* (Cambridge, MA 1975) 147–54

66 William Dummer Powell 'First Days in Upper Canada' quoted in Craig *Upper Canada* 281

67 Speech quoted in *York Gazette* 1 Apr. 1808

68 Ibid.

69 34 Geo. III (1794), c. 2 (UC)

70 38 Geo. III (1798), c. 6 (UC); Cartwright Memorandum 1801

71 William Renwick Riddell *The Life of William Dummer Powell* (Lansing, MI 1924) 10, 91–5, 114, 141; Riddell *Legal Profession in Upper Canada* 27; Lillian F. Gates *Land Policies of Upper Canada* (Toronto 1968) 46–7, 56–8

72 The Journals of the Assembly and the Legislative Council for the period 1792–1812 have been published in the *Sixth, Seventh and Eighth Reports of the Bureau of Archives for the Province of Ontario, 1909–11* (Toronto 1910–12); 'Journals' June 1801 *Sixth Report* 230; 'Journals' *Seventh Report* 145; Cartwright Memorandum 1801; Riddell *Life of Powell* 92–3.

73 Allcock to Hunter, letter on the bill to permit seizure and sale of land in satisfaction of judgment, 12 June 1801, PAC MG11 CO42 Vol. 328

74 Allcock to Hunter, letter on the Feme Couverte Bill, 12 June 1801, ibid.

75 51 Geo. III (1811), c. 3 (UC)

76 The court records are found in OA RG22 Series 3 III-B and, besides the Docket Books Vols 46–7, include the Clerk's Entries of Proceedings 1803–13 Vols 38–40 (hereafter Clerk's Entries) and the King's Bench Term Books 1794–1812 Vols 55–62 (hereafter Term Books); because most of the records of the Midland

District were kept in a regional office after 1797, they have not survived; see also the Cartwright Letterbooks, *Upper Canada* and *York Gazette* 1793–1812 and the *Kingston Gazette* 1810–12.

77 *Bliss* v *Street* (1799), Term Book Vol. 58

78 *Upper Canada Gazette* 30 Nov., 7 Dec. 1799; Cartwright to Elmsley 26 Dec. 1799 Letterbook II; Allcock to Hunter 12 June 1801

79 'A Friend to Justice' *Upper Canada Gazette* 2 May 1800; Cartwright Memorandum 1801

80 Elmsley quoted in Gates *Land Policies of Upper Canada* 47; Elmsley to Russell 26 Nov. 1797 in Cruikshank *Correspondence of Peter Russell* II 25–7

81 William Renwick Riddell 'Thomas Scott, the Second Attorney-General of Upper Canada' *Ontario Historical Society Papers and Records* XX (1923) 126, 128, 138; Scott to Hunter 4 Aug. 1801, PAC MG11 CO42 Vol. 328; Allcock to Hunter, letter on the bill to permit seizure and sale of land after judgment, 12 June 1801

82 Cartwright Memorandum 1801; Elmsley to Hunter 11 July 1801, PAC MG11 CO42 Vol. 328; 'Journals' *Sixth Report* 229–31, 305–6, 309; 'Journals' *Seventh Report* 143; Allcock's seat in the Assembly was unusual in Upper Canada, but Elmsley's position as Speaker of the Legislative Council was not. Members of the judiciary continued to fill this overtly political role until 1843.

83 Allcock quoted in Cartwright Memorandum 1801

84 Thorpe to the Secretary of State 14 Aug. 1807 *Report of the Canadian Archives, 1892* (Ottawa 1893) 105–8

85 Allcock to Hunter 12 June 1801

86 *Gray* v *Willcocks* Term Books Vol. 59, 16 Nov. 1803; Vol. 60, 6 Nov. 1805 and 13 July 1809; Cartwright to James McGill 26 July 1809 Letterbook VI

87 Clerk's Entries Vols 38–40

88 Elmsley to Russell 26 Nov. 1797 in Cruikshank *Correspondence of Peter Russell* II 29; Holdsworth *History of English Law* IX 256–7

89 34 Geo. III (1794), c. 4 (UC); 37 Geo. III (1797), c. 13 (UC); 43 Geo. III (1803), c. 3 and c. 8 (UC); 47 Geo. III (1807), c. 5 (UC); 'A Man of No Trade or Profession' *Kingston Gazette* 13 Nov. 1810; William Renwick Riddell *The Bar and Courts of Upper Canada or Ontario, Part I, The Bar* (Toronto 1928) 73

90 Minutes of the Assizes 1795–1812, OA RG22 Series 3 III-B Vols 153, 155–6, 162

91 Blackstone *Commentaries* III 397–8

92 34 Geo. III (1794), c. 4 (UC); 37 Geo. III (1797), c. 4 (UC); General Rule Nov. 1803, Term Book Vol. 56; Minutes of the Assizes Vols 156 and 162

93 William Tidd *The Practice of the Courts of King's Bench and Common Pleas in Personal Actions* 7th ed. 2 vols (London 1821) I 598–9; Elmsley to Russell 26 Nov. 1797 in Cruikshank *Correspondence of Peter Russell* II 29–31

94 Blackstone *Commentaries* III 303; Docket Books Vols 46–7

95 Goebel *Law Practice of Alexander Hamilton* I 19; 37 Geo. III (1797), c. 6 (UC)

96 37 Geo. III (1797), c. 4 (UC); Elmsley to Russell 26 Nov. 1797; 38 Geo. III (1798), c. 6 (UC)

97 Ibid.; Elmsley to Russell 11 Aug. 1798 in Cruikshank *Correspondence of Peter Russell* II 244; Elmsley to Smith 18 Feb. 1798 in Smith Papers Toronto Public Library; 41 Geo. III (1801), c. 9 (UC)

98 Dey Gray Accounts Vols 5–6

99 Term Books Vols 55–7; Docket Books Vols 46–7

100 Lower *British America and the Timber Trade* 45–7; Adam Shortt 'The Economic Effect of the War of 1812' in Morris Zaslow, ed. *The Defended Border: Upper Canada and the War of 1812* (Toronto 1964) 296–302; Cartwright to James McGill 26 July 1809 Letterbook VI; Docket Books Vols 46–7

101 Riddell *Legal Profession in Upper Canada* 174–7; *York Gazette* 9 Mar. 1808

102 Ibid.; Cartwright to Allcock 14 Mar. 1807 and Cartwright to Strachan 15 Mar. 1808 Letterbook II; Sherwood's proposals and their implications are discussed more fully in Wylie 'Civil Courts in Midland' 260–5.

103 Cartwright to Allcock 14 Mar. 1807

104 'Journals' *Eighth Report* 205–6, 212–13, 240; 'Journals' *Seventh Report* 307, 309, 311, 316–18

105 Cartwright to Strachan 15 Mar. 1808

106 Gates *Land Policies of Upper Canada* 65–74

107 Ibid. 75–7; Memorandum of William Dummer Powell, nd, *Report of the Canadian Archives* 36

108 William Renwick Riddell 'Mr. Justice Thorpe, the Leader of the First Opposition in Upper Canada' *Upper Canada Sketches* (Toronto 1922) 57–74; Harry H. Guest 'Upper Canada's First Political Party' *Ontario History* LIV (1962) 275–96

109 Firth to Edward Cooke 6 Feb. 1808, PAC MG11 CO42 Vol. 348; *York Gazette* 1 Apr., 7 Apr. 1808; Riddell *Life of Powell* 112

110 Craig *Upper Canada* 43–9; Alfred L. Burt *The United States, Great Britain, and British North America: From the Revolution to the Establishment of Peace after the War of 1812* (Toronto 1940) 247–50

111 Wilson 'Enterprises of Robert Hamilton' 2–8, 158–9; for a detailed analysis of the situation in Midland, see Wylie 'Civil Courts in Midland' 323–36.

112 Jackson *Political Situation of Upper Canada* 10–11; (Richard Cartwright) *Letters from an American Loyalist in Upper Canada to His friend in England on a Pamphlet Published by John Mills Jackson* (York 1810) 43–4

113 Minutes of the Assizes Vols 153, 155–6, 162; Docket Books Vols 46–7

114 These events may be traced in the Journals of the Legislative Assembly and

Council in the *Sixth, Seventh and Eighth Reports of the Ontario Archives*; the relevant acts are 44 Geo. III (1804), c. 3 (UC) and 50 Geo. III (1810), c. 9 (UC); a fuller discussion of the situation and a more complete listing of authorities is given in Wylie 'Civil Courts in Midland' 277–82.

115 John Bruce Walton 'An End to All Order: A Study of Upper Canadian Conservative Response to Opposition, 1805–10' (Master's thesis, Queen's University 1977) 28–9

2

Legal Education in Upper Canada
1785–1889:
The Law Society as Educator

G. BLAINE BAKER

In the common law world the bar, together with legislatures, courts, executive branches of government, and the public service, is an essential agency of the law. The ways lawyers structure and utilize law as a form of social intelligence are largely a product of the way they are socialized through law training. In the geographic area now known as Ontario, legal education has been exclusively or principally the prerogative of the Law Society of Upper Canada for almost two centuries. The development of the Society's role as legal educator in the period between 1785 and 1889 is the focus of this essay. It describes the design and administration of the various components of legal education in Upper Canada, attempts to divine the pedagogic and social values that the 'Convocation of Benchers' of the Law Society intended to further through law training, and considers the local and comparative efficacy of the Society's approach to legal education. An attempt also is made to specify the kind of additional information that would be necessary to respond more adequately to general questions about élite formation in Upper Canada, the social origins of law students, effects of changes in the nature of law practice upon legal education, the excess of educated men that plagued mid-nineteenth-century Canada, and the occupational prestige of Upper Canadian lawyers.

The period between 1785 and 1889 was crucial in the development of legal education in Ontario. Although there were licensed advocates and laymen performing the law role in the 'Upper Country' before 1785, that year saw the promulgation of the first operative regulation about the training of Canadian lawyers. Lieutenant Governor Henry Hamilton's 'Ordinance concerning Advocates' required that persons seeking to practise law in old Quebec serve no less than five years' apprenticeship and pass a bar admission examination. This framework for Canadian legal education was reproduced in the 1797 Law Society Act and refined through rules, resolutions, and standing orders passed thereunder by Convocation. By 1889 most elements of legal education in nineteenth-century Ontario had passed their peak and were fading. More significant was the adoption that year of the milestone recommendation of a Law Society committee that responsibility for law training not be delegated to or shared with the province's universities. This affirmation of the Society's statutory monopoly over legal education determined the shape that training for the practice of law would take in Ontario until 1957.

From the beginning the Law Society of Upper Canada conceived of itself as, and tried to act like, an educational institution with the training of aspiring lawyers and their admission to practice as its main responsibilities. Through its first half-century approximately ninety-five per cent of the business of Convocation had to do with legal education.[1] The 'licence' awarded by the Society at the conclusion of five years' study as a legal apprentice was referred to exclusively as the 'Diploma of Barrister-at-Law,' and practitioners regularly alluded to the Law Society as their 'professional *alma mater*.'[2] A principal reason for the construction of Osgoode Hall in the 1820s was to house students and provide a physical plant for this educational institution; the courts did not sit regularly at Osgoode Hall until at least 1846.[3] The popular press adverted to the Law Society as a 'university,' and Convocation generally was anxious that its admission and graduation policies coincide with such schools as the University of Toronto.[4] The Society consistently allocated larger funds to its legal education programs than to all other activities combined. Members of Convocation and the laity regarded the Society as more than a mere certifying agency.

The bar admission examination administered between 1831 and 1889 included liberal arts and legal subjects. Attendance at classes or lectures first was required in 1832. Although the attendance requirement waxed and waned regularly between 1832 and 1889, this school-related component of legal education was present from a comparatively early date. 'Term-keeping duties' inaugurated in 1828 required students-at-law to attend court in the provincial capital on a daily basis, typically for a year and a half of their apprenticeships, and to take notes on cases argued. In practice this meant that all law students spent no less than two-fifths of their training in Toronto, which made them eligible to attend lectures, classes, or club meetings required by the Society; yet it also meant that concentration of these resources in the capital did not prevent persons not apprenticed in Toronto from partaking of the Society's structured programs.

From the perspective of the 1980s these features of Upper Canadian legal education may not add up to full-fledged schooling in a university environment, but in the context of pre-Confederation Upper Canada or from the standpoint of contemporaneous English and American developments, legal education in Upper Canada was highly distinctive. The Law Society was a seriously educative enterprise whose informal methods achieved education without formal schooling. Moreover, this solid base and the traditions associated with it enabled law, unlike medicine, dentistry, engineering, or teaching, to resist association with Ontario's universities until the mid-twentieth century.

A second theme of this essay is that one consequence of the Law Society's self-image as an educational institution is that it makes little sense to contrast law office training with university schooling in law in the Upper Canadian setting. If asked about this modern antinomy, a Bencher of the 1830s or 1840s either would have responded that the Society's students-at-law received academic instruction in a school setting or that Convocation's program was neither fish nor fowl but involved the generation of the professional élite noted 100 years later by John Porter.[5] Two aspects of this academic / professional contrast function here as subthemes. In the final analysis it was Ontario's universities and not the Law Society which argued most strenuously in favour of the legal profession retaining exclusive responsibility for legal education; the pressure to create university-related law schools which climaxed in the 1860s and 1880s was more a product of regional self-interest than pedagogical debate or institutional jealousy. A second subtheme is that the form of law training which evolved in Upper Canada between 1785 and 1889 was more intensive and more sophisticated than that which existed in England, in most American jurisdictions, or in other British colonies. Institutionalization of legal education of the sort that occurred in Nova Scotia, Massachusetts, New York, and England in the 1870s and 1880s could not have occurred in late-nineteenth-century Ontario because it already had happened over roughly eighty years under the auspices of the Law Society.

The nineteenth-century American pattern was that comparatively rigorous and innovative programs of legal education and bar admission that had developed slowly and deliberately in the colonial era were disassembled during the antebellum period. New England Bar meetings disintegrated after 1810, the first generation of university-related law schools was moribund by 1820, and most jurisdictions abolished bar admission requirements; nominal forms were all that was left in the few states that retained standards. Similarly, English legal education had been in decadent chaos since the Glorious Revolution of 1688. Admission to an Inn of Court during the eighteenth and most of the nineteenth centuries was predicated principally upon eating the requisite number of dinners with its Benchers. Feverish manoeuvering and grand plans were necessary in the late nineteenth century both in Britain and the United States to revitalize law study in a way that would make it compatible with current social, economic, and ideological trends. Few of these ebbs or flows occurred in Upper Canadian legal education.

A third theme of this essay relates to the politics of legal education. At no point during the period under consideration did more than twenty per cent of the Society's members practise law in Toronto. The proportion of students from the provincial capital was also consistently less than a fifth of each class. To conclude that these figures merely mirrored demographic patterns would miss the point. As the nineteenth century progressed, an increasingly sharp split developed between Toronto and provincial interests. Regional self-interest was most clearly articulated in debates about the creation of county law library associations in the 1860s, the abolition of the term-keeping requirement and the enactment of statutory amendments, which required the election of Benchers on a regional basis in the early 1870s, and the delegation of legal education to Queen's, Western, and Ottawa universities in the 1880s. By the fourth quarter of the nineteenth century regionalism shaped much of the Society's politics. The politics of Convocation in turn exerted control over pedagogy in the post-1870 period at least equal to the domination of principle and commitment to education qua education of the first two-thirds of the century. The politics of legal education speak directly to the evolution of Canadian federalism and the allocations of power associated with it.

A fourth theme is that a striking continuity of goals, forms, and personalities characterized the development of legal education in Upper Canada between 1785 and 1889. This continuity dictated the topical rather than chronological organization of the essay. By 1832 each element of Upper Canadian legal education was in place. Changes that occurred between 1832 and 1889 are better characterized as fine-tuning than major additions to or revisions of the early scheme. While Upper Canada of the 1830s was qualitatively different from Ontario of the 1880s, legal education during the same periods was not nearly so different as social transformation in the province might lead one to expect.

Entrance examinations were introduced in 1819; the last major restructuring of entrance requirements occurred in 1832. Apprenticeships for those admitted as students became obligatory in 1800 and did not change during the period under consideration, except that they were reduced in length for university graduates in the late 1830s and 1840s. Term-keeping was not modified significantly during its forty-year lifetime which ended in 1871. Between 1832 and 1889 the Society's classes and lectures were operated variously by its law clubs, Convocation or its 'Law School,' and the province's colleges. Though attendance requirements occasionally went into remission, the program of formal tuition was not significantly more intensive in the 1880s than it had been in the 1860s, the 1840s, or the 1830s. In many respects it was less intensive. Similarly, Convocation's periodic revisions of bar admission reading lists and adjustments to the mode in which the examination was conducted were minor changes in contrast with those occurring in English and American bar admission régimes during the nineteenth century. In short, there is little indication that the dynamics of Upper Canadian law training changed much in response to external influences such as alterations in the nature of legal practice as the nineteenth century advanced.[6]

This striking continuity of forms was achieved by and is reflected in incremental transfers of control of the Law Society's educational enterprise from one generation of Upper Canadian lawyers to the next. Dr William Warren Baldwin became the twenty-sixth member of the fledgling Law Society in 1803. His eleven-year treasurership in the 1820s and 1830s witnessed the introduction of most of the components of legal education described in this essay. Yet half a century after his father's call to the Bar, Robert Baldwin, president and instructor of the Society's first compulsory law class of the 1830s, remained one of the leading forces in the development of Upper Canadian legal education. Chief Justice John Beverley Robinson, in whose courtroom term-keepers sat, dominated the Upper Canadian judiciary from 1829 to 1863. Hugh Nelson Gwynne served as the Society's Entrance Examiner, Librarian, and Secretary for thirty years from 1842 to 1872. William Hume Blake was admitted to the Society from the fringes of Upper Canada (Adelaide Township, London District) in 1835 and became the province's first university teacher of law in the 1840s. On the eve of Confederation, Bencher and law lecturer Adam

William Warren Baldwin, Treasurer, The Law Society of Upper Canada
1811–15, 1820–1, 1824–8, 1832–6
Oil portrait by George Théodore Berthon (The Law Society of Upper Canada)

Crooks resigned briefly from Convocation and from his lectureship when certain Benchers criticized 'the Blakes' scheme' for law training.[7] Hume's son Edward Blake was the Society's Treasurer during the turgid debates about decentralization and delegation of law-teaching responsibilities to universities in the late 1880s.

Admittedly, elements of discontinuity and change also were present. New problems such as the over-supply of lawyers arose and provoked responses. The establishment of liberal arts colleges resulted in disagreement about the recognition of their degrees. Yet when the Upper Canadian record is viewed from a comparative perspective, it is clear that discontinuity and change were much less severe than existing scholarship has allowed or companion social histories might suggest.

A final theme of this essay is that the Benchers thought they were building an élite, which accounts for their preoccupation with admission and training. It also helps to explain the Society's self-image as an educational institution; it was hoped that an 'academic pedigree' would provide credibility to the members of this non-commercial, Tory élite. The promotion of law clubs for students, creation of a scholarship program based on merit and need, and especially construction of Osgoode Hall to accommodate law students were three of the instruments used by the Society to promote development of its élite.

In the context of debates about the construction of the Hall and the appropriate mode of law training, Archdeacon John Strachan in 1826 wrote to the Lieutenant Governor, Sir Peregrine Maitland, that:

There are, it is believed between forty and fifty young gentlemen in the Province studying for the profession of Law – a profession which must, in a country like this, be the repository of the highest talents. *Lawyers must, from the very nature of our political institutions – from there being no great landed proprietors – no privileged orders – become the most powerful profession, and must in time possess more influence and authority than any other.* They are emphatically our men of business, and will gradually engross all the colonial offices of profit and honour. *It is, therefore, of the utmost importance that they should be collected together ... become acquainted with each other, and familiar, acquire similar views and modes of thinking,* and be taught from precept and example to love and venerate our parent state.[8]

If one is seeking to create a self-reinforcing and cohesive élite, eighty per cent of whose prospective members are scattered throughout the villages and backwoods of a province, it seems highly appropriate to collect them together in a central hostel where, for a portion of their studies, they 'become acquainted with each other' and 'acquire similar views and modes of thinking.' The response of the Ontario Bar to the rise of a competing commercial élite between 1880 and 1920 indicates that notions about élite-building persisted into the early twentieth century.[9]

For the first half-century at least, the construction of Upper Canada's legal élite was neither an exclusively English, metropolitan, nor family enterprise. Recitals about the ancestry and places of origin of aspiring law students contained in petitions for admission to the Society reveal that a disproportionately large number of applicants were of Irish birth or descent.[10] Indeed, many of these expatriate Irishmen went on to become pillars of the provincial legal or political establishment. Yet the Irish were regarded as an inferior ethnic group in Upper Canadian society and sometimes were ostracized. What is known about the few who secured status through the accumulation of wealth in commercial activity suggests that this was a route preferred by those of Scots, American, or French background.[11] It bears repeating that until at least 1889 the vast majority of the Law Society's students came from places outside Toronto; the homes of many of them were on the geographic frontiers of Upper Canadian civilization. Moreover, before mid-century the occupations of the parents of many candidates admitted as students-at-law were catalogued in the 'Minutes' as ones like blacksmith, wharfinger, farmer, stonemason, or labourer. Through its first half-century, the ranks of Upper Canada's legal élite were relatively open, and the occupational status of lawyers was not exclusively an inherited one. Yet admission to the Society as a student always resulted in an instantaneous change of formal status. In the 'Certificates of Admission,' the 'Petitions for Call,' the 'Diplomas of Barrister,' and virtually all other documents related to legal training, law students always were referred to as 'gentlemen.'[12]

Investment capital was sparse in Upper Canada during much of the period under consideration.[13] When capital resources and patrimonial opportunities are scarce vehicles of upward social mobility, persons with this ambition often seek to maximize their potential by capitalizing on their human resources. Indeed, it has been said that the unremitting grind of the barrister's life in nineteenth-century Britain ensured that few wealthy men would pursue law as a career.[14] The Upper Canadian evidence suggests either that notwithstanding Convocation's views, law was a distinctly middle-class enterprise and that movement in and out of the legal profession was an instrument of class reproduction rather than class mobility or, that if law in fact achieved the gentrified status to which the Benchers aspired, a legal education offered opportunities for upward social mobility to Upper Canadians of low and middling estate.[15] Questions about who actually entered law study, the class mobility or continuity provided by a legal education, and the occupational status of lawyers deserve detailed studies of their own.[16]

By about 1860 the emerging legal élite entered a period of consolidation or retrenchment which coincided roughly with a general rise of liberalism in Upper Canada. Prior to mid-century the profession expanded at roughly three times the rate at which it is expanding in the 1980s. Barriers to entry rose in the 1850s, and the number of students admitted (measured on a per capita basis) dropped sharply. Failures on entrance and bar admission examinations became common, and politicians and journalists accused the Society of 'monopolistic tendencies.'[17] Criticisms of the practice of admitting talented but impoverished students became commonplace in the legal community.[18] 'Impeachments' of members of the Law Society also increased dramatically in number. The first fifty-odd years saw three disbarments; in one judicial term in 1850 Convocation heard five applications for suspension or disbarment.[19] Further evidence of consolidation is the fact that the names of members of the third and fourth generations of the profession reveal intermarriage among families ensconced in this élite, and the appearance on the 'Books' of the names of sons and grandsons of members of the Society who sought membership in the legal fraternity. The Blake-Cronyn-Elliott family is one example of this phenomenon; the Baldwin-Sullivan-Robinson dynasty is another.[20] These events suggest that the caste was beginning to close ranks and that the occupational status of lawyers was becoming hereditary. Consolidation or achievement of the goal of creating a credible non-commercial élite also is indicated by the enrolment at mid-century of students like Thomas Galt, Henry Cawthra, Alexander Wood Strachan, and Delos White Beadle. Although recitals in open Convocation of the occupations of parents became less regular after about 1848, occupational statuses such as physician, gentleman, banker, and retired military officer were beginning to appear by that date.

Legal education in Upper Canada was designed to generate a self-conscious and literate social élite which apparently had, at least for its first half-century, relatively open ranks.[21] The notion of an educational institution awarding the Diploma of Barrister-at-Law after five years of comparatively intensive training was intended to give social and professional credibility to this emerging élite with membership based on ability and merit, not on wealth or birth. As innumerable nineteenth-century commentators noted, education, occupational status, and manners distinguished the Upper Canadian gentleman, since land was so easily acquired and commercial opportunities were few.[22]

CREATION OF THE LAW SOCIETY OF UPPER CANADA

A series of influences determines the nature of a law student's training: the most obvious include the structure of the legal system in a jurisdiction, the organization of its legal profession, and the demands placed upon the system and the profession by the society they serve. An Act for the better Regulating the PRACTICE of the Law in 1797 set out the general contours of Upper Canada's legal profession and training for its Bar.[23] It established the Law Society of Upper Canada as a self-governing body with exclusive control over the admission of barristers and solicitors and legal education. There is little indication that the act was informed by much economic or regulatory theory; the Legislative Assembly retained authority to engage in rate-making for the profession and some aspects of discipline remained the prerogative of the courts.[24] Since its empowering statute was grounded in social and pedagogic theory, the Law Society cannot be said to have been a self-regulating professional body in the full-blown twentieth-century sense.

The blueprint set out in the Law Society Act was similar to that provided for the Upper Canadian medical profession by the Physicians' and Surgeons' Act of 1795.[25] However, because there was insufficient medical presence to organize a Board of Surgeons under that statute, the Law Society stands alone in Canada as one of the common-law world's oldest self-governing professions with statutory mandates. Its organic law predates the English Apothecaries' Act of 1815, which is thought by many historians to have provided the model for nineteenth-century professional organizations.[26]

With respect to legal education, the Law Society Act specified that prospective barristers would be required to spend five years enrolled on Convocation's 'Books'; prospective solicitors had to spend three years as articled clerks. Later, additional and more particular requirements were added to flesh out the basic structure established in 1797. To appreciate the basis and import of decisions taken by the Legislative Assembly and later by the Law Society regarding legal education, one must understand something about the eighteenth-century pedagogic and legal heritage of each group represented by those who participated in these early processes of institutional design. Gad Horowitz's observations that the vernacular of colonial societies and institutions is often more distinctive than it first appears, and that events which surround their creation go far to account for that which is peculiar to them, seem particularly compelling in the case of the Law Society.[27]

The Law Society Act put the finishing touch on a six-year legislative program of erecting a judicial system for the infant province; no less than a quarter of the laws enacted between 1791 and 1797 concerned court structure, civil procedure, and legal services. English officials, members of the Legislative Assembly, and persons practising law in the province framed these enactments. Chief Justice William Osgoode, Attorney General John White, Lieutenant Governor John Graves Simcoe, President Peter Russell, and Chief Justice John Elmsley were the relevant officials. The Bar of Upper Canada numbered about twenty through the 1790s and was composed of French Canadian advocates and notaries, United Empire Loyalist licensees, and expatriate English barristers. There also were numerous untrained and unlicensed attorneys-in-fact regularly performing the law role, whose presence influenced the form taken by the organized Bar.[28]

To the early processes of institutional design English officials brought their commitment to the creation of a provincial aristocracy and their reverence for things British. Expatriate American colonials contributed a market for legal services, certain seaboard notions about the role of law and lawyers in North American society, and knowledge of the workings of the progressive colonial Bar meetings. The pre-existing French Canadian legal presence reinforced English and American preferences for an integrated bar with higher standards of admission than those in vogue in Britain or under government licensing schemes in the second Empire, and provided a Canadian precedent for what otherwise might have been rejected as an onerous or premature régime of law training.[29] The result of this confluence of traditions was the refinement and perpetuation of a distinctive Upper Canadian vernacular in law training and governance of the profession in the century that followed.

One must begin with conventions inherited as a result of the Quebec Act of 1774. A small group of Quebec-trained civil lawyers resided in the Upper Country after about 1730.[30] Owing to English case law and the Quebec Act, the French Canadian version of the Coûtume de Paris with which these lawyers were familiar remained in force in the Upper Country until 1792.[31] There was resort to civilian principles even after the arrival of the Loyalists, and cases often went from places as remote as Detroit to the superior courts in Montreal.[32] Walter Roe, the most prominent representative of this Québécois presence, received his legal education in

Montreal under the traditional French Canadian system and was called to the Bar of old Quebec in 1789. Roe, one of fifteen charter members of the Law Society, was number three on the 'Books' after Attorney General White and Solicitor General Robert Isaac Dey Gray, and was one of the six inaugural Benchers of the Society. William Dummer Powell, another influential member of the province's early legal community, was called to the Bar of Quebec in 1779, practised in Montreal with James Monk for a decade prior to his migration to Upper Canada, and administered the Coûtume de Paris for three years as Chief Justice of Common Pleas at Detroit.

In the early years royal ordinances applicable to New France prohibited professional lawyers from operating in the colony.[33] Canada's first structured program of legal education was initiated by Louis-Guillaume Verrier, an expatriate Parisien, in 1733.[34] Verrier's lectures led directly to the inauguration in 1744 of a system of licensing those who received his certificate to act as 'assessors' before the Sovereign Council and the lower courts of New France. Although Verrier disbanded his school in 1758, and despite the disruption of the French Canadian Bar by the introduction of English martial law in 1760, this system of licensing by the executive on successful completion of a structured academic program was established firmly by the time of the Conquest.

The granting of a number of royal commissions to practise law by Governors James Murray and Guy Carleton prior to the enactment of the Quebec Act notwithstanding, Verrier's certified assessors continued to constitute an influential group which pressed for the cessation of licensing untrained favourites of the English Crown and a return to the system of granting licences to practise on completion of formal legal training. Certified assessors from the pre-Conquest period petitioned Lieutenant Governor Hamilton and Baron Dorchester unsuccessfully to reopen Jesuit College in Quebec City and to include a professorship of law; in the 1780s Montrealers of French descent lobbied without effect for the creation of 'Collège Clarence' and expansion of the Collège de Montréal, both of which would have included professorships of civil law.[35]

French Canadian activists realized qualified success in 1785. A controversy about granting notaries' and advocates' commissions to the same applicant climaxed in 1784 when Alexandre Dumas, an unsuccessful merchant and ironmaster, was granted an advocate's licence in addition to the notarial commission he already held.[36] All fifteen French Canadian members of the Quebec Bar petitioned the administration demanding more rigorous rules about admission to law practice. An Ordinance concerning Advocates, Attorneys, Solicitors and Notaries, and for the more easy collection of His Majesty's Revenues was the response. Its partial reinstatement of the system of structured law training that had prevailed between 1733 and 1758 was thought necessary because 'the welfare and tranquility of families and the peace of individuals require as an object of the greatest importance that such persons only should be appointed to act and practise as barristers, advocates, solicitors, proctors and notaries who are properly qualified to perform the duties of those respective employments.'[37] Thenceforth no one was to be permitted to practise law without serving five years under a written contract with some duly admitted member of the legal profession in His Majesty's Dominions or six years with a clerk or registrar of the Court of Common Pleas or Appeals in Quebec. Candidates also were required to take examinations set by 'a group of the most able barristers, advocates or attorneys' and held in the presence of the Chief Justice of Quebec or at least two judges of the Courts of Common Pleas. The Law Society's rules seven and nine of 1800 provided for a similar five-year apprenticeship, and a bar admission examination later became the second cornerstone of legal education in Upper Canada.

The Ordinance of 1785 remained the controlling instrument of the legal profession in Lower Canada until 1849, when the provincial Bar was incorporated as a self-governing agency with three regional sections.[38] In Upper Canada it was suspended for two years in 1794 and repealed in stages in 1797 and 1798.[39] Three Upper Canadians commenced their local legal training under the Ordinance: John Ten Broeck, Walter Butler Wilkinson, and William Weekes, who were apprenticed to Attorney General White. However, all three students were admitted to practice by the Law Society and not by the Upper Canadian judiciary under the law of 1785.[40] There is no record of any student in the Upper Country being examined by the judges during the nine-year period that the old Quebec Ordinance was in full effect. None the less, early Convocations regularly recurred to this régime as a model in the design of the Society's rules.

A second ingredient in the provincial recipe for law training was 5500 Loyalists who settled in the 1780s in what was to become Upper Canada. American immigration to the province is relevant to the development of legal education for three reasons. First, until at least 1820 the majority of Upper Canadians were of American birth or extraction; this ethnic make-up was as true for the legal profession as it was for the population at large.[41] Second, the Loyalists anticipated continued enjoyment of common law customs and institutions; much of the legislation passed by the Assembly in its first decade was responsive to this sentiment. Finally, and most important, at the inaugural meeting of the Law Society held in 1797 at Wilson's Hotel, Newark, no less than five of the ten practitioners in attendance were American.[42] Nicholas Hagerman appears to have been called to the Bar of New York. William Dummer Powell began his legal training in Boston under Loyalist Attorney General Jonathan Sewell but completed his apprenticeship with an English barrister and later was admitted to the Middle Temple and the Bar of Quebec. William Weekes, who was both admitted to the Law Society and called to the Bar in 1799, is reputed to have apprenticed in the New York City law offices of Aaron Burr prior to his departure for Canada. Weekes quickly became the most prominent and busy member of the Upper Canadian Bar. Christopher Robinson, a licensee under the Judicature Act of 1794, was a Virginian Loyalist and Angus Macdonell had spent time in the seaboard colonies.[43]

At least 130 lawyers left the United States as Loyalists; a number of these jurists migrated to the districts that were to become Lower Canada, Nova Scotia, and New Brunswick.[44] The Upper Country, which was less developed, tended to attract farmers from New York, New Jersey, and Pennsylvania.[45] It is highly relevant to the political and economic history of the province, and to the Law Society's perception of its role as the procreator of a Tory social élite, that Americans who settled in Upper Canada came from moderately undeveloped portions of the seaboard colonies and that their backgrounds were agrarian. Land and not capital became the socio-economic basis of Upper Canadian society. Toryism of a Georgian variety became ensconced as the dominant ideology. The resulting anti-republican, anti-liberal climate provided an ideal atmosphere for the generation of a social élite composed of lawyers that secured its position through education, tradition, and social behaviour rather than through the accumulation of land or economic capital.[46]

In the first years following the Treaty of Versailles of 1783, disputes that arose among Loyalists in the Upper Country were settled by their retired military officers according to 'principles of equity and justice.' Commissions later were given to these officers so 'that they might preserve the peace and settle minor disputes.'[47] By 1786 the volume of litigation initiated by expatriate Americans had increased dramatically; in 1788 four regional Courts of Common Pleas were established to meet this need.[48] Although a sizeable number of suitors appeared in these courts on their own behalves, there was considerable reliance on non-professional attorneys-in-fact.[49] The appearance of this unauthorized Bar was one indication that Upper Canada's need for legal services had outstripped its supply of lawyers.

The Legislative Assembly's response to this problem was the Judicature Act of 1794, section two of which authorized Lieutenant Governor Simcoe to license as many British subjects 'not exceeding sixteen in number as he shall deem from their probity, education and condition of life best qualified to act as Advocates and Attorneys, in the conduct of all legal proceedings in this Province.' This enactment, which also introduced English civil procedure, was the linchpin of the plan evolved by Simcoe and Chief Justice Osgoode to bring 'the judicial structure of the province more closely to that of the mother country.' These British officials intended that the intricacies of common law pleading would prevent laymen and lawyers-in-fact from performing the law role, thereby facilitating the emergence of licensed lawyers. Members of the province's nascent merchant class, the proponents of republican values in Upper Canada, objected to the Judicature Act as an undue promotion of élitism.[50]

The Judicature Act also suspended the Ordinance of 1785 insofar as it had provided for training and examination of law students. Within two years the licences contemplated by the act had been granted, mostly to retired military officers; several who applied were rejected. No more than eight of these licensees carried on active practices. Upper Canada's legal profession thus became an eclectic but somewhat gentrified group by 1797; many of its members had limited formal training in law.[51]

In addition to generating demands for legal services, the Loyalists promoted the reception of English law, as the preambles of Upper Canada's reception statutes make clear. Although the Property and Civil Rights Act and the Criminal Law Reception Act were designed principally to supplant the Quebec Act, they helped to induce the rapid emergence of a class of indigenous lawyers.[52] The holus bolus reception of English law distinguishes Upper Canada from colonies of the first Empire such as Rhode Island, Connecticut, and Massachusetts, where the common law was not received in the early period and in some cases was not received at all.[53] The development of diverse local customs was not conducive to the rise of an integrated, centralized bar and produced different markets for legal services and patterns of legal training than did the monolithic reception of English law in Upper Canada. Moreover, the common law received in Upper Canada was moving rapidly away from the semi-feudal institution it had been in the early seventeenth century when the seaboard colonies were in their formative stages.[54] The role of lawyers in the new province therefore was potentially different from their counterparts in the seaboard colonies. Most important, English legal literature of the sort required to support an integrated bar, effective delivery of legal services, and formalized training in law was more readily and widely available in the early years of the nineteenth century than it had been at comparable stages in the development of the seaboard bars.[55] In short, the attributes of the legal system received were as relevant to the rapid rise of the Upper Canadian Bar and the development of its régimes of law training as was the mere fact of reception.

The American presence in Upper Canada also resulted in the importation of ideas about the role of lawyers that had developed over the course of a century and a half. On the eve of the Revolution the colonial American Bar was relatively well educated and had become an important element in commercial life. By 1750 the Boston Bar, for example, was a Harvard-dominated élite, while fifty per cent of the lawyers practising in New York in the 1770s held college degrees. The English Board of Trade ranked this group as inferior only to large-scale landowners in social status and above New York's burgeoning merchant class. A seven-year apprenticeship was the rule in that province. Many late eighteenth-century colonial lawyers were North American-born but had spent time at the Inns of Court.[56] Moreover, the colonial merchant class created a continuing market for legal services related to business paper, shipping, and insurance.[57] As a result of the relative pervasiveness of the professional legal presence in pre-Revolutionary American society and the extent to which their services were regarded as indispensable by the citizenry, expatriate Americans in Upper Canada were acclimatized to the notion of a distinctive bar with training appropriate to the dispensation of moderately sophisticated legal services.[58]

Two other characteristics of the Loyalists and late Loyalists distinguished them from the first arrivals in other British North American colonies and facilitated the early emergence of an Upper Canadian legal caste. Upper Canada was not created in the religious or revolutionary fervour that characterized the settlement of Massachusetts, Georgia, Maryland, or Pennsylvania. As a result, the developing legal profession never had to compete with a clerical élite to the same extent as the legal profession in certain seaboard colonies.[59] The hostility towards lawyers associated with Utopian régimes was not a part of the Upper Canadian experience. Moreover, since there was no merchant or planter class in early Upper Canada, there was no commercial élite to be offended politically by the rise of a powerful and well-organized bar as had been the case in Virginia and the Carolinas.[60] These features of Upper Canadian society remained prevalent for at least fifty years and clearly encouraged the rise of an integrated and powerful provincial Bar.

The British Crown regularly dispatched lawyers to Upper Canada to implement imperial policy. In the aftermath of the American Revolution, the mother country was particularly interested in keeping a tight rein on Canadian developments, and from the beginning its officials assumed a higher profile than they had in the former colonies. Through the export and employment of trained lawyers the Crown influenced the design and growth of the Upper Canadian Bar.

The first Chief Justice, William Osgoode, resided in Upper Canada between 1792 and 1794 when most of the judicial infrastructure was put in place. He was a graduate of Harrow and Oxford, had been admitted to Lincoln's Inn, and practised six years at the English Chancery Bar. He favoured a provincial bar built on the English model but with higher standards of admission. As Chief Justice, Speaker of the Legislative Council, and leading adviser to Lieutenant Governor Simcoe, Osgoode was well placed to affect legislation and policy. He also influenced the nomination of his successor. Although the heir apparent was Justice W.D. Powell, whose first legal training had occurred in Boston, followed by practice in Montreal, Osgoode insisted upon the appointment of the English lawyer, Middle Templar John Elmsley.[61]

John White, the first Attorney General, also was English. An Inner Templar who arrived in Upper Canada in 1792, White was outspoken in his criticism of legal services rendered through the 1790s by lay attorneys. He favoured the creation of a graded bar closely modelled on the Inns of Court and the Society of Gentlemen Practitioners. White was the driving force behind the nascent Law Society of Upper Canada.[62]

Colonel Simcoe, the first Lieutenant Governor, was not a lawyer but was compulsively English. He regarded the establishment of a system of professional education and the duplication of English customs as instrumental to his goal of fostering political attitudes along British rather than American lines. The cultivation of an aristocracy and the promulgation of English institutions were principal values underlying what Simcoe did and said, including his promotion of the legal profession. Although he failed to organize a full-service university on the model of medievel Oxford, his program did result in the chartering of the Law Society.[63]

The Society's organic law was passed during the tenure of President Russell, Simcoe's successor. Solicitor General Gray advised Russell that the object of the legislation was 'to secure to the Country a learned and honourable body of Professional Men to assist their fellow subjects, and to support the Constitution.' No person was to be awarded the Society's degree 'without having been regularly educated and duly called to the situation.' Gray speculated that the scheme would ensure that persons educated in Upper Canada would become the dominant members of the élite, a result he regarded as highly desirable.[64] Simcoe shared this concern about creating a high-quality, all-Canadian bar, complemented by a respectable and well-trained judiciary, in order to prevent appeals to Great Britain. For Simcoe, reliance upon the Judicial Committee of the Privy Council would be burdensome and would 'appear to the Inhabitants of the United States as Badges of inconvenient Subjection.'[65]

Although the Law Society bore some resemblance to the Inns of Court, it was essentially a hybrid whose English parentage was somewhat recessive. In particular, its internal structure and its treatment of legal education differed in several crucial ways from the Inns familiar to White, Elmsley, Russell, and Osgoode. Until 1753 when William Blackstone delivered the first of what later became the Vinerian Lectures in common law at Oxford, the Inns of Court had been the only English fora for formal training in the common law. However, the eighteenth-century Inns were primarily social and disciplinary bodies in which instruction had ceased and examinations were perfunctory. The significant features of the Inns of Court familiar to Upper Canada's English bureaucrats were their academic decadence, gentlemanly atmosphere, and monopoly over legal services.[66]

Attorney General White opposed the adoption in 1799 of the Society's first two rules about legal education, which eventually patterned law training more after the old Quebec and New England models than after legal education at the Inns of Court. The Upper Canadian judiciary, seventy-five per cent of whom had English backgrounds or legal training, refused to ratify these rules. As Bencher Robert Baldwin noted in 1833, it was no coincidence that the majority of Convocation's regulations about law training passed thereafter were disguised as 'resolutions' or 'standing orders' which did not require the approbation of the Society's official visitors, many of whom were English during the period about which Baldwin spoke.[67]

Comments made in Convocation respecting the origins of the Society provide additional insight into the genealogy of the Law Society and the extent to which its programs were patterned after those of the Inns of Court. In the process of impeaching James Doyle in 1833, a select committee on Doyle's case reported that 'this Society is to every extent one of the Inns of Court in the Mother Country.' The committee concluded that the Law Society's authority regarding admission, call, and expulsion could best be understood by reference to old texts on the Inns.[68] Convocation, however, disputed this determination by seizing upon Lord Mansfield's 1780 judgment in *Regina* v *Gray's Inn* which indicated that the prerogative writs did not lie against the Inns of Court since they were voluntary societies and not bodies corporate, and that redress against them had to be by application to the judges as official visitors.[69] As the Benchers noted, the Law Society was, and is, a body corporate whose power flows from the legislature and is not delegated to it by the judiciary. Accordingly, when Convocation in 1840 had to consider again the Society's constitution, its counsel, Toronto Chancery lawyer Robert Easton Burns, cited with approval Bartholomew Thomas Duhigg's 1806 treatise on the Irish Inns of Court and concluded that 'the Law Society of this Province appears ... to stand upon a footing more analogous to the King's Inns of Ireland than to the Inns of Court of England.'[70] On other occasions the Benchers recurred to old practices related to 'the Irish degree of Barrister-at-Law.'[71]

Rules, resolutions, and orders promulgated by Convocation and particularly regulations regarding legal education magnified differences that existed at the outset between the Law Society of Upper Canada and the English Inns of Court. While the structural similarities are superficially compelling, substantive counterparts are limited. Indeed, developing differences were not lost on British lawyers. By the mid-nineteenth century the editor of the English *Law Times* remarked that with respect to legal education, 'young Canada has taken the lead of old England.'[72]

Upper Canada's legal profession emerged in one decade. American colonials brought to the new province a market for legal services and certain kinds of notions about the role of law and lawyers in North American society. Seaboard lawyers informed Convocation with knowledge of the colonial Bar meetings. British officials contributed their belief in the importance of a provincial aristocracy and institutions modelled loosely along English lines. French Canadian influence led to the perpetuation of a statutory requirement of supervised legal training followed by a mandatory bar admission examination. The 1797 Law Society Act was the result of this convergence of traditions. Over the next ninety years, Upper Canadian engineers implemented the design of these early architects.

ELEMENTS OF NINETEENTH-CENTURY LEGAL EDUCATION

Section five of the Law Society Act established bar admission regulations for the fledgling profession. Persons seeking a call to the Bar had to register on the Society's 'Books' for five years and be at least twenty-one years of age at the time of their admission to practice. There was no requirement that aspiring barristers be apprenticed to a member of the profession, but section six specified that prospective solicitors serve three years under articles of clerkship.[73] Convocation was rigid and meticulous in its enforcement of these formal provisions. Many calls to the Bar were postponed when the Society discovered that the applicants had not spent a full five years enrolled on its 'Books.'[74] Each student also had to pay £10 for admission to the Society, £20 for his call to the Bar, and £5 in annual dues. The Treasurer was empowered to lend money to impoverished students to defer this expense, and other members of the Society sometimes acted as bondsmen for aspiring barristers, so that impecunious applicants would not be barred from the profession.[75]

The Society's second operative Convocation in the fall of 1799 framed rules seven and nine, which remained cornerstones of legal education until the mid-twentieth century. Proposed by Solicitor General Gray, these rules fused training for the profession and required all law students to complete an apprenticeship. In the early years laymen regarded the apprenticeship as onerous; it was alleged that the mandatory training period protected the monopoly of the few, discouraged an increase in the supply of lawyers, and blocked the road to the Bar for all but the most ambitious young men.[76]

These criticisms notwithstanding, the Society regularly raised its barriers to entry. An entrance examination which included Latin and English literature was introduced in 1819; the difficulty of this examination and the number of subjects covered were increased at several junctures, mostly before 1842. Term-keeping and a bar admission examination, which tested candidates' 'legal attainments and general competence to discharge duties,' supplied additional structure.[77] First and second intermediate examinations which students were obliged to take at specified intervals were added in 1832, 1868, and 1872. The inauguration in the 1830s of classes, lectures, and club meetings sponsored by the Society further enhanced the educative quality of law training and diminished the importance of rote apprenticeship. These components of nineteenth-century legal education constitute Upper Canada's bar admission régime in the broad sense, since failure of any element resulted in being enjoined from trying the bar admission examination. Each facet of the program is treated topically in the pages that follow, moving through the requirements as a student-at-law or articled clerk would have progressed. Until about 1870 Convocation's animating goal was to perpetuate and refine a system with roots to 1797, worked out in the early nineteenth century, and in large measure implemented by 1832.

ENTRANCE REQUIREMENTS AND PRE-LAW TRAINING

During the first twenty-two years of the Society's existence, students were not obliged to satisfy preliminary educational requirements. Although there were formal requisites such as being at least sixteen years of age (eighteen after 1861), paying the admission fee, and engaging a principal, the early emphasis was upon social and ethical criteria: the Society was to be composed of 'honourable' men. Persons licensed to practise in England, Scotland, Ireland, or another British North American province could be admitted upon 'production of testimonials of good character and conduct.'[78] The 'Affidavits of Admission' submitted by the prospective principals of Walter Butler Wilkinson of Cornwall and Levius Peters Sherwood of Brockville, the Society's first students, recited that the applicants were 'qualified by education, principles and habits of life' to be admitted as students-at-law. Similar ritualistic recitals appeared in most early petitions for admission and later became a mandatory part of the entrance process.[79]

In practice, the Treasurer put petitions for admission on Convocation table with 'his reports thereon and thereunto annexed.' These essentially formalistic reports included statements that a 'Notice of Presentation for Admission' had been tendered in a timely manner, that all rules and standing orders of Convocation had been complied with, and that no notice of objection to the admission of the candidate had been received. The posting of lists over the 'northern fireplaces in Convocation Chamber and in the Common Hall [at Osgoode],' naming all those who had filed their term's notice, facilitated such objections.[80]

Through most of the antebellum period, indeed through much of the nineteenth century, candidates for admission to American law schools and state bars also were required to be of good moral character and of a certain age. School-related entrance qualifications did not become common until early in the twentieth century.[81] In Upper Canada the Law Society imposed preliminary education requirements after 1819. Applicants for enrolment had to do written translations of parts of Cicero's *Orations* and satisfy Convocation of their 'acquaintance' with Latin and English composition in any way the Benchers specified.[82] No reason appears in the 'Minutes' for this change in policy, which was promoted by Attorney General Robinson, Solicitor General Henry John Boulton of the

Middle Temple, and Dr Baldwin. Although twelve to fifteen students were then being admitted annually, concern about the size of the profession did not develop for another decade, Convocation had not disciplined any student, the Society had not disbarred anyone, and there is no indication that practitioners were dissatisfied with the general education of their students. Indeed, half a century later Ontario's medical doctors were still engaged in bitter debates about whether similar entrance requirements should be adopted.[83] Following promulgation of the Law Society's 1819 rule, and prior to raising these standards in 1825, four applicants failed the entrance examination. David Lockwood Fairfield of Hallowell, who was to be apprenticed to Simon Washburn, a prominent member of the York Bar and a popular principal, failed three times due to 'lack of education.'[84]

Upon the urging of James Buchanan Macaulay and Dr Baldwin, Convocation made the entrance examination more difficult in 1825: 'in future the Student on his examination will be expected to exhibit a general knowledge of English, Grecian and Roman History, a becoming acquaintance with one of the ancient Latin poets as Virgil, Horace or Juvenal and the like acquaintance with some of the celebrated prose works of the ancients such as Salest or Cicero's *Offices* as well as his *Orations* or any Authors of equal celebrity which may be adopted as the standard Books of the several District Schools – And it will also be expected that the Student will show the Society some reasonable portion of mathematical instruction.'[85] Before the next major change in entrance examinations in 1832, a handful of applicants failed to satisfy the Benchers with their preparation, typically due to lack of familiarity with the classics.[86] One student applying for a second time was admonished for his poor showing in history and geography but was admitted; another applicant was advised 'to resume his studies.'[87] The Examiners regularly instructed those who failed to 'kindly call again next term' and unsuccessful candidates often were admitted at a later date. In the face of an increasing failure rate, Middle Templar and Law Reporter Thomas Taylor unsuccessfully brought a motion in 1826 to relax entrance requirements. The concession was to forward the descriptions of the Society's entrance standards to the Masters of the District Public Schools.[88]

The first Monday and Saturday of each judicial term were 'examination days.' Entrance examinations were administered orally in full Convocation; questions were put by or through the Treasurer. Appointment of days and times for examinations, attendance of all Benchers, and strict adherence to rules was supposed to 'excite a feeling in the minds of students, of the necessity of study, as well as correct conduct; and tend materially to raise the general character of the profession.'[89]

The social prerequisites for admission also were made more rigorous in the late 1820s. Solicitor General and future Chief Justice of Newfoundland, H.J. Boulton, introduced a rule to the effect that:

no person shall be entered on the books of the Society as a Student unless he presents to the Society at or before his examination written declaration upon honour by one Bencher or two barristers that the person so applying for admission is properly known to him or them; and that such applicant is in his or their opinion qualified by principles, education and habits of life to become a Member of the Society.[90]

This declaration was to serve 'not merely as an introduction to Convocation ... but as a pledge from the member giving it that the Candidate for admission is by character and by habits a proper person to be admitted into the Society. It ought, therefore, always to be procured from some gentleman to whom the Candidate has been previously known, as it might probably otherwise not be received.'[91] A companion regulation promulgated four years later required that prospective students give one term's notice of their intention to apply, specifying 'particulars of the family residence and connections.' Its purpose was to 'give the Benchers ample opportunity of making the necessary inquiries' and to ensure that 'every facility for acquiring the necessary information would be afforded when a stranger offers himself.'[92] According to Treasurer George Ridout, students' 'habits of conduct and character' were important subjects of inquiry and enabled the Society to consider the propriety of admitting particular applicants.[93] Although there is no indication that this scrutiny ever resulted in a candidate's rejection, it must have constituted a considerable barrier to entry.

The declaration by one Bencher or two barristers gave rise to disagreement among members of the Society. Robert Baldwin's 'Committee on Revision of the By-Laws' determined in 1832 that such certificates were undesirable because they were 'very frequently given as a matter of course,' and tended to interfere with Convocation's assessment of a candidate's suitability. Baldwin feared that on occasions when students failed the entrance examination, the declarations added 'to the unpleasantness of being obliged to reject the candidate, an apparent disregard of the Certificate of those by whom he was recommended.' The committee's view later was adopted by Convocation; 'the admission or

The Honourable Robert Baldwin, CB, Treasurer,
The Law Society of Upper Canada 1847–8, 1850–9
Oil portrait attributed to George Théodore Berthon
(The Law Society of Upper Canada)

rejection of the party presenting [the Certificate] would nevertheless depend, at least as to his education, wholly upon the view which those to whom his examination was entrusted, took of his qualifications.'[94] As a result of this change of policy, the admissions process became more open, and failures of the entrance examination became common.

The Society found administration of admission requirements time-consuming. This problem also was taken up by Baldwin's Committee on Consolidation and resulted in publication of an 'Appendix of Forms' to 'prevent the inconvenience and delay which have sometimes occurred from the papers of Candidates for Admission and Call being incomplete.'[95] However, by the late 1830s, ten or a dozen applications for admission each term was the rule, and formal streamlining of the process became an inadequate solution. Moreover, the Benchers had become dilatory and disorganized; many entrance and call examinations were postponed due to want of a quorum in Convocation.[96] As a result, Convocation agreed to appoint an examiner in order to 'establish a more uniform system of Examination of Candidates for Matriculation as Members of this Society.'[97]

Hugh Nelson Gwynne, a classicist from Trinity College, Dublin, and brother of Justice John Wellington Gwynne of the Ontario Court of Common Pleas and later the Supreme Court of Canada, was retained as Examiner in the summer of 1842. He had been a master in Upper Canada College. During his thirty-year tenure he also served the Law Society as Secretary, Librarian, and Sub-Treasurer. There are many accounts of Gwynne's rigour and eccentricity.[98] It has been said that during the age in which he held sway he was the most notable character of Osgoode Hall. On occasion, applicants petitioned Convocation for reexamination on the basis that they were 'made nervous' or 'intimidated' by the Examiner.[99] At the Trinity Term 1843 entrance examination, for example, Gwynne failed every candidate. However, he did not have much direct impact upon the Society's education policy. With the exception of a minor restructuring of entrance examinations he orchestrated in 1842, Gwynne was merely a conscientious and imposing minister of Law Society policy. Part of his salary was paid by the initiates; each person trying an entrance examination was required to provide him with 20s.[100]

The Benchers first discussed the division of entering students into classes in 1832. A 'Select Committee on Improvements in the Mode of Conducting Examinations' consisted of George Ridout, Middle Templar Dr John Rolph, and Robert Baldwin, all of York. Since 'the evils of the present system which leaves the young man of the first talents and most persevering Industry undistinguished from the least talented and industrious of his Fellows will be readily seen and acknowledged,' the committee recommended that the range of pre-law study of the candidates should be translated into membership in one of three classes.[101] This system continued until 1877. With respect to the advanced class, the committee concluded that 'no young man within whose reach such advantages are placed [a Collegiate education, good natural abilities, and laborious industry] *ought* to commence the study of Law at an earlier age [20] or until he has fully availed himself of such means of intellectual improvement.'[102] Convocation's goal therefore was not merely to reward those who were better prepared than their confreres, but to emphasize that prospective law students were to take advantage of all opportunities afforded by their families' geographic and economic station in life. Less privileged candidates were welcome at a younger age, notwithstanding failure of opportunity, so long as they had done what they could. In view of the substantial differences in the books upon which the categories of applicants were examined and the four-year age differential among the entering classes, the intimation must have been that less advantaged persons who showed promise would benefit from early admission to the Society. The sons of Upper Canadians of low estate were not to be judged by the same standards of education and duty as the sons of gentlemen.

The most advanced class, 'Optime,' signified 'the greatest chance of success in the profession.' Members of this class were to be twenty years of age, have had some collegiate education, and be of good natural ability and 'laborious industry.' They were required to pass entrance examinations in English, Latin, and Greek languages, geometry, algebra, moral philosophy, metaphysics, rhetoric, belles lettres, geography, astronomy, and history. Tests in trigonometry and mechanics were added later. The Society conceded that 'in the present State of the Province, but few may perhaps be able to prepare themselves to pass such an examination [however] the ambition to attain it will materially improve the education of that part of our youth in general who are intended for the profession.'[103] Although several persons tried, no applicant ever was admitted to the Optime Class.

The 'Senior' Class was for those who had availed themselves of 'the ordinary opportunities for improvement' available in the province. The committee believed that with industry, 'and no one without industry can become a lawyer,' virtually anyone could qualify for this class by age eighteen. There were examinations in English and Latin, and either geometry, algebra, and moral philosophy, or Greek, geography, astronomy, and history.[104] Approximately a third of the Society's students were Seniors.

Admission to the 'Junior' Class required 'the smallest quantum of Education which can under any circumstances whatsoever justify the reception of Young Men as candidates for the profession.' This included 'only such acquirements as [the Society] conceived absolutely indispensable,' namely English and Latin, and either mathematics and geography, or history.[105] The majority of the Society's initiates were Juniors.

As a result of these changes in admissions policy, applications lagged through the 1830s, and failures at the entrance examination became common. However, many persons who were able to hurdle the Law Society's barriers to entry remarked about the ease with which they were able to do so. Patrick McGregor of Kingston spent only ten weeks in 1834 preparing for the preliminary examination. The entrance papers of Donald Wellington Bruce Macaulay of Cornwall filed in 1833 simply recited that he had studied Latin and Greek classics, mathematics, and geography in the District Public School of the Eastern District under the Reverend Hugh Urquhart. Moreover, most of the second generation of Upper Canada's judiciary (Chief Justices Robinson, Macaulay, McLean, Cameron, Harrison, and Spragge) were admitted to the Society as students on the basis of preliminary education acquired in the province.[106] Access to the Society apparently was not as difficult as the formal prerequisites might lead one to believe.

Obviously, the ease of access to elementary and secondary education in Upper Canada related directly to the Law Society's admission standards. Convocation considered its feeders to be such schools as Upper Canada College, Upper Canada Academy, Grantham Academy, and the various District grammar schools. Modifications of the rules about admissions, including Robert Baldwin's *1833 Rules*, routinely were forwarded to the presidents, principals, and masters of these schools.[107] From the 1840s, as the number of grammar (or High) schools multiplied, the requisite preliminary education became increasingly available, and by the 1870s even very small urban communities had high schools which could provide the standard general education required by the Law Society.[108]

The second quarter of the nineteenth century witnessed the appearance in Upper Canada of liberal arts colleges such as King's, Trinity, Queen's, and Victoria. The Law Society was apparently unwilling to make any special concessions to the graduates of these new colleges, but the Legislative Assembly insisted it do so. Laws of 1837 and 1847, modelled after a similar Lower Canadian statute, required Convocation to reduce the period of tuition for certain college graduates from five years to three 'in consideration of the learning and abilities requisite for the taking such [college] degree' and in case graduates 'may be deterred by the length of service required for the admission [to the practice of law].'[109] Even when the second of these reforms was enacted, fewer than ten per cent of the Society's students held college degrees.

The Benchers interpreted the provincial acts narrowly, declining to apply them to schools or degrees not specifically mentioned. This resulted in dissatisfaction among Queen's graduates, since they were not covered by the 1837 statute. Moreover, Convocation refused to extend to university graduates any benefits not expressly granted by the Assembly. In particular, until 1871 university degree holders had to take the Society's entrance examinations like other candidates; even after that date the waiver of entrance examinations for college graduates excited opposition from some Benchers.[110]

The only significant gesture the Society made to the colleges was the creation in 1846 of a fourth category of entering students, the 'University' Class. Applicants were examined on materials roughly analogous to those for candidates for the Senior Class. After 1856, students admitted to the University Class were ranked on the basis of their performance on the entrance examinations, and these rankings were published.[111]

The Law Society's pre-1871 failure to extend any faith or credit to college degree holders provoked at least two kinds of reactions among laymen. College lecturers often were anxious that their curricula and reading lists conform with the admission requirements. At the other end of the spectrum John Langton, Vice Chancellor of the University of Toronto in the early 1850s, complained bitterly about Convocation's breach of the spirit of the permissive laws about university graduates.[112]

Following the reforms of 1837 and before mid-century, half a dozen college graduates entered the Society's program. However, during the 1850s the percentage of students admitted who held university degrees increased dramatically. At least sixty were accepted; by the end of the decade almost two-thirds of the Society's students were university alumni. The percentage of candidates admitted as college graduates declined during the 1860s such that in the first University Class taken in without having to try the entrance examination in 1872, there were seven university degree holders; fifty candidates had applied for admission, seventeen were failed by Examiner George Mountain Evans, and twenty-six were admitted without university training. These statistics are typical of the 1870s and 1880s.

Permissive rules applicable to university graduates were extended in 1877 to college students who had taken examinations in subjects covered by the Society's entrance examination. A new group of applicants thus became eligible to study law without passing through Convocation's screening process.[113] Over the next twelve years the proportion of aspiring lawyers who took advantage of this reform was about equal to those admitted as university graduates. Through the late 1870s and 1880s the number of candidates accepted on the basis of the entrance examination was consistently larger than the total of university graduates and those whose examinations were waived, and often was three times the size of the latter two groups combined. Enrolment in a general college program appears to have been regarded as a simple alternative to a legal education throughout most of the nineteenth century.

The mode in which the entrance examination was conducted, but not its content, also changed significantly towards the end of the period under consideration.[114] In 1871, parallelling changes in the examination for call, the entrance test was divided into written and oral parts. The written portion was standardized in each term and was graded by the Examining Committee out of 1000; the oral examination was conducted in Latin and graded out of 300. Passage of the written test became a prerequisite to taking the oral examination.[115]

The University of Toronto used the same admission examinations as the Law Society after 1878 and shared responsibility for their administration. This arrangement was the result of a combined protest by the Minister of Education, the Examiners for Matriculation, and the Senate of the University of Toronto regarding the 'want of uniformity' between the university and the Law Society with respect to entrance examinations. The university argued that lack of standardization caused inconvenience for the masters of collegiate institutes and high schools. A joint committee established to co-ordinate examinations, to which Convocation dispatched five of its law lecturers, agreed that the university should hold the Easter and Trinity term examinations, while the Society would host those held in Michaelmas and Hilary terms.[116]

The Law Society's academic and social prerequisites to admission reflect several themes of legal education in Upper Canada. As early as 1797 social and ethical criteria were emphasized. While the satisfaction of these prerequisites was superintended variously by Convocation, selected

Benchers, the Society's Examiner, the 'Standing Committee on Legal Education,' and the 'Sub-Committee on Examinations,' the means used to gather information about a candidate's family, social status, and preliminary education did not vary significantly after 1832. Requirements related to literacy and erudition were introduced in 1819 and intensified in the second quarter of the nineteenth century. The failure rate on the examination to test these acquirements increased dramatically in the 1850s and levelled off at about fifty per cent by 1880. For over seventy years, the minimum preliminary education requirement remained the colonial version of a classical education that could be acquired readily in the province's grammar schools after about 1840. In short, the content of the entrance examination which William Renwick Riddell's classmates took in the 1880s was not substantially different from that taken by John Alexander Macdonald and Oliver Mowat in the 1830s. Problems related to the admission of university graduates arose in the late 1830s but were not addressed coherently by the Law Society until the 1870s. A forty per cent reduction in the period of apprenticeship and the 1872 waiver of entrance examinations notwithstanding, the proportion of university alumni admitted to the Society's program peaked in the 1850s and declined steadily until 1889. At least until mid-century, a number of the applicants admitted to law study were of low estate and primarily from rural areas. Regional patterns of entry did not change much over time, except that the percentage of students from the southwestern counties increased sharply in the 1830s.

To complete a study of admission policies and their effect, one would want to know more about the social backgrounds of law students and the proportion of those admitted in each period who came from private schools, public schools, colleges, or no school. How did the formal barriers to entry translate into actual social or academic barriers to entry for young Upper Canadians? The Law Society's records reveal total numbers of failures in each period and that the entrance examination was not merely the bête noire of Smiths and Jones; Oslers, Vankoughnets, Boultons, and Buells failed too. However, neither the 'Minutes' nor the 'Books' provide sufficiently regular information for systematic statements about these matters. Information that is available points in several directions. Convocation clearly was attempting to align its behaviour with its understanding of how universities admitted students. A striking continuity of policies and forms also characterized the admissions process. Finally, the application of different barriers to entry to divergent groups of candidates suggests a desire to further meritocracy.

APPRENTICESHIPS

Histories of legal education in the common law world often focus upon a perceived transformation from training through apprenticeship to formal schooling in a university. Yet when one surveys the common law empire of 1700 or 1820 one discovers that only a small minority of jurisdictions required periods of apprenticeship for law students. In 1763 the Inns of Court adopted a five-year apprenticeship requirement, but it was not enforced systematically. Neither the Society of Gentlemen Practitioners nor its successor, the English Law Society, imposed articles of clerkship.[117]

In the eighteenth-century American colonies alternative routes to the Bar included self-education through independent study, scribing in the office of a court clerk, reading at an English Inn of Court, enrolling in a colonial college that offered instruction in law, and apprenticing in a practitioner's office. A few colonies such as New York, New Hampshire, and Massachusetts prescribed apprenticeships.[118] During the nineteenth century, however, even the custom of apprenticing fell rapidly into disfavour, chiefly as a result of the liberalization or removal of bar admission requirements. In most nineteenth-century American jurisdictions few candidates for admission to the Bar served any kind of coherent apprenticeship, and the vast majority clearly were not required to do so.

The transition in law training more often has been from no systematic pattern of training or bar admission to formalized schooling, rather than from apprenticeship to schooling. In Upper Canada, with the possible exception of the 1797–1832 period, neither mode of law training ever existed in a discrete or exclusive form and the transition, if any occurred, was not sequential. Pioneering university law teachers like Christopher Columbus Langdell in the 1870s and Cecil Augustus Wright in the 1940s developed the ahistorical theory about transformation from mere apprenticeship to formal schooling to further their political or pedagogical goals. Because this characterization does not describe a general phenomenon, it is inappropriate to measure Upper Canadian developments against it.

Upper Canada required apprenticeship for articled clerks after 1797 and for students-at-law after 1800. For about three decades it was the heart of Convocation's law-training operation. The theory of the early Benchers seems to have been that their dozen law offices would function as the 'regional colleges' of Convocation's educational enterprise, rather like medieval Oxbridge. Practitioners took this posting seriously during the early years; pre-Union Upper Canadian lawyers often read law with their students. Early petitions for award of the Diploma of Barrister routinely recited the name of the office in which the student received his 'professional education.'[119] However, aspects of legal education grafted onto this model in the 1820s and 1830s diminished the importance of apprenticeship. Participation in York-based law clubs which originated in 1821 and became a *de jure* obligation in the next decade, intermediate examinations, and the reading of mandatory texts (the availability of which often was limited to Toronto) all subtracted from time students spent in the offices of their principals, particularly when they were indentured to provincial practitioners.

Section four of the Law Society Act empowered each member of the Society to take one student-at-law. Since many of the licences to practise dispensed by Simcoe and Russell under the Judicature Act of 1794 expressly withheld the privilege of taking apprentices, this portion of the Law Society Act probably was permissive rather than restrictive. Legislation of 1803 permitted practitioners to take two students and allowed the Solicitor General and Attorney General to instruct three apprentices. A companion statute promoted by Sheriff Alexander C. Macdonell and merchant Richard Cartwright, which empowered Lieutenant Governor Peter Hunter to license six lawyers following a cursory examination by Chief Justice Henry Allcock of Lincoln's Inn, was enacted because 'great inconvenience has arisen and is now experienced ... in several parts of this Province, from a want of a sufficient number of persons duly authorized to practice the profession of the Law, and unless the number can be speedily increased, justice will in many places be with great difficulty administered.' This recital, together with petitions received by the Legislative Assembly, suggests that once again the need for legal services had outstripped the supply of lawyers and helps to account for the enactment of both 1803 laws without apparent opposition.[120] Further amending legislation of 1807, which remained in force at least until 1889, permitted each practitioner to take four apprentices.[121]

These limitations on the number of students lawyers were authorized to instruct were fundamental to the development of legal education in Upper Canada. They go far to account for the province's failure to produce the private or law office schools common in early nineteenth-century America, which provided the womb for university law schools.[122] The restrictions also explain some of the basic differences between Upper Canadian legal and medical education. In medicine, where limitations on apprentices did not exist, office schools on the American model flourished.[123] Restrictive provincial laws prevented law offices from providing a similar bridge between rote apprenticeship and university-centred schooling in law and helped to ensure the continuing domination of Osgoode Hall. An aspiring Upper Canadian barrister was primarily a student of the Law Society; there were no direct contractual undertakings between students-at-law and their principals. Although the name of one's master was recorded in documents like the 'Personal Report of the Student to the Treasurer,' the terms of a student's service were specified exclusively in Convocation's regulations.[124] An Oxford County apprentice observed in 1861 that 'the majority of law students get no salary [during their apprenticeships].' Yet some Upper Canadian law students were being paid by their principals as early as the third quarter of the nineteenth century. Nathaniel Francis Hagel, who apprenticed at Woodstock and Toronto in the 1860s, received a wage of $5-15 a month from his principals. In other cases parents and guardians actually paid as much as £120 to obtain positions for their sons and wards in prestigious law offices. Indeed, it has been said that it was a great favour for prominent Upper Canadian lawyers to receive students without fee.[125]

Naturally, some practitioners took apprentices more regularly than others. Until about 1820 Levius Peters Sherwood of Brockville was a popular principal. During the 1820s and early 1830s Dr William Baldwin and Robert Baldwin of York took students more often than other members of the Society. Later in the 1830s Miles O'Reilly of Hamilton and Marshall Spring Bidwell and Simon Washburn of York regularly served as principals. In the following decade Law Reporter Henry Sherwood of Brockville, George Stephen Jarvis of Cornwall, and Rolland McDonald of St Catharines instructed large numbers of students.

Apprenticeships often were split between two or more principals during the second and third quarters of the nineteenth century. The first mention of this phenomenon appears in the 'Minutes' for 1832 and followed imposition of the requirement that students keep term at York.[126] In practice, this regulation obliged students to spend about the last year and a half of their apprenticeships in the capital and apparently required those not indentured at York (which became Toronto in 1834) to shift apprenticeships. This reform affected many students since about eighty per cent of Upper Canada's law students were not apprenticed in the capital at this time, and since Convocation was scrupulous and uncompromising in its enforcement of term-keeping duties and attendance at Toronto law lectures when attendance was mandatory. During the first two or three decades that splitting apprenticeships became necessary, there was little evident opposition from the Bar, which is surprising since the ratio of country to Toronto practitioners was about five to one during this period and the proponents of the program were Torontonians. Moreover, when serious resistance to the centralization of law training at Toronto began to develop in the 1870s, the ratio was still at least four to one.[127]

The Law Society insisted that when students were not keeping term, attending lectures, or taking examinations they be at the disposal of their principals. Numerous applicants were rejected when it appeared to the Benchers that their attention would be diverted by other commitments, such as teaching.[128] Similarly, Convocation refused to call candidates whose apprenticeships had been interrupted by other activities, such as employment or travel. Phillip Fergusson Hall's application for call was rejected because he had been in debtors' prison at Kingston for part of his apprenticeship.[129]

What students received in exchange for commitment of labour and capital to apprenticeship is difficult to determine. Accounts of the experience that survive tend to be anecdotal, self-congratulatory, or critical. In any event, the records are sparse and not necessarily representative. Although nineteenth-century periodicals contain numerous letters from law students and editorials decrying the tedium, long hours, and lack of intellectual challenge associated with legal apprenticeship, criticism tended to surface when other aspects of the Society's law-training programs were in temporary remission, namely 1848–50 and 1878–89.[130] Typical of this criticism were comments contained in a memorial from the Osgoode Club, a voluntary association of law students, presented to Convocation in 1849:

The Office of Attorney or Solicitor is now the only Law School for the great majority of the Law Students in [Canada West], their only teachers, men whose business precludes them from imparting regular systematic instruction even when qualified by nature and education to perform the function of that office. The consequence is that the Law Student's instruction is almost necessarily confined to the formal business of the Office, and the routine of the practice of the Courts, and appears better adopted to make him a kind of superior copying machine, or an adept in chicane, or at best a mere sciolist, than a scientific Lawyer.[131]

Thirty years later Thomas Ambrose Goreham reported that his apprenticeship was spent 'learning where the clients of [his] principal lived or, when [he] was of more sedentary disposition, learning to copy letters and to reduce legal scrawl to legibility.' John Edwin Farewell spent most of his

Toronto apprenticeship in the 1860s 'serving subpoenas and assembling evidence.' And another commentator concluded as a result of an early oral history project that 'in [the period before 1890] most students-at-law in Ontario had been laboriously occupied in the transcription of pleadings, contracts, letters and the like.'[132]

However, biographies of eminent Upper Canadian lawyers and reported cases in which the scope of a legal apprentice's authority to act was litigated imply that some students did more than transcribe letters and serve subpoenas. During his training in the Kingston law offices of George MacKenzie in the 1830s, for example, John A. Macdonald ran errands, searched titles, transcribed documents, and made pressed copies of correspondence on the wetted tissue leaves of letter-books. He also opened a branch office for his principal in Napanee, thirty miles from Kingston. Although Macdonald received regular instructions from MacKenzie by horseback courier, he appears to have run the daily affairs of the Napanee office. In the third year of his apprenticeship, the future Prime Minister took charge of Lowther P. Macpherson's Hallowell-Picton law office while Macpherson recovered abroad from bronchitis. He returned to MacKenzie in Kingston just before the end of his apprenticeship and took Oliver Mowat as his first student two weeks before he was called to the Bar.[133] In the nineteenth century all Upper Canadian Queen's Bench, Common Pleas, and Supreme Court motions were heard at Toronto. Motions regularly were the occasion of relatively sophisticated legal arguments. Since students-at-law often were assigned to appear on these applications, and because provincial practitioners habitually retained Toronto firms to argue Chambers motions, the opportunities to acquire this kind of experience must have been considerable for students apprenticed to Toronto lawyers who did extensive agency work or had large Chambers practices.

The regulations of Convocation relating to apprenticeship made no mention of serving one's principal in ways not related to the practice of law. Conversely, the indentures of colonial American law students often specified such duties, as well as avoidance of places that might bring a master's name into disrepute, maintaining confidentiality, and abstention from matrimony and fornication. Perhaps as a result, Upper Canadian students-at-law often had leisure time. Charles Durand, who apprenticed at Robert Berrie's Hamilton law offices in the 1830s, reported that 'although writing [my principal's documents] as my duties required me to do, I found time to write books about various things, a book on birds and one on trees, several on poetry, and a great many political letters in the

Hamilton Free Press.' Other students read novels, history, biography, economics, and politics as often as they read law.[134]

The surroundings in which Ontario's law students worked in the nineteenth century were substantially different from those in which they work in the late twentieth century. George MacKenzie's branch office in Napanee was in the corner of a country store crowded with stoves, hardware, pork barrels, cloth, and kegs of beer. In other jurisdictions lawyers typically worked at home and their apprentices often boarded with them. Although it is known that half the lawyers practising in Hamilton in the 1850s worked in their own homes and that students Macdonald and Mowat boarded with their Kingston principals in the 1830s, foreign models yield an hypothesis which is untested with respect to Upper Canada but which is highly plausible.[135] The general lay-out of offices seems to have been to line the walls of one or two rooms of a house with 'pigeon-holes' in the manner of an old post office. This mode of decorating provided a filing system; one pigeon-hole was assigned to each client and typically contained the client's will, the deed to his land, his mortgage, and any relevant trust instruments.[136]

The only significant formal change in apprenticeship requirements during the period under consideration was the reduction in 1837 and 1847 of the term of service from five years to three for certain university graduates. The introduction of a similar provision in England in 1793 notwithstanding, the precise precedent for this enactment probably was an analogous Lower Canadian statute.[137] The noteworthy features of the plan were that it was introduced by the Legislative Assembly in response to agitation by college administrators, that none of the other components of law training was reduced proportionately (which meant that members of the University Class, for example, spent only about a year and a half under full-time apprenticeship), and that Convocation's hostility to these régimes was expressed in its formalistic construction of the relevant provisions. The 1837 act applied only to King's College and the universities of the United Kingdom. The trustees of Queen's College pressed the legislature in 1847 for extension of this statutory privilege to Queen's graduates. When they were joined by the trustees of Victoria College, a law was passed providing advanced standing at Osgoode Hall for alumni of both schools and future degree-granting colleges in Canada West.[138]

The plans of King's, Queen's, and Trinity administrators notwithstanding, few students took immediate advantage of the acts to reduce their tuition at Osgoode Hall. Through the 1840s fewer than ten per cent of the

Society's initiates held college degrees. The percentage peaked in the late 1850s at about sixty and declined through the 1860s and 1870s until it rested around thirty for the fourth quarter of the nineteenth century. Declining percentages of university graduates who sought admission to the Society in the 1870s must be considered together with the resolution which waived the entrance examination for collegians who had taken tests in the relevant subjects elsewhere. As well, the rules of the Society's second School (1872–8) provided a reduction in apprenticeship of up to eighteen months for those who attended its lectures.

The Benchers first interpreted the statutes of 1837 and 1847 liberally by permitting the Society's students to study for college law diplomas simultaneously and by applying the reduction to anyone who earned a degree during the first three years of his enrolment on Convocation's 'Books.' During the 1850s about fifteen students took advantage of this régime, many of whom became prominent members of the Upper Canadian Bar.[139] However, by 1860 the Society had grown sufficiently antagonistic to this practice that it successfully entreated the Legislative Assembly to pass a law requiring consecutive rather than concurrent studies for those who sought to reduce their legal apprenticeships.[140] Further, it adopted a literal interpretation of the laws of 1837 and 1847 by deeming 'college graduates' to mean graduates of courses other than law. Presumably Convocation was seeking to undercut developing college law programs and to affirm its long-standing policy that law students devote all their time to the Society's training programs. After 1860 petitions for advanced standing were treated individually with varied results.[141] Motions made in Convocation in 1879 and 1880 by Bencher and Ontario Minister of Education Adam Crooks, which specified that all law degrees would count for the purpose of reducing apprenticeships, were defeated.[142]

Apprenticeship was the background against which law training occurred in Upper Canada. From an early date its contours were dictated more by Convocation's requirements than by the proclivities of particular principals, and by the 1830s office routine was so interrupted by other aspects of the Society's program that the role of principals receded further, and apprentices looked to Convocation to equip them to succeed in the developing school-related components of their training.

To round out this essay one would want to know whether apprenticeship was organized in any manner by Upper Canadian principals, whether there was a pattern of learning to it, or whether it was wholly ad hoc. No doubt some structure was imposed by the impending bar admission examination, which always was divided into subject areas and obliged students to be familiar with legal and liberal works set out on reading lists published and updated periodically by Convocation.[143] These reading lists were not short; in the 1830s they normally consisted of eighteen or twenty titles, and by 1890 comprised twenty to twenty-five legal works plus the statutes and case reports of Ontario and all liberal arts titles relevant for purposes of admission to the Society. First and second intermediate examinations, which students were obliged to take at specified intervals during their apprenticeships, date from 1832 and assumed considerable relevance in the 1860s. Here too, lists of mandatory readings were published by Convocation. These tests also must have had the effect of structuring students' apprenticeships. Moreover, term-keeping, participation in the Society's clubs and classes, and attendance at lectures must have organized and diminished office duties. Accordingly it would be an overstatement, except perhaps with regard to the Society's first three or four decades, to say that apprenticeship was the heart of its law-training operation. However, a clearer picture of legal education in Upper Canada will emerge from a specialized study of this component of the program.

TERM-KEEPING

Between 1828 and 1871 law students were required to keep judicial terms at Toronto during their apprenticeships. Before 1857 they were obliged to spend 'four terms at the least' attending court and to stay in residence at Osgoode Hall; after 1857 the tuition was two terms.[144] Keeping term entailed sitting in the back bench of courtrooms and taking notes on cases argued. This requirement had no precise English or North American antecedents, although it was somewhat similar to 'walking the wards' of a teaching hospital in the wake of a professor-physician as was done by certain nineteenth-century medical students.[145]

Term-keeping was the earliest formal aspect of the Society's curriculum that compelled students to spend part of their training in the provincial capital; in 1828 about eighty per cent of these students were not indentured at York. Although this reform had an enormous centralizing effect in that it translated into spending roughly a year and a half of the five-year program in the capital, its adoption did not provoke opposition, perhaps because it was not unprecedented. Voluntary aspects of the Society's program such as the Junior Advocates' Society had, since 1821, attracted large numbers of out-of-town students to its fortnightly meetings at York. [146] Term-keeping was a central component of law training in Upper Canada, since it meant that at all times almost half the Society's students were resident in the capital and therefore eligible and able to attend the law classes that developed in the 1830s and 1840s. Its staggered abolition in 1869 and 1871 coincided with the reintroduction of a series of law lectures in order to coerce continued student presence in Toronto by attaching certain benefits to attendance.

Resolutions adopted by Convocation in 1829, 1830, and 1831 specified term-keeping obligations. On the first and last day of the relevant judicial terms, each student had to report personally and in writing to the Treasurer, who recorded this event in his day-book. This formality was aimed at students who did not 'reside at the seat of the Court and Society' and was intended to compel their attendance at court. Students also had to autograph daily a register kept in each courtroom; signing on alternate lines was a common subversion of the ritual, designed 'to enable those visiting Toronto Island or Niagara Falls to sign in later.' When court was in session, students occupied narrow, sloping desks installed by the Society at the back of each Chamber. [147]

A few candidates missed their calls to the Bar due to improper term-keeping. The 'Minutes' contain seven petitions to Convocation asking for special consideration in view of the writers' failure to satisfy the formal requirements; the one that was granted was brought by a provincial student who recited difficulty of travel as the basis for discretionary treatment. [148]

Between roughly 1832 and 1851 students keeping term, attending law lectures, or taking the Society's examinations (as well as provincial barristers) boarded in Osgoode Hall; indeed, Convocation resolved that no persons other than members of the Society would be permitted to reside at Osgoode. When the decision was taken in 1826 to build the Hall, the accommodation of students-at-law was cited as a principal reason for construction. [149] The idea of housing students in an official hostel probably was drawn from British habits. For centuries English students-at-law had spent their legal training in residence at the Inns of Court. The editor of the *Kingston British Whig* referred in 1830 to Osgoode Hall as 'the Inner Temple of the Province.' [150] When seeking to build a self-reinforcing and cohesive élite, it was highly appropriate to feed and house its initiates in one building. [151] There was great need for a law hostel in Upper Canada of the late 1820s since most of the Society's sixty-odd students were scattered around the province. Until the inauguration of term-keeping the only scheduled occasions upon which they met each other were trips to the

Osgoode Hall, main entrance cow gates, c1857
(Panda Associates Photography and Art Services, Toronto)

capital to try the Society's entrance examinations. After the promulgation of the term-keeping rule but before the opening of the Hall in 1832, provincial students were obliged to board at diverse locations around York. The extent to which Osgoode Hall became the focal point of the Upper Canadian legal fraternity is indicated by the facts that until the turn of this century, business cards of Ontarian lawyers often recited 'Osgoode Hall' as an address, and that despite actual domicile, they could sue or be sued at the seat of the Society.[152]

Students in residence at Osgoode Hall were obliged to bring their own bedding, towels, and candles but were provided with furnished rooms and a steward who would clean one pair of boots for each boarder daily. John Molloy, formerly an attendant on the SS *Royal William*, became the Hall's first full-time steward in 1844. During his thirty-four-year tenure Molloy also assisted Hugh Gwynne in the administration of entrance examinations. The 'Reports of the Committee on Oeconomy' reveal that the Hall was run at a loss, partly as a result of the provision of these services. Another problem was that the room, board, and wine accounts of residents often went unpaid. Students were the worst financial offenders; in one twelve-month period in 1834–5, £45 was left unremitted by term-keepers and examination-sitters.[153]

Convocation assumed primary responsibility for disciplining students staying at Osgoode Hall. Since there was no Discipline Committee for students or barristers until 1877, even minor breaches of etiquette went directly to the Benchers. On one occasion in 1836 Convocation admonished a group of students for sneaking wine and liquor into their rooms. As a result, one Walter McKenzie was expelled from the Hall following prolonged deliberation by Treasurer Robert Baldwin Sullivan and Attorney General Robert Sympson Jameson. McKenzie grieved that the expulsion would be 'a deadly blight' on his record. On another occasion two students were censured for assaulting each other on the lawn of the Hall. The Society used this event to warn its initiates that Convocation's authority 'over the moral conduct of the Students of the Law resident in Osgoode Hall is not confined to the precincts of [that] Square but extends to all parts of the province.'[154]

Charles Durand, a legal apprentice of the 1830s, provided further flavour of the environment at Osgoode Hall during the early years of term-keeping:

An incident occurred to me as a student, going up the old stairs ... in the old East wing of Osgoode Hall – William Warren Baldwin ... although called a reformer, yet was a haughty, prejudiced, Protestant Irish gentleman, and wonderfully set in all his ways and notions of propriety towards young men and law students ... We met halfway up these stairs, [I] going up, he coming down; and although accustomed to be courteous to my superiors, not then knowing him or who he was, I did not take off my hat to him. He spoke out angrily: 'Sir, why do you not take off your hat?'[155]

Durand's remarks are typical of others that appeared in the records; the credibility of Upper Canada's legal élite was to flow from its members' education, principles, and habits of life. Writing in 1873, local historian Dr Henry Scadding concluded that the 'great expense lavished on Osgoode Hall' was justified by the atmosphere the Society had been able to generate; 'the effect of [the Hall], kept in its every nook and corner and in all its surroundings in scrupulous order, is invaluable, tending to refine and elevate each successive generation of our young candidates for the legal profession and helping to inspire among them a salutory *esprit de corps.*'[156]

The life of an Upper Canadian student-at-law in residence at Osgoode Hall differed from that of his English counterpart at an Inn of Court. In England the 'keeping of exercises' and the 'sharing of commons' with members of the relevant Inn were obligatory. Novices at the Inns typically were required to eat three dinners in each of four judicial terms during their five-, seven-, or ten-term careers as students. Throughout the eighteenth and nineteenth centuries traditional forms of instruction such as mooting, bolting, and reading were not relied upon; the sharing of commons and the keeping of exercises were the only vestiges of the traditional curriculum that remained.[157] Neither the keeping of exercises nor the sharing of commons was followed at Osgoode Hall. The model for the Hall may have been English but the substance of that which emerged was Upper Canadian.

Term-keeping was indigenous to legal education in Upper Canada. It brought the Society's students into immediate contact with each other and the Bench and Bar in order, as Archdeacon Strachan urged, to become 'familiar [with each other], acquire similar views and modes of thinking, and be taught from precept and example to love and venerate our parent state.' Collecting students together at Osgoode Hall not only exposed them to judicial decisionmaking and supplied an additional formal, centralizing component to legal education, but also was intended to assist law in becoming 'the most powerful profession [which would] in time possess more influence and authority than any other.' Term-keeping was abolished in stages in 1869 and 1871 as a result of reforms that created the second 'Osgoode Hall Law School' and sought to attract students to Toronto for an eighteen-month term during their studies by offering a reduction of apprenticeship equal to time spent attending lectures.[158]

LAW CLUBS, CLASSES, AND LECTURES

After the construction of Osgoode Hall and the introduction of term-keeping, Convocation's sponsorship of law clubs was a third mechanism used to cultivate the provincial legal élite. These clubs passed into and out of existence between 1821 and 1889 and were known variously as the Junior Advocates' Society, the Trinity Class, the Osgoode Club, the Osgoode Hall Literary and Debating Society, and the Osgoode Hall Legal and Literary Society. They were designed to foster a spirit of professional camaraderie among students and to provide fora where the attention of future lawyers could be focused upon political and legal issues, thereby promoting the growth of like notions about the social role of law and lawyers. Most important, the clubs were conceived of as classes in which initiates received tutoring from the Bar and undertook essays and examinations. Occasionally they also developed their own interests and provided vehicles through which student activists campaigned for changes in the Society's education policies and attempted to police the quality of apprenticeship received by provincial law students. Upper Canada's law clubs therefore provided a meeting ground for the Law Society's social and educative functions.

The province's first law club was the Junior Advocates' Society formed at York in 1821. Promoted by student Robert Baldwin, the Society met fortnightly at Russell Abbey and, although membership was voluntary, attracted representatives from all parts of the province. At one 1823 meeting, for example, there were nineteen law students in attendance, fourteen of whom did not come from York. This turn-out represented about eighty per cent of the Society's students. The Junior Advocates' Society functioned like a miniature Convocation with Law Society-like procedures and an imposing slate of officers that included Benchers, the Keeper of the Great Seal, the Treasurer, the Advocate, and the Prothonotary. Its agendas specified arguments on points of law and renderings of mock judgments in the tradition of English moots. At an early meeting whose minutes have been preserved by David Breckenridge Read, three cases argued in King's Bench that day were scrutinized, and a Bencher lectured about scholarly and disciplined approaches to law study. A

John Hillyard Cameron, Treasurer, The Law Society of Upper Canada 1859–76
Oil portrait by George Théodore Berthon (The Law Society of Upper Canada)

similar organization of Kingston students created in 1822 carried on after the Junior Advocates' Society disbanded in the late 1820s or resolved itself into its successor, the Trinity Class, in 1832.[159]

The Trinity Class played a more important role in the evolution of legal education in Upper Canada than its predecessor. It was initiated pursuant to a restructuring of law training by Robert Baldwin and George Ridout, which also introduced the bar admission examination, classes of incoming students, and intensified entrance requirements. The Trinity Class régime required participation in classes and lectures, and provided for intermediate examination of certain law students during their apprenticeships. Although neither coherent nor regular intermediate examinations prevailed until the late 1860s, the seeds of this component of legal education also lie in the Baldwin-Ridout reforms of 1832.

A permissive rule of Convocation of Hilary Term 1832, which received immediate assent from the judges, empowered the Benchers to create Trinity Classes whose exercises were to consist 'in the reading of Essays composed by the Students themselves; in the discussion of points of Law either in the shape of cases or of questions; in the discussion of questions of general, constitutional and international Law; in stated examinations of the Students in standard Authors in different branches of the Law; and in the pursuit of any other branch of useful knowledge, which may be appointed in the Order of Convocation.' The Classes were to meet 'eight times a year at the least' under the direction of their Presidents, who were to be Barristers-at-Law appointed by the Society. The Benchers' justification for this innovation was that 'in the present more advanced state of the Profession in this Province it is highly expedient and necessary to provide for a more regular and systematic attention on the part of those who are preparing for the Bar to those studies proper to the profession.'[160] Convocation's authority to operate a law school therefore dates not from 1862 or 1889, as generally has been supposed, but from Hilary Term 1832. The school-related components of the Trinity Class constitute the first generation of a tradition of law lecturing in Upper Canada that was perpetuated by Hume Blake in the 1840s, Dr George Skeffington Connor and Philip Michael Matthew Scott Vankoughnet in the 1850s, and John Hillyard Cameron, Alexander Leith, Adam Crooks, Thomas Moss, and James Bethune in the 1860s and 1870s.

Later in 1832 the Benchers particularized the Trinity Class rules. All legal apprentices residing within ten miles of York were obliged to participate in its activities. In addition to weekly exercises assigned by the Trinity instructors, students were to meet for periods of at least six days each, four times a year. Barristers also were encouraged to take part in the class; their tuition was 10s. for admission and 5s. per term. The annual examination was held at Christmas and tested students' knowledge of William Blackstone's *Commentaries on the Laws of England*, William Selwyn's *Abridgment of the Law of Nisi Prius*, Samuel March Phillipps' *Treatise on the Law of Evidence*, and selected aspects of the municipal law of England and Upper Canada. Questions were put by the President of the class and Barristers in attendance. Robert Baldwin, who had been Student Treasurer of the Junior Advocates' Society prior to his call to the Bar in 1826, became the first President of the class.[161]

The Trinity Class was well received. In 1834 and 1839 members petitioned for its expansion and the appointment of a full-time President.[162] The fact that attendance was not mandatory for those who lived more than ten miles from Toronto notwithstanding, students apprenticed to provincial practitioners regularly took advantage of its organic resolution which enabled them to be admitted to its exercises. Moreover, students keeping term at Osgoode Hall were deemed to be 'resident in Toronto' and therefore were required to participate. In short, the Law Society's first formal school-related initiative was ambitious, welcomed, and coincided precisely with the opening in 1832 of the seat of its 'university,' Osgoode Hall. In many ways Upper Canada's law clubs were the bridge between apprenticeships and formal training that was provided by the private law office schools of the United States. The general pattern for the 1820–89 period was that voluntary student organizations tended to wax when formal classes and lectures were waning.

The tradition inaugurated by Robert Baldwin and his Trinity Class of the 1830s was perpetuated by Hume Blake following his appointment in 1843 as first Professor of Common and Civil Law in the University of King's College, Toronto.[163] Blake was an expatriate Irishman who had been admitted to the Bar in 1838 after apprenticeship in the Toronto offices of Simon Washburn, a popular principal of the period. At the time of his appointment he was solicitor to the Law Society, Judge of the Surrogate Court of the Home District, and practised in the capital with Blake, Morrison, and Connor. During his five-year lectureship he became a Bencher of the Law Society and Upper Canada's sixth Queen's Counsel.[164] Writing to his predecessor, Robert Baldwin, Blake described his part-time teaching post as 'not lucrative, but honourable and gives one a standing at the profession.'[165] He lectured twice a week in the early morning. Substantively, he treated practical topics like contracts and partnership, sometimes through the case method of instruction. One of his students has stated that Blake 'never qualified before any decision, English or Canadian. If he thought the judgment unsound reasoning, he did not hesitate to say so and urge the students to examine for themselves.' There also is evidence that Blake emphasized American decisions and those of Lord Mansfield.[166] Most of those who attended Blake's lectures were also candidates for the Society's Barrister-at-Law degree and were classified by King's as 'occasional students.' They could elect to complete the college diploma in law, but fewer than ten per cent of them did so. Indeed, a salient feature of Blake's Chair was that it was regarded by Convocation as a Law Society initiative. Although the proposal for King's College announced in 1826 mentioned professorships of law and courses in civil and public law, its Royal Charter of 22 March 1827 did not specify degree-granting power in law. Events of the early 1850s would confirm that college instruction in law could proceed only with Convocation's blessing; permissive amendments to the University of Toronto's Charter eventually made in 1887 were necessary for that school to award law degrees without the Law Society's acquiescence.[167]

Ill health obliged Blake to resign from his lectureship in 1847. Although William Henry Draper and James Christie Palmer Esten filled in for him, the lectures were cancelled in 1848. None the less, Hume Blake was to influence the development of legal education in Upper Canada for at least another decade. Not only was his Chair later accepted by his business partner and brother-in-law, Skeff Connor, but Blake served simultaneously as Chancellor of the province and the University of Toronto in the 1850s and provided an important link between the Law Society and local colleges during the crucial years of their development. Moreover, he was succeeded as University Chancellor by his colleague at the Chancery Bar and long-time President of the Osgoode Club, R.E. Burns.

Perhaps the greatest compliment to Blake's skill as a teacher was the founding of the Osgoode Club in 1849 as a voluntary organization of Upper Canadian law students and the pressure it exerted on the Benchers to continue his project. In February 1849 the Osgoode Club memorialized Convocation:

[Since 1832] this Province has rapidly advanced in all that was then justly considered as in the preamble to [the 1832 Rule and Particular Order creating the Trinity Class of Students] ... while the facilities of obtaining a legal education have not increased in a corresponding ratio – if at all. And students of the Laws are now for the most part left to grope their way through the intricate labyrinth of legal science, almost without a clue to guide their steps. Many efficient schools have been established for instruction in Theology and Medicine while the Sister Profession – no less learned – no less difficult of acquisition – and no less useful and necessary, has, *save such provision as has been made in the University of King's College, suffered in this respect a total neglect* ... [accordingly], being convinced that these objects can only be secured by a more systematic and thorough legal education on the part of those who are preparing themselves for the Bar, than is now generally obtainable in this Country with its very limited facilities, have lately organized into an association under the name of 'Osgoode Club' for the purpose of advancing legal education.[168]

The petition went on to explain that the Club held weekly meetings for discussion of legal matters and original essays, emphasized that its membership was large and broadly based, since students then generally spent the last year and a half (keeping term) if not the whole of their apprenticeships in Toronto, and asked that this new law club be recognized as a continuation of the Trinity Class. More specifically, the Club requested the appointment of a law lecturer to replace Blake, reinstatement of intermediate examinations, assignment of essays, award of prizes for student achievement, and prescription of a more detailed course of studies. The Osgoode Club was attempting to function as a conduit between the pre-1828 model of simple apprenticeship and the attenuated and insecure development of structured schooling in law.

The Osgoode Club's 1849 petition was referred to a Law Society committee composed of George Ridout, Treasurer John Godfrey Spragge, and Vice Chancellor J.C.P. Esten.[169] This milestone committee announced no formal response for four years. Informally, Convocation successfully encouraged its members to perpetuate Blake's casual association with the colleges. In 1852, for example, the Benchers were able to note with approval that 'Professor' Skeff Connor of the bars of Ireland and Upper Canada was lecturing on evidence at the University of Toronto. On the same occasion, Convocation remarked that John Hawkins Hagarty was lecturing on contract law, P.M.S. Vankoughnet was teaching equity jurisprudence, and J.H. Cameron was conducting a real property course, all at Trinity College. Each of these lecturers was a Queen's Counsel and a prominent member of the Toronto Bar. Hagarty became a judge in 1856 and later served nineteen years as Chief Justice of Ontario. Vankoughnet was appointed Chancellor of Upper Canada in 1862, a position which he occupied until his death in 1869. Cameron was a Bencher of the Law Society, Commissioner for the revision of the provincial statutes, Reporter to the Court of Queen's Bench, founding editor of the *Upper Canada Queen's Bench and Practice Court Law Reports* and *The Upper Canada Jurist*, and author of two Canadian legal digests. The courses conducted by these men corresponded to the subject areas treated by the bar admission examination of the day.[170]

The Ridout-Spragge-Esten Committee tabled its recommendations in Convocation in September 1854. The Osgoode Club was vindicated in every respect. The Society resolved to create a series of formal law lectures, attendance at which by all students keeping term was to be mandatory.[171] It was announced in *The Official Gazette* and a special pamphlet that an agreement had been reached in 1853 by the provincial Superintendent for Education, the Benchers, and the Legislative Assembly, which recited their support for the proposition that responsibility for legal education in the District of Canada West properly belonged to the Law Society. Professorships of law, 'except insofar as they may form part of the general system of liberal education,' were to be abolished in the teaching part of the University of Toronto on 1 January 1854. The University was allowed to continue awarding the degree of Bachelor of Civil Law, and students were permitted to sit the University's examinations following attendance at lectures and thereby proceed to the BCL and Barrister-at-Law degrees simultaneously. Treasurer Robert Baldwin was to become a member of the Senate of the University of Toronto.[172]

From the students' point of view key features of the system of lectures formalized in 1854 were that attendance was compulsory, apprenticeships could be shortened by earning the college law degree during the first three years of enrolment on Convocation's 'Books,' and the attendance requirement provided yet another opportunity for the Society to observe its initiates' personal qualities. Compulsory attendance at Law Society lectures remained the rule until 1868 and was enforced rigorously. Lecturers were obliged to call the class roll at each session and to fail late or absent students. This requirement generated dissatisfaction and caused difficulty for numerous students. One provincial apprentice complained that 'it is hardly possible to conceive a greater humbug, than the present system of compulsory attendance of law students on the lectures in Toronto.' Other students who petitioned Convocation for special treatment on the basis of difficulty of transit or regional disparity met with mixed responses. For example, one Grey County apprentice was granted term in 1854 when poor steamship connections at Collingwood caused him to miss several lectures, and eight students from the southwestern counties were forgiven absence in 1855 when they pleaded transportation difficulties. However, two Belleville students who missed one class due to 'gales on Lake Ontario' and several London apprentices who were a few minutes late for the first lecture of term in 1855 were obliged to attend another set of lectures. Conversely, classes missed due to illness gave the Benchers little difficulty; term regularly was granted.[173] Emerging discontent with centralization of legal education at Toronto in the 1850s represents the beginning of a trend which assumed landslide proportions in the years following Confederation. Convocation's early response to those who regarded centralization as a monumental 'humbug' also anticipated a trend – indecision.

The number of students who enrolled simultaneously in the University and on the Law Society's 'Books' and thereby qualified for abbreviated apprenticeships was small. Eventually the provincial government eliminated this option in 1860 by requiring consecutive rather than concurrent enrolment.[174] Another aspect of the 1854 plan, which was widely utilized, was that candidates for the University law degree were not required to attend college lectures; moreover, passing grades on the Law Society's examinations were accepted in lieu of University results. Perhaps its mere design accounts for the popularity of this prerequisite. In any case, this approach was the inverse of that adopted at a later date in Manitoba, Nova Scotia, and New Brunswick, where completion of university law school courses was accepted by the governing bodies of the legal profession in lieu of apprenticeship and passage of a bar admission examination.[175]

The Law Society's lectures of the 1850s were held in the early morning to accommodate office duties and term-keeping. There were typically two class hours a week in each of two subjects. Courses offered included simple contracts, executors and administrators, bills of exchange and promissory notes, agency, criminal law, pleading, evidence, partnership, mortgages, and torts. According to one participant in these programs, classroom sessions often were supplemented by ad hoc moots in the relevant subject areas. Cases would be assigned to teams of three students a few days in advance of evening hearings before leading members of the Toronto Bar.[176] These sessions, together with classroom attendance, provided the Society with yet another opportunity to observe and cultivate the 'principles and habits of life' of aspiring barristers. Students' behaviour at classes sometimes was 'censured' and on one occasion the admission to practice of one Joseph Ryan was postponed for three months when it was discovered that he 'personated Mr. Cicolari at lectures.' The

Benchers implored their examiners and lecturers to be vigilant regarding student breaches of etiquette.[177]

From Convocation's perspective the compulsory lectures initiated in 1854 had numerous implications. For the first four years instructors served gratuitously. Toronto practitioners Secker Brough, Samuel B. Freeman, Miles O'Reilly, Oliver Mowat, D.B. Read, Adam Wilson, and George A. Phillpots each delivered a series of lectures during the early years. As time passed the personnel of the School was transformed, but Samuel Henry Strong, John T. Anderson, Alexander Leith, Edward Blake, and Adam Crooks were names that appeared regularly on the teaching rolls.[178] Blake, the son of William Hume Blake, went on to become Premier of Ontario, Minister of Justice for Canada, Irish Nationalist member of the British House of Commons, and a prominent counsel in Canadian constitutional matters before the Judicial Committee of the Privy Council. Leith was an Upper Canadian treatise writer whose best-known works are Ontario editions of Blackstone's *Commentaries* and Joshua Williams' *Principles of the Law of Real Property*. Crooks later served variously as Attorney General, Treasurer, and Minister of Education for Ontario. Strong became Vice Chancellor of Ontario, Puisne Justice of the Supreme Court of Ontario, inaugural Justice of the Supreme Court of Canada, Chief Justice of Canada, and an Imperial Privy Councillor.[179] In 1858 Lewis Wallbridge, later Chief Justice of Manitoba, and William Buell Richards, Puisne Justice of the Upper Canadian Court of Common Pleas and sometime Chief Justice of Canada, became the Law Society's first salaried lecturers in law.[180]

In 1861 the twenty-nine-year existence of these school-related components of Upper Canadian legal education was formalized when Convocation resolved that all students-at-law should be obliged to attend 'lectures, readings, and mootings, and otherwise' at the Law School of Osgoode Hall; their tuition was to 'be conducted by four lecturers of the Degree of Barrister-at-Law to be designated respectively the Reader on Common Law, the Reader on Equity, the Reader on Commercial Law and the Reader on the Law of Real Property. Such Readers to be elected annually, and to be paid a yearly salary of one hundred and fifty pounds.'[181] Great care should be taken not to overstate either the form or substance of this gesture. In form, it was framed as a resolution; the statutory instrument upon which its legal validity rested was the February 1832 Rule which empowered Convocation to create classes. Moreover, this resolution did not represent a new or definitive step in substance. It added nothing to the program of law lectures that had been in operation at least since 1854 and provided for a régime of schooling less onerous than that of the Trinity Classes of the 1830s and 1840s. Lectures were still one hour in duration four mornings a week. The lecturers remained part-time instructors. Clearly, Convocation was not creating a 'school' and was not creating anything new.

The 1861 resolution is problematic. It had been drafted by the Committee on Legal Education in the mid-1850s but not tabled for six years. The best explanation for the Society's confirmation of its lecture program probably has to do with events then transpiring in Kingston. In 1860 the Board of Governors of Queen's University retained several Kingston practitioners as part-time lecturers in law.[182] Queen's new Bachelor of Laws program was advertised in the *Kingston Daily News* in February 1861 and the first lectures in its Law School were held later that year.[183] Queen's inquired whether the Law Society would accept work done in its Law School as a substitute for keeping term at Toronto; this inquiry was answered in the negative in September 1862. Convocation instructed Treasurer J.H. Cameron to write to the Board of Governors of Queen's specifying that the Society would not relax the term-keeping or lecture rules for Kingston students, not accept work done at the Queen's Law School as a substitute for its own programs, and not amend its rules or resolutions to promote the Queen's project. This rebuff notwithstanding, classes continued, and Queen's first graduation was held in April 1863; five students were awarded the degree of Bachelor of Laws and Prime Minister John A. Macdonald was made an Honorary Doctor of Laws. However, due to failure of recognition and financial instability, law courses at Queen's were cancelled in 1864.[184]

The Law Society's lecture program was terminated in June 1868. A terse note in the *Canada Law Journal* (New Series) recited financial difficulties as the reason for the 'School's' closure.[185] The Society's accounts for the period indicate that the amount paid in scholarships and Lecturers' salaries ($1725) was roughly equal to income from student fees and exceeded the total of other expenditures. Moreover, neither inability to attract outstanding Lecturers nor student dissatisfaction account for the School's closure. Lectures were popular even among students not obliged to attend, and the curriculum was progressive. In the winter of 1866, for example, a Dr Berryman taught medical jurisprudence, and J.T. Anderson regularly lectured on torts in a period when that subject had not yet emerged as a coherent category of the common law.[186] Indeed, in the Benchers' 'Decennial Report to the Treasurer' of February 1871, the operation of the lectures was described as the Society's greatest achievement of the 1860s.[187] A cynical explanation for Convocation's posture might be that once the threat of competition from a real university ended, the Benchers allowed their own program to lapse.

Convocation's resolution of 1862 and the Benchers' rejection of the competing Kingston project were landmark events. They signalled the rise of dissatisfaction among provincial practitioners with the concentration of most aspects of legal education in Toronto. This theme, which has to do with the politics of legal education, was surprisingly absent from debates about law training which occurred throughout the first sixty-five years of the Society's existence, but came to dominate in the fourth quarter of the nineteenth century. Arguments about the post-1867 creation of county law libraries to complement the Society's Great Library at Osgoode Hall, the abolition of term-keeping in 1869 and 1871, and the franchisement of Western, Ottawa, and Queen's law schools in the 1880s all reflect this theme. While the decentralization that eventually resulted from these debates may have been desirable, the rise of positions informed only by regional self-interest and the dislike for 'Hogtown' in the years following Confederation is difficult to explain. Indeed, the same phenomenon was rampant in the medical profession. These developments may have been responses to massive reallocations of power associated with the advent of Canadian federalism, which transferred authority from local agencies to provincial capitals as regularly as it seconded heretofore provincial powers to Ottawa.[188]

In 1872 Convocation resolved to re-establish its law lectures under the aegis of the 'Osgoode Hall Law School.' Although the Lecturers of the 1860s had remained on the Society's payroll as Bar Examiners, no classes had been given since 1868. The mode in which the lectures were re-established reflected the growing dissatisfaction of provincial practitioners with the Toronto wing of the Law Society and was merely part of a larger overhaul of the legal education program. Treasurer Cameron, who had taught in the Trinity Class of the 1850s, and Thomas Moss, who had lectured for the Society in the 1860s, were dominant voices in Convocation at this time and prime movers behind the re-establishment of law lectures.[189]

As in the Society's earlier programs, there were no full-time instructors, and classroom sessions occupied only one hour each morning. The 'school year' ran from November to April inclusive and tuition was by way of lectures, discussions, and examinations. The distinguishing feature of this series of lectures was that attendance was voluntary. However, in a throw-back to the 1850s, benefits were attached to participation: apprenticeships could be abbreviated by six, twelve, or eighteen months, contingent upon regular attendance and acceptable examination results; and successful completion of the Lecturer's examinations enabled candidates to avoid the Society's intermediate examinations. For the first time in forty-five years Upper Canadian law students were not obliged to spend significant portions of their apprenticeships in the provincial capital. The educational policies of the Society were being affected by the politics of regional self-interest in Convocation. Moreover, this 'School' had greater independence from Convocation than had been the case in the earlier lecture programs. Curriculum, examination policy, and teaching materials were determined by a council composed of the Society's Treasurer, the Chairman of the Legal Education Committee, and the President of the School. The term of appointment for Lecturers was extended to three and later four years. Most important, Convocation delegated all of its authority regarding scholarships, intermediate examinations, honours, certificates of fitness for attorneys, and the degree of Barrister-at-Law to this faculty.[190]

The founding faculty of 1872 was Alexander Leith, James Bethune, Zebulon Aiton Lash, and Thomas Moss. William Mulock joined the teaching staff in 1874 and Thomas D. Delamere and Thomas Ewart were appointed in 1876.[191] Each of these men was committed to a program of formal instruction in law. Leith had lectured for the Society since 1862 and was President of the School. Moss also had lectured in the 1860s, was an outspoken proponent of re-establishing lectures, and succeeded Leith as President in 1876. Ewart and Delamere offered their lectures gratuitously for four years following the program's termination in 1878. Courses always revolved around material relevant for the bar admission examination. The Junior Class was for beginning students and the Senior Class was for students who had attended the Junior lectures or completed two years of apprenticeship. Lecturers were obliged to advertise their course outlines and book lists in provincial and Toronto newspapers at least one month in advance of term.[192]

During the early years student enthusiasm ran high; in the first term of the program's operation, for example, 100 pupils enrolled. However, participation quickly declined. In 1875 attendance averaged twenty-nine at the Senior Lectures and thirty at the Junior Lectures. Few candidates took advantage of the opportunity to be forgiven Convocation's examinations by trying those administered by the lecturers; in 1875 the total was twenty-seven. By 1877 interest in the program was lagging and Convocation resolved to abolish the lectures.[193]

The motion 'to abolish the Law School or to ensure its more efficient operation' was brought by John Douglas Armour of Cobourg and Stephen Richards of Toronto two weeks after Cameron's retirement. In the first instance it was defeated. Three days later Thomas Hodgins, also of Toronto, gave notice of motion to affiliate the Law School with the University of Toronto. Hodgins' motion was tabled (for ten years) and the Armour-Richards motion was reintroduced and passed in a modified form that called for a committee to evaluate the program.[194] It was as a result of the adoption of this Committee's 'Report' that the lecture series was terminated. One is driven to conclude that Cameron's personal interest in legal education was responsible in no small measure for the law schooling regimes of the 1860s and 1870s.

Four explanations have been advanced for the closure of the Society's second School.[195] A first is that the School was not financially viable. While no figures are available for 1878 or for the 1872–8 period, the 'Report of the Finance Committee for 1876' indicates that the Society's annual income was approximately $15,000 and the value of its assets was about $30,000. Most of this income was composed of student fees, which included tuition fees in the School. The amount spent on the operation of the lectures, $4120 annually, was less than that appropriated to grounds-keeping at Osgoode Hall, heating and lighting the Hall, or library acquisitions.[196] Lack of financial viability had little to do with closing the School.

A second explanation is that the approach of its Readers was insufficiently theoretical. This hypothesis is less than persuasive. The most practical courses were the best attended and, when medical jurisprudence was offered, fewer than twenty students attended.

A third account of the reasons for Convocation's closure of the School is that the Readers were underpaid and therefore took their teaching duties lightly. Every Lecturer was paid $800 for each six-month period; the President was paid $1000 a year. By way of comparison, the Society's full-time law reporter was paid $800 per annum in the 1870s.[197] The scale of remuneration for lecturers seems generous. Moreover, student comment indicates that the lectures were well received by those who attended.

A final explanation for the closing of the second School is that it was excessively popular with the Society's students. Indeed, this was the explanation offered at the time by Convocation's critics. It was alleged that provincial practitioners exerted pressure upon the Benchers to terminate the lectures when they noticed that the abolition of term-keeping notwithstanding, many students gravitated towards the provincial capital to capitalize on the reduction in apprenticeship offered to those who attended the lectures. For a number of reasons, this explanation is as unsatisfactory as the others. In 1879 there were 1020 lawyers in active practice in Ontario. Two hundred and sixty of them practised in Toronto. There were 580 students on the 'Books' of the Society, 366 of whom were not apprenticed to Toronto practitioners. In 1877 the maximum regular attendance at Junior and Senior Lectures combined was sixty-five. The total of those who sought to reduce their apprenticeships by attending lectures and taking the Schools examinations in 1877 was forty-four.[198] Attendance patterns are inconsistent with claims that the lectures' perpetuation of a Hogtown law school provoked provincial interests to have them aborted. Moreover, those who promoted their abolition in Convocation were mostly Toronto lawyers.

The best conclusion is that confusion caused Convocation to abolish its second Law School. The Society was anxious to preserve its jurisdiction but wholly uncertain how to do so. Benchers of the late 1870s and 1880s were under fire from many quarters. The recently created county law library associations were seeking greater autonomy. Certain university administrators were pressing the Society to divest itself of its monopoly over legal education. Provincial practitioners had become increasingly critical of Convocation's centralizing tendencies in all aspects of its affairs. Upper Canadians were watching the rapid rise of the American university-based law schools, sometimes with envy and sometimes with anxiety. Students were highly critical of the post-1872 lack of structure in the Society's legal education program. The Benchers were becoming increasingly concerned about the Society's financial stability. As a result of debts incurred in the reconstruction of Osgoode Hall, Convocation's annual revenues then barely exceeded its annual expenses and measures such as the discontinuation of the *Supreme Court Reports* and tapping an independent water supply had been taken.[199] Finally, since 1872, legal education in Upper Canada had been less structured than at any point in the previous half century. The most important aspect of the Law Society's affairs had become the most confused. In short, the Law Society of Upper Canada was having an identity crisis which would not be resolved for at least ten years.

Student petitions to Convocation calling for the re-establishment of lectures became a commonplace.[200] The bar journals and the popular press of the period are replete with letters and editorials criticizing the Benchers and bemoaning the state of legal education in Ontario.[201] Writing in 1880, two commentators alleged that the province was at a standstill in legal education while American law schools turned out 'men who guide half the councils of the world.'[202] Another young Ontarian lawyer branded the Society's actions as short-sighted, selfish, and ignoble; 'their attitude is as false to ancient legal tradition as to the modern spirit.' The same writer accused provincial Benchers of indulging their selfish desire to kill the program of legal education merely to maintain their equality; 'in a fit of rampant localism they stabbed the young institution.'[203] Students-at-law argued that the wealth of the Law Society was generated largely by student fees (which was true), but that no service was provided to legal apprentices in return (which also was more or less true).[204] The editor of the *Canada Law Journal* (New Series) asked, 'has it ever been suggested that of all courses of study, that of law stands out so pre-eminently easy that no ... assistance is a requisite?'[205] In the face of this criticism Convocation was immobilized. The Select Committee on Abolition of the Law School remained alive but did nothing. A Finance Committee recommendation that money be appropriated to add lecture rooms to Osgoode Hall was rejected. A Legal Education Committee proposal that Examiners be paid more money, since this would 'probably have the effect of ... giving voluntary law lectures by some if not all of the examiners,' was ignored. Yet another motion to affiliate the defunct School with the University of Toronto was defeated.[206]

Following the termination of lectures in 1878, the legal education program was kept alive by the Osgoode Hall Legal and Literary Society, a voluntary association of law students founded in 1876. As had happened on at least two other occasions in Upper Canadian history, a law club filled the gap created by a failure of formal schooling.[207] Even before 1878 the Legal and Literary Society had been encouraging the writing of student essays, cultivating public speaking and reading, and generally promoting the scholarly study of law. After the termination of the Society's lectures in 1878, it intensified its programs through sponsorship of lectures by prominent members of the Toronto Bar, conducting examinations, and awarding prizes. In the 1880–1 academic year, for example, it organized thirty-two law lectures by eight Toronto lawyers. The students' estimate had been that thirty of their classmates might attend each classroom session, but Lecturer Thomas Ewart reported to Treasurer Edward Blake in 1880 that many more than thirty students attended; all seats were always occupied and sometimes all standing room was taken.[208]

Convocation was supportive of the Legal and Literary Society and seems to have been content to let it operate both as a surrogate law school and a gentlemen's club for students. The Benchers provided prizes for distribution by the club in its lecture programs and freely allowed the club to use the Great Hall for public meetings, the dining room at Osgoode for monthly dinners, and the Benchers' Chambers for special occasions.[209] These quarters apparently enabled the club to carry on elegantly. Convocation even offered to construct a tennis court on the lawn of Osgoode Hall for the Legal and Literary Society in the 1880s.[210]

Most important, the activities of the Osgoode Hall Legal and Literary Society led directly to the re-establishment by Convocation of its formal law lectures in 1881 and their perpetuation in a somewhat diminished and uncertain spirit until 1889.[211] This step was the result of joint counsel of the Legal Education Committee and the Finance Committee that mounting public and student criticism should be allayed, and was regarded as an interim measure. Attendance at lectures was voluntary and free. The curriculum continued to revolve around the subjects relevant for the bar admission examination, and the format remained that of the 1860s and 1870s, namely one one-hour lecture each day.[212] Student participation in the program was unimpressive, at least in numbers, and according to the editor of *The Canadian Law Times* the interest of Convocation and of the Bar was negligible. Although the few students who did attend the lectures published a letter of appreciation addressed to Convocation in the *Canada Law Journal* (New Series), Chairman Thomas Hodgins reported to the Benchers in 1883 that 'the attendance has been very irregular and unsatisfactory as to numbers considering the very numerous signatures to the petition for re-establishing the Law School, it is very disappointing to find so few students availing themselves of the lectures.'[213]

From all appearances the development of law schooling in Ontario was at a standstill. However, through the 1880s much was going on *in camera*. The criticisms of the editor of *The Canadian Law Times* were misplaced. Convocation's concern about legal education reached a level of intensity in that decade unparalleled for at least half a century before or after that time.

A special committee was struck in 1880 'to encourage legal studies by law students in various parts of the province.' Chaired by Treasurer Blake, the Committee tendered its 'Report' in the form of a motion passed in June 1881. The rule which resulted provided that local associations like the Osgoode Hall Legal and Literary Society were to be founded around the province wherever there were enough students and at least one barrister prepared to lecture; that this program was to be directed by the 'County Library Aid Committee'; that eighteen one-hour lectures at least were to be delivered each term, and that written examinations comprising twenty-four or more questions were to be administered; that the Society would finance these 'branch law schools' provided there were no less than twelve students in regular attendance; and that the purpose of the program was 'the extension of the legal knowledge, and the cultivation of the powers of reasoning, speech and composition of the members by the delivery of lectures, holding of exams, preparation and reading of essays and by arguments on legal questions.'[214] Book prizes were to be awarded to leading students. Three features of this plan were significant. First, it was to be implemented by way of 'local option'; the Society would promote branch law schools only if asked to do so. Second, the mandate of the proposed campuses was almost identical to that of the Trinity Class of 1832. Finally, this rule is the key which has been missed by all commentators on the rise of local and university-related law schools in late nineteenth-century Ontario. Members of the Middlesex, Frontenac, and Ottawa Law associations who sought to create local law schools in the 1880s were not challenging the authority of Convocation but merely seeking to bring themselves within the scope of this permissive rule.

In December 1884 Albert Oscar Jeffrey, Secretary of the Middlesex Law Association, petitioned Convocation to apply the Rule of 1881 to the newly formed London Law School. A special committee was formed and, in February 1886, a motion by Thomas Hunter Purdom of London to allow Western University to conduct the Law Society's courses and examinations was carried. It also was resolved to permit the University of Toronto to do the same.[215] These developments encouraged other Ontario schools to establish faculties of law; Queen's, Victoria, and Ottawa universities took steps to create or revitalize law schools in the 1880s. Moreover, some Benchers took advantage of the Law Society's indecision to encourage it to go much further than merely acquiesce in these schemes; for example, William R. Meredith of London and Toronto urged that Convocation take affirmative steps to establish Law Society schools outside Toronto and that two examination centres be established, one in eastern Ontario and one in the southwestern counties.[216] Pressure to decentralize had peaked.

In response to regional and university pressure, and acknowledging that law training in Ontario was out of control, the Society took a second definitive step in February 1888. A 'Committee on the Establishment and Maintenance of a Law Faculty' was struck.[217] The event that overcame the Benchers' inertia was the receipt of a letter from Registrar Alfred Baker of the University of Toronto inviting 'the Law Society of Upper Canada to cooperate with it in considering the question of the establishment of a Teaching Faculty of Law in the University.'[218] Baker's proposal called for a four-year law course; two years were to be spent at Osgoode Hall and two were to be spent in the University's Bachelor of Laws program. The new Committee was to 'consider submissions from all universities and local law associations in the province.' The importance attached by Convocation to this problem is indicated by the fact that its membership reads like a 'who's who' of late nineteenth-century Ontarian lawyers.

The Committee's total membership was sixteen; nine of the delegates were Toronto practitioners. Briefs were heard from Queen's, Trinity, Victoria, and Ottawa universities, and from the Law Library Association of Frontenac. George Monro Grant, Principal of Queen's, argued that the Society should retain control of legal education but require an arts degree as a condition of admission to study. Trinity College also argued in favour of the Society retaining exclusive control of legal education on the theory that the integration of law training into the universities would damage the arts faculties and threaten academic Bachelor of Civil Law programs with 'heightened professionalism.' C.F. Marson of Ottawa University was amenable to the proposal so long as it extended to all Ontario colleges. The Law Library Association of Frontenac rejected any delegation of the Law Society's authority as 'wrong in principle' but opined that it could live with the plan if it was applied to all universities and the tuition was not shortened. The University of Toronto was the only Ontario college that was much interested in operating a law school, despite the Law Society's overtures.[219]

The Committee recommended to the Benchers 'that it is not expedient at present to express an opinion as to the desirability of entering into arrangements with any university for the joint education of students, nor to shorten in any way the period of study or service of students. It is expedient to continue and reorganize the Law School; and to appoint a President who shall have supervision and general direction of the School.' Convocation adopted this recommendation by a one-vote margin, provincial Benchers tending to vote against it. A companion motion which sought to reduce the number of compulsory courses for provincial students from two to one was defeated by a similarly narrow vote with about the same regional split.[220] After sixteen years of debate Toronto interests prevailed, and law training in Ontario emerged in a more certain and structured condition than it had enjoyed since 1872. This resolution determined the form that legal education would take in Ontario until 1957. The post-1889 lecture program was to be compulsory. Toronto students were obliged to take three courses, while provincial students were to attend two series of lectures. For the first time the School's presidency was a full-time teaching position; it was offered initially to Puisne Justice S.H. Strong of the Supreme Court of Canada and then to W.A. Reeve of Napanee.[221] The plan drew immediate criticism from practitioners who alleged that it was insufficiently structured, and from provincial law students who objected to the attendance requirement and renewed centralization that it contemplated. In response to condemnation Treasurer Blake urged Convocation to modify the program. A suggestion by Charles Moss that students be forgiven their office duties during the teaching term was adopted. T.H. Purdom and W.R. Meredith of London proposed that existing university law schools be constituted branch law schools. The distinguished criminal counsel, Britton Bath Osler of Dundas and Toronto, promoted an amendment to this motion that substituted 'Local Law Association' for 'Law School.' In response Edward Martin of Hamilton drew the attention of Convocation to the 1888 resolution, and the Osler-Purdom-Meredith proposal was rejected. However, a middle ground advocated by Byron Moffat Britton of Kingston and Charles Moss that students be credited by the Society on a course-by-course basis for work done in pre-established law schools was adopted.[222]

Principal Reeve's first assignment was to visit 'New York, Massachusetts and other places as may be deemed desirable, for the purpose of acquiring information on the Law School systems adopted at those places.' Reeve spent two months touring the United States with Bencher Edward Martin and soon-to-be Chief Justice of Ontario, Charles Moss. At Columbia this group conferred with Professor of Criminal and Tort Law, George Chase; at Harvard they met Law Librarian John Himes Arnold; at Yale they visited with Dean Francis Wayland; and at Boston University they met Edmund Hatch Bennett.[223] Ironically, as recently as 1876, the fledgling American schools had been asking Treasurer J.H. Cameron for advice.[224] The speed with which the tables turned is merely further evidence of the deterioration in Upper Canadian legal education since the 1870s. Even Ontario's most junior counsel had noticed that graduates of these American schools played prominent roles. Nicholas Flood Davin and T.A. Goreham had grasped, if only intuitively, the massive social challenge facing Ontario's legal educators in the fourth quarter of the nineteenth century and the extent to which a program eminently suited to Upper Canada of the 1830s quickly was being eclipsed by its modern American analogues. What they had not grasped was the phenomenon of non-transferability of law-related institutions. [225]

In New York, Connecticut, and Massachusetts, Reeve observed a major renaissance in university-based law training. Harvard was then the foremost of a handful of older American university law schools that had survived the levelling effects of the antebellum period. [226] Christopher Columbus Langdell, who became Dean of Harvard in 1870, generally is credited with revitalizing American legal education. His inauguration of the case method of instruction, Socratic teaching, and the view of law as a science (the primary materials of which are decided cases) has become famous. Langdell and his disciples gave law training a singular credibility in the emergence of professionalism in post-Civil War America by transforming law from a mere trade into a craft or science, and by ensconcing legal education in the university. With increasing frequency, the American university was regarded by the expanding middle class as the primary avenue to respectability, social status, and professional rewards. [227] Emerging big business also 'demanded of the bar knowledge and skills not within the sonorous phrases of the "constitutional lawyer" of mid-century or the blackletter learning of the conveyancer'; Langdell courted this new market, too, and filled the rapidly expanding ranks of Wall Street, LaSalle Street, and Chestnut Street firms with his university law school 'scientists.' [228]

By the time Reeve, Moss, and Martin toured the American law schools the pre-eminence of the Harvard model was assured. There were then over seventy university-related law schools in the United States, and Columbia and Michigan each enrolled over 600 law students. The typical law school curriculum had been extended to three years, graduate legal studies programs were developing, and elective courses abounded. [229] This American renaissance was commanding the attention of the common law teaching world. Writing in 1899, English constitutional scholar Alfred Venn Dicey stated: 'the professors of Harvard, have, throughout America, finally dispelled the inveterate delusion that law is a handcraft to be learned only by apprenticeship in chambers or offices.' Similarly, English political theorist Viscount James Bryce concluded in 1895 that he did 'not know if there is anything in which America had advanced more beyond the mother country than in the provision she makes for legal education.' [230] Reeve, Moss, and Martin were watching the birth of the modern

American law school. Although they could not have known it then, many of the cultural, economic, and political factors that led to this institutional response would push the Law of Society of Upper Canada to engage in new exercises in institutional design in the decades that were to follow.

Reeve structured his inaugural address of 1889 around American developments and emphasized three distinctly Langdellian points. He argued first for the value and necessity of academic studies in law, second for the use of contracts as the first law school course, and finally 'for the cultivation of reasoning faculties'; ... 'to be compelled to think is the paramount need of the student-at-law,' said he, 'and the oral examination by the lecturer of the student from day to day ... [is a better method of securing this object] than a steady adherence to the plan of reading or delivering uninterrupted lectures.'[231] At the end of its first century, the Ontario Bar was becoming colonial. The sophisticated and highly distinctive Ontario vernacular in law teaching developed carefully by Dr William W. Baldwin and Robert Baldwin, Hume Blake, and J.H. Cameron, who clearly sensed that it was special to be an Upper Canadian, was being rejected before a viable substitute had been identified.

The modifications of the Society's classes and clubs that occurred in the fourth quarter of the nineteenth century signal that 1889 was a watershed in the history of Upper Canadian legal education. As one scholar has noted, at the end of the century the Law Society sat Janus-like with the Tory values of Upper Canada behind it and the emerging values of an urban, industrialized culture ahead.[232] Simcoe's notions of an aristocratically organized society topped by a class of lawyers whose social status was to flow from 'education, principles, and habits of life,' and whose professional mission would be to protect that which was distinctive about the Upper Canadian community from 'inconvenient subjection,' were losing their grip on the legal world.

As early as 1822 gentlemen's clubs of law students had flourished in York. These organizations not only participated extensively in doctrinal education but also facilitated social intercourse among law students. The Upper Canadian legal fraternity that they fuelled was a small and relatively close-knit group from which regional and professional differences of opinion were surprisingly absent for the first sixty-odd years. However, by the fourth quarter of the nineteenth century the force of Archdeacon Strachan's imperative that law students spend time together to ensure that they would become a unified, coherent, and self-reinforcing group had withered. This change was reflected in the abolition of term-keeping in 1869 and 1871, the suspension of compulsory lectures in 1868, and the creation of regional law clubs in the early 1880s. The emphasis of Simcoe, Gray, the Baldwins, and other early Benchers upon education also fell into disfavour at this time. Convocation remained jealous of the Society's prerogative as a pioneering educational institution, but its constructive exercise of this mandate quickly was being surpassed in the last decades of the nineteenth century by developments in American universities and the province's liberal arts colleges. At certain junctures law clubs filled gaps in legal education by functioning as surrogate law schools, and in doing so they kept alive the notions of law schooling articulated by Robert Baldwin and Hume Blake. Convocation guarded its jurisdiction anxiously to the end of the century, but in the post-Confederation period it failed to notice that social change in Ontario meant that neither its mission nor the means it had evolved to execute that mission could be carried forward without rationalization.

SCHOLARSHIPS AND INTERMEDIATE EXAMINATIONS

Additional structuring of the education of the Upper Canadian law student occurred through the imposition of interim examinations which students were obliged to take at specified points in their apprenticeships. These tests were initiated with the Trinity Class reforms of 1832 but had limited relevance until 1861. Throughout the 1830s certain students were obliged to submit to examinations 'as to their professional attainments' every Christmas. As was the case with the entrance and call examinations, reading lists were published by Convocation. In 1833, for example, the assigned texts were Blackstone's *Commentaries*, Selwyn's *Nisi Prius*, and Phillipps' *Evidence*.[233] The reason for this reform was that the Benchers wanted 'to provide for a more regular and systematic attention on the part of those who are preparing for the Bar to those studies proper to the profession.' However, this aspect of the program faded when the Trinity Class evolved into Blake's lectures at King's College.

Intermediate examinations were revived as a non-compulsory scholarship competition in 1861 which made available cash prizes to top achievers in each of the first four years of the program. Again, a number of relevant texts were specified. The purpose of awarding scholarships was 'to ensure further excellence' and Convocation specified that 'cases of rich and poor were to stand equally.'[234] This initiative was consistent with the Society's perception of itself as an educational institution and provided an additional potential source of income for less advantaged apprentices. Yet over the years, 'a totally insignificant number of students' participated; in

1865 the scholarship program was cut back to two prizes and in 1880 it was abolished.[235]

The reintroduction of a full-blown system of intermediate examinations was one of the measures taken in 1868 in association with the suspension of compulsory law lectures. Edward Blake hoped that the intermediate examinations, which were taken in the third and fourth years of the apprenticeship (the second and third years in the case of university graduates), would salvage some of the structure lost through the suspension of compulsory lectures. Reading lists which bore considerable resemblance to the syllabi of deposed lecturers were published.[236] Like the post-1871 entrance examination and examination for call, the intermediate examinations were composed of two parts, namely written and oral components. Good work on the thirty-question written portion permitted candidates to be forgiven the oral component of the test. Although no student failed the first set of intermediate examinations, the failure rate was about twenty per cent through the 1870s and 1880s. The consequence of failure was that the candidate had to try the relevant series of tests again the next year, which meant that each unsuccessful attempt added one year to the length of one's law studies.

The intermediate examinations added considerable structure to the Society's law schooling program since their effect was to spread the reading of material necessary for call to the Bar over a three- or five-year period. Although their inauguration was consistent with the Society's self-image as an educational institution, they also were products of the regional dissatisfaction of the 1860s and 1870s that impugned numerous Toronto-based aspects of legal education. Presumably intermediate examinations also enhanced apprenticeship to the extent that they further integrated office training with the reading of mandatory texts.

BAR ADMISSION EXAMINATIONS

A bar admission examination was the last hurdle for the Upper Canadian student-at-law. These tests always involved a trip to the provincial capital, since they never were held outside Toronto. Introduced in 1831, the bar examination was a product of the period in which Robert Baldwin and Dr William W. Baldwin were the principal architects of legal education and was designed to test students' knowledge of 'the material relevant for the purposes of the entrance examination, the principles of the law of England, the science of special pleading, the law of evidence, the law of trials at *nisi prius* and the practice of the Courts.' Convocation declined to specify categories of success on the examination for call to the Bar 'in deference to the practice which obtains in most Universities.'[237]

The inauguration of bar examinations coincided roughly with the Benchers' first expression of interest in the number of lawyers practising in the province. Following instructions 'to set the rolls right' and take a census of practitioners, Robert Baldwin's Committee on Consolidation reported in 1832 that the records of the Society were kept in such an 'inaccurate manner' that it was compelled to rely upon the 'Rolls of King's Bench' and recollections of lawyers and old inhabitants of the province in compiling its lists of students, practitioners, Benchers, and judges. Indeed, there is no indication before 1830 that the Society knew or cared how many persons it had graduated or how many practising lawyers there were in Upper Canada.[238] Throughout the nineteenth century increases in bar admission standards and numbers of practitioners disbarred coincided somewhat with bouts of concern about overcrowding in the legal profession.

Legal texts upon which students were examined for the purpose of bar admission were specified by Convocation as early as 1831, and candidates routinely recited titles they had read in their applications for call to practice. A recital contained in the 1832 call papers of Allan McDonell of Hamilton was typical of others which accompanied early petitions for permission to write the bar examination. McDonell had read history, poetry, geography, and natural history. His knowledge of trials at *nisi prius*, special pleading, and the practice of the courts had been drawn from Blackstone, Selwyn, Phillipp, Joseph Chitty's *Treatise on Pleading*, and William Tidd's *Practice of the Court of King's Bench and Common Pleas*.[239] Like other students of the 1830s, McDonell submitted to an oral bar examination before full Convocation.

No student failed the bar admission examination during the first nine years that it was administered, with the result that twenty-five to thirty students were called to the Bar each year. During the 1840s half a dozen students failed their bar examinations, and there was some correlation between having tried the entrance examination more than once and failure of the bar examination. Still, the number of failures before mid-century was trifling.

Failure rates increased radically in the 1850s. At mid-century the Society had no precise statistics about the legal population of the province; the only censuses taken since Baldwin's tabulations of 1832 had been contained in reports by the Society's Committee on Oeconomy filed in 1840 and 1842.[240] The next formal census was not taken until 1873, although Upper Canadian law lists were published commercially as early as 1856.[241] Lack of precise statistics notwithstanding, comments about the large size of the profession came from many quarters in the 1850s. Examiner Gwynne expressed concern when twenty candidates applied for entrance in a single term and stated that the country was 'going mad' when this number jumped to forty in the next term. In 1859 an early local historian declared that 'if [lawyers] go on increasing and multiplying as they are now doing, they will in the end, ruin themselves and the country too! Our young gentlemen should begin to turn their attention to some other occupation.'[242] The excess of educated or professional men in mid-nineteenth-century Upper Canada is a theme that runs through the primary and secondary literature. Whether there was actual overcrowding in the mid-century legal profession deserves a study of its own, but certainly some lawyers and lay persons perceived it to be the case.[243]

Against the background of statements by Benchers to the effect that 'there is now [1848] no want of gentlemen of the bar in any of the Districts,' it probably was no coincidence that failures on the bar admission examination began to occur at the rate of one each term; five lawyers were disbarred or suspended from practice in one term of 1850 and, most important, the Society resolved to intensify the requirements for call.[244] Oliver Mowat, a prominent member of the Chancery Bar, was the Chairman of a landmark committee struck to achieve this end. Pursuant to Mowat's recommendations, which went into effect in February 1855, two classes of admission to practice were created, a 'simple call' and a 'call with honours'; a written component was added to the oral examination; an 'Examination Board' of Benchers drafted new questions for each term; the written tests were taken one day before oral examinations, passage of the written test being a condition precedent to taking the oral test; written examinations were five hours in length; and the oral portion was held in public. New lists of mandatory reading materials for the examinations were published.[245] Although the assigned texts varied, this general structure prevailed until 1889. The only significant modification, which affected one or two students each term, specified that candidates who achieved more than sixty-seven per cent on the written test would be forgiven the oral examination.[246]

The implementation of the 'Mowat Rule' provided one of the few occasions upon which the popular press scrutinized the Law Society's activities. The *Daily Colonist*, a moderate Conservative Toronto newspaper, saluted Convocation for its interest in excellence among its students and competence at the Bar but added that the reforms were not unprecedented; the Society was merely bringing itself into line with other university faculties.[247] In practice, academic excellence translated into a considerable increase in the number of unsuccessful attempts to pass the bar examination. The first term the new rule was in effect, for example, the number of applicants admitted to practice dropped from twenty to three.[248] Thereafter, the failure rate ranged from twenty to fifty per cent and a large number of those who sought to be called 'with honours' were simply 'passed.' By the third quarter of the nineteenth century the preferred solution for those who were apprehensive about their ability to complete the program and pass the bar examination was to withdraw. Through the 1880s, for example, almost fifty per cent of those admitted as students followed this course which, when combined with failure rates on the bar examination, meant that only a third of those admitted to law study were actually called to practice.

Bar examinations held between 1855 and 1889 were conducted by the Society's lecturers or its examiners. Each of the four lecturers-examiners was responsible for one of the subject areas upon which students were examined, namely commercial and maritime law, real property, equity jurisprudence, and criminal and tort law. At mid-century, Thomas Moss, Alexander Leith, Michael Anderson, Edward Blake, Adam Crooks, and Vice Chancellor William Proudfoot were regular Examiners. Their positions were regarded as prestigious and lucrative. Convocation regularly advertised vacancies in its Examination Board in *The Globe*, *The Mail*, and *The Telegram*; following a September 1879 advertisement for an examiner in equity and real property, the Benchers received seventeen applications; in response to a December 1879 tender, they received fifteen applications for four positions.[249]

The five-hour written portion of the examination contained thirty-five short answer questions. On the commercial and maritime law portion of the 1858 examination, one of seven questions on Sir John Barnard Byles' *Treatise on the Law of Bills of Exchange* was whether the payment of a bill at maturity by anyone other than the acceptor would destroy its negotiability. The property law component of the test required students to explain the nature of a treasure trove by drawing on their knowledge of Blackstone's *Commentaries*.[250] Students found the questions difficult and the atmosphere surrounding the examinations intimidating. Perhaps as a result, students Calvin Brown and Edward Chadwick wrote the first Canadian 'hornbook,' a collection of Law Society examination questions, which was recommended strongly by the *Upper Canada Law Journal* (Old Series) to their classmates.[251] The Society's examiners and lecturers also regularly published compilations of their lecture notes and examination questions.[252] More important, they often wrote leading Upper Canadian treatises or institutional works on their subjects.[253] In keeping with nineteenth-century patterns throughout the common law world, a local treatise-writing tradition developed to service the Upper Canadian Bar, despite its small size (which ranged from 140 to 1200 during the relevant period).[254] The Law Society's lecturers created and maintained this tradition, which was consistent with the Bar's perception of Osgoode Hall as an academic institution. Indeed, the tradition of scholarly writing by 'near-academics' was in many respects stronger in nineteenth-century Ontario than it has been in the twentieth century. This is yet another aspect of the history of the Ontario Bar that deserves specialized study. For present purposes the salient point is that the academic activity of Upper Canada's early law lecturers and examiners extended beyond the classroom.

As alternatives to passing the Law Society's bar examination on completion of a five-year program of apprenticeship, term-keeping, lectures, and intermediate examinations, one could be admitted to practice on the basis of membership in certain foreign Bars, or licensed by the executive branch of government. These methods were used frequently in the early period but less regularly after about 1830.[255] Section five of the Law Society Act specified that English, Scots, Irish, or British North American lawyers could be admitted to practice in Upper Canada provided they produced 'testimonials of good character and conduct.' Amending legislation of 1822 specified that only lawyers from foreign jurisdictions 'in which the same privilege would be extended to Barristers from [Upper Canada]' would be entitled to reciprocal admission to the Law Society.[256] In the years that followed the stipulation about reciprocal privileges seems to have been ignored by Convocation, especially when the applicants were expatriate Lower Canadian or Irish lawyers. However, during the 1840s and early 1850s a dramatic increase in the number of immigrant English lawyers caused the Benchers to consider the admission of foreign lawyers with greater care, ostensibly because the Inns of Court long had refused to recognize the Society's degree. In 1855 Convocation dispatched Chief Justice Robinson to England to inquire into the attitudes of the Inns towards the Society. Although he was complimented by Privy Councillors on the quality of Upper Canadian lawyering observed in cases on appeal to the Judicial Committee, he was not able to extract any commitments from the Benchers of the Inns of Court.[257]

After about 1850 applications for admission to practice in Upper Canada by foreign lawyers routinely were treated as questions of *reciprocal privilege*, perhaps as a consequence of the Society's general concern about the rate of growth of the Upper Canadian legal profession at mid-century. Criticism of the 'defective training' of other British North American and especially English lawyers became commonplace.[258] Lawyers from the maritime provinces, for example, were denied admission in almost every case; failure of reciprocity was typically the reason cited.[259] However, Quebec lawyers, many of whom migrated to Ontario in the years immediately following Confederation, generally were admitted to the Law Society without question.[260] The Benchers appear to have regarded the Canadas as a single whole, unified by the St Lawrence waterway. In view of Convocation's antipathy towards extraprovincial common lawyers, its support of an 1876 Nova Scotian Barristers' Society proposal, spurred by the creation of the Supreme Court of Canada, that a 'Dominion Law Society' be formed was uncharacteristic.[261] More consistent with its traditional posture was unqualified opposition to a similar proposal for the United Canadas vetted in 1841.[262] The motivation for the 1876 federalist stance was twofold. Certain Benchers, such as John A. Macdonald and Oliver Mowat, were proponents of a unified, pan-Canadian bar.[263] Other Ontario lawyers had begun to comprehend the Society's potential role as 'legal colonizer' of the developing western territories.[264] In any case the 1876 Nova Scotian proposal came to nought, at least until the Canadian Bar Association was founded in 1914.

Government licensing of Upper Canadian lawyers provoked consistent opposition from the Society.[265] The Benchers' most common argument, which also was used in cases of unauthorized practice, was that government licensing made a mockery of Convocation's whole program of legal education.[266] Their motivation for opposing executive licensing and the admission of foreign lawyers is difficult to determine. The profane explanation would be grounded in protectionism and institutional jealousy. Yet due to continuity at the Bar the sacred aspects of the project, first articulated by Simcoe, Osgoode, Gray, and Strachan, remained omnipresent for a century. Since the Law Society's mission was the cultivation of a social élite, persons born and educated in the province were to predominate.[267] Whatever the explanation for the Benchers' behaviour, they were essentially successful in discouraging the granting of executive licences and limiting the scope of reciprocal call. At least ninety-five per cent of those admitted to the practice of law in the province before 1889 passed through Convocation's training program; foreign lawyers composed most of the other five per cent.[268] Successive generations of legislators seem to have been content to permit the Law Society to operate as the exclusive architect of Upper Canada's legal profession.

During the period in which Convocation was steadily increasing its bar admission requirements, most American states were disassembling standards for call to the Bar that had been developed during the colonial era.[269] These divergent approaches reflect differing attitudes about the appropriate place of lawyers in a social hierarchy. Similarly, the Law Society of Upper Canada was not much influenced by the rising culture of professionalism of the late nineteenth century or the institutionalization of legal education that occurred in England, Nova Scotia, Massachusetts, and New York at that time. It was the decadent and disorganized state of the American Bar that made the professionalization of law and law study an urgent matter in the last quarter of the nineteenth century. The birth of the modern American schools and the transformation of legal education they effected was possible and necessary only because these university-related law schools were born in the wreckage that Jacksonian democracy had made of bar admission requirements and legal education between 1800 and 1860. Partially as a result of the linear development of legal education in Upper Canada, only in 1797 was it thought necessary to make a definitive break with the past. The linear and cumulative manner in which the Law Society's program was developed resulted in a continuity unparalleled in American or British jurisdictions.

CONCLUSION

Writing in 1871, the Editor of the *Canada Law Journal* (New Series) speculated that there was no part of Ontario's statute books which was more convoluted and misunderstood than the acts and statutory instruments related to entry into the legal profession.[270] The system of law training to which this commentator was referring was structured by diverse regulations and policies of Convocation and was neither simple nor unoriginal. Unlike the ease with which R.C.B. Risk's mid-century American lawyer could have understood and coped with the organization, structure, and doctrine of Upper Canadian law, incredulity might more accurately describe his response to conditions precedent to the practice of law in the province.[271] Indeed, records abound of the disbelief of English barristers faced with the Law Society's program of legal education.[272]

At least until 1889 the Law Society of Upper Canada was much more than a mere certifying agency. Seriously educative programs were comparatively complex in design and administered methodically. Through its curriculum of entrance examinations, apprenticeship, term-keeping, intermediate examinations, clubs, classes and lectures, and a bar examination which included legal and liberal studies, the Society not only executed its mandate as legal educator but also attempted to cultivate a coherent and self-reinforcing legal élite. Convocation conceived of this social engineering function as no less important than its basic law-training operations. Yet throughout most of the nineteenth century the Society's admissions policies were designed to promote meritocracy; the emphasis at all stages of law study was on the processing and development of human raw materials rather than the raw materials per se. Moreover, the marriage of social and pedagogic goals often enabled Convocation's informal methods to achieve education without formal schooling.

In many ways the Law Society's regulations and policies about legal education seem extraordinary, given their massively centralizing effect and the manifest difficulty of travel in pre-Confederation Upper Canada. Although statements to the effect that no less than ninety-five per cent of Convocation's business concerned law training emphasize the Society's perception of its role in the community as educator, they divert attention from the human commitment necessary to make the system work. After 1831 convocations were held sixteen times a year and each one lasted several days. In keeping with the geographic distribution of Upper Canada's lawyers, many Benchers were provincial rather than Toronto practitioners. It often took over a week for Benchers like Walter Roe and Angus Macdonell to travel from their homes at Detroit and Cornwall to the Society's post-1800 seat at York. When one reflects upon travelling time necessary to get to and from the provincial capital, together with time spent in Convocation, it becomes clear that at least one-third of a Bencher's time was allocated to Society business and not to his own practice.

Throughout most of the period under consideration Upper Canada's frontier was a 500-mile-long east-west axis. Yet the places of origin and employment of the province's lawyers provide little sense of either physical expanse or an immediate frontier. Although persons from 'the front' predominated for the first half century, there were lawyers in active practice at Peterborough, Bytown, Perth, and London by 1835.[273] By the last decade of the century towns on the new fringes of Ontario society such as Bracebridge, Huntsville, Parry Sound, Fort William, North Bay, Sault Ste Marie, and Rat Portage had burgeoning bars.[274] The Law Society's presence was felt from one end of the province to the other.

Owing to the educational standards imposed by Convocation, 'backwoods' practitioners were not the 'constitutional lawyers' of the American frontier.[275] These were men who had jumped through Hugh Gwynne's Irish classical hoops, sat in King's or Queen's Bench for 'four terms at the least,' and observed Chief Justice Robinson render judgments about which Privy Councillor Sir Edward Ryan was 'most strong and emphatic in his praise.'[276] These were also men who had attended the law lectures of future Attorneys General, sometime Chief Justices of Ontario, Manitoba, and Canada, and leading Toronto commercial lawyers. Many of them had lodged as students in the splendour of Osgoode Hall and shared commons not unlike those shared at the Hall by the Prince of Wales in 1860 and the delegates to the Quebec Conference in 1864. When Convocation quipped that its authority was not limited to the precincts of Osgoode Square but extended to all parts of the province, it might well have said 'influence.' The achievements of the Law Society and its near domination of all aspects of lawyering in Ontario for almost two centuries must be a phenomenon very close to the heart of the Upper Canadian experience.

The most striking conclusion to be drawn from this consideration of one aspect of the Law Society's activities is that except in the period of gestation the direct influence of Britain, the United States, and Lower Canada was far less important than internal and indigenous influences. One sees neither pronounced hostility to American agencies of the law nor unqualified enthusiasm for the English model. The Society assigned American treatises to its students and encouraged the use of American legal materials through spokesmen no less eminent than Oliver Mowat.[277] Convocation expressly declined to follow most practices of the Inns of Court and refused to admit English barristers to practice on the basis of their 'defective training' while blithely admitting lawyers from certain other British North American provinces. Even those who occupied the highest echelons of the Upper Canadian legal élite, such as Chief Justice Robinson, spoke very favourably about the comparative quality of the Upper Canadian Bar, notwithstanding their avowed concern about maintaining a British connection. What one does see in this microcosm of Upper Canadian society is a principled commitment to, and a quiet confidence in, a distinctively Upper Canadian institution. Indeed, no enterprise remotely comparable to the Law Society developed in any American jurisdiction. Moreover, legal education is an aspect of Upper Canadian life in which 'time lag,' apparent in some facets of the province's socio-legal development, did not pre-empt creativity. Gad Horowitz's hypotheses that the vernacular of colonial institutions is often far more distinctive than it appears at first blush, and that events which occur at the outset go far towards explaining the development and perpetuation of that vernacular, are highly applicable to legal education in Upper Canada.

On the first of July 1867 Confederation was an accomplished fact. The Law Society's recruitment and training programs for law practice and for the perpetuation of a legal élite were at their peak. They had not yet been diluted or disorganized by the politics of regionalism, the rise of liberalism, the impact of English and American influences, or the diminution of the social role of lawyers which soon would be wrought by industrialization, urbanization, and the expansion of commerce in Ontario.[278] American notions like professionalism, republicanism, and scientism still made little sense in Upper Canada's stubbornly Georgian legal community. The message emerging from specialized studies of Upper Canadian professional life is that Ontario did not become a colony until the twentieth century. This is precisely the pattern that is revealed in the development of legal education. It appears to be a general pattern among the Upper Canadian professions, but it is one which is only beginning to be examined. At any point before the fourth quarter of the nineteenth century, Simcoe, Osgoode, and Gray would have been delighted by the achievements of Convocation. The educative enterprise founded by their delegates at Newark in 1797 had effectively resisted the 'undue subjection' about which these early institutional designers worried.[279]

Although the history of Ontario's legal profession is essentially social history, it seeks to divine the role of one of the principal agencies of the law, the Bar, in processes of social and legal change. To date, Canadian historians have largely ignored the history of the legal profession. The explanation for this posture is not obvious. Even if one concedes that legal infrastructures played a secondary or perhaps passive role in the development of Ontario, it does not follow that the role of the legal profession in Upper Canadian society was inconsequential. Moreover, as James Willard Hurst has properly suggested, studies of the interrelatedness of legal and social transformation must be informed by detailed analysis of various agencies of the law and their participation in processes of social change.[280] In sum, there need be nothing trivial or limited in the kinds of questions one poses when studying the legal profession, whether one focuses upon training for the bar, horizontal and vertical distributions of lawyers in society, the kinds of jobs that lawyers actually do, or the ways in which they structure and utilize law as a form of social intelligence.

The Law Society of Upper Canada is probably unequalled in the common law world, not least because it was an exclusive agency of law training for almost two centuries. Like most élites, it did things informally in private; public meetings were reserved for self-affirmation, rhetoric, and other forms of self-justifying public statements.[281] Convocation provided a private setting in which the Benchers did things informally, confident that their comments would remain *in camera*.[282] Convocation Chamber might just as well have been John Beverley Robinson's drawing room. Accordingly, the Society's records of the role it performed in the nineteenth-century experience of professionalization, industrialization, and urbanization provide a unique point of access to the participation of the Bar as an agency of the law in processes of change common to the nineteenth-century legal history of English-speaking peoples. Upper Canada offers not merely a useful case study of the Canadian experience, but also a highly potent microcosm of the role of the legal profession in modern socio-legal reform.

NOTES

Research for this essay was initiated in 1978 under the auspices of Columbia Law School's graduate seminar on legal education; I am grateful for the guidance and encouragement provided in the initial stages by members of that School's professorial staff. Rande Wilfred Kostal, LLB, of McMaster University lent helpful research assistance in 1980, and Robert D. Gidney of the Faculty of Education, University of Western Ontario, contributed constructive criticism of an earlier draft. My greatest debt is to the Law Society of Upper Canada and particularly to Kenneth P. Jarvis, QC, and John D. Honsberger, QC, who provided access to the unpublished minutes of Convocation of the Society, 1797–1890. These minutes were the principal primary resource for this study. For the period under consideration they are recorded in eight volumes of the 'Journal of Proceedings of the Convocation of Benchers of the Law Society of Upper Canada' (hereafter 'Minutes') and number some 5000 pages. There are several respects in which the 'Minutes' are imperfect. Volumes IV, VII, and VIII, which deal with the periods between Feb. 1857 and Dec. 1864, and May 1881 and Dec. 1889, are unavailable. Therefore I used the unpublished 'Librarian's Book of Exercises' and the 'Rough Minute Book of Convocation' (hereafter 'Rough Minutes') in which notes were entered prior to transcription into the formal 'Minutes.' *The Upper Canada Law Journal* (hereafter UCLJ) and the *Canada Law Journal* (hereafter CLJ) published sketchy summaries of Convocations held between 1861 and 1889. There is also *The Journal of Proceedings of the Convocation of Benchers of the Law Society of Upper Canada* 3 vols (Toronto 1885–1904) (hereafter *Journal*), which covers the 1879–1904 period. After 1855 certain issues related to legal education were dealt with by a standing committee. Its 'Reports' and some of its debates were reproduced in the 'Minutes,' but the Committee did not preserve records of its daily business. The third defect of the 'Minutes' is that often they contain little detail or are inaccurate. At least until 1832, entries were somewhat formalistic and repetitive. Errata were common throughout the period under consideration. The Benchers recognized these problems and formed special committees in 1831, 1837, 1858, and 1874 to examine the 'Minutes,' 'Common Roll,' and 'Barristers' Roll' (hereafter 'Books') and to consolidate the Society's rules, orders, and resolutions. Robert Baldwin's 'Committee on Consolidation' of 1832 published 500 copies of *The Rules of the Law Society of Upper Canada* (York, UC 1833) (hereafter *1833 Rules*). Baldwin annotated and updated his own copy of this manual to about 1855. I am grateful to John Honsberger for facilitating access to this copy, which has since been deposited in the Public Archives of Ontario (hereafter PAO). Financial information was drawn from the 'Grande Ledger of the Law Society of Upper Canada' (unpublished, Osgoode Hall, Toronto).

1 Matters which occupied the balance of Convocation's time included banking arrangements, maintenance of gravestones of deceased treasurers, and landscaping Osgoode Hall. Since standing committees were not used until the 1830s and not used extensively until the 1870s, most of the Society's business passed through Convocation during the period under consideration. Debates tended to be wide-ranging and rarely occurred in the context of framing a particular rule or resolution.

2 See 'Robert Baldwin to Convocation' (1833) 'Minutes' I 416; *Rules of the Law Society of Upper Canada* (Toronto 1859) 57.

3 'Minutes' I 65; 'Minutes' II 533, 612

4 See 'The Law Society of Upper Canada' *Toronto Daily Colonist* reproduced in UCLJ I (OS 1855) 31–2. See also 'Minutes' I 384; 'Minutes' VI 227–8.

5 See J. Porter *The Vertical Mosaic: An Analysis of Social Class and Power in Canada* (Toronto 1965).

6 Since little has been written about the nature of nineteenth-century Canadian law practice, it is impossible to consider the impact of shifting demands for legal services upon the evolution of legal education in much detail. See S. Raymond *Law and MacInnes* (Welland, Ont. 1952); D.H. Tees *Chronicles of Ogilvy, Renault 1879–1979* (Montreal 1979); A. Graydon *Some Reminiscences of Blakes* (Toronto 1970).

7 'Adam Crooks to Convocation' (1866) 'Minutes' v 88–9

8 Reproduced in J.R.W. Gwynne-Timothy *Western's First Century* (London, Ont. 1978) 428 (italics added)

9 See J.F. Newman 'Reaction and Change: A Study of the Ontario Bar, 1880 to 1920' *University of Toronto Faculty Law Review* xxxii (1974) 51; E.B. Campbell *Where Angels Fear to Tread* (Boston 1940).

10 The ratio of Irish to English and Scots immigrants at mid-century was about 2-1-1 (Canada *Censuses of Canada 1665 to 1871* iv [Ottawa 1876] 136). The ratio for purposes of admission to the Law Society was more like 4-1-1.

11 See R.T. Naylor *The History of Canadian Business 1867–1914* 2 vols (Toronto 1975); D. McCalla *The Upper Canada Trade 1834–1872: A Study of the Buchanans' Business* (Toronto 1979).

12 Compare M.B. Katz 'Occupational Classification in History' *Journal of Interdisciplinary History* iii (1972) 63.

13 See H.C. Pentland *Labour and Capital in Canada, 1650–1860* (Toronto 1981) 130–75.

14 W.J. Reader *Professional Men: The Rise of the Professional Classes in Nineteenth-Century England* (London 1966) 54. For similar descriptions of the Upper Canadian experience see UCLJ iv (OS 1858) 219–20; CLJ i (NS 1865) 144.

15 The latter pattern of social mobility contrasts with that of other nineteenth-century North American jurisdictions. Compare G.W. Gawalt *The Promise of Power: The Legal Profession in Massachusetts 1760–1840* (Westport, CT 1979); M. Bloomfield *American Lawyers in a Changing Society, 1776–1876* (Cambridge, MA 1976); J.S. Auerbach *Unequal Justice: Lawyers and Social Change in Modern America* (New York 1976) 14–101.

16 Compare D.R. Keane 'Rediscovering Ontario University Students of the Mid-Nineteenth Century: Sources for and Approaches to the Study of Going to College and Personal, Family and Social Backgrounds of Students' (PHD thesis, University of Toronto 1981).

17 See W.R. Riddell *The Bar and the Courts of the Province of Upper Canada or Ontario* (Toronto 1928) Pt i *The Bar* 95–106.

18 See CLJ i (NS 1865) 54, 79, 138, 221.

19 See 'Minutes' iii 224–30.

20 See E.M. Chadwick *Ontarian Families: Genealogies of United Empire Loyalists and Other Pioneer Families of Upper Canada* (Lambertville, NJ 1970).

21 The Society admitted its first Canadian native student (Solomon White) in the 1860s, its first black student (Delos R. Davis) in the 1870s, and its first female students (Clara Brett Martin and Eva Maude Powley) in the early 1890s.

22 See C.P. Traill *The Backwoods of Canada* (London 1836) 3–4, 81–2.

23 37 Geo. iii (1797), c. 13 (UC). Confirmed and 'made perpetual' by the Law

Society Amendment Act, 2 Geo. IV (1822), c. 5 (UC). See also *Mandamus in re Lapenotiere* (1848), 4 *Upper Canada Queen's Bench Reports* (New Series) (hereafter UCQB) 492, at 495 per Robinson CJ.

24 Although the parliamentary debates for the 1797 session have been lost, it is clear that the Legislative Assembly made early and regular use of its residual regulatory authority. See Fees and Costs of King's Bench Act, 44 Geo. III (1804), c. 3 (UC); Fees and Costs Amendment Act, 50 Geo. III (1810), c. 9 (UC); Court of King's Bench Act, 2 Geo. IV (1822), c. 1 (UC), ss. 44–5; Riddell *Bar and the Courts* Pt I *The Bar* 60–7, 102–5. Compare T. Johnson *Professions and Power* (London 1972).

25 35 Geo. III (1795), c. 1 (UC)

26 55 Geo. III (1815), c. 194 (UK). See A.H. Manchester *A Modern Legal History of England and Wales 1750–1950* (London 1980) 51.

27 See Gad Horowitz *Canadian Labour in Politics* (Toronto 1968) 3–57.

28 See Ontario Bureau of Archives, ed. *Records of the Early Courts of Justice of Upper Canada (Reports of Cases in the Court of Common Pleas for the Districts of Hesse, Mecklenberg (Kingston), and Luneberg, 1789–94)* (Toronto 1918).

29 Compare J.M. Bennett and J.R. Forbes 'Tradition and Experiment: Some Australian Legal Attitudes of the Nineteenth Century' *University of Queensland Law Journal* VII (1971) 172.

30 See J.-E. Roy *Histoire du notariat au Canada* 4 vols (Lévis, Qué. 1899–1901) I 370–1; A. Vachon *Histoire du notariat canadien 1621–1960* (Québec 1962) 9–76.

31 See *Calvin's* case (1608), 77 *English Reports* (hereafter ER) 379; *Blankard v Galdy* (1693), 90 ER 1089; Quebec Act, 14 Geo. III (1774), c. 83 (UK), ss. 8, 11; Property and Civil Rights (Reception) Act, 32 Geo. III (1792), c. 1 (UC).

32 See W.R. Riddell *Michigan under British Rule: Law and Law Courts* (Lansing, MI 1926) 45, 211.

33 See B.A.T. de Montigny *Histoire du droit canadien* (Montreal 1869) 576; E. Lareau *Histoire du droit canadien* 2 vols (Montreal 1888–9) I 255.

34 See E. Fabre-Surveyor 'Louis-Guillaume Verrier' *Revue d'histoire de l'Amérique française* VI (1952–3) 159.

35 See L. Lortie 'The Early Teaching of Law in French Canada' *Dalhousie Law Journal* II (1976) 521, 524–6.

36 See J.-E. Roy *L'ancien Barreau au Canada* (Montreal 1897) 72–91.

37 25 Geo. III (1785), c. 4 (Que.), preamble. Reproduced in *Ordinances Made and Passed by the Governor and Council of the Province of Quebec, 1763–1791* 2 vols (Ottawa 1917) II 165

38 See An Act to Incorporate the Bar of Lower-Canada, 12 Vict. (1849), c. 46 (Can.).

39 Judicature Act, 34 Geo. III (1794), c. 4 (UC); Law Society Act, s. 8; Notaries Public Act, 38 Geo. III (1798), c. 2 (UC)

40 'Minutes' I 6–7, 11

41 W.T. Easterbrook and H.G.J. Aitken *Canadian Economic History* (Toronto 1955) 152, 154, 273

42 'Minutes' I 1

43 See W.R. Riddell *The Life of William Dummer Powell, First Judge at Detroit and Fifth Chief Justice of Upper Canada* (Lansing, MI 1924); W.S. Wallace 'William Weekes' in *The Macmillan Dictionary of Canadian Biography* (Toronto 1978) 876 (hereafter MDCB); R.E. Saunders 'Christopher Robinson' in *Dictionary of Canadian Biography* IV (Toronto 1979) 677 (hereafter DCB); W.R. Riddell *The Legal Profession in Upper Canada in its Early Periods* (Toronto 1916) 11, 151–85.

44 See L. Sabine *The American Loyalists, or Biographical Sketches of Adherents to the British Crown in the American Revolution* 2 vols (Boston 1847) II.

45 See G.M. Craig *Upper Canada: The Formative Years 1784–1841* (Toronto 1963) 8.

46 See T. Cook 'John Beverley Robinson and the Conservative Blueprint for the Upper Canadian Community' *Ontario History* LXIV (1972) 82 (hereafter OH).

47 See Riddell *Michigan* 45.

48 Courts of Common Pleas Act, 29 Geo. III (1788), c. 3 (Que.)

49 Riddell *Michigan* 63; Riddell *Bar and the Courts* Pt I *The Bar* 41–2

50 See Craig *Upper Canada* 30; 'Richard Cartwright to John Graves Simcoe,' E.A. Cruickshank, ed. *The Correspondence of Lieut. Governor John Graves Simcoe, with Allied Documents Relating to His Administration of the Government of Upper Canada* 2 vols (Toronto 1923–31) II 270.

51 See A. Fraser, ed. *Records of the Early Courts of Justice of Upper Canada* (Toronto 1918).

52 Criminal Law Reception Act, 40 Geo. III (1800), c. 1 (UC)

53 See B.A. Black 'The Constitution of Empire: The Case for the Colonists' *University of Pennsylvania Law Review* CXXIV (1976) 1157.

54 See P.S. Atiyah *The Rise and Fall of Freedom of Contract* (Oxford 1979).

55 See G. Ridout, ed. *A Catalogue of Books, Belonging to the Law Society of Upper Canada* (York, UC 1829); 'Minutes' I 6; 'Registry of Donations to the Society' (unpublished, Osgoode Hall, Toronto). See also J. Parrish 'Law Books and Legal Publishing in America, 1760–1840' *Law Library Journal* LXXII (1979) 355; W.H. Bryson *Census of Law Books in Colonial Virginia* (Charlottesville, VA 1979); H.A. Johnson *Imported Eighteenth-Century Law Treatises in American Libraries 1700–1799* (Knoxville, TN 1978).

56 See P.M. Hamlin *Legal Education in Colonial New York* (New York 1939); R.B. Morris *Studies in the History of American Law with Special Reference to the*

Seventeenth and Eighteenth Centuries (New York 1959) 62–8; E.A. Jones *American Members of the Inns of Court* (London 1924).

57 See J. Goebel jr and J.H. Smith, eds *The Law Practice of Alexander Hamilton: Documents and Commentary* 5 vols (New York 1964–81).

58 Petitions received by the Legislative Assembly reflect this dependence, and cases decided by the Courts of Common Pleas between 1788 and 1796 reflect this sophistication. See Riddell *Michigan* 73–264, 268–355; W.N.T. Wylie 'Instruments of Commerce and Authority: The Civil Courts in Upper Canada 1789–1812' in this volume.

59 No doubt the clergy occupied a very important position in early Canadian society, but its relations with the legal community are better characterized as co-operative than competitive. Indeed, bishops Jacob Mountain and John Strachan were promoters of legal education. See S.B. Frost *McGill University for the Advancement of Learning 1801–1895* (Montreal 1980) I 51.

60 Compare A.G. Roeber *Faithful Magistrates and Republican Lawyers: Creators of Virginia Legal Culture, 1610–1810* (Chapel Hill, NC 1981).

61 See W.R. Riddell 'William Osgoode – First Chief Justice of Upper Canada 1792–1794' CLT XLI (1921) 278, 345; W. Colgate, ed. 'Letters from the Honourable Chief Justice William Osgoode' OH XLVI (1954) 77, 149; A.R.M. Lower, ed. 'Three Letters of William Osgoode – First Chief Justice of Upper Canada' OH LVII (1965) 181.

62 See 'Minutes' I 6; W. Colgate, ed. 'The Diary of John White, First Attorney-General of Upper Canada (1791–1800)' OH XLVII (1955) 147; E.G. Firth 'John White' in DCB IV 766.

63 See W.R. Riddell *Life of John Graves Simcoe* (Toronto 1926).

64 'Robert I.D. Gray to Peter Russell,' 1 Aug. 1797, E.A. Cruickshank and A.F. Hunter, eds *The Correspondence of the Honourable Peter Russell* (Toronto 1932) 236–7

65 Cruickshank *Correspondence of Lieut. Governor John Graves Simcoe* I 4

66 See G.C. Brauer *The Education of a Gentleman: Theories of Gentlemanly Education in England, 1660–1775* (New York 1959); D. Duman 'Pathway to Professionalism: The English Bar in the Eighteenth and Nineteenth Centuries' *Journal of Social History* XIII (1980) 615; W. Prest *The Inns of Court under Elizabeth I and the Early Stuarts 1590–1640* (Totowa, NJ 1972).

67 Baldwin, *1833 Rules* 60. See also C.H.A. Armstrong *The Honourable Society of Osgoode Hall* (Toronto 1952) 15.

68 'Minutes' I 440, 478 et seq.

69 *Regina* v *Gray's Inn* (1780), 99 ER 227. See also A.H. Marsh 'Visitors and Their Jurisdiction' CLT XV (1895) 173.

70 'Minutes' II 276–7. See B.T. Duhigg *History of the King's Inns: or, Account of the Legal Body in Ireland, from Its Connexion with England* (Dublin 1806).

71 See 'Minutes' II 276. There are insufficient secondary resources to pursue this Irish or 'British' comparison in detail.

72 Reproduced in UCLJ V (OS 1859) 97. See also ibid. 149 and UCLJ VI (OS 1860) 4 for a similar statement by the editor of the English *Solicitors' Journal*.

73 Prior to 1822 one could be admitted to the Law Society as an attorney before being awarded the Diploma of Barrister, since the term of clerkship for attorneys was three years while the period of apprenticeship for barristers was five years. Section 3 of the Law Society Amendment Act (1822) extended the tuition for articled clerks to five years and transferred control over that branch of the profession to the Court of King's Bench. Before 1822, one could be an attorney without becoming a barrister. Nevertheless, the vast majority of pre-Union Upper Canadian lawyers were both. Although the Law Society attempted unsuccessfully to persuade its visitors and the Legislative Assembly to separate the profession fully in 1830, 1839, 1840, and 1841, it was effective in policing the monopoly of its barristers in the superior courts. See *In re Lapenotiere*, above note 23; *In re Brooke* UCLJ X (OS 1864) 49; *In re Judge of the County of York* (1877), 31 UCQB 267. Authority to admit attorneys was redelegated to the Society by the Admission of Attornies Amendment Act, 20 Vict. (1857), c. 63 (Can), ss. 3–7, 19. Convocation merely rendered its regulations for students-at-law applicable to articled clerks and dispensed 'certificates of fitness' which graduates took to the judges to be admitted to practice in the courts as attorneys. Even in the 1822–57 period when training attorneys was the prerogative of the courts, the judges routinely imposed educational requirements similar to those stipulated by Convocation. See *In re Hagarty* (1842), 6 UCQB (OS) 188; *In re Holland* ibid. 441; *In re Macara* (1844), 2 UCQB 114; *Ex parte McIntyre* (1852), 10 UCQB 294; *In re Patterson* (1859), 18 UCQB 350. Accordingly, it is inappropriate for this essay to treat articled clerks differently from students-at-law.

74 Applicants also were rejected on the basis of being less than sixteen years of age. See 'Minutes' I 94–5, 146; 'Rough Minutes' IV 202; UCLJ IX (OS 1863) 196.

75 See Rule 3, 37 Geo. III (1797), Trinity Term; Rule of 1 and 2 Wm IV (1831), Trinity Term; 'Minutes' I 90; 'Minutes' III 289, 302.

76 The Rules are reproduced in Riddell *Legal Profession* 12. On the disapproval of laity see Riddell *Bar and the Courts* Pt 1 *The Bar* 58–67.

77 'Minutes' I 166

78 Law Society Act ss. 1, 8

79 'Jacob Farrand to Convocation'; 'Angus Macdonell to Convocation' (1801) 'Minutes' 16–7. See also Rule 22, 9 Geo. IV (1828), Easter Term; 'Minutes' I 133.

80 Baldwin *1833 Rules* 61; *Rules of the Law Society* 19

81 See W.R. Johnson *Schooled Lawyers: A Study in the Clash of Professional Cultures* (New York 1978).

82 Rule 18, 60 Geo. III (1819), Hilary Term, 'Minutes' I 51

83 See *The Medical Register for Upper Canada, 1867* (Toronto 1867); *Journals of the Legislature of Ontario 1868–9*, 13 Nov. 1868.

84 'Minutes' I 55, 62, 68

85 Ibid. 102

86 See ibid. 158, 166, 193.

87 See ibid. 189, 464.

88 Ibid. 114, 142

89 Baldwin *1833 Rules* 59

90 Rule 22, 9 Geo. IV (1828), Easter Term, 'Minutes' I 133

91 Baldwin *1833 Rules* 65

92 'Report of the Committee on the Examinations for Admissions and Calls' 1 July 1831; 'Minutes' I 207–9, 227

93 Ibid. 208

94 Baldwin *1833 Rules* 59

95 'Minutes' I 208. See also 'Minutes' II 179. These forms can be found at the end of Baldwin *1833 Rules*.

96 The delegation of 'the whole executive government of the Society' to the Standing Committee on Oeconomy in 1839 reflected the magnitude of this problem. Its apparent source was that Osgoode Hall was leased to the provincial government and the 93rd Highlanders for five years following the Rebellion of 1837.

97 'Minutes' II 238

98 For a description of Gwynne by someone who knew him see J.C. Hamilton *Osgoode Hall: Reminiscences of the Bar and Bench* (Toronto 1904) 25–6. On his eccentricity see ibid. 26–35.

99 See, for example, 'Minutes' III 546.

100 'Minutes' II 404. George Mountain Evans, who replaced Gwynne in 1872, did not acquire Gwynne's notoriety. He also was easier on the candidates than his predecessor had been. See 'Minutes' VI 185, 300. See also G.M. Rose 'George M. Evans' in *A Cyclopaedia of Canadian Biography, Being Chiefly Men of the Time* (Toronto 1886) 426.

101 'Minutes' I 390

102 Baldwin *1833 Rules* 62 (italics in original)

103 'Report of the Select Committee on Improvements in the Mode of Conducting Examinations' 16 Nov. 1832; 'Minutes' I 381–4

104 Ibid. 384–7. See also 'Minutes' II 601. After 1855, lists of books relevant for the entrance examinations routinely were published in the UCLJ (OS) and later in the CLJ (NS). See UCLJ I (OS 1855) 60, 120, 180, 240.

105 'Minutes' I 387–91

106 See D.G.Kilgour 'A Note on Legal Education in Ontario 125 Years Ago' *University of Toronto Law Journal* XIII (1959) 270 (hereafter UTLJ); 'Minutes' I 430; D.B. Read *The Lives of the Judges of Upper Canada and Ontario from 1791 to the Present Time* (Toronto 1888) 124, 148, 161, 300–3, 366, 406.

107 See, for example, 'Minutes' I 453–4.

108 See R.D. Gidney and D.A. Lawr 'Egerton Ryerson and the Origins of the Ontario Secondary School' *Canadian Historical Review* LX (1979) 442 (hereafter CHR).

109 Admission of Barristers and Attornies Amendment Act, 7 Wm IV (1837), c. 15 (UC); Act Respecting Barristers-at-Law, 10 and 11 Vict. (1847), c. 29 (Can.); Act Respecting Attorneys-at-Law, ibid. c. 30 (Can.). Compare An Act Concerning Persons to be Admitted to Practise the Law, 6 Wm IV (1836), c. 10 (LC), s. 2.

110 See 'Edward Martin to Convocation' (1880) 'Minutes' VI 485; 'John Crickmore to Convocation' (1880) ibid. 492.

111 See 'Minutes' II 607, 609; 'Minutes' III 546, 563.

112 See 'A. MacNab [Principal, Victoria College] to H.N. Gwynne' (1844) 'Minutes' II 575; J. Langton *Early Days in Upper Canada: Letters of John Langton from the Backwoods of Upper Canada and the Audit Office of the Province of Upper Canada* W.A. Langton, ed. (Toronto 1926) 283.

113 'Minutes' VI 122–7

114 Compare CLJ IX (NS 1873) 72, 100, 136; CLJ XVII (NS 1881) 92, 280, 296. Indeed, motions to add French, German, and natural philosophy to the entrance examinations routinely were defeated. See 'Minutes' II 605; 'Minutes' VI 498.

115 See 'Minutes' VI 345, 429, 512.

116 Ibid. 227–8

117 See P. Lucas 'William Blackstone and the Reform of the English Legal Profession' *English Historical Review* LXXVII (1962) 456, 477, 480; M. Birks *Gentlemen of the Law* (London 1960) 132–205.

118 See Hamlin *Legal Education* 35–8, 47–8; A.-H. Chroust *The Rise of the Legal Profession in America* 2 vols (Norman, OK 1965) I 30–7.

119 See *Rules of the Law Society* 53; D.G. Creighton *John A. Macdonald: the young politician* (Toronto 1952) 22; Hamilton *Osgoode Hall* 151.

120 See Attorneys' and Clerks' Act, 43 Geo. III (1803), c. 8 (UC); An Act to Authorize the Governor to Licence Practitioners in the Law, 43 Geo. III (1803), c. 3 (UC), 'recital.' See also 'Minutes' I 6–7, 11, 287–9; Riddell *Bar and the Courts* Pt I *The Bar* 59; Quarter Sessions Amendment Act, 41 Geo. III (1801), c. 6 (UC). See also R. Gourlay *Statistical Account of Upper Canada* 3 vols (London 1822) I 234–5.

121 Practitioners' and Clerks' Act, 47 Geo. III (1807), c. 5 (UC)

122 A.Z. Reed *Training for the Public Profession of the Law* (New York 1921) 45, also 431–3

123 See R.S. Harris *A History of Higher Education in Canada, 1663–1960* (Toronto 1976) 64–5, 84–5, 161; G.P. de T. Glazebook *Life in Ontario: A Social History* (Toronto 1968) 74, 114.

124 By contrast, articles of clerkship of prospective Upper Canadian attorneys were contracts between the student, his parents, and the solicitor to whom he was articled. They routinely specified that the student would 'well, faithfully and diligently serve, ... readily and cheerfully obey and execute his [principal's] lawful and reasonable commands,' pay for any damage caused, keep his master's secrets, and refrain from embezzlement. See Law Society of Upper Canada *Curriculum of the Law School* (Toronto 1891) 48.

125 See UCLJ VII (OS 1861) 276; CLJ I (NS 1865) 23–4, 220–1; CLJ XVI (NS 1880) 121–2; Hamilton *Osgoode Hall* 149; R. St G. Stubbs *Lawyers and Laymen of Western Canada* (Toronto 1939) 23.

126 'Minutes' I 254. See also ibid. 271; 'Minutes' II 28; *In re Patterson* and *Ex parte McIntyre* above note 73.

127 In Feb. 1840, for example, 37 of the 183 members of the Law Society practised in Toronto. In 1879 260 of the Society's 1104 members practised in the capital. See 'Minutes' II 236; 'Minutes' VI 392.

128 'Petitions of John Lawe [sic] for Admission to Convocation' (1825–7) 'Minutes' I 100, 123

129 'Petition of John Lyons for Admission to Convocation' (1819) 'Minutes' I 93; *Ex Parte Lyons* (1824), *Taylor's Reports* (hereafter TR) 171; 'Minutes' I 147; 'Petition of James Glass for Admission to Convocation' (1878) 'Minutes' VI 179; UCLJ X (OS 1864) 82; CLJ V (NS 1869) 280; Law Society Amendment Act (1822) s. 3. Compare *In re Hagerty* above note 73.

130 See, for example, UCLJ VII (OS 1861) 135; CLJ XVIII (NS 1882) 122, 349–50; L. Lelan 'Law and the Study of Law' *Canadian Monthly* II (1878) 190 (hereafter CM).

131 'Minutes' III 129–33. Compare S.B. Frost and D.L. Johnston 'Law at McGill: Past, Present and Future' *McGill Law Journal* XXVII (1981) 31, 32–4 for contemporaneous developments in Canada East.

132 T.A. Goreham 'The Law Student's Grievance' CM IV (1880) 287; J.E. Farewell

'The Student at Law in the Early Sixties' CLT XXXV (1915) 52; O.M. Biggar 'Legal Education Again' *Canadian Bar Review* I (1923) 846 (hereafter CBR)

133 See Creighton *John A. Macdonald* 22, 25; J.P. Macpherson *Life of the Right Honourable John A. Macdonald* 2 vols (St John, NB 1891) I 82; *Regina v Bidwell* (1827), TR 487 (Simon Washburn's office); *In re Brooke* above note 73.

134 See C. Durand *Reminiscences of Charles Durand, of Toronto, Barrister* (Toronto 1897) 76; Creighton *John A. Macdonald* 26; Hamilton *Osgoode Hall* 150–2; CLJ XVII (NS 1882) 149.

135 See Creighton *John A. Macdonald* 25; M.B. Katz *The People of Hamilton, Canada West: Family and Class in a Mid-Nineteenth-Century City* (Cambridge, MA 1975) 22.

136 'I saw this set-up in 1960 at the offices of an Orillia law firm that was a successor to "Evans," founded before Confederation, which had occupied the same physical plant for several generations.' Simcoe County Court Judge A.M. Carter to the author 2 July 1980

137 Advanced standing or reduction of apprenticeship also was extended to students who fought in the War of 1812 and the North-West Rebellion of 1885. See Barristers, Attornies and Law Students Relief Act, 55 Geo. III (1815), c. 3 (UC), ss. 2, 3; *Journal* I 166, 172. See also above note 109.

138 See D.D. Calvin *Queen's University at Kingston, 1841–1941* (Kingston, Ont. 1941) 210–12; also A. Morel 'Maximilien Bibaud, fondateur de l'Ecole de droit' *Revue Juridique Thémis* II (1951–2) 9.

139 Edward Blake, Charles Moss, D'Alton McCarthy, William Ralph Meredith, and Zebulon Aiton Lash all began their legal careers with one foot in Osgoode Hall and the other in the provincial university. See R.A. Falconer 'Establishment of a Faculty of Law within the University of Toronto' CLT XXXIV (1914) 149, 150; Hamilton *Osgoode Hall* 155–6.

140 An Act to Amend An Act Respecting Barristers at Law, 23 Vict. (1860), c. 47 (Can.); An Act to Amend An Act Respecting Attorneys at Law, 23 Vict. (1860), c. 48 (Can.). Compare An Act Respecting the Bar of Lower Canada, 29 Vict. (1866), c. 27 (Can.) s. 28.

141 See 'Minutes' III 269–70; 'Minutes' VI 194, 200, 318.

142 'Minutes' VI 437, 451, 493

143 In the 1830s the subject areas were Greek and Latin, mathematics, history, geography, and English composition, together with the laws of England, the rules of evidence, procedures at *nisi prius*, and the practice of the courts. By mid-century they had crystallized into liberal studies, commercial and maritime law, real property, common law, equity jurisprudence, and criminal and tort law.

144 See 'Minutes' I 130; 'Minutes' V 399. See also Riddell *Legal Profession* 51.

145 Compare Frost and Johnston 'Law at McGill' 31; E.C. Surrency 'Law Reports in the United States' *American Journal of Legal History* xxv (1981) 49, 50–2 (hereafter AJLH); Riddell *Legal Profession* 107–21. Colonial and nineteenth-century American law students sometimes attended superior court sessions and made manuscript notes of cases, but these reports were intended for use in future practice. Public law reporting in Upper Canada was initiated five years before term-keeping. See An Act Providing for the Publication of Reports of the Decisions of His Majesty's Court of King's Bench in this Province, 4 Geo. IV (1823), c. 3 (UC).

146 See Read *Lives of the Judges* 450–61.

147 See 'Minutes' I 160, 163, 216; Farewell 'Student-at-Law' 52, 53–4. Term-keeping desks can still be seen in Queen's Bench Courtroom Four at Osgoode Hall.

148 'Minutes' II 103–4, 191, 209–10, 260–4, 343

149 See Baldwin *1833 Rules* 19; 'Minutes' I 50, 102, 111. The other reasons for construction were to provide a place for the Society to transact business and to house a communal law library. Only as a result of the provincial government's contribution to additions to the Hall in 1845–6 did the Benchers offer accommodation for the courts. Even then, the Society was the government's landlord. See 'Minutes' II 533, 612; An Act to Provide for the Accommodation of the Courts of Superior Jurisdiction in Upper Canada, 9 Vict. (1846), c. 33 (Can.), s. 1.

150 Attorney General Robinson, one of the promoters of Osgoode Hall, spent 1815–17 and 1822–3 in England and was explicit that the Society should be housed in a manner similar to that of the Inns of Court. He was admitted to Lincoln's Inn in 1823. Bencher Adam Wilson, who oversaw the 1857 additions to the Hall, also conceived of it as a 'temple of justice' along English lines. See R.E. Saunders 'Sir John Beverley Robinson' in DCB IX 678; Hamilton *Osgoode Hall* 3; Riddell *Legal Profession* 76–7.

151 James Sterling Young has demonstrated that early nineteenth-century political party allegiance and legislative power blocs often were attributable directly to the Washington, DC, hotels at which lawmakers stayed and the taverns they frequented. See Young *The Washington Community 1800–1828* (New York 1965).

152 See *Smith* v *Rolph, One, & C.* (1825), TR 272; G.A. Johnston 'The Law Society of Upper Canada 1797–1972' *Law Society of Upper Canada Gazette* VI (1972) 1, 2.

153 See 'Minutes' II 58–61, 70–1; 'Minutes' V 534; Baldwin *1833 Rules* 88–90; Hamilton *Osgoode Hall* 36–42; Law Society of Upper Canada *Osgoode Hall: A Short Account of the Hall 1832–1932* (Toronto 1932).

154 See 'Minutes' I 138, 343, 467; 'Minutes' II 44–5, 46–57.

155 Durand *Reminiscences* 128
156 H. Scadding *Toronto of Old, Collections and Recollections* (Toronto 1873) 102
157 See V.K. Gay 'Courtesy and Custom in the English Legal Tradition – On Dining at Gray's Inn' JLE XXVIII (1976) 181.
158 See 'Minutes' v 181; Attornies Amendment Act, 32 Vict. (1869), c. 19 (Ont.).
159 See Read *Lives of the Judges* 450–61; E. Gillis, 'Legal Education in Ontario – An Historical Sketch' *Canadian Law Review* IV (1904) 101–2; Riddell *Legal Profession* 43; D.B. Read 'The Law School of Osgoode Hall, Toronto' *Green Bag* III (1891) 264–6
160 Baldwin *1833 Rules* 12–13
161 See ibid. 33, 68–9, 71; 'Minutes' I 327–9, 412.
162 See Riddell *Legal Profession* 33; Johnston, 'Law Society' 4.
163 The Chair had previously been declined by Attorney General William Henry Draper, a leading Toronto commercial counsel and prominent Family Compact Tory. See Harris *History of Higher Education* 66–72.
164 Baldwin *1833 Rules* 158, 165a, 187. See generally D. Swainson 'William Hume Blake' in DCB IX 55.
165 Metropolitan Toronto Library Board, Baldwin Papers, 'W.H. Blake to R. Baldwin' 19 May 1848. John D. Blackwell kindly provided this reference, together with that which appears in the following note.
166 See PAO 'Blake Family Papers' W.H. Blake's lecture notes, Feb. 1846; J. McG. Young 'The Faculty of Law' in W.J. Alexander, ed. *The University of Toronto and Its Colleges, 1827–1906* (Toronto 1906) 151; Read *Lives of the Judges* 273; Hamilton *Osgoode Hall* 137; G. Blaine Baker 'A Note on the Migration of Upper Canada's Law Libraries' *Law Society of Upper Canada Gazette* XIV (1980) 362, 364.
167 See An Act Respecting the Federation of the University of Toronto and University College with Other Universities and Colleges, 50 Vict. (1887), c. 43 (Ont.), ss. 5 (1) (5), 35, 53 (1).
168 'Minutes' III 129–33 (italics added)
169 Ibid. 133–4
170 See ibid. 347 et seq.; 'The Late Mr Justice Conner [sic]' UCLJ IX I (OS 1863) 115; D. Swainson 'John Hillyard Cameron' in DCB X 118; W.S. Wallace 'Sir John Hawkins Hagarty,' 'Philip Michael Matthew Scott Vankoughnet' in MDCB 323, 854.
171 'Minutes' III 416–17
172 Ibid. 397–8; Toronto University Amendment Act, 16 Vict. (1853), c. 89 (Can.), ss. 18–19, 32; Young *University of Toronto* 153
173 See 'Minutes' III 426–7, 457, 490–2, 574; UCLJ V (OS 1859) 129, 164–5; UCLJ VII (OS 1861) 276.
174 See above note 140.

175 See Hamilton *Osgoode Hall* 155–6; Reed *Present-Day* 345, 365. Compare J. Willis *A History of the Dalhousie Law School* (Toronto 1978) 19–45.

176 See Farewell 'Student-at-Law' 51, 54.

177 See 'Minutes' III 574; 'Rough Minutes' IV 103, 116, 233; 'Minutes' VI 727; *Journal* I 175–7.

178 'Minutes' III 537, 571; 'Rough Minutes' IV 144, 165, 171, 175, 188, 196, 299

179 See J. Schull *Edward Blake: The Man of the Other Way (1833–1881)* (Toronto 1975); W.S. Wallace 'Adam Crooks,' 'Sir Samuel Henry Strong' in MDCB 184, 804.

180 'Rough Minutes' IV 107, 120, 132; UCLJ IV (OS 1858) 60. Wallbridge also was an examiner in the Victoria University Law School (1864–92) in the 1860s. See C.B. Sissons *A History of Victoria University* (Toronto 1952) 124.

181 'Rough Minutes' IV 196

182 See H.M. Neatby *Queen's University: To Strive, To Seek, To Find and Not To Yield* F.W. Gibson and R. Graham, eds (Montreal 1978) I 106–7.

183 *Kingston Daily News* 6 Feb. 1861

184 'Rough Minutes' IV 223. See also Calvin *Queen's University* 212.

185 CLJ IV (NS 1868) 134. See also 'Minutes' V 174.

186 See 'Minutes' V, 43, 65, 142, 333; Farewell 'Student-at-Law' 52.

187 'Minutes' V 289. See also CLJ VII (NS 1871) 91–2. Similar rhetoric, both published and unpublished, was a commonplace in the period. See R.T. Walkem *A Treatise on the Law Relating to the Execution and Revocation of Wills, and to Testamentary Capacity* (Toronto 1873) 'author's preface.' See also 'John A. Macdonald to Convocation' 16 May 1876, 'Minutes' V 632–3; 'J.H. Cameron to Convocation' ibid. 635; CLJ XII (NS 1876) 158–60.

188 Compare H.V. Nelles *The Politics of Development: Forests, Mines, and Hydro-Electric Power in Ontario 1849–1941* (Toronto 1974); D.C. Masters *The Rise of Toronto, 1850–1890* (Toronto 1947).

189 'Minutes' V 416. For Cameron's inaugural address in this series of lectures see CLJ IX (NS 1873) 105.

190 'Minutes' V 416–17, 420, 495, 500; 'Minutes' VI 16; CLJ IX (NS 1873) 4

191 'Minutes' V 420, 533

192 Ibid. 416; 'Minutes' VI 16, 32–5

193 See 'Minutes' V 551; 'Minutes' VI 116, 146; Gillis 'Legal Education' 102; CLJ XIV (NS 1878) 69.

194 'Minutes' VI 2, 4, 21, 129

195 See CLJ XIV (NS 1878) 69; Gillis 'Legal Education' 105; N.F. Davin 'Legal Education' CM IV (1880) 287; CLJ XVI (NS 1880) 119; Lelan 'Law and the Study of Law'; B.D. Bucknall, T.C.H. Baldwin, and J.D. Lakin 'Pedants, Practitioners and Prophets: Legal Education at Osgoode Hall to 1957' *Osgoode Hall Law Journal* VI (1968) 137, 153–7.

196 'Minutes' v 421; 'Minutes' vi 84, 366. By far the greatest drain on the Society's resources was publication of the law reports.

197 See 'Minutes' v 420, 437.

198 See ibid. 551; 'Minutes' vi 116, 392.

199 See 'Minutes' v 102, 586; 'Minutes' vi 4, 534–5, 558–60; CLJ vii (NS 1871) 92–3; CLJ xii (NS 1876) 187–8; CLJ xiv (NS 1878) 68; CLJ xvi (NS 1880) 119–20, 121–2; CLJ xvii (NS 1881) 282; Journal i 109; N.F. Davin and T.A. Goreham 'No Law School' CM iv (1880) 119; An Act Respecting the University of Toronto, 36 Vict. (1873), c. 29 (Ont.), s. 45; R. McCormick 'The Libraries of the Law Society,' LSUCG vi (1972) 55.

200 See for example 'Minutes' vi 449–50; Journal i 106.

201 See for example CLJ ix (NS 1873) 154; CLJ xviii (NS 1882) 349; CLJ xxii (NS 1886) 273.

202 Davin and Goreham 'No Law School' 119

203 Davin 'Legal Education' 237

204 Journal i 106. See also Davin and Goreham 'No Law School'; Goreham 'Law Student's Grievance' 531.

205 CLJ xvii (NS 1881) 111

206 'Minutes' vi 469, 534–5

207 See generally CLR v (1906) 122–4; CLJ ix (NS 1873) 7.

208 See 'Minutes' vi 580, 614.

209 See ibid. 580–98; Journal i 111, 157, 183. The Law Society was not as generous in the case of other clubs. See 'Minutes' iii 485, v 286, vi 462.

210 See Hamilton Osgoode Hall 185; Journal i 183.

211 For the promoters and lecturers, see Journal i 106, 130, 195, 213. A two-year sunset provision was built into the resolution recreating the lecture program. The School had to be continued by special orders of Convocation in 1884, 1886, and 1888. See ibid. 130, 148, 192, 212, 244. For the courses offered see ibid. 130, 213, and Law Society Curriculum 20.

212 Journal i 130, 192

213 Journal i 116. Average total attendance was about eight per cent of Ontario's students-at-law and was therefore about twenty per cent of students apprenticed in Toronto. Accord CLJ xxiv (NS 1888) 419

214 'Minutes' vi 589, 689, 699. See also CLJ xvii (NS 1881) 282.

215 Journal i 157, 183–4. See also Gwynne-Timothy Western's First Century 421–8; Hamilton Osgoode Hall 133–4.

216 See Journal i 157; Sissons History of Victoria 124; G. Caron 'The Faculty of Law at the University of Ottawa' UTLJ xii (1958) 292; C. Franklin Universities and Colleges of Canada (Toronto 1976) 385.

217 Journal i 213, 233

218 Ibid. 147, 213
219 Ibid. 234–8. The Editor of *The Canadian Law Times* also opposed affiliation with the universities. See CLT VIII (1888) 69. For mention of earlier university reluctance to teach law see UCLJ V (OS 1859) 245.
220 *Journal* I 263, 266 (as amended)
221 Ibid. 287. There was considerable controversy about whether a Canadian or an Englishman would make the most appropriate principal. See for example CLT IX (1889) 356.
222 See CLT VIII (1888) 151, 172, 238; *Journal* I 273–6; 297.
223 *Journal* I 274, 277, 288, 292
224 See 'Minutes' V 187; 'Minutes' VI 142, 507. See also CLJ XVII (NS 1881) 93–4.
225 Davin and Goreham 'No Law School' 119
226 See L.M. Friedman *A History of American Law* (New York 1973) 142–6, 265–82, 525–38; R. Stevens 'Two Cheers for 1870: The American Law School' *Perspectives in American History* V (1971) 403; Johnson *Schooled Lawyers* 58–119.
227 See generally B.J. Bledstein *The Culture of Professionalism: The Middle Class and the Development of Higher Education in America* (New York 1976).
228 J.W. Hurst *The Growth of American Law: The Law Makers* (Boston 1950) 260
229 See J. Goebel jr *A History of the School of Law: Columbia University* (New York 1955); A.E. Sutherland *The Law at Harvard: A History of Ideas and Men, 1817–1967* (Cambridge, MA 1967) 162–205; E.G. Brown *Legal Education at Michigan, 1859–1959* (Ann Arbor, MI 1959).
230 A.V. Dicey 'Teaching of English Law at Harvard' *Harvard Law Review* XIII (1899) 422; J. Bryce *The American Commonwealth* 3 vols (New York 1888) II 623
231 W.A. Reeve 'Inaugural Address to the Law School' CLT IX (1889) 242, 245–7, 248, 252–3
232 Newman 'Reaction and Change' 53. See also Bucknall et al. 'Pedants, Practitioners and Prophets' 160–84.
233 Baldwin *1833 Rules* 70–1
234 See 'Rough Minutes' IV 209, 289–91; UCLJ VII (OS 1861) 140; UCLJ IX (OS 1863) 145.
235 'Report of the Select Committee on Scholarships to Convocation' (1880) 'Minutes' VI 552. See also 'Rough Minutes' IV 227, 242, 259, 261; 'Minutes' V 40, 98.
236 See 'Minutes' V 174, 345, 387. See also Attorneys-at-Law Amendment Act, 31 Vict. (1868) c. 23 (Ont.).
237 'Minutes' I 384, 390
238 Ibid. 284. Compare *Nagle* v *Kilts* (1825), TR 269, 270 where Baldwin himself urged King's Bench to relax certain rigid English rules due to 'a want of professional advice' in parts of the province.

239 'Minutes' I 396–8
240 'Report of the Committee on Oeconomy to Convocation' 'Minutes' II 236, 384. See also W.C. Keele 'Attornies and Barristers' in *The Provincial Justice or Magistrate's Manual* (Toronto 1835) 'appendix.'
241 'Minutes' v 439; J. Rordans *The Upper Canada Law List and Solicitors' Agency Book* (Toronto 1856)
242 Hamilton *Osgoode Hall* 147; E. Ermatinger *Life of Colonel Talbot and the Talbot Settlement* (Toronto 1859) 169–70. Compare *Morin* v *Wilkinson* (1850), 2 *Grant's Chancery Reports* (hereafter Gr. Ch.) 157; *O'Keefe* v *Taylor* ibid. 95; *Gray* v *Springer* (1855), 5 Gr. Ch. 242, where Chancellor Blake alluded to a lack of professional legal advice in certain transactions.
243 In Hamilton a fifty-five per cent increase in the number of lawyers and doctors occurred in the decade between 1852 and 1861. See Katz *People of Hamilton* 55, 72. Compare F. Ouellet *Lower Canada 1791–1840. Social Change and Nationalism* (Toronto 1980) 171–7, 363.
244 'Minutes' II 497; 'Minutes' III 224–30. See also UCLJ I (OS 1855) 162–5; UCLJ II (OS 1856) 49–50; UCLJ III (OS 1857) 76–7; UCLJ VII (OS 1861) 140–1; UCLJ IX (OS 1863) 135–6; CLJ I (NS 1865) 24–6, 53, 79, 311; CLJ III (NS 1867) 113; CLJ IV (NS 1868) 162.
245 'Minutes' III 413–16. See also UCLJ I (OS 1855) 59–60.
246 'Minutes' v 135
247 'Law Society of Upper Canada' above note 4
248 'Rough Minutes' IV 237
249 See 'Minutes' VI 414, 462, 469.
250 Any of these questions could appear on an Ontario law school examination in the 1980s. See 'Minutes' v 57. See also UCLJ I (OS 1855) 216; UCLJ V (OS 1859) 30–1, 55–7, 79–81, 102–3; UCLJ VI (OS 1860) 30–3, 78–9; UCLJ VII (OS 1861) 28–30, 197–8, 225–7, 253–5, 308–10; UCLJ VIII 2–4, 87–8, 145–6.
251 C. Brown and E.M. Chadwick *Osgoode Hall Examination Questions, Given at the Examinations for Call With and Without Honours, and for Certificates of Fitness, With Concise Answers, and the Student's Guide; A Collection of Directions and Forms for the Use of Students-at-Law and Articled Clerks* (Toronto 1862). See also UCLJ VIII (OS 1862) 140.
252 See J.E. McDougall *Law Lectures on the Subjects of Torts and Negligence* (Toronto 1882); D.B. Read *Lectures on the Judicature Act* (Toronto 1881); H.N. Roberts *Examination Questions and Answers on Harris' Criminal Law* (Toronto 1889); J.S. Ewart *Examination Questions on Blackstone's Commentaries* (Toronto 1863).
253 See A.H. Marsh *History of the Court of Chancery, and the Rise and Development of the Doctrines of Equity* (Toronto 1879); H.N. Roberts *Law of Wills* (Toronto 1892); T.W. Taylor and J.S. Ewart *Practice of the Supreme Court of Judicature for Ontario* (Toronto 1881); R.E. Kingsford *Manual of Evidence in Civil Cases*

(Toronto 1889); A. Leith *Williams' Real Property: Adapted to Ontario* (Toronto 1881); R. Sullivan and C. Moss *Commercial Law for Upper Canada* (Toronto 1866); R.E. Kingsford *Manual of the Law of Landlord and Tenant* (Toronto 1896).

254 See A.W.B. Simpson 'The Rise and Fall of the Legal Treatise: Legal Principles and the Forms of Legal Literature' *University of Chicago Law Review* XLVIII (1981) 632.

255 Between July 1797 and Feb. 1840 436 persons were called to the Bar of Upper Canada; 247 of these lawyers held the Society's Barrister-at-Law degree; 199 of them had been admitted as foreign lawyers or government licensees. However, of the 183 lawyers *living* in the province in 1840, 176 had been students of the Society. 'Minutes' II 238.

256 Law Society Amendment Act (1822) s. 2. See also An Act to Establish a Court of Chancery in This Province, 7 Wm IV (1837), c. 2 (UC), s. 22; An Act to Facilitate and Encourage the Study of the Law in This Province, 13 Vict. (1850–1), c. 26 (Can.).

257 See C.W. Robinson *Life of Sir John Beverley Robinson Bart, C.B., D.C.L., Chief Justice of Upper Canada* (Edinburgh and London 1904) 375, 389.

258 See, for example, UCLJ III (OS 1857) 76–8.

259 See 'Minutes' II 339, 476, 533, 551, 580, 584, 607–12 (Newfoundland); 'Minutes' V 32 (New Brunswick); ibid. 210 (Nova Scotia).

260 See 'Minutes' I 6–7, 19; 'Minutes' II 156, 160, 199, 535; CLJ V (NS 1869) 114; CLJ VII (NS 1871) 7; CLJ VIII (NS 1872) 263.

261 'Minutes' VI 14. See also 'Dominion Law Society' CLJ XII (NS 1876) 271; CLJ (NS 1877) 9–10.

262 See *Journals of the Legislative Assembly of the Province of Canada* (Toronto 1841) 355, 405.

263 See G.P. Browne, ed. 'Hewitt Bernard's Minutes of the Quebec Conference, 10–29 Oct. 1864' *Documents on the Confederation of British North America* (Toronto 1969) 120.

264 See generally D. and L. Gibson *Substantial Justice: Law and Lawyers in Manitoba 1670–1970* (Winnipeg, Man. 1972); A. Watts *Lex Liberorum Rex: History of the Law Society of British Columbia, 1868–1973* (Vancouver, BC 1973); W.H. McConnell *Prairie Justice* (Calgary, Alta. 1980) 13–6, 20–1, 35–7, 63, 68, 79, 88, 189–91, 209, 216.

265 See 'Minutes' II 73; 'Minutes' V 11, 107–8; *Journal* I 143, 301; 'Proceedings of the Legislative Assembly' *Ontario Archives Reports* VI (Toronto 1909) 112–13; *Ontario Archives Reports* VII 87–9; Licensees' Act (1803); Court of Chancery Act (1837), ss. 12, 22.

266 See for example 'Minutes' III 54.

267 Convocation also resolved at an early date that no applicant would be admit-

ted to law study without declaring on his honour that he intended to remain in Upper Canada and that his purpose in law study was to become a
'resident practitioner.' 'Minutes' I 36. See also King's Bench Act (1822), s.
44.
268 For lists of Upper Canadian lawyers admitted to practise by special acts before
1855 see G.W. Wickstead, ed. *Index to the Statutes in Force in Upper Canada
at the End of the Session of 1854–5* (Toronto 1856) 402; G.W. Wickstead, ed. *Table
of the Provincial Statutes in Force or Which Have Been in Force in Upper Canada in
Their Chronological Order* (Toronto 1856) 145.
269 F.S. Smith 'Admission to the Bar in New York' *Yale Law Journal* XVI (1907)
519; Farmer 'The Bar Examination and Beginning Years of Legal Practice in
North Carolina, 1820–1860' *North Carolina Historical Review* XXIX (1952)
159
270 'How to Become a Lawyer in Ontario' CLJ VII (NS 1871) 229
271 See R.C.B. Risk 'The Law and the Economy in Mid-Nineteenth-Century
Ontario: A Perspective' in D.H. Flaherty, ed. *Essays in the History of Canadian
Law* 2 vols (Toronto 1981–3) I 88, 120. See also W.R. Riddell *A Philadelphia
Lawyer in Canada in 1810* (Toronto 1928).
272 See Lord Durham *The Report of the Earl of Durham* (London 1902) 121–3;
Kilgour 'Note on Legal Education' 270; *Law Times* XXVIII (1856) 85; *Re de Sousa*
(1885), 9 *Ontario Reports* 39.
273 See Keele *Provincial Justice* 'appendix.'
274 See H.R. Hardy, ed. *The Canadian Law List* (Toronto 1893) 18–32.
275 Compare D.H. Calhoun *Professional Lives in America: Structure and Aspiration,
1750–1850* (Cambridge, MA 1965); W.F. English *The Pioneer Lawyer and Jurist
in Missouri* (Columbia, MI 1947).
276 Robinson *Sir John Beverley Robinson* 375, 389
277 O. Mowat 'Observations on the Use and Value of American Reports' UCLJ III
(OS 1857) 35. See also 'Minutes' III 500; 'Minutes' V 187; 'Minutes' VI 322,
507; UCLJ III (OS 1857) 16; note 245 above.
278 See W.R. Riddell 'The Lawyer' CLT XXVII (1907) 785, 787; Bucknall et al.
'Pedants, Practitioners and Prophets' 160–85; Newman 'Reaction and
Change.'
279 Compare R.D. Gidney and W.P.J. Millar 'The Origins of Organized Medicine
in Ontario, 1850–1869' (unpublished manuscript 1981); C. Berger *Imperial-
ism and Nationalism, 1884–1914: A Conflict in Canadian Thought* (Toronto 1969).
These conclusions contrast starkly with those of other commentators who
have argued that in endless cases Upper Canadians were very 'British'
and that the province was merely an intellectual and legal colony of the
mother country. See A.B. McKillop *A Disciplined Intelligence: Critical Inquiry*

and Canadian Thought in the Victorian Era (Montreal 1979); Risk 'Law and the Economy' 107–8; B. Laskin *The British Tradition in Canadian Law* (Oxford 1968).

280 Hurst *Growth of American Law* esp. 3–19, 439–460
281 See S. Botein 'Professional History Reconsidered' AJLH XXI (1977) 60.
282 See 'Minutes' v 101. Indeed, the Benchers' jealous guarding of privacy resulted in their remarks remaining confidential for over a century.

3

'The Ten Thousand Pound Job': Political Corruption, Equitable Jurisdiction, and the Public Interest in Upper Canada 1852–6

PAUL ROMNEY

'The Ten Thousand Pound Job' was a highly profitable speculation in City of Toronto debentures that was undertaken in 1852 by Francis Hincks, premier and finance minister of the Province of Canada, and John George Bowes, mayor of Toronto. It has most often been noticed as one of several scandals that marred Hincks' premiership (1851–4). Upon close investigation, it illuminates various subjects: the practical and ethical problems posed by the advent of business enterprise on an unprecedented scale in the form of railways; the nature of politics and public morality in Upper Canada, and above all in Toronto, its economic and political metropolis; and (not least) the functioning of the law both as a code embodying basic social values and as a complex of institutions designed to arbitrate disputes according to those values. The affair touched many aspects of Upper Canadian public life at a time of rapid change both within the colony itself and in its relations with the British Empire.[1]

THE HISTORICAL CONTEXT

In Upper Canada between 1825 and 1850 the social changes wrought by British immigration imposed great strains on the colony's fragile political structure. In 1837 the body politic was shattered by rebellion, and in the following decade it underwent a metamorphosis. The union of Upper and Lower Canada in 1841 broke the political monopoly of the old provincial oligarchy, the Family Compact. The British government tried a while longer to keep the executive branch of the government independent of the legislature and primarily responsive to imperial rather than local needs, but by the end of the decade it had abandoned its effort to maintain economic dominance over the colonies by political means.

During the early 1850s the politics of Upper Canada were fluid and amorphous as politicians struggled to adapt themselves to the new order. The old Reform party, its great goal achieved, split into factions distinguished by their views on the province's political and religious institutions. The 'Grits' admired American political institutions and opposed any state funding of religious organizations, including church schools. George Brown led a faction that was also voluntarist in ecclesiastical policy but was devoted to British political institutions and the imperial tie. The Hincksite rump, like the Brownites, held that responsible government was the last word in political organization; but the Hincksites were loath to end state aid to religious institutions, either from conviction or else from fear of jeopardizing the alliance with the Lower Canadian Bleus that kept them in power. The Conservatives were also divided. A pragmatic wing was eager to forge a link with the Hincksites and Bleus which would provide access to political power, while a 'High Tory' faction still resented the union of 1841 and the advent of responsible rule. The latter disliked the Bleus for being French, Roman Catholic, and suspect in their devotion to the empire. Associated with the Conservatives were the Orangemen, whose ranks were correspondingly split into pragmatically and ideologically inclined wings.[2]

Underlying the political chaos at mid-century was the economic ferment of unrestrained growth in the nineteenth-century 'boom-and-bust' style. Upper Canada was dominated by immigrants who had come there to grow rich. The means employed by the most enterprising were sometimes far from proper. The oligarchic propensities of the Family Compact itself had stemmed as much from economic interest as from political idealism: one of its main objects had been to promote Toronto's economic dominance over the colony as a whole, a goal which reflected the guiding principle of the empire, the maintenance of economic dominion by political means.[3] After the oligarchy had been politically dispossessed, the tone of provincial society remained one of unbridled materialism. 'Oh for a Canadian nationality which would ameliorate the unmitigated selfishness which pervades the land!' exclaimed George Brown (himself immigrant, businessman, and politician) in 1847.[4]

Economic aspirations helped to shape the new political alignments. The Hincksites comprised those reformers who held that, now that responsible government had been won, economic growth must be the main goal of politics. The coalitionist Conservatives were those who felt that the struggle over political organization was now a dead issue and it was time to join the Hincksites in promoting economic expansion. This pragmatic conservatism was epitomized by Sir Allan MacNab, former last-ditch defender of the old order, who in 1854 was to preside over the first Conservative-Hincksite-Bleu ministry. As he plunged into a variety of squalid business deals, MacNab pithily summed up his new political priorities in the phrase: 'All my politics are railroads.'[5]

Railroads were the leading edge of economic growth. They promised undreamed-of prosperity to those who could use them as instruments of economic control; but they also rendered everything uncertain by linking rival centres of power in new and unstable relationships. Toronto and Hamilton vied for supremacy in Upper Canada by means of railroads; Montreal sought to dominate both by the same means. MacNab had first sought social advancement as an auxiliary of the Family Compact. Now that the oligarchy's institutional predominance was shattered, he was eager to challenge their city's mastery from his own base of Hamilton, wielding the mighty weapon of railroads by which one might dominate an empire more effectively than politics had ever allowed. For men like MacNab, politics became above all a process of promoting the right railroads.[6]

The 'Ten Thousand Pound Job' caused such a stir at least in part because it touched so many of these volatile elements of Upper Canadian public life. John George Bowes personified the pragmatic, entrepreneurial conservatism that wished to combine with the Hincksites and Bleus. His speculative partnership with Hincks prefigured, in a sense, a political alliance that was already in the air, although it was not to be consummated until 1854. The speculation itself seemed to many observers to epitomize the lax approach to public morality that might be expected of men who made a virtue of opportunism in politics and business alike; but others dismissed Bowes' critics as envious quibblers who feared the new social and economic order that was bringing men like him to the top. For his part the mayor justified his actions by claiming that their main object had been to promote the construction of a railway which would benefit the citizens he was elected to serve. In deciding how far this motive purified the impugned facts, Chancellor William Hume Blake and his colleagues in the courts of Chancery and Appeal found themselves obliged to consider how far 'railroads' should be not only the politics but the law of Upper Canada. They also had to decide the extent to which the fiduciary conception of government implicit in the concept of 'responsible government' should be applicable to municipal officials. Their differing opinions mirrored conflicting conceptions of the dictates of public morality at a particular time and place, but the doctrinal issues they addressed are still controversial today.

THE BACKGROUND OF THE SCANDAL

The debentures involved in the scandal had been issued in aid of the Ontario, Simcoe and Huron Railroad (commonly known as the Northern) under authority of a by-law of 28 June 1852, which carried into effect two earlier resolutions of the Toronto city council. The first resolution, passed in November 1850, had granted the Northern £25,000 in debentures, provided that the company built its line along the whole of the city's waterfront and set up a passenger terminus on a certain lot in the city centre. A second resolution of August 1851 had lent the railway another £35,000 in bonds on the same conditions. Gift and loan were to be granted in a ratio of £1000 for every £10,000 spent on building the line, the first £10,000 to be paid over when £100,000 had been invested.[7]

The first £10,000 of debentures were issued under the by-law on 15 July 1852, but almost at once the plan had to be altered.[8] The provincial government held a lien on the line in return for aid given under the Railway Guarantee Act of 1849, and the railway was therefore unable to give the city adequate security for its £35,000 loan. The railway contractors, an American firm called Story & Co., were pressed for funds and needed more than the £25,000 worth of bonds to which the railway was entitled by the 'gift' resolution of 1850. Negotiations therefore were resumed to see if the city might help the line on other terms.[9] Bowes worked out an agreement with the Northern which the city council ratified by a resolution of 29 July 1852. Under this arrangement the railway renounced its right to the gift and loan, and the city consented to buy £50,000 of Northern stock at par from the contractors provided that the conditions attached to the earlier bargain were also applied to the new one. The city paid for the stock by issuing its own debentures to the amount of £50,000. £10,000 worth (as noted) had already been issued when the resolution confirming the new agreement was passed; the rest followed between August and November 1852. These £50,000 worth of Toronto debentures were the bonds that figured in the 'Ten Thousand Pound Job.'[10]

The bonds, which carried six per cent annual interest, were redeemable after twenty years. In fact, though, they were redeemed in November 1852: the same month in which the last of them had been issued. The reason was that they were illegal. The by-law of 28 June under which they had been issued was informal in two respects: it had been passed without either the three months' public notice or the five per cent sinking fund required by the general municipal law of Upper Canada.[11] This irregularity had arisen from a conflict of legislation, because the special act empowering the city to aid the Northern had not demanded either provision. Nevertheless, doubts as to the by-law's legality had been expressed even before its enactment, and the city's finance committee had sought opinions from two Toronto attorneys. Both found it defective, but it was passed none the less because Story & Co. were anxious for funds to pay pressing bills.[12] Joseph Curran Morrison, a director of the Northern who was soon to become Solicitor General for Upper Canada, expressed a different view of the law, and Mayor Bowes assured Story & Co. that if the by-law did prove to be invalid the city would take other steps to meet its obligation. The railway's directors for their part readily assumed full responsibility for any complications that might arise should the bonds be declared illegal.[13]

At the time it was supposed that, if the bonds were in fact illegal, the government would simply authorize a bill to legalize them. From Bowes' negotiations with the ministers, however, a different scheme emerged. Bowes told the city council that Premier Hincks was unwilling to permit simple legalization because it would leave the bonds unsecured by a sinking fund. But the city had £50,000 of debt falling due in January 1854, and the government would support a bill empowering the municipality to consolidate its debt by issuing debentures for £100,000, half of which would be used to redeem the irregular bonds and the rest to pay off the expiring debt. A sinking fund would be required, but one of only two per cent instead of the five per cent fund imposed on municipal bond issues in aid of railways.[14]

Encouraged by Bowes, council decided on 23 August to petition the legislature for the proposed consolidation act. The city solicitor drew up a bill and sent it to Quebec, where it was introduced into the Legislative Assembly on 22 September. Six days later, Thomas G. Ridout, Cashier of the Bank of Upper Canada, conveyed to the city's finance committee an unprecedented offer from unnamed parties in England to take the whole £100,000 loan at par, provided the city accepted its illegal bonds at face value in part payment: that is, the city would receive £50,000 in cash, plus the bonds.[15]

Toronto's debentures always sold at a substantial discount in Canada, and the prospect of their commanding par on the London market was most gratifying. The committee gave no thought to other ways of raising the £100,000 loan. The consolidation bill was rushed through a complaisant legislature and received royal assent on 7 October.[16] On the eighteenth, the city council passed a by-law formalizing the resolution of 29 July by which it had bought the Northern stock. On 1 November it enacted another to issue £100,000 in new debentures and to redeem the illegal bonds as the Toronto Consolidation Act directed.[17] The mayor, as the city's agent under this second by-law, thereupon accepted the British offer for the loan. Story & Co. had been helped over their troubles; the building of the Northern was proceeding smoothly; the city had been able to negotiate an enormous loan at par; and, best of all, Toronto securities for the first time were recognized on the London money market. Then the rumours began to spread.

In mid-December, shortly before the civic elections, anonymous placards were posted in Toronto, insinuating that Story & Co. had realized only £40,000 on the prematurely redeemed bonds and that the remaining £10,000 had gone to other parties, one of whom was Bowes.[18] They did not stop Bowes' re-election to council, nor his re-election as mayor by the new council.[19] Just before the mayoral election the charges had come before the retiring council when Councillor Charles Romain, the mayor's ally, had obligingly asked him if it was true that Story & Co. had been bilked of £10,000. Bowes assured the council that the contractors had realized the bonds' full value. When one of Bowes' enemies asked if he had not made £4,000 profit on the debentures, the mayor gave specific and circumstantial reassurances that he had not. Bowes' supporters were able to return him to the mayoralty with a clear conscience.[20]

But not all the council members, nor all the citizens, were partisans of Bowes. The handsome, swaggering Irish Methodist was a man of great energy and charm, but his words and deeds made him almost as many enemies as friends. His personality and political style symbolized changes in Toronto society that many powerful citizens disliked. He was the second Irish mayor of Toronto, but the first had been a gentleman. He was the second merchant to be mayor, but the first had been a Scot and an Anglican. He had done more than any other man to bring Toronto into the railway era, persuading the wealthy electors who were entitled to approve or reject money by-laws by referendum to authorize large-scale municipal aid to both the Northern Railroad and the Toronto & Guelph. To those citizens, however, to whom the railway was a necessary evil rather than a splendid opportunity (and there were many such among Toronto's élite), the man who had persuaded them of its necessity symbolized the insecurity of an era of rapid change. Even among those who embraced the railway as an engine of civic and personal enrichment, some disliked Bowes' ostentatious pose as a 'self-made' man, his demagogic cultivation of lower-class Irish support (irrespective of religion), and his propensity to tweak the noses of Toronto's patricians in public.[21]

Thus when Alderman John Bell, a wealthy Liberal lawyer, moved for a select committee of inquiry into the circumstances surrounding the issue and sale of the illegal bonds, it was not surprising that the motion was defeated only after acrimonious debate. Rumours were cited to the effect that Bowes had shared the alleged profit with Hincks and other parties: James Cotton, a government contractor, was named by some, and an anonymous official of the Bank of Upper Canada was also implicated. The mayor closed the debate at last by warning that '*he would make it a personal matter* with any man who pressed it further,' a remark which one newspaper interpreted as a promise of 'pistols for two and coffee for one.'[22]

Still the rumours persisted. Nearly 500 petitioners, including many of Toronto's leading citizens, besought council to investigate the scandal and take action in Chancery, if the truth could not be otherwise discovered, or at least to authorize private citizens to sue Bowes in the city's name. Alderman Bell moved an immediate committee of the whole on the petition, and Bowes' friends could fend it off only by conceding the select committee they had refused two weeks earlier.[23]

PROCEEDINGS IN COUNCIL: AN ATTEMPTED WHITEWASH

During these early weeks of 1853 no definite bill of particulars was presented against Bowes but only a profusion of sometimes contradictory charges, which were fed by the administrative irregularities in which the affair abounded.[24] Apart from the defects in the by-law of 28 June, these concerned the manner in which the bonds had been issued. The first £10,000 worth had not gone out until three weeks after the by-law's passage, but the rest had been emitted far in advance of the one-to-ten ratio prescribed therein.[25] The last £7000 worth had actually been issued ten days after the Toronto Consolidation Act had become law and had then been redeemed in apparent contravention of the act, which provided for the redemption of bonds issued 'heretofore.' Even more odd was the fact that none of the bonds had been given to Story & Co., as might be expected: they had all been deposited in the Bank of Upper Canada instead.

It was easy to surmise that the early delay had been engineered to give Bowes and his partners time to raise the purchase price, and that the later acceleration reflected a wish that the whole amount be issued before the Consolidation Act became law; but why had the bonds been deposited in the Bank? One hypothesis stated that the Bank had loaned the funds used to buy them on security of the bonds themselves. These possibly illegal instruments could have been acceptable as security only if Bowes had officially assured the Bank that they would be legalized if necessary; and, if Bowes himself was one of the buyers, such assurances were a clear abuse of his office for private gain. More lurid still was the rumour that the Bank had advanced the £40,000 purchase price not from its own funds but either from the government's account at Hincks' order or from the city's at Bowes': a flagrant abuse of trust by the guilty party.

Even those who suspected Bowes of sharp practice were far from sure who had lost by it. It was generally agreed that the city had issued bonds with a face value of £50,000, that Story & Co. had sold them for £40,000, and that soon afterwards their latest owners had surrendered them to the city at par. But to whom did the £10,000 profit made thereby belong: to the city, or to the contractors? Some argued that the city had intended to aid the Northern Railroad to the extent of £50,000 cash and that only the bonds' illegality had prevented the contractors from selling them at par. If this were so, the contractors had been robbed of £10,000. Others contended that the bonds' illegality had not affected their value but that Story & Co. had sold them to Hincks and Bowes at a discount in return for improper favours. In this case the profit should revert to the city, which would have been the victim of a breach of trust by Bowes. It was also suggested that, even if Bowes had bought the bonds from Story & Co. legitimately, he had committed a breach of trust by not telling the council that the contractors were ready to sell at eighty, thereby giving the city a chance to buy back its own bonds at the discount price that he and his partners had paid.

The question of whether the city had a claim to the £10,000 was later to figure in the equity pleadings. Regardless of that question, however, it was alleged that the city had certainly lost by the deal in one respect. The profit had been made by exchanging the defective bonds, bought for £40,000, for securities worth £50,000 issued under the Toronto Consolidation Act. But half of the £100,000 loan negotiated under the act in November 1852 was destined for the redemption of existing debt which did not fall due until January 1854. For more than a year, then, the city would have to pay interest at six per cent on both the new debt and the old.

Against this plethora of charges Bowes' supporters contended that there were no grounds for complaint whether he had bought the bonds or not.[26] Neither the public nor the contractors had been cheated by the deal. Eighty was known to be the going rate for city debentures with twenty years to run, and Story & Co. had been very happy to sell at that rate because they had needed cash to pay for a shipment of very cheap iron then in transit from England. To assert that the bonds had deliberately been made illegal in order to prevent their sale outside Toronto, and to link their issue with the later passage of the Toronto Consolidation Act as elements in a plot to defraud the public, was to make a 'gratuitous inference.' The charge that the Consolidation Act had compelled the city to pay double interest on £50,000 for more than a year was greatly exaggerated. Ten thousand pounds of the old debt had been redeemed early and the Bank of Upper Canada was allowing four and a half per cent interest on another £20,000, reducing the city's burden on that amount to seven and a half per cent. Most of the last £20,000, on which the city *was* paying double interest, was accounted for by city notes of small denomination which were coming in for redemption day by day.

Both sides stated theoretical positions on the breach of trust issue right from the start. Bowes himself stated, while denying any part in the deal, that once the debentures had been paid to Story & Co. at par, what had happened to them was none of the city's business: the contractors could sell them to whomever they liked. He himself, though mayor, had a perfect right to deal in Toronto securities in his private capacity as long as he did not defraud the city in doing so. He added, however, that 'from his peculiar situation, he had made it an invariable rule to make all his purchases through an agent, at a fee of ½ per cent.'[27] The *British Canadian* countered with the argument that there was 'a wide distinction between a private citizen trading in city securities, and the Mayor who may be regarded in the light of a Trustee of those securities – in intimate communication with the Government – forewarned of their intentions with reference to the Consolidated Loan Fund Act, and the influence that Act would have on those very securities with which he claimed a right to deal for his personal benefit.'[28] Since Bowes denied any interest in the transaction, no one suggested that his right to deal in city bonds might depend on whether the city benefited by his actions. The mayor laid the ground for such a defence, though, by stressing the advantages the city had reaped from the affair. It had faced the prospect of having to issue new debentures at a discount of twenty to thirty per cent to redeem the debt expiring in January 1854. Instead, at a trifling cost in extra interest payments, it had been able to issue them at par.

The evidence heard by the select committee sustained many of the arguments offered in Bowes' defence. Its report stated that Story & Co. had received their full entitlement of debentures and had sold them quite legitimately at eighty, the going rate. It cleared Bowes of any part in the deal and said that the city had not been harmed by it. But for good reasons the report carried no conviction. The witnesses had not been sworn to their testimony and had received written notice of the committee's questions; those who knew most had refused to testify at all. James Cotton, the contractor implicated by rumour in the deal, attended the committee but would not answer its questions. Alderman John Hutchison, who lived with Cotton, was willing to prove the mayor's complicity, but only in a court of law. On top of all this, the committee contained a majority of Bowesites. Four of the seven had recently supported Bowes' re-election as mayor, and these four imposed the report on the anti-Bowesite minority.[29]

Even this result was not reached without an embarrassing misadventure, for which Bowes himself was to blame. The committee had asked him three questions designed to find out if he expected to profit, or had already profited, from Story & Co.'s sale of the bonds. At first he had refused to answer either in person or in writing, and his refusal had provoked one of his supposed supporters to vote for a text stating that the committee had been unable to conduct a serious inquiry because it had lacked the power to subpoena. This defection extracted a single written sentence from the reticent mayor: 'I introduced the Contractors to the Bank of Upper Canada and rendered them any assistance in my power in the negociation [sic] of the £50,000 Debentures, but received no remuneration present or prospective therefor.'[30] Bowes' reply was a masterpiece of evasion, since it *appeared* to deny that he had bought the bonds but did not actually deny it; but it gave the scrupulous Bowesite, Councillor Alexander Macdonald, an excuse to vote for the report exonerating the mayor, which the committee adopted at the last minute and presented to council.

The revelation of these facts sparked off a torrid debate in council which lasted until three AM. The anti-Bowesite minority walked out in disgust, leaving the mayor's friends to write their own version of the business into the minutes, but the scandal was far from done with.[31] Press interest in

Toronto's municipal affairs had already reached an unprecedented height as *The Globe*, the *Daily Patriot*, and the *British Canadian* each devoted several closely printed columns to reports and editorials. The last-named published all its coverage, plus a verbatim account of the select committee's evidence, in two pamphlets.[32]

As might be expected, the initial response of the Toronto papers to the scandal reflected their political leanings. The *Patriot*, which was owned by Aldermen Ogle Gowan and Samuel Thompson, Bowes' most prominent defenders, acclaimed the proceedings as 'a full, complete and triumphant vindication of RIGHT and TRUTH, against the assaults of CALUMNY and FALSEHOOD.'[33] Gowan was the veteran leader of Upper Canada's Orangemen and the chief spokesman of the 'pragmatic' wing of the Order that was willing to combine politically with the Hincksites and Bleus. He was in short a politician of the same sort as Bowes (and, for that matter, the same sort as Hincks: another Irish Protestant who had from time to time employed a similar sort of demagogic blarney on behalf of the Reform party).[34] The Hincksite *Leader* did not report the council proceedings, but it announced Bowes' exoneration and quoted freely from a long exculpatory rider to the select committee's report, which had been added in council on Gowan's motion after the anti-Bowesites left. The Irish Catholic *Toronto Mirror* also nailed its colours to Bowes' mast, no doubt influenced by the fact that the mayor was friendly to Roman Catholic interests while his leading assailants were fiercely anti-Catholic.[35]

Three newspapers that later condemned Hincks and Bowes at this time sat on the fence. The Grit organ, *The North American*, reported the debates and criticized Bowes, but the Grits were uneasily allied with the Hincksites and held two cabinet portfolios, so their metropolitan standard-bearer ignored the premier's rumoured involvement except to say: 'We should hope at all events that the Inspector General had nothing to do with it.' The moderate Scottish conservative, Hugh Scobie, seems to have ignored the affair in his *British Colonist* (some issues of the paper are missing, but we may note that Scobie had been a great booster of the Northern). William Lyon Mackenzie, the rebel leader of 1837, also said little at this point in his brand-new *Weekly Message*: knowing how political malice could masquerade as moral outrage, he said later, he had refused to sign the petition against Bowes.[36]

Mackenzie's old friend, James Lesslie, had no such scruples. The sternly voluntarist Scottish Reformer had stood fifth in the list of petitioners for an investigation, and his *Examiner* (ironically enough, a paper founded fifteen years earlier by Hincks) reflected his outrage. Two other papers expressed similar disgust: George Brown's *Globe* and the conservative *British Canadian*, which was probably owned by former Solicitor General John Hillyard Cameron, a High Tory who had challenged Bowes for the mayoralty in 1852. Both papers stressed the inconclusiveness of the city council's investigation and the need for recourse to Chancery, where the facts could be elicited under oath; and this was in fact the next step in the affair. Five of the petitioners for the abortive inquiry entered a bill of complaint against the mayor alleging fraud and breach of trust and asking that he be ordered to pay his profit over to the city.[37]

Before examining the trial, it is worth noticing one or two points emerging from this stage of the debate that help to elucidate later events. One is the uncertainty about the market value of Toronto debentures. Strong testimony to the effect that one per cent per annum (ie, twenty per cent over twenty years) was a normal rate of discount was contradicted by the striking fact that someone had bought the city's consolidated loan at par. Since it was impossible that identical securities could at once be worth eighty and par, the discrepancy led to wild speculation as to how the £10,000 profit had been extracted from the deal.

In fact, though, the bonds issued under the by-laws of 28 June and 1 November were *not* identical, and the difference was crucial. Toronto securities were potentially more valuable in London than in Canada, especially in large amounts such as £50,000 or £100,000, because the London money market was much larger. It later appeared that the illegal bonds had been replaced with new ones under the Consolidation Act not merely to force early redemption of the former but also to procure their exchange for *sterling debentures with interest payable in London.* Such securities were more enticing to British investors than Canadian currency debentures payable in Toronto because the charges involved in converting the interest (and in due course the principal) to sterling and remitting it to London fell on the municipality instead of the investor. The bonds issued under the debt consolidation by-law of 1 November 1852 were the first Toronto securities ever issued in sterling.

Early in 1853 few participants in the uproar over the debenture scandal seem to have known of the difference this made to the value of Toronto bonds. Even Thomas G. Ridout of the Bank of Upper Canada later testified in court that he had not known it.[38] Bowes, it would appear, was one of the few Torontonians who had. While this information as to the higher value of sterling bonds contradicted charges that Francis Hincks had obtained par for the city's consolidated debt only by using his official influence (and doubtless in return for improper favours to the obliging

British purchasers), it would enable Bowes' critics to argue that the mayor might have had the bonds in aid of the Northern issued in sterling in the first place, so that the profit he and Hincks had made on them might have accrued to the city or to Story & Co. instead.

It is also significant in retrospect that in the debate on the committee report Samuel Thompson, chairman of the finance committee and co-owner of the *Patriot* with Ogle Gowan, had felt compelled to review other measures the city might have taken to pay off its expiring debt. Bowes had claimed that his negotiation of the £100,000 loan had saved the city from having to issue bonds at a twenty to thirty per cent discount in order to redeem the debt. Now Thompson admitted that William Cawthra, the Toronto financier, had been ready to renew his £20,000 loan to the city at par, while John Crawford and James H. Hagarty, Toronto attorneys acting as agents for a third party, had offered a loan of £25,000 for thirty years at the cost of a mere £625 in commission and expenses. Thompson gave reasons for preferring the English loan: Crawford and Hagarty had demanded their small commission, while Cawthra had wanted to renew his lien on certain city property, a condition that Thompson said was detrimental to the city's credit.[39] Cawthra himself, however, later maintained in court that his lien did not harm the city's credit and that the main reason why Toronto bonds sold at a discount in Canada was that they carried only six per cent interest, while the prevailing rate in the Toronto market was seven per cent.[40] In any case, Thompson had had to admit that the city could have raised £45,000 in Toronto, virtually at par, without paying any double interest or the expenses entailed in the issue of sterling securities. Later it would emerge that the holders of the other large loan falling due in January 1854 (an amount of £10,000) would have been happy to renew it, too, at par.[41]

PROCEEDINGS IN CHANCERY: OPPORTUNISM UNMASKED

Traditionally, proceedings in equity were initiated by presenting a *bill* which recited the defendant's alleged misdeeds, posed *interrogatories* to him based on those allegations, demanded his *discovery* of documentary evidence (specified or other) that might bear on the suit, and prayed for whatever remedy the plaintiff thought fit. The bill also had to state the plaintiff's claim to standing, where this might be in doubt. The defendant was then obliged to enter an *answer* which responded specifically to each interrogatory posed in the bill, although it might also include a general statement of his case which stated facts omitted from the bill. If these proceedings disclosed wrongs that differed from those alleged in his bill, the plaintiff could amend it to take account of the discovered facts. If the defendant contradicted any of the plaintiff's allegations, the plaintiff could join issue by making *replication*, which the defendant again answered.

This procedure gave the plaintiff in equity a great advantage over his counterpart at common law; for, until the middle of the nineteenth century, a defendant in a civil action at common law could be compelled neither to testify, nor to discover documentary evidence, to his detriment. In a court of equity the defendant had to do both, unless he managed to avoid the obligation by one of two ploys. He might enter a *demurrer*, by which he admitted the bill's allegations without prejudice in order to challenge the suit's basis in law (strictly speaking, in equity). Alternatively he might enter a *plea*, by which means he could state new facts which, had they been stated in the bill, would have made it demurrable.[42]

The plaintiffs' bill in *Paterson v Bowes* charged that Bowes had made an arrangement with Story & Co. on behalf of the city to buy from them Northern Railroad stock of £50,000 nominal value for £40,000. City of Toronto debentures of £50,000 nominal value had been issued and deposited with the Bank of Upper Canada as security against payment of the purchase price. The city had then raised a loan of £100,000 upon legislative authority, £40,000 of which had been used to pay for the Northern stock. But Bowes had led the city council to believe that he had agreed to pay £50,000 for the stock, and he had had the city chamberlain pay that amount into the Bank of Upper Canada to redeem the bonds deposited as security for the purchase price. The Bank had turned the extra £10,000 over to the mayor (although under circumstances that freed it from any liability), and he continued wrongfully to hold it to his own use. The bill sought discovery of the circumstances under which this had happened and restitution of the £10,000 to the city.[43]

These allegations were not a statement of what the plaintiffs thought had actually occurred. They were a schematic account of the suspected transaction couched in terms that established Bowes' role as the city's agent and the city's claim (as against any that Story & Co. might have) to the £10,000 that Bowes had allegedly misappropriated. Rather than answer the various allegations, though, Bowes chose to demur. He cited various grounds, the chief being the plaintiffs' want of standing. They had claimed standing on the following grounds: that as ratepayers they were members of the municipal corporation; that their interest was identical with that of all the other ratepayers; that the ratepayers numbered several thousand and there was no way of legally ascertaining the will of the majority in the matter; and that the city council, being misled by the mayor, had refused either to take action itself on the corporation's behalf or to authorize others to take such action. Bowes demurred that the plaintiffs had made no case for withdrawing the council's right to act as it saw fit, and that in any case the proper way for them to have proceeded was by filing an information with the provincial Attorney General.[44]

The court easily dismissed all the grounds of demur except those relating to the form of the suit. The allegations against the mayor amounted to a dereliction of an agent's duty to his principal that was obviously cognizable in equity. The funds used in the stock purchase were administered by the city council in trust for the corporation, and to argue that the council had discretion in the matter was therefore tantamount to maintaining that trustees could condone a breach of trust by one of their number. Only the question of the plaintiffs' right to proceed directly against Bowes, rather than through the Attorney General, caused the court any difficulty; but sufficient precedent was found to let the suit proceed.[45] Bowes thereupon filed an answer to the bill, stating such of the facts as did not harm his case but saying nothing about what Story & Co. had done with the bonds, except that they had 'appropriated the same as to them seemed fit.'[46]

All proceedings in equity had traditionally been conducted in writing, but the streamlined procedure of the court of Chancery as reformed by William Hume Blake in 1849 provided for viva voce hearings.[47] Blake's reforms exposed his fellow countryman Bowes to a day of excruciating public humiliation. The plaintiffs' leading counsel was Oliver Mowat, soon to be one of the closest political associates of Bowes' arch-enemy, George Brown. His relentless interrogation, pressed with Presbyterian zeal, squeezed from the defendant one damaging admission after another. Bowes' counsel were John Wellington Gwynne and George Skeffington Connor, both Irish Protestants like Bowes and Hincks, both moderate reformers of the 'railroads' persuasion like the latter. They did the best they could, but their frequent challenges to the propriety of Mowat's questions were invariably decided in the plaintiffs' favour.[48] The mayor was forced to admit that, in partnership with another, he had indeed bought the illegal bonds from Story & Co. A profit of more than £8000 had been made on them, half of which had gone to his firm of Bowes & Hall. The illegal issue and redemption of the last £7000 worth of bonds after the Consolidation Act had alone involved the city in a loss of £1400, which had gone to him and his confederate. 'And so it went,' reported *The Globe* gleefully, 'the Mayor shrinking and guilty, endeavouring to avoid answering, aided by his lawyers – the Counsel for the public, strengthened by the vigour and spirit of the bench, forcing unwilling replies.'

At last Bowes, 'deserted by his lawyers, who could no longer bear up against the firmness of the Court,' twice refused to name his partner in the deal. The court declared that he must speak or go to prison but it adjourned to give him time to think it over. He was eventually allowed to complete his testimony without divulging his partner's identity, and it was left to T.G. Ridout of the Bank of Upper Canada to name him as Francis Hincks. Hincks had paid for the bonds with drafts on a London bank and, while arranging the financing, had got the Bank of Upper Canada to advance the price to Story & Co.

Bowes conceded as little as he could. He had asserted, for instance, that Story & Co. had offered to sell him the bonds only on 30 June, two days after the authorizing by-law had been passed, whereas he later would be forced to admit that their letter of 30 June had merely formalized an earlier bargain. This point was important, as Chancellor Blake emphasized in his judgment, because it proved that Bowes might well have procured the by-law to facilitate the 'job.'[49] Bowes also claimed that before making the agreement he had reported to the finance committee the contractors' willingness to sell at eighty, but the committee had refused to think of the city's buying its own bonds back at a discount because to do so would harm its credit. Later certain members of the committee would swear that Bowes had only mentioned the matter informally to two or three members without either suggesting means by which the city might raise the money to buy the bonds or revealing that he planned to do so on his own account.[50]

Bowes claimed to have bought the bonds only because he had thought it would harm the city if £50,000 of its securities were put on the market by Story & Co. at a time when it was trying to raise an equal amount to pay off its expiring debt. 'My exertions to keep them out of the market were made without the expectation at that time of making much by them,' he said, 'although I knew that I would not lose anything.' This was a very dubious statement, as Mowat well knew. The city could easily have raised the necessary funds at par, and in due course he would call witnesses to prove it.[51] In order to test Bowes' motives, Mowat demanded that he produce his correspondence with Hincks. Bowes had to admit that he had destroyed it; some, perhaps, even after the suit had begun. It was his practice to destroy all letters marked 'private,' he said, although he would have preserved these had he known they were necessary to the suit. Asked why he and Hincks had tried to keep the deal secret, Bowes denied any wish on his part to do so.

Bowes' and Ridout's testimony on the genesis and execution of the debenture deal, though very damaging to the defendant, disproved some of the plaintiffs' bill. A three-month adjournment ensued while the bill was amended and Bowes responded. The amended bill took a different tack from the first, soft-pedalling the possibility of positive fraud and stressing the case for breach of trust. The plaintiffs dropped the charge that Bowes, after arranging for the city to buy Story & Co.'s Northern stock for £40,000, had misrepresented the purchase price to council in order to inveigle the city into paying out an extra £10,000 which he had then pocketed. Instead, they accused him of abusing his authority and influence as mayor to involve the city in a series of transactions which had netted him and Hincks a profit of £10,000 at the city's expense. Bowes had bought the illegal bonds at eighty, they alleged, when he knew they could command par or even a premium in London and could have been sold at more than eighty even in Canada. He had urged council to pass the by-law of 28 June despite its dubious legality and had delayed the bonds' emission for three weeks thereafter to give Hincks time to raise funds in England to buy them. When the gift and loan arrangement enshrined in the by-law fell through, Bowes had saved his speculation by arranging for the city to buy the contractors' Northern stock at par, even though it was worth less than fifty at the time: that is, he had procured the issue of £50,000 of city bonds to pay for stock worth less than £25,000.[52] Instead of devising an arrangement to save the city the disputed sum of £10,000 as he might have done, he had used his official influence to promote the steps by which he and Hincks had procured that sum for themselves, and in doing so he had concealed material facts from the city council.[53]

In his answer Bowes sought as usual to justify his actions by stressing how much they had benefited the public. The by-law of 28 July had been passed at the railway's behest, not his. Both that by-law effecting the gift and loan, and the stock purchase later substituted for it, had served the best interests of city and railway alike, and Story & Co. had got the best possible price for the bonds they received for the stock. To have bought that stock at its market price, instead of at par, would only have hurt the railway's credit, whereas one object of the stock purchase had been to boost it. Bowes denied responsibility for any delay in issuing the bonds and claimed that his public office had constituted no bar to his legitimate purchase of them. He had never let his private interest influence his public conduct, and the city council had given every aspect of the matter due deliberation.[54]

When the trial resumed in December 1853, each side summoned witnesses to prove its contentions. The plaintiffs called several members of council to testify that Bowes had energetically promoted the various actions taken by the city and that they would have been less hasty in complying with his suggestions had they known of his personal interest. Story & Co.'s Toronto agent testified that the delay in issuing the irregular bonds after 28 June had been partly due to the absence of the mayor, who had to sign them. On the subject of the Consolidation Act, both Samuel Thompson and Alderman Joshua Beard swore that Bowes had told them at the time that it was Hincks who had insisted on the bonds being replaced rather than legalized. Beard also said that the mayor had specifically credited Hincks with the act's speedy passage, while Thompson (now thoroughly disenchanted with his old leader, Bowes) expressed his resentment at having a sinking fund imposed on the city by an act passed (as he put it) for Hincks' and Bowes' private purposes.[55] All this evidence strongly suggested that Bowes had misled his colleagues on council and that both he and Hincks had used their official influence to promote their private profit.

The plaintiffs also tried to prove two more difficult points. One was their charge that Bowes had known of the potential value of Toronto securities on the London market and could have sold the bonds issued in aid of the Northern there on the city's behalf. To this end Bowes was asked to produce his correspondence with two residents of England to whom he was known to have written about marketing Toronto debentures there. Strange to tell, these letters had all been destroyed, and the letter-book that might have duplicated some of them was missing. The plaintiffs were able, however, to produce a copy of a letter to Bowes from one of his correspondents, John Henry Dunn, former Receiver General of Upper Canada and the united Canadas. From the questions that Mowat based on this letter it seems clear that Dunn had offered to negotiate the securities and had held out hope of obtaining a high price for them. Bowes asserted, however, that Dunn's offer had been so 'unsatisfactory' that he had not even submitted it to the city council.[56]

The plaintiffs also tried to prove that the scheme to profit from the defective bonds had been set on foot long before the end of June 1852, when the by-law authorizing their issue had been passed. To this end they called their most sensational witness: James Cotton, the government contractor said to have joined Hincks and Bowes in the deal. Cotton testified that Bowes had told him very early in 1852 that a 'speculation' might be made in the debentures and before the end of March had asked him to join in. The two had had to call in Hincks in order to finance the deal, but Bowes had also told Cotton that it was a good idea to give Hincks a stake so that he would favour the debt consolidation bill. Bowes had spoken cynically of his motive in telling the finance committee that Story & Co. were ready to sell at eighty: 'They [the municipality] were not in a position to buy the debentures, but he would ask them, so that they could not afterwards find fault.' He had planned to delay the issue of the bonds to give Hincks time to arrange financing. Cotton's testimony confirmed some of the worst suspicions of Bowes' and Hincks' enemies, and the defence would take great pains to discredit it. 'The evidence given by Mr. Cotton ... it was fit to watch narrowly and receive cautiously,' the Judicial Committee of the Privy Council later remarked, but they went on to note that it was by no means entirely unsupported.[57]

The case for the defence was of course shaped by that of the plaintiffs. It had been proved that Bowes had purposefully promoted, both by what he had said and what he had concealed, certain public acts which had allowed him to make a profit of more than £4000. His attorneys would have to wait until closing arguments to assert that his behaviour did not constitute a breach of trust. The immediate task was to disprove the darkest allegations against him: that his conduct had been motivated more by self-interest than by public duty and had sacrificed the common good to his private profit.

The defence had already got some of the plaintiffs' witnesses to admit that both the Northern stock purchase and the later debt consolidation had benefited the city.[58] Now they produced testimony that the deal had aided the contractors. Various witnesses declared that Story & Co. had received a fair price for the illegal bonds, while Joseph C. Morrison, by now both Solicitor General for Upper Canada and president of the Northern Railroad, stressed the difficulty of selling so large an amount of securities in Toronto at a higher rate than eighty (a point also gained from financier William Cawthra during cross-examination). Morrison stated that in June 1852 a director of Story & Co. had asked *him* to sell the bonds on commission, and the director in question testified that the contractors had received Bowes' offer to buy them only on 27 June, the day before the by-law was passed. This testimony suggested that there had been no long-standing commitment to sell the bonds to Bowes. Morrison also defended the debt consolidation by saying that he and William Henry Boulton, MPP for Toronto, had pushed it through without Hincks' help.[59]

In order to disprove the charges of deep conspiracy between Hincks and Bowes, it was above all necessary to discredit Cotton's evidence. To this end the defence sought to cast doubt on his motive for testifying against the mayor. Cotton had had a furious row with Bowes in November 1852 when the Toronto & Guelph Railroad, of which Bowes was president (representing the city, the largest shareholder), had rejected his tender for construction in favour of a substantially higher one by Gzowski & Co.[60] During cross-examination Cotton had been quite ready to admit his animus against the mayor both on this score and because Bowes had cast doubts on his financial competence to fulfil the contract.[61] He had also asserted that Hincks and Bowes had 'chiselled' him out of his share of the profits from the 'Ten Thousand Pound Job.'[62]

The defence wanted badly to prove that Cotton had authored the anonymous placards exposing the deal. They wished to argue that it was unlikely that a partner in a secret speculation would jeopardize his profit by exposing it: thus Cotton could not have been a party to the debenture speculation and if he had lied about that there was no reason to believe anything else he said. During cross-examination Cotton denied any blame for the placards and claimed to have been out of town when they were posted. His housemate, Alderman Hutchison, also denied responsibility but admitted that his and Cotton's clerks might have had something to do with the placards.[63] Now the defence called two city councillors to testify. George Platt stated that he had seen Cotton in Toronto on the day the placards had appeared and on several days immediately before and after that. Charles Romain's evidence was more direct. He claimed to have seen Cotton keeping watch that night while his and Hutchison's clerks were posting a placard. Two days later he had challenged Cotton about it and the contractor had denied being there. But because Cotton had then granted Romain a favour that he had hitherto refused, the effect of the interview had been to confirm rather than to dispel Romain's suspicions.[64]

Cotton unsuccessfully sued Romain for insinuating that he had tried to bribe the latter into silence. Romain and his witnesses may well have lied in court, but the impression lingers that Cotton had indeed been responsible for the placards.[65] Yet that impression will scarcely bear the interpretation that Bowes' attorneys wished to place on it. The evidence that Cotton was at first a party to the 'Ten Thousand Pound Job' is strong.[66] He emerges from the record as a proud as well as a covetous man, and he may well have thought £2000 or £3000 so easily come by well spent in sinking Bowes, whom he blamed for his failure to win the Toronto & Guelph construction contract.

The last witness for the defence was Francis Hincks.[67] The court had to wait a whole month for his testimony. Living outside Upper Canada, he could not be summoned to Toronto to testify and had to be examined at Quebec. His evidence conformed to the general thrust of the defence case, depicting him and Bowes (he denied that Cotton had ever been involved) not as venal conspirators but as astute opportunists who had advanced rather than hurt the public interest. Bowes had proposed the deal to him only on 24 June 1852, Hincks said: he could not have done so much earlier because Hincks had only returned from a lengthy trip to England on the thirteenth. The mayor had planned to get the Bank of Upper Canada to finance the deal, but Hincks had insisted on obtaining support from London, where money was cheap and he could get a twelve-month loan at five per cent. The interest rate was important, Hincks explained, as he had planned to dispose of the securities in small parcels over the year, taking advantage of a rise in their value which he had expected and which had in fact occurred. The idea of including the bonds in a city debt consolidation had been (he claimed) a later brainwave which took advantage of the bonds' illegality and Hincks' own belief that he could sell Toronto sterling debentures in London at ninety-five. He had in fact managed to dispose of them at ninety-seven, and any loss the city would suffer by having to pay interest in sterling was offset by the fact that he and Bowes had given the municipality £50,000 cash out of the proceeds, themselves absorbing the 'loss' incurred by their failure to sell the loan at par.[68]

Hincks firmly denied any understanding with Bowes to use their influence in parliament and council respectively to promote the requisite legislation; nor had he used his influence to procure financing in London. He defended the debt consolidation (which had been expedited without his aid, he claimed) and pointed out that irregular bonds issued in aid of the Northern by the County of Simcoe had been legalized by another act of the same session. As to the financing, Glyn & Co. had given him a five per cent loan at a time when the bank rate was two and a half per cent: he could have got such terms as a private citizen. To confirm this he produced a letter from the British bank (unsolicited, he said) attesting to the straightforwardness of the deal and the adequacy of the security given for the loan.

Cross-examination posed few problems. When challenged about the secrecy observed by himself and Bowes, Hincks said that it was normal in such business and particularly requisite in this case because of the enmity of certain newspapers towards him. Bowes had invariably declared his readiness to conduct the deal in the open, and when Hincks had heard of his breach with Cotton he had authorized him to tell all, imagining that Cotton would do so anyway. His correspondence with Bowes, he said, had been destroyed as was usual in such affairs, but he also stated rather inconsistently that Bowes had specially asked him to do so.[69] Was there a letter-book? Alas, Hincks (like Bowes) had mislaid his letter-book, but he was sure it contained none of the correspondence in question. Finally he opined that he and Bowes would have made just as much money on the illegal Canadian currency bonds as they had on the sterling securities: the benefits of the Consolidation Act had therefore accrued entirely to the city.

The last evidence had been heard. The legal process advanced towards final arguments in June 1854 and judgment in October. The court found unanimously for the plaintiffs, ordering Bowes to disgorge his share of the profits (plus accumulated interest) with costs. The judgment was confirmed on appeal, with two dissenting opinions, and finally by the Privy Council, to which body the pertinacious loser ultimately took his quest for vindication and profit.

THE GUILT OF HINCKS AND BOWES

Before reviewing the reasoning underlying the judgments in the various courts, we must consider what had actually been proved against Bowes (and, by implication, against Hincks). The question of moral turpitude is relevant because there was sufficient novelty in the case to permit the argument that it did not come within the precedents governing breach of trust. In deciding whether to apply the rule that had evolved from earlier cases, several judges took into account both the effects of the defendant's actions and his motives in undertaking them.

Clearly no deep design to defraud was proved against Bowes and Hincks. Story & Co. had lost nothing by the debentures' illegality and had not given the speculators a £10,000 bribe in return for improper favours. Neither the city's nor the government's credit had been used to buy the bonds. Bowes could reasonably claim that to have bought the contractors' Northern stock at the market rate, which was virtually nil, would have defeated the city's object (which was to promote the railway) by damaging the railway's credit. He could not therefore be said to have manoeuvred the city into paying too much for the stock in order to ensure that the maximum amount of bonds was issued to buy it. The charge that Hincks had used his official influence to obtain more than the market price for Toronto's consolidated loan debentures was contradicted by the even higher price they had since commanded on the London market.

On the other hand, Bowes had undoubtedly pressed the passage of a presumptively illegal by-law at a time when he had had a personal interest in its enactment, having contracted with Story & Co. to buy the bonds to be issued under it. It was, moreover, vital to his interest that the by-law *should be illegal*, for only thus could the city be compelled to redeem the bonds prematurely, thereby aiding his and Hincks' speculation. In pressing council to this action he had assured it that there would be no trouble in getting the bonds legalized by act of parliament if necessary, although he knew that he and Hincks had no intention of doing so because they planned to have the defective bonds replaced with sterling securities. When the Northern had proved unwilling to give the city the security required for the £35,000 loan, Bowes had actively promoted the agreement to substitute the stock purchase for the gift and loan, thereby ensuring that at least £50,000 worth of illegal bonds would issue to his benefit and not only the £25,000 worth to which the railway was entitled under the 'gift' resolution of 1850. The debt consolidation, which Bowes had promoted with as much deceitful enthusiasm as the earlier bond issue, had been utterly unnecessary because the city could easily have borrowed at par in Toronto the full £50,000 due for redemption in January 1854. Bowes had lied repeatedly to his council colleagues both during and after the fact. Hincks for his part had used his official influence improperly in promoting the debt consolidation and probably in financing his and Bowes' purchase of the bonds on an unsecured loan.

But all these malfeasances might possibly be palliated by the plea that the deal had benefited the city. Bowes and Hincks might argue that it had been necessary to pass the by-law of 28 June as quickly as possible because Story & Co. were in desperate need. They could excuse the stock purchase resolution of 29 July on the same grounds. They could claim that the debt consolidation was justified by the advantage to the city's credit of having financial standing in the London money market. The plaintiffs, in their bid to prove Bowes guilty of moral turpitude, therefore laid great stress on showing that he could have had sterling securities issued to aid the Northern in the first place, and that he had promoted the issue of Canadian currency bonds solely so that he could benefit by their illegality to force their premature redemption and replacement by the more valuable sterling bonds.

In order to prove this point the plaintiffs had shown that Bowes had first tried to negotiate a loan in London at par through the agency of the Bank of Upper Canada and had then turned to J.H. Dunn, who had offered to market Toronto securities but on terms that the mayor had thought unsatisfactory.[70] But Bowes had also written to someone else on the matter: Thomas Wilson, formerly of the Commercial Bank of Toronto and Kingston. No details of this correspondence emerged in the viva voce hearings, because Bowes had destroyed his copies, but when Wilson read of the case in England he sent copies to one of the plaintiffs and they were admitted in evidence. These letters show that in April 1852 Bowes had known quite well that Toronto securities might command par or near it in London, and that on 10 June, less than three weeks before the by-law was passed authorizing the debentures in aid of the Northern, he had written to Wilson of his intention to 'make those Debentures payable in London, and have them negotiated by an agent appointed by the Corporation, and hand their value in cash to the Railway Company, and thus prevent the credit of the City being injured by entrusting the sale of its bonds to unskilful hands, or their being forced into the market by needy railway contractors.'[71]

Why did Bowes not carry out this plan? Were the contractors' needs so urgent that there was no time to negotiate sterling bonds? It is hard to believe that interim financing could not have been arranged until the bonds were marketed: the Bank of Upper Canada was dominated by directors and shareholders who had an intimate personal interest in the completion of the Northern because they owned large quantities of land on or near its route, and it had certainly had £40,000 at hand to help Hincks and Bowes buy the illegal bonds.[72] Much was made of the Wilson correspondence by judges who found against Bowes: by Blake in Chancery, Draper in Appeal, and their lordships of the Privy Council. The two judges who found in his favour ignored its importance.[73]

The evidence that Bowes had known of the potential value of Toronto bonds in London sustained the following argument.[74] If in the summer of 1852 the market value of Toronto Canadian currency debentures with twenty years to run was eighty, the city might be deemed, by issuing £50,000 nominal value in aid of the Northern Railroad, to have intended to give aid to a cash value of £40,000. But if sterling bonds had been issued and sold in London at or near par, the city could have extended that aid while incurring a debt of little more than £40,000. In withholding his special knowledge and encouraging city council to incur the larger debt so that he and Hincks could make a profit, Bowes had committed a breach of trust that was more than merely technical.

As for Hincks, his guilt may be thought greater because his authority was greater. The judges said nothing about it, perhaps because he was not a party to the cause, but his avoidance of pursuit at law was no vindication of his actions. A recent sympathetic biographer has pointed out that Hincks 'lived in an age that was only starting to clarify its ideas on conflict of interest. Only a few years previously the province's receiver-general had been permitted to invest the public funds in his custody for his own private profit.'[75] True, but Hincks had risen to eminence as a leader of a party that professed a superior public morality to that which had prevailed under the old régime. As William Lyon Mackenzie told the Legislative Assembly's select committee of investigation into the charges against the Hincks administration in 1854–5, 'I had always understood Mr. Hincks, through his *Examiner* and his *Pilot*, to be decidedly opposed to allowing Members of the Government to use their official position to gain ... wealth by gambling or speculating in the public Debentures, or using the Legislature as a means of private gain to themselves, through its sanctioning such speculations and jobs.'[76]

Mackenzie did not wait until Hincks had testified before denouncing him, but George Brown let the premier condemn himself by his own words. *The Globe* then scrutinized Hincks' evidence closely, highlighting many equivocations and discrepancies. It stressed the contradictory reasons he had given for destroying his correspondence on the matter and the curious fact that he had mislaid his letter-book: businessmen simply did not destroy correspondence with their bankers, or with partners in important deals, unless they had something to hide.[77] It scoffed at his claim to have exerted no official influence in dealing with Glyn & Co., who had advanced a loan to buy the illegal bonds on no better security than the bonds themselves: they would hardly have done so unless Hincks had assured them that the bonds would be validated. Aldermen Thompson and Beard had both sworn that Bowes had ascribed the debt consolidation scheme to Hincks, who had discountenanced simple legalization of the bonds; and it was inconceivable that Hincks, as premier, had had nothing to do with the haste with which the Consolidation Act had been passed. His claim that he and Bowes could have made as much on Canadian currency as on sterling bonds was a barefaced lie: the conspirators had sold the latter in London at ninety-seven, while Toronto debentures with twenty years to run had never sold higher than ninety in Canada and had reached that level only since, and because of, the sale of the consolidated debt in London.[78]

Yet some of the evasions by which Hincks defended the debt consolidation were detected neither by *The Globe* nor by the plaintiffs' counsel at

Quebec, Andrew, later Sir Andrew, Stuart. Hincks sought to justify the act on three grounds: first, that similar acts had been passed in the same session on behalf of Montreal, Kingston and Hamilton; second, that the Hamilton and Kingston acts, like Toronto's, had empowered those cities to redeem bonds recently issued in aid of railways; and third, that the propriety of legalizing Toronto's initial bond issue in aid of the Northern was proved by the legalization of defective County of Simcoe bonds issued for the same purpose. All three arguments were misleading.

There were three reasons why the other cities' debt consolidations could not justify Toronto's. First, Hamilton and Kingston did not petition for consolidation until after the Toronto act had set a precedent. Montreal's petition was brought up only three days after Toronto's, but its bill did not receive second reading until four weeks after Toronto's had become law.[79] Second, Toronto's consolidation at least was unnecessary, because the city could have raised more than enough to redeem its expiring debt at par. Even if the city could not have done so, there was no reason to include in the consolidation the bonds issued in aid of the Northern, which still had twenty years to run. Finally, Hamilton's and Kingston's railway bonds were included in their debt consolidations because they bore an onerous five per cent sinking fund; the Toronto bonds bore no sinking fund at all.[80] Hincks might perhaps have argued that it was good policy to require municipalities to secure their debt by a two per cent fund, because sinking funds were a cornerstone of his financial policy; but he did not in fact take that ground.[81]

For Hincks to cite the legalization of the County of Simcoe bonds to justify legalizing Toronto's was even more brazen, although the plaintiffs' counsel missed the point. The illegal Toronto bonds were *not* legalized: they were superseded by the debt consolidation. Indeed, Solicitor General Morrison, president of the Northern, had testified that he had intended to legalize the Toronto bonds along with Simcoe's until the consolidation scheme had cropped up, whereupon he had dropped the Toronto bonds from his bill.[82] But Stuart let Hincks off the hook when he asked him whether, in fairness to Bowes or to himself, he could have opposed an act legalizing the defective bonds. Hincks was able to reply that, since both the Northern and the contractors had been assured that steps would be taken to validate the bonds if they turned out to be illegal, any honest man must have supported such a measure as a matter of course. 'I consider that opposition to such a measure would be an act of fraud,' he proclaimed.[83] But if Stuart had asked Hincks why, instead of legalizing them, they had been included in a debt consolidation, Hincks could have replied only that it had been done to let him and Bowes make a large profit on them.

Hincks seems to have lied, too, about James Cotton's part in the deal. He admitted talking to Cotton about it once, but only because Cotton was acting as Bowes' messenger on that occasion, not because he was a partner.[84] Other evidence belied this assertion. In a letter of 9 August 1852 Hincks had told T.G. Ridout of the Bank of Upper Canada that the illegal bonds had been, or would be, deposited at the Bank by 'Mr. Cotton or Mr. Bowes.'[85] When Bowes had been asked about this reference to Cotton, he had replied simply that he did not know what it meant.[86] Obviously Hincks could not answer thus. He said instead that he had told Ridout in an earlier letter that Bowes would handle the deal, but Bowes had later 'expressed a wish that he (Mr. Bowes) should not be known as concerned … at the Bank of Upper Canada, and had said that he would therefore get Mr. Cotton to transact any business to be done there with regard to the delivery of the bonds … In a subsequent letter I mentioned to Mr. Ridout that the bonds would be deposited there by Mr. Cotton or Mr. Bowes.'[87]

This is hard to believe. If Cotton was to deliver the bonds solely to obscure the mayor's connection with the deal, why should Hincks have mentioned Bowes at all in his letter of 9 August? Besides, both Bowes and Hincks had sworn that the mayor had always been ready to transact the affair in the open and that secrecy had been preserved only for Hincks' sake. These statements are obviously incompatible with Bowes' supposed desire to keep his own part secret from the Bank. These contradictions make Hincks' letter of 9 August the best evidence there is that Cotton was an original partner in the deal.

A hypothetical reconstruction of the affair might suppose that Bowes had invited Cotton to take part in the speculation because of the latter's influence with Hincks, which was necessary to market the bonds in London on the speculators' behalf and to secure the illegal bonds' replacement by sterling securities. The mayor testified that he had gone to Hincks as a 'friend,'[88] but the latter said in his memoirs that his 'personal acquaintance' with Bowes at that time was 'but slight' (ex parte evidence, admittedly, and uttered more than thirty years after the event; but at least the memoirs in general show that Hincks had a good memory or good sources of reference).[89] Cotton, a government contractor, was identified in the press at the time as a 'friend' of Hincks, and he was also a political ally of Bowes (it appeared later that the two had shared the legal costs involved in challenging W.H. Boulton's return in 1851 as MPP for Toronto).[90] What better intermediary could there be between Bowes and the premier he wished to interest in the deal? Had Bowes not later fallen out with Cotton over the Toronto & Guelph construction contract, the debenture speculation would never have come to light.

This finding does not mean that either the buyers or the vendors of the bonds were committed to the deal before Bowes and Hincks clinched their partnership in Quebec on 24 June 1852. Bowes may well have pursued the plan of issuing sterling securities on the railway's behalf (as indicated in the Wilson correspondence) right up to that time. Likewise, Story & Co. may have been looking for a better buyer (as Morrison's evidence suggested) right up to the last minute. But Cotton's evidence shows that Bowes had envisaged the action eventually taken for weeks, if not months, before the deal was actually concluded.

EQUITABLE DOCTRINE AND THE 'TEN THOUSAND POUND JOB'

The argument in *Toronto* v *Bowes* revolved about two basic questions. Was the defendant in his capacity as a member of the city council (the directorate of the municipal corporation), a trustee of the corporation property? If so, had his conduct in the debenture speculation constituted a breach of trust? These questions involved the court in the intricacies of what was then, and still is, a rapidly evolving area of law: that pertaining to fiduciary relations.

The law of fiduciaries regulates the relationships that arise when one person is invested with the power to act on behalf of another. Its object is to prevent the former from using that power to enrich himself unjustly at the latter's expense. The historical prototype of such relationships was that between a trustee and his beneficiary, or *cestui que trust*. In this case the fiduciary was formally invested with the legal ownership of the trust property, subject to the proviso that the property in question was to be administered for the sole benefit of the *cestui que trust*. As time passed, judges in equity found themselves obliged to determine cases involving a profusion of relationships that were more or less analogous to this one: relationships such as those between solicitor and client, and agent and principal. These relationships did not necessarily entail the vesting of legal ownership in the fiduciary, but they did entail his investiture with the power to act on another's behalf and frequently to use that other's property in doing so. When disputes arising from such relationships came before the courts, judges naturally tended to apply to them the principles that had been devised to govern the paradigmatic relationship between trustee and *cestui que trust*.[91]

The temptations inherent in the fiduciary position, and the difficulty that often attended the attempt to discover and prove a breach of duty, induced the courts from the late seventeenth century on to favour a preventive approach to the protection of the beneficial interest. Increasingly severe constraints were imposed on dealings between the fiduciary and either his trust itself or its beneficiary; and the courts went beyond this to adopt rules that sometimes threatened to hamper the fiduciary unduly in his conduct of his own affairs, or even to deter him from actions that might benefit his trust.[92] In the leading case of *Keech* v *Sandford* (1726), a trustee was prevented from taking for his own benefit a lease of property which the lessor had previously refused to renew to the trust.[93] In its anxiety to enforce a rule that would forestall the creation of conflicts between a trustee's interest and his duty, the court rejected both the defence that the trustee had acted in good faith (having first sought renewal to the trust) and the defence of 'impossibility': that is, that a fiduciary might legitimately acquire for himself a benefit which the trust had enjoyed but was incapable of retaining, or – by extension – which it desired but was incapable of obtaining.

In the following century or so, the preventive constraints on the trustee's freedom of action were progressively extended to other fiduciary positions, and the rule against unjust enrichment was generalized to the point that virtually no benefit obtained (even from third parties) by the use of fiduciary powers, or which passed from the trust to the fiduciary without a great lapse of time, could be retained by the fiduciary for his own use. In such cases the court was liable to declare the benefit a *constructive trust*: that is, to rule that the fiduciary *should* have acquired it for his beneficiary rather than for himself and must therefore be held to have done so. Only the prior, fully informed, and uncoerced consent of the beneficiary could legitimize the fiduciary's self-enrichment in such a manner; but a heavy onus of proof was placed on the fiduciary which could rarely withstand challenge by the beneficiary. The courts' suspicion of this means of purifying such gains is illustrated by the growth during these decades of the doctrine of 'undue influence.' By the terms of this doctrine, a person who acquired an advantage from another by means of what was deemed to be illicit suasion was liable to be construed by the court as the latter's trustee in respect of the advantage, although no fiduciary relationship had previously existed between them.[94]

The rules regulating fiduciary relations had several possible applications to the 'Ten Thousand Pound Job.' The plaintiffs asserted that Bowes, as a member of the city council, was in effect the corporation's trustee, and that as such he had set up an unconscionable conflict of interest merely by buying City of Toronto debentures, the debts of his trust.[95] Less extremely, it could be argued that he had done so in two other ways: first, by agreeing to buy bonds which the council had not yet decided to issue and then urging their issue; and second, by urging upon council, once the bonds were his, measures designed to increase their value. In addition to these conflicts of interest as a member of council, there were possible breaches of duty deriving from Bowes' specific agency in dealing with the railway, the contractors, and the government with respect to the debentures on the city's behalf. By negotiating the issue to Story & Co. of bonds he had previously agreed to buy from them once issued, had he become the secret purchaser of property he was commissioned to sell on the city's behalf? By negotiating under the by-law of 1 November to redeem the illegal bonds of which he was an owner, had he made himself the secret vendor of property he was authorized to buy? Such acts were breaches of the fiduciary duty that the agent to sell and the agent to buy owed their respective principals.

Yet while the case presented analogies with many of the leading cases that had defined fiduciary duty, it differed from them enough to make it debatable whether the precedents damned or favoured Bowes. The plaintiffs cited several strong judgments on breach of trust relating to individual fiduciaries and the directors of both municipal and non-municipal corporations.[96] The defendant denied their relevance. His counsel argued that a municipal council member was a trustee only for the faithful application of corporate property to the purposes designated by law, and Bowes had caused no property of the city of Toronto to be applied to unauthorized purposes. The bonds he had bought were not the city's property but Story & Co.'s, which they might sell to whomever they pleased. Bowes could not have promoted the city's purchase of them, because the city had not had the purchase price to hand. As to the question of agency, he had never been expressly appointed the city's agent; but neither could he be considered its implied agent, since he had never had the power to make an agreement that bound the city. The only exception was Bowes' role in the redemption of the illegal bonds under the by-law of 1 November, in which he had been the city's express agent under the by-law; but this had represented the mere ministerial performance of a duty imposed on the city by the Consolidation Act.

Finally, Bowes' conduct at every stage of the impugned transaction had benefited the public interest. The by-law of 28 June and the resolution of 29 July had merely effectuated a prior commitment to the railway, and both had given vital aid to an important public purpose. Bowes' prior agreement to buy the bonds issued under their authority was likewise justified. The legalization of the irregular bonds, like the by-law authorizing their issue, had been an obligation of honour. The debt consolidation by which it had been done had been beneficial to the city's credit.[97]

These considerations had no influence on those judges who wanted to apply the general rule, as all three Chancery judges did with great rigour. They found that Bowes as a council member was indeed the city's trustee in the sense asserted by the plaintiffs, and furthermore that he had exercised a particular agency, albeit implied, by his various negotiations on the city's behalf.[98] On this basis they found that Bowes had placed himself in breach of his duty by agreeing before 28 June 1852 to buy from Story & Co. the bonds that were issued under the by-law of that date. After that date, his promotion of measures to ensure the bonds' issue and their replacement by sterling securities had entailed a further conflict of interest. By concealing his interest in the issue of the illegal bonds and his knowledge of the potential value of Toronto debentures in London, Bowes had infringed the rule of fair dealing that alone could purify transactions between principal and agent. Vice Chancellor John Godfrey Spragge went so far as to say that even the fullest disclosure of his interest to the city council would not have purified Bowes' position, because they were merely his fellow agents, his principals being the ratepayers of the municipality.[99]

In finding against Bowes, the equity judges stressed the basic principles at issue. The rule that barred a trustee from acquiring a personal interest in his trust, noted Chancellor Blake, was 'founded upon principles of reason, of morality, and of public policy. It has its foundation in the very constitution of our nature, for it has been authoritatively declared that a man cannot serve two masters ...' The temptation inherent in trusteeship was so severe, especially since the discovery of wrongdoing was often so difficult, that only an absolute ban on a trustee becoming personally interested in his trust could protect the sanctity of fiduciary relations.[100] Spragge was equally definite:

The question is not whether he allowed his private interests to warp his judgment, and to prevail over the duty which, as an agent, he owed to the city – a question impossible to solve – but whether, by his agreement for the purchase of the debentures, he raised up a private personal interest in himself which conflicted or might conflict with the interests of the city. No other rule would be a safe one; for when a man views his duty to another through the medium of his private interests, it is human nature that his vision of the former should be imperfect, if not distorted.

The application of the rule might sometimes have borne hard on men who had done no moral wrong, but it was 'essential to the keeping of all parties filling a fiduciary character to their duty, to preserve the rule in its integrity, and to apply it to every case as it arises, which justly falls within its principle.'[101]

Only in the Court of Error and Appeal did the defendant find sympathetic ears. Chief Justice John Beverley Robinson delivered a seventy-six page judgment which, while not denying the validity of the principles cited in the court below, questioned whether they had been properly applied to John George Bowes. Noting that the case at issue, while analogous to cited precedents, differed from them significantly as to facts, he argued that though the language of the rule invoked was comprehensive, it must be taken as applying only to cases like those which had evoked it. Bowes' case could not be *assumed* to come within the rule, therefore, but must be judged by the facts.

Robinson made his point by fastening on the plaintiffs' argument that Bowes had placed himself in breach of trust merely by buying the bonds of his municipality. The Chancery judges had not discussed this contention specifically but had seemed to accept it tacitly by stating the relevance of certain precedents that dealt with fiduciaries in a position analogous in this respect to Bowes': namely, assignees in bankruptcy and executors who had bought on their own account the debts of estates under their administration.[102] Robinson devoted a good thirty pages to refuting the relevance of the analogy. East India Company directors, he noted, were not barred from holding their company's bonds. A recent imperial statute acknowledged the right of municipal council members in Britain to hold the bonds of their municipality, and he assumed (though lacking 'particular information on the point') that in Canada such a practice was as common as it was (hitherto) unchallenged. He posited an analogy between municipal councillors and members of a government or legislature, who he did not think were debarred from holding securities issued by the state upon legislative authority. Reducing the analogy to absurdity, he noted that, strictly applied, it would bar a bank director from possessing the note issue of his bank, which was a pledge of its credit similar to a debenture.[103]

Having argued that the 'two masters' rule could be applied only with reference to the facts, Robinson proceeded to review them in a way calculated to show that Bowes had done nothing which contravened his duty as the city's fiduciary. He had not traded in the city's property, nor with its funds. He had bought its bonds from a third party and with no detrimental consequences to the municipality, which would have had to pay the same amount of interest at the same intervals, and ultimately to redeem the bonds for the same sum at the same time, no matter who owned them. He had not bought them at a price made lower by their illegality. Even if Bowes had concealed from council his knowledge of Story & Co.'s readiness to sell the bonds at eighty, the fact was irrelevant: the city could not properly have bought up its own bonds at a discount even if it had had £40,000 available. To say that Bowes should have used his influence with Hincks for the city's rather than their own benefit was quite unreasonable because it was by no means clear that Hincks either would or could have employed his influence with his English friends on such terms. There were no grounds, then, for saying that Bowes' profit was the city's loss. As to the later passage of the Consolidation Act, it was not permissible to impugn an act of parliament by surmising that it had been passed under undue or corrupt influence; but there was no evidence that Bowes had exercised such influence in any case.[104]

Finally, Robinson sought to refute the argument that Bowes was guilty of a conflict of interest in urging and voting on the measures by which he had realized his profit. Members of legislatures were not blamed for similar actions, so why should municipal legislators be blamed for them? In this regard, as in the case of breach of trust in general, the case must be judged on the facts, which he argued were in Bowes' favour.[105]

Robinson's construction of the facts was as favourable to Bowes as that of most of his brethren was detrimental. He consistently ignored the effect of Bowes' agreement to purchase the illegal bonds prior to issue upon the defence that he had bought from a third party, not from the city. He studiously overlooked the evidence that Bowes had not needed to go through Hincks to market Toronto bonds in London and could therefore have had sterling bonds issued in the first place.[106] He also cited the legalization of the Simcoe Railroad bonds to justify the Toronto debt consolidation: a flimsy argument, as we have seen.[107]

Robinson carried only one colleague on the Court of Error and Appeal with him: Archibald McLean of the Court of Queen's Bench.[108] The other three common law judges who rendered judgment found no more difficulty in applying the 'two masters' rule to the case than any of their colleagues in Chancery.[109] William Henry Draper, newly appointed Chief Justice of the Court of Common Pleas, repeatedly stressed the irrelevance of the question of whether Bowes' actions had served the city's best interests.[110] Robert Easton Burns of the Queen's Bench made the same point about the appellant's motives: 'The question never is, whether the agent has acted faithfully, but is, whether his position is such that he may act otherwise.'[111] William Buell Richards of Common Pleas quoted at length from a recent English judgment applying these principles to officers of corporations.[112]

Their judgments varied in detail both from each other and from those in Chancery, however. Those given in lower court had focused on Bowes' acquisition of an interest in the illegal bonds prior to the passage of the by-law authorizing their issue, but these appellate decisions laid equal or greater stress on his position under the Toronto Consolidation Act and the by-law that had given effect to it. Burns in particular, himself an equity lawyer before his elevation to the bench, reserved his opinion on whether Bowes' original purchase of the illegal bonds had placed him in breach of trust and concentrated instead on the later steps in the speculation. He noted that the by-law of 1 November, which had authorized the issue of sterling bonds under the Consolidation Act, had made Bowes the city's agent to sell the new bonds and to negotiate with the owner of the illegal bonds for their redemption. Rejecting the defence that Bowes' actions under the by-law had been mere ministerial performance of a duty imposed on the city by the legislature, Burns concluded that, at that point if not earlier, Bowes' interest was in conflict with his duty because he was himself part owner of the bonds. His *interest* was to have the bonds redeemed immediately at par, even if it meant selling the consolidated loan debentures at a heavy discount in order to do so. His *duty* might have been to negotiate with the owners of the illegal bonds to secure a discount for redeeming them prior to term, or even to refuse to redeem them prematurely at any discount.[113]

This rather abstract reasoning was heavy with irony, since it took at face value the statute and the by-law that Bowes and Hincks had procured to realize their profit. They had intended all along that the city should take the illegal bonds at par in part exchange for the consolidated loan debentures, but in order to set off the process that summoned forth the offer in those terms from 'unnamed parties in England,' it had first been necessary to have the city petition for a debt consolidation act. The city had petitioned on 23 August 1852; the 'anonymous offer' had been conveyed to council on 28 September; the Consolidation Act had become law on 7 October and the by-law to issue sterling debentures had followed on 1 November. But the language of the act had reflected the terms of the petition of 23 August, which had been framed by (or for) a city council ignorant of the 'English offer' that was to come. It therefore spoke not of redeeming the illegal bonds with new bonds at par, as the 'English offer' proposed, but of raising money by the issue of new bonds and using it to redeem the illegal bonds.

Draper had commented acidly on this inconsistency between the language of the act, and of the by-law that gave effect to it, and the intentions of their procurers, rightly concluding that it could only have resulted from a design to mislead the council.[114] Burns knew this as well as Draper, but he decided to take the statute at face value, applying to it Robinson's maxim that an act of parliament could not be impugned by surmising that it had been passed under improper influence. Robinson had opined that the legislature must have intended the illegal bonds to be redeemed at par: a correct opinion in that the legislature had no intention that could be distinguished from that of the two men behind the legislation. But Burns found in the language of the act a discretionary power to negotiate terms with the owners of the illegal bonds: a power which it was Bowes' duty as the city's agent to exercise against his private interest as an owner of the bonds. Had Bowes revealed his interest as he should have, Burns noted, 'the Common Council might have thought it more prudent to appoint some other person as agent ...'[115]

Whereas the Chancery judgments had focused on the earlier stages of the debenture speculation and those in Appeal on the latter, the Privy Council judgment of 1858 stressed Bowes' continuous dereliction of duty throughout the affair. Their lordships expressed 'some surprise that there should not have been a unanimous affirmance of the decision of the Court of Chancery,' and they went out of their way, like Blake four years previously, to contradict the defendant's claim that the impugned transaction had not harmed the city.[116] Bowes had told Thomas Wilson of his intention to have the bonds in aid of the Northern issued in London in sterling, they noted, but after his meeting with Hincks at Quebec on 24 June Canadian bonds had been issued, which the two men had bought and had later had replaced by the more valuable sterling bonds of the consolidated loan issue. This was how the disputed gain had been made, 'and it would probably be wrong to assume that this was made merely at the expense of the Contractors, but be nearer the truth to say, that it was made at the expense of the Corporation ... who would not have found it necessary to issue so many debentures on the English as on the Canadian plan.'[117]

Their lordships also followed Blake in stressing the irrelevance of these facts to their decision.[118] The key consideration was Bowes' position in June 1852. 'He may not have been an agent or trustee within the common meaning or popular acceptation of either term, but he was so substantially; he was so within the reach of every rule of civil jurisprudence, adopted for the purpose of securing, so far as possible, the fidelity of those who are entrusted with the power of acting in the affairs of others.' As the city's accepted agent in its dealings with Story & Co., it had been his duty 'not to place himself voluntarily in a position in which, while retaining the office of Mayor, he would have a private interest that might be opposed to the unbiassed [sic] performance of his official duty.' From the time he agreed to buy the illegal bonds from Story & Co., he had 'stood, as to the debentures, in the position of the Contractors.' From then on, in dealing with Story & Co. on the city's behalf, he was dealing with himself.[119] The court reserved judgment on the general question of whether a municipal council member was competent to buy from third parties bonds previously issued by his municipality.[120]

THE UNDERLYING DEBATE ON PUBLIC POLICY

Underlying the factual analysis and the conflict of views over the relevance of precedent was a debate on the requirements of public policy with respect to the case. Robinson and McLean recognized as clearly as their colleagues the human fallibility that the preventive rule was designed to counteract, but they were unwilling to apply the rule so as to deprive Bowes of a profit he had made by a deal which (as they saw it) had caused no private loss and considerable public benefit.

It was not that they approved of what Bowes had done. Robinson at least condemned the deal as 'one which had far better not have taken place.' He declared that a court of equity might well have refused to countenance Bowes' deal by helping him to possess his profit had he sued for it, and that it might even have enjoined him from suing for his profit at common law.[121] But given that Bowes *had* possessed his profit, Robinson could see no grounds on which he could properly be deprived of it for the sake of the City of Toronto, when the obvious and only losers of the sum in question (he held) were Story & Co., who were very grateful to Bowes.

Robinson's decision has recently been cited as evidence of a striking shift in the attitude of members of the old Family Compact toward entrepreneurship.[122] Peter Baskerville bases his interpretation on R.C.B. Risk's analysis of judicial attitudes towards economic issues in mid-nineteenth-century Upper Canada. Risk has observed that, while the judges of the time shared their American counterparts' preference for legal interpretation that favoured the rights of 'dynamic' over 'static' property (to use Willard Hurst's formula), the Upper Canadians were less ready to break with precedent in order to enlarge the field of action open to entrepreneurs. They felt themselves bound by English case law, which they recognized was not necessarily appropriate to Canadian conditions, but they were unwilling to pre-empt the legislature in remedying the problem.[123] Thus Robinson's judgments included 'some short statements of dissatisfaction with doctrine, the need for certainty, and economic need and policy, that were more numerous than the general appearance of the judgments suggest[s],' but these obiter dicta 'did not affect the reasonings or outcomes except in the few cases for which the precedents permitted a choice.' Risk has detected a contrast between Robinson and Blake, who was also respectful of precedent but showed more 'determination to shape the law to Canadian needs and conditions.' Blake's 'public speeches stressed freedom; Robinson stressed duty.'[124] Yet in the 'Ten Thousand Pound Job,' Baskerville suggests, it was Robinson who opted for freedom and Blake for duty.

In the context of Robinson's usual bias, Baskerville interprets his decision as reflecting the old ruling oligarchy's acceptance of new economic and political realities. During their heyday they had sought to foster slow and steady economic growth, using the power of the state to further enterprises in which they were interested and to advance Toronto's metropolitan dominance over Upper Canada. They had discountenanced speculative enterprise as the source of an instability dangerous to the body politic. But their old body politic had been metamorphosed, substantively by the rapid economic and population growth that had begun about 1830, and formally by a process that had started with the union of the Canadas in 1841 and ended with the advent of responsible government a few years later. They no longer possessed the institutional power to assert their metropolitan supremacy and now faced a competitor, in Allan MacNab's Hamilton, whose dynamic methods put the Toronto entrepreneurs at a disadvantage. In an era when 'politics' meant 'railroads,' Toronto too must have its railroads; and if speculations like the 'Ten Thousand Pound Job' were necessary to procure them, so be it.[125]

Baskerville quotes Robinson to the effect that, since transactions such as Bowes' had been common throughout the province, to brand them as illegal would take the commercial world quite by surprise. Neither Canadian nor British transportation routes had been advanced wholly by the votes of persons who had no interests that might conflict with their public duty.[126] 'It would be a very slowly progressing country, I apprehend,' he quotes Robinson as saying, 'in which all public enterprises and improvements should be left to be suggested and advanced by those who neither had, nor believed they had, any personal pecuniary interest in pushing them forward, or who, while they were intrusted with the public duty, acquired no interest which could be affected by the course which they might publicly take on such occasions [as I now allude to].'[127] Baskerville concludes that Robinson's judgment reflected his dismay at Toronto's parlous economic position, a dismay which impelled him in this particular case to abandon his normal approach.

This is a suggestive interpretation, but it is not beyond challenge. For one thing Baskerville fails to grasp the complexity of Robinson's argument. He quotes, as though they justified the debenture speculation as a whole, remarks which refer only to the hypothetical question of whether Bowes was in breach of trust *merely by buying the debentures of his municipality*. It is only such purchases as these which Robinson avers are widespread, and the discountenancing of such purchases which he thinks would surprise the world of commerce. It is the notion of banning the promotion of measures in legislatures and municipal councils by members with *any personal interest at all, irrespective of its nature*, that he addresses in the quotation which Baskerville generalizes by truncating it. The quoted remarks do *not* apply to the debenture speculation in its entirety, and Baskerville's misunderstanding of Robinson's views leads him wrongly to conclude that the Chief Justice was 'unequivocally supportive of all of Bowes' activities.'[128]

On the other hand, Robinson *did* defend the speculation, and he did so with arguments that contain a strong dash of 'instrumentalism': the innovative approach to legal interpretation whereby the judge accorded an authority above that of precedent to what he saw as social needs, on the presumption that by doing so he was enacting the communal will.[129] Thus Robinson accepted the mayor's 'laissez-faire' defence that Story & Co., as owners of the illegal bonds, were entitled to sell them to whomever they pleased; and he also, as Baskerville notes, defended the speculation as a whole by contending that it had helped Story & Co. surmount their liquidity problem: 'It was only by some such train being laid in advance of legislative measures as was laid by the defendant and Mr. Hincks, under the stimulus of personal gain, that the difficulty could have been met at the time; [at least, whether it could have been managed otherwise or not, can only be conjectured].'[130]

Yet Robinson's foray into instrumentalism was not a bold one. He did not proclaim the case as one governed by precedents which he none the less rejected as inapplicable to current Canadian conditions: he laboured instead to portray it as one of the few for which, in Risk's words, 'the precedents permitted a choice.' True, one might ascribe his circumspection to the natural ambivalence of a judge to whom an instrumentalist approach did not come readily, but who felt driven, perhaps unconsciously, to contradict his 'formalistic' instincts by what Baskerville calls the 'disorientation of Toronto's metropolitan development, as measured by its limited success in railway promotion.'[131] Moreover, in so far as a municipal council member had never been declared in breach of trust under analogous circumstances, this was indeed a case for which the precedents allowed a choice. Yet it is precisely here that the argument for Robinson's instrumentalism breaks down. Until recently, English municipal corporations had been governed by privileged oligarchies which were held in law to have the same rights over the corporation's property as a private person had over his personal property. The notion that municipal property was held in trust for the citizens had grown up only over the last quarter century.[132] Yet instead of exploiting the opportunity that these circumstances offered, Robinson embraced the new doctrine concerning the fiduciary position of municipal council members.[133] Having done so, he could deny that Bowes' case presented a valid analogy with precedents relating to private fiduciaries and directors of non-municipal corporations, and could argue that the debenture speculation had fulfilled a valuable public purpose, only by ignoring evidence that other judges stressed heavily to Bowes' detriment: the evidence that Bowes had known of the potential value of Toronto sterling bonds in London and had had another agent than Hincks available to market them there. Robinson did not confront this evidence but sidled by it, dismissing the argument it sustained (in the qualifying clause that Baskerville omits) as 'conjectural.'

The basic flaw in Baskerville's interpretation is that, while it recognizes the exceptional nature of Robinson's judgment, it underestimates the aberrancy of his reasoning. Acute in detail but strangely rambling in structure, Robinson's decision was based on a strikingly narrow construction of the facts: one which accepted the defendant's invitation to consider the propriety of each fact in isolation without asking how far their conjunction pointed to a corrupt scheme by Bowes (let alone a corrupt conspiracy between Bowes and Hincks). Why should Robinson undergo such contortions of intellect, consciously or unconsciously, to justify the 'Ten Thousand Pound Job'?

Robinson certainly had reason to rejoice in the building of the Northern. It was not only a Toronto enterprise but a Simcoe County one, and the Robinson family had large estates in Simcoe County. In fact the Chief's sons, James Lukin and John Beverley, jr, had earlier taken part in an abortive scheme to promote the line by a most blatantly speculative venture: a lottery.[134] Yet nothing Robinson might say or do to Bowes' detriment in February 1856 could have any effect on the line, which was a fait accompli. Furthermore, railways epitomized the irresistible social and economic forces that had overthrown the Tory ideal of an ordered agrarian society which Robinson espoused, while Bowes, the 'self-made,' demagogic Irish mayor and avid railway booster, personified the changes that had ended the Family Compact's domination of Toronto society.[135] Even if Robinson was grateful to the ex-mayor for his energetic promotion of the line, it is not easy to see why he should have undergone, either deliberately or by unconscious compulsion, the twists of reasoning that were necessary to save Bowes his speculative gains.

The key to Robinson's thinking can be found in the fact that his disagreement with his colleagues concerned the extent to which the general rule should be applied to municipal council members, whose position he equated with that of public officials in general. Ignoring the nature of the bond speculation to do so, Robinson argued that the rule must be applied more leniently than in other cases, since municipal councils, like legislatures, were naturally and desirably filled with men who had a strong personal interest in the economic advancement of the polity they served, and if such men were barred from promoting and voting on any measure in which they had such a personal interest, nothing would get done.[136] His confrères, who did not ignore the nature of the speculation, noted the magnitude of the property entrusted to individual municipal councils and the even greater magnitude of municipal property as a whole in a province which, since the comprehensive municipal legislation of 1849, was studded with county, city, town, and village municipalities from one end to the other. These municipalities, moreover, could only operate through trustees.[137]

It is easy to pick holes in Robinson's reasoning: there is, of course, a large difference between a *legislator* who presses a measure in which he has a personal interest and an *executive* who uses his authority to commit his trust to a deal which redounds to its loss and his personal gain. But what was the underlying cause of Robinson's confusion? There is a clue in the Privy Council's strong rejection of the idea that a municipal council's deliberative character might afford its members some of the privileges of legislators. 'The Common Council of Toronto cannot in any proper sense of the term be deemed a legislative body; nor can it be so treated,' they asserted. 'The members are merely delegates in and of a Provincial town for its local administration. For every purpose at present material, they must be held to be merely private persons having to perform duties, for the proper execution of which they are responsible to powers above them.'[138] The key word here is 'responsible.' It alerts us to the likelihood that, underneath Robinson's superficially progressive, 'instrumentalist' wish to free elected officials from the harsher constraints of fiduciary obligation for the sake of promoting economic growth, there lurked a deeply conservative impulse to vindicate privileges which Robinson himself had once enjoyed, but which the trend to 'responsible' government had recently all but eradicated in England and Upper Canada alike.

Both in Britain and the colonies, responsible government accompanied the fruition of a Lockean theory of representative government which envisaged the public official as a trustee empowered by the public to act for society's benefit.[139] This essentially fiduciary interpretation was quite different from the old view of public office as an appurtenance of superior social rank and as a sort of property, which might properly be subjected to entrepreneurial exploitation by its owner. This old view had begun to fade in England only towards the end of the eighteenth century; and in the sphere of municipal government, as we have seen, it had been effectively superseded by the fiduciary conception only in the 1830s.[140] Upper Canada was backward by comparison with the mother country, and Chief Justice Robinson and his colleagues of the Family Compact had administered it for decades under the old system that countenanced the application of public executive authority to the holder's personal enrichment. Under this system, in fact, Robinson's brother Peter had defalcated to the extent of more than £10,000 as Commissioner of Crown Lands.[141] The Chief's attempt to justify the 'Ten Thousand Pound Job' was probably rooted, consciously or unconsciously, in an impulse to vindicate the system under which public officials like Peter Robinson had been free to exploit their offices entrepreneurially, so long as they could balance the public books at the end of the day.

Such exploitation of office was, after all, only an analogy of the Family Compact's exploitation of their collective, oligarchic power to promote the dominance of their metropolis. Robinson might probably have justified both instances of entrepreneurial exploitation of political power by arguing that their beneficiaries were the members of the community best fitted by breeding and intelligence to possess political power, and that they wielded it in the best interests of the community as a whole. Such a view was, of course, quite incompatible with the 'two masters' rule and the Christian dictum that underlay it.[142] In resisting the application of the equitable rule to Bowes, Robinson was registering a perhaps unconscious protest against the new ideal of political organization that had superseded his own.

CONCLUSION

Chief Justice Draper began his judgment with a 'historical' preamble which noted that since its first recognition the 'two masters' rule had been more and more widely applied 'in proportion as the number and development of the variety of cases which it was found necessary to subject to it, have demonstrated its soundness and the impossibility of preventing wrong without giving it the utmost force, and the widest extension.'[143] In response to Robinson's conservative argument that the rule had never been applied to a case like the present, Draper in effect replied that changing times were constantly throwing up new ways of doing wrong, and the rule must be flexibly applied to meet new exigencies.

Such an approach to equitable jurisdiction was especially apt for a society in rapid transition. The advent of railways had plunged Upper Canada and its municipalities into the dangerous waters of large-scale enterprise and international finance. Municipal councillors elected to mend pot-holes floundered out of their depth and eagerly accepted the informed guidance of an expert like Bowes. When their pilot was rumoured to be in league with the sharks, they did not know what to do; and those who best understood what was happening were too often in league with the sharks. On the Toronto City Council of 1853, Bowes' staunch ally C.E. Romain was a paid agent of Gzowski & Co., the Toronto & Guelph Railroad contractors.[144] Samuel Thompson, who as chairman of the finance committee sat with Bowes on the Toronto & Guelph board, was offered a £500-a-year post in Montreal when the railway was absorbed by the Grand Trunk in April 1853 and given a £500 gratuity when he turned the job down.[145] With this sort of influence being brought to bear on municipal councillors, it would have been highly impolitic for the court to apply the 'two masters' rule laxly.

If the judges did not restrain officials from abusing their public position for private gain, no one was likely to do so; for public and political reaction to the affair was confused and ambiguous. After Bowes' exposure in court in September 1853, he had to face a motion of censure which gave rise to protracted and acrimonious debate. Seven successive amendments were discussed and defeated, and it became clear that Bowes had lost the support of two or three council members who had backed him during the select committee controversies eight months previously. Even so, the amendment finally passed was more acceptable to Bowes' supporters than to his enemies, eight of whom resigned in disgust.[146]

At the next municipal elections, Bowes' opponents did notably better than his friends, but two of the leading 'corruptionists' (as The Globe called them), Ogle Gowan and Charles Romain, headed the poll in their respective wards.[147] Worst of all from The Globe's point of view, Bowes himself, who had not sought re-election to council, came first of five candidates (all Conservatives) who contested Toronto at the general election of July 1854. The man who sustained the adverse decrees of the courts of Chancery and Appeal was an MPP playing an important role in consolidating the alliance of the Conservatives with the Hincksites and Bleus under the premiership of Sir Allan MacNab. In 1856 he was re-elected to the city council, and from 1861 to 1864 was mayor once more.[148]

Bowes' continuing political success was compounded of a canny blend of 'Gowanite' Orange and Roman Catholic support, the latter acquired by vociferous devotion to the cause of separate schools, and both probably enhanced by his disreputability.[149] The lower classes often admire white-collar crime, especially when it is committed against the rich. The same plebeian voters who elected the 'self-made' Bowes to parliament in 1854 had three years earlier returned the famously bankrupt William Henry Boulton: a scion of the Family Compact, to be sure, but a glad-handing devotee of horse racing and the music hall who played to the plebeian gallery much as Bowes did. These voters probably saw little distinction between the 'Ten Thousand Pound Job' and the way a financier like William Cawthra made his money. They would have made money that way themselves if they could, and it hurt people less than foreclosing on mortgages.[150]

Such voters probably sympathized with their spokesman, Ogle Gowan, when he denounced one of Bowes' chief assailants as a 'pettifogging lawyer, who preferred quibbles to facts,' adding that 'the days of quirks and quibbles had passed away, and that the present times were those of business realities.'[151] This crude echo of MacNab's catchphrase, 'all my politics are railroads,' might also have found favour with Chief Justice Robinson, since it also echoed the cry used to discredit the cause of responsible government in the 1830s and 1840s, when the reformers' ideals had been dismissed as mere 'quirks and quibbles' that were distracting the country from its proper concern, the pursuit of economic growth.

The patrician Robinson might also have found common ground with Bowes' plebeian admirers in agreeing with *The New York Herald*'s comment on the scandal. Recalling the still recent days when Upper Canada had been dominated by officials 'holding half-a-dozen berths, appropriating stray townships, allotting water rights to their sons, plunging their arm to the elbow in the public coffers, and growing fat off the cream of the land,' it noted that Hincks was more responsible than anyone else for Canada's economic boom and concluded: 'We cannot bring ourselves to blame him for having invested his money judiciously.'[152] Robinson might have thought the *Herald*'s description of the Family Compact's heyday a trifle tendentious, but its conclusion came very close to his own belief that it was all right for public officials to do well by doing good.

The *Herald*, it is true, based its remarks on the incorrect premise that Hincks had not been shown to have used his official position to his personal advantage; but this error merely highlights the true extent of the changes the paper made so much of. Under the old régime an oligarchic élite entrenched in authoritarian institutions and sustained by an alien (ie, English) doctrine of prescriptive right had entrepreneurially exploited their monopoly of political power on two levels: they had collectively sought to extend their economic control throughout the province, and they had individually exercised their respective offices to their private advantage. But even before Upper Canada's creation in 1791, a new idea had appeared to challenge the old doctrine of aristocratic élitism that underlay the British political structure on which the colony's was modelled. This new idea was laissez-faire, the creed of free enterprise, which held that each individual's informed pursuit of his own interest conduced to the common good. Upper Canada's liberation first from the Family Compact and then from imperial political dominance released the forces of free enterprise in the colony. The new creed sustained a new élite recruited according to new standards, and – lo and behold – a system in which officials had used their public position to 'appropriate stray townships' became one in which they used it to make 'judicious investments.'

The existence of a court of Chancery which chastised excesses of entrepreneurial zeal might be cited to contradict this view. There is no doubt that the court worked well in the 'Ten Thousand Pound Job,' within the scope of its jurisdiction. It had allowed private citizens, as members of the municipal corporation, to bypass a refractory city council and press suit against Bowes, until a new council took the suit over to prevent its being jeopardized by the plaintiffs' possible lack of standing. Its flexible rules, so different from the rigid forms of the common law courts,[153] had let the plaintiffs use an inaccurate bill of complaint to force disclosure of malfeasance by the defendant under oath and then amend their bill to conform to his evidence. Above all, it had extended the scope of the municipal official's fiduciary responsibilities.

But while it certainly benefited the public to have municipal property brought under the full protection of the preventive rule that guarded other trusts, the court of Chancery remained above all an institution to protect the rich from the depredations of the rich (or else from those of their own agents). The costs of the proceedings (including both appeals) came to more than £2000, of which little more than half was recoverable from Bowes.[154] They had been undertaken only because private individuals were willing to bear those costs; for, even when the city took over the suit early in 1854, it did so only on condition that the original plaintiffs indemnify it against any costs it might incur.[155] Bowes' speculation foundered in Chancery partly because he had thoughtlessly taken his profit from funds in which rich men felt a particular interest: the scandal erupted at a moment when merchants felt aggrieved by a new municipal assessment law, recently carried through by Hincks, which they felt discriminated against them.[156] It foundered too because Bowes himself personified social and economic trends that were obnoxious to many of the city's élite.

In any case, although Hincks' gains were no less ill gotten than Bowes', the law did nothing to stop Hincks escaping with his share of the boodle: a fact that emphasizes the limits of the courts' efficacy in enforcing a fiduciary conception of public office. Mackenzie reported in his *Weekly Message* that the mayor's pursuers had at first sought to sue Hincks too, but he had had to be left out of the case because the court had no control over him.[157] This may have been because he was a resident of Lower Canada who had performed all his acts in aid of the speculation at Quebec; but it may also reflect the fact that his official position afforded him the privileges that Robinson had vainly tried to extend to Bowes.[158] Indeed, Chief Justice Draper may have had Hincks in mind when, in refuting Robinson's analogy between municipal officers and members of the legislature, he added: 'Besides, considerations of the highest constitutional policy intervene to prevent such an inquiry into the motives of a member before any tribunal but that of public opinion.'[159]

However, we have noted the unreliability of public opinion in this respect, and the same weakness was evinced (as might be imagined) by Hincks' fellow politicians. After Hincks resigned as premier in September 1854, his part in the 'Job' was one of several charges of misconduct investigated by select committees of both houses of the legislature; but in a legislature dominated by the new coalition he had nothing to worry about. George Brown contrived to have the whole of the evidence in the scandal entered into the record of the Assembly's committee, but neither committee found any more to blame in the debenture speculation than in other improprieties which were less well documented. Hincks spent most of the next fifteen years as a colonial governor in the Caribbean. He returned to Canada in 1869, graced with the accolade of knighthood, to become Sir John A. Macdonald's minister of finance.[160]

Even so, the fact that wronged citizens received any justice at all made the 'Ten Thousand Pound Job' exceptional in the history of Toronto's early encounters with the railway interest. Two other incidents in 1853 showed that the law's impotence and the politicians' reluctance to chastise Hincks were more typical of the sort of protection the public interest might expect. The terms of the Grand Trunk's merger with the Toronto & Guelph Railroad obliged Gzowski & Co., the Toronto & Guelph contractor, to offer to buy at par all municipally owned Toronto & Guelph stock, which could however be swapped for Grand Trunk stock instead at the owner's option. Toronto would have been far better off selling its £100,000 in stock to Gzowski, and Bowes advised the city council to do so; but misleading rumours abounded as to potential value of Grand Trunk stock, and Bowes' rumoured part in the 'Ten Thousand Pound Job' made the council distrust his advice. Gzowski & Co.'s agent, Councillor Romain, urged acceptance of the stock swap, while Gzowski himself gave contradictory information to the committee set up to look into the matter. Compelled by the terms of Gzowski's offer to decide in haste, before they could obtain the needed information, the council chose the stock swap, which ended in the city's loss of £52,000.[161] Later in the year the city was forced to accept Gzowski & Co.'s high tender to build its waterfront esplanade because the council's ratification of the Grand Trunk-Toronto & Guelph merger without obtaining guarantees that the line would pass through downtown Toronto allowed Gzowski to threaten to bypass the city should his tender be rejected.[162] In neither case did the law offer the public interest even the partial protection afforded in the 'Ten Thousand Pound Job.'

The juggernaut was simply too strong. The railway interest represented an unprecedented concentration of economic power; and to colonial politicians, who generally speaking had little understanding of the world of international finance which had suddenly embraced them so tightly, the railway builder seemed to have the power of life and death. He came among the competing business communities of Canada like the white man among warring native tribes: his friendship promised prosperity, his enmity meant despair. Even where the will to resist was present, the know-how was lacking; but as long as he kept the chief and one or two of the smarter braves on his side, he could have the whole tribe eating out of his hand most of the time.[163]

This situation was easily achieved. At a time when municipal and provincial legislators were unsalaried and even cabinet ministers' pay was low, the railway interest had something to offer almost everyone who counted: the Legislative Council's committee on the charges against the Hincks administration recommended that cabinet ministers be paid well enough that they did not need to engage in private business while in office.[164] One waterfront proprietor in Toronto, saddled by legislation with a large share of the cost of building the esplanade across his water-lot, grumbled in 1855 that every lawyer in town was in Gzowski & Co.'s pocket.[165] Alderman John Beverley Robinson, jr had alleged a year earlier that the whole Legislative Assembly was in the pocket of Gzowski's principal, the Grand Trunk.[166] Yet the railway interest's greatest asset was not its ability to buy up lawyers or bribe private members, but its claim on the allegiance of cabinet ministers. When the city tried in 1855 to denounce the esplanade contract with Gzowski & Co., the government brought it to heel within weeks by means of punitive legislation.[167]

The Grand Trunk's easy command of lawyers and politicians calls to mind the 'Wisconsin Purchase' of 1856, in which a railroad company bought up a governor, a judge, and most of the state legislature with parcels of company bonds ranging from $10,000 to $50,000 and talked farmers into buying its stock with mortgages on their property. The project collapsed; the mortgages passed into the hands of the financial institutions that were the company's primary creditors; and the law's preference for the rights of the innocent purchaser for value prevented it from affording the duped farmers any relief from the demands of the new mortgage holders.[168] This scandal was much more spectacular than any that occurred in Canada during this period, but it suggests a conclusion that is applicable to Canada, too. Where economic power and political corruption went hand-in-hand, and judges were unwilling to take the initiative in adapting the law to new conditions, legal proceedings could at best palliate the resulting injustices.

NOTES

I would like to acknowledge Professor Michael Bliss's useful critique of an earlier draft, the valuable advice of Professors T.G. Youdan and R.C.B. Risk, and the gracious help of the City of Toronto Archives and the Metropolitan Toronto Library.

1 Notices of the scandal include Nicholas Flood Davin *The Irishman in Canada* (London and Toronto 1877) 282–3; Samuel Thompson *Reminiscences of a Canadian Pioneer for the Last Fifty Years* (Toronto 1884; new ed. Toronto 1968) 206–8; Sir Francis Hincks *Reminiscences of His Public Life* (Montreal 1884) 355–7; Gustavus Myers *A History of Canadian Wealth* (Chicago, IL 1914; new ed. Toronto 1972) 192–4; R.S. Longley *Sir Francis Hincks: A Study of Canadian Politics, Railways and Finance in the Nineteenth Century* (Toronto 1943) 238–9; W.G. Ormsby 'John George Bowes' in *Dictionary of Canadian Biography* IX (Toronto 1976) 76–7 (hereafter DCB); Ormsby 'Sir Francis Hincks' in J.M.S. Careless, ed. *The Pre-Confederation Premiers: Ontario Government Leaders, 1841–1867* (Toronto 1980) 177–8, 184; Barrie Drummond Dyster 'Toronto 1840–1860: Making It in a British Protestant Town' (PH D thesis, University of Toronto 1970) 345–9; Peter A. Baskerville 'The Boardroom and Beyond: Aspects of the Upper Canadian Railroad Community' (PH D thesis, Queen's University 1973) 172–206.
2 J.M.S. Careless, *The Union of the Canadas: The Growth of Canadian Institutions 1841–1857* (Toronto 1967) 166–94; Dyster 'Toronto 1840–1860' 350–86
3 Peter A. Baskerville 'Entrepreneurship and the Family Compact: York-Toronto 1822–1855' *Urban History Review* IX 3 (Feb. 1981) 15–34
4 Careless *Union of the Canadas* 165
5 Peter A. Baskerville 'Sir Allan Napier MacNab' in DCB IX, 524; Dyster 'Toronto 1840–1860' 370–1
6 Baskerville 'Entrepreneurship and the Family Compact' 21–2; Baskerville 'Boardroom and Beyond' 19–132; Baskerville 'Sir Allan Napier MacNab' 519–27; Dyster 'Toronto 1840–1860' 295–315
7 A *debenture* is an IOU which promises repayment of a loan at the expiry of a

specified period and states the interest due from time to time thereon. Debentures were also commonly called *securities* or *bonds*. A transaction made in such bonds at face value was said to have been made at *par*; one at a twenty per cent discount at *80*; one at a similar premium at *120*; and so on. By-law No. 184; Toronto City Council Minutes 25 Nov. 1850, 18 Aug. 1851, City of Toronto Archives (hereafter Council Minutes)

8 Great Britain, Privy Council, Judicial Committee, Indian and Colonial Appeals Heard in 1857 (vol. 1), *Bowes v City of Toronto*, Plaintiffs' Bill (hereafter PC Bill) 70 (Exhibit R). The Privy Council material also contains the *Cases* of the Appellant and the Respondents. There are two other official accounts of the pleadings, testimony, and exhibits. One is *In the Court of Error and Appeal: John G. Bowes, Appellant, and the City of Toronto, Respondents* (Toronto 1854). The other is Canada, Legislative Assembly, *Journals* XIII (1854–5) (hereafter JLAC), Appendix AAAA (Report and Proceedings of the Select Committee on Charges against the Late Administration), Appendices 3 and 4 (hereafter Appendix AAAA). The only copy I have seen of the former (at Metropolitan Toronto Library) is mutilated, and the latter is unpaginated. I have therefore chosen to cite the Privy Council material (available on microfilm at the City of Toronto Archives) and also, wherever possible, a newspaper reference.

9 *Toronto Daily Patriot and Express* 31 July 1852 (hereafter *Patriot*); *Semi-Weekly Leader* 3, 6 Aug. 1852; *Globe* 12 Jan. 1854

10 Toronto, City Council *Report of the Select Committee Appointed to Inquire into the Issue and Sale of City Debentures in 1852, with the Evidence* (Toronto 1853) 36–7 (hereafter *Report of the Select Committee*)

11 A *sinking fund* is a special capital fund built up to provide for repayment of a long-term debt.

12 Upper Canada Municipal Act, 12 Vict. (1849), c. 81, s. 177 (re sinking fund); Toronto, Simcoe and Lake Huron Railroad Amendment Act, 13 & 14 Vict. (1851), c. 113; UC Municipal Corporations Amendment Act, 14 Vict. (1851), c. 109, s. 16 (re notice). James H. Hagarty thought the by-law defective on both counts, Oliver Mowat only for want of notice. PC Bill, 89–92

13 *Report of the Select Committee* 41–2; *Globe* 15 Sept. 1853, 12 Jan. 1854; *Daily Leader* 12 Jan. 1854

14 *Report of the Select Committee* 44–6; *Patriot* 26 Jan. 1853; *Globe* 22 Dec. 1853; *British Colonist* 23 Dec. 1853

15 PC Bill 80–1, 88–9; *Patriot* 26 Aug. 1852

16 *Globe* 1 Feb. 1853; *Report of the Select Committee* 45–6; Toronto Consolidation Act, 16 Vict. (1852), c. 5

17 By-laws Nos 190, 192

18 *Report of the Debate in the City Council on Monday, January 24th, 1853, in reference*

to the £50,000 City Debentures (Toronto 1853) 9 (hereafter *Report of the Debate ... Jan. 24th*)

19 *Patriot* 5 Jan. 1853; *British Colonist* 18 Jan. 1853

20 *Patriot* 17 Jan. 1853

21 Ormsby 'John George Bowes'; Davin *Irishman in Canada* 279–82; Dyster 'Toronto 1840–1860' 304, 306, 308–9, 337–9; *British Colonist* 21 Jan. 1853; *Patriot* 5 Nov. 1852, 18 Jan. 1853

22 *Report of the Debate ... Jan. 24th*; *Patriot* 26 Jan. 1853

23 *Patriot* 9 Feb. 1853; *Globe* 10 Feb. 1853; Council Minutes 7 Feb. 1853; *Report of the Select Committee* 3–5

24 This summary is based on *Report of the Debate ... Jan. 24th*; *Globe* 26 Jan., 1 Feb., 10 Feb. 1853; *Patriot* 26 Jan., 9 Feb. 1853.

25 PC Bill 69 (Exhibit N). By 1 Dec. 1852 the total expenditure on the railway was less than £350,000: *Hamilton Gazette* 16 Dec. 1852.

26 This summary is based on the sources cited in n24, and *Patriot* 28 Jan. 1853.

27 *Patriot* 26 Jan. 1853. Cf. Bowes in ibid. 17 Jan. 1853.

28 *British Canadian* 26 Jan. 1853

29 *Report of the Select Committee*, passim; *Patriot* 24 Feb. 1853; *Globe* 24 Feb. 1853; Council Minutes 17 Jan. 1853

30 *Report of the Select Committee* 52, 54–5, 59

31 *Globe* 24 Feb. 1853; *Patriot* 24 Feb. 1853; Council Minutes 21 Feb. 1853

32 *The Report of the Debate in the City Council on Monday, February 21st, 1853, on Bringing up the Report of the Special Committee Appointed to Investigate in Reference to the Issuing of the City Debentures* (Toronto 1853) (hereafter *Report of the Debate ... Feb. 21st*); and see n18.

33 *Patriot* 23 Feb. 1853

34 Hereward Senior 'Ogle Robert Gowan' in DCB x (Toronto 1972) 309–14; Dyster 'Toronto 1840–1860' 378–86. For Hincks, see Ormsby 'Sir Francis Hincks' passim.

35 *Semi-Weekly Leader* 25 Feb. 1853; *Toronto Mirror* 25 Feb. 1853

36 *North American* 3 Feb. 1853; *Mackenzie's Weekly Message* 10 Feb., 3 Mar. 1853; *Journals of the Legislative Council of Canada* XIII (1854–5) (hereafter JLCC), Appendix 2, 29; Dyster 'Toronto 1840–1860' 304. Hincks' official title was Inspector General of Public Accounts.

37 *Report of the Select Committee* 4; *Examiner* 2 Feb. 1853; *Globe* 24 Feb. 1853; *Report of the Debate ... Feb. 21st* 33–7; Edith G. Firth, ed. *Early Toronto Newspapers, 1793–1867* (Toronto 1961) 24; Council Minutes 19 Jan. 1852. The five plaintiffs were David Paterson, Arthur Lepper, Hugh Miller, and Robert Sargent, all merchants, and Jonathan Watson, leather dealer: *Globe* 12 Oct. 1853.

38 PC Bill 16–17; *Patriot* 17 Dec. 1853
39 *Patriot* 24 Feb. 1853
40 PC Bill 24; *Globe* 22 Dec. 1853
41 PC Bill 36 (evidence of G.P. Ridout); *British Colonist* 23 Dec. 1853
42 George Spence *The Equitable Jurisdiction of the Court of Chancery* (London 1846–9); F.W. Maitland *Equity: A Course of Lectures*, ed. A.H. Chaytor and W.J. Whittaker, rev. John Brunyate (Cambridge, Eng. 1949) 1–14; John Sidney Smith *A Treatise on the Practice of the Court of Chancery*, 2nd American ed., David Graham, jr (Philadelphia 1842). See also *Jowitt's Dictionary of English Law*, 2nd ed., John Burke, 2 vols (London 1977) I 113, 590–1, 622, II 1370–1, 1550–1.
43 *Paterson* v *Bowes* (later *City of Toronto* v *Bowes*) (1854), 4 *Grant's Chancery Reports* 170, at 170–4 (hereafter GCR)
44 Ibid. 175–7
45 Ibid. 177–98. Before the suit came to judgment, this cause of objection was to be eliminated by a new city council's decision to take the suit over from the plaintiffs. *Globe* 8, 13 Feb. 1854
46 PC Bill 5–7
47 John D. Blackwell 'William Hume Blake and the Judicature Acts of 1849: The Process of Legal Reform at Mid-Century in Upper Canada' in David H. Flaherty, ed. *Essays in the History of Canadian Law* 2 vols (Toronto 1981–3) I 132–74
48 For Mowat, see Margaret A. Evans 'Oliver Mowat: Nineteenth-Century Ontario Liberal' in Donald Swainson, ed. *Oliver Mowat's Ontario* (Toronto 1972). For Gwynne and Connor, see Davin *Irishman in Canada* 577–8, 604–5; Dyster 'Toronto 1840–1860' 300, 317; David B. Read *The Lives of the Judges of Upper Canada and Ontario, from 1791 to the Present Time* (Toronto 1888) 328–36; R. Lynn Ogden 'George Skeffington Connor' in DCB IX 151. Mowat's colleague as counsel for the plaintiffs was Philip VanKoughnet, a Conservative of 'High Tory' background: see Read *Lives of the Judges* 314–27; W.L. Morton 'Philip Michael Matthew Scott VanKoughnet' in DCB IX 803–4. The ensuing account of Bowes' and Ridout's testimony on 12 and 13 Sept. is based on PC Bill 11–16 and *Globe* 13 Sept., 15 Sept. 1853 (editorial quotations from *Globe* 13 Sept.).
49 PC Bill 17–18; *British Colonist* 20 Dec. 1853; 4 GCR 489, at 498–503
50 PC Bill 22, 25, 33 (evidence of Bowes, Hutchison, Beard, and Thompson); *Globe* 22 Dec. 1853; *British Colonist* 23 Dec. 1853
51 See above, 155; PC Bill 24, 29, 36 (evidence of Cawthra, McCord, and G.P. Ridout).
52 For the pros and cons of this issue see *Report of the Select Committee* 36; PC Bill 23 (evidence of Hutchison); *Patriot* 24 Feb. 1853.

53 PC Bill 1–3; *Globe* 12 Oct. 1854

54 PC Bill 8–10; *Globe* 2 Dec. 1853

55 PC Bill 22–35; *Globe* 22 Dec. 1853; *Daily Leader* 22, 23 Dec. 1853; *British Colonist* 23 Dec. 1853

56 PC Bill 18–19; *Daily Leader* 17 Dec. 1853; *Patriot* 17 Dec. 1853; *British Colonist* 20 Dec. 1853. Bowes testified that he had thought Dunn's offer unsatisfactory because Dunn had not expected to get par for the bonds. In the event, neither could Hincks.

57 PC Bill, 19–22; newspapers as in n56; *Bowes v City of Toronto* (1858), 11 *Moore's Privy Council Reports* 463 (hereafter MPCR: reprinted 14 *English Reports* 770, at 505)

58 Citations as in n55

59 PC Bill 36–44; *Globe* 12, 13, 14 Jan. 1854

60 *Globe* 11, 13, 18 Nov., 18, 23 Dec. 1852; *Patriot* 20 Dec. 1852

61 PC Bill 20. Cotton sued Bowes for slander on this account: *Globe* 7 May 1853.

62 PC Bill 22; newspapers as in n56

63 PC Bill 23; *Globe* 22 Dec. 1853; *Daily Leader* 22 Dec. 1853

64 PC Bill 42–4; *Globe* 12, 13 Jan. 1854

65 *Globe* 23 Jan. 1854

66 See below, 169.

67 Hincks' evidence is printed in PC Bill 46–60, *Daily Leader* 27 Feb. 1854 and *Globe* 1 Mar. 1854.

68 Since Bowes and Hincks made a joint profit of £8247 and must therefore have disposed of the consolidated loan for £98,247 plus whatever bank charges were levied on the deal, it is hard to see why Hincks talked of selling the loan at only 96 or 97.

69 See also below, 167 and n77.

70 See above, 160, and *Daily Leader* 23 Dec. 1853.

71 PC Bill 76 (Exhibit B in Crooks' affidavit). The entire correspondence is printed in *Daily Colonist* 18 July 1854.

72 Dyster 'Toronto 1840–1860' 264–76, 302–9

73 See below, 175, 177, 181; also 4 GCR 489, at 511–13, and 6 GCR 1, at 88.

74 11 MPCR 463, at 522–3. It is also hinted at in *Globe* 15 Sept. 1853 and ibid. 2 Mar., 28 Aug. 1854.

75 Ormsby 'Sir Francis Hincks' 172

76 Appendix AAAA, question 334

77 *Mackenzie's Weekly Message* 1 Dec. 1853; *Globe* 1 Mar. 1854; the *Daily Leader* of 2 Mar. 1854 replied that the destruction of such correspondence was 'a practice not less general than it is correct. To what purpose would any man of honorable feelings accumulate piles of private correspondence?'

78 *Globe* 1 Mar., 2 Mar. 1854
79 Montreal Consolidation Act, 16 Vict. (1852), c. 26; Kingston Consolidation Act, 16 Vict. (1852), c. 32; Hamilton Consolidation Act, 16 Vict. (1853), c. 95. The passage of each may be traced in JLAC.
80 Hamilton City Council Minutes, City of Hamilton Archives, 31 May, 18, 20 Aug., 13 Dec. 1852; ibid. 28 Feb., 7 Mar. 1853 (microfilm at Ontario Archives). A deputation of the Kingston city council was in Quebec to try to persuade the government to reduce the city's tax burden at the very time the Toronto Consolidation Act was passed: *Weekly British Whig*, 8 Oct., 19 Nov. 1852.
81 Ormsby 'Sir Francis Hincks' 158–9
82 PC Bill 40; *Globe* 12 Jan. 1854; Andrew F. Hunter *A History of Simcoe County* 2 vols (Barrie, Ont. 1909) I 166; County of Simcoe, Council Minutes 1852, October Session, Appendix 19–20 (copy at Ontario Archives)
83 PC Bill 56–7; *Daily Leader* 27 Feb. 1854
84 PC Bill 47–8
85 Ibid. 93
86 Ibid. 18; *British Colonist* 20 Dec. 1853
87 PC Bill 54
88 As n86
89 Hincks *Reminiscences* 356
90 *Globe* 15 Jan., 9 May 1854. Cotton is identified as a 'government contractor' in the Toronto city directories of 1850/1 and 1856.
91 J.C. Shepherd *The Law of Fiduciaries* (Toronto 1981) 12–20
92 A modern but historically rooted discussion of this still lively problem is Gareth Jones 'Unjust Enrichment and the Fiduciary's Duty of Loyalty' *Law Quarterly Review* 84 (1968) 472–502. See also Shepherd *Law of Fiduciaries* 71–8, 273–302.
93 25 *English Reports* 223. See also Shepherd *Law of Fiduciaries* 19, 76–7, 118–19, 303–8; and Maitland and Brunyate *Equity* 80–1.
94 Shepherd *Law of Fiduciaries* 19; Maitland and Brunyate *Equity* 80–4. A leading mid-nineteenth-century authority is Joseph G. Story *Commentaries on Equity Jurisprudence* 4th ed., 2 vols (Boston and London 1846) I cap. 7.
95 4 GCR 489, at 489–90; *Globe* 1 July 1854. The noun *fiduciary* was not used at this time as a general term, and Bowes was always discussed as the city's *agent* or *trustee*.
96 They were discussed in the judgments in Chancery and in Appeal: 4 GCR 489; 6 GCR 1.
97 The defendant's case in Chancery is summarized in 4 GCR 489, at 491–3. The argument in Appeal is printed in a 115-page pamphlet, of which there is a copy at Metropolitan Toronto Library (title-page missing). This extensively anno-

tated document was probably the working copy of one of Bowes' counsel. It is cited below as 'Argument.' The defendant's argument in Appeal was also serialized in the *Daily Leader*, starting 7 Sept. 1855. See also the Appellant's case in the Privy Council (see above, n8).

98 4 GCR 489, at 505–8, 515–16, 519–21

99 Ibid. 527–8

100 Ibid. 504, 505

101 Ibid. 525–6 (my italics), 530

102 Ibid. 503, 518, 523

103 6 GCR 1, at 7–36, 53–4

104 Ibid. 17, 36–44, 54–63

105 Ibid. 44–7

106 So, of course, did the defendant: see 'Argument' 87–92, 94–6, 103–4, where this evidence is relevant but ignored. McLean, J, also overlooked it: 6 GCR 1, at 98.

107 6 GCR 1, at 60–1; and see above, 168–9.

108 6 GCR 1, at 92

109 The Court of Error and Appeal consisted of the judges of Queen's Bench, Chancery, and Common Pleas, with the CJQB as their president (in this case, Robinson). James Buchanan Macaulay, CJCP, retired during the case, so only five common law judges rendered judgment in it. The constitution of Upper Canada's superior courts at this time is discussed in Blackwell 'Blake and the Judicature Acts.'

110 6 GCR 1, at 86, 88

111 Ibid. 106

112 Ibid. 112–13

113 Ibid. 100–7. Burns' views on the earlier transactions are couched in rather obscure language but seem to have been as follows. Bowes was not at fault in merely agreeing to purchase, prior to the passage of the by-law authorizing their issue, the bonds to which Story & Co. were entitled under the resolution of 1850 that granted the railway £25,000 in debentures. He *was* at fault in buying them with the secret knowledge that he could make the city redeem them to his own profit prior to term. As to Bowes' buying the bonds issued under the stock purchase agreement (which could also be seen, though not unarguably so, as merely fulfilling an earlier commitment by the city to the railway), Burns expressed no opinion as to the mere purchase, but here too he discountenanced the purchase with a view to premature redemption. Ibid. 103, 106

114 Ibid. 89–90

115 Ibid. 104

116 11 MPCR 463, at 516–17
117 Ibid. 522–3; and cf. 4 GCR 489, at 511–13.
118 11 MPCR 463, at 519–20; and cf. 4 GCR 489, at 511.
119 11 MPCR 463, at 518
120 Ibid. 525
121 6 GCR 1, at 9, 24
122 Baskerville 'Entrepreneurship and the Family Compact' 25–7
123 R.C.B. Risk, 'The Law and the Economy in Mid-Nineteenth-Century Ontario: A Perspective' in Flaherty, ed. *Essays in the History of Canadian Law* I 100–7. See also James Willard Hurst *Law and the Conditions of Freedom in the Nineteenth-Century United States* (Madison, WI 1956) 23–9.
124 Risk 'Law and the Economy' 115–16
125 Baskerville 'Entrepreneurship and the Family Compact' passim
126 Ibid. 26, at nn66 and 67
127 Ibid. 26, quoting 6 GCR 1, at 16. Baskerville omits the words in brackets.
128 Baskerville 'Entrepreneurship and the Family Compact' 26
129 Morton J. Horwitz *The Transformation of American Law, 1780–1860* (Cambridge, MA 1977) 1–30
130 6 GCR 1, at 43, quoted in Baskerville 'Entrepreneurship and the Family Compact' 26 (words in brackets omitted)
131 Baskerville 'Entrepreneurship and the Family Compact' 27
132 Sidney and Beatrice Webb *The Development of English Local Government, 1689–1835* (London 1963) passim; Sir William Holdsworth *A History of English Law* vol. XIV, ed. A.L. Goodhart and H.G. Hanbury (London 1964) 232
133 6 GCR 1, at 52–3, 66–8
134 Dyster 'Toronto 1840–1860' 302–4
135 Terry Cook 'John Beverley Robinson and the Conservative Blueprint for the Upper Canadian Community' *Ontario History* LXIV (1972), 79–94 reprinted in J.K. Johnson, ed. *Historical Essays on Upper Canada* (Toronto 1975) 338–60
136 6 GCR 1, at 15–17, 46–7, 63–7
137 Ibid. 90, 115; 4 GCR 489, at 506–7, 531
138 11 MPCR 463, at 524. Cf. *Parsons v London* (1911), 25 *Ontario Law Reports* 172, at 179.
139 See Shepherd *Law of Fiduciaries* 27–8, where *Toronto v Bowes* is cited.
140 Blackstone classed offices as *incorporeal hereditaments*: Robert Malcolm Kerr, ed. *The Commentaries on the Laws of England of Sir William Blackstone, Knt* 4th ed., 4 vols (London 1876) II 31.
141 *The Arthur Papers*, ed. Charles R. Sanderson, 3 vols (Toronto 1959) I, 9–12, 64–5, 209–11, 221–2
142 'No man can serve two masters: for either he will hate the one, and love the

other; or else he will hold to the one, and despise the other. Ye cannot serve God and mammon.' Matthew 6:24. It is noteworthy that the one judge who concurred in Robinson's view of the case, Archibald McLean, was a contemporary of his who like him had been born in Upper Canada. Draper had reached high political office in the last years of the old province, but he was a decade younger than they and had grown up in England. The other five judges were younger still, and three of them were also British in background. Read *Lives of the Judges* 158–75, 222–36, 263–313; George Metcalf 'William Henry Draper' in Careless, ed. *Pre-Confederation Premiers*; Bruce W. Hodgins 'Archibald McLean' in DCB IX 512–13; Donald Swainson 'William Hume Blake' in ibid. 55–60; Brian H. Morrison 'Robert Easton Burns' in ibid. 108–9; Robert Hett 'James Christie Palmer Esten' in ibid. 244–5; W. Stewart Wallace, ed. *The Macmillan Dictionary of Canadian Biography* 4th ed. rev. by W.A. McKay (Toronto 1978) 700–1, 788.

143 6 GCR 1, at 77
144 *Patriot* 15 Jan., 17 Jan., 18 Jan. 1853; *Globe* 15 Feb. 1854
145 Thompson *Reminiscences* 206
146 Council Minutes 19, 26 Sept., 14, 17 Oct. 1853; *Patriot* 12, 27 Oct. 1853; *Globe* 12 Oct. 1853; *Daily Leader* 5, 12, 18 Nov. 1853
147 *Globe* 3, 24 Nov., 31 Dec. 1853; ibid. 4 Jan. 1854
148 Ibid. 31 July 1854; Dyster 'Toronto 1840–1860' 455–7
149 Dyster 'Toronto 1840–1860' 386–91, 455–7
150 Ibid. 374–8; Hereward Senior 'William Henry Boulton' in DCB X 79–81; G.P. de T. Glazebrook 'William Cawthra' in ibid. 155
151 *Patriot* 24 Feb. 1853
152 Quoted in *Toronto Mirror* 7 Oct. 1853
153 F.W. Maitland *The Constitutional History of England* (Cambridge, Eng. 1908) 468–70; and refs above, n42
154 City of Toronto Archives RG2 B, Finance Committee Communications, 1865: 14–14i, comprises correspondence about the payment of costs. Item 14d is the complete bill of costs.
155 *Globe* 8, 13 Feb. 1854; Council Minutes 11 Feb. 1854
156 *Globe* 24, 26 Aug. 1852; *Patriot* 3, 4 Mar. 1853
157 *Mackenzie's Weekly Message* 1 Dec. 1853
158 Although Hincks had continued to represent the Upper Canadian county of Oxford, he had resided in Lower Canada since 1844. Ormsby 'Sir Francis Hincks' 156–8, 163, 166, 178
159 6 GCR 1, at 87
160 Ormsby 'Sir Francis Hincks' 183–8. The reports are cited above, nn10, 38.
161 *Patriot* 9, 18, 24 May 1853; Dyster 'Toronto 1840–1860' 340–1

162 *Patriot* 17 Oct. 1853
163 Robert S. Hunt *Law and Locomotives: The Impact of the Railroad on Wisconsin Law in the Nineteenth Century* (Madison, WI 1958) 72, 80–1, 90–1, 157–8, 172–3; Hurst *Law and the Conditions of Freedom* 83
164 JLCC XIII, Appendix 2, xiv
165 Dyster 'Toronto 1840–1860' 317 cites *Globe* 4 July 1855. See also Francis N. Mellen 'The Development of the Toronto Waterfront during the Railway Expansion Era, 1850–1912' (PH D thesis, University of Toronto 1974) 29–78.
166 *Globe* 26 Apr. 1854
167 Mellen 'Development of the Toronto Waterfront' 49–52
168 Hunt *Law and Locomotives* 3–65

4

Nineteenth-Century
Canadian Rape Law
1800–92

CONSTANCE B. BACKHOUSE

In his history of English criminal law Sir James Fitzjames Stephen, the
eminent Victorian, slighted important aspects of women's legal history: 'I
pass over many sections punishing particular acts of violence to the
person, and in particular the whole series of offences relating to the
abduction of women, rape, and other such crimes. Their history possesses
no special interest and does not illustrate either our political or our social
history.'[1] Contrary to Stephen's claim, nineteenth-century rape law provides a wealth of rich information about the roles assumed by men and
women, attitudes towards sexuality, and changing views about a woman's
right to sexual self-determination. The omission of rape from historical
analysis has been a serious oversight, especially in view of the consequences for the nineteenth-century victim. Short of murder, rape was the
most serious crime that could be perpetrated upon the female sex.
Canadian writers often referred to the crime as an 'outrage.' The
newspapers of the day frequently refused to print the details of the
charge, classifying them as 'unspeakable.' The editors of an 1862 issue of
The Upper Canada Law Journal concluded that the loss of a woman's
reputation defied computation: 'The consequence at times is a life of
prostitution, loathsome disease – in a word, a living death.' Not only was
the woman affected, but her family as well was injured: 'Nothing is so
destructive of domestic comfort and earthly happiness as the ruin of a
fond daughter or a loved sister. The contemplation of it is awful. The
realization of it is maddening. The complication or miseries which arise
from this cause cannot be computed.'[2]

A study of the law of rape as it evolved in nineteenth-century Canada reveals much about the status of women and raises many complex questions. Whose interests and what objectives did this area of law serve? Did the legal system view rape as a crime against the woman herself, or was the law intended to protect a particular form of male property, that is, the father's or husband's right to the ownership of a daughter's or wife's reproductive capacity? Did legislatures which passed increasingly detailed statutory codes against sexual assault of women perceive the crime differently than the judiciary? What values and attitudes were associated with the prohibition of sexual assault? Was Canadian rape law different from that of England? How did rape law change during the nineteenth century? What significant changes occurred in the definition of the crime, in the types of charges laid, in the rates of conviction, and in the penalties handed out? Who were the rapists, and who were the rape victims who brought their cases to court? And finally, what light does this shed on nineteenth-century perceptions of women? Although one cannot satisfactorily answer all of these questions in a single essay, they are the ultimate concerns of historical investigation on this important topic.

EARLY ENGLISH INFLUENCE 1800–60

For the first half of the nineteenth century Canadian rape law simply reflected the law as it existed in England. In 1800 the legislature of Upper Canada enacted legislation proclaiming that the province would adopt the criminal law of England, as it stood on 17 September 1792.[3] Eighteenth-century English rape law had evolved from the early common law felony of rape, which was punishable by death.[4] Sir William Blackstone's account of the origin of the crime in Jewish law indicates that rape was initially viewed as a crime against male property rights in women: '[B]y the Jewish law, [rape] was punished with death, in case the damsel was betrothed to another man; and in case she was not betrothed, then a heavy fine of fifty shekels was to be paid to the damsel's father, and she was to be the wife of the ravisher all the days of his life ...'[5]

The first English statute to deal with the crime of rape reduced the offence from a felony to a form of trespass in 1275, lowering the penalty to a maximum of two years and a fine.[6] The statute stated that 'none shall ravish nor take away by force any maiden within age (neither by her own consent, nor without) nor any wife or maiden of full age, nor any other woman against her will.'[7] Although there was no indication why the legislators decided to reduce the severity of the crime, later commentators noted that the experiment was unsuccessful. Blackstone claimed that 'this leniency [was] productive of the most terrible consequences.' Perhaps in response, the crime of rape was soon restored to a capital felony.[8] The law of rape remained substantially unaltered until 1576 when offenders lost the right to plead benefit of clergy and the age limit for consensual sexual intercourse was lowered to ten years. Whereas the 1275 statute had prohibited the ravishing of maidens under twelve years, (whether they consented or not), the statute of 1576 provided the death penalty for carnal knowledge of girls below the age of ten.[9] Blackstone explained the rationale behind the prohibition of sexual relations with such girls: 'the consent or non-consent is immaterial, as by reason of her tender years she is incapable of judgment and discretion.'[10]

By the close of the eighteenth century, English statutory law did little but set the penalties for rape. The prohibited act was to 'ravish,' 'rape,' and 'unlawfully and carnally know.' It remained for the common law to clarify the definition. Sir William Russell, the author of a widely cited treatise published in 1819, defined rape as 'having unlawful and carnal knowledge of a woman, *by force and against her will.'* Edward East, another of the early treatise writers on English criminal law, stated in his *Pleas of the Crown* in 1803, that it was 'no mitigation of this offence that the woman at last yielded to the violence if such her consent were forced by fear of death or duress. Nor was it any excuse ... that the woman consented after the fact ... nor that she was first taken with her own consent, if she were afterwards forced against her will.' East noted that it had previously been thought that if the woman conceived a child as a result of the act, there was no rape, since the conception was proof of her consent. However, East stated that it was now admitted on all hands that such an opinion had no foundation in reason or in law.[11]

As to the character of a rape victim, Blackstone dealt with the question of whether a prostitute or 'common harlot' was capable of being raped. He noted that the civil law refused punishment 'for violating the chastity of her, who hath indeed no chastity at all, or at least hath no regard to it.' However, the law of England was not so harsh: 'It therefore holds it to be felony to force even a concubine or harlot: because the woman may have forsaken that unlawful course of life.' According to East, it was proper to direct this type of information to the attention of the jury, especially in doubtful cases where the woman's testimony was not corroborated by other evidence. William Eden, the English author of a criminal law text published in 1771, outlined the requirement for corroborating evidence. In a somewhat contradictory fashion, he stated that 'the offence of rape is secret in its kind, and generally confined to the knowledge of the party injured ... The charge, however, is in most cases supported by the collateral, and concurrent testimony of time, place, and circumstances; and the mere affirmative oath of the woman is rarely thought sufficient to convict.'[12]

In England a number of factors were considered important in determining the truth of the woman's claim: 'If the witness be of good fame, if she presently discovered the offence, and made pursuit after the offender; if she shewed circumstances and signs of the injury, whereof many are of that nature that only women are proper examiners; if the place where the fact was done were remote from inhabitants or passengers; if the offender fled for it ...' On the other hand, East further noted that the following factors afforded a strong presumption that the testimony was feigned or contrived: 'If she be of evil fame and stand unsupported by other evidence; if she concealed the injury for any considerable time after she had opportunity to complain ... again, if the place where the fact was supposed to be committed were near to the persons by whom it was probable she might have been heard, and yet she made no outcry; if she gave wrong descriptions of the place.'[13] Operating upon the popular premise that women would make malicious and false complaints, Sir Matthew Hale, author in the late seventeenth century of *The History of the Pleas of the Crown*, cautioned that the heinousness of the offence had the potential to transport the judge and jury to an over-hasty conviction: 'It is true rape is a most detestable crime, and therefore ought severely and impartially to be punished with death; but it must be remembered, that it is an accusation easily to be made and hard to be proved, and harder to be defended by the party accused, though never so innocent.'[14]

Eighteenth-century English law contained a series of offences parallel to rape which dealt with the abduction of unmarried women from the lawful custody of their fathers for the purpose of marriage or defilement. The first statutory prohibition was passed in 1285, when it was made a crime to abduct an heiress for the purpose of marriage. However, if the abductor paid for the marriage, it was valid, although he could still be imprisoned for two years. If he was unable to satisfy the marriage price, he was imprisoned for life.[15] A variety of statutes enacted during the next several hundred years forbade, with increasing detail, the abduction of heiresses.[16] The preambles stated that ravishment and abduction of ladies and daughters of noblemen was becoming more prevalent and more violent in every part of the realm.[17] The thrust of such legislation was to protect the father's property interest in his daughter. Paternal control was necessary in order to establish marriage alliances and to protect the

204 CONSTANCE B. BACKHOUSE

females of the family from the sexual advances of social inferiors. The father had the right to sue the offender. The violation was abduction against the father's will; the consent of the woman was immaterial. The legislation provided that she would be disinherited and disentitled to all her claims against her family's property. These statutes were enacted to protect the property of the wealthy class. Abduction and defilement of women who had no property interests fell outside the scope of the legislation. Recognizing how closely this crime was tied to property rights, a commentator of the day stated: '[B]y confining the offence to women of estate only, moral principles are made to yield to political considerations; and the security of property is deemed more essential than the preservation of female chastity ... This act we find makes the property of the woman the measure of the crime ...'[18]

Such was the body of English law that the legislature of Upper Canada purported to receive in 1800. During the first half of the nineteenth century, the legislature, by and large following the example of the English parliament, passed several statutes which related to the crime of rape. An 1833 reform statute abolished benefit of clergy and reduced the number of capital offences. Abduction of an heiress, formerly a capital crime, was removed from the list of capital offences. Rape and carnal knowledge of a girl under ten years, however, remained capital felonies.[19] In 1841 the first major criminal statute enacted in the Province of Canada repealed all earlier legislation regarding offences against the person and attempted to consolidate and codify the law under one statute. Persons convicted of the crime of rape and persons who unlawfully and carnally knew and abused any girl under the age of ten years were to suffer death as felons. Carnal knowledge of a girl above the age of ten and under the age of twelve years was a misdemeanour, punishable by imprisonment for such term as the court should award.[20] This new provision restored the age limit for statutory rape found in the 1275 statute.

Although rape itself was not defined, the 1841 legislation set forth a new statutory definition of the proof required for conviction: 'It shall not be necessary, in [cases of buggery, rape, and of carnally abusing girls under the respective ages specified], to prove the actual emission of seed in order to constitute carnal knowledge, but the carnal knowledge shall be deemed complete upon proof of penetration only.'[21] Prior to this, the English cases had ruled on this issue in a contradictory manner; some courts required proof of emission but others did not.[22] This legislative clarification marked one of the first significant departures from the view of rape as a crime against a form of male property. The latter analysis of rape law required that the woman's reproductive capacity be impaired; thus ejaculation and the potential of pregnancy were critical to the definition of the crime. The amending section claimed that the reason for the change was that offenders had frequently escaped conviction because of the difficulty of proof.[23] Yet the crime was now beginning to be perceived as a violation of the woman, rather than primarily as a potential interference with the line of descent. Only limited records survive from the Canadian legislative materials of this time, so it is difficult to know whether the legislators themselves recognized the significance of this enactment. There was only one indication that anyone was aware that substantive changes were involved. William Henry Draper, then Attorney General for Upper Canada, proposed that the bill be delayed for a year because the alterations proposed 'were so extensive, and would so materially alter the criminal law of Upper Canada that he could not consent to its passing into a law ...'[24] No other legislators spoke on the issue, and it is probably safe to assume that most were unaware of the changes the bill would create. In fact the legislation was virtually a perfect duplicate of an earlier English reform statute of 1828. Home Secretary Robert Peel, who introduced the English legislation in the House of Commons, said that the bill would not affect the substance of existing law and therefore he did not anticipate any opposition to it.[25]

The Canadian consolidation of 1841 also codified the law with respect to the abduction of women. It prohibited anyone from taking away or detaining an heiress *against her will* 'from motives of lucre ... with intent to marry or defile her.' The stipulation that the abduction be contrary to the woman's will seems to indicate that this section was meant to protect women rather than the father's interest in the woman's property. As such, this seems to complement the new provisions on proof in the act. However, section 20 made it clear that parental protection was still foremost in the minds of the legislators: '[I]f any person shall unlawfully take, or cause to be taken any unmarried girl, being under the age of 16 years, out of the possession, and against the will of her father or mother, or of any other person having the lawful care or charge of her, every such offender shall be guilty of a misdemeanor, and being convicted thereof, shall be liable to suffer such punishment, by fine or imprisonment or by both, as the Court shall award.'[26]

While the 1841 legislation seemed to be expanding the provisions on abduction to include all young women, regardless of their property interests, the clear intent was to protect parental property rights. The consent of the daughter was irrelevant; the issue was whether the taking away was done without the consent of the parents. The debate in the English House of Commons concerning the counterpart section of the 1828 English statute indicated that this section was inspired by 'the unfortunate case' of Miss Ellen Turner, who had been abducted by Edward Gibbon Wakefield and compelled 'by fraud and intimidation' to marry him. Wakefield was sentenced to three years, and William Turner, presumably Miss Turner's father, brought a petition to parliament to declare the marriage null and void.[27] There is no indication that the Canadian legislators believed there was a particular need for this provision; they were simply enacting duplicate legislation based on the earlier English precedent.[28]

In 1842 the Canadian legislature provided for the punishment of the crime of assault with attempt to commit rape.[29] The courts were directed to sentence offenders to a term of hard labour at the penitentiary in Kingston not to exceed three years, or imprisonment in any other prison for a term not to exceed two years. This charge became common in many cases of rape where the evidence was not sufficient to prove the full offence.[30] The difficulty of securing convictions in cases of rape presented a continuous problem throughout the nineteenth century.

DEPARTURE FROM THE ENGLISH LEGISLATIVE MODEL 1861–80

The 1860s witnessed the first Canadian legislative initiative not uniformly modeled upon the example set by the English parliament, which in 1861 had enacted another major criminal law consolidation statute. The counterpart Canadian act was passed in 1869. Alexander Campbell, Postmaster General of Canada, described it as 'the fruit of seven or eight years' attention to this subject by a commission of eminent men in England, which was considered to be 'as safe a starting point as they could get for the preparation of criminal laws.'[31]

While the Canadian statute resembled the English legislation in many respects, there were some significant differences. One major distinction involved the penalty for the crime of rape. The English statute abolished the death penalty and substituted a maximum penalty of penal servitude for life. It also abolished the death penalty for statutory rape. Carnal knowledge of a girl under the age of ten years was given the same, lighter penalty as for the crime of rape. Carnal knowledge of a girl over the age of ten and under twelve years was to be made a misdemeanour punishable by penal servitude for three years with or without hard labour.[32] The debates do not disclose why the English parliament decided to lower the penalty in this respect. However, a political battle had been raging in England since the beginning of the nineteenth century to reduce the number of capital offences, and by the 1840s some social reformers and politicians had begun to demand the complete abolition of the death penalty.[33] Presumably the English legislators eliminated the capital penalty for rape and statutory rape in response to this growing movement. The Canadian legislation retained the death penalty for rape as well as for statutory rape upon a girl under the age of ten. Similarly, it also provided a harsher penalty for statutory rape of a girl over ten and under twelve years: imprisonment in the penitentiary for a term not exceeding seven years and not less than two years, or imprisonment in any other jail for any term less than two years, with or without hard labour.[34]

The discrepancy in the rape penalties did not go unnoticed by the members of the Senate of Canada. During debate on the bill, Jonathan McCully of Nova Scotia pointed out that capital punishment had been 'banished' from the offence of rape in England 'for many years,' and he questioned whether such a severe penalty was required in Canada. His question went unanswered. Some Senators did argue that English laws were not suitable for Canadian society. John Sewell Sanborn of Quebec claimed that English laws were 'unsuitable to this country and cannot as a general rule be imported into our prevailing systems without great danger.' Robert Duncan Wilmot of New Brunswick echoed this view, objecting that the importation of English policy was wrong in principle and would not prove satisfactory. Campbell, the moving force behind the bill, protested that the greatest care had been taken to strike out everything that was not adapted to Canada: 'It was not a complete adoption of the English laws, but these bills were prepared after a careful examination of them and an adoption of those portions which were applicable to Canada.'[35]

The other distinction between the Canadian and English legislation concerned the issue of proof. While the English statute merely re-enacted the statement that it was not necessary to prove the actual emission of seed, but only proof of penetration, the Canadian law went further in section 65: 'it shall not be necessary to prove the actual emission of seed in order to constitute a carnal knowledge, but the carnal knowledge shall be deemed complete on proof of any degree of penetration only.' This provision was probably enacted to deal with the question of whether it was necessary to prove the rupturing of the woman's hymen in order to secure a conviction for rape, a question unsettled in English jurisprudence. Some cases had held that if the hymen was not ruptured, there was not sufficient penetration to constitute the offence; other cases had concluded that the least degree of penetration was sufficient, even though 'it might not be attended with the deprivation of the marks of virginity.'[36]

The problems of proof, even though alleviated somewhat by the earlier stipulation concerning emission, apparently had not been solved. Permitting even the slightest degree of penetration to complete the act was an attempt to secure more convictions, and another illustration that the Canadian legislature was coming to view rape as a crime against women rather than against male property rights in women's virginity. This statutory provision, however, still did not eliminate the difficulty of securing convictions. A trial judge, in a case decided as late as 1891, made reference to the difficulty of proving actual penetration in this class of offence.[37] Prosecutors and juries customarily resorted to the alternative of charging or convicting rapists under lesser offences such as indecent assault, assault with intent to commit rape, and common assault.

In 1873 parliament on its own initiative amended the rape legislation once more. Although the death penalty was specifically retained, the statute added as an alternate life imprisonment or imprisonment for any term not less than seven years.[38] While the penalty remained much harsher than it was in England, both in terms of the maximum and minimum sentences, the legislature appeared to be relenting somewhat with its express recognition of a possible prison sentence for rape. The statute also altered the maximum penalty for the offence of 'assault upon any woman or girl with intent to commit rape.' The previous penalty under the 1842 legislation had been a maximum of three years. The 1873 statute raised the penalty to a maximum of seven years, indicating a general intent to treat sexual assault more harshly. This was likely a response to the difficulty of proving the full offence of rape. Recognizing that many of those convicted of the attempt had in fact committed the act, the legislators wished to provide for harsher sentences.

This 1873 legislation also indicated once again that a shift was beginning to take place in how society viewed the crime of rape. Historically, the view was that men held property rights in women and that the value of this property was diminished if the woman had sexual relations with someone other than her husband. Ownership implied exclusivity, and sole control over the woman's potential for child-bearing. By the 1860s and 1870s, however, the criminal law was moving to extend a higher degree of protection to women's rights in their own sexual integrity, and the stricter sentences for lesser offences reflected this. The complete offence of rape, with its connotations of interference with male property interests in women's reproductive capacity, was decreasing in importance. Simultaneously, the actual sexual assault, regardless of penetration, was being viewed more seriously.

There was yet another distinction between English and Canadian legislation during this period. Between 1875 and 1880 the English parliament moved to provide stricter sanctions against the crime of statutory rape. In 1875 An Act to Amend the Law Relating to Offences against the Person both increased the penalty for certain acts of statutory rape and raised the age of consent.[39] Previously, carnal knowledge of a girl under ten had been a felony with a maximum penalty of life imprisonment; carnal knowledge of a girl over ten and under twelve had been a misdemeanour with a maximum punishment of three years' imprisonment. The new statute made carnal knowledge of a girl under twelve years a felony punishable with life imprisonment and added a new offence of carnal knowledge of a girl above twelve and under thirteen years, which was to be a misdemeanour with a maximum of two years' imprisonment. The motivation of the proponents of the legislation was paternalistic – to extend the protection of the criminal law to a larger class of young women. William Thomas Charley, who introduced the bill, initially set the age of consent at fourteen years. He argued vociferously for this change: 'There were now young girls left at the mercy of every scoundrel who was base enough to take advantage of their youth and innocence. Was it just, was it fair, was it statesmanlike, to exclude from the protection of the law girls of so tender and critical an age?' Many MPs maintained that the age should remain at twelve. Richard Assheton Cross justfied this compromise on the age of thirteen, noting that it was an age which was frequently used in other statutes, such as the Factory acts and the Elementary Education Act, as the age at which childhood ended.[40]

In 1880 the English parliament tackled the question of establishing an age of consent for the offence of indecent assault. P.A. Taylor asked the Secretary of State for the Home Department whether he was aware of a case of indecent assault on a girl of six years of age, where no conviction was obtained because the prisoner pleaded consent. The Stockport magistrate, in dismissing the charge, had declared that it was a 'miscarriage of justice.' Sir William Harcourt replied that he believed the state of the law to be unsatisfactory and that he would endeavour to effect a remedy. That year a bill was introduced to abolish the defence of consent to a charge of indecent assault upon a child under the age of thirteen. Several members of the House of Commons opposed the measure. Charles Nicholas Warton argued that no cases were ever tried before juries in which the prejudice against the prisoner was so fearful as in these cases of assaults upon young persons: 'Even if the person charged were innocent, it was scarcely possible to get an acquittal when a little girl was in the witness box.' Warton attributed this in part to the existence of societies which were 'maintained by bringing charges of this description.' He claimed that they gave themselves 'grand names and issued prospectuses, in which they said they never failed to get a conviction, and that was true for they did this by tampering with the medical witnesses.' Warton's conclusion reflected an inherent class bias: 'It was well known,' he said, 'that amongst the lower classes acts of indecency were very common; and children, owing to their condition of living, became familiarized with these acts at a very tender age.' George Woodyatt Hastings argued that a charge of indecent assault might mean very little, 'indeed, no more than lifting up the clothes.' Hastings cited a case where a man had been indicted under the old statute with respect to a girl under twelve, who was actually pregnant when she came to the witness box. 'Now, it would be very hard that a charge of this kind should be brought by a girl sufficiently developed in body to become pregnant and that a man should not be allowed to plead in defence that the act was done with her consent,' he claimed. 'It was really appalling to hear the number of child-prostitutes in the country ... was a man to be placed in peril by the evidence of such persons and prohibited from pleading consent?'[41]

The debates surrounding this bill illustrated the polarizing of public opinion around the need to protect children from sexual relations. On the one hand, there were charitable organizations forming to eradicate the problem, and legislators were beginning to respond to their lobby. On the other hand, there were those who felt the legislation was unwarranted, that it would entrap men who were seduced by 'wileful' young girls, and that the prostitutes and lower class girls who would utilize such legislation were not in need of criminal law protection. The bill also continued the trend away from viewing the crime of sexual assault as an attack upon male property rights. The primary rationale behind the statutory rape legislation had been to protect the virginity of young girls. This bill expanded the protection of the criminal law to encompass other forms of sexual conduct with young girls. Sexual assault was coming to be seen as a crime against the woman rather than an interference with a father's control of his daughter's virginity. Despite the strong opposition, those lobbying for expanded protection won in this instance. The 1880 Act to Amend the Criminal Law as to Indecent Assaults on Young Persons heralded the beginning of a new era of 'morals legislation' which would become increasingly the subject of attention and debate throughout the rest of the nineteenth century.[42]

In Canada this phenomenon did not appear until the mid-1880s. Previously neither the lobby groups nor the legislators seemed to be particularly concerned about increasing protection against sexual assault upon young girls. To the contrary, as the English parliament increased the penalties and raised the age of consent, the Canadian parliament passed a law to lower the penalty for statutory rape. In 1877 An Act to Amend the Act Respecting Offences against the Person removed the penalty of capital punishment from the offence of carnal knowledge of a girl under the age of ten, substituting life imprisonment with a minimum term of five years. Edward Blake, Minister of Justice, stated that the intent was to lower the penalty in order to secure more convictions. The capital penalty, he observed, prevented the obtaining of convictions, although few offenders were hanged even when convicted.[43] This argument was not applied to the offence of rape. The death penalty remained in force for that offence, even though presumably convictions were no easier to obtain for rape than for statutory rape.

During the 1860s and 1870s Canadian rape law began, in part, to take on its own distinctive character. In contrast to English law, Canadian legislation set forth harsher penalties for rape. Proof of penetration to any degree was sufficient for conviction, whereas in England some courts still required evidence of penetration sufficient to rupture the hymen. Canadian legislators moved to increase the penalty for the lesser offence of assault with intent to commit rape. English legislators increased the penalty for statutory rape, raised the age of consent, and abolished the defence of consent for the offence of indecent assault upon women under the age of thirteen, just as Canadian legislators were lowering the penalty for statutory rape.

One can argue that these differences were relatively minor and that the majority of Canadian legislators and citizens may have been unaware that their rape law was developing differently than in England. However, there is enough substance to the distinctions to warrant some analysis. Why did parliament decide to retain the death penalty for rape and statutory rape despite relaxation of the English criminal penalties? The Canadian press of the time followed and reported upon the debates in England and the United States on principles of penal philosophy and practice; articles about the virtues of capital punishment and imprisonment appeared regularly.[44] However, the movement for social reform of the criminal law may not have been as strong in Canada as in these other jurisdictions. Furthermore, there is some evidence that Canadian attitudes towards crime and punishment were becoming harsher. Jerald Bellomo has noted that in the 1830s and 1840s there was a great perceived increase in crime. John Beattie has found that there appeared to be 'an alarming increase in crime' in the 1840s coupled with a very great increase in the number of inmates in the Kingston penitentiary. Indeed, between 1842 and 1845 the prison population tripled.[45] Earlier, more lenient attitudes towards crime changed as the populace became more concerned with social order in the face of an influx of immigrants. Strong measures, including retention of the capital penalty, may have been intended to check the threat to traditional values posed by the new immigrant population.

Retention of the capital penalty may also have been a response to a concern over the incidence and severity of rapes committed in Canada. The number of cases reported in the law reports are of little assistance; no cases of statutory rape and only four cases of rape appear to have been reported prior to 1869.[46] However, examination of the surviving Minute Books kept by the Courts of Criminal Assize (Court of Oyer and Terminer) and the County Court Judges' Criminal Court Minute Books of the province of Ontario for the period 1840 to 1892 reveals approximately 330 cases of rape, statutory rape, assault with intent to commit rape, and indecent assault which went to trial.[47] Given the stigma attached to a victim of rape, it is likely that there were many more victims who refused to come forward and participate in the criminal process.[48] These numbers seem to indicate that rape was far from being an uncommon crime and may explain retention of the harsher penalty.

Explanations for the legislative differences regarding proof of penetration and statutory rape are more elusive. Perhaps the socio-economic situation in Canada, with large segments of the country still primarily rural and pioneer-like in setting, permitted a more individualistic, less sex-stereotyped view of women. The crime of rape was beginning to evolve from its historical origins as an offence against male property rights in women's chastity. Increasingly it became viewed as a crime against women's own sexual integrity; the Canadian legislative amendments allowing proof of a lesser degree of penetration and the stricter penalties for the lesser offence of sexual assault illustrated this trend. At first glance the movement in England towards an expansion and strengthening of the law against statutory rape and sexual assault upon young girls would seem to contradict this analysis. Why did the Canadian legislators not follow this lead?

The distinction had, perhaps, to do with the alleged consensual nature of these offences. The crimes of statutory rape and indecent assault upon a girl under the age of consent were strict liability offences. The mere act of sexual contact constituted the crime, whether or not the woman consented. In essence, this legislation was paternalistic in nature, stipulating that for the protection of young women, men could not engage in sexual conduct with them, consensual or otherwise. In a more rural society children would be expected to grow up more quickly and shoulder adult responsibilities from an early age. The modern concept of childhood as a separate stage of development was a notion that did not exist in pre-industrial society.[49] In Canada, the processes of industrialization and urbanization came relatively late, at least in comparison with England and the United States. The major era of industrialization did not begin until the 1880s, and in 1881, 74.35 per cent of the population was still classified as rural.[50] Possibly the Canadian legislators at this stage did not see the need to strengthen and expand criminal sanctions for consensual sexual conduct with young girls.[51] Furthermore, the lobby forces that had organized in England to pressure for these changes did not spring up so quickly in Canada. It would take another decade before similar sentiments were expressed and debate was joined on this issue in Canada.

RESPONSE OF THE JUDICIARY:
A RESTRICTIVE APPLICATION OF RAPE LAW

When the Canadian judiciary came to interpret the statutory provisions concerning the crime of rape, they followed English precedent extensively and gave no indication that they thought there was any distinction between Canadian and English law on the subject.[52] It was in the application of the law of rape that its scope became restricted. Case by case the decisions carved away at the broad statutory language until rape laws came to be applied within only a very narrow range of situations.

Standards of Force, Resistance, and Lack of Consent

One of the most interesting series of Ontario cases concerned the interrelated issues of force, resistance, and lack of consent. S.R. Clarke, a barrister-at-law of Osgoode Hall, in his 1872 treatise on Canadian criminal law defined rape as 'having unlawful and carnal knowledge of a woman by force against her will.'[53] The phrases 'by force' and 'against her will' would seem to indicate that the facts to be proved were that the act had occurred with a certain degree of force and violence, and that the woman had not consented to the penetration. However, the judiciary was reluctant to convict unless the victim had put up a strong show of resistance. The 1866 case of *R.* v *Fick* provides the best illustration of this attitude.[54] The prosecutrix, named Wealthy Tutty, lived with her husband and daughter in the county of Norfolk in Ontario. The rape took place while Tutty's husband was away in Windsor. Tutty testified at trial that the prisoner, who apparently was a man she had been acquainted with previously, came to her house, bolted the door without her knowledge, and ordered her to go into the bedroom. Although she testified that she got away from him two or three times, he managed to drag her to the bedroom and throw her on the bed. Tutty continued: 'I raised to try and get up two or three times, but I was so exhausted that I had no strength to help myself. He had connection with me, as a man with a woman. I did not scream before he got what he wanted, because I thought I could get away from him. I fought as long as I could, and when I could do no more, I had to scream. I called to my little girl. I screamed until the child came in.' At trial Chief Justice William Buell Richards directed the jury that they 'had a right to expect some resistance on the part of the woman, to shew that she really was not a consenting party.' D.B. Read, QC, counsel for the accused, appealed the conviction, arguing that the Chief Justice should have cautioned the jury that they must be satisfied that Tutty was overcome by physical violence or terror. There was no mark of physical violence left upon her, and Read claimed that she had not made any real effort to escape from the house and only cried out when discovered. In fact, the accused alleged that he had had a previous sexual relationship with Tutty, that on this particular occasion she had again agreed to sexual intercourse, and that she and her husband had then tried to blackmail him for money. When he refused to pay, he maintained that Tutty and her husband had charged him with rape.[55]

Justice Adam Wilson, who delivered the appeal decision, refused to quash the conviction, stating that the evidence was sufficient to warrant a conviction for rape. Nevertheless, he accepted Read's argument concerning the resistance standard: 'The woman [must have] been quite overcome *by force or terror, she resisting as much as she could,* and resisting *so as to make the prisoner see and know that she really was resisting to the utmost;* and that if this degree of coercion by the prisoner, and resistance by the prosecutrix, have not been proved, the crime of rape has not been committed.'[56]

The requirement for evidence of resistance was readily accepted, even by the prosecutors of the day. In the trial of Robert Johnson in the county of York on 12 October 1866 on a charge of assault with intent to commit rape, Barbara Ann Pifer testified that Johnson had attempted the crime on the evening of 10 June in the woods near her home.[57] The newspaper account of the trial reported that Pifer's own testimony, as well as that of two witnesses (one of them for the Crown) who saw the parties in the woods about the time of the occurrence, proved that she 'had not cried out, nor made any proper resistance.' The Crown prosecutor, in response to this evidence, decided not to seek a conviction, and the prisoner was found not guilty.

In another trial in the county of Renfrew in 1883, the defence counsel argued for an acquittal on the grounds that the fifteen-year-old victim did not resist to the utmost.[58] Antoine Legacy had been charged with raping Maggie C. Wilson as she was walking from her father's residence to a friend's farm. Wilson testified that Legacy made indecent proposals to her and that when she tried to run away, he chased her and threw her on the ground. When she started to scream, Legacy covered her mouth and threatened to strike her, although he never did. 'He was too strong for me,' she testified, 'and he succeeded in outraging my person.' Upon cross-examination Legacy's lawyer asked her why she had not scratched him. However, a neighbour testified that when Wilson escaped from Legacy, she ran to his farm and arrived 'crying, screaming, and going into fits.' Several men who worked with Legacy testified that Wilson was 'decent or reputed to be so.' Despite the strong arguments of the defence counsel that Wilson's resistance had not been forceful enough, Legacy was found guilty and sentenced to ten years.

Several years later, in a trial in the county of York, the resistance standard was again raised, although on the facts, the jury had little difficulty convicting. Hannah Walls charged that Henry Waggstaff had raped her on the evening of 7 July 1887, as she was returning home from a meeting of the Salvation Army.[59] When the accused attempted to take liberties with her, Walls testified that she told him to stop or she would scream murder. When he 'threw up her clothes,' she screamed until a James Hodge, who was drinking in a hotel approximately 100 yards away, came to her rescue. Walls testified that Waggstaff had torn the buttons off her drawers and kicked them down to her feet. She claimed that he accomplished his purpose, although she tried her utmost to prevent him. The court concluded that Walls had made sufficient resistance, although the conviction was for 'assault with attempt to commit rape' rather than the full offence.

Another important case, heard in Toronto in 1888, dealt with a father-daughter rape. Jeannie Cardo testified that her father came home late one night and beat his wife so severely that she fled the home, leaving behind her three children. Cardo made Jeannie, the eldest child, come out with him to look for his wife. When they did not find her, he returned home and made Jeannie go into his bedroom, where he raped her three times. Jeannie claimed that her father told her there was no use in screaming. Cardo seemed to recognize the atrocity of his acts, since he also told her: 'You are ruined for life. This is a terrible thing to do to my own daughter. Do you know I could get twenty years for this?' When she reported this, in tears, early the next morning to her next door neighbour and her mother, charges were laid immediately. The accused's lawyer submitted that it was through solicitation, and not from fear, that Jeannie had permitted the sexual connection, and that Cardo therefore could not be convicted of rape. Justice Hugh MacMahon disagreed: 'The prisoner Cardo had, on that night at least, created terror in his household, because he had beaten and driven his wife from the house; and he told the prosecutrix, when out with her endeavouring to find his wife, that he would whip her within an inch of her life if he got her.'[60] The court determined that there was ample evidence for the jury to conclude that Jeannie submitted out of fear. The conviction was allowed to stand, despite the lack of overt evidence of resistance. The incestuous nature of the crime may have been the underlying reason behind the decision.

The requirement for evidence of resistance was further illustrated quite starkly by judicial rulings on cases where the accused had sexual intercourse with a woman by impersonating her husband. One early case in Upper Canada, reported in 1855, involved a situation where the accused climbed into bed with a woman while she was asleep without waking her, as if he had been her husband. As he was attempting to have sexual intercourse with her, the woman awoke, discovered the intruder, and made her escape. He was charged with assault with intent to commit rape. The jury convicted the accused at trial, but on appeal Justice William Henry Draper, the former Attorney General, quashed the conviction. Citing a number of English decisions which he felt he ought to follow, Draper concluded that 'there was danger in implying force from fraud, and an absence of consent, when consent was in fact given, though obtained by deception.'[61] Obtaining consent through fraud and deception was clearly insufficient to convict for rape. There had to be force and a certain degree of resistance registered. This was recognized to be the clear state of the law by all of the Canadian treatise writers of the time.[62] A woman had to resist; the only exception involved women incapable of resisting. H.E. Taschereau, author of one of the first treatises on Canadian criminal law (and later appointed the fourth Chief Justice of the Supreme Court of Canada), noted that if a man had or attempted to have connection with a woman while she was asleep, it was no defence that she did not resist, since she was incapable of resisting. In this situation, he concluded, a man could be found guilty of rape or an attempt to commit rape.[63] Apparently the treatise writers, all men of eminent legal reputation, saw nothing wrong with this narrow application of the rape law.

Cases involving mentally handicapped women also focused on the ability of such women to express consent or resistance. In *R. v Connolly* (1867), the accused had been caught in the act of attempting to have sexual intercourse with a married woman who for some years had been considered insane. Justice John Hawkins Hagarty stated that in the case of rape 'of an idiot or lunatic woman, the mere proof of the act of connection will not warrant the case being left to the jury; there must be some evidence that it was without her consent.' If she was incapable of expressing consent or dissent, or of exercising any judgment on the matter because of her imbecility, the act would amount to rape. However, if she gave her consent 'from animal instinct or passion' it would not be rape. Hagarty noted that there was no evidence whatever as to the woman's general character for decency or chastity and nothing to raise a presumption that she would not consent to the alleged outrage upon her. The report continued: 'There was no evidence in this case except the prisoner's admission; and a medical man testified that she was a fully developed woman, and that strong animal instinct might exist notwithstanding her imbecile condition.' Despite the prosecutor's protest that according to this analysis 'every idiot found on the street might be ravished with impunity,' the court quashed the conviction. Perhaps anticipating the need for legislation, Hagarty noted that there was no statute which declared the fact of 'criminal connection with an idiot or lunatic to be an offence, as in the case of children of tender years.'[64]

It was left to the legislators to broaden the protection of the rape laws to cover women who submitted because of fraud or mental handicap. In 1886 parliament made it a misdemeanour, punishable with a maximum of two years, to have or attempt to have carnal knowledge with 'any female idiot or imbecile woman or girl, under circumstances which do not amount to rape, but which prove that the offender knew at the time ... that the woman ... was an idiot or imbecile.' In 1887 the Ontario legislature enacted another statute dealing with carnal knowledge of women in asylums.[65] This legislation may have made little difference. In 1892 George Warr was charged under the federal legislation with 'unlawful knowledge of an idiot or imbecile woman.'[66] There was medical testimony that the woman was in fact an imbecile and that the doctor had found evidence of sperm inside her. Several other witnesses testified that Warr had claimed he had sexual intercourse with the woman, but that she was willing. Warr was acquitted.

In 1890 parliament passed legislation dealing with the situation of the woman who submitted because of fraud. The law stated that 'everyone who, by personating her husband, induces a married woman to permit him to have connection with her, is guilty of rape.' Not all of the legislators were in favour of the amendment. Peter Mitchell, member of parliament for Northumberland, stated that in his view such legislation was unnecessary: 'If a woman does not know whether her husband or someone else is in bed with her, it is a strange thing.'[67] Mitchell was apparently unfamiliar with the circumstances of the case which had inspired the statute. With the passage of this amendment, however, the legislators appeared to be carving away at the very strict standard of resistance set out by the courts; they wished to broaden the coverage of the rape laws to provide protection to women who did not put up resistance either through mental incapacity or because of trickery on the part of the rapist.

A pattern had begun to emerge where judges interpreted rape law so as to give it a narrow application, while the legislators, perhaps in response to these decisions, began to enact statutory amendments to expand the scope of the law of rape. Why were the judges restrictive in their holdings? One reason may have been that as the final interpreters of the criminal law, judges felt compelled to exercise great caution before convicting, especially in capital cases. However, on the whole the judiciary in nineteenth-century Canada can be characterized as conservative. Jennifer Nedelsky, in a study of judicial rulings on the law of nuisance between 1880 and 1930, concluded that Canadian judges exhibited a consistent stance of conservatism, even during Canada's major period of industrialization, when the pressure for judicial innovation must have been particularly strong. 'The full explanation,' she concluded, 'must ... take into account [the judiciary's] actual relation to and attitude towards the legislatures, and [their] position in the Canadian social structure.'[68] Their attitudes also reflected a very traditional view about women. My own earlier study on nineteenth-century Canadian custody law uncovered a marked distinction between the attitudes of the legislature and the judiciary over the question of whether mothers should be granted custody of their children. Throughout this period the legislatures increased the rights of mothers to custody, while the judges interpreted the legislation so as to restrict maternal access:

With several notable exceptions, it seems clear that as compared with the legislature the Ontario judiciary took a cautious stance on the issue of expanding mothers' rights to custody ... It has been suggested that this conservatism may have been based on Canadian reliance on English precedents which retarded the development of a creative judiciary. While this may account for some of the conservatism in custody law, the likelier explanation is that most of the judiciary were unsympathetic to the notion of increased rights for mothers to the custody of their children. The majority of the reported decisions during this period illustrate a desire to preserve patriarchal control and a reluctance to undermine the father's authority in the family.[69]

Although, not surprisingly, judges left no written records outlining their views on sexuality, their legal decisions indicate something about their opinions. The proper role for women, as they would likely have seen it, was to remain safely in the home, surrounded by family responsibilities, protected by their fathers and husbands from all forms of non-marital sexual contact. The chaste woman would never be exposed to the danger of rape and, should the unthinkable happen, she would resist to the utmost. She would be overcome only through overwhelming physical force. The judges would probably have had little compassion for a woman who succumbed through misguided ignorance.

Some of the legislators obviously shared this perspective, but, in the majority, the elected politicians were beginning to enact legislation in response to changing notions about the roles of the sexes. In the 1860s and 1870s a whole new Victorian sexual ideology was emerging. Medical and religious leaders espoused the view that women were inherently passionless in matters of sexuality.[70] William Acton, a prominent English physician, wrote that 'the majority of women (happily for them) are not very much troubled with sexual feeling of any kind.'[71] Representatives of the clergy began to move away from sermons on the immorality and carnal desires of women as descendants of Eve. In deference to the new predominance of women in their congregations, ministers portrayed women as highly moral, intellectual beings. Passionlessness, modesty, and demureness became the quintessential female virtues.[72] Even the novels read by women of the time were undergoing a dramatic transformation. The popular seduction novel was almost completely overtaken by a new genre of fiction. In these novels the hero was no longer the typical, dashing, libertine vagabond, but instead the older, more intellectual, responsible, and respectful gentleman.[73] While men were not viewed as passionless, they were increasingly subjected to strict prohibitions against sexual promiscuity. The growing middle class labelled sexual promiscuity as an aristocratic excess. Male sexual self-control was prescribed to instil an ethic of discipline which would result in greater economic productivity for the nation.[74] These new attitudes were beginning to affect how society viewed the crime of rape. Men who departed from the standard of self-control set for them were to be censured and punished severely. Passionless women, on the other hand, who were the victims of force, deceit, or their own misguided ignorance, deserved compassion, understanding, and the full protection of the criminal law. The legislators, more in tune with and responsive to these new attitudes, moved to expand the coverage of rape laws.

Fear of False Complaints

Throughout the nineteenth century members of the bench expressed their concern that malicious women might make false complaints of rape. Fear that women might use criminal charges of rape as a tool of vengeance, or to protect themselves when discovered in the act of consensual intercourse, may explain the reluctance of the judges to apply the rape laws except in the clearest of circumstances. In the early case of *R. v Francis*, Justice Draper noted that situations might arise, 'however extreme, when a detected adultress, might, to save herself, accuse a paramour of a capital felony.' One such case, at least according to the verdict of the jury, occurred in 1882 in Toronto. Caroline Mercer, a married woman, charged William Stead, a married man who lived near her, with rape. According to her evidence, Stead raped her while her husband was out putting a horse to pasture. Justice John Douglas Armour cautioned the jury that such charges sometimes arose from motives of malice. In his charge he stated that it would not be safe to convict on such evidence, 'for it was apparent that had the husband not returned at the critical moment, nothing would have been heard of the charge.'[75] Stead was acquitted.

Compounding the fear of false complaints was the belief that juries were overly anxious to convict in charges of rape. The editors of *The Upper Canada Law Journal* stated in an 1866 editorial:

[B]ut every man is fully alive to the risk he runs from the fact that, if a woman takes it into her head to charge him with an indecent assault, the chances are ten to one that he will be found guilty, no matter how strong may be the proofs of his innocence, or how weak the evidence against him. To be accused of such an offence is to be condemned. The chivalrous male juror feels that woman, as the weaker vessel, requires special protection; and his notion of specially protecting her is to accept, in the face of all evidence, whatever charges she may like to bring against her male oppressor.[76]

This assumption was entirely unfounded in fact. The Ontario court records which have been preserved and summarized in Table 1 indicate that few charges of rape resulted in conviction.

In the face of this evidence, why did judges and law journal editors express such concern over the dangers of unwarranted convictions? Were they unaware of the pattern of low conviction rates? Presumably judges and lawyers were in a unique position to witness the frequency of acquittals on charges of rape. Did they believe all the acquittals were justified, and furthermore, that some of the few men convicted were not guilty? If so, they would have had to believe that rape was an extremely uncommon occurrence. In part, their opinions reflected a form of reverse paternalism. Sensitive to the ethic of chivalry which was fostered between the sexes, the legal community feared that male jurors would overreact to charges of rape and seek to punish the male even where the evidence did not warrant it. The statements made by the judges and legal writers, however, illustrated little concern over the rights of men accused of rape; the predominant attitude expressed was hostility towards women.

Reputation of the Victim

In adjudicating rape cases, the courts often turned their attention to the reputation and character of the complainant. Although the decisions stated that this evidence related to questions of credibility and consent, it is clear that the courts were unwilling to extend the protection of the rape laws to women of doubtful reputation. The landmark decision was the Quebec case of *Laliberté* v *The Queen* in 1877. When the complainant testified that, prior to the alleged rape, she had not had sexual relations with any man, the accused's counsel asked her the following question: 'Do you remember your being in the milk-house of Clovis Guilmette with the two Malhoits, one after the other?' The Crown prosecutor objected to the question, the judge sustained the objection, and the jury convicted. On appeal, the Supreme Court of Canada directed that the conviction be quashed and discharged the prisoner. The court concluded that it was

TABLE 1
Prosecutions for Rape in Ontario 1840–92

Decade	1840s	%	1850s	%	1860s	%	1870s	%	1880s	%	Total	%
Rape convictions	0	0	2	10	13	17.6	9	16.1	25	32.4	49	21.5
Convictions for lesser offences	0	0	5	25	13	17.6	6	10.7	9	11.7	33	14.5
Not guilty	1	100	9	45	33	44.6	28	50	34	44.2	105	46
Sub-total	1	100	16	80	59	79.8	43	76.8	68	88.3	187	82
No record of disposition	0	0	4	20	15	20.2	13	23.2	9	11.7	41	18
Total	1		20		74		56		77		228	

Source: surviving County Court Judges' Criminal Court Minute Books and Courts of Criminal Assize Minute Books 1840–92, Archives of Ontario Record Group 22 proper to permit these questions to be asked. Chief Justice Richards stated: 'When the prisoner admits the improper connection; but contends that it was with the consent of the prosecutrix, the fact that she had had connection with other men at no distant time would, to the unprofessional mind, seem a fact proper to go to the jury and relevant to the question whether the connection complained of was against her will or not.' Justice Taschereau added that the trial judge was wrong in rejecting the question, 'which was manifestly calculated to affect the character, and as a consequence, the credibility of the prosecutrix in a case of rape, where her chastity was in question.'[77]

The case of the 'Sayer Street Outrage,' as it was dubbed by the newspapers, presented a clear indication of the court's lack of sympathy with women of unconventional morals. Charges of rape were laid against Robert Gregg and three other men, stemming from an incident of gang rape in Toronto on 13 December 1858.[78] The victim was Ellen Rogers, an unmarried woman living in a common law relationship with a gambler who rarely returned home before 2:00 or 3:00 AM. On 13 December, at midnight, Ellen was disturbed by a knock on the door. When she looked out, she saw 'sixteen or seventeen boys outside.' They told her they wanted to come in to get something to drink. Ellen testified that she knew most of the men, that they had been in her house before, but that she had never had sexual relations with any of them. When she refused to allow them in, they broke down the door. She told the court that while one of them held her down, four proceeded to rape her. At trial, defence counsel for Robert Gregg, Henry Eccles, QC, pointed out that his client was from a respectable family, whereas the complainant's reputation was such that no reliance could be placed upon it: 'let a woman be ever so abandoned, she was entitled to the protection of the law; but ... though she was entitled to the protection of the law, she was not entitled to credit; and no jury could feel justified in convicting on the bare assertions of those who, while telling their story, themselves admitted that they were of the loosest grade and character.' Eccles reminded the jury how easy it was for women such as these to seduce misguided young men and then to turn upon them. He concluded that it was evident that this affair was a fabrication, and that the prosecution had been instituted for purposes of extorting money from those accused.

The jury took only a short while to return their verdict of not guilty. A newspaper reported that the announcement was received 'with loud cheering and other demonstrations of pleasure by the audience. It was some time before order was restored ...' Ellen Rogers was extremely upset by this verdict, and when the prosecutor called her as a witness in his next charge against Gregg of burglary and break and enter arising out of the same incident, she took the stand in tears and told the court she did not think it was any use giving evidence, since the lawyers and witnesses had all said she was not worthy of belief. According to *The Globe*, she appeared to be very angry and 'harangued' the court, stating: 'If I am unfortunate, I am not to be murdered by any set of men, surely.' Upon a second verdict of not guilty on this charge, the judge discharged the prisoners, expressing a sincere hope that they would lead such a life in the future as would show that they had benefited from their very narrow escape.[79] The judge evidently believed the men were in fact guilty but he was clearly not unsympathetic with the verdict.

Juries also refused to convict when there was evidence that the complainant had been drinking at the time of the incident. In the case of *The Queen v Edwin Cudmore* the accused was charged with raping Mary Jane Stennett in Toronto on 5 August 1864.[80] The woman testified that she had been at a tavern that evening, dancing and engaging in other amusements with the accused and others. Shortly after ten, she left to return home in the company of two young men. On her way the accused overtook her on horseback. He dismounted, seized her, carried her into the bushes, and raped her. The two young men who had accompanied Stennett testified that she resisted and screamed. The accused's lawyer told the jury that Stennett was a person of easy virtue, given to drink, and one that would barter her chastity. The jury refused to find Cudmore guilty.

The Ontario case of *The Queen v John English* resulted in a similar holding.[81] Eliza Miller testified that she had stopped at William Bell's tavern to warm herself before the fire, when the accused sat down beside her and offered her a glass of brandy. Approximately fifteen or twenty minutes after she drank it, she told the court that she 'became sick and stupid, and the prisoner then violated her against her will.' Upon cross-examination by R.A. Harrison, the accused's lawyer, it appeared that she had ordered three glasses of brandy herself. The jury took little time to return a verdict of not guilty.

Canadian courts appeared to be reluctant to convict for rape unless the victim appeared to be a virtuous and upstanding woman. Indeed, it is somewhat surprising that cases such as the 'Sayer Street Outrage' and some of the others cited above ever went to court at all.[82] By and large the victims in rape charges that came to trial were either young, unmarried women still living with their fathers, or married women. Most were women dependent on a father or husband; the parents or husband in many cases seemed to be the instigators of the charge.[83] The few examples of independent women making complaints of rape, such as Ellen Rogers' case, resulted in acquittals. The argument made earlier, that women in a newly developing country were viewed as more independent and given greater legal protection for their rights to sexual self-determination, clearly did not operate here. Women were allowed a greater measure of freedom and licence, but this extended only so far. A woman who strayed beyond the bounds of propriety found herself at the mercy of whichever men chose to take advantage of her. The development of Victorian sexual ideology may have reinforced this view, operating to the severe detriment of a woman who did not fit the mould of the passionless female. She found herself an outcast, viciously attacked by the community, and denied protection of the rape law which, after all, was meant for the virtuous woman, living her life in modesty and above reproach.

Who were the men accused of sexual assault in nineteenth-century Canada? Insofar as the reported cases and records from the Ontario Archives reveal, most of the female complainants were assaulted by men they knew.[84] In many cases the accused was a family member. Fathers, uncles, and brothers-in-law were most often mentioned. In many cases the accused was a neighbour. Often they were men employed as labourers by the woman's husband or father to work on the family property. In one case the accused was the woman's schoolteacher; in another, the woman's attending physician.[85] The rapes generally occurred in the woman's home, in a field, or in other uninhabited areas near her home. Numerous cases involved multiple offenders rather than a single accused. It is unfortunate that there is little or no evidence readily available about the social background of the men charged with rape or about the motivations underlying their crimes.

As for the sentencing patterns, where these were recorded, they showed a trend towards greater leniency in rape cases. Based on Ontario archival records from 1840 to 1892, until the 1870s the only penalty handed down was death. Prior to 1873 the crime was a capital one. The court was required to hand out a death penalty; the accused was then required to make application for pardon to have the sentence commuted. During the 1870s the death penalty was still handed out, but sentences of life, eight years, and seven years, were seen. In the 1880s and early 1890s there were no records of capital sentences and few of life. The typical sentence for rape was then seven to ten years, with one anomalous penalty for eighteen months. The sentence for the lesser offences of assault with intent to commit rape, indecent assault, attempted rape, and common assault remained fairly uniform, ranging between several months and several years during the 1840s to 1890s. The records for the sentences for statutory rape were too few to give much evidence of a pattern at all.

STATUTORY RAPE CASES:
ANOTHER EXAMPLE OF LEGISLATIVE/JUDICIAL DIFFERENCES

The reported statutory rape cases illustrate the confusion surrounding the intent of the legislation. A property analysis of the crime suggests that the legislation was designed to protect the status of virginity and thus only the act of intercourse was prohibited. Indecent assaults and attempts to commit sexual intercourse were not prohibited per se, since such treatment did not affect the reproductive capacity of the girl. The opposite view was that the intent of the statute was to protect young girls from all sexual contact, whether this amounted to actual sexual intercourse or not. The tension between the conflicting views surfaced once again in the difference between the views of the legislators and the judiciary. By and large the judiciary maintained the property analysis, but the position was not completely uniform.

In *R.* v *Connolly* (1867), Justice Hagarty delivered a judgment in *obiter* in which he stated that just as the defence of consent was immaterial in a statutory rape case, it was also immaterial where the charge was an attempt to commit statutory rape. Consent was a defence for the offences of assault with intent to have carnal knowledge of a girl under twelve, indecent assault or common assault.[86] Allowing the defence in the latter group of charges illustrates a property analysis of the crime; however, Hagarty departed from the property analysis in his decision regarding the attempted rape. An attempt would no more interfere with virginity than the other lesser offences. The legislature responded quickly and enacted Hagarty's decision in the 1869 statute.[87] Section 53 provided specifically for the offence of attempt to have carnal knowledge of any girl under twelve years, with a maximum penalty of two years.

The Quebec case of *R.* v *Paquet* in 1883 was the first reported case to deal with the new legislation. Paquet was charged with an attempt to commit rape on a girl under twelve years. The defence attempted to prove that the girl had had sexual connection with other young persons and had consented to sexual relations with the prisoner. Stating that the evidence of consent was irrelevant in this charge, Justice Thomas Kennedy Ramsay explained: 'The principle seems to be that the consent of a child under twelve years of age being immaterial if the crime of rape was complete, it necessarily follows that consent to the preliminary attempt is immaterial. Were it otherwise, we should have an innocent attempt to commit a felony, which would be absurd.'[88] However, Ramsay took care to point out that the defence of consent was material on a charge of indecent assault.

It was left to the legislators to extend the prohibition to include consensual sexual conduct short of the act of intercourse and the attempt to commit it. As mentioned previously, the English parliament responded in 1880 with legislation stating that consent was not a defence to indecent assault of a girl under thirteen. The Canadian parliament, slower to act on statutory rape than its English counterpart, did not pass similar legislation until 1890. Three reported cases from Manitoba applied this legislation in 1891.[89] While the decisions all concluded that consent was no longer a defence to indecent assault upon a girl under the statutory age (by then raised to fourteen years), the judge in the case of *R. v Brice* exhibited some reluctance to let the legislation put an end to the issue. Although Justice Joseph Dubuc stated that section 7 of the 1890 act applied, he went on to consider the factual evidence of the girl's consent. The prosecutor had argued that her tacit consent to the indecent assault should be considered as a mere submission without any voluntary act on her part. Dubuc concluded that 'the consent of a girl of such tender age who, very likely, ignored the gravity of the act done to her, should be considered more properly as a mere submission, immaterial to the offence, and insufficient … in … law.' However, he added, 'I am not entirely free from doubt on the matter.'[90]

The same pattern was beginning to appear in cases of statutory rape as in cases of rape. The judiciary applied the legislation narrowly, and the legislature was the activist in the expansion of the law of statutory rape. The one new feature was that Canadian legislators were much slower to act than their English counterparts in this area. This difference cannot be explained by arguing that statutory rape was a non-existent problem in Canada. The court records contain twenty-four trials on the charge of statutory rape in Ontario between 1840 and 1892, two charges of assault with intent to commit statutory rape, and one of attempted statutory rape. The lag in the response of the Canadian legislators may be attributable to the slower development of the organized lobby of those advocating 'morals legislation,' as well as to the environment of the newly developing Canadian society, which prevented an extended childhood and forced young girls to take on adult responsibilities at an early age.

THE MORALS CRUSADE:
A MOVE TO PROTECT WOMEN AND GIRLS FROM SEXUAL ABUSE

During the 1880s a vociferous public lobby grew up in England to eliminate juvenile prostitution and what was referred to as the 'white slave
trade,' the exportation of young girls to foreign countries for the purpose
of prostitution.[91] In 1881 a Select Committee of the English House of Lords
investigated the matter at length and recommended legislation. Although
bills were introduced several times, none of the initial legislation was
passed. According to the pro-reform lobby, the defeat of the early legislation was due to active opposition from a group of 'notorious evil-
livers.'[92] Josephine Butler and W.T. Stead, the editor of the *Pall Mall
Gazette*, headed the campaign in support of the legislation. When Stead
himself arranged to procure a young girl for the purpose of sexual
relations to show how easily this could be accomplished, and then
published an account of the venture in his *Gazette*, the English parliament
had to act.[93]

Supported by religious leaders and the upper middle-class women of
the day, parliament in 1885 passed An Act to Make Further Provision for
the Protection of Women and Girls, the Suppression of Brothels, and
Other Purposes. It dealt in the main with the procuring of women for the
purposes of prostitution, but the statutory rape provisions are of more
interest for the purposes of this essay. Previously, carnal knowledge of a
girl under twelve had been punishable with life imprisonment; carnal
knowledge of girls twelve to thirteen had been punishable with a maximum of two years. The new legislation made the defilement of girls under
thirteen punishable by life, and the defilement of girls aged thirteen to
sixteen punishable with a maximum of two years.[94] The offence of abduction of an unmarried girl from the lawful custody of her parents was
changed to cover all girls under the age of eighteen (where previously the
age limit was sixteen). Parliament was responding to the continuing
pressure to raise the age of consent and to increase the penalties for
statutory rape. Some of the legislators, however, expressed concern over
false complaints and the potential for extortion. In response, the statute
contained an express statement that mistake of fact would furnish a
defence. If the accused 'had reasonable cause to believe' that the girl was
above the statutory age limit, he could not be convicted.

The Canadian parliament was soon faced with a similar lobby organized
by a Montrealer, D.A. Watt.[95] Newspaper columns began to reflect public
concern about sexual assault of young women. The Toronto *Globe* repor-

ted in October 1887 that the following statement had been included in the grand jury presentment: 'The number of cases of indecent assault upon girls of tender years appears to be on the increase, through which, in several instances, severe injury has been inflicted on the children, and the jurors would strongly recommend that in addition to imprisonment the application of the lash should in all cases be inflicted, in hopes that the law may become a terror to such evil-doers.'[96] Religious leaders also urged increased protection for young women; the General Assembly of the Presbyterian Church passed a resolution in favour of extended criminal legislation to prevent the sexual exploitation of young girls.[97] John Charlton, MP for Norfolk North, was one of the main supporters in the House of Commons. He presented petitions 'from thousands of ladies praying for' swift passage of the legislation to protect women from sexual exploitation and claimed that the 'Christian and moral sentiments of Canada' were enlisted in favour of the law. The Canadian legislators also explained that their decision to enact such a measure was in part based upon the British and American example. Referring to the existence of such a law in England and in the adjoining American states, Senator Alexander Vidal reminded his colleagues that in 'nearly all civilized countries, women and girls have a measure of protection thrown over them by the law of the land' whereas 'Canada [stood] almost alone in having no sufficient provision for their protection.'[98]

As a result, parliament passed a rash of statutes from 1885 to 1890.[99] The legislation dealt with procuring offences but also raised the age of consent in statutory rape to fourteen years.[100] The major innovation was to create the offence of seduction. The act of 1886 made it a crime to seduce and have illicit connection with any girl of previously chaste character who was above the age of twelve and under the age of sixteen. It also prohibited seduction of an unmarried female of previously chaste character and under the age of eighteen, under promise of marriage. The maximum penalty for these offences was two years.[101] In 1887 the provision on seduction under promise of marriage was altered to raise the age of the woman to twenty-one, so long as the seducer himself was over twenty-one.[102] In 1890 the seduction of a ward or female employee became an offence.[103]

The criminalization of seduction moved the law of sexual assault far beyond earlier requirements that the attack occur with violence and that women resist to the utmost. Women were to be protected from non-marital sexual intercourse regardless of the methods by which the seducer sought to accomplish his goal. The law was to provide increased protection for certain women – those under the statutory age who were also of previously chaste character. There was a strict prohibition against sexual relations with these women under sanction of the criminal law; society was prepared to impose its own notions of when sexual relations were proper.[104] Why did the legislators perceive the need to create a blanket prohibition against seduction of these women? The emerging sexual ideology provides some explanation.[105] As women came increasingly to be understood as lacking in all sexual desires – essentially passionless – responsibility for the act of seduction was laid at the foot of the male. Acton wrote that since women were sexually passive beings, the man must have initiated all instances of seduction.[106] This view fed the notion that it was men who should be punished for acts of non-marital intercourse, whereas the women should be seen as unfortunate, even tragic victims of circumstance.

The belief that women were lacking in sexual feeling may have caused the legislators to perceive the crime as that much more of a violation – the ultimate intrusion – and thus deserving of stricter criminal sanctions. However, only young, passionless women were to be protected. The young girl was viewed as inherently pure and uncorrupted. Those women who were no longer chaste were denied protection of the criminal law. Having experienced non-marital intercourse, such women were no longer considered passionless.[107]

In addition to changing views about women's sexuality, there may also have been another explanation for the criminalization of seduction. Large numbers of women were moving into the cities from rural areas and from Europe. Living away from home, removed from parental control and surveillance, these women were prime targets for seduction. This legislation may have been enacted, in part, to protect these women from sexual contact outside of marriage.

The parliamentary debates on seduction also shed some light on the attitudes of the day towards women and sexuality. Those who supported the legislation believed that a fall from virtue was the most disastrous fate that could be visited upon a young girl. Senator Vidal claimed that such an injury to a virtuous young woman was 'worse than death itself.'[108] MP John Charlton argued from a broader, societal perspective: 'The degradation of women is a crime against society. The pure Christian home is the only safe foundation for the free and enlightened State. Vice in the shape of social immorality is the greatest danger that can threaten the State.'

Not everyone was so impressed with the need for such protective legislation. Indeed, Charlton himself alluded to the opposition when he told the House that his introduction of such legislation had caused him to be 'subjected to many gibes and some abuse; I have been characterized as the apostle of cant, I have been accused of legislating for the purpose of creating brazen females.'[109] The forces of opposition had several major arguments. They cautioned that no law of man could make an impure woman virtuous. Senator Alexander W. Ogilvie of Quebec put the position in the following manner: 'I do not think we can legislate people into virtue and morality. I think the proper place to inculcate morals in the minds of the youths of both sexes, and especially the female sex, is in the family circle, in the Sunday School, in the church and in the public school ... [T]his Bill is an insult to the morality of the sex in Canada. A virtuous woman as a rule can protect her own honour.' Senator Henry Kaulback of Nova Scotia expanded on this view:

A good woman knows she is the guardian of her honour and lives above suspicion. Pure, modest women need not the protection of the law to guard their honour, and no man looking on one surrounded by purity can have evil thoughts ... A woman surrounded with the safeguard of her own virtue is seldom or never improperly approached and when she is approached violently there is already on our statute book a criminal law ample and sufficient to protect her. The moment we impress upon the minds of the community that woman is not the guardian of her own honour, that she requires a law of this kind to protect her against unchastity, that moment we are endangering the best interests of society and gratuitously insulting the whole female sex.[110]

There was also grave concern that the seduction and statutory rape laws permitted women to practise extortion. Senator Thomas R. McInnes of British Columbia provided one vivid hypothetical example: 'Take for instance a young man of fifteen or sixteen who is sole heir to a large property, and a designing girl of nineteen or twenty seduces him and then takes an action against him for seduction ... [T]he boy would have no alternative but to leave the country, or be imprisoned in the penitentiary, or what is worse, to condone the offence by marrying her.' McInnes continued on a rather defensive note: 'I have a couple of sons ... and we do not want to see them marry characters of that kind and bring them to our homes to be treated as we should treat daughters-in-law and members of our families.' Turning the focus back to the responsibility of women, McInnes concluded: 'While I desire to see the mantle of protection thrown around those who ought to be protected, I cannot close my eyes to the fact that if guardians, parents, and especially mothers, exercised more care and more authority over their daughters, there would be fewer of these abominable cases of seduction throughout the country.'[111] In essence, McInnes maintained that sexual matters were the responsibility of the individual rather than a matter for societal intervention. The obligation for purity was allocated to women; they were to protect themselves, and mothers were to protect their daughters. Senator Alexander Campbell based his opposition to the legislation on quite another footing. He stated that any woman who deserved sympathy would not enter the court out of an overwhelming sense of shame. Charlton agreed that in a majority of cases, this might be true. Yet he urged enactment in order to provide redress for those who chose nevertheless to seek legal assistance.[112]

The debate over the criminalization of seduction was not restricted to the House of Commons and the Senate. The editors of the law journals also ventured to state their opinions. The Montreal-based *Legal News* suggested that the tables be turned and that women also be subjected to criminal prosecution for seduction. Attempting to strike a humorous vein, *The Legal News* reported that under an old New Jersey statute women had been liable to charges of witchcraft if they seduced a man or betrayed him into matrimony 'by virtue of scents, cosmetics, washes, paints, artificial teeth, false hair or high-heeled shoes ...'[113] The editors of the *Canada Law Journal*, however, actively supported the criminalization of seduction as a response to 'one of the crying evils of the day.' The problem was that even if both parties were equally guilty, society treated them totally differently: 'The man practically goes unpunished; he is scarcely tabooed in society; in fact, his companions think him rather a fine fellow ...; while the unfortunate woman bears the whole burden, becomes an outcast, is driven from home, disgraced and ruined, to bear her trial alone, overwhelmed by an agony of shame, that too often ends in some hideous crime or piteous suicide.' In fact, the article continued, these women ended up in reformatories, havens for fallen women, Magdalen asylums, police cells, and city morgues. Urging speedy adoption of the legislation, the journal stated: 'The present state of the law of seduction ... is not only a disgrace to humanity, but causes a financial burden to the country and to charitable citizens.'[114]

The legislators' positive response to the campaign for morals legislation illustrated once again that they wished to provide additional protection for women, and especially for young girls, from sexual relations. The concern, however, was clearly a paternal one; believing that the loss of virtue was a mortal blow to women, they extended the statutes to provide increasing protection. One suspects that much of this legislation was merely hortatory and without any real force. When even the major proponents of the legislation agreed that most victims would be too ashamed to come to court, it is difficult to imagine that any of the politicians expected the law reform to alter the situation dramatically.

When the female complainants did bring their cases to court, they once again encountered a sceptical judiciary, which appeared to be fairly hostile to the new seduction legislation. The *Canada Law Journal* noted that the views of judges against enactment had been influential: 'Some of our judges, viewing the subject only from the standpoint of seduction cases brought before them by those, who, as a rule, are *not* the class that require protection, have, by their remarks in Court, helped to lead astray public thought on this matter.'[115]

Faced with the reality of legislation, the bench proceeded to interpret it very restrictively. The case of *The Queen* v *Walker* dealt with a charge of seduction under promise of marriage.[116] Donald Walker of Medicine Hat had allegedly seduced Fanny Ford Small, an unmarried woman under twenty-one years and of prior chaste character. Since he was engaged to her at the time, the jury convicted him. On appeal, Justice Hugh Richardson concluded that the legislation was not intended to prohibit all sexual relations during the period of engagement; instead, the seduction had to be effected by making a promise of marriage: '[W]e think the expression "under promise of marriage" qualifies "seduces," that is, shows the means by which the seduction is effected.' Unless the seduction was accomplished by means of a promise of marriage, the accused should have been acquitted. The court ordered a new trial. The pattern of restrictive judicial decisions continued to limit the impact of the newly enacted morals legislation.

CODIFICATION 1892

In 1892 parliament enacted the first Canadian Criminal Code. It was based upon a draft code prepared by a Royal Commission in Great Britain in 1880, on Stephen's *Digest of the Criminal Law* of 1887, George Burbidge's *Digest of the Canadian Criminal Law of 1889*, and Canadian statutory law.[117] Senator William Miller stated, upon introduction of the bill, that this was not a new set of criminal enactments, but simply what it purported to be – a codification of the laws as they already existed.[118]

There were, however, two substantial changes to the law of sexual assault enacted in the code. First, another seduction offence was added – the seduction of females who were passengers on ships. Masters, officers, or other seamen who committed this offence, and were not redeemed by eventual marriage to the seduced women, were liable to a term of one year and a fine of $400. This section was apparently thought necessary to protect helpless female immigrants, who were believed to be at the mercy of the officers and crew of the ships carrying them to Canada.[119] Second, parliament codified a complete definition of rape for the first time. It was defined as 'the act of a man having carnal knowledge of a woman who is not his wife without her consent, or with consent which has been extorted by threats or fear of bodily harm, or obtained by personating the woman's husband, or by false or fraudulent representations as to the nature and quality of the act.'[120] The expanded notion of lack of consent went further than previous legislation. Again, the legislators appeared to be attempting to cover more coercive sexual behaviour with the criminal law. On the surface, they were moving even further away from the standards for resistance formulated by the judiciary. Not only did the definition refer to fear of bodily harm but also to threats. The legislators recognized that although a woman might consent to intercourse, this might amount to mere submission. Where submission was obtained forcibly or in some cases fraudulently, the act still amounted to rape. The new provision with respect to 'false and fraudulent representations as the nature and quality of the act' presented a significant alteration to the common law. Burbidge wrote in 1890 that if the woman gave her permission to the act of sexual intercourse, the act did not amount to rape, 'although such permission may have been obtained by fraud, and although the woman may not have been aware of the nature of the act.'[121] Statutorily reversing this rule, the legislators continued to participate in the trend towards expanding the law of rape to include a broader range of coercive sexual behaviour.

The new definition also codified the spousal immunity from rape charges. There had been no Canadian cases on point, and the immunity was assumed to be based upon an early treatise by Sir Matthew Hale, who had stated that a husband could not be guilty of rape committed upon his lawful wife, 'for by their mutual matrimonial consent and contract the wife hath given up herself in this kind unto her husband, which she cannot retract.'[122] Burbidge pointed out that Hale gave no authority for this assertion; Burbidge was clearly of the opinion that the position was not without some difficulty: 'It may be doubted, however, whether the consent is not confined to the decent and proper use of marital rights. If a man used violence to his wife under circumstances in which decency, or her own health or safety required or justified her in refusing her consent,

I think he might be convicted at least of an indecent assault.'[123] Nevertheless, with the codified immunity, parliament unequivocally chose the Hale position as the correct one, which seemed to depart from the legislative trend towards expanding the scope of rape law.

To some extent codification of spousal immunity appeared to fly in the face of Victorian sexual ideology. Authors of medical treatises and marriage advice manuals were promoting sexual self-control, even within marriage. They wrote and lectured about the dangers of excessive or too-frequent coitus.[124] The ideology of female passionlessness fostered the view that women had the right to refuse their husbands' sexual demands. Daniel Scott Smith has documented the growing popularity of this view:

Dio Lewis claimed that marital excess was the topic best received by his female audience during his lecture tours of the 1850s [through the United States]. The Moral Education Society, according to Lewis, asserted the right 'of a wife to be her own person, and her sacred right to deny her husband if need be; and to decide how often and when she should become a mother.' The theme of the wife's right to control her body and her fertility was not uncommon. 'It is a woman's right, not her privilege, to control the surrender of her person'; she should have pleasure or not allow access unless she wanted a child.[125]

Despite these new attitudes about a wife's right to sexual autonomy, the legislators enshrined a legal requirement that women submit to their marital duty. Perhaps members of parliament, concerned about these new ideas, wished to shore up male marital privileges.[126] Legislative immunity also indicated that parliament – itself so much in advance of the courts – still retained some of the same type of analysis and thinking that viewed rape as a crime directed against a form of male property. Since a husband and wife were legally one person, the crime of rape between spouses was impossible. Remnants of the ancient origins of the law of rape resurfaced even as the legislators moved increasingly towards the expansion of rape law to protect the rights of women.

CONCLUSION

At the beginning of the nineteenth century rape was viewed as a crime against a species of male property – potential interference with a wife or daughter's reproductive function. As a result the crime was not complete without an act of sexual intercourse and ejaculation. As the century progressed, the law began to move away from this property conception of rape law. The requirements for ejaculation, rupturing of the hymen, and finally even penetration were dropped as the definition of rape was altered and other, lesser offences of assault with intent to commit rape, and indecent assault were created. This change signified that rape was no longer conceived of solely as a crime against property; instead, the law was beginning to recognize that women deserved protection from sexual abuse in their own right, that they were entitled as individuals to sexual autonomy. The law of rape evolved past requirements for physical violence and resistance to encompass other forms of sexual coercion such as fraud and taking advantage of the mentally disabled. Finally seduction itself was criminalized.

While this evolution indicated that women were beginning to escape categorization as male property, it did not represent a true liberation. Instead, the predominant thrust of late nineteenth-century rape law was paternalistic. Seen as vulnerable, corruptible, and most important, passionless, women required protection from the evil designs of male sexual predators. Obviously this view was not subscribed to by all; the judges and a minority of the legislators expressed reluctance to expand the criminal law to encompass more instances of sexual contact. Judges gave the new legislation as restrictive an interpretation as possible. Those who spoke against reform in parliament insisted that women themselves should retain the responsibility for their own sexual purity. Yet the legislation was passed, and the overriding theme became a paternalistic, almost condescending concern to provide chaste women with legal protection from illicit sexual contact.

The transformation of rape law from conceptions of property to paternalism was not monolithic. The codification of spousal immunity at the end of the century stands out as a striking illustration that property notions remained firmly embedded in the law of rape. The tensions between the property analysis and the paternalistic thrust of the new legislation were vividly highlighted in the legislative decision to enact the blanket exception for marital sex. Presumably the notions of property still attached to the status of marriage overrode the desire to protect women's right to sexual self-determination.

Contrary to the views expressed by historians of the criminal law such as Stephen, the history of rape law is of great significance.[127] It provides an abundance of information about the values and attitudes surrounding sexual assault in the nineteenth century, the similarities and differences between Canadian and English legal developments, continuing tensions between legislators and the judiciary, and the status and role assigned to women in a developing Canadian culture. When comparable research has been done in the United States, it will be important to examine whether or not the American experience with rape law reflects the findings of this essay.

NOTES

I would like to acknowledge my appreciation and indebtedness to Stephanie McCurry, who acted as my research assistant on this article, and to Diana Majury, whose interpretation, analysis, and support were fundamental to the development of my thinking on the history of rape.

1 J.F. Stephen *A History of the Criminal Law of England* 3 vols (London 1883) III 117–18

2 *Upper Canada Law Journal* VIII (1862) 309 (hereafter UCLJ)

3 An Act for the Further Introduction of English Criminal Law into Upper Canada, 40 Geo. III (1800), c. 1, s. 1. The date 17 Sept. 1792 was chosen because it was the day on which the first session of the Legislature of Upper Canada opened. The desire for English laws and institutions had been a significant factor in the creation of Upper Canada and the wholesale adoption of English criminal law was not surprising.

4 William Oldnall Russell *A Treatise on Crimes and Misdemeanours* 3d ed. 2 vols (London 1843) I 675; Matthew Hale *Historia Placitorum Coronae: The History of the Pleas of the Crown* 2 vols (London 1736, reprinted London 1971) I 627

5 William Blackstone *Commentaries on the Laws of England* 4 vols (London 1765–9; facsimile ed. Chicago 1979) IV 210

6 Statute of Westminster I, 3 Edw. I (1275), c. 13

7 The age referred to here was the age of twelve, the age at which a woman could consent to marriage.

8 Blackstone *Commentaries* IV 212; Statute of Westminster I, 13 Edw. I (1285), c. 34

9 Statute of Westminster VI, 18 Eliz. I (1576), c. 7. For the sake of clarification, the term 'statutory rape' will be used to designate such forms of sexual relations with girls under the age designated by the relevant statute.

10 Blackstone *Commentaries* IV 212

11 Russell *Crimes and Misdemeanours* I 675 (emphasis added); Edward Hyde East *Pleas of the Crown* 2 vols (London 1803, reprinted London 1972) I 444–5

12 Blackstone *Commentaries* IV 213; East *Pleas of the Crown* I 445; William Eden *Principles of Penal Law* (London 1771) 236–7

13 East *Pleas of the Crown* 445, 446

14 Hale *Pleas of the Crown* 1 635–6

15 Statute of Westminster 1, 13 Edw. 1 (1285), c. 35

16 Statutes of Westminster 11, 6 Rich. 11 (1382), c. 6; 31 Hen. vi (1452), c. 9; 3 Hen. vii (1487), c. 2; 4 & 5 Philip & Mary (1557), c. 8; 39 Eliz. 1 (1597), c. 9; and 26 Geo. 11 (1753), c. 33

17 See, for example, preamble to 6 Rich. 11 (1382), c. 6; 3 Hen. vii (1487), c. 2; and 4 & 5 Philip & Mary (1557) c. 8.

18 H. Dagge *Considerations on Criminal Law* (London and Dublin 1772) 378–9, quoted in Leon Radzinowicz *A History of English Criminal Law and Its Administration from 1750* 4 vols to date (London 1949–) 1 441

19 An Act to Reduce the Number of Cases in Which Capital Punishment May Be Inflicted, 3 Wm. iv (1833), c. 3. While the legislation itself mentioned nothing about the removal of the offence of abduction of an heiress from the list of capital crimes, Chief Justice John Beverley Robinson noted this in his charge to the Grand Jury of the Home District, Apr. 1833 (York, Upper Canada 1833) 31. For a discussion of the background behind the legislative reform of 1833, see John D. Blackwell 'Crime in the London District, 1828–1837: A Case Study of the Effect of the 1833 Reform in Upper Canadian Penal Law' *Queen's Law Journal* vi (1981) 528 (hereafter QLJ).

20 An Act for Consolidating and Amending the Statutes in This Province Relative to Offences against the Person, 4 & 5 Vict. (1841), c. 27, ss. 16, 17

21 Ibid. s. 18

22 See, for example, Russell *Crimes and Misdemeanours* 1 679–86 and East *Pleas of the Crown* 1 439–40.

23 Ibid. 4 & 5 Vict. (1841), c. 27, s. 18

24 *Debates of the Legislative Assembly of United Canada* ed. Elizabeth Nish (Montreal 1970–) 1 713

25 An Act for Consolidating and Amending the Statutes in England Relative to the Offences against the Person, 9 Geo. iv (1828), c. 31; *Hansard Parliamentary Debates* 2d Series v. 17 (1827) 934–5. The only relevant difference between the two statutes concerned the penalty of transportation; this was not included in the Canadian legislation.

26 4 & 5 Vict. (1841), c. 27, s. 19 (emphasis added), s. 20

27 *Hansard Parliamentary Debates* v. 17 (1827) 787, 1133; v. 18 (1828) 1174

28 The simple adoption of English statutes was a common practice in nineteenth-century Canada. See for example Constance B. Backhouse 'Shifting Patterns in Nineteenth-Century Canadian Custody Law' in David H. Flaherty, ed. *Essays in the History of Canadian Law* 2 vols (Toronto 1981–3) 1 212–48.

29 An Act for Better Proportioning the Punishment to the Offence, in Certain

Cases, and for Other Purposes Therein Mentioned, 6 Vict. (1842), c. 5, s. 5. This legislation also dealt with the crime of assault with intent to commit buggery.

30 In *John v The Queen* (1888), 15 *Supreme Court Reports* 384 (hereafter SCR), the Supreme Court of Canada specifically concluded that on an indictment for rape, the accused could be convicted of the lesser and included offence of assault with intent to commit rape. This lesser offence, the court stated, was merely an attempt to commit the felony charged.

31 An Act to Consolidate and Amend the Statute Law of England and Ireland Relating to Offences against the Person, 24 & 25 Vict. (1861), c. 100; An Act Respecting Offences against the Person, *Statutes of Canada*, 33 Vict. (1870), c. 20; *Debates of the Senate of Canada* (1867–8) 320

32 Ibid.; 24 & 25 Vict. (1861), c. 100, ss. 48, 50, and 51

33 See Anthony H. Manchester *A Modern Legal History of England and Wales 1750–1950* (London 1980) 244–9.

34 Ibid.; *Statutes of Canada*, 33 Vict. (1870), c. 20, ss. 49, 51, and 52. A number of the provisions relating to sexual assault against women were identical. Specifically, both statutes created the new offence of 'indecent assault upon any female,' and 'attempt to have carnal knowledge of any girl under twelve years of age,' with a maximum of two years' sentence (Canada, s. 53; England, s. 52). Procuring defilement of a woman under the age of twenty-one was made a misdemeanour, punishable with a maximum sentence of two years (Canada, s. 50; England, s. 49). The existing abduction offences were added to by a series of new provisions: abduction of an heiress under the age of twenty-one against the will of her father (Canada, s. 54; England, s. 53), and forcible abduction of any woman with intent to marry or carnally know her (Canada, s. 55; England, s. 54). Those guilty of abducting heiresses were specifically disentitled from taking any property in which the woman might hold an interest (Canada, s. 54; England, s. 53). Although the legislation had provided that only a capital penalty could be handed down, the Crown retained the right to extend clemency and reduce the death penalty.

35 *Debates of the Senate of Canada* (1867–8) 320–3

36 Horace Smith *Roscoe's Digest of the Law of Evidence in Criminal Cases* (10th ed. London 1884) 901–2

37 *R. v Bedere* (1891), 2 *Ontario Reports* (hereafter OR) 189

38 An Act to Amend the Act Respecting Offences against the Person, 36 Vict. (1873), c. 50, s. 1

39 An Act to Amend the Law Relating to Offences against the Person, 38 & 39 Vict. (1875), c. 94, ss. 3 and 4

40 *Hansard Parliamentary Debates* 3d Series v. 223 (1875) 917–18; v. 226 (1875) 866–8

41 Ibid. v. 254 (1880) 1662; v. 255 (1880) 1083–6

42 An Act to Amend the Criminal Law as to Indecent Assaults on Young Persons, 44 & 45 Vict. (1880), c. 45

43 An Act to Amend the Act Respecting Offences against the Person, 40 Vict. (1877), c. 28, s. 2; *Debates of the House of Commons of Canada* III (1877) 319 (hereafter *House of Commons Debates*)

44 J.M. Beattie *Attitudes towards Crime and Punishment in Upper Canada, 1830–1850: A Documentary Study* (Toronto 1977) 1–2

45 J. Jerald Bellomo 'Upper Canadian Attitudes towards Crime and Punishment, 1832–1851' *Ontario History* 64 (1972) 11–26; Blackwell 'Crime in the London District' 528; Beattie *Attitudes towards Crime and Punishment in Upper Canada* 29. See, however, Terry Chapman 'The Measurement of Crime in Nineteenth-Century Canada: Some Methodological and Philosophical Problems' in Louis A. Knafla, ed. *Crime and Criminal Justice in Europe and Canada* (Waterloo; Ont. 1981) 147, regarding the difficulties of assessing the incidence of crime in this era.

46 *R. v Francis* (1855), 13 *Upper Canada Queen's Bench Reports* (hereafter UCQB) 116; *The Queen v Chubbs* (1864), 14 *Upper Canada Common Pleas Reports* (hereafter UCCP) 32; *R. v Fick* (1866), 16 UCQB 379; *R. v Connally* (1867), 27 UCQB 317. Very few decisions were reported or published before 1850. Decisions of the Upper Canada courts were first collected and published in 1824. Various reporters were appointed from 1824 onwards, although for years they were not paid, and the work was often discontinued for stretches of time. (William R. Riddell *Legal Profession in Upper Canada* [Toronto 1916] 108)

47 Archives of Ontario (hereafter AO) RG22 County Court Judges' Criminal Court (hereafter CCJCC) Minute Books and Courts of Criminal Assize Minute Books 1840–92. The statistics cited are drawn from these Minute Books, located in the Archives of Ontario. This essay is concerned with the period 1840 to 1892, although records are available from 1792 to the present. The records are not complete, some having been destroyed by fire or simply lost. The case files used are from the Criminal Indictment records also located at the Archives of Ontario. Like the Minute Books, they have survived only intermittently. The case files which are available contain some of the testimonies of the accused, complainant, and witnesses.

48 Modern estimates indicate that the actual number of rapes is from five to ten times greater than the number reported to the police (Lorenne Clark and Debra Lewis *Rape: The Price of Coercive Sexuality* [Toronto 1977] 40). Although there is no nineteenth-century research with which to compare this data, most of the reasons which keep victims from reporting the crime of rape would presumably have been present in the nineteenth century. C.S. Clark, newspaper-

man and author of a book titled *Of Toronto the Good: A Social Study*, published in 1898, gave a striking account of the drawbacks of reporting rape in the nineteenth century:

> Some years ago two boys, cousins, committed rape upon a girl who was the sister of one and the cousin of the other. They were arrested, tried, convicted and sentenced to two years in the Penitentiary. The result is that those boys when they got out, did not return to the place where the disgrace occurred, but are today respectable citizens while the girl is still unmarried, and even to this day she and her family are looked at askance for an act that happened twenty years ago. Was it any benefit to that girl to have those boys punished? Would it not have been far better to have let the matter drop than press it to a conclusion? That girl is disgraced forever, she will never be married, and simply because her father, a hot-headed English ignoramus determined to punish those boys. [(Toronto 1898) 110–11]

49 Neil Sutherland *Children in English-Canadian Society: Framing the Twentieth-Century Consensus* (Toronto 1976); Philippe Ariès *Centuries of Childhood: A Social History of Family Life* (New York 1962)

50 G.W. Bertram 'Economic Growth in Canadian Industry, 1870–1915' and K.A.H. Buckley 'Capital Formation in Canada, 1896–1930' in W.T. Easterbrook and M.H. Watkins, eds *Approaches to Canadian Economic History* (Toronto 1967); H.T. Naylor *History of Canadian Business 1867–1914* (Toronto 1975); *Census of Canada 1921* (Ottawa 1924) I 3

51 R.C.B. Risk has commented in 'The Law and the Economy in Mid-Nineteenth-Century Ontario: A Perspective' in Flaherty, ed. *Essays in the History of Canadian Law* I 112: 'The frontier conditions did create distinctive needs for law, but the response came from legislation, not common law, because the needs were appropriate for legislative responses, not common law.'

52 Indeed, treatise writers in Canada quoted directly and at length from the English treatises and interspersed English and Canadian case references. Russell and Hale were the two most often mentioned.

53 S.R. Clarke *A Treatise on Criminal Law as Applicable to the Dominion of Canada* (Toronto 1872) 264. He cites Russell *Crimes and Misdemeanours* I 675 as authority for this statement.

54 *R. v Fick* (1866), 16 UCQB 379

55 Ibid. 380–8

56 Ibid. 383, emphasis in original

57 This case is not reported, but records are available at the Archives of Ontario. AO RG22 York County Minute Books, 12 Oct. 1866, *The Queen v Robert Johnson*. The case is also discussed in the Toronto *Globe*, 13 Oct. 1866, 2.

58 AO RG22 Renfrew County Minute Books, 4 Oct. 1883, *The Queen* v *Antoine Legacy*

59 AO RG22 York County Minute Books, 4 Oct. 1887, *The Queen* v *Henry Waggstaff*

60 R. v *Cardo* (1888), 17 OR 11, 12–14

61 R. v *Francis* (1855), 13 UCQB 116, 117

62 S.R. Clarke *Treatise on Criminal Law* 264–5; G.W. Burbidge *A Digest of the Criminal Law of Canada* (Toronto 1890) 248–9; H.E. Taschereau *The Criminal Law Consolidation and Amendment Acts of 1869, 32–33 Victoria for the Dominion of Canada* (Montreal 1874–5) I 309

63 Taschereau *Criminal Law* 310

64 R. v *Connolly* (1867), 26 UCQB 317, 318–25

65 An Act to Punish Seduction and Like Offences, and to Make Further Provisions for the Protection of Women and Girls, 49 Vict. (1886), c. 52, s. 1(2); An Act for the Protection of Women in Certain Cases, *Revised Statutes of Ontario*, 1887, c. 249. Section 1 stated: 'No person shall at any time or place within the precincts of any institution to which *The Prison and Asylum Inspection Act* applies, unlawfully and carnally know any female who is capable in law of giving her consent to such carnal knowledge while she is a patient or is confined in such institution.' The penalty was a maximum of two years' imprisonment less a day (s. 2). As this appeared on the surface to be criminal legislation, questions must be raised about its constitutionality.

66 AO RG22 York County Minute Books, 7 Jan. 1892, *The Queen* v *George Warr*

67 An Act to Further Amend the Criminal Law, 53 Vict. (1890), c. 37, s. 14; *House of Commons Debates* XI (1890) 3165.

68 See Jennifer Nedelsky 'Judicial Conservatism in an Age of Innovation: Comparative Perspectives on Canadian Nuisance Law 1880–1930' in Flaherty, ed. *Essays in the History of Canadian Law* I 283, 312.

69 See Backhouse 'Nineteenth-Century Canadian Custody Law' 226–7

70 See Nancy F. Cott 'Passionlessness: An Interpretation of Victorian Sexual Ideology, 1790–1850' in Nancy F. Cott and Elizabeth H. Pleck, eds *A Heritage of Her Own* (New York 1979) 162–81; Daniel Scott Smith 'Family Limitation, Sexual Control, and Domestic Feminism in Victorian America' in Cott and Pleck, eds *Heritage of Her Own* 222–45

71 William Acton *The Functions and Disorders of the Reproductive Organs in Childhood, Youth, in Adult Age and in Advanced Age, Considered in the Physiological, Social and Moral Relations* (London 1865) 112

72 See Cott 'Victorian Sexual Ideology' 222–45.

73 See Nina Baym *Woman's Fiction: A Guide to Novels by and about Women in America, 1820–1870* (Ithaca, NY 1978).

74 Cott 'Victorian Sexual Ideology' and Smith 'Family Limitation, Sexual Control, and Domestic Feminism'

75 *R.* v *Francis* (1855), 13 UCQB 116–17; AO RG22 York County Minute Books, 11 Oct. 1882, *The Queen* v *William Stead; Globe,* 12 Oct. 1882

76 (1866), 2 UCLJ (New Series) 234

77 *Laliberté* v *The Queen* (1877), 1 SCR 117, 118, 130, 143

78 AO RG22 York County Minute Books, 6 Jan. 1859, *The Queen* v *Robert Gregg et al.; Globe* 14 Jan. 1859

79 *Globe,* 14 Jan. 1859

80 AO RG22 York County Minute Books, 19 Oct. 1865, *The Queen* v *Edwin Cudmore*

81 AO RG22 York County Minute Books, 18 Apr. 1866, *The Queen* v *John English; Globe,* 19 Apr. 1866

82 This point deserves further research. The present article focuses on nine-teenth-century rape law from the perspective of legislative and judicial decisions. It would be extremely useful to know more about who typically laid charges of rape, what role the police played in investigation and prosecution, and the conduct of the Crown attorneys in such matters. Presumably some of the individuals involved in these initial levels of law enforcement believed that these women were raped and that their cases should go forward for prosecution. Their attitudes about the crime of rape may have been somewhat different from those of judges and jurors.

83 This conclusion is drawn from an analysis of the reported cases and the surviving court records from the Ontario Archives as listed in note 47.

84 The reported cases and case files from the Ontario Archives have so few details concerning the relationship of the rapist to the victim that it is difficult to draw firm conclusions. However, the Ontario records are useful, due to the large population living in Ontario at the time, relative to the population in Canada as a whole: the population of Ontario in 1891 was 2,114,321, almost forty-four per cent of the national total.

85 *R.* v *James Chute* (1882), 46 UCQB 555; *Re Weir* (1887), 14 OR 389

86 The case dealt with assault with intent to ravish an idiot; the analysis concerning statutory rape was therefore merely an aside and had no binding authority. *R.* v *Connolly* (1867), 26 UCQB 317, 323.

87 An Act Respecting Offences against the Person, *Statutes of Canada,* 33 Vict. (1869), c. 20, s. 53

88 *R.* v *Paquet* (1883), 9 *Quebec Law Reports* 351

89 An Act to Amend the Criminal Law as to Indecent Assaults on Young Persons, 44 & 45 Vict. (1880), c. 45; An Act Further to Amend the Criminal Law, 53 Vict. (1890), c. 37, s. 7; *R.* v *Chisholm, Jacob's Case* (1891), 7 *Manitoba Law Reports*

(hereafter MLR) 613; *R.* v *Chisholm, Hammond's Case* (1892), 12 *Canadian Law Times* 26 (Occasional Notes); *R.* v *Brice* (1891), 7 MLR 627

90 *R.* v *Brice* (1891), 7 MLR 627 at 631–2

91 This essay will not focus on the problem of prostitution, the resulting reform movement, and the legal response. These must be the subject of another inquiry. Insofar as the morals crusade had an impact on the rape laws, however, it will be examined.

92 Frederick Whyte *The Life of W.T. Stead* (London 1925) I 160

93 Stead took care that he was never alone with the girl, and that she was always supervised by a matronly woman, so that no hint of impropriety would attach to him.

94 An Act to Make Further Provision for the Protection of Women and Girls, the Suppression of Brothels, and Other Purposes, 48 & 49 Vict. (1885), c. 69; ibid. ss. 4 and 5

95 See D.A. Watt *Moral Legislation: A Statement Prepared for the Information of the Senate* (Montreal 1890); Watt *Moral Legislation: A Statement Prepared for the Information of the Senate* (Montreal 1892)

96 *Globe,* 8 Oct. 1887

97 *House of Commons Debates* v. 1 (1885) 619

98 Ibid. v. 1 (1886) 441; *Debates of the Senate of Canada* (1886) 364–7

99 An Act Further to Amend an Act Intitled 'An Act Respecting Offences against the Person,' 48 & 49 Vict. (1885), c. 82; An Act to Punish Seduction and Like Offences, and to Make Further Provision for the Protection of Women and Girls, 49 Vict. (1886), c. 52; An Act to Amend the Act Respecting Offences against Public Morals and Public Convenience, 50 & 51 Vict. (1887), c. 48; An Act to Amend the Criminal Law, 53 Vict. (1890), c. 37

100 An Act to Amend the Criminal Law, 53 Vict. (1890), c. 37, ss. 3, 7, and 12

101 An Act to Punish Seduction and Like Offences, and to Make Further Provision for the Protection of Women and Girls, 49 Vict. (1886), c. 52, ss. 1, 2, and 8

102 Ibid. 50 & 51 Vict. (1887), c. 48, s. 2

103 Section 4 read: 'Everyone who, being a guardian, seduces or has illicit connection with his ward, and every one who seduces or has illicit connection with any woman or girl of previously chaste character and under the age of twenty-one years who is in his employ in a factory, mill, or workshop, or who, being in a common employment with him, in such factory, mill, or workshop, is, in respect of her employment ... under ... his control or direction is guilty of a misdemeanour and liable to two years imprisonment.' 53 Vict. (1890), c. 37. This essay will not further explore the provisions on seduction of a servant. However, the debates in the House of Commons and Senate on this measure constitute an interesting source of information concerning the

plight of female employees of the time and societal attitudes. See Constance B. Backhouse and Leah Cohen *The Secret Oppression: Sexual Harassment of Working Women* (Toronto 1979).

104 The link between rape and seduction was rarely acknowledged explicitly. When lobbyists and legislators addressed the need to create the crime of seduction, they made virtually no reference to the law of rape or its deficiencies. It is fascinating to speculate that the advocates for the new seduction legislation were responding to perceived weaknesses in the rape law, and yet felt compelled to couch their arguments around the law of seduction. Rape may have been simply too indelicate to discuss publicly. The likelier conclusion is that most lobbyists and legislators never considered the overlap between the two areas of law.

105 There has been relatively little research on Canadian views about sexuality in the nineteenth century. Most of the sources cited here are American or English. Michael Bliss has concluded that the Canadian experience was similar to that of the United States. (Michael Bliss 'Pure Books on Avoided Subjects: Pre-Freudian Sexual Ideas in Canada' in Canadian Historical Association *Historical Papers* [Ottawa 1970] 90)

106 William Acton *Prostitution, Considered in Its Moral, Social, and Sanitary Aspects, in London and Other Large Cities, with Proposals for the Mitigation and Prevention of Its Attendant Evils* (London 1857) 173

107 This type of thinking is evident from the following statement: 'Women's desires scarcely ever lead to their fall for the desire scarcely exists in a definite and conscious form, till they have fallen. In men in general the sexual desire is inherent and spontaneous and belongs to the condition of puberty. In the other sex, the desire is dormant, if non-existent, till excited by actual intercourse.' (*Westminster Review* [1850] 456–7, in E.M. Sigsworth and T.J. Wyke 'A Study of Victorian Prostitution and Venereal Disease' in Martha Vinicus, ed. *Suffer and Be Still: Women in the Victorian Age* [Bloomington, IN 1972] 82)

108 *Debates of the Senate of Canada* (1886) 476

109 *House of Commons Debates* v. 1 (1886) 441–2

110 *Debates of the Senate of Canada* (1886) 367–8

111 Ibid. 432. The concerns McInnes expressed may have been based, in part, upon the rather flamboyant personality of his offspring. One of his sons, Thomas Robert Edward McInnes, managed to live his life in a most unusual manner. Educated at the University of Toronto and Osgoode Hall, Thomas Robert was called to the bar but never engaged in the practise of law. Instead, he took part in the Yukon gold rush, lived for a number of years in China, and is chiefly remembered for the many volumes of poetry he published (W. Stewart Wallace, ed. *The Macmillan Dictionary of Canadian Biography* 4th ed.

rev. by W.A. McKay [Toronto 1978] 459). The legislators eventually sought to eliminate the potential for false complaints by requiring corroborating evidence in every case (An Act to Punish Seduction and Like Offences, and to Make Further Provision for the Protection of Women and Girls, 49 Vict. [1886], c. 52, s. 5). L.H. Davies, MP for Queen's, PEI, opposed this requirement, describing it as a 'monstrous' attempt to 'nullify the Bill': 'We know that practically, it would be impossible to get this corroborating evidence in ninety-nine cases out of a hundred.' (House of Commons Debates v. 1 [1886] 706)

112 Campbell's statement is from a reference made by John Charlton, House of Commons Debates v. 1 (1886) 442.

113 Legal News (Montreal 1886) IX 49. The New Jersey statute referred to was not cited.

114 (1882) 18 Canada Law Journal 151

115 Ibid.

116 The Queen v Walker (1893), 1 Territories Law Reports 482

117 The Criminal Code, 1892, 55–6 Vict. c. 29; House of Commons Debates v. 1 (1892) 1312. See also Graham Parker, 'The Origins of the Canadian Criminal Code' in Flaherty, ed. Essays in the History of Canadian Law I 249–80.

118 Debates of the Senate of Canada (1892) 390. In fact, during the debate on the Code, when J.J. Curran, MP for Centre Montreal, moved to amend the age of consent from fourteen to sixteen in the statutory rape provisions, he was outvoted. Curran told the House that he was requesting this amendment upon the suggestion of a society in Montreal which had a great interest in this law. Sir John Thompson, who introduced the bill, disagreed with the proposed age change. He told the House of Commons that he did not think it was wise to accede to the wish of the philanthropic gentleman from Montreal. He referred to a 'remarkable case' in Winnipeg a short while previously, in which a man had been sentenced to a long term of imprisonment and to be whipped, when it was proved that the female complainant was under fourteen. The woman in question, however, was also a 'notorious prostitute.' He concluded that: 'If we extend the age to sixteen, we shall be punishing offences against young women, while this clause is really intended to punish those who commit offences against children.' (House of Commons Debates v. 11 [1892] 269, 4225)

119 Ibid.; Criminal Code, s. 184; House of Commons Debates v. 11 (1892) 2972

120 Ibid. Criminal Code, s. 266

121 Burbidge Criminal Law of Canada 249

122 Hale Pleas of the Crown I 629

123 Burbidge Criminal Law of Canada 249

124 Smith 'Family Limitation, Sexual Control and Domestic Feminism' 233–5

125 Ibid. 233–5; Dio Lewis *Chastity, or Our Secret Sins* (New York 1888) 18; Henry C. Wright *Marriage and Parentage* (Boston 1853) 242–55

126 It is noteworthy that women did not yet have the right to vote or to sit in parliament. The lack of any direct female influence on the legislative process may explain, in part, why spousal immunity was enshrined in the new code.

127 Stephen *History of the Criminal Law* III 117–18

5

Law and Ideology:
The Toronto Police Court
1850–80

PAUL CRAVEN

Out of an interest in the history of labour law, I began some time ago to investigate the Ontario Master and Servant Act of 1847. I completed what was essentially a statutory history of that act and an interpretation of its policy, and then turned to examine its administration by the Toronto Police Court, a tribunal that had both a large caseload and an extensive group of surviving records.[1] Part of this research involved looking in the local newspapers for accounts of master and servant cases, and it quickly became apparent that the Toronto press devoted a great deal of space to coverage of the city police court.

This reportage is interesting for a number of reasons. First is its extent: a regular Police Court column appeared in *The Globe* and *The Leader* practically every day, and while it was often quite short this was by no means always true, particularly in the 1860s and 1870s. Second, the reporters give detailed information about a substantial proportion of the cases heard by the court, which forms a very useful supplement to the quantitatively exhaustive but qualitatively skeletal information provided by the court's formal records. But it is two other aspects of the press coverage that really led to the writing of this essay.

Quite apart from the cases themselves, the reporters have a great deal to say about the court's ambience: they comment on its physical surroundings, the peculiarities of the presiding magistrate and other functionaries, the spectators, and the judicial process. In this, reports of the police court differ enormously from the press treatment of tribunals like the assizes or the recorder's court, which are confined to simple and straightforward reports about the charges laid, the evidence heard, and the sentences handed out. Beyond this, the Police Court reports are unique not only for *what* they say about the court, but for *how* they say it, not just in the irreverence which contrasts so markedly with reports of superior tribunals, but in the pervasive use of metaphor and figurative language in describing and commenting on what went on there.[2]

It occurred to me that the material exists for writing a detailed descriptive account of the workings of the Police Court, a useful enterprise because so little is known about the history of these inferior tribunals which constituted the broad base of the judicial pyramid. But to attempt just this would be to ignore a problem and an opportunity. The problem is that the richest source of evidence – the newspaper accounts – is clearly not a neutral one. Yet this also presents an opportunity, for it seems likely that in the frequency of its reporting, in its broad choice of what to report, and perhaps especially in its style of reporting, the press was responding to an as-yet-undefined need in the consciousness of its readers. To be sure, it might be said that the Police Court columns were the mid-Victorian equivalent of the modern comic strip, leavening the daily diet of parliamentary debates and reprinted foreign news with a quotient of sheer amusement, but this seems only half an answer. The Police Court column was often funny, but it was sometimes quite maudlin in its seriousness. And in any event, enough analysis has been written of such hardy standbys of popular culture as comic strips, romantic fiction in women's magazines, and children's stories to suggest that these ephemera often incorporate important societal themes, some of which may be persistent and others more narrowly confined to a particular place and time. If there is any virtue to these speculations, it might repay analysis of the Police Court reporting for what it can tell us about the social uses of the experience of the legal process, and for the characterization of what I have come to call the 'social imagination' of mid-Victorian Torontonians.[3]

In pursuing these lines of thought, it occurred to me that there was a partial analogue to my enterprise in Douglas Hay's seminal essay on the English criminal assizes in the eighteenth century. Hay focused on the law as a system of legitimating ideology, arguing that social order was imposed in that grossly inequitable society not by a regular police force and standing army, but by a 'spirit of consent and submission' fostered in the public ceremonial and ritual aspects of the administration of the criminal law. My evolving view of the Police Court and the press reports corresponds to Hay's analysis on a number of points. Like him, I am concerned with the ambience of a court rather than with the law as a body of substantive doctrine. Similarly, my view, like his, is turning to the uses of law – more exactly, of the vicarious experience of being brought to law – in a broadly ideological sense, seeing it as contributing most generally to legitimation and consent, more narrowly, as he puts it, to 'vindicate or disguise class interests.'[4]

Yet in several respects my enterprise differs from Hay's. Leaving aside the great differences between the eighteenth-century English Midlands and mid-nineteenth-century Toronto, or between the criminal assizes and the Police Court, two seem especially important. The first is that for Hay the ideology of the law was aimed first and foremost at the oppressed and exploited victims of eighteenth-century society, while my evidence is about how the law was vicariously experienced, through the newspapers, by a rather different social stratum. We do not know enough about newspaper readership in mid-Victorian Toronto, but it is safe to say that it was concentrated in the city's middling and upper strata, the 'respectable classes' as they often called themselves, and not among the impoverished and the unwashed. It would seem to follow that legitimation, if that was what was involved, would take a different form. Second, Hay did not engage, as I am forced to by their nature, in a critique of the neutrality of his sources. He found it possible to write about the assizes: I am conscious that in writing about the Police Court I am mostly peering through the tinted spectacles of the newspaper reporters and inevitably assimilating their astigmatism to the view I portray. I have therefore to find a way to write about both the Police Court and its depiction by the press, but the former will always be a partial account (in both senses). For these reasons, and for other less significant ones, this essay does not amount to a comparison with Hay's. It is, rather, an investigation that shares some of his methodological and theoretical concerns and goes part of the distance in parallel.

Nevertheless, one feature of Hay's analysis survives more or less intact in this essay. He characterizes the consent-commanding ideology implicit in the practice of the assizes under three heads: majesty, justice, and mercy. He is silent as to whether he considers this trilogy to have been peculiar to the English eighteenth century: one would have to hypothesize that any account of the ideological contents of law would have to be at least partly bound in time and space. I have chosen, however, to use these heads to organize my account of the ambience of the Police Court, both because majesty, justice, and mercy seem to me to resonate even today with frequently expressed, almost commonsensical, and therefore deeply rooted values about the nature of the Anglo-Canadian legal system, and because that trilogy had its faint echoes in the newspaper stories of what went on at the Police Court.

The essay begins with an institutional account of the development of the Police Court and its jurisdiction in the context of the other local courts. The second section uses the newspaper columns and other sources to explore the ambience of the court, employing Hay's ideological trilogy as its organizing principle. Next is a discussion of the uses of metaphor in the press accounts, and finally I address more directly the uses of the vicarious experience of being brought to law, as portrayed by the newspapers, as aspects of legitimation in mid-Victorian Toronto.

TORONTO'S LOCAL COURTS: DEVELOPMENT AND JURISDICTION

The origins of the Toronto Police Court are bound up in the history of municipal institutions in Ontario and complicated by a plethora of statutes touching both the office of justice of the peace and the machinery of local government. This is not the place to explore either subject in depth: there are books waiting to be written on both of them. The most that can be done here is to sketch the historical development in outline, clearing up some of the muddle in the existing literature, and supplying the background for a study of the court after 1850. Essentially, the story is one of the separation of legislative, administrative, and judicial functions and the distribution of the latter among various tribunals.

From the beginnings of settlement in what is now Ontario, local administration was in the hands of the magistracy. Justices of the peace were appointed by the Lieutenant Governor and qualified to exercise their commissions by meeting certain property requirements and swearing an oath of office. They performed a variety of legislative, administrative, and judicial functions. A large number of enabling statutes specified the powers and responsibilities of justices acting alone, in pairs, and sitting as a quorum of the district magistracy in the Court of General Quarter Sessions of the Peace. To take only a few examples of these various functions and capacities, an act of 1792 empowered justices in quarter sessions to tender, contract for, and establish a district jail and courthouse, establish jail rules, and hire a jailer. Legislation the following year permitted individual justices in districts with fewer than five Anglican ministers to solemnize marriages, and empowered any two justices to call parish meetings, serve as returning officers in the election of local officials, and supervise local assessment rolls and tax collection. In 1794 justices in quarter sessions became responsible for granting and regulating liquor licences.[5]

In their judicial capacity, the magistrates received complaints, took informations, issued warrants and summonses, and conducted trials. Minor criminal offences could be tried summarily by two justices, while the quarter sessions received bills of indictment from its grand jury in more serious cases and proceeded to try many of them (most frequently cases of simple larceny and assault) before petit juries. The quarter sessions also bound over prisoners charged with the most serious crimes to the assizes and, in this era of private prosecutions, took securities from their accusers to appear against them. The justices had essentially no civil jurisdiction, except for their power to order the payment of withheld wages under the Master and Servant Act, although sitting as commissioners of the Court of Requests they presided over the precursor of today's Small Claims Court.[6]

The criminal jurisdiction of the magistracy was the subject of an enormous volume of legislation, much of it hidden in minor clauses of various statutes. It was partially consolidated in an 1832 act which supplied general forms of conviction and other administrative and jurisdictional guidance. Legislation in 1834 established a scale of fees and provided for summary trial in petty trespass and other offences. The distinction between grand and petit larceny was abolished in 1837, with the effect of enlarging the criminal jurisdiction of the quarter sessions. By an 1841 act, justices were obliged to make returns of their summary convictions to quarter sessions, and another act of the same year sought to reform the law on examination of the accused and setting of bail by the justices, along with a great number of additional changes in the administration of criminal justice. Other statutes of that year consolidated and amended the laws respecting larceny, malicious injuries to property, and offences against the person. Much more legislation followed, culminating in 1852 with two acts which attempted to codify the duties of justices acting out of sessions with respect to summary proceedings and indictable offences: these were accompanied by an act to protect justices from vexatious actions launched against them. Shortly after Confederation, the Dominion parliament sought to codify these and related matters on similar principles; in the interim, of course, other legislation had further complicated the picture.[7] Finally, the justices had a general responsibility to preserve the peace and maintain order, epitomized by what is probably their best-known duty: 'reading the Riot Act' on occasions of public disorder.

The first justices in the vicinity of York were sworn in in 1796. Until the town's incorporation as the City of Toronto in 1834, the local magistracy, meeting in the Home District quarter sessions, was responsible for local government. Its legislative and administrative jurisdictions were enlarged in 1817 by a statute giving quarter sessions the power to regulate such matters as street repair, paving and lighting, fire-fighting, nuisances, and so on, and to raise money by assessment for local improvements. The quarter sessions could establish fines for breach of these 'police' regulations.[8]

It was not long before York's unpaid, part-time justices found the duties of local government overly burdensome. In 1816 they memorialized the Lieutenant Governor to consider 'the expediency of appointing (after the example of our Sister Province) some one discreet and intelligent Magistrate, who, with an adequate Salary, would undertake the superintendance of the District Police, and, at certain hours daily, attend to all such matters as may come within the jurisdiction of the Commission [of the Peace for the Home District].' The executive was sympathetic to this request, but the legislature ignored it. A similar memorial in 1827, calling for the appointment of a 'Chairman of the Quarter Sessions, with a Salary equal to a recompense for his daily attendance on the duties of Police Magistrate,' met the same fate. In 1833, on the eve of incorporation, the legislature defeated a bill to the same purpose which had been introduced by York Sheriff William B. Jarvis.[9]

In common with other justices in the province, York's magistrates exercised their judicial functions singly, in pairs, and in quarter sessions as the law required; their enforcement of local regulations was presumably conducted summarily, probably by a single justice sometimes assisted by others. In 1826 they established a police office at which, as they informed the Lieutenant Governor in their 1827 memorial, 'they respectively engaged to give their daily attendance at fixed hours in weekly rotation, and appointed a Clerk, whose services were to be paid by the fees authorized by law, if sufficient, otherwise the deficit to be supplied from the Town Treasury.' The justices warned that this arrangement was bound to fail for want of sufficient time to attend on their parts. If it in fact succeeded in whatever measure, this initiative marked the inception of the local police court.[10]

The structure of local government changed markedly with the incorporation of Toronto in 1834. The city was to be governed by a common council of two aldermen and two councilmen for each ward elected on a restricted franchise by the male householders of each of the four (subsequently five) wards: council would elect one of its aldermen as mayor.

There were higher property qualifications for aldermen than for council-men, and the former served ex officio as city justices of the peace. Council was empowered to make by-laws on a large variety of subjects, and these were to be enforced, subject to fine or imprisonment, by the mayor or any alderman. The jurisdiction of the Home District quarter sessions over the city was transferred to a Mayor's Court, occasionally referred to as the 'City Quarter Sessions.'[11]

As its surviving records show, the Mayor's Court closely resembled quarter sessions in both procedure and jurisdiction. The crucial difference was that it lacked legislative authority: by-laws were to be made by the elected council, not by the magistrates in sessions assembled. The mayor presided over the court with at least one alderman, although occasionally a second alderman substituted for the absent mayor. It was held four times each year for a week or so at a time, and there was usually a special session in late December for the sole purpose of ballotting for jurors for the coming year. It tried criminal offences within the jurisdiction of the quarter sessions, most frequently larceny and assault (more often the latter than the former in its early years, with the proportions reversing by the 1850s), and it bound persons charged with more serious offences over to the assizes. It heard appeals from convictions in the police court and received grand jury presentments on such matters as the state of the jail, the provision for lunatics, and the condition of the city's sidewalks. It also issued tavern licences. In fine, the Mayor's Court was the city equivalent of the quarter sessions and did not, as is sometimes represented, concern itself with the enforcement of by-laws or the exercise of the jurisdiction of justices out of sessions (acting alone or in pairs).[12]

The latter fell to the Police Court, the descendant of the police office of 1826, where the mayor and aldermen attended singly or in pairs on a daily basis to try minor ciminal offences and by-law infractions summarily. By 1836 at the latest, the police court had acquired regular premises of its own, for in that year the council's Standing Committee on Public Build-ings reported that 'it would be attended with considerable advantage towards keeping order and Regularity in the Police Court were the bar removed nearer to the Magistrates Bench so as to allow the Public to approach within hearing of the Proceedings also with a view to prevent the Confusion attendant upon the accused, the Witness and the Audi-ence crowding indiscriminately around the Clerk's Table.'[13]

The Mayor's Court, with its grand and petit juries, was a court of record; the Police Court, like other courts of summary jurisdiction, was not, and if records were kept for this period they have not survived. Thanks to the commissioners appointed by the provincial legislature to report on election riots in the city, however, a tabulation of offences tried in Toronto in 1840 has come down to us, and it helps to clarify the nature and business of the two local courts. First, it is plain that the people listed in Table 1 were charged in the first instance at the police office. This almost certainly means that they were brought up before the mayor or an alderman sitting in his ex officio capacity as police magistrate at the Police Court. It is equally probable that the same official was responsible for the summary disposal of cases, and for the majority of them this likely occurred then and there. The police magistrate would have investigated charges of indictable offences, and upon finding a prima facie case to have been made out he would have bound the defendant over to the mayor's court or the assizes. So 'disposed of summarily' in the 1840 tabulation must have included cases that were discharged for want of prosecution, indictable offences where the magistrate found insufficient evidence to commit the accused for trial, and summary cases that were dismissed on their merits, as well as summary convictions. It probably also included cases that were discharged for want of jurisdiction and related reasons. To take one example, in the 1840s magistrates could not convict summarily on a charge of larceny: simple larceny could be tried by quarter sessions, otherwise it was an offence for the assizes. It would seem to follow that the forty-three cases of larceny disposed of summarily were discharged for insufficient evidence, want of prosecution, or similar reasons; in other words, that they were not tried by the police magistrate.

A large number of the most common offences fell within the Police Court's sole jurisdiction: breach of statute and city law, licensing offences, drunk and disorderly, prostitution, simple trespass, and threatening. The Police Court had by far the largest caseload by virtue of its jurisdiction over these petty offences, and because it saw and examined everyone who was charged with an offence in the city. The Mayor's Court, by contrast, had little enough to do. In any event it sat only fifteen or twenty days in the year. As Canada's first legal historian, the pseudonymous versifier 'Plinius Secundus' seems to imply, the true significance of the court may have been the opportunity it afforded to reaffirm ceremonially the judicial authority of the municipal corporation:

> TORONTO has a Court, tis said
> SHERWOOD, the Mayor, is now the head
> With Court of Aldermen, to judge
> All wicked cheats, prevent all fudge;
> Four times a-year, to punish sinners,
> Justice to grant, and eat good dinners.[14]

TABLE 1

Persons tried for offences committed in Toronto 1840

Nature of offence	Charged at police office	Committed to assizes	Tried at mayor's court	Disposed of summarily
Assault	213	—	4	209
Assault with firearms or deadly weapons	2	2	—	—
Assault with intent to commit buggery	1	1	—	—
Assault upon constables in the execution of their duty	5	5	—	—
Burglary	5	2	—	3
Breach of provincial statutes and city laws, for which penalties under twenty shillings were inflicted	118	—	—	118
Contempt, refusing to give evidence	3	—	—	3
Disorderly conduct (whores, rogues, and vagabonds)	317	—	—	317
Disorderly houses (for keeping)	7	—	—	7
Drunk in public streets, unable to take care of themselves	157	—	—	157
Enticing soldiers to desert	2	2	—	—
Buying soldiers' necessaries	2	—	—	2
Distilling without licence	1	—	—	1
Keeping billiard tables without licence	4	—	—	4
Pedding without licence	2	—	—	2
Selling spirits without licence	32	—	—	32

TABLE 1 (*concluded*)

Nature of offence	Charged at police office	Committed to assizes	Tried at mayor's court	Disposed of summarily
Larceny	126	50	33	43
Receiving stolen goods	4	—	1	3
Frauds	2	1	1	—
Rape	1	1	—	—
Riot	9	2	—	7
Threatening personal violence	61	—	—	61
Trespassing upon private property	17	—	—	17
Selling poison contrary to statute	1	—	—	1
Uttering forged money	5	4	—	1
Practising medicine contrary to statute	1	—	—	1
TOTAL:	1098	70	39	989

'I certify this to be a correct Return of all the Trials before the Mayor and Magistrates of the City of Toronto, during the year 1840 ... CHAS. DALY, Clerk of the Peace, City of Toronto.'

Source: Canada (Province), Legislative Assembly, *Journals*, 4–5 Vict., 1841. Appendix S, appendix C. I have combined the figures which in the original are reported separately for males and females, and have corrected two obvious errors in the figures (involving the transposition of one numeral). The original characterization of the offences has been retained.

It will not do, however, to draw too strict a line between the Mayor's Court and the Police Court. After all, the same civic officials presided over both, so that we should not be surprised if, for example, petty offenders who were apprehended during the Mayor's Court sittings might find themselves taken there rather than to the police office for summary judgment, perhaps because the Mayor's Court was the only place a competent official could be found that day. This at any rate seems to explain what occurred on one occasion in December 1834 when Mayor William Lyon Mackenzie and one of the city aldermen were presiding at the Mayor's Court. They had tried, with all the dignity of grand and petit juries, cases of larceny, assault and battery, and riot and tumult, and had committed a prisoner accused of grand larceny to the assizes. Then in the midst of things, perhaps while a jury was out considering its verdict, 'the court received the information of Thomas Grey against Owen Killam for Drunkenness: Committed to Jail for two nights and to be then discharged.'[15] Such incidents were very rare, however, and the informality that the odd occurrence reveals is to be attributed to the fact that one man filled two offices, rather than to any confusion about the respective jurisdictions of the two courts.

The city fathers might accept that the occasional Police Court matter would arise in the Mayor's Court so long as they presided over both. But they were prepared to oppose vigorously any outside interference with their prerogative. In 1845 the provincial legislature entertained a bill to amend the Toronto incorporation act and among its provisions was one for the appointment of a recorder in the city. Toronto council immediately resolved that were such an officer to be appointed, he should merely carry out the duties of a district (subsequently county) court judge in the city, and nothing more:

we deem it an interference with our own rights & duties and with those of our constituents and therefore decidedly protest against the Said Recorder being empowered or allowed to preside at the meetings of the Mayor & Aldermen, for granting Tavern licenses, or for any other purpose, and to his presiding at, or having anything to do with the City Police court, and we also object to the Said recorder, being armed with the power of appointing a Clerk, or of dismissing at his pleasure certain other officers of the Corporation.

Because by investing the Recorder with the proposed power of presiding on all occasions, when the Mayor & Aldermen or any part of them may meet, for public business, you reduce the Mayor, for the time being, from the condition of Chief Magistrate, to that of mere chairman of the meetings of the common council, while the Aldermen are reduced to the condition of mere assistants or official associates to the Said Recorder.

Because by giving the Said Recorder the power of appointing an officer to discharge the duties of the Clerk of the Peace and Police Court leaving to the present officer, merely the duties of clerk of the common council, you interfere as it appears to us quite unnecessarily with the power heretofore possessed by the corporation, who are alone accountable to the constituency of the city for the due execution of the duties of Said officer, and for the appropriation of the public money for the payment of the Same.

We are further of the opinion that if a Recorder is to be appointed, that appointment ought to be vested in the corporation as it is in all the large city's of the Mother Country, and not in the executive government for the time being, as in the proposed Bill.[16]

It is noteworthy that nowhere in this diatribe did council concern itself with protecting the jurisdiction of the Mayor's Court, except in the granting of tavern licences. Perhaps its members felt that the court was a time-consuming anachronism, and one they would be well rid of. In any event, few aldermen presented themselves at its judicial sessions, which were typically attended by the mayor and but a single associate. It was a different story when the court convened to distribute tavern licences: these sessions were well attended by the aldermen, eager, no doubt, to further their constituency work. The idea that a salaried recorder might be appointed to take over the judicial burden of the Mayor's Court seems not be have bothered council in 1845. Perhaps the growing city with its proliferation of institutions offered sufficient opportunities for eating good dinners without the quarterly Mayor's Court.

In the event, an amendment to Toronto's incorporation act in 1846 made provision for a recorder. He was to be an Upper Canada barrister of at least five years' standing with a salary of £200 per annum paid out of the city funds. His jurisdiction was to be equivalent to that of quarter sessions, which is to say the same as the Mayor's Court, and he was granted the power to license taverns that had previously been the province of the mayor and aldermen. The major concession to the council's protests, and it was a significant one, was the proviso that no recorder would be appointed by the provincial government until council passed a resolution declaring such an appointment to be necessary. Until that occurred, the Mayor's Court was to continue. Over the course of the next five years several attempts were made in council to have such a resolution passed, but opponents of the measure (or, as it would appear, of the chief candidate for the recorder's position) managed to have it either side-tracked or defeated. Toronto was not to have a recorder until 1851.[17]

In 1849 the legislature considered a bill that would consolidate and amend all the municipal government legislation in Ontario. Toronto's city council appointed a select committee, chaired by Mayor George Gurnett, to examine the proposal: it reported against several of the provisions. It objected to the reduction in the number of aldermen for each ward from two to one and to a number of clauses affecting property qualifications for municipal officers and the city franchise. It also expressed a good deal of concern about the sections of the bill that dealt with the local courts.

The committee opposed the £250 minimum salary provided for the recorder, arguing that it was 'altogether disproportionate' to his duties, and suggesting that if the recorder were made to perform the duties of a circuit judge the salary might be appropriate. The bill provided for the appointment of a salaried police magistrate when one might be required, and the committee objected to the proviso that he be a barrister of three years' standing. In its view there were, 'as is very well known, many unprofessional men in the Country who are at least equally qualified to discharge the duties of Police Magistrate … it is inexpedient to fetter the hand of the Executive by any such restriction.' The committee wanted the police magistrate to be subject to the same property qualification as aldermen. It was especially hostile to a provision that would permit the offices of recorder and police magistrate to be combined in one person:

That a magistrate who has examined – heard the evidence against a prisoner – and committed him for trial, from the Police Office (of course under a conviction of the guilt of the Prisoner) should afterwards preside as the Judge to try that prisoner for the same offence, is surely incompatible with that purity in the administration of Justice, which requires, and assumes, that such Judge shall come into Court with a mind, not only unprejudiced and unbiassed, but un-imbued with any previous knowledge of the cases he is to try, and, of any other information on the subject, than such as shall then and there be adduced in evidence before the Court.

The committee's chairman, a non-barrister, but a man who combined long experience as a city justice of the peace with the ability to meet the aldermanic property qualification, was subsequently to be appointed the city's first stipendiary police magistrate.[18]

The select committee's report was adopted by council and sent to the provincial government, but the objectionable parts of the bill were retained in the Upper Canada Municipal Corporations Act of 1849. It provided that on the request of any incorporated town or city, the provincial government would appoint a stipendiary police magistrate, whose salary of £100 or more was to be paid from the municipality's funds. The police magistrate would be a justice of the peace ex officio, with power to try offences against by-laws and all other offences over which one or two justices had jurisdiction, assisted, when two justices were required, by one or more of the city's regular magistrates. The act provided for the erection of a Recorder's Court, with the powers of quarter sessions, in each city. The mayor was to preside, assisted by one or more aldermen, until such time as the city council resolved for the appointment of a stipendiary recorder by the provincial government. The bill's provisions for the salary and qualifications of the recorder and the option of combining his job with that of the police magistrate remained intact. The stipendiary police magistrate, where appointed, was to have the tavern-licensing power.[19]

Thus the 1849 act contemplated the erection of Recorder's and Police courts in each city, presided over by provincial appointees who were to be paid by the city. The judicial authority of the justice of the peace was distributed between these courts, the Recorder's Court inheriting the jurisdiction of the quarter sessions and the police court that of the justice out of sessions. The immediate consequence for Toronto was that the Mayor's Court was renamed the Recorder's Court, but continued just as it had in the past until a police magistrate was appointed, when the administrative jurisdiction to award tavern licences passed to that office, or a recorder was appointed, which changed the bench but left jurisdiction and procedure intact. The legislative and local administrative functions of the old quarter sessions had been passing in stages to the elected council, and with this act that transfer was almost complete. The sole vestiges of the old administrative role were the tavern-licensing power, in exercising which the police magistrate remained subject to local by-laws, and the shared responsibility of recorder and police magistrate to supervise the police force by virtue of their power to suspend its members. Toronto's first stipendiary recorder, George Duggan, and its first stipendiary magistrate, George Gurnett, were both appointed in 1851. Both had been aldermen and both had aspired to the mayoralty: Gurnett had succeeded in 1837 and again in 1848–50.[20]

The Municipal Corporations Act received numerous technical amendments in 1850 and 1851, among them one restoring the second alderman in each city ward. By the 1851 act the provincial executive was empowered to appoint the city's recorder to sit as county court judge in the city division, and this elision of the two posts was emphasized by an 1866 statute specifying that recorders held their office during good behaviour, subject to the same impeachment procedure as county court judges. Recorder Duggan served in that capacity until 1868, when he was raised to county court judge. December of that year saw the last judicial session of the Toronto Recorder's Court. It tried persons charged with larceny, burglary, assault, wounding, and felony, and heard a number of appeals against convictions by the police magistrate, the majority of them in liquor licensing cases. The Recorder's Court convened in January 1869, but only to ballot for grand and petit jurors for the superior courts. After the list of names selected, its clerk wrote, 'Here ends the Recorders Court.' Its functions passed to the city division of the county court, with Duggan remaining on the bench. The new version of the Municipal Corporations (UC) Act, in 1866, had provided that every city should be a county of its own for municipal and for certain specified judicial purposes, while in 1869 a Dominion statute empowered recorders and county court judges to do alone anything that might be done by two justices of the peace, and enabled them to conduct summary trials of several offences formerly within the jurisdiction of the quarter sessions and assizes, upon the consent of the accused.[21]

The police magistrate's jurisdiction was also affected by legislation after 1851. The 1866 municipal act made it exclusive by barring other local justices from adjudicating cases except in his absence or by his request. The 1869 consolidations and revisions of the law relating to justices out of sessions applied to him, as did the juvenile offenders legislation of the same year. The most significant change came in 1875, when a speedy trials act permitted stipendiary magistrates to try any offence within the jurisdiction of quarter sessions summarily, on the consent of the accused. By virtue of this, the Toronto Police Court was to become the busiest criminal court in the province.[22]

Something of the nature and extent of the Police Court's business from 1850 to 1880, the period considered in this essay, is indicated by Tables 2 and 3, based on the annual reports of the Toronto police chief. The tables report the 'crime statistics' in five-year intervals: full data to carry the series back to 1854 unfortunately are not available. The local newspapers did publish summaries of the missing report for that year but they were internally inconsistent, and the figures reported by *The Globe* and *The Leader* differed in several particulars. The two papers did agree, however, that the total number of offences heard before the police magistrate was

TABLE 2
Toronto Criminal Statistics 1859–79: offences for which persons
were brought before the police magistrate

Offence		1859	1864	1869	1874	1879
Vagrancy[1]	N	—	141	228	401	255
	%	—	4.0	5.8	6.5	3.9
Drunk/disorderly	N	2266	1876	1836	3080	2836
	%	49.3	52.6	46.9	49.6	43.3
Licensing offences[2]	N	81	196	343	88	416
	%	1.8	5.5	8.8	1.4	6.3
City by-law	N	380	253	345	1027	957
	%	8.3	7.1	8.8	16.5	14.6
Larceny[3]	N	731	287	326	560	661
	%	15.9	8.0	8.3	9.0	10.1
Assault[4]	N	453	273	294	456	449
	%	9.9	7.7	7.5	7.3	6.9
All other offences	N	682	540	542	601	980
	%	14.8	15.1	13.8	9.7	15.0
TOTAL OFFENCES		4593	3566	3914	6213	6554

Source: compiled from Toronto City Council Minutes, Report of the
Chief Constable, various years
Notes: 1 Vagrancy was not a category of offence in 1859. 2 These
are mostly offences against the liquor laws, but other licensing
offences may be included in some years. 3 Includes suspicion of
larceny. 4 Excludes assault against a police officer.

3364, and in both accounts 'drunk and disorderly' amounted to roughly
forty per cent of the total. *The Leader* account suggests that a smaller
proportion of cases were withdrawn, dismissed, or discharged than in
later years, and this is consistent with the trend apparent in Table 3.[23]
Something must be said about the nature of these figures. They were
typically reported as statistics of 'crime,' showing the number of 'offenders' apprehended or summoned by the city police. It is evident, however,
from Table 3 that a very large proportion of the so-called 'offenders' were
not convicted. Some proportion of the offences were not in fact crimes: the
statistics included entries for non-payment of wages under the Master
and Servant Act, an offence that was clearly not criminal, and it would be
difficult to characterize such by-law offences as failing to clear snow from
the sidewalk as figuring in the annals of crime. What these statistical
returns really indicate is appearances before the police magistrate, and
the persons appearing were not always apprehended by the police or
summoned by them, except to the extent that private complainants (for

TABLE 3
Toronto criminal statistics 1859–79: disposition by police magistrate

Disposition		1859	1864	1869	1874	1879
Convicted (sentenced or bound to peace)	N	2499	1833	1707	3137	3087
	%	65.6	51.4	43.6	50.1	47.1
Committed for trial	N	81	100	203	230	105
	%	2.1	2.8	5.2	3.7	1.6
Dismissed/withdrawn/discharged	N	1227	1633	2004	2846	3362¹
	%	32.2	45.8	51.2	45.8	51.3
TOTAL		3807²	3566	3914	6213	6554

Source: compiled from Toronto City Council Minutes, Report of the Chief Constable, various years

Notes: 1 No 'dismissed' category was separately reported in 1879. 2 784 cases listed as 'remanded or postponed' in 1859 are eliminated from this calculation. This leaves a discrepancy of 2 cases between this total and the total in Table 2.

example, workers seeking unpaid wages under the Master and Servant Act) laid their complaint before the police magistrate or his clerk, who then issued a summons which was delivered by a policeman. Thus the statistical returns give inflated impressions of the volume of crime, the number of offenders, and the workload of the police force. A certain amount of cynicism about the data is appropriate, given the provenance of the reports and their principal purpose, the justification of ever larger appropriations for the force.

The chief constable occasionally supplied explanations for various statistics. In 1869 he commented that the number of persons summoned or arrested had decreased considerably since the previous year, due largely to a reduction in drunk and disorderly conduct: 'I attribute the diminution of offences against law and order to the successful working of the Vagrant Act, which was passed during the last session of the Dominion Parliament, and which, if strictly enforced, will tend more to the prevention of crime than any acts hitherto passed by the Legislature.' He attributed the large increase in by-law offences in 1879 to the unusual number of 'snow cases' that year. In his 1866 report he noted a substantial increase in the number of offences against the liquor licensing laws, attributing it to the fact that the police department had taken over the job of enforcing those provisions from the inspector of licences. This was a comment, then, on more efficient policing rather than on an increase in the actual level of offences. He did not comment on the dramatic fall-off in such cases in 1874, however. Some of the chief constable's explanations seem to bear realistically on the figures he presented; others seem specious and self-serving.[24]

Nevertheless, the statistics reported in Tables 2 and 3 are useful in showing the caseload of the police court and the principal matters with which it dealt. There is obviously ample scope in the surviving records of this court for detailed quantitative research on crime, policing, and the local administration of justice. Such questions do not figure very prominently in the remainder of this essay, however. Instead, it is concerned with the ambience of the court, with the ways in which it was perceived and interpreted by the newspapers, and with the place of these perceptions and interpretations in the mid-Victorian social imagination.

THE AMBIENCE OF THE COURT

Majesty

The eighteenth-century assizes described by Hay conveyed the lesson that the law was majestic through the pomp and ceremony that attended the opening of the sessions, the spectacle of ritual and dress, the eloquence of judge and counsel, and the awful sublimity of the ultimate pronouncement of sentence on those who were to hang. By contrast, there was little that was majestic about the Toronto police court.

To begin with, its physical surroundings were better calculated to inspire nausea than awe, less by virtue of any criminological theory of deterrence than because the city council, always anxious to minimize the tax bill, sought to keep maintenance and building costs to a minimum. Thus in April 1854 city council heard a representation from police magistrate George Gurnett that 'the Police Office, particularly when occupied by a considerable number of persons, many of whom are in an uncleanly condition, became so fetid and oppressive as to be palpably and seriously felt by all who inhale it, and especially by that gentleman himself, and that his medical adviser ... ascribed his recent indisposition to that cause.' A month later council voted $30 to make repairs. The court was held in a room at City Hall overlooking the main fruit and vegetable market, which contributed its share to the noise and effluvium. In 1861 Gurnett, still concerned about the 'atmosphere ... exceedingly deleterious and prejudicial to the health of the parties whose duties require their attendance therein,' prevailed upon council to move his court to the hall of the old Mechanics' Institute building. Once all the furniture had been transferred to the new location however, the magistrate was prevented from using it pending further deliberations in council. In the meantime he held court in what had been his private office, a room about ten feet square: 'The Magistrate occupies a seat at a table in front of the door, while the Clerk is crowded into a corner, and has an article like a packing-box for a desk. Standing on the floor in front of the 'bench,' or ranged round the room, are to be seen Aldermen, Councilmen, policemen, prisoners, witnesses and the general public, with a couple of reporters vainly endeavouring to take notes amid the general confusion.'[25]

The final move to the Mechanics' Institute did not come until September 1863, but Gurnett was no longer alive to enjoy it. There were still many defects and within a year a new ventilator had to be installed. Complaints about the effects of the general stench upon public health were still aired regularly, although when they reached the council agenda early in 1866, one alderman complained that it was the first he had heard of the problem. Council permitted certain improvements, including a coat of paint, but put off others 'to a more convenient season.' More substantial and apparently satisfactory renovations were conducted later that year, and the fact that Gurnett's successor, Alderman George Boomer, had died in the interim to be succeeded by Alexander MacNabb, suggests either that new brooms swept clean in the literal sense, or that council was momentarily shocked into releasing funds by fear that the unsanitary conditions of the court had contributed to the incumbent's demise: as late as 1877 *The Globe* was attributing the high rate of judicial mortality to the foul air in courthouses.[26]

Despite the 1866 renovations, by 1869 the police commissioners were negotiating to transfer the police court to the old Recorder's Court quarters in the County Council building: 'The present Police Court and offices become unfit for occupation in summer, owing to the presence of the stable for the fire-engine horses underneath. The Council have refused to remove these, and the Commissioners take the only course open to them – to leave.' The court remained in its old quarters, notwithstanding the fire horses or the large hole 'in which a man might be buried,' which had appeared in the sidewalk immediately outside. 'The place smells like a pest-house from the stables underneath, the strong-scented many inside, the privies behind, and the conglomeration of dirt and filth of all kinds deposited in front and rear of the court house building.' A general renovation was authorized in April 1871, but the spring cleaning was less than thorough. 'The cage has been scoured,' *The Globe* reported, 'and the accumulated dirt of many months has been partially washed away, but the vile odours resulting from defective ventilation still remain.' Police Magistrate MacNabb, 'overcome by the bad air,' announced in December 1873 that 'the stench of the place was most abominable' and barred spectators from the court. Two months later the Chairman of the Board of Health stepped in, giving orders 'for a plentiful supply of chloride of lime with which the place is to be sprinkled every day to destroy the noxious effects of the poisonous atmosphere which exists. The use of the disinfectant has to a certain extent made the place more bearable, but the place is a disgrace to the city, and should be done away with as a court for the majesty of the law to be exercised in.' Two weeks later the pestilence was unabated, and lawyers scheduled to appear stayed away until the very last moment, some of them having to be sent for before charges could be heard.[27]

Magistrate MacNabb could tolerate only a few weeks of this, declaring early in June that he would not hold the court in its usual place until improvements were made: in the meantime he toured the police stations, dispensing justice on his daily rounds. This had relatively instant effect. On Christmas Eve *The Globe* was able to report the laying of the cornerstone for a new building to house the police court and the fire department: it took pains to point out that the latter's stable was to be 'entirely separated from the other portions of the building.' The new court was opened for business early in February 1876, and the press was generally approving of all features except the accommodation supplied for the reporters themselves. Only one serious cause for complaint remained: whenever the bells of St James' Cathedral chimed, the court had to suspend its proceedings on account of the deafening noise.[28]

The physical inadequacies of its various quarters aside, other features of Police Court life hardly contributed to an air of majesty. Hay makes much of the robes, furs, and wigs with which the functionaries of his assizes bedecked themselves. There was nothing of this in the Police Court, whose magistrates did not require counsel to wear robes. A minimal standard of propriety was, however, expected: on one occasion Gurnett found it necessary to reprimand a barrister, saying 'you should not come here attired like a waiter at an hotel.' Similarly, the learned eloquence of counsel and judge in Hay's assizes had no counterpart in the Police Court, where tempers seem frequently to have been lost and magistrates usually had little patience with lengthy disquisitions. The worst offender in this respect was the barrister R.M. Allen, who made the magistrates' lives miserable throughout much of 1857 with his allegations of a judicial conspiracy against him. On one of these occasions the mayor, sitting in place of Gurnett, was led to comment that the magistrates had formed the collective opinion 'that your conduct in the matter throughout, has been very disgraceful.' This led to the following exchange:

Mr. ALLEN. – I respectfully submit you are not competent to give an opinion upon my professional conduct.
The MAYOR. – I cannot allow you to proceed, Mr. Allen. I decline arguing with you.
Mr. ALLEN. – I repudiate your authority to criticize my conduct as a barrister.
The MAYOR. – It will be for barristers to say that.

Then in 1859 a quarrel between Allen and James Boulton led to the first of these 'legal luminaries' rising in open court to call the second a 'd—d coward' and challenge him to a duel. 'Not alone do scenes of this nature occur very frequently, but the Magistrate himself has often to submit to the insults of these gentlemen.' When Allen repeated his antics before magistrate Boomer in 1864, he was fined for contempt. 'Hardly a day passes without a *fracas* occurring in this court between the lawyers,' *The Globe* complained, 'and it is high time that something was done to stop the disgraceful scenes.'[29]

A year later, the same newspaper concluded that the problem was a thing of the past. 'Professional bickerings were at one time rampant, and the magistrate required the tact and skill of "a country dominie" to keep the unruly "limbs of the law" within the bounds of decency and self-respect, but latterly a trifling "scene" only now and again occurs.' This may have been somewhat premature, as a *Leader* report for 1869 suggests. Magistrate MacNabb had adjourned a case until the attendance of a particular witness could be arranged, whereupon counsel demanded to know the witness' name and whether he had been subpoenaed to appear:

His Worship – you have no right to ask that question, Mr. McKenzie.
Mr. McKenzie with great warmth asserted his right not only as a Queen's Counsel to appear and defend or prosecute a prisoner, but also to put any pertinent questions connected with the case in which he was engaged.
His Worship retorted as warmly that he had no right, but was there by courtesy – a courtesy which had always been extended by him, and which therefore had been greatly abused and misconstrued.
A lengthy wordy war ensued, which was ended by the adjournment of the case until Thursday.[30]

Nor were the police magistrates especially interested in the technical niceties. This tendency was most pronounced in the person of Colonel George T. Denison, who became police magistrate after MacNabb's resignation in May 1877. Denison had no use for precedents. 'To save time,' he recalled, 'I used to chaff lawyers wanting to read them, saying, "Why read me another judge's opinion. If it agrees with my view, what is the object? If it takes a different view, why should I follow another man's mistakes?"'[31]

Denison's concern with saving time points to another contrast with Hay's assizes, where effective stage management could endow the awful moment of pronouncing sentence with the maximum of suspense and emotional impact, contributing materially to the experience of the law's majesty. In the Toronto Police Court there was little time for such high drama. It was not unheard of for as many as eighty cases to be considered and disposed of in a single day. Some flavour of the pace of the proceedings is captured in this reporter's reconstruction:

SERGEANT – *solemnly* – bring in the next prisoner.

SOMEBODY ELSE – Quickly and mixing up the Christian surnames – 'Srynohalran,' which being interpreted, may or may not be held to mean 'Sarah Anne O'Halloran.' Srynohalran is brought into court.

1ST REPORTER – What's the name? Did you catch it?

2ND DITTO – Why, no.

1ST DITTO – Bother!

2ND DITTO – Ask somebody. Ssshssh (in a shrill whisper). Say, Boardman, what's the prisoner's name?

BOARDMAN – Don't know. (Turns away thoughtfully and considers).

1ST REPORTER – Look here. I *must* get that name.

POLICE MAGISTRATE – Next case.

SERGEANT – Mumble, mumble, mumble.

BOARDMAN (to 1st Reporter) – What was that woman fined?

2ND REPORTER (disdainfully) – Pooh! who cares.

1ST REPORTER – Oh don't bother, I haven't even got her name yet, and here's the next case.

POLICE MAGISTRATE – (To witness who is whispering in his ear.) – 'You say that the prisoner' – mumble, mumble, mumble – and writes rapidly.

1ST REPORTER – Joyfully seizing the pause rushes precipitately to the Clerk's desk to get the name of the last prisoner.

CLERK & MAGISTRATE – (Simultaneously) – Five dollars or (mumble) days – can't give it you now; don't you see I'm busy – wait til after the court. Nexpresar.

REPORTER confusedly retreats and is appalled to see another wretched being placed in the prisoner's box. Being a new hand he desperately dashes his pencil on to the ten inch board which serves for a desk and fervently ejaculates 'I'm blest; what a Court!'

2ND REPORTER, consolingly – Nothing when you're used to it. Take it coolly. It's the same every day. You'll catch something or other bye and bye, and can easily imagine the rest; why its –

A VOICE, apparently underground or up in the ceiling, or somewhere far off – mumble dollars or thirty mumble.[32]

The press itself hardly contributed to the aura of the court. *The Globe* once remarked rather hypocritically that the fact that police courts were 'not very suggestive of that dignity and majesty which usually attach themselves to the administration of the law,' was due in some degree 'to that class of American journalists who, in their "enterprising" efforts to amuse their readers, have made this tribunal a special fountain from which has flowed the bucolic streams of the most ghastly humour that ever deluged a laughter loving people.' This was the same paper that could on another occasion pose the query 'whether the Court is a place where bad jokes are perpetrated, and justice burlesqued, or a place where offenders are placed on their trial for public offences, and then and there awarded the punishment due to their sins.' The press was less prone to hold the magistrates in awe than in ridicule. Thus MacNabb was variously referred to as 'the pascha' and 'the khadi,' while his surrogate, Alderman John Baxter, was 'His Serene Highness' or 'His Serenity.' On one occasion *The Globe's* police reporter was inspired to this piece of Tennysonian doggerel:

Up near the justice seat, where the reporters meet,
in paper collars neat, gathered the lawyers; but in
the vestibule, which to its best was full, stood
Drummers top-sawyers. And from the seat on high,
where with a beaming eye, the beak sat to try, all who
had blundered, came the old sentence that leads to
repentance, $3 or 20 days, while the crowd wondered.[33]

Occasionally this general sport of twitting the magistrate and his court gave way to more serious attacks. During the interregnum of Boomer's final illness, when his duties were carried out by Aldermen Vance and Canavan, *The Globe* alleged 'that the Police Magistrate is utterly unable to perform the most ordinary duties of his office, and the law which he administers is daily brought into contempt by his incapacity ... The Attorney General knows as well as we do how dangerous it is in this country to bring the administration of justice into popular contempt; and we assure him it is done daily in the Police Court of this city.' The Tory *Leader* actively campaigned against MacNabb's appointment, saying 'he is of a dismal disposition, and is nursing the bitterness of the curse of deferred hope.' Were he to get the job, the newspaper charged, it would be due solely to the exertions of his brother-in-law, a Reform member of the legislature. 'If we must have a Clear Grit appointed, let us have one who is respected.' During the Toronto printers' strike of 1872, when *The Leader* alone among the local newspapers supported the strikers' cause, it was especially vociferous in attacking MacNabb for the sentences he awarded to printers convicted under the Master and Servant Act. Under the heading, 'Judicial Tyranny,' it compared him to 'the infamous Judge Jeffreys,' accused him of 'vindictiveness of purpose,' and convicted him of 'haughtiness of manner and brutality of language.' In 1875, angered by MacNabb's leniency towards prisoners who committed their offences while under the influence of liquor, *The Globe* let it be known that 'the vagaries of our Police Magistrate are becoming so offensive and so frequent that they call for very thorough investigation at the hands of his superiors – His rulings have been so often grotesquely absurd, and his sentences so conspicuous in their lenity, and severity too, that one has often wondered how he ever was thought of for such a place, and still more how he has managed to keep that place so long – Very much, we believe, through the misdoings of this official, Toronto has become a hissing and a bye-word throughout the Province.'[34]

The various magistrates occasionally attempted to discipline the reporters but with little success. When Vance ventured to remark on some inaccuracies, he was more or less flatly contradicted. On one occasion MacNabb lectured the Police Court reporters for having questioned his judgment in a bawdy house case, threatening to exclude them from the court if similar insinuations were made in future. *The Globe* made light of the rebuke, referring to the magistrate as 'His Mightiness' in a report under the headline, 'A Breeze in the Police Court.' *The Leader* went so far as to read the bench a lecture in return:

however wise his worship might be as a magistrate, he was not competent to instruct reporters for the press in their duties, and he [the reporter] certainly would give little heed to lectures from the bench upon that point. It was a matter altogether foreign to the business of the court, and in England stipendiary and other magistrates frequently avowed that they could exercise no supervision or control over the reporters of the press and could have nothing whatever to do with them. The same doctrine held good here ... Such lectures were simply waste of words, for his worship could not expect that the reporters would pay the slightest attention to them. The matter then dropped.[35]

What little dignity might have been left to the court after its physical shortcomings, lawyers' tantrums, and press japes was further diluted by the antics of its spectators. Hay reports of his assizes that 'tradesmen and labourers journeyed in to enjoy the spectacle, meet friends, attend the court and watch the executions.' The Toronto Police Court was the common resort of the unemployed and, to the despair of the public health authorities, the unwashed. 'If there is one place more than another which is a somewhat sure indication of the state of the labour market, it is a police court, for whenever there is a slackness of trade, the police court is always attended by a large crowd of spectators.' Until 1865, when it was finally forbidden, the hangers-on crowded even inside the bar, making it 'almost impossible for either barristers or the reporters of the city dailies to attend to their business, or for the magistrate to hear the various cases properly.' *The Globe* engaged in phrenological speculations about the onlookers and sketched their characteristics:

All classes are represented. Bounty jumpers dressed to perfection in their latest style, with patent leather boots, and breeches with a check as large as a good sized plate, a gold chain dangling across a flashy vest and rolls of greenbacks sticking out of their pockets; young lads who are galloping along the road to sin; old men whose 'sands of life will soon run out,' and others who have brought themselves to the lowest ebb of poverty by their love of alcohol. Ex-gaol birds also put in an appearance, and with a decided compassion for the prisoner in the dock they vent their hatred of the magistrate with a muttered curse.

This was not a passive audience. The crowd cheered its heroes, hissed its villains, and left its seats to clap acquitted comrades on the back. Nor was it an all-male company. Particularly when a charge of soliciting was to be heard, the court would be crammed with 'Babylonians' in full regalia. From time to time a magisterial warning that unless the noise subsided the court would be cleared produced a version of order, but the lull was always temporary. The crowd's purpose in attending was complex: partly for warmth, partly for comradeship, and, in great part, for sheer fun.[36]

Some idea of this aspect of the court may be gained through an account of Alexander MacNabb's rather quixotic sortie against the unwashed in the early months of 1869. Among the collections of Irish hovels and tenements that were to be found in the city's side streets and back alleys, two had achieved some prominence for their rivalry. The inhabitants of Stanley and Dummer streets formed a regular part of the audience at the Police Court, and both groups had natural leaders jocularly referred to as their mayors. For some time MacNabb had been deploring the presence of 'so many lazy, good-for-nothing loafers hanging round this Court from day to day, to the number of 200 to 300,' and early in February 1869 he was sufficiently disgusted to attempt a remedy. He ordered the police to admit to the court only those who had business to transact and others who were dressed respectably. This announcement was met with 'rebellious groans,' and the following day 'the Mayor of Dummer street, determined not to forego his customary morning's amusement, appeared in full toggery – black swallow-tail and black pants, with his face cleanly washed, and nicely shaved, looking the very picture of modesty, sobriety and innocence.' Then for several days it appeared that MacNabb's stratagem might be effective. The rival mayors, 'thoroughly disgusted at the ostracism of their fellows,' stayed away. But MacNabb shortly left on one of his numerous vacations, and his surrogate, Alderman Baxter, concerned about the legality of excluding the public from the court, relaxed the rule. 'The Stanleyites and Dummeronians who have no such "rig" in which to vest themselves are jubilant, and earnestly pray that Mr. MacNabb's advent may be indefinitely prolonged.' When MacNabb returned he had to rescind the order. The Stanleyites and Dummeronians had no hard feelings:

The crowd outside this morning awaited the arrival of his Worship with great impatience. It was rumoured that he was going to try the 'Velocipede,' and Mayor Murphy got the b'hoys together to notice the working of the machine. It did not arrive, however, but his worship did on foot, and was lustily cheered as he passed along, when it was understood that the unfavourable weather and the disgraceful state of the streets had prevented him from making trial of this model locomotive.

What magisterial 'ukase' failed to accomplish was supplied some months later by defects in the Police Court's plumbing. 'The court room was as cold as charity is said to be, and the regular hangers-on cleared over to the assizes, which is kept warm and comfortable.'[37]

Justice

This second component of the ideology of eighteenth-century English criminal law was founded, in Hay's analysis, on the constitutional principles that offences must be fixed, rules of evidence carefully observed, and the bench both learned and honest. It was put on public display at the assizes through judicial solicitude for the rights of the accused and an extreme regard for procedural formalism. The lesson that English justice was impartial and no respecter of persons was inculcated by the widespread publicity afforded the occasional sensational case in which men of rank and wealth were convicted of serious offences and treated with exemplary severity. While Hay notes the gradual emergence in the eighteenth century of a conception of justice as 'rational, bureaucratic decisions made in the common interest,' he stresses that Englishmen on the whole continued to think of justice in personal terms, 'and were more struck by the understanding of individual cases than by the delights of abstract schemes.'[38]

In many respects the appearance of justice was as significant in the proceedings of the Toronto Police Court as in the eighteenth-century English assizes. There are clear parallels to be drawn; but there are also important reservations to be made. A matter of emphasis must be decided. When the press criticized the Police Court system for failing to realize the objective of impartial justice, which is of more importance: the alleged failure, or the scales in which it was measured? It is at any event necessary to remember, in what follows, that justice remained a compelling by-word for all that it was occasionally more honoured in the breach.

That procedural formalism was not the strongest suit of the Police Court has already been suggested. Informality had several aspects. It was inherent in the court's heavy caseload and the rapid pace of proceedings that this necessitated. It was reflected in the magistrates' impatience with the long-winded arguments of some members of the bar. Sometimes this informality was carried to unusual extremes. 'Business was speedily despatched this morning, there being no lawyers, no reporters and no audience. His worship [MacNabb] being bent upon a day's pleasure of another kind, and unable to secure the attendance of his worthy deputy, who had a "previous engagement," visited the different police stations at six a.m., had the prisoners before him, and then and there, without interventions of any kind, pronounced their doom.' Procedural defects were sometimes cured by higher courts. Thus in March 1869 *The Globe* reported that two prisoners had been released by Judge Wilson on an application for *habeas corpus* on defects in the warrants of commitment. Where the city bylaw prescribed penalties for offenders found drunk and disorderly in a public place, the warrants failed to specify 'and disorderly.' In one of the cases Judge Wilson decided that a police station was not a public place for the purposes of the bylaw. *The Globe* suggested that there were some fifty prisoners in the city jail on defective warrants.[39]

While the Police Court was normally the scene of quick justice, complaints were occasionally heard about excessive remands and adjournments. These were particularly pronounced in MacNabb's court. 'Many, indeed most, of the parties who move in a respectable sphere complain loudly of the protracted consideration given to their cases by the police magistrate,' reported *The Leader*, 'but their protestations are to little purpose. Until his final decision is given he is as absolute an autocrat in his own court, as any Czar or Amurath who ever lived, and prisoners generally fare worse who by themselves or through their counsel declare they are ready for trial, and wish to have their cases decided without an adjournment.' But justice delayed might be justice denied, and MacNabb in particular was found wanting for his irregular hours and frequent vacations. The fall of 1869 saw a regular press campaign on these points. It began with *The Globe*'s complaint that 'the crowd at the Police Court this morning were kept waiting upwards of half-an-hour. It was surmised that the wet weather had probably detained His Worship, but the weather was also an additional reason in the mind of those attending why they should be kept in the rain as short a time as possible.' Then *The Leader* noted that 'the Police Magistrate has gone to London – his deputy cannot be found; and, consequently, the services of [Alderman Riddell] had to be brought into requisition. Fortunately for him, the calendar was a light one, and none of the prisoners were charged with either murder or robbery. It was Alderman Riddell's maiden session, so to speak, and he was very merciful.' A few days later *The Globe* was acid in its comments about MacNabb's lateness, which in this instance amounted to his non-appearance. Alderman Riddell finally appeared to replace him an hour and a half after official opening time.[40]

In *The Globe*'s litany of charges against MacNabb in 1875, his frequent absences and their consequences for the availability of justice played a part:

He has been in the habit of taking holidays at all times of the year, – stumping the country sometimes for teetotalism, and sometimes for railways, whose bonuses were secured, if all accounts were true, by the liberal employment of bad whiskey and other equally objectionable stimulants. Had he on these occasions left any decent substitute in his place, the public might have been thankful for the change. But it is notorious that those who were promoted to the honour have not only been ludicrously and profoundly ignorant of the very first rudiments of the English language – in fact, unable to understand the simplest terms in not only medical testimony, but in testimony very much more intelligible. If anything could bring our Police Court into more absolute contempt than that into which it has fallen in its now normal condition it would be to have such exhibitions as were made, for weeks upon weeks, of ignorance, insolence, and general incapacity, in the course of the present summer. It was a place, then, to make those who had the veriest smattering of law stand aghast, and those who had still the least remnant of shame hang down their heads. And it is so still.

In this light, the boast of Colonel Denison, MacNabb's successor, that he had 'never been one second late in going on the Bench in the morning' and had never missed a day in more than forty years assumes a significance that at first glance might seem unwonted.[41]

It was not merely the alleged incompetence of aldermanic replacements that threatened justice but their partiality as well. Until 1851 the functions of police magistrate were carried out by the mayor and aldermen sitting in their capacity as city justices of the peace. In that year the position of stipendiary police magistrate, appointed by the provincial government but paid by the city, was created. Aldermen retained the right to sit with the magistrate, however, and, as we have seen, were called upon to serve in his absence. This system gave rise to several problems. Aldermen were jealous of their judicial power, they were prone to intervene on behalf of their political supporters, and they sought on occasion to use the power of the purse to control the stipendiary magistrate. All of these had the potential to bring justice into disrepute.

Conflicts over the judicial power of the aldermen were most pronounced in the early years of the stipendiary system. Thus in 1855 one Alderman Carr arrested and imprisoned three suspects in a hotel robbery. When they were brought before Gurnett, the stipendiary magistrate, he released them on bail pending trial. It appears that the three left town. Carr was enraged and moved in council for the production of the documents in the case. Gurnett replied explaining his actions and noting that the papers 'had most unaccountably disappeared from the files in the Clerk's office.' This hardly satisfied the alderman, who 'stood up [in council], and with much indignation, said it was a piece of impertinence, or something very nearly allied thereto, for the Police Magistrate to send such a document to that Council ... Such a thing was, he thought, a disgrace to the city ... He was surprised that Mr. Gurnett should again attempt to rule that Council in the way he had always ruled it – as Police Magistrate and as Mayor of the city. But he, for one, was determined to do his duty fearlessly; and he would not submit to be ruled by any one.' All this was to little avail: council at this point went into committee of the whole on the Bill for the Reorganization of the Fire Brigade, and the matter seems to have been dropped.[42]

Aldermanic interference on behalf of constituents was a more serious and frequent matter, and one that persisted as an intrinsic part of the Police Court system until at least the late 1870s:

Were a stranger to look at the bench some morning he would suppose that all the judicial wisdom of the land was situate in the craniums of those who are seated there right and left of the Police Magistrate. Far from it however. The centre gentleman is the respected Police Magistrate, who rattles through his work in a business-like manner, and with an amount of discretion and good judgment highly creditable; but the 'associates,' as they are politely termed, are nothing more or less than a few of our city fathers who have come on the bench, either that the *hoi polloi* may see that they are attending to their magisterial duties or are on hand to influence the bench in behalf of a 'decent fellow' who 'voted for me' at the last election, but who unfortunately managed, at a 'late hour last night' to knock an unoffending citizen down and nearly kill him.[43]

The Globe was urging the abolition of the magisterial jurisdiction of aldermen as early as 1865, when it took Vance and Canavan to task for releasing a local distiller on bail. 'Why these two men should have thought proper to interfere in the case, when the assault charged upon Halliday was committed more than 200 miles away, and far enough beyond the magisterial jurisdiction of Toronto aldermen, we are unable to say.' This instance, *The Globe* complained, was 'only one of scores of illustrations of the evils of the present system ... For years it has been the practice of certain aldermen to interfere in this way, and release friends who happened to fall into the hands of the police.' But it was not only when they took their seats on the bench that the aldermen interfered in the impartial administration of justice: they relied as well on their control of the magistrate's salary to influence his decisions. 'For a magistrate to be dependent on a city council for the amount of his stipend is an arrangement almost certain, more or less, to affect his independence,' hinted *The Globe*, 'or to lay him open to the suspicion of his independence being affected.' Once again in this respect Colonel Denison appears (at least in his own recollections) as the great reformer:

For the first few days after my taking up the work the entrance to my private office was blocked in the morning by a number of plaintiffs and defendants, intending to continue a custom which had been long in existence, of interviewing the Police Magistrate about their cases beforehand. They were usually provided with letters from aldermen telling the magistrate what to do in their cases. I stood in front of my door and as each letter was handed to me I opened it in the presence of the others, glanced at it hurriedly, and told the bearer to tell his alderman to come and give his evidence in open court under oath, and I would then tear the letter up in the presence of them all. As the aldermen at that time had the control over my salary, I felt it necessary to take a very firm stand at the outset. It only took about a week to stop that practice.[44]

Another feature of the aldermanic system, and one from which Denison was seemingly not exempt, was the practice of petitioning the council executive for remission of fines imposed by the police magistrate in bylaw cases. Although the city solicitor had given it as his opinion that council had no power to remit fines in most circumstances, the question remained an open one. Petitioners could be persistent:

Some weeks ago I spoke to you about a poor German named Hains who was fined because his wife sold a glass of lager beer which had been left after one of the club meetings held at his house. I also explained the hardship of the case to the Finance Committee and was under the impression that the fine ($11½) with the exception of that part going to the Informer would be remitted. I have just been informed however that a summons has been issued against Haines [sic] and I fear the poor people will have all their earthly goods seized unless you will be kind enough to being the matter before the Committee again ...

Well into the Denison magistracy, the executive committee of council was corresponding with the police magistrate requesting details of convictions where petitions for remission of fines had been received. Unfortunately, Denison's replies have not survived.[45]

The city fathers' occasional willingness to forego fines must be set against their vigilant attention to Police Court finances. They were reluctant to dip into the treasury to maintain the court's fabric, as has already been seen, and they were correspondingly eager to ensure that none of the court's receipts should escape the Chamberlain's grasp. From time to time the latter predilection led to muted aspersions on the honesty of the magistrate and his subordinates. News that the auditors had discovered serious shortfalls in the court's account led to an attempt to launch an investigation of 'malfeasance, breach of trust or other misconduct' at a council meeting in January 1867. The question was postponed until the full report had been printed, but in the meantime the press had a field day with the revelations of what *The Globe* repeatedly referred to as 'gross irregularities' in the way the Police Clerk, J.F. Nudel, kept his books. When the matter came to council again in March, there was another attempt to institute an immediate investigation. But the report had not yet been printed, and several aldermen pressed for delay. A motion to this effect was adopted, although not until it was admitted that the auditors' report had been 'mislaid.' Were the report not to be found, predicted one member at the close of the debate, the charges would never be investigated. Events proved him correct.[46]

A year later the issue was joined again, although under slightly different circumstances. One of the city's numerous publicans charged that MacNabb was in the habit of splitting the fines received in liquor cases between himself and George Mason, a private detective who specialized in acting as informer (and, it would appear, provocateur) in violations of the liquor laws; he had a small sideline in bawdy-houses cases as well. The charge was brought before city council, where a battle ensued over whether it should be referred to the Recorder's Court. MacNabb's supporters opposed the motion on the grounds that he was 'one of the most upright and efficient incumbents of that position'; his detractors supported it because he made 'unjustifiable attacks on the professions, members of the [city] corporation, and ministers of religion.' The matter was compromised with an amendment asking the Recorder to investigate all charges against all city officials – and this six months before the Recorder's Court was to be abolished.[47]

The inquiry began late in June with MacNabb's preliminary objection that the court had no jurisdiction over him. Recorder Duggan ruled that he had jurisdiction, treating the city corporation as the prosecutor, but counsel for the city declined to press the charges. The investigation was postponed two or three times at the request of the tavernkeeper who originated the affair. It ultimately collapsed because the latter insisted on having all charges against city officials heard, as the council resolution had provided, while the Recorder refused to entertain any charges but the one initially made against MacNabb. *The Globe*, which at this point was supporting MacNabb, crowed that the prosecution was a farce and the charges against the police magistrate 'virtually declared to have been without foundation.' It would be closer to the truth to say that the investigation was simply inconclusive; that it had fallen victim to the usual obscurantist machinations within council. Detective Mason received his come-uppance several weeks later at the hands of MacNabb's surrogate, Alderman Baxter, who had supported the stipendiary magistrate during the council debate. When Mason refused to yield two arrest warrants against bawdy-house keepers to the police for execution, Baxter committed him for contempt and sent him to the cage for an hour while the warrant was being made up. Mason was 'led away ... gnashing his teeth in the most savage manner, and growling under his breath like an encaged hyena.' It was surmised that his motive in retaining the warrants was to extort payments from the accused in return for withholding his testimony.[48]

This was hardly the end of the affair. In November 1869 two aldermen briefly tried to open an investigation into renewed charges of peculation in the Police Court, but without success. Then in 1871 George Mason himself applied to council for permission to examine the Police Court books, alleging that sums due him as informer were not being paid: in 1873 he launched a suit against the city for the money he alleged was owing. In the meantime council ordered an independent audit of the Police Court accounts for several years past, but it appears that this initiative was not wholeheartedly supported by the whole body, for there is correspondence from the auditor, W.R. Hughes, complaining that the Mayor was attempting to deprive him of his office and bookshelves. This investigation appears to have dragged on in a dilatory fashion for several years. In 1876 a correspondent wondered aloud in the columns of The Globe, 'what has become of the Police Court books and their auditors?' The following year MacNabb communicated to the 'Official Investigation Committee' his thoughts about how Police Court records might be kept, along with other reforms. Once again, however, the issue of possible malfeasance was never resolved, for early in May MacNabb resigned.[49]

What part the renewed investigation played in this decision cannot be satisfactorily determined. MacNabb gave as his reason for stepping down the inadequacy of his salary. But it is noteworthy that in the council debates of 9 and 20 April, when salaries for the year were being determined, no attempt was made to increase the police magistrate's stipend, although such motions were made on behalf of almost every other civic official and were in many cases successful. MacNabb had put in a written request for a salary increase in January, pointing out that the jurisdiction of his court had been enlarged in 1875 so that he had power to try prisoners on any charge within the jurisdiction of the quarter sessions, providing the accused consented: this had 'greatly increased my duties and is a great saving to the City saving the expense of trial by Jury.' Moreover, he complained, Gurnett had received at least $600 a year in salary and fees more than he was receiving. Council's conspicuous silence on this matter seems significant, as does the fact that MacNabb did not appear in court on the Monday following the Friday on which the salary bill was adopted, nor on any subsequent day: his resignation was formally received by council on 7 May. It is possible that the city politicians chose to prod MacNabb into resigning on the face-saving issue of his salary rather than drag out a series of charges against him in the wake of the official investigation. *The Globe*, as has already been seen, was armed with a quiver of complaints against him, and none of the papers expressed any surprise or curiosity at his resignation.[50]

On 9 May *The Globe* offered some thoughts on the proper qualifications for a new magistrate, including an increase in salary, and when it said that 'it is indispensable that the City Magistrate should be one against whom slander itself has breathed no suspicion; whose name could never be associated with the idea of a bribe, and who could not only say "these hands are clean," but could have both friends and foes implicitly to believe that they were,' it was rather transparently reflecting on MacNabb's alleged shortcomings. Once again the self-congratulations of his successor may be taken as an allusion to MacNabb's contrary propensities. 'The question of salary did not weigh with me a particle,' wrote Denison. 'I have always felt that the pecuniary side of any question should not be allowed to have undue weight ... I refused, as I have said, to act as president or director of any company ... I also decided to take no fees. I have a great aversion to the fee system; in time it is sure to bring the pendulum off the plumb. A man acting in a judicial capacity should have nothing to affect him, pecuniarily or otherwise, in deciding either way.'[51]

That procedural formalities were frequently shunned in the Police Court, and that the honesty and independence of its magistrates were rather readily thrown into question, suggest some significant differences between it and the eighteenth-century assizes. Some other features of Hay's delineation of justice are really not susceptible to comparison. The ideological importance he ascribes to the occasional punishment of upper-class offenders has no obvious counterpart in the Police Court, unless we are to stretch the point to include the outraged protestations of leading citizens who were fined for failing to clear the snow from the sidewalks outside their homes: it can be imagined what delight such scenes must have afforded the Stanleyites and Dummeronians. But the magistrates, at least when they were acting in their judicial, as opposed to their ministerial, capacity, had nothing to do with very serious crimes. In some other respects, though, the Police Court conception of justice did seem to run in tandem with Hay's assizes.[52]

The eighteenth-century judges' concern with protecting the rights of the accused certainly had its counterpart in the Police Court, at least in the public statements of its officials. MacNabb felt some discomfort at having to act as 'advocate, judge and jury' in many cases and suggested the appointment of a prosecuting attorney to relieve him of the conflict. Denison relied heavily on his intuitions as to whether the accused was guilty or not, rather than on 'weighing and balancing the evidence.' When neither intuition nor evidence served, however, 'I give the prisoner the benefit of the doubt, if I am still doubtful.' While these statements hardly show the magistrates bending over backwards to be fair to the accused, they do suggest that they understood justice to include a degree of solicitous concern for the rights of the prisoner. Their willingness to adjourn hearings to permit the attendance of witnesses and to extend the 'courtesy' of representation through counsel, both of which have already been instanced, are more tangible indications of the same thing. Unfortunately, the detailed accounts of particular determinations that can be garnered from the press are not very helpful in assessing this issue. That in itself may be of some significance, of course, from the standpoint of understanding the ideology that legitimized the law. We are on somewhat firmer ground in attempting to characterize the practice of justice in the Police Court, as between 'rational, bureaucratic decisions made in the common interest,' and a personalistic conception determined more 'by the understanding of individual cases than by the delights of abstract schemes.' But here we are on the borderline between justice and mercy, and before proceeding it is as well to consider that final component in Hay's ideological trinity.[53]

Mercy

The availability of the pardon permeated eighteenth-century criminal law and contributed enormously, in Hay's analysis, to its legitimation. The closest equivalent in the Toronto Police Court was likely the remission of fines by council, a matter we have already discussed. But in the same area and of greater significance was the wide discretion exercised by the magistrate in sentencing offenders. Whatever limits the case law might have attached to the magistrate's discretion to dismiss a case, it is evident that personalistic and indeed paternalistic considerations were deeply embedded in magisterial practice. Magisterial leniency served as an object lesson in the law's mercy, that it could understand force of circumstance in bringing citizens to the breach and was prepared to show forgiveness in the face of repentance.[54]

The largest single category of offenders brought before the police magistrate was the 'drunks and disorderlies,' and some of their experiences will serve to illustrate this aspect of the law. Consider the cases of two 'respectable topers' who appeared before MacNabb on the same August day in 1868. The first denied that he had been drunk, 'but admitted that he might have been a little overcome, and probably, under the excitement, had rather disturbed the peace.' MacNabb declared that he had no sympathy with the likes of him and sentenced him to pay $5 or spend fifteen days in jail. The second well-dressed offender 'admitted his offence, alleging in excuse that he was just out from England, and was not aware of the effects of the liquor sold here.' In the face of this admission of guilt, MacNabb discharged him with a warning to leave Canadian whiskey alone. Similar circumstances prevailed with MacNabb a few months later:

George Fowler, an agriculturist, who had left his fruitful fields and lowing herds to study human nature in the city's throng, had, in the pursuit of his investigations, been obliged to make an experiment as to the relative strength of forty-rod and tangle-leg, the result of which experiment staggered him. As he was a philosopher, the Pacha discharged him, with instructions to return to his native vale, where magistrates cease from troubling and peelers are unknown.[55]

Nor was it merely the respectable and propertied who on occasion found themselves the subject of magisterial benevolence. 'Old offenders' were sometimes discharged upon their promise to leave the city forthwith. Alternatively, when they pleaded readiness to leave town as soon as the weather made it possible, they might be remanded (presumably in custody) until the elements were favourable. The magistrate's willingness to extend mercy sometimes seems to have had more to do with his own circumstances than those of the accused. On one red-letter day in 1865, when the dock was almost empty and the clerk 'came within an ace of having to invest a dollar and honour the Magistrate with a pair of white kids,' there was a single drunk called upon to appear. Alderman Vance, 'who had a streak of pity for the old reprobate, kindly dismissed him with instructions to shun whiskey, and try even at this late day, with his face furrowed by the ravages of drink, to become a decent member of society.' The Leader ascribed Alderman Baxter's benevolence on another occasion to his recent vacation:

He has had a lengthened sojourn among the Redskins – camping out under the broad canopy of heaven by night; luxuriating in fishing, bathing, mining exploration and agricultural prospecting by day – and pronounces the country around the Upper Lakes fertile, luxuriant and rich in the extreme. This perhaps accounts for the extreme leniency the worthy justice showed towards several of the very hard cases brought up before him, and his disinclination to enter upon serious business until after visiting his friends, and hearing how his colleagues at the City Hall have faired [sic] and been working during his absence.[56]

Sometimes judicial leniency could be abused, however. Thus Magistrate Boomer announced from the bench his intention of inflicting fines in every case where the costs might be collected: 'He had been lenient lately, but order must be kept in the city, and he would deal severely with all offenders against whom a charge has been sustained.' In a similar vein MacNabb marked his accession to the magistracy 'in a praiseworthy and businesslike manner, in giving the vagabonds and disorderlies who haunt the city plenty of time to repent within a pristine looking building.'[57]

In 1875, as we have seen, The Globe attacked MacNabb for his leniency in sentencing prisoners who committed their offences while under the influence. The newspaper postulated that the magistrate's personal predilection for a prohibitory liquor law disposed him to deal lightly with offenders on the theory that 'the citizens may become so disgusted with everything connected with whiskey that they will vote Prohibition pure and simple.' It seems more likely, however, that MacNabb's practice was not the 'deliberately arranged Machiavellian plot' that The Globe claimed to discern, but a merciful exercise of discretion in sentencing that differed only in degree, if at all, from that of his predecessors. Nor was his successor any different in this respect. Denison's comments on the Toronto Ministerial Association's lobbying of the police commission, for example, are scathing: 'I have found many of these really worthy people, in well-meaning enthusiasm, and forgetting the example of their Master, who told the woman to go and sin no more, urging the most severe punishments on people who, if erring, were certainly unfortunate and to be pitied.' What may have been at issue, for both *The Globe* and the Ministerial Association, was precisely a conception of justice as rationally and bureaucratically administered on behalf of the larger (ie, 'respectable') community, as opposed to the benevolent paternalism of the magistrate who put the circumstances of the individual case before the abstractions of the law. Certainly this is hinted at in *The Globe's* complaint against MacNabb: 'We in our simplicity have been in the habit of thinking that a judge's business was to adminster the law as he found it – not to exercise the dispensing power of the Sovereign in order to set it aside, or the enacting power of the Legislature in order to have it changed.'[58]

If the newspapers stood ready to condemn the exercise of magisterial discretion as a deviation from even-handed formalism, rather than to celebrate it as the triumph of compassion over unfeeling rigidity, their stance was not without a certain ambivalence. For these same newspapers, as we shall see, frequently exhorted their readers to feel pity for the 'unfortunates' who occupied the police court dock. In the admittedly unusual circumstances of the 1872 printers' strike, *The Leader's* attack on MacNabb ended by predicting that 'the Police Magistrate must feel – if he has any such noble trait as feeling in his constitution – that there is reserved a day not far off, which will bring to his conscience the reproach of administering justice without mercy.' Indeed, there was a measure of ambivalence, although of a somewhat different cast, in what the press had to say about majesty and justice as well. The administration of the law *ought* to have been majestic, but it assuredly was not. Justice was certainly looked for, but often in vain. Thus what Hay discerned to be the first two components of the ideology of the law in the eighteenth century retained a certain poignancy in the Toronto Police Court reportage of the nineteenth. The difference was this: that what in the earlier period was taken to have real presence had now become a more shadowy and insubstantial ideal from which the perceived reality was distressingly distant. It would be a mistake to say, then, that the ideological configuration which Hay found so pronounced in perceptions of his assizes was wholly lacking where the Toronto police court was concerned. By the same token, however, the pointed contrast of the real with the ideal in press reports of the Police Court could hardly be taken to legitimize its conduct in the way in which active perceptions of majesty, justice, and mercy fostered consent and submission to the eighteenth-century terror.

In part this difference is an artifact of an important divergence between this analysis and Hay's. He was concerned to explain the apparent submission of the 'mass of unpropertied Englishmen' to the criminal law, while this treatment of the Police Court has relied very heavily on reports in the local press. But the Toronto press was not addressing an audience of the unpropertied: their experience of the Police Court was not mediated by newspaper reportage; it was direct, for they were the typical accused, or the Stanleyite spectators, or both. The newspapers' readers, who only saw the court through the reporters' eyes, belonged to a different stratum. They were the 'respectable and well-conducted portion of the community' who, *The Leader* considered, desired efficient policing of their city.[59] There will be more to say about the 'respectable classes' below: here it is necessary only to bear in mind that if the newspaper reports of the Police Court constituted a form of ideology, its intended consumers were not the equivalent of Hay's dispossessed. Thus far we have dealt for the most part with *what* the newspapers had to say to their readers about the Police Court. If we are to penetrate to a fuller understanding of the ideological bearing of those reports, we must shift focus somewhat and turn in our analysis from what the newspapers had to say to *how* they went about saying it. Here we must consider a metaphor and its audience.

THE POLICE COURT AS THEATRE

City council, neither for the first nor the last time, was debating the goings-on in MacNabb's office. The mayor was vainly trying to cut off discussion, when Alderman Strachan insisted on taking the floor. 'But I want to know from the Chairman of licenses,' he protested, 'whether there are licenses for the exhibitions reported at the Police Court. The curtain is reported to rise and drop daily. Can the Council not get a ticket to the show?'[60]

No metaphor was used more persistently by the newspapers to describe the Police Court than that of the theatre. Commenting on the adjournment of an important case, *The Leader* recorded that it 'was only formally opened – the afterpiece and farce being postponed.' When the reporters prefaced their lists of the day's appearances with a general commentary on some aspect of the court, they generally marked the transition with the formula, 'the curtain rises,' or, 'the play commences,' and, as we have seen, their reports sometimes took the form of dialogues, with full stage directions. The court was said to be a place where justice was 'burlesqued' and where 'scenes' were played. *The Globe* once ran a piece of more than 1500 words, devoted to exploiting the metaphor. 'Much more might have been said of the Police Court,' it concluded, 'but perhaps enough has been given to show that one need not go to New York or London to see what is styled in popular parlance – "Low Life" as it may be seen in all its degradation, and misery, and vividness, any morning in the Magistrate's room in Court street.'[61]

The theatre, of course, is not an uncommon metaphor for many aspects of social life; indeed, it might be argued that it is a metaphor in reverse, for one of the functions of theatre is to represent life. Again, the fact that it came so readily to hand could be taken merely to underscore how trite and cliché-ridden much nineteenth-century journalism was. But we might arguably go behind this view and take the reporters at their word. For we have already seen that the Police Court was crowded with spectators, who saw it as a show; and something of the same fascination must have gripped the newspapers' respectable readership, those who would never permit themselves to be seen mingling with the Court Street rabble, if we are to explain the amount of space devoted almost daily to court report-age. If the metaphor is to be accepted, then, we might proceed within its terms to ask what species of theatre this was, and what its audience found there to attract it. The answers to these questions should inform the earlier one: what ideological uses were made of the Police Court experience?

While the reporters wrote in passing of 'burlesque' and 'farce,' their more detailed musings on the workings of the Police Court show these terms to be inadequate in describing the genre. In some respects the court was seen to display a rapid succession of circus acts and music hall turns. What all of these have in common is the stock simplicity of stereotyped characters. The portrayals of the Police Court, as we shall see, relied heavily on this convention. But taken as a whole, its dramaturgy belonged to a single identifiable genre (and one that frequently incorporated bur-lesque, farce, the circus, and the music hall). The Police Court was a theatre of life, and its repertoire consisted in the main of melodrama.

As many recent writers on the subject have noted, melodrama today is frequently a term of abuse. That is not the sense intended here. Instead, melodrama may be seen as a legitimate literary genre, of which there are superb examples as well as bad ones, with its own conventions and form. Its characters are essentially types: they are 'monopathic,' to use the language of one critic; 'the characters have no interior depth, there is no [internal] psychological conflict ... What we have is a drama of pure psychic signs,' to quote another. The conflict that actuates melodrama, then, is not an interior one, a warring within the self – this is one of the features distinguishing the genre from tragedy – but is externalized. Melodrama is an expressionist form and its conflict is Manichaean: the extremes of good are pitted against the extremes of evil, and no compromise is possible between them. Melodrama is the drama of secular morality, and its central thrust is to 'locate and articulate the moral problems in which it deals':

Ethical imperatives in the post-sacred universe have been sentimentalized, have come to be identified with emotional states and psychic relationships, so that the expression of emotional and moral integers is indistinguishable. Both are perhaps best characterized as moral sentiments. ... The play's outcome turns less on the triumph of virtue than on making the world morally legible, spelling out its ethical forces and imperatives in large and bold characters.

'They are sermons in dialogue,' wrote an early critic. 'If they are not a true picture of life, they show, at least, what life itself ought to be.'[62]

Certain expressionist conventions characterized melodrama as a theatre of excess, of the larger than life. Histrionics and broad gesture are part of the stereotype of this theatre of stereotypes. It was enlivened by the antics of clowns (frequently stereotypical Irishmen and Negroes in the American examples) and the plot was moved along by a succession of improbabilities, to be resolved more often than not by the forced coincidence of a recognition scene or the timely intervention of a deus ex machina. The pleasures of melodrama resided in the release of pure emotion, for which the various characters stood as simple signs, and in the imaginative liberation from the anxieties of choice and self-doubt afforded by the conventional externalization of inner conflict. Only in melodrama is man essentially 'whole' and uncomplicated; only in melodrama can moral conflict be resolved through emotional release. Melodramatic resolutions tend to be comfortable ones: 'The issue here is not the reordering of the self, but the reordering of one's relations with others, with the world of people or things; not the knowledge of self but the maintenance of self, in its assumption of wholeness, until conflicts are won or lost.' The appeal of melodrama as a cultural form, and its limitations, can be seen in this contrast with other genres:

The fall of the tragic hero brings a superior illumination, the anagnorisis that is both self-recognition and recognition of one's place in the cosmos. Tragedy generates meaning ultimately in terms of orders higher than one man's experience, orders invested by the community with holy and synthesizing power. Its pity and terror derive from the sense of communal sacrifice and transformation [cf. Hay's assizes]. Melodrama offers us heroic confrontation, purgation, purification, recognition. But its recognition is essentially of the integers in combat and the need to choose sides. It produces panic terror and sympathetic pity, but not in regard to the same object, and without the higher illumination of their interpenetration. Melodrama cannot figure the birth of a new society – the role of comedy – but only the old society reformed. And it cannot, in distinction to tragedy, offer reconciliation under a sacred mantle, or in terms of a higher synthesis. A form for secularized times, it offers the nearest *approach* to sacred and cosmic values in a world where they no longer have any certain ontology or epistemology.[63]

The final section of this essay must return to questions of cultural criticism. The task here, though, is to re-examine the Police Court reportage to show how its use of the theatrical metaphor leads to its generic identification with melodrama, considering questions of characterization, of conflict, of resolution, and of the 'moral sentiments.' But a word of caution is required. The police court was not a theatre: it was only, and metaphorically, *like* a theatre. Metaphors inform but they can also mislead. We would search in vain for a complete realization of the melodrama in the proceedings of the Police Court. What was most lacking, of course, was the fully worked-out plot. To yield to the metaphor, what the Police Court offered was not the whole play but merely certain scenes. Those scenes, however, were unmistakably samples of the genre, and the observer, so long as he was attuned to the formulaic regularities of the type, could sufficiently imagine the drama of the whole.

We have already met one troupe of stock characters, the clowns. They were generally graced with the features of one or another stereotype: the bibulous, garrulous Irishman; the naïve hayseed; the comic Negro.[64] But from time to time the reporters managed to convey their sense that there was something more at issue in the Police Court than the comic low life interlude. Thus *The Globe's* police court reporter commented on those who attended the theatre to laugh and to thrill at absurd plots, grotesque dénouements, and predictable pratfalls: 'But the strange thing is that, as a rule, those people, and many people besides, fail to see anything interesting in the many-phased life which is plotting or scheming, or groaning, or sinning, or dying around them on every side.' The writer went on to contrast the drama of real life with the 'absurdities' of the theatre: but the incidents of real life, as he listed them, read more like a catalogue of stock items in the melodramatic horde. 'The history of the haggard despairing wretch, who rises of a morning and blows his brains out; or the plot of the scheming financier, who by some adroit manipulation at one sweep sends poverty, and sorrow, and woe into the abode of the widow or orphan; or the snivelling fool, whose life is one long series of foolish bets; or the poor, homeless, friendless, hopeless wretch, who prowls about the streets in the dark cold nights, with her hand against every man, and every man's hand against her – are objects which are of very little interest to them, but after all they form an essential part of what goes to make up life.' There are a number of points about this extraordinary sentence which deserve consideration.

First, of course, is the virtual hopelessness of the attempt to contrast life and the theatre, when life itself is presented in the full bloom of the rhetoric of melodrama. For these are not people the reporter is describing, but the stereotyped characters of the stage. They are precisely 'mono-pathic signs,' standing for one or another of the moral sentiments, as the very nouns and adjectives employed make plain. The cardboard cut-outs bear their labels plainly: Weakness, Villainy, Helplessness, Foolishness, Innocence Defiled. By the same token, they are less characters than they are extreme situations. And each entry in the catalogue calls up a story, each captures a scene from the melodrama. Nor should it escape our attention how this catalogue incorporates the stock stage directions and attitudinizing. But what is perhaps most noteworthy – and it is a point to which we shall have to return – is the reporter's last statement: 'they form an essential part of what goes to make up life.' There is no possibility of change; the universe is fixed in its constituents. The characters are objects of 'panic terror' or of 'sympathetic pity,' and for this alone, he plainly implies, they require our interested observation.

His failed contrast between the theatre and life at an end, the Police Court reporter proceeds to portray some of the action and dialogue. But once again his rhetoric is purely melodramatic, and he is concerned to draw the same responses from his audience as any playwright in the genre. Take just one example from the several he provides; the next prisoner has been called to enter the dock:

This is a girl of sixteen, whose form, and face, and eyes, and hair combine to make her positively beautiful – and when she appears, a stranger would naturally enquire, What can that young creature have been about to make her liable to be brought up here? But it is the old, old story. 'She's only two days out of gaol; and last night she was very drunk and riotous, your Worship, and using very profane language on the street.' Poor thing! she, too, begs hard for a 'chance' – and who would refuse her one, if there was any hope for her getting out of the fatal vortex in which she stands? But how can she? She gets a chance and descends the stairs, and 'she calls for help, but there is none to save her.' The world's sympathies are hermetically sealed against her, and the only resort she has is to throw herself once more into the foul dens always ready to open their doors to such as her.

Once again a pasteboard silhouette, and an assurance that change is not to be looked for. And so it goes with the entire list: the hardened prostitute; the habitual drunkards; the 'most terrible and startling object of all ... a young man, well educated, well trained, and once a well-beloved son; he might have been an ornament to his family and a useful and respectable member of society, but how terribly he has thwarted his destiny'; the wife beater; the gambler; the 'rough'; and the children: 'their position is, in the circumstances, the most natural thing in the world.'

Nor was this the only exercise of its sort. Seven years later *The Globe* published another column which had much the same things to say: the same contrast between superficial hilarity and 'unqualified wretched-ness,' the same catalogue of stereotypes (this time, subspecies of the genus 'drunk'); the same emphasis on female virtue defiled ('those depraved wretches whom to call woman would be to outrage every sentiment associated with that name'); the same 'terrible sight' of the respectable fallen. The only novelty to enter this account is the picture of the Police Court as 'a half-way house at which young men not irretrievably lost make up their minds either to turn back or to join the regular army of drunks' – and here, the melodramatic scene is made complete with the addition of 'a pale-faced, respectable looking woman, dressed in black, standing among the unwashed crowd behind the bar, and regarding the case with the painful anxiety with which only the mother of perhaps a widow's only son can regard what is to her and to him such a momentous issue.'[65]

Full-dress essays like these were admittedly few. On the one hand they are exceptional; on the other, they provide the matrix into which we may fit the less-considered remarks and incomplete sketches which proliferate in the daily Police Court columns. When the categories have been assimilated, small allusions illuminate a universe of understanding: the drunk, 'whose grey hairs were a sorrowful spectacle in the prisoner's dock'; the respectably dressed mechanic of whom the magistrate remarked, 'it was disgraceful to see a man of the prisoner's appearance in the dock'; the woman who patiently waits, 'to get a warrant against a cowardly son, who has so far forgotten himself as to strike his mother'; the 'apparently exceedingly modest young woman, clad in half-mourning,' but charged with prostitution. The language of the Police Court reporters was the language of melodrama, and the sense that they made was in their appeal to the melodramatic imagination. It remains to consider what purposes this served.[66]

IDEOLOGY AND CULTURE IN MID-VICTORIAN TORONTO

We enter now upon what must be the most tentative phase of this inquiry, the attempt to chart the structures of the mid-Victorian social imagination. There are few signposts to aid us here, for not only is there little Canadian scholarship to draw upon for this purpose, but the available language of analysis itself seems crude and inadequate. Ideology, with its connotation of a systematic and holistic body of thought, may be too constraining a concept, while at the other extreme culture seems too diffuse.

The most sophisticated attempt to discover a language for such a project is surely Raymond Williams', whose phrase, 'structure of feeling of the period,' manages both to capture the regularity and pervasiveness with which certain cultural themes appear and to emphasize that what is often at issue is not so much explicit doctrines of social thought as a 'pattern of impulses, restraints, tones,' of nuance and affect. But Williams' phrase has clustered about it its own connotations – of an analysis grounded in studies of imaginative literature and focusing on intergenerational differences – that make it less than wholly satisfactory for our purposes. These purposes are twofold: we must first seek to understand how the respectable Torontonians of our period made sense of the society in which they lived, and then step back to inquire with the advantages (and limitations) of hindsight what sense that sense may have made. To put it somewhat differently, the first step is to describe some elements of a world-view; the second, to assess what ends these may have served. With this we shall have returned to the question of ideology, at least to the extent that the term implies that particular interests are served, that ideas or modes of thought have a social function.[67]

The contemporary project of making sense of one's society was perhaps especially pressing for the Victorians. Indeed, a pre-eminent international student of the period, Asa Briggs, has suggested that 'Victorianism' itself is best seen as 'an attempt to come to terms with a society still in flux ... to uphold values, including old values, which often seemed precarious and insecure; to discover and perpetuate elements of permanence in the world; and to provide elements of unity where very frequently there was division of interest.' Undeniably, Torontonians experienced rapid and often disquieting change in the period considered here. It had its material indices in the near trebling of the city's population between 1850 and 1880, and in its transformation from a commercial and service centre to an industrial metropolis. It had its social counterpart in the respectable classes' explosion of concern about urban crime, poverty, and ignorance, and in the institutional remedies they erected to meet them. Central to this changing image of the society, according to Susan Houston, was the 'critical transition from a perception of the seasonality of poverty to an apprehension of a permanent class of dependent urban poor,' a transition which has elsewhere been explained in terms of the experience of coping with the massive Irish famine immigrations of the late 1840s. What makes the new perception so critical to an understanding of the period is the 'gulf' that it seemed to reveal 'between the respectable classes who define what society is and the disreputable elements who exist beyond their reach.'[68]

Closely related to this new perception of their society as a house divided was a fundamental ambivalence experienced by its respectable members. In seeking to make sense of their situation, they found themselves equating the very forces which they believed must make for progressive social change with the sources of social disorder and threat. Elsewhere I have suggested this to have been the case in attitudes towards the propertyless labourer: an ample supply of wage workers was considered to be the sine qua non of future prosperity, while at the same time the unpropertied were viewed as potentially criminal for lack of a stake in the social order. Alison Prentice makes much the same point in her study of Ontario school reformers in this period:

They believed that vast numbers of Upper Canadians had come to the country ignorant; that the increasingly urban environment somehow encouraged their depravity; and that the growing competitiveness of the economy, the need for local self-government and the threat of crime, meant that Upper Canada could no longer allow them to remain in this state. But the glorious future held out for Canada was nevertheless one of growth: economic growth, the growth of population, cities and towns. If rapid growth and change, immigration and urbanization were the root causes of apathy and social disorder in the province, most educators did not wish to dwell on this fact. These, after all, were the very changes that they were busy promoting.[69]

Two avenues were followed to explain away this contradiction that lay at the heart of the mid-Victorian world-view. The first was to turn attention away from the material changes in the society as causes of social unrest by emphasizing instead 'human weakness and inadequacy.' Thus Houston notes that with the realization that there existed a permanent pool of the unemployed, a new social category, 'pauperism,' was invented to explain and confine it. 'Unlike poverty, which is a material condition, pauperism denotes a moral and psychological state which simultaneously explains the phenomenon it defines ... Certainly, by the 1860's Torontonians regarded the problem of urban poor to be of *class* in scale and scope, although not in any modern sense a problem of industrial and economic organization. While the scale was one of class, the condition of the individual members of that class stemmed not so much from sociological causes as from their individual moral qualities.' The second avenue intersected the first: it was the strategy of resolving the contradiction by transcending it through the creation of institutions – schools, prisons, reformatories, asylums – that 'ought to be and could be better than the society which created them.'[70]

During the period of this study, 'the social landscape of Ontario was fundamentally transformed ... by the setting in place of institutional structures which both mirrored and maintained distinctions of social class and condition. Institutions classified their inmates, frequently creating whole new categories of social beings and patterns of behaviour by virtue of their existence ... Upper Canadians started to erect the scaffolding of a modern society by objectifying fundamental structural inequalities in institutions for all sorts of people and problems.' But as this project proceeded, it came to centre on shaping children, particularly the children of the poor, in the respectable image of the desirable citizen. It seemed so much easier to form the next generation than to reform the existing one. 'The training and disciplining of children ... appeared the only effective antidote to what reformers regarded as the moral weakness endemic to the lowest elements in society which endangered the social order.' What of these children's parents? More explicitly repressive solutions seem to have been found for the problem of the irredeemable present generation. Concern about the innate criminality of the unpropertied worker was met by the re-enactment in 1847 of a master and servant law that provided imprisonment for disobedient employees. The Toronto police force was reorganized and placed on a professional and militaristic basis in the 1850s. Indeed, the reorganization of the Police Court, with the appointment of a full-time stipendiary magistrate in 1851, and such subsequent reforms as the appointment of a regular deputy and the broadening of the court's jurisdiction, might well be seen as aspects of this larger pattern.[71]

These concerns, ambiguities, and responses can be situated within a

broader setting. The predominant cultural mode of mid-Victorian Ontario, as William Westfall has argued, was romanticism, an outlook founded in dualism and yearning towards transcendence. The principal duality
was that of the real and the ideal, the mundane and troubling world of
everyday life contrasted with the what-might-be. In the third quarter of
the nineteenth century this romanticism was built on individualistic
premises, reflected in the evangelical movement as well as in the emphasis
on personal responsibility that motivated the categorization of such social
problems as 'pauperism.' Later, in the emergence of the Social Gospel and
other forms of sociological reformism, it was to be transformed in its
emphasis to the collectivity. Romantic dualism appealed because it took
into account the respectable classes' profound disquiet with many of the
features of the world as it was: 'obsessive materialism,' the increasingly
patent division of society between propertied respectability and filthy
poverty, the growth of crime. Dualism provided a dramatic and, as I shall
argue shortly, an essentially comforting, framework within which to
express these accumulated concerns and fears. Thus the pursuit of
material well-being was set in opposition to spiritual and intellectual
attainment: the issue was one as between barbarism and civilization. 'In
the turmoil of business, in the scramble for wealth and power, how are the
affections neglected! How do we trample upon man's higher and nobler
nature!' Similarly school reformers equated the conflict of virtue and vice
with the dualism of education and ignorance, as in Egerton Ryerson's
claim that to fail to send children to school was to 'train up thieves and
incendiaries and murderers.'[72]

Melodrama was an obvious expression of this dualistic romanticism,
and it is within this cultural mode that the representation of the Police
Court as melodrama becomes explicable. The lessons of melodrama, as we
have seen, went to the reordering of one's relations with the world, to the
recognition of Manichaean conflict, and to the need to choose sides. But
melodrama was not concerned with reshaping the world or the self: above
all it was a drama of *recognition*. What the respectable readers of *The Globe*
and *The Leader* found in the Police Court column was, first of all, a picture
of 'low life' that was contrasted with, and in direct opposition to, the lives
they led themselves. They were afforded the opportunity to experience
'panic terror' and 'sympathetic pity,' not to mention a good deal of
laughter, and all of these emotions served further to set apart the world of
the Police Court from the world in which they moved. Above all, then,
they received daily affirmation of their comfortable place in the social
order, and a justification of it in the irreconcilability of opposites. For

these readers, the Police Court melodrama legitimized their social situation, because it transcended in its externalized Manichaean conflict the contradictions within their society and the doubts and disquiets within themselves.[73]

These considerations should help us to understand why it was that the press, in all its descriptions of the Police Court, consistently refused to countenance the possibility that it might serve as an agent of individual or social reform. Vice, said the reporters, forms 'an essential part of what goes to make up life'; it is the 'most natural thing in the world.' 'One might as well impress a man with the necessity of paying his tailor's bill as try to reform some of those bright blossoms of poverty, drink and misery, who daily frequent our Police Court.' The only exceptions to this rule were those of the respectable accused: the young man of good education who stood at the crossroads when he stood in the dock; the well-dressed mechanic who had no business appearing on a drunk and disorderly charge. One of the social functions of the Police Court, as it was portrayed by the newspapers, was to mark off the gulf between the respectable and the disreputable. A member of the respectable classes might totter on the brink of the abyss – and here, it will be recognized, I am using a favourite metaphor of the temperance proselytizers – and he might save himself or he might fall. A secondary purpose of the reportage was to exert moral pressure on the readership to choose sides clearly and keep to the right: one useful index of the effectiveness of such pressure is the anguished appeal, rarely successful, to keep names out of the papers. But its principal purpose was to underline the recognition of separation between the respectable and the disreputable. There was, after all, no ladder upward from the abyss.[74]

Police Court reporting, then, took its place amid all the other manifestations of the mid-Victorian social imagination which I have discussed. It transcended the contradiction between the real and the ideal by joining in the postulate of a great gulf between two moral orders in society and firmly reinforced its readers' identification with the elect. It remains here to consider a final problem: the scope of 'respectability' itself, and hence something of the dimensions and meaning of mid-Victorian understandings of class divisions.

'Respectability' was compounded of both moral and material constituents. Material definitions seem to have been uppermost in the mind of one travel writer in 1840, who said of Toronto that 'a great portion of its inhabitants are respectable, which, according to the witness upon a late trial, is anyone who keeps a one-horse chaise.' If this was a common understanding at the time, by mid-century the idea had become more complex. It was associated with such character traits as modesty, honesty, and kindness but, as Prentice suggests of the attitudes of the school reformers, 'visible signs too were necessary': 'The manifestations of respectability that they praised and promoted were refined manners and taste, respectable religion, proper speech and, finally, the ability to read and write proper English. In addition, both the concept and actual possession of private property were sometimes portrayed as distinguishing not only civilized from savage societies, but within a given social order, the respectable from the lower classes.'[75]

The word could be made, then, to embrace a broader segment of society than terms like 'middle class' or 'élite.' It incorporated professionals, merchants and manufacturers, small retailers, independent farmers, artisans, and skilled mechanics. It excluded, for the most part, unskilled workers, farmhands, domestic servants, casual labourers, and the impoverished lower orders in general. In the context of rapid social change, as Prentice points out, traditional occupational distinctions could become blurred, so that in the continuing process of technical adjustments to the concept's scope such indicia as the nuances of Police Court reportage played their part.[76]

Hay's account of the eighteenth-century English assizes postulated an ideological use of the practice of the law in legitimizing a system of rule based ultimately on terror to the dispossessed. This essay, on the other hand, has concentrated on the usefulness of one form of portrayal of the law in fostering the complacency of a group who, if they were not entirely society's oppressors, were certainly not its principal victims. We might characterize the rhetoric of melodrama in the Police Court reportage as being essentially ideological, to the extent that it served to vindicate the respectable classes to themselves and disguise the role of straightforward exploitation in generating social inequality. We can say little, though, about the non-respectable, whose direct experience finds few interpretable echoes in the Police Court columns: we cannot extend our analysis of a legitimizing function for the respectable to include the disreputable as well.

But perhaps this is to miss the point and to fall into the melodramatic snare of straining at extremes. For if we leave aside the 'miserable wretches' with whom the papers made such play, and look instead at the 'respectable classes' themselves, we may be closer to the ideological import of the reportage. In positing the dualism and dramatizing it in their columns, the newspapers were not only offering a form of self-justification for the respectable classes. They were at the same time forging and reinforcing that very category and endowing it with a special unity. But that unity was essentially specious. Farmer and merchant, manufacturer and skilled worker did not cohabit in easy amicability. They did not constitute a single social class with common interests and mutually compatible aspirations. No one knew this better and denied it more vociferously than the publisher of *The Globe*, George Brown, whose shop was struck by the local printers' union four times between 1853 and 1872 and who prosecuted employees before the police magistrate on several occasions in our period, in one case launching criminal conspiracy charges against the printers' vigilance committee. The printers, who had organized their union in 1832 'in order to maintain that honourable station and respectability that belongs to the profession,' had turned the rhetorical tables on their employer in an 1845 strike, claiming to 'maintain that which is considered by all the *respectable* proprietors as a fair and just reward.' But the pursuit of respectability and its most important material manifestation, home ownership, showed itself time and again to be an often effective obstacle to the emergence of working class consciousness in mid-Victorian Toronto. It certainly contributed to the failure of the nine-hour movement in 1872 as John Battye, quoting Oshawa and Hamilton newspapers, explains:

The acquisition of his own home was paraded before the workingman as being "the short road to independence." With such an acquisition the workingman was "strengthened in the consciousness of the possession of property" and he began "to experience the self-reliance and prudence of the capitalist." More importantly, such individual ownership was claimed as being desirable "because it aimed to make every man a capitalist instead of robbing those who are." Thus the illusion could be fostered of the workingman as capitalist, which was only a step from suggesting that the interests of the workingman and capitalist were identical.[77]

Perhaps the fundamental ideological significance of the Police Court reportage, then, was in its reiteration of a grand, melodramatic, and in the final analysis quite empty, antagonism of respectable and miserable, to substitute for the far more real and threatening conflicts that the evolving industrial society embodied. To this extent, the newspapers were eminently Victorian in Briggs' sense that they sought 'to provide elements of unity where frequently there was division of interest.' To this extent at least, the reportage was truly ideological, as Hay uses the term. 'The

Theatre, as affording representations of life, is very good in its way,' remarked George Brown's *Globe*, 'but the life it represents is rather an imaginary kind of substance, and bears very little relation to the actual course of affairs of the world.' If our speculations are not entirely wrong-headed, the same must be said of *The Globe* and its contemporaries.[78]

NOTES

An earlier version of this essay was presented to a seminar at the University of Winnipeg. I should like to thank the seminar participants for their helpful comments, as well as my colleagues, Doug Hay, Susan Houston, John Hutcheson, Peter Oliver, Dick Risk, Nick Rogers, and Tom Traves, all of whom read the paper in draft and made welcome suggestions. Of course, I remain responsible for its shortcomings. Rose Hutchens supplied dedicated research assistance, and The Osgoode Society provided generous financial support.

1 Paul Craven 'The Law of Master and Servant in Mid-Nineteenth-Century Ontario' in David H. Flaherty, ed. *Essays in the History of Canadian Law* 2 vols (Toronto 1981–3) I 175–211
2 This essay is based on two Toronto newspapers, *The Globe* and *The Leader*. Other Toronto newspapers, and newspapers in other Canadian and American cities, carried similar police court coverage. It appears to be one of the phenomena of the growth of a popular press in North America in the second half of the nineteenth century. For *The Globe*'s contemporary comment on the genre, see page 270 below.
3 For an intriguing glimpse of the place of such other nineteenth-century newspaper preoccupations as macabre deaths, bizarre accidents, and natural disasters in the social imagination of the time, see James F. Reaney 'Myths in Some Nineteenth-Century Ontario Newspapers' in Frederick H. Armstrong et al., eds *Aspects of Nineteenth Century Ontario: Essays Presented to James J. Talman* (Toronto 1974) 253–66.
4 Douglas Hay 'Property, Authority and the Criminal Law' in Douglas Hay et al., eds *Albion's Fatal Tree: Crime and Society in Eighteenth-Century England* (London 1975) 17–63
5 32 Geo. III (1792), c. 8 (jail and courthouse); 33 Geo. III (1793), c. 5 (marriages), 33 Geo. III (1793), c. 2 (parish meetings); 33 Geo. III (1793), c. 3 (assessment rolls and tax collection); 34 Geo. III (1794), c. 12 (tavern licences)
6 For the order to pay wages, see Craven 'Law of Master and Servant'; for

the court of requests, see J.H. Aitchison 'The Courts of Requests in Upper Canada' in J.K. Johnson, ed. *Historical Essays on Upper Canada* (Toronto 1975) 86–95.

7 2 Wm IV (1832), c. 4 (forms of conviction); 4 Wm IV (1834), c. 17 (fees); 4 Wm IV (1834), c. 4 (petty trespass); 7 Wm IV (1837), c. 4 (larceny); 4 & 5 Vict. (1841), c. 12 (returns of convictions); 4 & 5 Vict. (1841), c. 24 (administration of criminal justice); 4 & 5 Vict. (1841), c. 25 (consolidation re larceny); 4 & 5 Vict. (1841), c. 26 (malicious injuries to property); 4 & 5 Vict. (1841), c. 27 (offences against the person); 16 Vict. (1852), c. 178 (summary convictions); 16 Vict. (1852), c. 179 (indictable offences); 16 Vict. (1852), c. 180 (vexatious actions); for the subsequent Dominion legislation, annotated for the use of the magistracy, see S.R. Clarke *The Magistrates' Manual* (Toronto 1878). The various magistrates' manuals furnish a useful (but not always unimpeachable) guide to the criminal jurisdiction of the justice of the peace; besides Clarke, they include W.C. Keele *The Provincial Justice* (Toronto 1835), with revised editions in 1843 and 1851, Richard Dempsey *Magistrate's Hand-Book* (Toronto 1861), John McNab *The Magistrates' Manual* (Toronto 1865), and William H. Kerr *The Magistrate's Acts of 1869* (Montreal 1871).

8 Edith G. Firth, ed. *The Town of York 1793–1815* (Toronto 1962) xlviii-xlix; 57 Geo. III (1817), c. 2

9 Edith G. Firth, ed. *The Town of York 1815–1834* (Toronto 1966) lxxii, and Documents G1 and G14

10 Ibid. Document G14

11 4 Wm IV (1834), c. 23: the Mayor's Court was referred to as the 'City Quarter Sessions' by Alderman (later Recorder) George Duggan in the typescript Toronto City Council Proceedings, Toronto City Archives (hereafter TCA), 15 Mar. 1847, minute #46.

12 The surviving records of the mayor's court are to be found at the TCA in Record Group 7, Series E. They consist of one volume of Proceedings, 2 June 1834–4 Sept. 1838, and rough minutes, which include detailed transcripts of evidence, for 1837–41 and 1843–6, together with lists of tavern licences and petit jurors for 1840. Firth, ed. (*York 1815–34* lxxix) appears to confuse the functions of the Mayor's Court and the police magistrate when she follows her correct assertion that the former supplanted the quarter sessions with the statement that in 1851 'a police magistrate was appointed to take over the judicial responsibilities of the mayor and aldermen.' In fact, the Mayor's Court was supplanted by the Recorder's Court, and the police magistrate exercised a separate jurisdiction, as is explained in detail below.

13 Typescript Toronto City Council Proceedings, TCA 18 Mar. 1836, minute #178

14 'Plinius Secundus' *Curiae Canadensis, or The Canadian Law Courts* (Toronto 1843) 36–7
15 Toronto Mayor's Court *Proceedings*, Dec. Session, 1834
16 Typescript Toronto City Council Proceedings, TCA 10 Mar. 1845, minute #19
17 9 Vict. (1846), c. 70; the battle over appointment of a recorder can be traced in the typescript Toronto City Council Proceedings, TCA: see, to list only the opening salvos by way of example, 25 Oct. 1847, #259; 1 Nov. 1847, #263; 3 Jan. 1848, #290; 17 Jan. 1848, #298; 3 Feb. 1848, #312. There is a short account of the political opposition to George Duggan's candidacy for the post in Barrie Dyster 'George Duggan' *Dictionary of Canadian Biography* x (Toronto 1972) 262–3.
18 Typescript Toronto City Council Proceedings, TCA 13 Feb. 1849
19 12 Vict. (1849), c. 80 repealed the existing municipal authorities legislation; 12 Vict. (1849), c. 81 replaced them with a single general statute, coming into force on 1 Jan. 1850.
20 There is a good deal of confusion in the secondary literature about the function of the recorder's court. In part this may arise because the recorder in Canada East, for example in Montreal, exercised many of the functions exercised by the police magistrate in Toronto. Jesse E. Middleton *The Municipality of Metropolitan Toronto: A History* 3 vols (Toronto 1923) II 777, is in error in stating that it tried 'infractions of City by-laws,' and Dyster 'Duggan' 263 also has it wrong in saying that it tried 'minor civil cases.' There is a similar confusion in dating Duggan's appointment. Middleton has him serving from 1850 to 1867, and this error is repeated in several other sources. It appears to have originated in a clerical error made in compiling early lists of the city officials, and repeated in subsequent updatings; thus *The Members of the Municipal Council and Civic Officials of the City of Toronto, from the Date of the Incorporation of the City in 1834 to the Year 1870 Inclusive* (Toronto 1870) has Duggan serving as recorder from 1850 through 1867: the correct dates are 1851 through 1868.

Duggan studied law in York, and was called to the bar in 1837. George Gurnett was not a lawyer; outside of politics he had been a newspaper proprietor (if that can be considered to have been outside politics). He was born in Sussex in 1791 or 1792, emigrated to Virginia in the mid-1820s, and moved to Upper Canada later in the decade. He was appointed a magistrate for the Home District in 1837, the year of his first mayoralty, and shortly afterward Clerk of the Peace for the district, an office which he filled until the year of his death. He resigned from his seat as alderman for St George's ward in Jan. 1851 to accept the appointment as first stipendiary police magistrate, serving in this post until his death in 1861. For details on his extra-magisterial career see

Frederick H. Armstrong 'George Gurnett' *Dictionary of Canadian Biography* IX (Toronto 1976) 345–6, and the entry on Gurnett in T. Melville Bailey, ed. *Dictionary of Hamilton Biography* 1 vol. to date (Hamilton, Ont. 1981) I 89.

21 13 & 14 Vict. (1850) c. 64; 14 & 15 Vict. (1851), c. 109; 29 & 30 Vict. (1866), c. 47. The surviving records of the Toronto Recorder's Court, comprising two volumes of Proceedings and a group of rough minutes, are in Public Archives of Ontario, Record Group 22. The first volume of proceedings, beginning in Dec. 1848, starts with the continuation of the mayor's court under its new name, but still presided over by the mayor and one or more aldermen. Duggan presided in the absence of the mayor on 16 Oct. 1850. The first session to be presided over by 'His Honor the Recorder' took place on 13 Jan. 1851, when Duggan sat with one alderman. They swore in the grand jury and adjourned until Apr. 29 & 30 Vict. (1866), c. 51 (new municipal corporations act); 32 & 33 Vict. (1869), c. 32 (Dominion legislation on summary trials by recorders and county court judges)

22 38 Vict. (1875), c. 47 (Dominion); George Taylor Denison *Recollections of a Police Magistrate* (Toronto 1920) 7–8 comments on the increasing volume of business in the Toronto police court from the time of his appointment in 1877 and compares it to the caseload of other provincial courts and the police courts of London, England. There exists a broken but extensive run of Toronto police court proceedings, the Toronto Police Register of Criminals (together with warrant registries and alphabetical indices of accused persons), housed at the Toronto City Archives and at the Toronto Police Museum.

23 *Globe* 28 Feb. 1855; *Leader* 28 Feb. 1855

24 Report of the Chief Constable, appendix to Toronto City Council *Minutes* 1869 TCA; ibid. 1879; ibid. 1866; ibid. 1874

25 *Leader* 3 Apr. 1854, 17 May 1854; *Globe* 21 May, 16 July, 28 Aug., 19 Sept. 1858, 6 May 1862

26 George Boomer was born in Ireland in 1819 and came to Canada in 1832. He was a barrister and formed a law partnership with George Skeffington Connor. Boomer served as city alderman and was appointed stipendiary police magistrate upon Gurnett's death, serving in that office until his own death in 1865. Alexander MacNabb was a Toronto barrister who became the city's third stipendiary police magistrate in 1866. He resigned from the office in 1877, and died in California in 1907. MacNabb occasionally appeared as counsel in the police court in the years preceding his appointment as magistrate and following his resignation. *Globe* 5, 8 Sept. 1863, 11 Aug. 1864; *Leader* 28 Apr. 1865; *Globe* 6 Feb., 26 July, 17 Sept. 1866, 27 June 1877

27 *Globe* 14 May 1869; *Leader* 26 Aug. 1869; *Globe* 4 Sept. 1869, 8, 13 Apr., 1871, 7 Nov. 1871, 8 Dec. 1873, 16 Feb., 1874, 4 Mar. 1874

28 *Globe* 5 June 1874, 24 Dec. 1874, 26 Aug., 1875, 10 Dec. 1875, 8, 9 Feb. 1876, 13
    July 1876
29 *Leader* 28 Aug. 1857, 12 Oct. 1857, 21 July 1859; *Globe* 23 Feb. 1864
30 *Globe* 17 May 1865; *Leader* 18 Aug. 1869: for more on Allen see, inter alia, *Leader*
    25 June 1857, 4 Aug., 8, 9, 10 Oct. 1857; *Globe* 14 Dec. 1858; *Leader* 3 July 1860
31 Denison *Recollections* 10. There are several biographical treatments of the
    extraordinary figure, Colonel George Taylor Denison, cavalry officer, author,
    imperialist, lawyer, and Toronto's police magistrate from 1877 to 1921,
    including David Gagan *The Denison Family of Toronto* (Toronto 1973) and Carl
    Berger *The Sense of Power* (Toronto 1970). For a highly coloured journalistic
    account of Denison's court in later years than those covered by this essay, see
    H.M. Wodson *The Whirlpool: Scenes from Toronto Police Court* (Toronto 1917);
    Wodson was police court reporter for the Toronto *Evening Telegram*. A recent
    appraisal of Denison's court, based largely on his memoirs and on news-
    paper reports, is G.H. Homel 'Denison's Law: Criminal Justice and the Police
    Court in Toronto, 1877–1921' *Ontario History* LXXIII (Sept. 1981) 171–86.
32 *Globe* 1 June 1864, 25 Sept. 1869
33 Ibid. 20 Apr. 1876, 27 Sept. 1869, 2, 9, 7 Nov. 1868: the reference to 'Dummers
    top-sawyers' is explained below.
34 *Globe* 16 Dec. 1865; *Leader* 20 Dec. 1865, 6 Jan. 1866; 4 Apr. 1872; *Globe* 15 Oct.
    1875. I intend to explore the magistrates' attitudes to trade unions and labour
    relations in general in essays on collective prosecutions of workers, and on
    master and servant in the Toronto Police Court, currently in preparation.
35 *Globe* 30 Dec. 1865, 8 May 1867; *Leader* 7 May 1867
36 *Globe* 26 Aug. 1875, 27 Mar., 1865, 16 May 1865; *Leader* 29 June 1868, 20 Jan.
    1869, 4 Feb. 1869; *The Globe*'s comment about 'all classes' must not be taken too
    literally, as the list quoted suggests.
37 *Leader* 27 June 1868, 4, 9, 10, 16, 17, 22 Feb., 28 Oct. 1869. For MacNabb's
    reflections on the advent of the bicycle, see *The Leader* 20 Apr. 1869. For more
    on the Irish 'mayors' see Denison *Recollections* 178; for a description of Stanley
    and Dummer streets see Susan E. Houston 'The Impetus to Reform: Urban
    Crime, Poverty and Ignorance in Ontario, 1850–75' (PHD thesis, University
    of Toronto, Toronto 1974) 262–3. In his Report for 1869, Toronto's Chief Con-
    stable noted that nearly two-thirds of those arrested for larceny were con-
    victed, 'but of these many have been brought before the Police Magistrate
    several times during the year, having committed petty thefts, but under
    a charge of larceny. I refer to the young denizens of Stanley and Dummer
    Streets, many of whom have been charged at the Police Court with larceny, or
    suspicion of larceny, but being mere children were discharged by the Magi-
    strate, from the fact of there being no place for their confinement, but the Gaol;

and to have sent them there to associate with hardened criminals, would not have bettered their moral condition. Nevertheless, these infants have tended to swell the register of larcenies in the records of the Police Department.' (Toronto City Council *Minutes* 1870, appendix, Report of the Chief Constable)

38 Hay 'Property, Authority and the Criminal Law' 39
39 *Leader* 17 Aug. 1869; *Globe* 1 Mar. 1869
40 *Leader* 31 May 1869; *Globe* 9 Sept. 1869; *Leader* 24 Sept. 1869; *Globe* 27 Sept. 1869
41 *Globe* 15 Oct. 1875; Denison *Recollections* 13–14
42 *Leader* 4, 5 Sept., 1855
43 *Globe* 17 May 1865
44 Ibid. 8 Nov. 1865, 30 Oct. 1875; Denison *Recollections* 6–7
45 *Toronto City Council Papers* (TCA) Finance Committee Communications (1871) item 25 (city solicitor); (1865) item 33 (Todd to Smith); Executive Letterbook (21 Feb. 1876–23 Dec. 1889) items 13, 102, 106, 109, 125, 156, 164, 174: see also *Globe* 20 Feb. 1866; *Leader* 30 Oct. 1866.
46 *Globe* 15, 16 Jan., 1867, 21 Mar. 1867; 1 Apr. 1868
47 Ibid. 10 Mar. 1868; section 380 of the 1866 municipal corporations legislation empowered recorders, upon resolution of city council, to 'investigate any matter to be mentioned in the resolution and relating to a supposed malfeasance, breach of trust or other misconduct on the part of any member of the Council or Officer of the Corporation ...' with all the powers of commissioners of inquiry.
48 *Globe* 25 June 1868; *Leader* 1 July 1868; *Globe* 1, 11 July 1868; *Leader* 5 Sept. 1868
49 *Globe* 17 Nov. 1868; *Toronto City Council Papers* Finance Committee Communications (1871) item 68 (Mason); ibid. (1873) item 127 (Mason), item 4 (Hughes); *Globe* 7 Sept. 1876 (and see 18 July 1876), 28 Feb., 2 Mar. 1877 (and see 4 Apr. 1877)
50 *Mail* 8 May, 10, 21 Apr. 1877; *Toronto City Council Papers* Finance Committee Communications, 3 Jan. 1877 (MacNabb): MacNabb had asked for a salary increase in 1870 (ibid. 11 Nov. 1870) saying: 'At the time the amount was fixed at the present rate it was understood that I could at the same time practice my profession but the business of the Police Court is so great that it is utterly impossible for me to do anything at my profession for the last two years.' This request was unsuccessful, and MacNabb raised the matter again once the new council took office, apparently with the same result (ibid. 1871, item 9).
51 *Globe* 9 May 1877; Denison *Recollections* 4–5. MacNabb took fees from Police Court clients, as he told the official investigation committee (*Globe* 2 Mar. 1877). After his resignation, council resolved to lobby the provincial government to have it pay the magistrate's stipend (*Globe* 15 May 1877); if the attempt was made, it failed. See Denison's *Recollections*, ch. 16, on this matter as well as

on his own difficulties with council over payment of his salary (his claim that it weighed 'not a particle' notwithstanding). In 1868 *The Leader* editorialized about the need to require a property qualification for the police magistrate (thus echoing council's concern of almost twenty years before): 'It is not seemly that men should sit upon the Police Court bench who are bankrupt. It is not right that the administrator of the law should have shown so little capacity for work as to be unable to keep himself free from the operations of the 91st clause' (ibid. 8 Dec. 1868). There is no suggestion elsewhere in the press that MacNabb was facing bankruptcy, so *The Leader* may simply have been setting up a hypothetical case. On the other hand, it would not be inconsistent with the other evidence were MacNabb finding himself in some financial straits, and the unsympathetic *Leader* was fully capable of exaggerating this in its continuing campaign against the magistrate. Beyond this, the comment goes as well to a view upon which *The Leader* and *The Globe* were agreed, that the Police Court ought to be conducted in a 'businesslike' manner: this view is discussed below.

52 Denison *Recollections* 28. The distinction between ministerial and judicial capacity is that between the justice of the peace's duties in indictable and in summary cases: McNab *Magistrates' Manual* 4–5.

53 *Globe* 2 Mar. 1877; Denison *Recollections* 11–12; Douglas Hay informs me that MacNabb's discomfort about his multiple roles had its counterpart in England, where judges complained about having to present the case against the accused (by interpreting depositions sent up without counsel) when their traditional role was supposed to be acting on the prisoner's behalf.

54 Hay ('Property, Authority and the Criminal Law' 40) includes the discretion of the justice of the peace to 'compose quarrels, intervene with prosecutors on behalf of culprits, and in the final instance to dismiss a case entirely' among the elements of mercy.

55 *Leader* 15 Aug. 1868

56 *Globe* 7, 2 Nov. 1868, 8 May 1867, 3 Sept. 1868

57 Ibid. 6 Oct. 1863, 21 Mar. 1866

58 Denison *Recollections* 58; for examples of his leniency towards various drunks who were sufficiently well known to figure as local characters, see ibid. 185 ff.

59 *Leader* 10 Oct. 1865

60 *Globe* 17 Nov. 1868

61 *Leader* 3 Sept. 1868; *Globe* 16 May 1865, 25, 27 Sept. 1869; *Leader* 29 July, 9 Oct. 1857; *Globe* 29 May 1869. The theatrical metaphor has also been used by legal historians: see, for example, A.G. Roeber 'Authority, Law and Custom: The Rituals of Court Day in Tidewater Virginia, 1720 to 1750' *William and Mary*

Quarterly xxxvii (1980) 29–52. Roeber characterizes court day rituals as 'dramaturgical exercises' and expands the metaphor by calling components of them 'overture,' 'set,' 'stage,' 'spotlight,' 'act,' 'scene,' and so on. But it is important to emphasize a crucial distinction between his essay and this one. Roeber's use of the theatrical metaphor does not (so far as he tells us) grow out of the perceptions of his subjects; instead, he employs it self-consciously to elucidate their experience. It is *his* metaphor, not theirs. By contrast, here we are seeking to explain why contemporary observers of the court used the metaphor: it is *theirs*, and the task this essay sets itself is to explore how they used it, and what their use of it may mean. To use the dramatic analogy as Roeber does can be very effective, but it is subject to the same criticism that is levelled here at the nineteenth-century newspapers: that metaphors conceal as well as reveal, and that the limits and ideological contents of such analogies require exegesis.

62 R.B. Heilman *Tragedy and Melodrama: Versions of Experience* (Seattle, WA 1968) 85; Peter Brooks *The Melodramatic Imagination* (New Haven, CT 1976) 35, 42; *American Magazine* (Oct. 1788), quoted in David Grimsted *Melodrama Unveiled: American Theatre and Culture 1800–1850* (Chicago, IL 1968) 229

63 Grimsted *Melodrama Unveiled* ch. 8; Heilman *Tragedy and Melodrama* 86; Brooks *Melodramatic Imagination* 205

64 The 'Negro element' is treated as a conventional figure of fun in Denison *Recollections* ch. 8.

65 *Globe* 20 Apr. 1876

66 Ibid. 9 Sept. 1869, 19 May 1865; *Leader* 15 Aug. 1868

67 Raymond Williams employs the concept analytically in *The Long Revolution* (London 1965) 64–88, and places it in the context of cultural theory in *Marxism and Literature* (Oxford 1977) 128–35. My comments here are grounded in the extended discussion of the concept and its limitations in his *Politics and Letters: Interviews with New Left Review* (London 1981) 156–74 and passim.

68 Asa Briggs *Victorians and Victorianism* (Saskatoon 1966) 15; Houston 'Impetus to Reform' 5 (and see 267–9); G.J. Parr 'The Welcome and the Wake: Attitudes in Canada West toward the Irish Famine Migration' *Ontario History* LXVI (June 1974) 101–13

69 Craven 'Law of Master and Servant' 191–6; Alison Prentice *The School Promoters: Education and Social Class in Mid-Nineteenth Century Upper Canada* (Toronto 1977) 59

70 Houston 'Impetus to Reform' 267; Prentice *School Promoters* 46

71 Houston 'Impetus to Reform' 9–10, 413 (and see 269: 'By the 1860s, in Upper Canadian cities, the focus of reform enthusiasm had turned to the possibility of extracting the children of the urban poor from their demoralized environ-

ment and thus simultaneously eliminating the future of the lowest classes and salvaging a generation of future criminals and wastrels from their destined disgrace.'); Craven 'Law of Master and Servant' passim; Houston 'Impetus to Reform' 73–6

72 The argument about romanticism draws on unpublished work by William Westfall. The quotations, to be found in Prentice *School Promoters* 48, 51, are from *The Canadian Gem and Family Visitor* (1849) and the *Annual Report for 1848* of the Department of Public Instruction.

73 For the identification of melodrama as a romantic genre see Brooks *Melodramatic Imagination* 21–2.

74 *Globe* 15 May 1865. Appeals that names not be published were commented upon in passing from time to time by the newspaper reporters. Wodson (*Whirlpool* 34–8) spent most of a chapter on the phenomenon in his account of the later years of Denison's court.

75 Henry Cook Todd (attr.) *Notes upon Canada and the United States* (Toronto 1840) 76; Prentice *School Promoters* 68

76 *School Promoters*, ch. 4 ('Occupations in Transition')

77 Gregory S. Kealey *Toronto Workers Respond to Industrial Capitalism 1867–1892* (Toronto 1980) 84–8; Paul Craven *'An Impartial Umpire': Industrial Relations and the Canadian State 1900–1911* (Toronto 1980) 167–9; John Battye 'The Nine Hour Pioneers: The Genesis of the Canadian Labour Movement' *Labour/Le Travailleur* IV (1979) 35

78 *Globe* 29 May 1869

6

The Kamloops Outlaws and Commissions of Assize in Nineteenth-Century British Columbia

HAMAR FOSTER

INTRODUCTION

On 31 January 1881 four young men were hanged at the prison in New Westminster, British Columbia, for the murder of John Ussher, a constable. Alex Hare and the McLean boys, Allan, Charlie, and Archie had been tried and found guilty nearly a year earlier, but the Supreme Court of British Columbia had declared that trial a nullity because no commission to hold a court of assize had been issued to the presiding judge. So the prisoners had to be tried, condemned again and, finally, executed. Those who watched, said a local newspaper, breathed a sigh of relief, and so no doubt did many others: the ranchers they had terrorized, the witnesses who, after testifying against them, had requested to be armed, and certainly the judges and politicians who had made the validity of their first trial an issue that occupied the public mind and purse for months.[1] The deaths of Alex Hare and the McLeans brought to an end what may have been the most undignified episode in the troubled and often rancorous history of British Columbia's judicial system in the nineteenth century. But what was truly remarkable about the case of the so-called 'Kamloops Outlaws' was that the jurisdictional error that wrecked the first trial had been predicted beforehand. The Supreme Court judges had told the government prior to the assize that they doubted it would be valid without a commission. Yet the government lawyers pressed on, forgetting, it seems, that the very men whose doubts they were choosing to ignore were the court in which this issue almost certainly would come to be resolved. Each side knew the other's position before this unnecessary battle began, and each could have prevented it. Instead, an intransigent government and an equally stubborn judge foisted an arcane question of jurisdiction upon the prisoners and their reluctant counsel. When Archie McLean, at sixteen the youngest of the outlaws, was led to the gallows, it is unlikely that he or any of his fellows understood why the law had had to try him twice. Aside from the government officials who prosecuted the case and the judges who opposed them, it is unlikely that anyone did.[2]

The history, jurisdiction, and status of assizes are not matters that command much attention today in the curricula of Canadian law schools, whatever their importance may have been in times past. An oblique reference in an old case studied for other reasons or a brief mention in a course on legal institutions is all that the student is likely to encounter.[3] Yet British Columbia still has something called assizes, and when the student, now articled, attends his first session, he may be surprised to hear the clerk of the Supreme Court loudly proclaim it to be a Court of Oyer and Terminer and General Gaol Delivery. Probably the student will be less concerned with the meaning of this phrase than with pronouncing it correctly, and will conclude that the clerk's words are no more than what they seem: a respectful but perfunctory acknowledgment of a practice once significant but now little understood, retained just in case one day something might turn upon it. Once, about twenty-five years ago, the relationship between the Supreme Court and the assizes did come up in a rather indirect way, but the judges who heard the case declined to go into the matter, noting that counsel had been 'unable to cite authority' on the point.[4] Slumbering in the Provincial Archives there was such an authority, but that is hardly the first place a busy lawyer would look and perhaps it is just as well.[5] For 126 pages the record of the *McLean* case drones on, unreported. It is a long lecture to an unrepentant Attorney General, a judicial 'we told you so' to a Canadian upstart who had ignored their earlier warning. The government was wrong, say the judges, to have insisted on proceeding with the assize without issuing a commission. An assize cannot be held without one, even if presided over by a judge of the Supreme Court. Reaching back 700 years to emphasize the difference between that court and a Court of Oyer and Terminer and General Gaol Delivery, they conclude that there must be a new trial. The law of nineteenth-century British Columbia, if unaltered by statute, was the law of England. These judges would have agreed with Pollock and Maitland that the small number of men who had created the common law in the twelfth and thirteenth centuries had made 'right and wrong for us and for our children,' even for those who toiled in the gold fields and trapped animals in the wilds of British Columbia.[6] But of course it was not quite as simple as that.

At least three themes weave their way through the complex tapestry of the *McLean* case. The most striking is the often intense animosity that existed between the judges of the Supreme Court and the Premier, George Anthony Walkem. Justice Henry Pering Pellew Crease and the Chief Justice, Matthew Baillie Begbie, had a low opinion of Walkem as a lawyer and little sympathy for his politics. Walkem was also Attorney General, and they saw his attempts to reform the administration of justice in the new province as a thinly veiled attack upon the independence of the judiciary. Begbie seems to have been more concerned with Walkem's competence than with his motives, but both judges looked to Ottawa for protection from what they saw as excesses of the provincial government. The Premier, for his part, appears to have regarded the judges as obstacles from the colonial period who did not understand the administrative problems of the day, and he therefore unwisely ignored their complaints. Faced with a hostile bench and a press largely in the hands of the opposition, Walkem should have trod carefully in a case that had excited and angered the public. That he did not is the central mystery of the affair.

A second theme is the extraordinary nature of criminal justice in British Columbia 100 years ago. It is true that the community was outraged by the murder of Constable Ussher and that there are occasional references in the records to fears that the McLeans might be lynched, both before and after the first abortive trial. But these references are exceptional. What the public and the press both seemed to want was the speedy resolution of the case by the law and all its imperial trappings. British Columbia's reputation for fast and fair trials had been established only twenty years earlier during the first gold rush, and the public expected no less in a case as important and unusual as this one.[7] Nowhere in the whole record does a serious criticism of Begbie and his court appear, nor is there any real indication that a lynch mob ever came close to being formed.[8] Instead, all the criticism is directed at Walkem and his government for failing to administer properly the very effective criminal justice system entrusted to them. Only once, in 1884, did an unlawful hanging take place, and as early as 1860 Begbie had felt able to boast that Sir William Blackstone 'was more regarded in his jurisdiction than Judge Lynch' – a reference to the rather different state of law and order in the gold fields of California.[9] But Blackstone and the assize system he described contributed to the problems in the *McLean* case, which saw the trial of four notorious killers overturned because of a point of law rooted in the Middle Ages and obscured by Confederation.

A final theme is the transition that British Columbia was going through in the last quarter of the nineteenth century. A fur-trading and gold mining colony was becoming a reluctant component of a modern federation, and in the process a way of life was passing into history, particularly for the native Indians and half-breeds of the remoter regions. Crease, who presided at both the McLean trials, dwelt at some length on this aspect of the case in his charge to the grand jury at New Westminster, even suggesting that the mixed blood and unfortunate family history of the McLeans was an important factor in their descent into crime.[10] But if the British Columbia of the gold rushes and fur trade had set its face against lawlessness and disorder, the British Columbia of Confederation and railroads was equally determined to present a civilized front to the world. The McLeans and their deeds were a blemish that had to be removed swiftly, legally, and in a manner that did credit to British – and Canadian – justice. For reasons that are even now not altogether clear, the resolution of the case was neither swift nor exemplary. But it was painfully, deliberately, interminably, legal.

EARLY BRITISH COLUMBIA

In the first half of the nineteenth century what is now British Columbia was the preserve of the great fur-trading companies and European settlement was sparse. Some of the trappers and traders took Indian women as wives, which brought some measure of permanence to what was otherwise a relatively transient white community; but by and large the men and their corporate masters were in the Pacific northwest to exploit its resources, not to found a colony. The children of these unions, at least before the white population began to explode in the late 1850s, lived lives relatively free of the pressures associated with being of mixed blood. But when the Hudson's Bay Company absorbed the Northwest Company in 1821, monopoly abruptly replaced competition and settlement began, slowly, to increase. Moreover, because the Hudson's Bay men tended to see themselves as representatives of the British Empire and believed in a 'managed, stable, socially stratified society,' they laid the foundations for a community quite different from that of the nation to the south, whose citizens by the 1840s were moving into the Oregon Territory in large numbers.[11] This latter development led the Company to establish

Fort Victoria at the southern end of Vancouver Island in 1843, just three years before the Treaty of Washington ceded all the land below the 49th parallel of latitude to the United States.

At common law the settlers who had trickled into the British possessions north of this boundary were deemed to have brought English law with them, but this was surely a proposition more theoretical than real when applied to a land without effective institutions to apply and enforce that law.[12] There were no colonies in the Pacific northwest at that time, and British justice within its ill-defined geographical limits must have seemed remote, at best. Perhaps worst off of all were the Indians, as an incident in the life of Donald McLean, father of the McLean brothers, amply demonstrates.[13] An employee of the Company, he married twice, first to a woman of Spanish-Indian descent and then to Sophia, a full-blooded Kamloops Indian who was the mother of the young outlaws. But his marriages provide a stark contrast to his other dealings with the native peoples of the area. In the fall of 1848 a rather mercurial and shiftless Company man had been murdered by a young Quesnel Indian named Tletlh, and the following January McLean was sent by his superiors to arrest him. When he arrived at Tletlh's village he confronted the man's uncle, demanding to know where the suspect was. When told that no one knew, McLean shot the uncle instead. His party then killed the man's son-in-law and wounded his step-daughter, killing her baby in the process. Yet no action was ever taken against McLean, who was to become a highly regarded member of the community and a chief trader for the Company. Typically, when some of the Chilcotin Indians under Chief Klatassin attacked a road building party in Bute Inlet in 1864, McLean was among the first to join the government forces sent to deal with the uprising. Shot in the back by one of the Indians he was stalking, he was the only government fatality.[14]

There is no evidence that such an extreme incident was typical of the pre-colonial period, but it is none the less disturbing. The imperial authorities had made some provision for the administration of criminal justice in the 'Indian Territories,' but the statutes designed to accomplish this reveal just how long the 'long arm of the law' really was in those days.[15] They authorized the Governor of Lower Canada and later 'His Majesty' to create justices in the Hudson's Bay lands and the Indian territories, but they had only limited jurisdiction and were expected to transfer all capital cases to Upper Canada, some 3000 miles to the east. A typical case occurred in 1842 when a number of men accused of murdering the son of the chief factor of the Hudson's Bay Company in the Oregon

Territory were sent to Canada for trial; there would be no assize judge in British Columbia – or New Caledonia, as it was then called – for another seventeen years.[16]

After the dispute over the Oregon Territory ended in 1846, however, the imperial authorities recognized that some more official form of government than Company rule was needed to prevent the whole Pacific northwest from being lost to the Americans. In 1849 this need was met by creation of the Colony of Vancouver Island. To encourage permanent growth the authorities granted the Company exclusive trading rights on the condition that it promote settlement. But neither this new status nor this new obligation really changed the character of the place, at least not right away: when the first governor arrived in 1850 he 'soon found that there were no public affairs to administer, no judiciary, no legislature and no colonists; all the inhabitants being connected with the company.'[17] Apparently the courts envisioned by the earlier statutes had never really been established. The hapless governor left less than a year later and was replaced by the man who was already the real power in the colony, the Chief Factor of the Company, James Douglas. Douglas had the status and credibility that his predecessor lacked, and was to rule the island and then the mainland for the next fourteen years.

By 1855 the white population of the whole area was not more than 1000, and even after several outbreaks of smallpox the Indians outnumbered the whites by about fifty to one. The Company had a number of trading posts on the mainland, including Fort Kamloops at the fork of the Thompson and North Thompson rivers, but there were probably no more than 200 Europeans manning them and each fort was quite isolated from the others. The Pacific northwest was still a remote backwater, a place where life for the native Indian inhabitants went on much as it had for centuries and where the small white community, 'isolated from the main currents of North American social and intellectual change, added a measure of rough gentility to the routine of the Hudson's Bay Company.'[18]

Gold changed all this. In 1858 thousands of miners, most of them veterans of the California rush nine years earlier who had arrived too late for the big strike, streamed into Victoria and headed across to the mainland in search of their fortunes. The result was considerable social dislocation, especially among the Indians, and by 1868 nearly half the native population had succumbed to disease.[19] But in the early days of the gold rush Douglas' most pressing concern was the effect of the large influx of American miners on British sovereignty over the area and the maintenance of law and order within it. He immediately proclaimed that all gold mines in the Fraser and Thompson districts were the property of the crown and even required all miners to purchase a licence in Victoria. But the gold was on the mainland, and the mainland was not part of the colony: Douglas' authority there was only that which he possessed as Chief Factor of the Company. His actions may not have been strictly legal, and the imperial authorities seemed to realize that something more was needed. As a result, Douglas and Matthew Baillie Begbie, a Chancery lawyer newly arrived from England to become the first judge, travelled from Victoria to Fort Langley in November of 1858 to proclaim the establishment of the mainland colony of British Columbia. They also proclaimed in force the English Law Ordinance, which provided that the civil and criminal laws of England in existence on 19 November 1858 applied to the new colony, insofar as they were 'not, from local circumstances, inapplicable ... [and until] such times as they shall be altered' by the crown, by Douglas, or 'by such other legislative authority as may hereafter be legally constituted in the said colony ...'[20] Although this ordinance did not distinguish between statute and case law, it confirmed the common law principle stated above and clarified it by adding a cut-off date. At about the same time the imperial parliament also provided that the earlier statutes dealing with the administration of justice in the Indian territories and the Hudson's Bay lands no longer applied to British Columbia.[21] Assuming local circumstances did not render it inapplicable, therefore, the English assize system appeared to be part of the law of the new colony.

There were now two British colonies bordering on the American territories in the Pacific northwest, each with its own finances and judicial system but presided over by the same man – Douglas. This anomalous situation came to an end in 1866 when the two were joined to form the united colony of British Columbia, and a new English Law Ordinance was passed which again adopted 19 November 1858 as the cut-off date. Subject to compliance with a general directive not to pass laws repugnant to those of the mother country, the partly appointed, partly elected legislative council had jurisdiction over criminal law and procedure, but made no move to legislate with respect to criminal assizes.[22]

In 1867, the year that the three eastern colonies joined to form the Dominion of Canada, British Columbia was not prospering. The gold rushes in the Fraser and the Cariboo had ended and the population was declining. The 12,000 non-Indians in the colony were still only half the native population and less than the number had been only nine years earlier, when in one year alone 25,000 miners had invaded the lower

Fraser. By 1867 most of these had left, and with the fur trade and gold mining clearly on the wane, the colonial administration began to look for solutions. One option was annexation to the United States, which purchased Alaska that year and was flexing muscles considerably strengthened by the massive northern victory in the Civil War. Joining the republic was not a course of action that appealed to the citizenry as a whole now that most of the Americans who had flooded into the colony during the gold rush had left, but for a time it was supported by at least two local newspapers.[23] The strongly pro-British faction, especially those who were former Company employees or held official positions, tended to want British Columbia to remain a colony, partly because they feared loss of employment and personal status if it did not. The only other option, which this faction also opposed until the imperial authorities expressed their preference for it, was confederation with the young Dominion of Canada. After much soul-searching and a long and sometimes bitter debate, the legislature resolved to do just that, if the terms were right.[24]

In return for the promise of a railway, a graving dock at Esquimalt, security for colonial officials, and sundry other benefits, the citizens of the colony on 20 July 1871 officially became Canadians, subject now to the laws of the Dominion as well as to those of the new province and the applicable English laws. In particular, the local legislators surrendered to Ottawa all jurisdiction over the appointment of superior and county court judges and over criminal law and procedure, although they retained legislative authority over the administration of justice in the province.[25] This division of responsibility was designed to meet the same problems faced by the Normans centuries earlier in medieval England – the reconciliation of central control with local administration and enforcement – but the way in which it was expressed ensured that sharply differing opinions could be held as to the extent of each level of government's authority over the administration of the criminal law. In the 1970s and 1980s the preferring of indictments by the Attorney General and his agents has become the bone of contention in this dispute; 100 years ago, it was the status of commissions of assize.[26]

COMMISSIONS OF ASSIZE

In medieval England royal authority made itself felt in the various counties through the offices of the sheriff and the coroner and through the regular visits of itinerant justices (or 'justices in eyre'). The latter were royal officials whose duties were as administrative as they were judicial and whose authority was contained in letters patent under the great seal of England. These 'commissions' authorized those named in them to do all manner of things and included jurisdiction over 'all pleas' whatsoever. The justices inquired into the way local officials had carried out their responsibilities, received presentments or accusations of wrongdoing and ensured that the proprietary rights of the crown were being observed. Every offence discovered and every failure of duty exposed meant fines or amercements for the crown, and for this and other reasons the institution was not popular.[27] Demands that eyres be held only once every seven years soon led to petitions for outright abolition, and by the middle of the fourteenth century they were no more.[28] What did survive and flourish, however, were lesser commissions which were to play as important a role in the legal system as the three central courts of Common Pleas, Exchequer, and King's Bench at Westminster. Indeed, just as the authority of Common Pleas to hear an action at common law came to depend upon the issuing of an original writ for each case, so the authority of the commissioners to hear cases depended upon their being named in the appropriate commission in the appropriate way.[29] The difference was that a judge of the King's Bench or Common Pleas was a judge with or without cases; a commissioner was a judge only for the life of his commission. It was the root of his authority, the source of his office and jurisdiction.

The earliest of these lesser commissions is probably the commission of assize, which authorized those named in it to preside in the countryside over disputes concerning the possession of land. These so-called 'possessory assizes' had a criminal aspect but were essentially civil, and eventually the 'justices of assize' were given jurisdiction to hear other civil cases as well if they were named in a commission of *nisi prius*.[30] The *nisi prius* system was another one of the ways in which the English legal system compromised central control and local administration. Pleadings in civil cases, wherever the cause of action arose, would be settled in one of the courts at Westminster, but it made little sense to have the jurors travel there from distant counties. Instead, the sheriff was ordered to send a jury to Westminster 'unless before' the date set for trial a commissioner of *nisi prius* visited the county where the case arose, and such a visit was soon the norm. Typically, then, a jury in say, Somerset, would decide Somerset cases, and their verdicts would be returned to Westminster where each would become a judgment of the central court in which the case had begun. The judge who presided over the case in the countryside might, for example, have been a Baron of the Exchequer, but he presided solely by virtue of his commission of *nisi prius*, and if the pleadings had begun in the Court of Common Pleas the judgment in the case would be a judgment of that court.

In criminal matters the situation was rather different. Neither the Exchequer nor Common Pleas had any criminal jurisdiction and the King's Bench heard criminal cases only at Bar, that is, as a court composed of all four judges. Consequently all serious criminal cases were heard by judges sitting as commissioners and such cases, unlike those at *nisi prius*, both began and ended in the countryside without reference to the central courts. The two most important types of criminal commission were *oyer and terminer*, which directed those named in it to 'hear and determine' all criminal cases in a particular county, and *general gaol delivery* which, as its name suggests, was confined to the processing of the inmates of particular jails. History, however, played a trick with these labels: the possessory assizes fell into desuetude, and the term 'assize' came to be associated with criminal as well as civil justice. As Sir Edward Coke put it, parliament had increased the authority of the justices of assize 'both in dignity and multitude of causes, yet they retain their first and originall name, albeit assizes are in these days very rarely taken before them.'[31]

The questions of law that could arise at *nisi prius* and the serious nature of the crimes tried by commissioners of oyer and terminer and gaol delivery led naturally to a perceived need for men 'wise and learned in the law.'[32] The judges of the central courts were the obvious candidates. As a result, although the need for travelling justice did not decline, the need for temporary ad hoc commissioners to dispense it did: by the end of the medieval period most commissioners were judges who, at least in criminal cases, exercised an authority as complete as that which they had when presiding at Westminster. Their authority, however, continued to depend not upon their office as judge but upon their temporary commissions. This may have made sense in the thirteenth century, but at a time when permanent judges had become the rule it seems difficult to defend. It is even stranger that the need for a commission should have survived the Judicature Act of 1873, and certainly there were those at the time who supposed it had not.[33] This statute was a major renovation of the English court system, and section 16 purported to transfer to and to vest in the new High Court of Justice all the jurisdiction that had resided in the courts 'created by Commissioners of Assize, of Oyer and Terminer, and of Gaol Delivery, or of any such Commissions.' But in law, practices die hard and caution is a byword: not only did commissions continue to issue after the Act but they were not abolished in England until 1971.[34]

The appropriateness of commissions in British Columbia first arose long before confederation with Canada, at a time when the mainland colony had not yet joined Vancouver Island and had neither an elected assembly nor the sort of hybrid council it would enjoy after 1866. In the period from 1858 to his retirement in 1864, Governor Douglas ruled British Columbia almost as a colonial monarch, ably assisted in most matters by Judge Begbie. Begbie was to become something of a legend during his thirty-six-year career, first as the only judge on the mainland, then as Chief Justice of the united colony, and finally as the first Chief Justice of the province of British Columbia. Especially in the colonial period he enjoyed a position of authority that was and is most unusual for a judge, and that may help to explain the position he was to take in the McLean case. He was of course never a candidate for office, but he 'became a political figure in the broad sense of that phrase,' advising on and even drafting colonial legislation, and, in the process, getting used to doing executive work and to doing it well.[35]

One of the first things to which he turned his attention was commissions of assize. Only a few months after his arrival in the colony Begbie made the first of his circuits in the interior, and he clearly assumed that the English assize system would apply in British Columbia just as it did in England. Certainly the only judge in the colony had to travel if justice were to be done in the scattered mining camps and Indian villages of the interior, and itinerant justice was nothing if not English. But in 1860 Begbie drafted and proposed a statute, the Gaol Delivery Act, designed to adapt the English assize system to the new colony and which in fact permitted the holding of courts of assize without commissions. Such a statute suggests that if the idea of travelling justice made sense in the local circumstances, that of commissioned judges did not. In England it was already peculiar that permanent judges should need temporary commissions; in British Columbia, which was not divided into counties and which had only one judge, it was absurd, particularly when the court of which he was the sole member had 'complete cognizance of all pleas, whatsoever,' the ancient formula for the plenary jurisdiction of the justices in eyre.[36]

It apparently did not occur to Begbie that local circumstances might render commissions 'inapplicable' under the terms of the English Law Ordinance or he would not have bothered to draft a statute to do the job. Yet he clearly felt that they were inappropriate in British Columbia. Writing to Governor Douglas after the Gaol Delivery Act had been disallowed by the imperial authorities, Begbie complained that the primitive state of communication and transport in the colony led to delays in the administration of justice that were only made worse by the need for special commissions for each assize. He knew that his legislation 'entirely contradicted the spirit and practice of Courts of Justice as administered in England' and probably was 'regarded with astonishment,' but it was 'expedient and necessary in the actual circumstances of the Colony.' Now that it had been disallowed, what was to be done? Ultimately, Begbie accepted a suggestion by Crease (who was then Attorney General) that commissions be issued permitting him to try offences committed at the date of the commission 'or within 6 months thereafter,' but he did so somewhat reluctantly, unsure of their legality. He even expressed a fear that he would voice again nearly twenty years later in the *McLean* case. 'It is by no means clear,' he wrote Douglas, 'that a sentence pronounced under such a commission would not be void ... and in such a case it is unnecessary perhaps to point out that all persons concerned in authorizing or executing a capital sentence would be legally guilty of murder.' Begbie's frustration with the imperial authorities for disallowing the Act permeates his letter to Douglas and was part of a larger concern that his position and authority be beyond question. Crease was to be equally adamant about this when he tried the McLeans, but in 1862 it was Begbie's turn: 'At the latest interview to which I was admitted with the Minister before leaving England I was informed in so many words that they wanted to send out a man who would not hesitate to try a criminal under a tree and hang him up to a branch of it, and that I was expected not to hesitate to do so. I believe that I shall always be found ready to act up to such instructions provided that I am legally authorized to do so, but it does not appear to be asking too much that my authority should be quite clear.'[37]

The practice of issuing commissions of assize was not affected by either the union of the colonies or by confederation with Canada, and it appears that all who were involved in the administration of criminal justice throughout these years assumed that commissions of assize were an integral part of the received English law that applied in British Columbia. Certainly it cannot be doubted that commissions were issued and read at each assize, although the government lawyers were to suggest otherwise during the *McLean* case, and once such a practice became entrenched it is not surprising that the legal mind might tend to conclude that only the legislature could dislodge it. But Confederation, even if it did not affect the issuing of the commissions, did affect their form. The division of authority over criminal justice that was a part of the bargain struck between the provinces and the Dominion was tantalizingly obscure about the precise location of executive authority, but the power to commute sentences was seen to have migrated to Ottawa even though the provincial government continued to issue the commissions and to announce the assizes. Consequently, a Dominion statute required judges presiding over criminal cases to make a report to the federal Secretary of State 'for the information of the Governor.'[38] This of course did not prevent a similar report from being made to the provincial authorities as well, but when the British Columbia government abruptly decided, in the *McLean* case, to make the commission itself returnable to Victoria, the judges protested and the fight was on. It was the new constitution as much as the old law of assizes that was at fault, but neither factor would have sufficed were it not for the strong personalities involved, who seem to have been preparing for just such a scrap for years. The result was a local quarrel between English trained judges who had been reluctant about Confederation and its Canadian proponents, and an Attorney General whose early career had been in Canada and who resented the judges' presumption of superiority. It was a combination that seems to have left little room for compromise.

One of the judges was of course Crease, who had been Attorney General of British Columbia for most of the colonial period and who was appointed a judge of the Supreme Court only two days after introducing the resolution to join Canada.[39] Given that he had previously been most unenthusiastic about Confederation, his conversion may not have been entirely unrelated to his judicial elevation. Crease, like Begbie, was an old hand at drafting statutes and had supervised both the 1871 and 1877 consolidations.[40] Also like Begbie he was used to wielding executive power and tended to be sceptical of the attempts of those he saw as lesser men to carry out reform of the legal system. Confederation had brought a measure of democracy that clearly did not appeal to him, and he saw many of those who held public office in the 1870s and 1880s as the unwelcome product of a 'rampant' universal suffrage.[41] This attitude may, perhaps, explain his reaction to a government bill that was sent to the judges in March 1877 for their 'unofficial' opinion. The bill, styled the Courts of Assize Act, provided for sittings of such courts 'with or without Commissions as to the Lieutenant-Governor may seem best.' If no commission were issued, the court was to be presided over by the Chief Justice or one of the other two judges, who would 'possess, exercise and enjoy all and every the like powers and authorities usually set forth and granted' in the old commissions. And if no member of the Supreme Court was available, the bill permitted county court judges and counsel 'learned in the law' – a time-honoured phrase – to preside instead.[42] Designed to remedy all the potential hazards of the commission system, this legislation appears to have been modelled on the English Judicature Act of 1873 and almost certainly on an even earlier pre-Confederation statute in Ontario.[43]

Thus three years before the first McLean trial the provincial government proposed an intelligent solution to the commissions problem, and given that Chief Justice Begbie had put forward a similar course of action some seventeen years earlier, a favourable reaction from the judges must have been expected. Yet the bill was withdrawn. It did not become law because the three judges, the same three who would later hold that the McLean trial was invalid because no commission had been issued, 'had reported against it.'[44] Crease, who was to try the McLeans as well as participate in the full court decision, wrote to Ottawa to explain that the judges had felt there was 'no necessity' for changing the existing law. Making reference to previous abuses that were 'not likely to recur,' he stated that 'the powers already existing in the hands of the Executive of the Province ... [are] already ample in that behalf for all the purposes of the administration of the law.'[45] There is no mention of constitutional problems with the proposed bill, no mention of the fate of Begbie's draft statute of 1860; instead, Crease's words point to a vague feeling that the change would somehow unduly increase executive power, something he clearly did not wish to see. Whatever the explanation for Crease's opposition, not to mention that of Begbie, the bill never became law. An even more curious incident soon followed.

Two years later almost to the day, the Supreme Court judges were once again asked, on very short notice, for their views on a piece of pending legislation. This time the proposed changes were even more ambitious, being in name and effect a Judicature Act for British Columbia.[46] One of its provisions especially interested and annoyed the judges: a clause providing for additional commissioners of assize. Just as in 1877, the judges replied that there was no need for such a clause, calling it 'nearly useless' and adding that 'its legality may be questioned,' presumably on constitutional grounds.[47] It would be much better, they went on, if the government declared 'the abolition of the continuous reiterated issue year after year of commissions of assize, nisi prius, oyer and terminer, etc.' The government, they argued, already had the power to fix the circuits and assizes, 'which, when fixed, the Judges of the Supreme Court *virtute officii* hold.'[48] What the judges meant by these words became a point of some importance in the *McLean* case, evoking as they did Coke's description of the King's Bench judges as 'sovereign justices of oyer and terminer' and strongly suggesting that such a judge presided at assize time by virtue, not of any commission, but of his office as judge.[49]

Yet what is truly remarkable is the ability of the judges to blow hot and cold. After they had seen a copy of the amended bill, which had taken into account nearly all of their recommendations and now contained a provision similar to that of the 1877 bill (permitting assizes to be held 'with or without Commissions ... as the Lieutenant-Governor may direct'), the judges again wrote to the government. They addressed themselves to Walkem, who as Premier and Attorney General was later to lead the government side in the McLean case and who was just the sort of democratic politician who aroused the ire of such as Crease. Walkem had been trained as a lawyer in Upper Canada and in his approximately twenty years at the British Columbia Bar he had never managed to earn the respect of either Crease or Begbie. The feeling was pointedly mutual, and could only have been exacerbated by the contents of their letter of 18 March 1879. In it, the judges graciously acknowledged the adoption of many of their suggestions in the new draft, and then – before protesting strongly about the rejection of one of them – proceeded to do an about-face on the question of commissions. Pleading the 'extreme haste' with which they had had to draft their response to the government's earlier request for advice, they urged that the clause permitting assizes to be held without commissions be dropped. They gave no other reason, although later they would say they had feared it was unconstitutional, and the clause remained. Had it been in force when the McLeans were tried, it, like the Courts of Assize Act of 1877, would have validated the assize.[50]

Such was the peculiar history of commissions of assize in British Columbia prior to 1880. On three occasions proposals had been made to abolish them or at least to permit the holding of assizes without them, and by March of that year such a provision had been enacted, but not proclaimed. Begbie's 1860 law had been disallowed, the 1877 Courts of Assize Act had been withdrawn on the advice of the judges, and the 1879 Judicature Act had permitted assizes without commission first at the request of, then over the objections of, these same judges. Throughout this period persons accused of serious crimes had been brought before the duly commissioned judges of assize, who sat in courts that rejoiced in the ancient titles of oyer and terminer and general gaol delivery, and who, berobed and bewigged, dispensed justice according to law before the trappers and miners and Indians who came to watch. The spectacle was not as elaborate as an English assize, but it was solemn enough. When Crease was in New Westminster in March 1880 to see that British justice was done to the McLeans, he charged the grand jury at length and 'in eloquent language' on the social causes of crime and the plight of the half-breed, and the members of that body not only returned true bills but also inquired into the state of the local hospital, lunatic asylum, and penitentiary and reported on the sanitary condition of the town.[51]

The remoter circuits were even more noteworthy, and two of these were the subject of comment by Justice John Hamilton Gray in the summer of 1877. Gray had been one of the fathers of Confederation in 1867 and was appointed the third judge of the Supreme Court in 1872, much to the consternation of Begbie and Crease.[52] He stressed the difficulties involved in travelling justice and maintained that they were 'almost incapable of being comprehended by those who live within the radius of a well-settled and well-organized community.' He continued:

the Judge who goes on one of those circuits must prepare for an expedition. There is not a spot on the whole route in which he can demand shelter or food ... the courthouse itself is the front of a grocery shop or a log hut improvised for the occasion ...

For six weeks in all weathers, his bed must be on the ground, his seat in the day on horseback, or in a canoe, his food sometimes dependent on the stream or bush, his only addressable companion the Court who accompanies him ... and his personal safety – next to the honesty of the guide who has charge of the mules, the packers and the train – [depends] upon the clearness of his own head and the steadiness of his own hand.

I have been on both these journeys. In the Kootenay case – going and returning – covering nearly a thousand miles on horseback ...[53]

Certainly British Columbia at the end of the 1870s was not the rough and ready place it had been at the height of the fur trade or during the gold fever that gripped the interior in the 1850s and 1860s, but it remained a frontier society. The English propriety of Victoria's drawing rooms and tea houses warily co-existed with the aboriginal ruggedness of most of the rest of the province, and one of the meeting places for these cultures was, it seems, the assize court room. They were to meet with considerable impact in the *McLean* case.

THE MURDER OF JOHNNY USSHER

In the winter of 1879 commissions of assize must have been the furthest thing from the mind of John Ussher, constable and government agent at Kamloops, some 300 miles northeast of the former colonial capital of New Westminster. He had made a little money in the Cariboo gold rush and had started on a new career as a rancher, but in his official capacity he was responsible for the jail, for assessing and collecting taxes, and generally for keeping order. He was also the Gold Commissioner, the Mining Recorder, and the Court Registrar, and, at forty, had recently married. Although he occasionally had to swear in a special constable and then endure a haggle over the expense with Victoria, normally he and the local Justices of the Peace were the only law in the district. Ussher appears to have been popular and as efficient as his common sense and meagre official budget allowed.[54] Slow to anger, he showed an unusual amount of patience when dealing with the exuberance of the McLeans and Hare, who so often ran afoul of the law. Reluctant to subject them to its full force and perhaps not certain that he could muster that force, he tried to get them to see the error of their ways by other means if he could. This generosity of spirit contributed to his death.

The three McLean boys were brought up by their Indian mother after the elder McLean had been killed in the Chilcotin in 1864.[55] The boys grew up wild and headstrong and in the company of their friend, Alex Hare, also a half-breed, soon began to cause trouble around Kamloops and Cache Creek. Acutely conscious of their racial heritage and with large chips on their shoulders, they were seasoned and even dangerous nuisances who, on one occasion, had shown their contempt by breaking out of Ussher's hopelessly dilapidated jail after he had imprisoned them on robbery charges. Their neighbours were becoming increasingly concerned, one writing to a friend that 'this is a fine state of things, to be terrorized by four brats who have threatened to burn the jail in order to destroy the records of their deeds. If these vagabonds are not either arrested or driven to American territory, it may become pretty hot for us ... I'm afraid it will end in something more serious, for the boys are armed to the teeth ...'[56] Such fears were not uncommon, and when William Palmer, a local rancher, discovered in November 1879 that his favourite stallion was missing, he immediately suspected the McLeans. When he came upon them a few days later and found Charlie McLean riding it, he hurried into Kamloops to report this to Ussher.

Palmer's complaint led to raising the reward already posted for the capture of the outlaws, and Ussher set out with a posse on the afternoon of Sunday, 7 December, to find and arrest them. In the posse were Palmer, Amni Shumway, a local packer who acted as guide, and of course Ussher himself. Along the way they were joined by two more men, John McLeod, a former policeman, and William Roxborough, who went along more to round up the stray horses and mules he looked after for the Canadian

Pacific Railway than as a real posse member. At least Palmer and Shumway had been sworn in as special constables, but none of them, except possibly Ussher, had reliable weapons and Shumway had none at all. Ussher, it seems, had not thought that the McLeans would put up a fight.[57]

About an hour before noon on 8 December the posse came upon the outlaws' camp. Almost immediately, the shooting started. McLeod was wounded by the first shot, and both he and Palmer discovered that their guns would not fire. Ussher, clearly still hoping that he could persuade the McLeans to give up and thus avoid further bloodshed, dismounted and went towards Alex Hare and Allan McLean, who had emerged from the woods. Shumway later swore that he had heard Ussher say, 'Surrender, boys, stop this shooting!' He heard no reply, but saw Hare, a pistol in one hand and a knife in the other, walk up to Ussher and throw him to the ground.[58] According to Palmer, Hare then 'jumped on top of him and used his knife and revolver, I couldn't say which. Mr. Ussher said, "don't kill me boys." Archie McLean then came from behind the tree with a revolver in his hands and either Charlie or Archie said "kill the son-of-a-bitch." Archie held the revolver about 18 inches from Ussher's head and fired.'[59] Shumway later deposed that he 'saw the smoke from the pistol' but that he thought it was Allan who had given the order to kill Ussher. After the shot was fired, he said, 'Ussher's feet rose up six or eight inches from the ground. I saw both Hare and Archie raise their pistols and aim blows at Ussher's head.' The outlaws then began shooting at the remaining members of the posse, who tried to return the fire but soon were forced to retreat and head back to Kamloops. They were now virtually without weapons, McLeod's horse had been shot, McLeod himself was wounded in the knee and the face, and Roxborough was not there: just before they had come upon the McLeans' camp he had gone off to round up some strays.[60]

The McLeans and Hare stripped Ussher's body, taking his overcoat, gloves, boots, and hat, and headed for the ranches of men with whom they felt they had other scores to settle. Some time after noon they arrived at the home of Thomas Trapp, a stock-raiser, demanding guns and ammunition. They told him they had killed Ussher and that they would kill anyone else who came after them. According to Trapp, 'Charlie was flourishing a hunting knife and said ... "Do you think that grey-headed son-of-a-bitch Judge Begbie will ever get the drop on me? They will never take me alive." He lowered his rifle ... and said a shot out of that would send [Begbie] straight to the right hand of Jesus Christ.' Rather omi-

Archie McLean in the yard of the New Westminster Penitentiary.
'Comparative youth is no excuse for the two youngest are the most
hardened desperadoes of the Gang' – report of the Trial Judge
to the Secretary of State, Ottawa, 12 December 1880
(Provincial Archives of British Columbia, Historic Photographs Division, #3390)

nously, they declared that they had 'made a beginning' and would make 'a clean sweep' if necessary.[61] The outlaws seemed to glory in what they had done, and in this way revealed how young they really were, all but Allan in their teens. Archie boasted that they could only die once, and Charlie told Trapp that his 'father had died in the face of cold lead and he was prepared to do the same,' not adding that his father had in fact been shot in the back by an Indian. Finally they left, but not before they had made Trapp promise that he would not inform on them. Surely they could not have put any stock in that.

Before they arrived at the ranch of Robert Scott, some three hours later, they quite needlessly killed again. Scott deposed that they had ridden up to his stable at about four in the afternoon, bragging of having killed Ussher and 'another man.' Knowing who lived in the vicinity Scott asked if it was James Kelly, the sheep herder, and Allan McLean said that he guessed it was, giving the unlikely excuse that the man had drawn a revolver on them.[62] He made a few more threats and told Scott that they knew another posse would soon be after them. Yet they were exultant that they had scattered Ussher's men and drawn blood. '"We have killed Ussher," Archie repeated, "upon my soul we have killed him." Hare then drew a dagger and said "there's the dagger that went through him and there's the blood on it." I could distinctly see the blood [Scott deposed], also spots of blood on his [Hare's] face. Archie held up his feet and said "there are Ussher's boots." Allan said "there are his horse, saddle and cantinas ..." [he then] pulled out a pair of handcuffs, and said, "there are the handcuffs that Ussher brought to put on me ... we have commenced our work now and want to go through with it."' Then they rode off.

After making an unsuccessful attempt to persuade the Nicola Indians, whose Chief, Chill-e-heetsa, was Allan's father-in-law, to join them in an uprising against the white community, the McLeans and Hare fled to a small log cabin at the foot of Douglas Lake to await the inevitable confrontation. It is surprising that they did not head south over the border, but Allan had been wounded by one of the few shots Palmer had managed before his gun jammed and was probably unfit for that sort of travel.[63] Back in Kamloops, a larger and better equipped posse was being organized under the leadership of Jonathan Edwards, one of the local Justices of the Peace. Earlier a small party led by Palmer and Shumway had gone back to the site of the ambush to retrieve Ussher's badly mutilated body, and when Palmer returned to Kamloops he joined the Edwards group and set out for Douglas Lake. By this time the public were aware of the murders and feelings were running high. On 10 December, the same day that the posse reached its destination, the *Mainland Guardian* reported that the killers were still at large, 'threatening to burn Kamloops and kill persons sent [after] them.' The government would be taking 'vigorous measures,' the editors assured their readers, but this supportive stance was dictated by the events of the moment and the paper would soon revert to form, launching a bitter and sustained attack on Walkem and his administration for its allegedly incompetent handling of the whole affair.[64]

The siege itself lasted only four days. It was the dead of winter, freezing cold and snowing, and the little cabin had very little food and fresh water. Attempts to scoop snow from the doorway were met by a blaze of gunfire, and by 12 December a force of over seventy-five ranchers and Indians surrounded the little log house, with more on their way: a contingent from Victoria had reached New Westminster and a smaller force under Senator Clement Cornwall, also a Justice of the Peace, had left Kamloops for Douglas Lake. The attackers were on the point of burning out the McLeans when Allan finally offered to surrender so long as they were not put in irons. Edwards and his men agreed, but as soon as the outlaws emerged from the cabin they were handcuffed and bound.[65]

Although the hunt was over, the recriminations began almost immediately. The government of Premier Walkem, said the press, had much to answer for. 'All this bloodshed and stress, and the very heavy expenses incurred,' accused the *Mainland Guardian*, 'might have been avoided if our model Government' had acted with dispatch and shown more concern for the needs of those charged with law enforcement in the interior. It went on: '[their] responsibility is very great, and we are sure that the people of this Province will not allow the blood of poor Ussher to appeal in vain to them. Mr. Walkem and his colleagues, we should think, have reached the end of their political existence.'[66] That was so much wishful thinking, but after the McLeans and Hare had been convicted of murder the Victoria *Colonist* agreed with this assessment of the situation, concluding that the lives of John Ussher and James Kelly were 'sacrificed on the altar of governmental parsimony.'[67]

Although most of the allegations that formed the basis of this charge were well known, what prompted the editorial in this case was evidence that had emerged at the trial; evidence, it must be said, of dubious admissibility. Both Thomas Trapp and Jonathan Edwards testified that eighteen months earlier a Kamloops grand jury had presented members of the 'gang' as being at large after breaking jail and accused them of killing cattle and stealing horses. The grand jury had also complained that the Kamloops jail was insecure, yet nothing was done. Trapp testified further that special constables had been appointed to arrest Allan McLean at that time, and that he had heard these were discontinued because the government had refused to honour their payment vouchers. Edwards also volunteered hearsay, testifying that he had 'heard that Ussher had written down to the authorities about the state of things [in Kamloops, but that] no action was taken by the Government.' The court was even told that Charlie McLean had bitten off the nose of a Siwash Indian and served several months in jail for this.[68] All of this hearsay, most of which was irrelevant and prejudicial, was grist for the journalists' mill: the Walkem government was not popular, and the 'Kamloops Outrage' provided those who opposed it with an excellent opportunity to call for the premier's head. When another publication tried to come to Walkem's defence by interpreting something Crease had said to the grand jury as exonerating the authorities, Crease took the first opportunity to set the record straight. The Victoria *Colonist* sniffed that it was 'greatly to be regretted that even the language of the judiciary should be distorted to answer the purposes of the government and shield them from the terrible responsibility which attaches to them in these deplorable cases.'[69]

The McLeans and Hare were returned to Kamloops after their capture and committed for trial, but not at Kamloops; the crime had horrified the local populace and hearts had hardened against the prisoners once the stories of their brutality began to circulate. Moreover, the Kamloops jail had failed to hold them in the past and the Justices of the Peace were afraid that they might escape again, or even that a lynch mob might break in. The trial would therefore take place in New Westminster, and they were to be taken there to be safely kept in the 'common gaol' until 'delivered in due course of law.' Two months later a notice of motion was filed by John Foster McCreight, prosecutor in the case and the first premier of British Columbia, seeking an order changing the venue to New Westminster. The Supreme Court judges, however, refused the application, perhaps thinking even then that if such an order could be made, only a commissioned assize judge could do so. Instead, the judges indicated to McCreight that such things were up to the Crown. When this became an issue at the trial, Crease ruled against the defence.[70]

About two weeks after their capture the McLeans and Hare arrived in New Westminster, somewhat the worse for wear after the long winter journey. The *Mainland Guardian* reported that 'the poor depraved wretches looked haggard and careworn. The hard trip appeared to have taken all the ferocity and blind rage out of them. Having crossed the ice, they were conveyed immediately by sleighs to the jail. A large crowd of citizens lined the street, anxious to have a look at the assassins as they passed up.'[71] They were lodged in cells to wait for the law to take its course, though no one knew at this point just how long that wait would be. On 17 February 1880, the day after the Crown's application to change the venue, an 'extra' issue of the British Columbia *Gazette* announced that a court of assize, nisi prius, oyer and terminer, and general gaol delivery would be held at New Westminster on Saturday 13 March, 1880.[72] The legal effect of this announcement would also be angrily debated before the full court.

THE SPECIAL ASSIZE AT NEW WESTMINSTER

On 8 March 1880 the Supreme Court judges in Victoria received from the Deputy Provincial Secretary a commission authorizing Crease to conduct the New Westminster Assize.[73] The next day Crease and Chief Justice Begbie each wrote letters addressed to the Provincial Secretary, T.B. Humphreys, expressing their concern, and Justice Gray followed suit the day after. The problem was the wording of the commission, which stated that it was returnable to Victoria rather than to Ottawa, even though the judges were under a statutory obligation to make their report to the Dominion. Begbie had objected to this change before, when a similarly worded commission had been issued for the Victoria assizes the previous November, and the government had relented. In his letter to Humphreys, therefore, he adverted to this and stated that he did not know what advantage the government saw in the change or why another attempt was being made 'at the last moment before the New Westminster Assize.' All three judges expressed the fear that the innovation might invalidate the commission and absolved themselves of all responsibility should that happen. Crease, in his letter, spoke of the 'grave doubts' entertained by all the judges and concluded that 'where men's lives are, as at this moment, immediately at stake [the judges] cannot conceal a sincere and conscientious anxiety that no change be made in the form of the commission hitherto used until, at least, the conclusion of the impending assize in New Westminster and the return of the Honourable Attorney-General shall have given time for a full consideration of so important a subject.'[74] This was not an unreasonable request, particularly in view of Walkem's absence from the province, and the government's refusal to grant it seems inexcusable.[75] When he received no answer Crease wrote again – he was nothing if not an indefatigable correspondent – declaring that to avoid any suggestion that the Supreme Court had caused any delay of justice he would proceed to New Westminster, but that he and his brother judges had not changed their minds about the new form of commission.[76]

On 11 March the judges received the government's response. The Provincial Secretary advised them that no change in the wording would be made and that the 'Committee of the Council' had been advised that no commission was necessary to try the McLeans. 'I am to add,' he concluded, 'that the Lieutenant Governor in Council has in consequence cancelled the commissions bearing date, the 9th of March, 1880.'[77] Why the government chose this moment to do by decree what they had been attempting for at least three years to do by statute is mystifying in the extreme, especially in a case in which their conduct had already been severely criticized. The public expected swift retribution for the McLeans, according to law, of course, but not if it meant their escaping on a 'technicality.' To add to the mystery, the Judicature Act was still in limbo, its provision for assizes without commission still unproclaimed nearly a year after its passage, and the judges were clearly signalling the government to tread softly. On 12 March Crease and Begbie promptly protested this new development. The Chief Justice informed Humphreys that Crease had left for New Westminster without a commission and he expressed a hope that the government was prepared 'for the contingency that the whole of the criminal trials, should any take place, would probably be questioned and possibly be held irregular and valueless.'[78] Crease, writing from New Westminster, told the Acting Attorney General, Eli Harrison, jr, that he was willing to do his duty but would take no responsibility for conducting an assize without a commission. He wrote again on the fourteenth and yet again on the fifteenth, finally requesting a hand-delivered acknowledgment. He received this the same day, but it gave no indication that his protestations had fallen on anything but deaf ears.[79]

The assize opened on Saturday the thirteenth. Although no commission was read, a grand jury was empanelled. Crease briefly reviewed some of the cases that would come before them, then adjourned court to Monday, when he would expand upon the real reason for the special assize, the *McLean* case. To require the outlaws to stand trial the grand jury had to find a true bill against them, that is, to find that the Crown had presented a prima facie case. This would not be difficult: the grand jury had before them the damning depositions taken by the justices of the peace at Kamloops. And when the trial itself began it moved along rails not unlike those of today, for reform of the criminal law is a slow process.

There were some differences, however, and at least three of them deserve brief mention. The most striking is that the accused could not give sworn evidence, although probably they could make unsworn statements from the dock which the jury might take into account.[80] This provision was unlikely to be of much help because they would not be under oath, nor subject to cross-examination by the prosecution. The prisoners also had no right of appeal if they were convicted, although as it turned out this too did not really matter in the McLean case. What may have, however, was the third difference. Today it is trite law that the Crown must prove guilt beyond a reasonable doubt, but a different rule applied in 1880 if the charge was murder. Once the prosecution had shown that the victim died as a direct result of the act of the accused, the law presumed the killing to have been intentional and therefore murder, unless the accused showed otherwise. This meant that the McLeans, unlike today, could not really challenge the Crown to 'prove it,' and Crease charged the jury accordingly.[81]

When Crease addressed the grand jury on 15 March, he did so in the style of his English predecessors, philosophising about the causes of crime, drawing moral lessons from the examples of the accused before him, and commenting sagely upon the troubled times in which he and the jurors found themselves. In the 'eloquent language' so admired by the editors of the *Mainland Guardian* he spoke to them about the McLeans and the prospects of those like them:

We are brought face to face with the condition of our numerous and growing half-breed population throughout the Country. What is their future? Sons of the hardy pioneer ... they fell into many of the habits of the natives among whom they lived and many a trapper and trader has owed his life to the fidelity and sagacity and courage of his Indian wife. The offspring of these marriages, a tall, strong, handsome race, combined in one the hardihood and quick perceptions of the man of the woods, with the intelligence and some of the training and endurance of the white man, which raised them into a grade above their mother's but yet not up to the father's grade. Quick shots, unrivalled horsemen, hardy boatmen and hunters, they knew no other life than that of the forest. They learned next to nothing of agriculture. They never went to school or had the semblance of an education and when the wave of civilization, without hurry, without delay, but without rest, approached, it met a restless, roving half-breed population, who, far from imitating did not even understand the resistless agency which was approaching them. So long as the white father lived the children were held in some sort of subjection, but the moment he was gone they gravitated towards their mother's friends and fell back into nature's ways ... The cases before us give a terrible illustration of my observations. Three young men in the opening prime of life, scarcely beyond the stage of youth, sons of a gallant man who was shot while serving the country in the Chilcotin Expedition, are now arraigned before you for the murder of a constable and another white man and several other crimes of nearly equal grade. No one becomes thoroughly bad all of a sudden ... Ask yourselves is it a magistrate the less or a constable the less at Kamloops that has caused or could have prevented these murders? Look deeper. What care, what education have they had whether from State or parents? There is no effect without a cause. Is there not little by little growing up among even our educated youth a spirit of misrule, an impatience of wholesome discipline and restraints of society and home? ...[82]

Whatever its other merits, this seems a convincing, almost sympathetic account of what was happening to a way of life that before the arrival of Crease and the generation before him was the only way of life in British Columbia. But it was irrelevant to what was to come. The McLeans and Hare had broken a law more fundamental than any contained in Crease's books, and that was all that mattered. Condemned as dangerous by the white community and rejected as foolish by the Indians, they stood in Crease's court charged with murdering one of the few men who had sympathized with them and perhaps even liked them. 'Mr. Ussher,' said William Palmer during the trial, 'was to my knowledge a protector to Hare on many occasions.'[83] Perhaps in some ill-defined way Alex Hare and the McLean brothers sensed that even help and protection from white society was fatal to that part of their inheritance about which they cared most; and when the Indians refused to join them they lost heart, retreating to the unprovisioned cabin at Douglas Lake where capture, or death, was a certainty. But if they did hate the white man, they at least came to regret what they had done. At the end of the first trial Hare thanked Crease and said death by hanging was for him 'a just and well-deserved sentence.' On the day of their execution, all four made statements to the same effect.[84]

On the first day of their trial, neither the accused nor their counsel were quite so docile. Before any evidence was led the trial jury had to be selected, and Theodore Davie, counsel for Alex Hare, moved to challenge the array. The Crown later successfully challenged one potential juror because he was opposed to capital punishment, but the defence motion was much more sweeping.[85] Davie argued that the prisoners were entitled to a trial by a jury of their neighbours, hence the panel or array from which this New Westminster jury was to be selected was insufficient in law. He made a forceful submission and seems generally to have handled the case well; afterwards, he would go on to become premier and to end his career as Begbie's successor as Chief Justice. But although the newspapers were aware of the problem with the commission and had already criticized the government on that score, neither he nor Norman Bole, counsel for the McLeans, raised this issue.[86] Instead Davie pressed his challenge to the array and throughout the affair never seems to have lost his conviction that it was the only point with any real merit. Citing Sir William Blackstone and other English and even American authorities, he submitted that the prisoners had to be tried by a Kamloops jury. The fact that the Crown had applied in February to change the venue, he argued, showed that the prosecution 'entertained the same opinion that I do now.' Unfortunately for Davie and his client British Columbia had yet to be divided into counties, and this division had been much of the rationale for the rule in England. McCreight, who was still in charge of the prosecution, therefore submitted that because the Supreme Court had jurisdiction throughout the province the common law rule did not apply.[87] Although the full court would later invalidate the whole trial because it took place not in the Supreme Court but in an assize court without commission, no one, including Crease, saw fit to make such an argument at this time.

In the course of his submissions McCreight also made a remark that seems an ominous foretaste of what would set off one of the most bitter exchanges before the full court a few months later. He suggested that if the defence argument were sound, the 'Indian murderers' recently brought from Barclay Sound to be tried in Victoria had themselves been murdered; although they were returned to Hesquiat and hanged there, they had not been condemned by a jury of their neighbours. McCreight did not add, as Walkem was to do in June, that the judge who passed sentence was also a murderer. Crease overruled the objection, and in doing so suggested that Hare originally had been content with the change because he was afraid of being 'lynched' in Kamloops. That of course had nothing to do with the jurisdictional issue, but Crease added that he thought the trial could not have been held there 'where perhaps every man has borne arms against the prisoners or certainly expressed most decided opinions respecting them.' No doubt the people of New Westminster shared those opinions. None the less, Crease concluded that a 'Kamloops jury would have made short shrift of the prisoners and so Hare and the McLeans must have thought when they asked to be tried [here] where as fair a trial as possible can be had.'[88] As it turned out, the New Westminster jury made equally short shrift of them.

The evidence at the trial followed closely the pattern of the depositions placed before the grand jury; its force was such that Davie and Bole were reduced, in their final submissions to the trial jury, to pleading for mercy. They occasionally clutched at other straws. Davie blamed the government – safe enough, if editorial opinion was anything to go by – for not providing the resources necessary to nip in the bud the McLeans' descent into lawlessness. Bole stressed that, although the Crown's theory was that the gun had been fired only inches from Ussher, there was no evidence of powder on his head. But there was little to be said. When on the third day Crease charged the jury, his bleak recital of the facts only emphasized the palpable lack of a defence, and was an invitation to convict. The law was clear: the prosecution had proved the killing and the burden was on the prisoners to show it was not murder. To do less than convict on that charge, Crease seemed to be saying to the jury, would be a woeful dereliction of duty and would let down not only those who had suffered at the hands of the prisoners but everyone who believed in British justice. 'Let it go out to the world that B.C. is a law-abiding country,' he urged them, 'let it be known that a dreadful murder having been committed, the people of the interior truly followed the genius and spirit of the law. They did not take the law into their own hands, they did honourably, and all honour to those brave men who during those cold, bleak December days, stood, night and day, sentinels around the beleaguered retreat of those prisoners, now before you ... Gentlemen of the jury, those men have done their duty, and it is now for you to do yours also.'[89] Earlier in his charge Crease had described the murder itself, and the Victoria *Colonist* reported that Alex Hare and Charlie had shown some emotion, but that Allan and Archie 'were unmoved, the former during the pathetic narrative yawning audibly and keeping his eyes fixed on the face of the judge with apparent unconcern and chewing tobacco vigorously.' The reporter thought Allan McLean 'a fitting prototype of Hugh, the half-gypsy, whose character Dickens so vividly described in *Barnaby Rudge.'*[90] The jury took twenty-two minutes to reach the expected verdict. The passing of the death sentence was adjourned to the last day of the assize, as was the ancient custom.

Before sentencing them the next morning Crease asked each of the prisoners whether he had anything to say. Originally, this had been done to give the accused an opportunity to claim benefit of clergy, but now it was simply a gesture. The three McLeans each made a few short and disjointed remarks, filling in a few details, quarrelling with certain items of evidence that must have seemed important to them but which no longer mattered and, in truth, never did. Only Alex Hare showed any bitterness. 'If I was not with the crowd,' he reflected, too late, 'I would not be here.'[91] Crease then passed sentence. It was almost as though he had memorized the exhortations of his eighteenth- and nineteenth-century predecessors and their apologists:[92]

After a long and patient trial, defended by able counsel, before a jury of twelve impartial men, you have been found guilty of a foul, atrocious murder, marked by peculiar brutality, and, in the case of one or perhaps two of you, aggravated by the additional stain of base ingratitude. Your life for some years previously had been that of outlaws and robbers – your hand against every man and every man's hand against you. Since then your life has been one continued course of blood and rapine. You became a terror to your neighbourhood and a disgrace to a province which is, and ever has been, pre-eminently peaceful and law-abiding. Until at last all your neighbours arose in arms against you to hand you over to that Law whose Majesty you had so offended. There is not *one* single redeeming feature, *one* extenuating circumstance to put forward in mitigation of your offence. A blacker record of crime in so young men I never saw.

You, Allan, not content with perilling your own life and steeping your soul in sin, instead of protecting, drew all your brothers into a similar danger with yourself and prostituted the hereditary courage of your race to the commission of violence and robbery and at last, murder, and became a band of outlaws chased about the Country like wild beasts.

And now you have to expiate your crimes with your lives, without a hope of mercy or the slightest chance of pardon. There is but one Hope left you now this side the grave. It is the Hope that by turning in sincere humility and penitence to The Almighty you might at The Throne of Infinite Mercy find forgiveness for your sins and crimes through that very Saviour who gave his Life, even for you, that sacred name whom you in your life have so often blasphemed.

Allan McLean, Charles McLean, Archibald McLean, Alexander Hare. The sentence of this Court is that you be taken from this place to the place whence you came and from thence to the place of execution and there that you be hanged by the neck until you be dead.

And may God have mercy on your Souls.[93]

Crease ordered the sheriff not to execute the condemned men before two calendar months had passed. This left him enough time to do what, arguably, he had been intending to do from the moment he decided to go to New Westminster and preside without a commission. On the same day, 19 March 1880, the witnesses presented their petition requesting firearms to the grand jury. No one, it appears, was willing to bet that the last had been heard of the McLeans and Hare.

HABEAS CORPUS AND THE FULL COURT

Ten days later Crease wrote to Attorney General Walkem to advise him that the report Crease was required as trial judge to make to the Secretary of State at Ottawa could not be completed without dealing with the issue of the validity of the assize. He reminded Walkem of the judges' continuing doubts, 'already so strongly but respectfully expressed beforehand to the government,' and repeated that he had presided at the assize 'under protest.'[94] Accordingly, the judges felt it their duty to give all the parties an opportunity to argue the point before the full court in the form of a rule nisi for a habeas corpus, in order that 'if possible, the doubt may be removed, and the validity of the trial, should such be the decision, established or otherwise as may be.'[95] No doubt Walkem felt the force of the 'or otherwise as may be,' but when Crease wrote in a similar vein to defence counsel he did not get the response he must have expected. Bole merely asked that notice of any such motion be served on him so that he might attend 'if advised.' Davie, who did not even reply until 7 April, seemed to view the suggestion as verging on maintenance.[96] 'I am not instructed,' he wrote, 'to take any proceedings on behalf of any of the prisoners.' Apparently they and their counsel were prepared to accept the verdict. 'Apart from this consideration, I cannot see that any practical good could result in the event of success in the suggested application.' He did, however, express a strong wish that his challenge to the array be brought to the attention of Ottawa when Crease filed his report, still believing in its merit and hoping that it might influence the Governor General to commute the sentence.

Davie was surely right about no 'practical good' resulting from the course of action Crease was proposing. At least there was none from the prisoners' point of view: if successful, a review would lead only to a new trial with the same result, and it is unlikely that Davie and Bole were enthusiastic about acting for a small fee or even no fee at all if the best that could be hoped for was delaying the inevitable. However, there may have been something in it for Crease and Begbie, who could well have been concerned that the conviction and execution of the McLeans and Hare without a commission might be a form of 'judicial murder.' There was some authority, including Blackstone, which suggested this was the law.[97] Moreover, McCreight had alluded to this possibility when arguing the challenge to the array and Begbie had expressed a similar concern years earlier when the Gaol Delivery Act was disallowed. But neither the government nor, it seems, the defence seemed interested in pressing the point.

Indeed, the government must have wanted nothing more than to let sleeping dogs lie. But Crease and his brother judges were losing their perspective and sacrificing common sense for an opportunity to win a long-standing quarrel with the government and to humiliate Walkem. Begbie and McCreight had first crossed swords years earlier in a case in which McCreight claimed that Begbie had grossly insulted him, and that 'His Honour would not dare to use the language outside the courtroom that he had used in it.' The case ended with McCreight requesting that the Registrar strike his name from the list of barristers entitled to practice on the mainland, and for years thereafter he confined his practice in protest to Vancouver Island.[98] Nor was there any love lost between Begbie and Walkem, whom both judges regarded as untrustworthy and incompetent. The animosity between Walkem and the Chief Justice stemmed from the latter's refusal to enrol Walkem as a barrister in the mainland colony because he had been trained in Canada. Begbie preferred English lawyers, and it took the intervention of the Colonial Secretary to overcome his intransigence.[99] Crease also had no time for Walkem and regularly complained in his correspondence that he was out to destroy the independence of the judiciary. He accused Walkem of deliberately keeping the public 'in the dark' about his plans for the judges and felt that much of the government's legislation was really designed to make the Supreme Court a mere 'appendage' of the executive. In his private letters he also accused Walkem of controlling a local newspaper – it certainly was not the Victoria *Colonist* or the *Mainland Guardian* – whose columns were 'calculated to make the judges appear ridiculous in the eyes of the public.'[100]

Yet whatever the reasons behind the judges' determination to force the issue, there is no doubt that the government had only themselves to blame for the fix in which they soon found themselves. Both sides seemed by the late spring of 1880 to be spoiling for a fight. By cancelling the commission, the Walkem government made one extremely likely; by going to New Westminster instead of refusing to preside, Crease made it inevitable.

If any hope remained after the trial was over, it ended with Walkem's response to Crease's letter of 29 March. 'After ascertaining the practice of Ontario,' he wrote on 8 April, the Lieutenant Governor had concluded prior to the New Westminster assize that he had no power to issue a commission. If the judges felt that they could not preside without one, they should have refused to do so, and the government would have 'accepted their decision with all proper respect' and sought Ottawa's advice on the matter. While Walkem did not share the judges' doubts about the validity of the trial, on behalf of the government, he begged 'to most respectfully disclaim any responsibility for Your Honour's act in trying and sentencing the prisoners, if these proceedings were illegal.' He then twitted Crease for not reserving the matter at the time if he had been so concerned about it and claimed that the government's position concerning the need for a commission was in fact consistent with that expressed by the judges themselves in their written response to the proposed Judicature Act of the year before. So far as he was concerned, Walkem concluded, it was now a matter for Ottawa, not the courts.[101]

It is difficult to imagine an attitude more carefully chosen to infuriate Crease. Not only did Walkem charge that if the trial were illegal the judges were solely to blame, thus ensuring that Crease could not let the matter drop, but by claiming that the Dominion government rather than the courts should decide what was clearly a question of law he must have confirmed all of Crease's darkest suspicions about Walkem's notions of judicial independence. 'Surely,' Justice Gray was to write in his judgment after the hearing before the full court, 'more unconstitutional doctrine never fell by accident from an Attorney General.'[102] Walkem was throwing down the gauntlet – or picking one up that he thought had been thrown down already. Crease's reaction was true to form: 'I observe that you now, on behalf of the Executive, allege a totally different ground for the non-issuing of a commission from that which was stated in the letter of the Provincial Secretary of the 11th March ... I cannot admit the accuracy of your recollection of facts, and entirely fail to perceive the cogency of your argument.'[103] These were the last words formally exchanged by the government and the judges outside the courtroom, where Begbie even more than Crease would challenge the accuracy of Walkem's facts and the cogency of his arguments. For the government, it was an inauspicious beginning.

On 21 March 1880 Crease made a preliminary report to Ottawa, advising the Secretary of State that he had been required to hold an assize without commission but that he would not mention this in his formal report on the trial, lest it weaken the effect of the verdict and sentence.[104] In the formal report Crease was unrelenting. There was not, he said, echoing the words he had used in passing sentence, a 'single alleviating circumstance connected with the cases, not one single redeeming feature in the horrid crime' committed by these 'desperadoes' which would justify him in suggesting 'the slightest mitigation of the terrible penalty of death.' Crease dwelt at length, as he was to do in his report on the second trial, on how the McLeans had nearly incited an Indian uprising, and he damned Archie and Alex Hare, the two youngest, as the worst offenders of the lot. It was Archie after all who had fired the fatal shot and Hare, for whom Ussher had performed many 'deeds of gentle kindness,' who had battered and stabbed him as he lay on the ground. 'There only remains,' he wrote at the end of the report, 'the references to His Excellency to pass upon the Case in exercise of the blessed gift of Mercy, and deeply pained and grieved I feel to be unable, conscientiously, to pray for the shedding of one scintilla of its rays upon the heads of any one of these unhappy hardened men.' To do otherwise would be only to encourage others 'similarly disposed' to act on the McLeans' example.[105]

Throughout April and May he engaged in a protracted correspondence with the Dominion government concerning the validity of the assize and the need for a reprieve pending the determination of that issue. When Ottawa finally agreed to pay the fees of defence counsel should they wish to challenge the conviction before the full court, Davie and Bole had a change of heart and commenced habeas corpus proceedings. Nominally a contest between the Crown and the prisoners, the hearing before the full court was really a dispute between the Walkem government and the judges. Given that the latter would now decide the point, the outcome was not difficult to predict.[106]

The argument began on 4 June and lasted a week. On 26 June all three of the judges delivered judgment in favour of the prisoners. The reaction of the press, or at least of a large part of it, was even more outraged than it had been after the outlaws had been captured. The *Mainland Guardian* bemoaned the fact that the 'unfortunate taxpayers of this province will be called upon to pay for the shocking blunder committed by our local government' and the Victoria *Colonist* railed bitterly against the 'meanness, stupidity, obstinacy and ignorance of the legal department of the Crown.'[107] In fact, the editorial writer of that paper quite lost control. The Supreme Court decision, he wrote, 'draws the pen through the proceedings instituted against the Kamloops outlaws ... and no decent excuse can be framed that will palliate the conduct of the Government.' He continued:

The English language does not contain words in which to frame an explanation that will be deemed satisfactory ... It is on record that the late government agent at Kamloops complained to the government that the gaol was insecure; that prisoners left it with ease; that the McLeans and Hare walked in or out as the whim seized them. The Grand Jury in the fall of 1878 presented the building as insecure, and the government agent offered, at an expenditure of $100, to make it secure, which small sum the government withheld ... After the arrest what followed? At an enormous expense, in the depths of a hard winter, the prisoners were conveyed under heavy guard to New Westminster, the superintendent of police was sent to the country to summon witnesses who were brought to the coast and kept at public expense for months awaiting the trial. Economy would have dictated that the trials be held in the district where the crime was committed, but like the orders given to Mr. Mould when old Anthony Chuzzlewit lay dead, there was 'absolutely no limit.' From the extreme of parsimony, the government plunged to the other extremity of wasteful extravagance ... [A] strange fatality would seem to dog the footsteps of this government. They appear utterly incapable of doing anything as it ought to be done ... From beginning to end ... they have acted with an utter disregard for the welfare of the public which will have to discharge all the liabilities incurred and bear all the burdens imposed due to the incompetency of their servants ... The officials responsible for the state of affairs which culminated on Saturday last should perform the political *hari-kari* and save the country the trouble and expense of doing it for them ...[108]

This certainly was no paper controlled by Walkem. But even the *Colonist* later reported that some thought the decision would be appealed and reversed, and the judges clearly expected an appeal.[109] It never came, and Begbie must have felt the victory complete when, within only a few years of the *McLean* case, all three of the government lawyers had been appointed to the Supreme Court. He was then able to note with some satisfaction that all of them had 'tried and sentenced prisoners under the Lieutenant-Governor's Commission without the least expression of doubt or hesitation.'[110] In fact, within days of handing down his judgment in the *McLean* case Begbie had an equally satisfying experience: he discovered a report in *The Times* of an assize in Hertford that very nearly miscarried a week earlier because of a defect in the commission. He promptly pasted the clipping in his Bench-book only a few pages after his notes on the McLean arguments conclude.[111]

The decision itself is long and complex, but the reasoning can be summed up in a single sentence. The trial had not taken place in the Supreme Court because the government had proclaimed a court of assize;

but the court was not a valid court of assize because Crease had no commission to hold one. Nor had the trial been removed into the Supreme Court by certiorari, where it could have been tried at Bar. The government put forward some good arguments and some unbelievably bad ones, but the judges were impressed by none of them. No doubt the unspoken premise of the government's position was common sense, but that is always a dangerous argument in a criminal case, especially when made by a litigant that had recently displayed such a glaring lack of it. McCreight, however, had argued this way when he addressed the jury in March. Simply apply common sense, he had said, scoffing at the defence, for the law was only common sense. And so he argued before the full court. The need for such a commission in British Columbia in 1880 violated common sense, hence there was no need for a commission. The logic is impeccable, but the premise was contradicted by experience. So the government had to resort to legal arguments.

These arguments were basically three, at least two of which would have commanded the respect of a court that had not become so intimately involved in the outcome of the dispute. The government's position was this: (1) that Crease as a judge of the Supreme Court lawfully presided in the assize court at New Westminster, notwithstanding he had no commission; (2) that if he could not preside without a commission, the trial was none the less valid because an earlier commission, dated 19 November 1879, was still in force at the time of the assize and Crease had presided by virtue of it; and (3) that if that earlier commission was no longer in force, the trial was still valid because it had taken place in the Supreme Court, not the assize court, before a Supreme Court judge. The first and third of these arguments had some merit, but Walkem and McCreight undermined them by making two further submissions that were remarkably ill advised, both legally and tactically. They argued, first of all, that the Lieutenant Governor had no power to issue a commission anyway, a position first advanced by Walkem in his letter to Crease of 8 April and, second, that as many as ninety-six of the 132 assizes that had been held in British Columbia had been held without a commission. The judges dealt with all these points in much the same way that Crease had predicted a Kamloops jury would have dealt with the McLeans.

The first of the Crown's three main arguments, said Begbie, was completely unsupported by authority. No English case had been or could be produced in which the Queen's Bench or a judge of that court had tried without commission a person committed for trial at the next sitting of a court of oyer and terminer, which was the court to which the prisoners had been committed. 'There is no such case,' he said, 'and neither has this court, or any judge thereof, any authority *mera virtute officii*, to preside in a court of oyer and terminer. No person, whether a judge of this court or otherwise, can do that without a commission.'[112] It was true that in the proceedings against the man charged in Ontario with the murder of D'Arcy McGee this point had arisen, and it was there held that the lack of a commission was not fatal; but in that province there was a statute that expressly provided for assizes without commissions.[113] There was a similar statute in British Columbia, but it was not yet in force, and this made the government's position doubly untenable. Begbie and his brother judges could argue, as Davie had when he pointed to the Crown's attempt to change the venue of the trial, that the Walkem administration's own action tended to show that they shared the doubts of the judges. If a statute was in the works, a statute was probably necessary to permit assizes without commissions.

Yet there were holes in all this. No statute existed that imposed the assize system on British Columbia, and Begbie could say that the prisoners had been committed to a court of oyer and terminer only because the forms prescribed by schedules to the Justices of the Peace Act (1869) made reference to such courts.[114] Indeed, the committals themselves made no such reference, saying only that the prisoners were to be held until delivered 'in due course of law.'[115] Begbie was attaching a great deal of significance to a couple of forms in a statutory schedule. Another difficulty was presented by the judges' memorandum of March 1879. In that document they had clearly said that they presided over the assizes *virtute officii*, yet when Walkem and Crease pressed this point Begbie replied that they had misinterpreted the memorandum. He did not explain how. Instead, he reminded them that the judges withdrew their recommendation that commissions be abolished because they feared that only the Dominion was constitutionally competent to do this. But when Walkem had the temerity to suggest there were no courts of oyer and terminer in British Columbia (another covert appeal to common sense), once again his own government's actions stood in the way. Who then was responsible for the announcement in the *Gazette* that such a court would be held at New Westminster? asked Begbie. That, replied Walkem, was 'merely an advertisement in a newspaper.'[116]

The Crown's second argument, that the assize was valid because it had been held pursuant to an earlier commission, gave the court no trouble at all. The older authorities were clear that such a commission was cancelled by the issue of a new one, and of course that is what the government had done on 8 March. The third argument, however, had more to it, and followed from Walkem's suggestion that there were no courts of oyer and terminer in the province. There was no need for them, he seemed to be saying, because the jurisdiction of the Supreme Court and its judges was ample. Although the argument was not made explicitly in Crease's Report of the case, the Crown must have been saying something like this. English law applies only if appropriate in local circumstances and not inconsistent with local statutes; the assizes are not appropriate and are rendered unnecessary by the wide jurisdiction of the Supreme Court as set out in a number of statutes, both federal and provincial.[117] Even if the judges of the King's Bench in England could not preside at assize time without a commission, Crease could: his court had jurisdiction over all crimes in the province and this jurisdiction could be exercised by a single judge. The words of Begbie, Crease, and Gray in their memorandum of 1879 suggested this as strongly as any 'advertisement in a newspaper' suggested the contrary.

This argument was persuasive, but it did not persuade. The judges were not in a receptive mood, and Walkem may have erred in placing too much emphasis on a Dominion statute declaring the wide jurisdiction of the Supreme Court when an earlier colonial law had been just as wide.[118] This enabled Begbie to point out that there was really no difference between the two, and he of course had long ago made up his mind that, in the colonial period at least, the commissioned assize system was the law of British Columbia. The question, Begbie said, was not whether the Supreme Court had jurisdiction to hear the case (it did), but whether the case had ever been brought before that court (it had not). The judge (Crease) and the court (oyer and terminer) did not match, and no one had made any attempt to remove the case by certiorari into the Supreme Court. It was the logic of English law and an English past, the literal terms of the original English Law Ordinance falling by the wayside. Just as a writ authorized a judge to hear a particular civil case, so a commission authorized him to hear a criminal one. An indictment would surely provide a better comparison, and of course there was an indictment in the McLean case. But at this point the argument begins to rotate wildly, for in Begbie's view the indictments were in the assize court (the schedule to the Justices of the Peace Act again) and Crease had no commission.

The judges, however, saved their real contempt for the government's contentions that the Lieutenant Governor had no power to issue commissions and that assizes had been held in the past without them. The first, said Begbie, was 'entirely irrelevant here' and 'not even incidentally relevant'; one could not meet the argument that the trial was invalid because there was no commission with the argument that the government could not issue one.[119] But it was Walkem's repeated assertion that most of the assizes in the past had been held without commissions that the judges found intolerable. He produced an affidavit of the Provincial Secretary that purported to show, year by year, that this was so. But when he reached 1879 he was interrupted by Begbie, who told him that a copy of the commission he had just declared non-existent was in the next room, and that if he looked there he would find it in a tin box.[120] Walkem seemed to be saying that if the official records did not indicate a commission, there had been none, or even that if there had been one in fact there was none in law – it is not clear. The judges would have none of it. They accused him of trying to persuade them that black was white, against the evidence of their senses, and condemned the affidavit as presenting legal inferences as facts. Yet Walkem stuck to his guns: ninety-six out of 132 assizes had been held without commission, he said, and '[that] is my broad proposition, whether I am right or I am wrong in my contention.'[121] This rather absurd statement was followed by an exchange that reveals the growing tension between the Bench and the government lawyers:

Crease: If the Attorney General is correct, then in the past prisoners have been murdered.
Walkem: No doubt about it.
Begbie: A very awkward position for the Crown Prosecutors.
Walkem: Fortunately, I did not pass sentence, My Lord.

What McCreight had touched upon in responding to the defence's challenge to the array was now out in the open. One can imagine that these words were said through clenched teeth, for it is not often that a Chief Justice and an Attorney General indulge in mutual accusations of official murder. If it was possible that the judges had any doubts left at all about the decision they would hand down, these must have been dispelled by this open suggestion that they might indeed be looked upon as judicial killers if the convictions should stand. Still, it is possible that Walkem thought this charge would make them cover up, retreat, and hold the assize valid to shield themselves from such accusations. If so, he badly misread his opponents, and worse was ahead.

Throughout the week-long hearing the lawyers for the Crown weaved back and forth between their submissions – or so it seems in Crease's Report – and even contradicted themselves. Perhaps the best job was done by the most junior member of the team, Alexander Rocke Robertson, who became the fourth member of the court only four months after his appearance in the *McLean* case and who died as a result of an injury suffered in a swimming accident barely a year later.[122] Robertson at least managed to stay clear of the sort of confrontations that occurred between his two learned friends and the Chief Justice, confrontations which soon degenerated into stalemate. When at last McCreight took his turn at bat, his attempt to reiterate Walkem's hopeless argument about all the assizes without commissions provoked the following outburst from Begbie: 'The statement is utterly untrue, it is the direct contrary to the fact and known to be so by everybody who ever attended in a court of criminal justice here – let one man be produced who ever was present when a court was opened without this commission. If you, Mr. McCreight, were in the habit of attending these courts, you would know that this is absolutely contrary to the facts. After what was said yesterday and the day before [Begbie is here referring to Walkem's arguments] it is stating what is wilfully contrary to reproduce this allegation.'[123] McCreight tried to smooth things over, but he too was a proud man, unwilling to forget past slights or to endure new ones. Asking to be allowed to proceed without interruption, he then expressed the hope that there would be no more angry words 'or we shall not get on.' Interrupted again by Begbie, he then indicated that he would sit down until the Chief Justice had finished. But when Begbie repeated his accusations, McCreight rose from his chair:

McCREIGHT: (rising rapidly) I deny –
CHIEF JUSTICE: You have sat down, sir, and you *shall* sit down. I will hear Mr. Robertson.
McCREIGHT: In accusing me of wilfully making a false statement you have said what is quite untrue and you have no right to make such an assertion.
CHIEF JUSTICE: Take your seat, sir. I will not hear you further.
McCREIGHT: (warmly) Indeed, I shall not –
CHIEF JUSTICE: You must apologize before I hear you again: (rising) the Court is adjourned until 11 o'clock tomorrow.
McCREIGHT: I will apologize only as far as to say that your statement was incorrect instead of being untrue.
CHIEF JUSTICE: I shall not hear you. The Court is adjourned until tomorrow when Mr. Robertson will proceed.[124]

Begbie was angry and flustered. He had not noticed that Robertson had left the courtroom, and that is why he had to adjourn. Now the same intransigence that had caused the original problem threatened to derail the hearing set to resolve it. Neither the Bench nor the Bar, it seems, were able to give in.

The next day McCreight tried to continue, but Begbie again demanded an apology. Instead, McCreight made the following statement:

I was told by your Lordship that I was making a statement that I knew to be untrue, and under the circumstances I think I have a right to ask you to apologize to me instead of my offering an apology to you ... I am a practitioner of some 20 years standing here, and if I am to be told these things whilst I am engaged in argument it is impossible for me to conduct a case properly or do justice to my client ... The privileges of a counsel are as important as those of a judge and should be observed ... I stand here now to vindicate the rights of counsel and I must state that I cannot possibly apologize for the language I made use of. I went as far as I could yesterday when I said your statement was incorrect instead of being untrue. I can go no further now and say that an apology is due to me.

Walkem then added the following: 'I have frequently had occasion to protest against the manner in which I have been treated by the Chief Justice, and I will state now, openly and without fear, that I would not be in politics today if I thought I could be decently treated by the Chief Justice. His treatment of Mr. McCreight yesterday was overbearing and tyrranical. No man of spirit could stand such treatment without resentment. I have resented it before and I resent it now.'[125]

The vehemence of these speeches clearly surprised and affected Begbie, although he noted in his Bench-book that Walkem's and McCreight's statements went on 'at length' and were, in his opinion, 'quite unjustifiable.'[126] But he was wounded. And when he protested, asking whether a barrister had ever left his courtroom or a conference with him without a smile, the Victoria *Colonist* reported that the Attorney General had grumbled under his breath that, if so, it was a smile of sarcasm. It is not certain whether Begbie heard this remark, but he would have seen it in the newspaper the next day. To his credit, he pressed the matter no further in court and told counsel to go on 'as if yesterday had never been.'[127] The hearing ended soon afterwards, and after a short interval judgment was rendered. The McLeans would have to be tried for the murder of Johnny Ussher a second time.

THE SECOND TRIAL

By November 1880 the newspapers were over the spasm of vituperation that had seized them after the full court decision had come down. But even after the second trial and conviction of the McLeans they once again expressed their impatience with all the 'haggling over law quibbles' by 'judges and lawyers and ministers.' The Victoria *Colonist* called it an 'extraordinary jumble' and one paper even warned that one more miscarriage of justice in the case would mean the McLeans would be shot before they could be hanged.[128] But the trial went as smoothly as the first had done, although now this was scarcely likely to be seen as any guarantee of its validity. The ubiquitous Crease presided once more, claiming that his remarks at the first trial had 'to some extent, been verified.' Theodore Davie, who had represented Alex Hare both in March and before the full court in June, did not appear this time,[129] and Norman Bole defended all the prisoners. He gamely argued that this trial, too, was invalid. It is not clear whether or not a commission was issued this time around, but the government must have been relying upon section 14 of the Judicature Act, belatedly in force as of 20 July, which permitted assizes with or without commission at the option of the Lieutenant Governor.[130] Bole submitted that this section was ultra vires of the legislature because it related to a matter of criminal procedure, and although Crease overruled this objection, he may well have had some sympathy for it. Indeed, he must have. In the hearing before the full court he and Begbie had given the judges' fears that such a provision was unconstitutional as the reason they had withdrawn their suggestion in the 1879 memorandum that commissions should be abolished. Only the Dominion, said Begbie, could accomplish that result.[131] Apparently Crease was not about to let such doubts sabotage the second McLean trial, which raises the issue of why he had been so eager to let similar doubts sabotage the first. Undaunted, Bole pressed on, claiming that a second trial would subject his clients to double jeopardy. He attempted to have them plead *autrefois convict*, that is, that they had already been tried and convicted for the murder of Ussher and could not in fairness be tried again. But as the full court had already ruled that the first trial was a nullity, Crease had no difficulty in holding that the McLeans and Hare had never been in jeopardy and dismissed this notion as well. After an almost *pro forma* challenge to the array which was also overruled, the trial began.[132]

And it was soon over, with the same result. The accused were then tried for the murder of James Kelly and convicted of that, as well. Not a man who could be accused of giving up without a fight, Bole trotted out the same preliminary objections – 'mooted' them in Crease's words – as he had made in the Ussher trial, and they were promptly overruled. Although he was given ample time to request that all these points be brought before the full court, he decided not to do so, contenting himself with requesting Crease to pass them on to the Secretary of State at Ottawa.[133] At the end of the assize both sentences were delivered at once, and this time the prisoners said nothing when invited to do so.[134]

In his report to Ottawa Crease repeated the recommendations he had made after the first trial that no mercy be shown to the McLeans and Hare. He again stressed that comparative youth was no excuse, for the two youngest were 'the most hardened desperadoes of the gang.' And now there was the murder of James Kelly to be considered, which was 'most unprovoked and cold-blooded, so little anticipated by the victim that when the body was discovered frozen stiff, one hand was still quietly reposing on his bosom under his plaid.' This of course was not what Allan had told Robert Scott.[135] Emphasizing and surely exaggerating how narrowly a general Indian uprising had been averted, Crease suggested that an important factor in this was the Indians' knowledge that the Dominion government would 'deal liberally with them in the matter of their reserve lands,' a sentiment that seems almost grimly humorous today.[136] But above all, he concluded, the McLeans and Hare had to be executed because that was what was expected. 'Any sign of what [the Indians] would consider as weakness in this matter is sure to be misconstrued. They cannot understand and cannot be made to understand the reason why the prisoners were not executed in March last.' Indeed, he added, even the whites would probably have lynched the outlaws had they not been assured that the law would be 'amply vindicated,' and all were looking 'anxiously for the result.'[137]

Two months later this vindication took place. The four condemned men seem to have accepted the inevitability of their fate and even its justice. It was over quickly, and death was probably almost instantaneous. Said the *Mainland Guardian*: 'With the exception of Charlie, who showed slight convulsions, they scarcely moved a muscle ... After the drop fell, something like a sigh of relief escaped from the spectators, who felt that innocent blood had been avenged, and the law vindicated. The McLeans and Hare are now no more, and although they have filled a large space in the minds of the public, they will, nevertheless, be soon forgotten.' The Victoria *Colonist* also ran a long description of the execution and the prison in which it took place.[138] Before he died, Allan McLean asked that none of his friends or relatives take revenge, and none did. But had the law truly been vindicated?

That the McLeans and Hare were murderers, there is no doubt. If one accepts the justice of capital punishment, at least in the context of the times, their punishment was deserved. They had a fair trial, in fact, two of them, and they were represented by competent counsel; in other parts of North America they might well have been lynched. And in some ways it is astonishing that such an elaborate system of justice should have flourished in such a young and potentially lawless part of the world. It is true that the McLeans and Hare were committed for trial by the same magistrates who had led the posse that captured them and that Crease had been both trial judge and 'appeal' judge in the same case. True it is as well that they could not testify under oath, had no formal right of appeal, and bore a burden of proof they would not have had to discharge today. But these defects, if that is what they are, were an integral part of the judicial system as it then existed, and to condemn them is to condemn that system as a whole rather than its disposition of the McLean case.

Yet in an equally important way the law was not vindicated at all. A senseless murder and its four young perpetrators were permitted to become an occasion for the continuation and escalation of a bitter and unnecessary quarrel between the judicial and executive branches of the government. It is difficult to know why Walkem persisted in holding an assize without a commission after the judges had expressed their doubts so unambiguously. Or as Justice Gray put it in his judgment in June, it is 'inconceivable, for what reason, on the very eve of one of the most important trials that could be held in the country, this sudden revolution in practice should have been adopted, notwithstanding the earnest and united representations of the Judges.'[139] Yet given these representations and the reasons for them, it is just as difficult to understand why Crease went to New Westminster and presided there, only to raise the issue after the fact. Viewed in this light, the squabble over commissions of assize that was the *McLean* case seems nothing more than a fight between two judges, Begbie and Crease, and a politician, Walkem, over who had the last word. How else can one explain the refusal to issue the commission and Crease's doggedness in bringing the matter to a head? The judges' dithering over the assize question between 1860 and 1879 almost seems a baited trap.

But of course it was not. It is too easy to read an evil intent into all these actions and to forget about the role that carelessness, human fallibility, and incompetence play in any judicial system. Walkem was out of the province when the final decision to proceed without the commission was made, and when he returned he may have felt it was too late to back down without losing face. He may also have been unduly encouraged by the wide statutory jurisdiction of the Supreme Court, by the judges' own suggestions that they thought commissions a nuisance, and by the able counsel at his disposal, McCreight and Robertson. No doubt he was influenced by his dislike of Begbie and Crease, no doubt he would have delighted in besting them; but perhaps the newspapers, who weekly charged him with the grossest incompetence, knew him best. Or, perhaps, in the heat of battle he simply lost all sense of proportion.

But the judges, who also lost their perspective, cannot enter a plea of incompetence. They were able lawyers and should have known better. Crease in particular behaved more like defence counsel than those who had been appointed to so act, and his zeal for battle seems to have taken over. No doubt all the members of the court had a passion for justice according to law and were troubled by the possibility that one of their number might have unlawfully sentenced four men to death. But that result could have been avoided if Crease had refused to preside. Moreover, the authorities did not dictate the conclusion that the three judges reached, they merely inclined towards it. No statute made the assize system applicable in British Columbia, and Confederation had cast some doubt upon whether the provincial practice had survived the BNA Act, especially in light of the recent Dominion statutes. But it was the old English law that appealed to Begbie and his court, and having kicked up such a fuss before the March assize, was it really open to the judges to conclude that they had raised a false alarm, even as the words of their memorandum on the Judicature Act were being hurled back at them?

They may also have felt that to permit the government to dispense with commissions without statutory authorization would be undesirable because it would remove the restraining hand of the legislature. It is difficult to say. But they could with some justification plead that this was how things had always been done, that they were simply sticking to the letter of the law and protecting the rights of the prisoners under the law. Justice Gray in fact quoted Lord Chief Justice Cockburn's famous words in *Martin v Machonochie* (1877–8), to the effect that the rules of criminal procedure are as much a part of the law as anything else, adding that 'these words should be written on the footsill of every court, so that when the vilest criminal crosses the threshold of the temple of justice, he may read there the majesty of his rights, and know that the decision which is to affect his fate will not be influenced by fear or favour, expediency or prejudice.'[140] Certainly no one could accuse the trial of the McLean brothers and Alex Hare of being overly expedient, nor can one say that the reasoning of the full court was clearly wrong. But in hard cases much more than the law determines the result, especially when a court has allowed itself to be drawn into the sort of contest that occurred here.

Begbie, for his part, summed up the successful argument for the defence as follows: 'The prisoners say, "I am to be tried by a court of oyer and terminer. You, not I, selected that court. You might have selected another court. That court cannot be held without a commission. You say that the Lieutenant Governor cannot issue the proper commission. You must find somebody then who can. If you cannot find anybody able to issue a commission, that only shows that you have summoned me before a non-existing, impossible court. With that I have nothing to do. You shall not send me to another tribunal than you have announced. I insist upon being tried before a legal judge." And I think he has a right thus to speak.'[141] That this was the view of the judges, passed on to defence counsel, and then restated by the judges, there is no doubt. But to imagine that the prisoners themselves were saying any such thing is absurd, as Begbie of course knew. They must have been bewildered by what was happening to them, and it is significant that even their own counsel hesitated to make these arguments. Neither Davie nor Bole were much interested in a point that could only delay the inevitable, and letting the matter drop may well have been kinder to the men in the New Westminster penitentiary, waiting to hang. It is difficult to avoid the conclusion, therefore, that the point of the exercise was not the vindication of the law but the vindication of the judges. Provoked by a headstrong Attorney General and not un-influenced by personal animosity, the judges allowed their respect for the rule of law to help them make a point, not on the prisoners' behalf, but at their expense. In short, the Indians of the interior are not the only ones who could not understand the reason why the McLeans and Hare had not been executed 'in March last.'

Walkem, McCreight, and Robertson all became judges of the Supreme Court within two years of the hearing before the full court, and it did not take long before the nature of judicial office asserted itself and they began to see many of the issues of the day affecting the court in much the same way as Begbie and Crease. Barely a year after the McLeans' execution the court and the Walkem government clashed again, this time over whether the judges or the government should make the rules of court.[142] The judges were adamant, but they were to lose this battle, just as, ultimately, they lost on the issue of the assizes. Both the law and history have forgotten their opinion in the McLean case and have instead affirmed the view that 'the administration of criminal justice devolves upon the provincial authorities'[143] Perhaps one of the most interesting aspects of the whole affair is that in British Columbia in 1880 this was not yet clear. All in all, the dramatis personae of the *McLean* case represented a goodly portion of the British Columbia establishment in the late nineteenth century. Norman Bole, in many ways the workhorse of the story, became a member of the Provincial Legislature and then a County Court Judge before retiring to resume private practice; the rest all moved in and out of the Cabinet and the Supreme Court. And as the editors of the *Mainland Guardian* had predicted, the outlaws, like the judges and lawyers, soon faded from memory. Their 'legend' still lingers in the interior of the province and in 1967 a song was written about them, but they are remembered for their bloody deeds, not for the legal niceties of their trial and execution.[144] Section 14 of the Judicature Act (1879) was amended in 1899 to abolish commissions outright, but four years later the original wording was restored and that is essentially how it reads today.[145] Commissions of assize are now a thing of the past, but assizes, uncertainty about the proper relationship between the judiciary and the executive, and deeply felt disagreements over the meaning of our constitution are with us still. *The Queen* v *The McLeans and Hare*, stripped of its frontier setting, is quite familiar after all.

NOTES

I wish to thank Mr Paul Williamson of Vancouver, BC, whose unpublished paper on the McLeans prompted the present essay, and Professor S.W. Jackman and Mr David Williams, QC, whose comments and criticism made it a better one than it would have been otherwise. I would also like to thank the staffs of the British Columbia Provincial Archives and of the Public Archives of Canada for their assistance. Finally, I am indebted to my friend and colleague, the late James E.R. Ellis, with whom I never once had a conversation that did not leave me wiser.

1 The spectators' reaction is reported in the *Mainland Guardian* 2 Feb. 1881. Provincial Archives of British Columbia (hereafter PABC) Roll 58A. The prosecution witnesses petitioned the New Westminster grand jury for firearms because they felt 'that in consequence of their testimony they had probably incurred the resentment of relatives or friends of [the] prisoners.' The grand jury recommended that this be done: Petition to the Grand Jury PABC Add MSS 54, Folder 5/32.

2 The *Mainland Guardian* covered the hearing before the full court in June 1880, its editors noting that they 'had but an indistinct idea of the true merits of the case.' But they did criticize the government lawyers for their 'rash and imprudent' language in court: *Mainland Guardian*, 16 June 1880. PABC Roll 58A

3 Eg, *Tuberville* v *Savage* (1699), 86 English Reports 684, a landmark in most first-year tort classes

4 *Regina* v *Auld and Auld* (1957), 26 Criminal Reports (hereafter CR) 266 (British Columbia Court of Appeal), considered recently in *Regina* v *Deol, Gill and Randev* (1980), 51 Canadian Criminal cases, Second Series (hereafter CCC(2d)) 40 (Alberta Queen's Bench)

5 *The Queen* v *Allan McLean, Charles McLean, Archibald McLean, Alexander Hare* 26 June 1880. PABC Add MSS 54, Folder 5/32

6 Frederick Pollock and Frederic William Maitland *The History of English Law before the Time of Edward I* 2 vols (Cambridge, Eng. 1895; Cambridge, Eng. 1968) II 674

7 See Barry M. Gough 'Keeping British Columbia British: The Law-and-Order Question on a Gold Mining Frontier' *Huntington Library Quarterly* (1974–5) 269–80.

8 Crease alluded to this possibility in discussing a defence challenge to the array at the first trial and a local newspaper made a similar comment at the conclusion of the second, but it is difficult to say how serious these speculations were. See text accompanying notes 88 and 128, below. Crease also suggested that a lynching could occur when he reported on the second trial to Ottawa. See text accompanying note 137, below.

9 Donald Fraser, writing in *The Times* (London), 15 Mar. 1860. Quoted in David R. Williams '... *The Man for a New Country*' (Sidney, BC 1977) 89, 99

10 See text accompanying note 82 below.

11 R. Cole Harris and John Warkentin *Canada before Confederation* (Oxford 1974) 289–90. See also Margaret A. Ormsby *British Columbia: A History* (Vancouver, BC 1964) chs 2 and 3.

12 For a statement of this principle, see William Blackstone *Commentaries on the Laws of England*, 4 vols (London 1765–9; facsimile ed. Chicago 1979) I, 104–5.

13 This incident is chronicled in Mel Rothenburger '*We've Killed Johnny Ussher!*' (Vancouver, BC 1973) 8–11, a popular and engaging account of the escapades of the McLean boys and Alex Hare. It is well researched, but part fiction.

14 For a description of this incident see Edward Sleigh Hewlett 'The Chilcotin Uprising of 1864' *BC Studies* (1973) No. 19, 50–72 and G.R.V. Akrigg and Helen B. Akrigg *British Columbia Chronicle 1847–1871* (Victoria, BC 1977) 297–305. The Indians apparently 'dreaded and hated' the elder McLean, calling him

'Kutschte te Kukkpe,' the 'fierce chief.' He was said to have killed nineteen Indians during his life, although this cannot be known for certain.
15 43 Geo. III (1803), c. 138; 1 Geo. IV (1821), c. 66 (UK)
16 R.G. Herbert 'A Brief History of the Introduction of English Law into British Columbia' *UBC Legal Notes* (1954) 94
17 F.W. Howay *British Columbia: The Making of a Province* (Toronto 1928) 105
18 Harris and Warkentin *Canada before Confederation* 294, 296
19 Ibid. 299
20 Proclamation of 19 Nov. 1858. See the Law and Equity Act, *Revised Statutes of British Columbia* (hereafter RSBC) 1979, c. 224, s. 2. There had been no such proclamation when the Colony of Vancouver Island was established, hence no clear cut-off date.
21 21 & 22 Vict. (1858), c. 99 (UK), repealing 43 Geo. III, c. 138 and 1 Geo. IV, c. 66 (see note 15 above) insofar as they applied to British Columbia. 12 & 13 Vict. (1849), c. 48 (UK) had done the same for Vancouver Island; see John C. Bouck 'Introducing English Law into the Province: Time for a Change?' *Canadian Bar Review* (1979) 74–87.
22 The colonies were united by virtue of 29 & 30 Vict. (1866), c. 7 (UK), and this second English Law Ordinance may be found in Laws of British Columbia 1871, No. 70. This removed any doubts that may have existed as to when English law ceased to apply on Vancouver Island. For the restrictions imposed by the imperial parliament upon colonial legislatures, see B.L. Strayer *Judicial Review of Legislation in Canada* (Toronto 1968) 6–7.
23 Harris and Warkentin *Canada before Confederation* 296, 307; W. George Shelton, ed. *British Columbia and Confederation* (Victoria, BC 1967) 15
24 See generally Ormsby *British Columbia* ch. 9 and Derek Pethick 'The Confederation Debate of 1870' in Shelton, ed. *British Columbia and Confederation* 165–94.
25 British North America Act, 30–1 Vict. (1867), c. 3 (UK), ss. 96, 91(27), and 92(14)
26 The leading modern case is *Regina v Hauser* (1979), 46 CCC (2d) 481 (Supreme Court of Canada), and the issue has not yet been finally resolved by the courts. In the nineteenth century, the judges of the Supreme Court in British Columbia took the view that theirs was a federal court, mainly because they feared provincial interference with the independence of the judiciary.
27 William S. Holdsworth *A History of English Law* 17 vols (London 1903–72, 7th ed. revised 1969) 1 268–9
28 Ibid. 1 271–2. In 1233 the men of Cornwall hid from the coming of the justices: Pollock and Maitland *English Law before Edward I* 1 202.

29 A writ was needed because originally a direct complaint to the eyre had been the proper course, and those who did not wish to wait for its visit were seen as seeking exceptional treatment and therefore as needing exceptional permission. See S.F.C. Milsom *Historical Foundations of the Common Law* 2nd ed. (London 1981) 34–6.

30 Statute of Westminster II, 13 Edw. I (1285), c. 30. See also Blackstone *Commentaries* III 59.

31 Edward Coke *The Fourth Part of the Institutes of the Laws of England* (London 1628, New York 1979) 161

32 J.S. Cockburn *A History of English Assizes 1558–1714* (Cambridge, Eng. 1972) 87. Blackstone notes (IV 267) that justices of the peace, prominent members of the local gentry, and serjeants at law were also named as commissioners, but most were serjeants or judges. In 1850 Parliament permitted Queen's Counsel to be named as well: *The Times* (London), 7 July 1880.

33 36 & 37 Vict. (1873), c. 66 (UK), s. 16. *The Times* (London) of 7 July 1880 expressed surprise that the legal view was that commissions were necessary even after the Act. See note 111 below and accompanying text.

34 19–20 Eliz. II (1971), c. 23 (UK), s. 1. See also John H. Baker *An Introduction to English Legal History* (London 1979) 20.

35 Williams *Man for a New Country* 148. In one memorandum Begbie even described himself as having advised 'the late Gov. Douglas as Attorney General as well as Judge.' Public Archives of Canada (hereafter PAC) RG 13 C-1, vol. 1418. I am indebted to Professor M.C. Friedland of the Faculty of Law, University of Toronto, for making me aware of the existence of this material.

36 Proclamation by Governor Douglas, 8 June 1859. Consolidated Statutes (British Columbia), 1877, c. 51. A reference to the Gaol Delivery Act of 1860 may be found in the Table of Reserved Bills and Disallowed Acts in RSBC, 1979 (Vol. 7, Appendix). The proposed act is not reproduced, but it is described there as a proclamation for the Speedy Trial of Persons Charged with Offences. It was proclaimed 23 April 1860, received in London 14 April 1861, and disallowed in May 1861.

37 Begbie to Governor Douglas, 18 May 1862. PABC Colonial Correspondence, File 142E. The Act was disallowed presumably because it was repugnant to the laws of the mother country (see note 22 above and accompanying text). After the passage of the Colonial Laws Validity Act in 1865, however, the likelihood of this sort of thing happening was greatly reduced; instead, the problem in 1880 was whether commissions were a matter of criminal procedure (and therefore under federal jurisdiction) or the administration of justice (provincial).

38 36 Vict. (1873), c. 3

39 Williams *Man for a New Country* 162. Begbie, who also had doubts about the wisdom of joining Canada, became an eloquent spokesman for the federal position in matters legal almost from the moment he became a Dominion judge (Williams ibid. 164). Like Crease, he saw Ottawa as a shield against the provincial government's attempts to administer 'his' court, and fought a losing battle to have the Supreme Court held to be a federal one. He was not quite as strident as Crease, however. Writing to Alpheus Todd about the *Thrasher* case [(1882) 1 *British Columbia Reports* 153] on 4 Feb. 1882, Crease warned Todd not to be surprised if he heard 'all sorts of observations against the judges in the local House here when it meets. It used to be the glory of Sir John's Government that the Ermine was never made a political engine of party warfare – that immunity clearly does not extend to B.C. The attempt here is simply and plainly to make the Supreme Court of Imperial descent a mere appendage to one department of a local government ... Whether it will succeed or not depends upon this case, and the sense of Justice of you good folks at Ottawa ... The recent legislation here of late years on Administration of Justice has thrown everything into confusion, and the judges who have *protested with both hands* on each year and occasion against it, are for some political object or other made the scapegoats. Like the returned Israelites of old we have to rebuild the walls of the City of Justice with arms in our hands. However, "che sara sara".' PABC Add MSS 54, Folder 14/76

40 Alfred Watts, QC 'The Honourable Sir Henry Pering Pellew Crease' *The Advocate* (1967) 5–6

41 Crease to Senator Clement F. Cornwall, 20 Apr. 1879. PABC Add MSS 54, Folder 13/71

42 Courts of Assize Act, 1877. PABC Add MSS 54, Folder 12/65. See also text accompanying note 32 above.

43 29 & 30 Vict. (1866), c. 40, s. 3

44 Notation in Crease's handwriting in the margin of the PABC copy of the bill. The third Supreme Court judge was John Hamilton Gray, as to whom see text accompanying note 52 below.

45 Crease to Edward Blake, Minister of Justice at Ottawa, 9 Mar. 1877. PABC Add MSS 54, Folder 12/65

46 The preamble stated it to be 'An Act to Amend the Practice and Procedure of the Supreme Court of British Columbia, and for Other Purposes Relating to the Better Administration of Justice,' and the corresponding sections of the imperial and Ontario statutes appear in the margin. It was enacted as the Judicature Act, 1879, and may be found in *Statutes of British Columbia* (hereafter SBC) 1879, c. 12, under 'Courts, Supreme.' Section 17, which transferred the rulemaking power from the judges to the Lieutenant Governor (a change

which thoroughly upset Crease and Begbie), came into effect immediately; the rest of the Act, including the section that permitted assizes without commission, did not come into force until 20 July 1880, and was thus of no help to the government in the *McLean* case.

47 Today the most likely constitutional argument might be that a province could not appoint such commissioners without violating s. 96 of the BNA Act. But in 1880 the argument was that commissions and commissioners of assize fell under s. 91(27) of the BNA Act, and hence were beyond the realm of the provincial authorities. See note 131 and accompanying text below.

48 Memorandum from the three Supreme Court judges to the Attorney General, 7 Mar. 1879. PABC Add MSS 54, Folder 5/34

49 Coke *Laws of England* 73. Coke, however, would have agreed with the judges.

50 The letter of 18 Mar. 1879 to Attorney General Walkem is in PABC Add MSS 54, Folder 5/34. The clause is presently the law in British Columbia (see notes 130 and 131 below) and its validity is unchallenged. Yet Begbie, in a memorandum he sent to the federal Minister of Justice in the spring of 1880, wrote that 'it seems clear that the clause is an interference with criminal procedure which is by the B.N.A. Act 1867 expressly reserved to the Dominion Legislature.' PAC RG 13 C-1, vol. 1418

51 *Mainland Guardian* 17 Mar. 1880. See also Victoria *Colonist* 16 Mar. 1880. PABC Roll 25

52 Alfred Watts, QC 'The Honourable Mr Justice John Hamilton Gray' *The Advocate* (1967) 59. They soon warmed to him, but at the time Begbie had told Crease that 'a third judge is as unnecessary as twenty-one wheels to a coach.'

53 Gray to Edward Blake, 12 July 1877. PABC Add MSS 54, Folder 12/66

54 This information is from Rothenburger *Johnny Ussher* 34.

55 Whether the defence of infancy was open to Archie was an important issue at the trial, and it turned upon whether he had been born at the time of the Chilcotin uprising. The testimony on this point conflicted somewhat, so Crease left the matter with the jury, indicating that there was evidence that Archie was over fourteen when he killed Ussher. Crease's notes of his jury charge, PABC Add MSS 54, Folder 6/34

56 *Colonist* 13 Dec. 1879. This letter was published in the *Colonist* a few days after Ussher's death but before the McLeans and Hare were captured. It was headed 'Prophetic Letter.'

57 At the trial in Mar. 1880, Palmer testified that Ussher had told him he thought 'there would be no trouble in arresting the men.' *Mainland Guardian* 17 Mar. 1880

58 Deposition of Amni Shumway, packer, sworn at Kamloops, 13 Dec. 1879. PABC Add MSS 54, Folder 6/34

59 Deposition of William Palmer, rancher, sworn at Kamloops, 13 Dec. 1879. PABC Add MSS 54, Folder 6/34

60 Deposition of William Roxborough, herder, sworn at Kamloops, 13 Dec. 1879. PABC Add MSS 54, Folder 6/34. McLeod's wounds were sufficiently serious that when he had to give evidence before the Kamloops magistrates five days later they came to his bedside, bringing the prisoners with them. As Palmer remembered it, the first shot 'cut the icicles off my whiskers and hit McLeod in the cheek ... McLeod couldn't use his weapon and I said to him, we are long enough here ... I was satisfied at the time that Ussher was dead ...' See note 59 above.

61 Deposition of Thomas Trapp, stock-raiser, sworn at Kamloops, 13 Dec. 1879. PABC Add MSS 54, Folder 6/34

62 Deposition of Robert Scott, farmer, sworn at Kamloops, 13 Dec. 1879. PABC Add MSS 54, Folder 6/34

63 Apparently a number of 'refugee' American Indians who resided at the head of Okanagan Lake also had urged Chill-e-heetsa to rebel, but 'with commendable foresight, he replied that he had no desire to accede to the proposal.' Victoria *Colonist* 19 Dec. 1879. Chill-e-heetsa participated in his son-in-law's capture, which indicates the degree to which the McLeans were caught between two cultures. Crease was later to make much of this ill-fated attempt at an uprising in his reports on the case to the Secretary of State at Ottawa: see text accompanying note 136 below.

64 *Mainland Guardian* 10 Dec. 1879

65 Rothenburger *Johnny Ussher* 100, 104–7

66 *Mainland Guardian* 17 Dec. 1879

67 *Colonist* 23 Mar. 1880

68 Ibid. 18 Mar. 1880

69 Ormsby *British Columbia* 269, 284; *Colonist* 19 Mar. 1880

70 This seems odd, because s. 11 of 32–3 Vict. (1869), c. 29 provided for applications for changes of venue. For a reason why the judges may have felt this section to be inapplicable, see text accompanying notes 87 and 88 below.

71 *Mainland Guardian* 27 Dec. 1879

72 PABC Add MSS 54, Folder 5/32

73 Ibid. T. Elwyn to the three judges, 8 Mar. 1880. The commission itself is to be found in PAC RG 13 C-1, vol. 1418.

74 Ibid. Crease to Humphreys, 9 Mar. 1880

75 Walkem was apparently in Ontario, and the press had only days before criticized him for his absences, remarking that this was 'not the first time this highly valuable functionary has thought proper to absent himself for many months at a time from his duties.' *Mainland Guardian* 10 Mar. 1880

76 PABC Add MSS 54, Folder 5/32. Crease to Humphreys, 10 Mar. 1880
77 Ibid. Humphreys to the three judges, 11 Mar. 1880
78 PABC Add MSS 54, Folder 5/32. Begbie to Humphreys, 12 Mar. 1880
79 Ibid. Crease to Eli Harrison, jr, 12, 14, and 15 Mar. 1880. The government presumably was in no hurry to proclaim the 1879 legislation because the judges had already expressed the opinion that it was unconstitutional (see note 50 above).
80 The incompetence of the accused to testify lasted until 1893 in Canada and until 1898 in England.
81 This rule was the law until *Woolmington* v *Director of Public Prosecutions* [1935] Appeal Cases 462 (House of Lords).
82 *Colonist* 16 Mar. 1880
83 *Mainland Guardian* 17 Mar. 1880
84 Hare's statement at the first trial is from Crease's Assize Book, 189. PABC. He also reported that Allan McLean 'kicked furiously at Palmer ... and Archie struck the constable a violent blow' as he left the court room at the end of the trial. 'They were overpowered.' At their execution ten months later Hare said he forgave everyone and thanked them for their kindness. 'I am guilty of the crimes laid to my charge and justly deserve the impending punishment.' *Mainland Guardian* 2 Feb. 1881
85 *Colonist* 17 Mar. 1880
86 On Davie see S.W. Jackman *Portraits of the Premiers* (Vancouver, BC 1969) 91–7; *Colonist* 11 and 12 Mar. 1880.
87 Crease's Notes of the Trial. PABC Add MSS 54, Folder 6/34. Davie made this argument in a later case and won. In *Malott* v *The Queen* (1867–89), 1 *British Columbia Law Reports* (hereafter BCLR) 207 and 212 (Part II), he submitted that his client could not be tried by a Kamloops jury for a crime committed in the Kootenay District. Justice Walkem (as he then was) rejected the argument at trial for the same reasons advanced by McCreight in the *McLean* case; but the full court, composed of Begbie, McCreight, Walkem, Crease, and Gray disagreed. They held that the Sheriffs' Act of 1873 divided the province into judicial districts and that this brought the case within the common law rule. Because no application to change the venue had been made, the prisoner had to be retried. This legislation was in force when the McLeans were tried. No mention is made of the contrary ruling in that case.
88 As to the propriety of moving accused persons so far from the scene of the offence, now see *Regina* v *Ittoshat* [1970] 5 CCC 159, assuming that it has survived the decision of the Supreme Court of Canada in *Rourke* v *The Queen* (1977) 35 CCC (2d) 129. The quotations are from Crease's Notes of the Trial. PABC Add MSS 54, Folder 6/34

89 *Mainland Guardian* 20 Mar. 1880

90 *Colonist* 19 Mar. 1880

91 Crease's Assize Book, 189. PABC

92 One such writer was Thomas Gisborne, whose *An Inquiry into the Duties of Men in the Higher and Middle Classes of Great Britain* (1794) reads like a primer for Crease's address. The relevant excerpt may be found in Douglas Hay et al., eds *Albion's Fatal Tree: Crime and Society in Eighteenth Century England* (London 1975) 28–9.

93 Crease's Notes of the Trial. PABC Add MSS 54, Folder 6/34. The underscoring is his.

94 PABC Add MSS 54, Folder 5/32. Crease to Walkem, 29 Mar. 1880

95 If the trial was invalid, the prisoners were being unlawfully detained and were entitled to habeas corpus. The procedure was for their counsel to obtain a rule nisi, ie, to obtain an order that they be released 'unless' at a set date the prosecution appeared to show cause why the order should not be granted. It was a barren remedy for the McLeans and Hare, however, because they were also being held pursuant to other valid warrants of committal, eg, for the murder of James Kelly. They were therefore not present in the full court when the case was heard.

96 PABC Add MSS 54, Folder 5/32. Bole to Crease, 31 Mar. 1880; Davie to Crease, 7 Apr. 1880. 'Maintenance' is the unlawful stirring up of litigation in which one has no legal interest. Davie of course did not actually accuse Crease of this.

97 'Thus, if any judgment whatever be given by persons, who had no good commission to proceed against the person condemned, it is void ... it being a high misdemeanor in the judges so proceeding and little (if anything) short of murder in them all, in case the person so attainted be executed and suffer death.' William Blackstone *Commentaries* IV 383–4

98 Patricia M. Johnson 'McCreight and the Law' *British Columbia Historical Quarterly* (1948) 144–5

99 Williams *Man for a New Country* 167. This incident led to the passage of the Legal Professions Act of 1863, but Begbie still refused to enrol Walkem until virtually ordered to do so by Douglas. See Alfred Watts, QC 'Mr. Justice George Anthony Walkem' *The Advocate* (1967) 178 and Jackman *Premiers* 33.

100 PABC Add MSS 54, Folder 13/71 and 14/76. Crease to Senator Cornwall, 20 Apr. 1879; Crease to Alpheus Todd, 4 Feb. 1882

101 PABC Add MSS 54, Folder 5/32. Walkem to Crease, 8 Apr. 1880

102 Ibid. Crease's Report of the judgment in *The Queen v McLeans and Hare* 108 (hereafter Crease's Report). It is interesting to note that James McDonald, the federal Minister of Justice, took a similar view of Crease's repeated requests that Ottawa intervene. In a report to Cabinet dated 11 May 1880 he remarks

that the 'learned Judge seems to think that it now devolves upon this Government to pass upon the validity or invalidity of the [McLean] trial ... In my opinion no such duty [exists] ... the only proper tribunal ... is the Court of British Columbia.' PAC RG 13 C-1, vol. 1418. If this is unfair to Crease, it is no more so than Gray's comment about Walkem.

103 Ibid. Crease to Walkem, 12 Apr. 1880

104 PABC Add MSS 54, Folder 6/33. Crease to Secretary of State, 21 Mar. 1880

105 Ibid. Folder 6/34. Crease to Secretary of State, 24 Mar. 1880. Crease's firm views were no doubt decisive in determining Archie's fate. The file respecting the case reached the Governor General's office only the day before the original date set for the execution, and Lord Lorne was clearly concerned about approving the execution of a fifteen-year-old boy. In a memorandum dated 18 May 1880 from the Governor General's aide to the acting Minister of Justice, Sir Alexander Campbell, the aide states that Lorne wondered whether Archie's age should 'be considered as pleading against the infliction of capital punishment.' PAC RG 13 C-1, vol. 1418

106 The *Colonist* published the exchange of letters that had taken place between the government and the judges prior to the assize under the heading, 'Sans Commission – Interesting Correspondence.' *Colonist* 22 June 1880

107 *Mainland Guardian* 3 July 1880; *Colonist* 27 June 1880

108 *Colonist* 27 June 1880

109 Ibid. 19 Nov. 1880; per Chief Justice Begbie in Crease's Report 1

110 Quoted in Williams *Man for a New Country* 175–6

111 Begbie's Bench-book, IX 510. PABC. *The Times* clipping stated in part that 'it was discovered by some blunder or other the name of the learned Baron was not on the Commission of Assize; so that he was not competent to hold the Assizes ... a singular illustration of the absurdity of relying on these obsolete commissions alone for the administration of justice at the assizes.' *The Times* (London), 7 July 1880. See also note 33 above.

112 Crease's Report 14–15

113 *The Queen* v *Whelan* (1868–9), 28 *Upper Canada Queen's Bench Reports* (hereafter UCQB Rep) 1. The statute was 29 & 30 Vict. (1866), c. 40, s. 3

114 32 & 33 Vict. (1869), c. 30, schedules o and s

115 Crease's Report 1–2

116 Ibid. 27, 29. It seems likely that what the judges meant in their memorandum of March 1879 was that they presided over the assizes *virtute officii*, only if the proceedings were not really 'assizes' but proceedings of the Supreme Court. They did not, however, make this sufficiently clear, and the distinction appears to have escaped the notice of the government lawyers. Clearly Begbie's experiences with the Gaol Delivery Act of 1860 had convinced him that

legislation was necessary to abolish commissions, and that after Confederation only the dominion government had that power.

117 37 Vict. (1875), c. 42 made a number of statutes passed between 1867 and 1870 applicable in British Columbia and provided that the British Columbia Supreme Court had the power to try and determine in due course of law all felonies therein specified, of which murder was one (s. 5). By virtue of a local statute passed in 1872 (Consolidated Statutes 1877, c. 56), the British Columbia legislature provided that the jurisdiction of the Supreme Court could be exercised by 'any one or more' of the judges of that court, something that had been unnecessary up to then because Begbie was the only judge.

118 Consolidated Statutes (British Columbia), 1877, c. 51. This is a proclamation by Douglas dated 8 June 1859. See note 36 and accompanying text above.

119 Crease's Report 16

120 *Colonist* 5 June 1880. Walkem seems the dishonest broker Crease thought he was on this point. He must have known of this commission because it was sent up to Begbie in a hurry due to a last-minute government decision to hold an assize there for political reasons.

121 Crease's Report 25

122 Alfred Watts, QC 'The Honourable Mr. Justice Alexander Rocke Robertson' *The Advocate* (1967) 142. Robertson was the first Canadian-born judge of the Supreme Court.

123 Begbie's Bench-book, IX 495. PABC

124 Ibid. and *Colonist* 9 June 1880. This account is a composite of these two versions of the exchange.

125 Johnson *McCreight* 148–9

126 Begbie's Bench-book, IX 495. PABC

127 *Colonist* 10 June 1880; Begbie's Bench-book, IX 495. PABC

128 The remarks about 'quibbles' and shooting are from the *Herald*, a 'government organ,' and are quoted in the *Colonist* 19 Nov. 1880.

129 It is not clear why. It brings to mind, however, a remark made by Crease in the course of his judgment in June. Commenting on Davie's unenthusiastic response to Crease's suggestion that the matter be argued before the full court, Crease muses, rather oddly in a judgment on a technical point of jurisdiction, that Davie's words were a 'euphemism probably for not paid for former or prospective efforts.' Crease's Report 87

130 B.C. *Gazette*, 17 July 1880. It is now section 30 of the Supreme Court Act, RSBC 1979, c. 397.

131 Crease's Report 29–30. However, in 1883 the Supreme Court of Canada affirmed the constitutional validity of s. 14 of the Judicature Act: *Canada Gazette*, 18 June 1883. Justice Walkem duly noted this in *Regina* v *Malott* (see

note 87 above). He held that not only could the Lieutenant Governor of British Columbia issue commissions but that s. 14 validly authorized assizes without them. See also *Sproul* v *The Queen* (1867–89), 1 BCLR 219 (Part II).

132 *Mainland Guardian* 13 Nov. 1880. See note 87 above.

133 Crease's Report to the Secretary of State at Ottawa, on the Trial of James Kelly, 13 Dec. 1880. PABC Add MSS 54, Folder 5/32

134 MG 17 Nov. 1880

135 See text accompanying note 62 above.

136 Crease's reference to liberal dealings is too close to the wording of Article 13 of the Terms of Union admitting British Columbia into Confederation to be accidental: Imperial Order in Council, 16 May 1871. As Colonial Attorney General, Crease had a large part in drafting these terms.

137 Crease's Report to the Secretary of State, 13 Dec. 1880. PABC Add MSS 54, Folder 5/32. Those 'looking anxiously for the result' included Mrs Crease's friends in Kamloops. In her diary for Monday, 18 Oct. 1880, she notes that 'Ladies express much interest in the cases – especially in young Hare and Hector McLean who they hope will be hanged!' Hector McLean was a brother charged with being an accessory after the fact. Notwithstanding the ladies' hopes, a jury acquitted him in separate proceedings some time later. (Mrs Crease's diary was kindly made available to the writer by Ms L. Lindley Roff, a family member.)

138 *Mainland Guardian* 2 Feb. 1881; *Colonist* 1 Feb. 1881

139 Crease's Report 109

140 (1877–8) 3 Law Reports, Queen's Bench Division 730, at 755; Crease's Report 110

141 Ibid. 16

142 See note 39 above.

143 These words are from the report of the Minister of Justice to Cabinet (note 102 above) and repeat almost verbatim the phrasing of s. 92(14) of the BNA Act. See also notes 26 and 131 above and *Di Iorio and Fontaine* v *Warden of Common Jail of Montreal and Brunette* (1976), 33 CCC (2d) 289 (SCC).

144 'Four Rode By,' by Ian Tyson

145 Supreme Court (Amendment) Act, SBC 1899, c. 20, s. 10; Supreme Court Act, SBC 1903–04, c. 15, s. 52

7

Private Rights and Public Purposes in the Lakes, Rivers, and Streams of Ontario 1870–1930

JAMIE BENIDICKSON

Government involvement in regulating the social and economic life of Ontario expanded dramatically in the final decades of the last century and the early decades of the twentieth. Legislative intervention and bureaucratic initiatives both at the departmental level and in the form of administrative agencies and commissions were increasingly frequent and varied in nature. The courts experienced severe challenges to their stature as principal institutions for resolving legal conflicts as a consequence of these developments, which included extensive legislation and the introduction of such agencies as the Hydro Electric Power Commission, workers' compensation boards, and railway regulation tribunals. An apparent diminution in the authority of the courts occurred as primary responsibility for decisionmaking was either removed from the judicial system in the case of certain types of long-established conflicts, or conferred directly on other institutions in the case of those conflicts which were regarded as newly created by modern conditions. In either form, the transition reflected an influential perception that the judicial process was ill suited to the determination of certain important public issues.

The new structures and procedures of public decisionmaking represented a remarkable transformation, reflecting the diversity and complexity of the urban, industrialized community that emerged alongside traditionally-rural Ontario society. This essay, by focusing on the relationship between changing economic activity and the emergence of new decisionmaking structures and processes, examines selected aspects of the shift in institutional responsibility that took place around the turn of the century. To illuminate this relationship, consideration is given to a variety of legal issues which affected the lakes, rivers, and streams of Ontario as a result of the activities of two important industries, the lumber trade and hydro-electric power production. The two industries, one dominating the nineteenth-century economy and the other expanding rapidly in the early years of the twentieth, placed extensive demands on provincial waterways. Some of these demands were common to both industries; others were distinctive to each.[1]

The competing interests of rival lumbermen provoked numerous conflicts about the use of provincial waterways in the nineteenth century. Two or more operators often claimed use of the same waterways to transport or to store logs. As Arthur R.M. Lower has written: 'Everything depended on seizing the proper moment and getting the logs down on the crest of the spring rise; for if they were allowed to float off into the swamps or low places or if the crest were missed they might have to remain in the woods for another season and the whole year's work be lost.'[2] Toll charges for the use of stream improvements were another source of frequent disputes, and competition in the exploitation of water power sites for saw mills and small manufacturing also gave rise to legal clashes. Although other legal disputes involving liability for lumber-related flooding, shoreline damage, and pollution affected elements of society outside the forest industry, conflict typically centred on competition between lumber companies whose interests in how water would be used were essentially similar. At the risk of oversimplifying, it may be suggested that legal conflicts arising from water use by the lumber trade were largely about which lumbermen would benefit from the use of Ontario's rivers, lakes, and streams, rather than about the manner in which water resources would be utilized.

The introduction and expansion of the hydro-electric power industry altered markedly the scale of industrial interference with provincial waterways. A different set of legal issues emerged. The range of interests directly affected by the manner in which provincial waters were used broadened significantly. The interests affected by the hydro industry's use of Ontario waters were not necessarily located on waterways, and their concerns were more likely to extend year-round in contrast to the typically seasonal nature of disputes raised by lumbermen's activity. Municipalities, for example, clashed with a variety of industrial water and power users over whether power production would be for 'public purposes' or for private development. Navigational interests became concerned about the inconvenience, if not the threat, posed by the need to draw off water from storage to maintain water power production levels through periods of low rainfall. Tourists and environmentalists found major dams objectionable for aesthetic reasons, because of shoreline flooding, and on account of suspected injury to spawning grounds. These differences in the type of water use, the range of interests affected, and the character of resulting conflicts were accompanied by an evolution in the legal framework – both doctrinal and institutional – for the resolution of disputes about the use of provincial water resources.[3]

The institutions primarily responsible for resolving conflicts about the use of water resources in the nineteenth century were the courts through their application of general principles to gradually changing circumstances and conditions. The judicial response may be examined in relation to emerging tension between 'property' and 'progress,' which was accentuated by industrial expansion and diversification.[4] Increasingly, regulatory agencies and the provincial administration assumed responsibility for managing conflict raised by the hydro-electricity industry. Public officials acquired extensive discretionary authority to obtain particularized solutions to water-use conflicts. This essay seeks to illustrate the general evolution in institutional responsibility and design and to suggest possible explanations.

The assumption by administrative authorities of increasing responsibility for the supervision of water use and management was a gradual and cumulative process rather than a sudden upheaval. To appreciate the process, it is necessary to examine a disparate array of events and issues, not all of which had the good grace to succeed each other in simple chronological order. For convenience, the material surveyed here is organized around the lumber trade and hydro. In connection with the lumber trade, the role of the judiciary and the legislature is examined in relation to water power privileges, stream improvements, toll charges, timber drives, and certain problems of liability arising where lumbermen clashed with other social interests. The hydro industry's impact on water law is then discussed with reference to water powers and provincial purposes, the ownership of the beds of navigable waters, the regulation of water power monopolies, including the regulation of production levels and pricing, the consequences of environmental awareness, and the complex challenges of managing multi-use international water basins. This sequence helps to demonstrate the growing complexity of legal issues and to illustrate the essay's central theme of diversity and innovation in the form of decisionmaking institutions. An attempt is also made to provide some explanation for this process of institutional diversification and in particular to relate that process to evidence of conflict between a judicial preference for the protection of established property interests and legislative encouragement of economic development and 'progress.'

THE COURTS AND THE LUMBERMEN

The principal legal conflicts arising from the lumber industry's use of rivers, lakes, and streams involved water power privileges, stream improvements, toll charges, timber drives, and liability for interference with navigation and shoreline property. For the most part such matters were internal to the forest industry itself; yet from the record of the industry's relations with the courts and the legislature regarding these issues, one may discern a recurring tension between the evident desire of legislators to promote economic development and the reluctance of the judiciary to endorse interference with established property interests. Occasional judicial efforts to balance and manage conflicting interests demonstrate recognition of the lumber industry's complexity and importance but also suggest limitations on the ability of courts to engage in such a role. This was especially true where the activities and interests of lumbermen had direct implications for other elements of the provincial community. Legislation and administrative procedures were contemplated or introduced in response to perceived limitations in the courts' ability to manage certain water-related lumbering conflicts.

Water Power Privileges and Judicial Balancing

Water power privileges were essential to several components of Ontario's nineteenth-century economy and particularly useful to the operators of saw mills prior to the mid-1870s, when steam became the more common form of power. The legal issues raised by water power privileges were well understood by mid-century and clearly addressed by the courts. In *Graham v Burr* (1853), the owner of a Humber River saw mill obtained an injunction to restrain a downstream proprietor from damming water back against a mill site on the upstream property. The defendant's unsuccessful arguments included the claim that no injunction should be granted because the fall of water at the upstream location was in any event inadequate for an efficient milling operation. Chancellor William Hume Blake was prepared to protect the property interest regardless of use or utility, while Vice Chancellor John Godfrey Spragge, recognizing that higher lumber prices might render commercial development of presently unprofitable locations quite attractive, was prepared to accept the plaintiff's assessment of his own property's usefulness. Vice Chancellor Christie Palmer Esten would have denied the injunction awarded against Burr. He rejected the principle that could protect Graham even though he made no actual use of the water or where he made only such use that 'his mill will not pay expenses, or more than pay expenses, or yield enough to make it worth any reasonable man's while to work it.'[5] R.C.B. Risk concludes that the Canadian courts' treatment of the principle of reasonable use presented in *Graham v Burr* shows that the judges 'feared monopoly, and were unwilling to sanction aggressive or innovative invasions of traditional property interests.'[6] Later cases suggest that the majority attitude favouring the security of property interests persisted in the courts, while the legislature took measures to further its competing preference for economic development and 'progress.'

An attempt was made in 1859 to pass legislation permitting mill owners to flood neighbouring lands and pay damages or compensation. John A. Macdonald opposed the bill as authorizing undue interference with private rights. Speaking in favour of the legislation, Oliver Mowat argued that the United States had benefited significantly from the adoption of similar principles and that residents of Upper Canada wanted such a statute: 'Nothing could be more just than that a party should be allowed to work a mill on giving proper compensation to those whose land was injured by any flooding that might result therefrom.' He was disturbed that an injunction would be available in Chancery for the slightest interference by flooding. Malcolm Cameron, taking a position that later achieved considerable prominence, suggested that the matter not be viewed as an issue between two private parties, but rather as a question of general public importance such as railways were. But the measure was defeated 44–38.[7]

Fifteen years after *Graham v Burr*, Mowat was Vice Chancellor and subject as such to the same constraints he had earlier lamented in the course of legislative debate. In *Dickson v Burnham* (1868), he declared that the builder of a dam which flooded upstream property would be liable to an action, 'even though the proprietor above him suffers no material injury, and though the mill of the trespasser is a public benefit.' The underpinnings of this position were concisely formulated: 'This rule follows from the sacred character which the law attaches to private property, property being one of the chief mainstays of society, and one of the most active agents in promoting civilization and national prosperity.' In reflecting upon the relationship between property rights and public objectives articulated through the parliamentary process, Mowat reaffirmed his approval of legislative intervention: 'This right of private property is made by Parliament to give way, on proper terms, and with proper precautions, in order to enable railways and canals to be built, and other objects of general utility to be accomplished; and I see no reason why the Legislature should not on the same principle make some provision of a like kind to encourage the building of mills and manufactories.'[8]

When Mowat left the bench to assume the premiership in 1872, he pursued these goals in the Water Privileges Act of 1873, an action which is best explained by viewing Mowat as a consistent proponent of economic development whose views on the primacy of the legislature as an agent of reform had constrained his judicial behaviour. The legislation conferred on developers the right to enter and examine lands potentially affected by the changes they contemplated and laid down elaborate procedures and guidelines under which interference or the right to 'take, acquire, hold and use' might be authorized by application to a County Court Judge and the measure of compensation settled.[9] The statute sought to maintain a balance between the stability demanded by holders of established rights on the one hand, and the transforming pressures introduced by subsequent developers, who hoped to modify local flow and storage patterns in order to exploit more fully the power potential of certain locations.

In contrast to the *ex post facto* determination of liability and compensation typically carried out by the courts, the new proceedings were intended to be anticipatory and facilitative. The judge's discretion to allow an application rested on his assessment or 'opinion' as to whether allowance 'is proper and just in all the circumstances of the case' and 'will conduce to the public good,' a concept not defined apart from its relation to the purposes of the legislation. The County Court Judge's decision could be appealed to the Court of Appeal, where 'any question of fact or other question shall be open to revision.' Yet there were substantive limitations on the applicability of this act. Without the owner's consent, there could be no interference with or injury to any 'occupied mill privilege' either upstream or down, and the act did not authorize any interference with navigation or the floating of logs.[10] Thus, despite the obvious indications that the legislature intended to promote effective use of provincial water power resources, there was considerable scope for judicial interpretation to tolerate a large degree of waste or inactivity.[11]

The judiciary's interpretation of the 'public good' and the meaning of 'occupied water privilege' indicated their continuing respect for established property rights. When the 'public good' was first examined in an application by the Parry Sound Lumbering Company for approval of a dam and reservoir development, Judge Ardagh likened his task to that of a legislator considering the power of eminent domain or expropriation. He narrowly construed the relevant 'public' to include primarily a few residents in the immediate neighbourhood of the reservoir who had raised objections and discounted claims made on behalf of the 150 or 200 employees of the lumber mill who were located at a distance of some twenty miles from the proposed flooding. Ardagh found that the employment supported at Parry Sound was 'a very indirect way of showing the "public good" of this mill,' because its products were readily available in the locality from other suppliers. This argument was used to distinguish American cases where particular mills 'qua mill' were found to be a 'vital necessity' in their districts.[12]

The potential implications of the Water Privileges Act were also sharply restricted in *Re Burnham et al.* (1895), a case decided one year before Mowat's retirement from the premiership. W.R. Meredith unsuccessfully argued that the legislation authorized interference with riparian rights in cases where this was necessary to ensure that valuable water powers would not be left in a state of only partial utilization: 'If the water power owned by one person is greater than is required for the actual commercial uses of that person, another person is entitled to come in and make use of the unused and therefore wasted excess.' In contrast, the court, by adopting a low standard extending the protection of the 'occupied water privilege' clause, sustained private property rights against the community interest in efficient water use: 'I think a privilege or power is occupied, if bona fide used to any considerable extent, even though capable of being used, far more extensively, either as to head, or as to the quantity of water.'[13] This judicial defence of established property rights was hardly an advance from *Dickson* v *Burnham* or *Graham* v *Burr*. The judiciary's reluctance or timidity to apply the Water Privileges Act as an effective tool for economic development was consistent with the uncertain treatment accorded stream improvements. This was another area where the cautious approach of Canadian courts to interference with property rights was in contrast with legislative encouragement of resource use.

Stream Improvements and Toll Privileges

Lumbermen's access to Ontario's waterways was a question of obvious importance in light of the considerable distances over which logs often had to be transported for processing. By the middle of the nineteenth century, Ontario lumbermen enjoyed a statutory right to use 'all streams in Upper Canada during the Spring, Summer and Autumn Freshets' in order to transport saw logs and other lumber.[14] An early decision, *Boale* v *Dickson* (1863), restricted the application of the relevant section 'only to such streams as in their natural state will, without improvements, during freshets, permit saw logs, timber, etc., to be floated down them.' Under this judgment the owner of stream improvements was entitled to reasonable remuneration for their use, a result that has been interpreted as suggesting 'a willingness to protect and encourage investment in stream improvements, and not permit free use of a valuable facility.'[15] The limiting view of the rights of lumbermen put forward in *Boale* v *Dickson* prevailed for nearly twenty years until forest industry rivals from the eastern Ontario community of Carleton Place appeared before Vice Chancellor William Proudfoot in 1880 seeking resolution of their conflicting claims over the use of tributaries of the Mississippi River. As Boyd, Caldwell and Company's 18,000 logs drifted downstream, Peter McLaren sought and obtained an injunction to prohibit their passage through his works at High Falls. McLaren, a riparian owner with substantial investments in stream improvements, asserted 'the absolute and exclusive right to the use of the [improved stream] for the purpose of floating or driving saw logs and timber down the same.'[16]

McLaren v *Caldwell* (1880–4) proceeded to the Court of Appeal, where Chief Justice Spragge explicitly stated what he believed the legislative preference to be: 'It is obvious ... that it was the policy of the legislature to encourage the lumber trade of the province.' He acknowledged that criticism might be made of the legislature for giving too much consideration to the interests of the lumbermen at the expense of riparian proprietors but that it was not appropriate for the courts to dispute the social balancing of the legislature: 'Our province is to construe the Act, and not to fail to give due effect to it under the idea that its provisions press over hardly upon one class of persons for the benefit of another class.' Justice Christopher S. Patterson expressed a similar attitude towards the burden on an improver whose efforts and investment rendered a stream fit for the use of lumbermen: 'It may be in appearance, and perhaps in reality, rather hard on the man at whose expense what was a highway only in legal contemplation becomes one fit for profitable use, to have to allow others to share in the advantage without contributing to the cost. That is, however, a matter for his own consideration when he makes the improvements.' Patterson also regarded his task as interpreting the statute in light of the legislative intention and appears to have been much influenced by a review of a series of related acts which led him to conclude: 'All these statutes proceed upon the assumption that the attribute of a highway, for at least one branch of commerce, [lumbering] attaches to streams of all degrees of size and volume.'[17]

The Supreme Court of Canada approached the question rather differently, with the result that the stream improver's interests were fully protected. Both Chief Justice William J. Ritchie and Justice John W. Gwynne insisted upon strict construction in the interpretation of statutes which encroached upon the rights of the subject. Ritchie wanted the legislature's intention 'clearly and unequivocally indicated' before he would recognize the effect of the enactment to confer on the public the right to use private property and the improvements made thereon by the proprietor thereof without making any compensation therefor,' while Gwynne was disturbed by 'the imputation of arbitrary interference by the legislature with the rights of private property.' Eventually, the Judicial Committee of the Privy Council reversed the Supreme Court decision and overruled *Boale* v *Dickson* on the ground that it did not seem that 'the private right which the owner of this spot claims to monopolise all passage there is one which the legislature were likely to regard with favour.'[18] Long before this, however, the provincial government had responded to McLaren's surprising success at trial by introducing the notorious Rivers and Streams Act.

The 1881 Act for Protecting the Public Interest in Rivers, Streams and Creeks explicitly rejected monopoly claims based on improvements made to otherwise non-floatable waterways. The statute proclaimed the rights of all users but supported investors by making the rights of users 'subject to the payment to the person who has made such constructions and improvements, of reasonable tolls.' During the debate Premier Mowat stated that the outcome at the trial level would seriously lessen the value of timber limits on which provincial revenues so largely depended. Crown Lands Commissioner Pardee echoed this theme, referring to the province's streams as natural highways and stressing the significance of a public interest in their use. Competition for timber licences upstream from an exclusively controlled river improvement could be seriously limited or even eliminated, thereby nullifying the considerable financial value of the bonus bidding system. The injunction granted by Proudfoot threatened to paralyse lumber activity along 234 Ontario streams in the same category as the Mississippi: 'The right of the licensee to use all such water-courses contiguous to his property, whether originally adapted for floating timber or capable of being made so by the construction of slides, the removal of obstacles to navigation or other improvements, is in fact essential to the utilization of timber growing on the higher and more remote areas, and its refusal would render lumbering over a large proportion of the public Domain an unprofitable pursuit.'[19]

Subsequent historical interest in the Rivers and Streams Act has customarily been associated with the case's role in federal-provincial relations, because the legislature's response to the trial level decision was repeatedly disallowed. For example, Christopher Armstrong has recently written: 'The rhetorical violence produced by the repeated disallowances of the Rivers and Streams Act can be explained partly by the pressure from competing private interests and partly by the desire of the politicians to make some capital.'[20] The legislature's commitment to economic development, which the Rivers and Streams Act and other water-related legislation illustrates, is equally relevant. The seriousness of the apparent threat posed by judicial attitudes to the aspirations of the legislature for economic progress and expansion should not be overlooked. To the suggestion that Macdonald as Conservative Prime Minister and Mowat as Liberal Premier responded to simple partisan urges in the rivers and streams disallowance struggle must be added the reminder that their substantive positions on property and economic progress were consistent. Macdonald who opposed water privileges legislation in 1859 as an undue interference with private rights now worked to protect McLaren's stream improvements, while Mowat who favoured water privileges legislation continued to advocate full and efficient use of provincial resources.[21]

One cannot conclude from *McLaren* v *Caldwell* alone that the courts either favoured or disapproved productive use of resources when that objective clashed with property interests. The case is at least an indication that the basis for doubt existed and that the legislature could not rely on the judiciary to foster provincial economic progress in clashes with property rights. There is also evidence of some impatience with the processes of the courts, which may have made other procedures and institutions more attractive by comparison. Opposition leader William R. Meredith was virtually alone in urging after the trial decision that the legislature await the courts' final decision about stream improvements.[22]

Closely related to the question of lumbermen's rights to use stream improvements for the purpose of floating logs to mills and markets was the issue of whether or not stream users would be liable to pay tolls to the owners of navigational improvements. The toll question was important to the lumber industry and for several reasons resulted in a significant amount of litigation. First, along certain waterways the dependence of lumbermen on stream improvements was unavoidable. Wherever tolls could be levied, they formed a recurring operational cost. Not infrequently, the users of stream improvements were in competition as lumbermen with the owners of stream improvements on which tolls might be collected. Natural variations in the floatability of streams and differences in legislative authority for toll collection are further possible explanations for the relative prominence of toll cases within the body of lumber industry litigation over water use.[23] Stream improvement operators derived their power to collect tolls from one of two statutory sources. Lumbermen or pulpwood companies who made improvements to render streams floatable for their own purposes were authorized to collect reasonable tolls from other users by the Rivers and Streams Act. A second statutory basis for toll charges occurred in legislation governing companies formed for the purpose of constructing works to facilitate timber transmission. Justice Cornelius Masten later described the underlying assumptions of the legislation: 'The legislature has considered it inequitable that persons who have not contributed to the cost of river and lake improvements should get the use and benefit of them without paying anything, and has passed the statute in question for a purpose which it deemed for the public good, namely, encouragement of needed improvements and equitable dealing between different classes of the community.'[24]

The provincial government comprehensively regulated timber slide companies, at least in comparison with other business enterprises. Legislation required incorporation, assurances about invested capital, and pre-charter consideration of the works proposed by the Commissioner of Public Works and municipal councils. This supervision and the mechanism for municipal participation were undoubtedly intended to have some effect as a means of controlling entry to a sector of the transportation industry, which was generally regarded as an important public service and one where local monopoly power would be a fact of geographic life. Tenure limitations provided further protection for the public.[25]

The 1888 application of the Rainy River Boom Slide and Navigation Company illustrates administrative procedure under the Timber Slide Companies Act and offers some insights about the way the applicants, the Premier, and provincial officials viewed the process. The promoters requested comprehensive powers to enable their company to engage in several aspects of the transportation sector on the grounds that this was necessary in the remote and undeveloped northern regions of the province: 'a pioneer in any kind of business who goes in to develop the resources of the country must take with him and be prepared to deal in almost everything wanted for himself, his work people and his business.' Although Premier Mowat was apparently unconcerned by the operational scope of the application, he objected to the geographical breadth and imprecision of the territorial limits which the applicants described in terms of 'adjoining waters,' and re-expressed the limits in order to confine the company's activities to the Rainy River 'and to rivers and streams in this province emptying into Rainy River.' Timber limit holders in the district were consulted about the charter proposal and the suggested toll.[26]

The review procedures are indicative of the manner in which the Ontario government approached its responsibility for early franchise awards. The approach appeared to be a pragmatic one, emphasizing the circumstances of the particular case. Insofar as the process indicated a governmental concern for a general or residual responsibility to safeguard public interests, this seemed to be confined to the interest of those directly affected, that is, existing timber operations. The principal criterion for decisionmaking was acceptance by those who would utilize the service and pay the tolls. Since that group could be identified relatively easily through other provincial records on timber licences, the process of consultation was potentially quite comprehensive. The review procedure encouraged affected timber operators to express their views, possibly in a manner more convenient to far-flung interests than a centrally-located hearing or a legislative discussion might have ensured. On the other hand, when a competing developer contested a timber slide application (as in fact the Rainy River proposal was), this particular form of decisionmaking might be susceptible to political considerations quite unrelated to the actual operation of the franchise, the fulfilment of conditions of service, or rates. Although executive or administrative processes led to initial decisions about the allocation of timber slide franchises, disputes arising from their operation were usually expected to come before the courts.

The awarding of franchises for the operation of timber slides represented an early Ontario experience with the allocation of control over certain kinds of water uses through executive or administrative processes. The actual rate setting or toll calculation function in the operation of the timber transport facilities was also in a transitional phase. Rate-setting criteria were being developed but were initially applied through the bureaucracy in the case of timber slide companies, while judges or stipendiary magistrates remained responsible for 'reasonable tolls' under the rivers and streams legislation.[27]

Provincial officials considering timber slide company tolls were apparently willing to circulate proposed tariff schedules for comment and review as a means of obtaining information on the reaction of the ultimate rate-payers.[28] However, if tolls were not set out in the letters patent, reasonably detailed legislative guidelines including the cost of the works, volume estimates of the various timber species expected to pass through the improvements, and the financial results of the previous season's operation were set out. Timber slide companies were required to publish their proposed toll schedules each year and to include them with annual reports submitted for inspection to the Minister of Lands, Forests, and Mines. Significantly, though, it was the Minister's responsibility to ensure that tolls had been fixed in conformity with the established guidelines and he was authorized to vary the proposed toll charges to ensure compliance. In the absence of notification of disallowance, the tolls proposed by the company 'shall be the lawful tolls for that year.'[29] The courts were consistently unwilling to interfere where toll rates had been set through the jurisdiction of the Crown Lands Commissioner. Non-compliance by the operator with statutory requirements such as annual reporting or charter conditions such as construction schedules had no impact on toll collection powers unless the Commissioner or Attorney General chose to act. Consequently the users of river improvements had limited opportunity to exercise legal leverage against those controlling timber slide franchises. On the other hand, 'reasonable tolls' under the rivers and streams legislation concerned with improvements to otherwise non-navigable or non-floatable waterways were to be fixed by application to a judge of the county or district court in the territory where the works were located. As the basic criteria for toll setting under the rivers and streams legislation were similar to those employed in the case of timber slide companies, it appears that judges were simply used for administrative convenience because of their availability. Yet the judges were also charged with considering 'such other matters as under all the circumstances may be deemed just and equitable,' and dissatisfied persons could appeal to the Divisional Court, where strict compliance with toll application regulations could be obtained. Thus tolls would not be given retroactive effect and, once fixed by application before a judge, would not be enforceable against lumbermen whose logs had previously been floated over the improvements.[30]

When in 1927 the Lakes and Rivers Improvement Act consolidated toll-setting procedures in one piece of legislation, appeal rights were expressly abolished, but formal notice and hearing requirements were introduced. As will be seen these steps were generally consistent with rate-setting practices for hydro-electric power and reflected a growing consciousness during the late nineteenth and early twentieth centuries that various decisionmaking functions had different characteristics that should be matched to the equally distinctive strengths and weaknesses of decisionmaking institutions such as the courts or the provincial administration.[31] Toll-setting was not the only function which provoked consideration of the comparative advantages and limitations of the courts.

Timber Drives, Flood Damage, and Procedural Expediency

The Saw Logs Driving Act (1887) addressed the problem of the frequent and inevitable clashes that arose when the downstream passage of one lumberman's timber was obstructed by the logs of another jamming the river, or when the logs belonging to two or more lumbermen became intermixed during the short timber driving seasons. The act imposed on lumbermen a duty to ensure the passage of their logs downstream. Timber drivers were instructed to 'make adequate provisions and put on a sufficient force of men' to break jams and remove logs from the shorelines 'with reasonable dispatch.' Generally, the statute required timber drives to be carried out 'so as not to unnecessarily delay or hinder' the progress of other drives or to 'unnecessarily obstruct' the use of the water for navigation or floating. These directions were obviously intended to promote the fullest utilization by numerous operators of the short-lived run-off water levels. But recognizing that opinions might differ about what was adequate, sufficient, reasonable, or unnecessary, the legislature specified procedures for resolving disputes outside the courts. The scheme encouraged self-help on the river, stressed direct party-to-party agreements to apportion costs, and intended arbitration to be the secondary and final resort: 'All claims, disputes and differences arising under this Act shall be determined by arbitration ... and not by action or suit at law or in equity.' In the case of intermixing, for example, where immediate separation of logs was inconvenient, the several owners were to 'put on a fair proportion of the men required' to conduct the drive. Costs were to be shared 'in such proportions as they may agree upon,' but in default of agreement, by arbitration. When one of the owners neglected to participate in the co-operative drive, the other(s) might lawfully make up the deficiency and conduct the drive 'with reasonable economy and dispatch,' in conformity with other statutory guidelines.[32] The Saw Logs Driving Act was responsive to the problems of delay and costs in the judicial process, factors which might be of particular concern where interaction between potentially conflicting parties was more or less continuous and variable.

Legislation dealing with flood damage in newly settled districts evidenced similar concerns about delay, costs, and general inconvenience. As enacted in the 1889 flood damage act, the process for resolving these disputes took into account features of claims in the more remote parts of Ontario likely to distinguish them from comparable flooding actions in long-settled sections. Procedures were established to facilitate prompt and economical resolution of complaints about overflowing occasioned by activity under the Timber Slide Companies Act or other lumbering operations. The responsible judge or magistrate was encouraged to proceed in a manner which 'will best facilitate the ends of justice and cause the least trouble and expense.' The approved investigative forum was a hearing rather than a formal trial. If required, hearings were to be scheduled with regard to 'the convenience of both parties and the possibility of their being able at the particular season of the year conveniently to procure the attendance of necessary witnesses,' a clear indication of the legislature's sensitivity to frontier economic conditions and the difficulties which stricter scheduling might impose. Although disputes closely resembled a *lis inter partes*, (conflict between parties), the judge or magistrate was authorized to visit the land in question 'before or after the hearing' and could act on the basis of his own inspection, judgment, and general knowledge as well as on the evidence. The explanation for this procedural flexibility is perhaps found in an anticipation of numerous apparently similar claims. By encouraging the judge or magistrate to inspect the individual sites and to apply his general knowledge and judgment to supplement other evidence, the legislature presumably intended to increase the suitability of the settlement awards to particular circumstances.[33]

Thus far the conflicts examined have been primarily within the lumber industry itself. It is necessary, however, to consider relations between the lumber trade and other sectors of the provincial community.

The Lumber Industry and Other River Users

Provincial legislation supported the forest industry's claim to use Ontario waterways to transport logs and accordingly permitted some interference with the activity of shoreline owners and other water users. Yet lumbermen were by no means fully insulated against challenges to their operations made through the courts on behalf of the wide range of non-lumbering interests dependent upon Ontario waterways. Disputes between lumber interests and navigation companies, for example, frequently reached the courts, although the basic issues involved were generally not difficult. In one of these cases the lumber company's attitude astonished the Ontario Court of Appeal: 'It is impossible to believe that the defendants could have considered themselves entitled to take exclusive possession of a portion of a great international river to prevent or seriously obstruct the plaintiff's steamer when engaged in carrying passengers, mails and goods, and to dislocate and injure their business with impunity.'[34] The issues in the navigation cases were generally amenable to judicial resolution, and there is no evidence that steps were ever contemplated to remove them from the courts. Knowledge of long-established and readily applicable principles was assumed. These could serve to encourage practical measures of avoidance by those whose activity might obstruct navigation.

The maintenance of liability for 'unnecessary damage' to shoreline property also qualified lumbermen's rights under the Rivers and Streams Act. The phrase was considered in Booth v Lowery (1917), which arose when a major timber drive seriously damaged a coffer dam built in connection with a federal public works project on the Montreal River. Both Justice Francis A. Anglin, who delivered the majority judgment, and Chief Justice Charles Fitzpatrick in dissent, were fully aware of the economic implications of the controversy and remarkably frank in discussing the financial implications facing a major, but then declining, river-using resource industry. The Chief Justice defended the public right of navigation against interference even from a dam supported by public funds though not expressly authorized by statute. The result, he noted, 'must seriously affect the interests of the large class engaged in the lumber business, the oldest and still one of the principal industries of this country.' He rejected the suggestion that the defendant lumberman should undertake 'perhaps at great expense and risk through delay, extraordinary precautions to ensure the safety of the structure.' Anglin, though, assumed that in completing his construction contract with the federal government, the plaintiff was carrying out a paramount right which the lumbermen, exercising their own rights, were 'bound to respect, at least to the extent of taking all practical precautions to avoid doing injury to the structure – even such as would involve expense, delay and risk of partial failure of the drive.' In short, the decision clearly involved the allocation of operating costs between different classes of river users.[35] Doubts about the institutional capacity or suitability of the judicial process to perform this balancing function led to some noteworthy innovations, as an unusual situation on the Ottawa River illustrates.

Lumber mill operators along the Ottawa River were in the habit of depositing mill waste including boards, bark, and sawdust in the river to the detriment of riparian and navigational interests. Indeed, Chancellor John A. Boyd in *Ratte* v *Booth* (1886), found evidence that 'this refuse accumulates in great floating masses, substantial enough occasionally for a man to walk upon.' Threats to the Ottawa River lumber mills in the form of actions for injunctions resulted in legislative efforts to restrict the availability of this particular legal remedy in certain circumstances. In 1885 the Mowat government introduced legislation to protect the owners or operators of saw mills who threw sawdust and refuse into the Ottawa River from actions for injunctions when the Lieutenant Governor determined that the public interest so required. Premier Mowat was initially of the view that 'the subject was of such a character that it would be difficult for the Courts to deal with it,' although he was prepared to leave such questions to the courts if suitable machinery could be designed. William Meredith, at this time leader of the provincial opposition, found the proposal very objectionable, among other reasons for the power it gave to the executive. In the long run, as we shall observe, executive power expanded greatly, but in 1885 the courts retained jurisdiction subject to the instruction that in an action for an injunction against the owner or occupier of an Ottawa River mill site, arising from the dumping of sawdust or other mill waste, they 'shall take into consideration the importance of the lumber trade to the locality wherein such injury, damage or interference takes place, and the benefit and advantage, direct and consequential, which such trade confers on the locality and on the inhabitants thereof, and shall weigh the same against the private injury, damage or interference complained of.' No doubt such legislation served as an effective deterrent to potential plaintiffs. The absence of reported cases makes an assessment of judicial reaction impossible, but the Ottawa River Act, whose principles were later extended to other regions of the province, does demonstrate the continuing willingness of the Ontario legislature to limit the judiciary's ability to protect traditional property interests in a manner that would impede the advancement of a major resource industry.[36]

Early twentieth-century evidence of the courts' willingness to tolerate some injury by flooding to upstream property interests is inconclusive. In numerous cases after 1900 riparian claims were brought for compensation and injunctions following the replacement of an earlier generation of dams which had fallen into disrepair or had been acquired by new owners. Such cases often involved the restoration of decaying beams, or the elimination of seepage to improve storage and power capacity, with the apparent result that upstream shoreline properties experienced heavier or more prolonged flooding. The frequent failures of plaintiffs in these situations at least raise the possibility that the courts were becoming more sympathetic to the needs of industrial water users. It seems, though, that river improvers were simply the beneficiaries of certain inadvertent procedural protections, since with the passage of time and the proliferation of separately owned dams on a given water system, the abandonment or deterioration of dams and other works as the local lumber industry declined, or the diversion or other alteration of stream flow, plaintiffs faced an increasingly complicated burden of causal proof.[37]

The general principle remained unchanged, and dam owners, whose works remained at the same height but held water more effectively, were not entitled to free enjoyment of new benefits where these involved prolonging the period of flooding or the flooding of greater areas. Even if the volume of water available for storage increased as a result of greater natural flow brought about by land clearing or the deterioration of abandoned lumber works, 'it is not a right of the defendants to take advantage of the increased flow if thereby they add to the burdens of the land of those above them.' On the other hand, the liability of the downstream mill owner or dam operator was not absolute; the use of a negligence standard protected dam operators from liability for temporary flooding resulting from unusual conditions. Thus the Gananoque Water Power Company, for which a standard of performance requiring it to lower water levels above a certain fixed point 'with reasonable expedition' was judicially determined in the early 1880s, was not held liable in 1901 when unusual and unexpected drainage conditions contributed to the flooding of more than thirty properties. Correspondingly, a northern Ontario power company was liable for damages where high water levels could be expected and 'the probability of danger was accentuated by the positive actions of those operating the dam.'[38]

In the case of claims for shoreline damage brought against lumbermen directly, there was some statutory protection in the Rivers and Streams Act. Justice William P.R. Street concluded in *Neely* v *Peter* that the legislation 'seems clearly intended to place the public advantage of allowing lumbermen to use rivers and streams as highways for carrying their logs to a market, above the private damage and inconvenience which may necessarily be caused to individual riparian proprietors by their doing so.' But an improvement company operating under the Timber Slide Companies Act for precisely the same purpose had to follow statutory procedures for expropriation to avoid liability and an injunction claim by flooded shoreline owners. Meredith, as Chief Justice, recognized the anomaly in this distinction between lumbermen and timber slide companies when he granted an injunction against an improvement company but suspended its operation for a year in order to enable the company to acquire the right to overflow the plaintiff's land by statute or otherwise.[39] The standard of negligence and the suspended injunction are two examples of judicial attempts to reconcile principles governing injury to traditional property interests with the pressing claims of economic development. These devices do not appear to have been widely used, however, and should perhaps be regarded as still experimental. Insofar as remedies are concerned, the more important development of this period was recognition of a need for more precise and detailed regulation or management powers than were previously available.

Conflicts with other interests using Ontario's rivers, lakes, and streams, which resulted from the ongoing operation of the lumber industry, tested the willingness, ability, and authority of the courts to lay down guidelines for management and regulation. The economic uses of Ontario waterways were either continuous, as in the case of navigation during periods of open water, or intermittent and recurring, such as timber drives. Moreover, these activities took place in a natural environment that was itself subject to marked annual and seasonal fluctuations. Thus, effective resolution of conflicts or avoidance of future clashes required remedial measures capable of responding on an ongoing basis to almost constant change. Members of the judiciary, who were either prepared to regulate lumbering and other operations on the water or to lament their inability to do so, explicitly and implicitly recognized this fact. After supporting the plaintiff's claim for an injunction in *Dickson* v *Burnham* and reviewing the general principle which should govern the defendant's use of his own water rights, Mowat appointed a surveyor to report on physical renovations to be undertaken by the defendant to avoid liability. An appeal from the decision at trial sustained the result in the case, while the precise operational directives were rejected: 'If it is the right of the defendant to redress the wrong in his own way, it is not for the court to direct him how he shall do it; and it follows that the Court cannot call in an expert to assist the Court to do that which it was not proper for the court itself to do.'[40]

Recurring difficulties and delays experienced by steamboat operators on rivers also used for floating timber led Justice Thomas Galt to recommend increased government regulation and ultimately resulted in legislation requiring lumbermen to use powered vessels to transport logs.[41] In *Booth* v *Lowery*, which was previously discussed for its relevance to the question of lumbermen's liability for property damage, Anglin ventured beyond a review of competing legal interests to outline procedures which verge on operational guidelines for river drivers. He noted, in particular, that it might have been appropriate to station men in positions where they could have prevented a jam from forming and that some of the boom upstream should have been kept closed until previously released logs had passed through the construction area.[42] These remarks are a further indication of the tentative introduction of a managerial dimension to the courts' supervision of water resource use.

The courts recognized the managerial function but also admitted their own limitations in performing it. Indeed, the courts were often unwilling and considered themselves poorly equipped to act in cases where the meeting point between those participating in different but legitimate activities was uncertain and where interaction was likely to be continuous. An example arose in *Ireson* v *Holt Timber Company* (1913), where the continuing use of rivers by lumber companies interfered with navigation and the shoreline access of riparians. Having lost a nuisance action and facing an injunction against further interference with the rights of the shoreline owners, the defendant lumber company sought some guidelines for identifying lawful means of continuing its operations. Justice William R. Riddell's legal response and refusal to contemplate the practicalities of a difficult situation were probably of limited consolation to the operator:

It is manifestly impossible for the Court to give specific directions to these defendants how they are to float their logs or arrange their booms – and it is equally impossible for the Court to determine in advance whether any particular method or arrangement will interfere with the plaintiff's rights. The defendants need not have any apprehension of anything like oppression. If they make an honest attempt to act in such a way as to give the plaintiff his undoubted rights, there will probably be no attempt to proceed against them for contempt – and, if such an attempt be made, a Court must be satisfied of a violation of the injunction before process will be awarded.[43]

One exception to judicial imprecision in the regulation of nineteenth-century water use is *Bradley* v *Gananoque Water Power Co.* (1901), where the court referred to an earlier decision directing defendant dam operators 'so as to keep and use their dam ... that the water shall not be raised by means thereof more than a half inch above the level marked by a certain bolt ... except during freshets and periods of overflow of the dam, and that at such periods it is the duty of the defendants, by means of proper waste gates, to lower the water to the level of half an inch above the said bolt with reasonable expedition.' A challenge to the adequacy of the defendant's performance after nearly two decades of operating under this early order revealed the strengths and suggested the limitations of judicial regulation. James Thompson Garrow of the Ontario Court of Appeal found that for flooding to have occurred but once in so long a period demonstrated the reasonableness of the dam operator's precautions up to that time and precluded liability. Yet the court also observed that 'proper waste gates' and 'reasonable expedition' prior to the flooding of 1901 might not be so thereafter. The court further remarked regarding any necessary physical alterations to the dam structure or its openings that these were 'a matter of mere expense, not of overwhelming amount' and the defendants would not be excused from making them by the need to remove their saw mill or to rebuild the dam: 'They have contracted to lower these waters with "reasonable expedition" which may mean as speedily as it can be done, not by the appliance which the defendants have, but by those which they ought to have and could have, by expending the requisite money, to save plaintiffs from injury.'[44] Whether or not this apparent exposure to open-ended and uncertain costs as well as possible dislocation could be borne by the nineteenth-century operators of saw mills and dams, it would be less easily accommodated by the large-scale developments and investments associated with the twentieth-century hydro-electric power industry.

The overall picture that emerges from this survey of the legal framework surrounding the nineteenth-century forest industry's use of Ontario's lakes, rivers, and streams is not entirely consistent. The diverse nature of the problems that had to be resolved and the unevenness of sources both complicate and limit the process of assessment. Yet general observations may be made and conclusions reached as to dominant trends. Legal conflict over water use during the late nineteenth-century lumber era produced frequent clashes between entrepreneurial initiatives and established property interests, the consequences of which for provincial economic development were at least partially understood by the judiciary. *McClaren* v *Caldwell* and *Booth* v *Lowery* are prominent but certainly not isolated examples of judicial recognition of the significance of particular decisions for the fortunes of the lumber trade. Though judicial preferences exhibited some variation, the underlying tendency, perhaps best illustrated in *Re Burnham*, was to recognize the claims of property and to leave decisions about the allocation and use of resources to the market or to the legislature. The courts thus exhibited a strong aversion to judicial lawmaking, a reluctance which was more pronounced where costs had to be distributed outside the lumber industry.

Legal disputes involving lumbering, though initially centred within the forest industry itself, increasingly involved other interests affected by the manner in which Ontario's water resources were used. The diversity of competing interests often required careful balancing and management which had implications for all water users, problems it was felt were best left to the legislature. The latter institution, as evidenced clearly by such legislation as the Water Privileges Act, the Rivers and Streams Act, and the Ottawa River Act, and implicitly in the Saw Logs Driving Act and legislation governing tolls, was anxious to foster productive use of Ontario's water resources by private interests. Most of this legislation assumed a continuing role for the courts in the application or administration of water law. But there were early indications, for example Mowat's initial inclination to employ executive authority to regulate the economic balance on the Ottawa River, that judicial decisionmaking would not always be regarded as suitable. And when specific operational guidelines appeared necessary, the courts tended to acknowledge their own limitations. All of this activity represented a conscious evaluation of institutions and deliberate efforts to adapt decisionmaking processes to the perceived qualities of the issues raised and the alternatives available. Judgments about the deficiencies or limitations of courts were based on both procedural shortcomings and grounds of philosophy or principle, with the overall result that administrative solutions became relatively more attractive for certain types of problems.

In the context of hydro-electric power, the legislature's desire to maximize a perceived public benefit was even more apparent. The legislature's acceptance of judicial decisionmaking became even more strained and a tendency emerged to resort to different institutional forms of decisionmaking. The importance of administrative decisionmaking in water management increased dramatically. Explanation for the use of regulatory and administrative institutions may be found partly in the nature of water management problems where ongoing and competing uses appeared to be more directly involved than in the lumber era, partly in the judicial response to those problems, and partly in contemporary attitudes quite unrelated to water law.

WATER POWERS AND THE PROVINCIAL INTEREST

The significance of provincial water powers in an era of rapid technological innovation in hydro-electricity generation and transmission was emphatically drawn to the Ontario government's attention in 1891. In his *Report on the Lakes and Rivers, Waters and Water-Powers of the Province of Ontario*, E.B. Borron reviewed the economic importance of electricity and its advantages to the province and identified a public interest in continuing control of the resource in light of future uses. The hydro production right was 'a franchise in which the people at large, now and hundreds of years hence, are and will be deeply, nay, vitally interested. It is one, consequently, in which the Rights of the Crown, or in other words, of the people, are to be most jealously and carefully guarded.'[45] The Crown Lands Department indicated that prompt utilization of available water power sites was desirable as a means of stimulating industrial development, particularly in the northern mineral sector. Water power, in effect, was regarded as the basis of a provincial industrial strategy by those who saw cheap power as the necessary foundation for saw mills, planing mills, pulp mills, and other woodworking industries together with mining operations and textile and chemical works.[46]

The Water Powers Act 1898

Borron's recommendation that legislative measures should be taken to establish state control was ignored until 1898, when a brief statute gave notice of the government's intention to safeguard public interests in future water power use by regulating the terms and conditions of private power development. The Water Powers Act authorized the Crown Lands Commissioner to reserve water powers and adjacent property from sale and to prepare regulations for approval by the Lieutenant Governor in Council establishing terms for the disposal and development of those water powers.[47]

Regulations appeared in the summer of 1898 applicable to those water powers with generating capacity, which even at low water would not fall below 150 hp. Henceforth water privileges and adjacent lands necessary for their development would be reserved from any grant or lease of crown lands and – subject to compensation – the right to flood portions of such leased or granted lands in order to develop a water power was also reserved, along with a right of road access to the power site. Reserved areas were available under separate lease arrangements. To ensure efficient and prompt performance in accordance with the objective of contributing generally to provincial economic growth – that is, providing the energy foundation for other industry – the regulations for leases required an advance description of the business expected to utilize the power produced and an indication of the rate at which power would be made available. To ensure that those seeking water power leases seriously intended to develop their sites, entry standards for the industry could be partially controlled by a requirement of proof of financial standing.[48] This was some assurance that the contemplated (and usually costly) works could be completed by the applicant.

In some cases an applicant intended to utilize the entire power capacity of the site for his own purposes. Applications of this nature could be approved, but where total water power production exceeded the developer's own requirements, service obligations were imposed. The surplus was to be made available to other parties on agreed terms, but in the absence of agreement, on terms and at rates to be fixed conclusively by Order in Council. The contrast may be noted here between tolerance of partial development of a power site under the Water Privileges Act as interpreted in Re Burnham and the provision for full utilization of the resource under the regulations of the Water Powers Act. The service requirements were a condition of the lease, and the Lieutenant Governor in Council assumed a residual responsibility to set rates.[49] Of the several hundred lease agreements contained in the Water Power Lease Books, most routinely employed the standard terms with only minor modifications. Standardized terms reduced the amount of bureaucratic effort necessary for processing and supervising leases and fostered awareness of the ground rules and conditions applicable to hydro-electric power development.[50]

An authoritative assessment of the overall effectiveness of the Water Powers Act and subordinate regulations would require consideration of a representative sample of issued leases and will not be attempted here. It is worthwhile, however, to illustrate the development of administrative procedures, problems of compliance, and the operation of ministerial discretion over leases.

In the Montreal River district of northeastern Ontario a striking geographical feature aptly known as 'The Notch' was looked upon as a promising (if challenging) water power location. E.H. Bronson, a prominent Ottawa Valley lumberman, was the first to apply for a lease on this site although he had no plans for immediate development and was advised by Premier George W. Ross that he could feel quite easy with regard to the right which priority of application had given him. A year later, however, the Commissioner of Crown Lands informed the applicant of procedures to be followed where there were several applicants for a lease: 'no definite action is taken until all parties are notified and a date arranged for the hearing of all the interests concerned. This policy will not be departed from.'[51] Two local residents obtained a lease of the water power in February 1907 and shortly thereafter assigned their rights to the Montreal Cobalt Power Company. The lease's original conditions included the requirement that annual rentals be paid and that the development of the first 1,000 hp be underway within a year. The principals of Montreal Cobalt dutifully reported their failure to perform the construction obligations as a consequence of the most unfavourable condition of the money markets and were granted a three-month extension with the possibility of a further short extension if progress could be demonstrated.

During the following years the Department of Lands and Mines received a succession of inquiries from other parties interested in undertaking development. Departmental officials corresponded intermittently with Montreal Cobalt Power and continued to advise other applicants up to 1911 that the Department was not aware that the development conditions of this lease had been complied with, but the power could not be dealt with until the lease had been cancelled. What appeared to be a decisive step was taken in December 1911 when the Minister notified Montreal Cobalt Power of his intention to cancel the lease unless reasonable cause was shown within ten days why this should not be done. Four months later a formal notice of cancellation was issued on the grounds that rental payments were in arrears and other conditions had not been fulfilled. The company was offered a further ten-day period to apply if it wished to be heard in the matter. These departmental procedures failed to induce the lessee to take any active steps or make any significant progress towards development. Finally, in January 1913, six years after the valuable lease had been granted, it was declared forfeited and cancelled by Order in Council. An almost instantaneous political response produced a legislative order for the production of all related correspondence, the series of documents on which this sorry tale is based. Political influence was very much available to water power leaseholders, no matter how flagrant their disregard or abuse of development conditions. The effect of public enforcement in this instance was not impressive.[52]

The scope of discretionary administrative authority exercised over the availability of water power leases was wide, as illustrated in the treatment of another northern Ontario site at Smokey Falls on the Sturgeon River. A group organized as the Smokey Falls Manufacturing Company first leased the site in 1904. Several individuals and the municipalities of Sturgeon Falls and North Bay later expressed interest in this water power. Both communities applied for the location on the assumption that the Smokey Falls Manufacturing Company had failed to comply with the prescribed conditions of the lease. The Minister of Lands and Mines initially encouraged North Bay officials to consider an alternative source of hydro-electric power for municipal and business purposes and eventually indicated his reasons for refusing the municipal operations. '[We] hope that in the spring that Sturgeon Falls Pulp and Paper Company will resume operations on a re-organized basis, and we have been holding this Smokey Falls power for that company as in order to make a success of their operation they must increase their capacity.' Precedence of application was of little value in circumstances such as this, where an undisclosed preference for a particular interest or purpose supplemented an expressed policy favouring development.[53]

As a result of the Water Powers Act and accompanying regulations, procedures and standards were theoretically in place to control the allocation of leases and several operational aspects of hydro-electric power production. Conflicts and problems continued to arise, however, with respect to the administration of the regulatory framework and its application to certain water powers in Ontario, especially those secured by private interests prior to the Water Powers Act. Conflicts affecting the scope or comprehensiveness of the applicability of the Water Powers Act demonstrated the continuing interaction of the legislative and judicial processes.

The application of the Water Powers Act to certain Ontario rivers depended upon the nature of the presumption regarding ownership of the beds of navigable rivers where shoreline property had been granted by the Crown. Control of a number of major hydro-electric power sites in the north depended upon determining whether the Crown was presumed to have granted or retained ownership of the stream beds when granting shoreline properties. In *Keewatin Power Company and Hudson's Bay Company v Town of Kenora* (1906), the issue was tested in a dispute involving the Winnipeg River.[54]

The ambitious municipal leaders of Rat Portage (later Kenora) were anxious to ensure that the electrical potential of Steep Rock Falls on the East Branch of the Winnipeg River would be utilized in a manner most advantageous to their community. Following unsatisfactory negotiations between private parties interested in immediate development of the site and the shoreline owners – the Hudson's Bay Company and the Keewatin

Power Company – town officials obtained powers to expropriate the necessary shoreline lands.[55] The community's actual water power lease was to be arranged under the Water Powers Act at a later date. The owners' opposition to municipal expropriation soon developed into a disagreement over property valuation, a matter to be settled by arbitration. The key question in the valuation became the nature of private rights in the river bed of a navigable waterway. This matter was brought before the courts for resolution.

From the outset the possibility of intervention by the Attorney General to represent provincial interests attracted attention on both sides. The Hudson's Bay Company's Land Commissioner wired Premier James Whitney to oppose rumoured provincial involvement in the case and received a critical response. 'Your telegram received,' stated the Premier, 'and I reply simply to draw your attention to the objectionable tone and language of it.' The rebuke could hardly have been unexpected. None the less, Leighton McCarthy, one of the Company's Toronto solicitors, continued to urge his client to adopt a firm stand for strategic purposes: 'the clearer Mr. Whitney and his government are shown that your company intends taking a strong position, I think the less trouble we will have with them.' Kenora officials, however, anticipated benefits from the Crown's direct participation and pressed for provincial action with qualified success. W.H. Hearst, who later became Premier, was delegated to represent the provincial interest. He travelled to Kenora with N.W. Rowell, counsel for the town and subsequently leader of the provincial Liberals, where *Keewatin Power Company and Hudson's Bay Company v Town of Kenora* opened before Justice Anglin on 12 July 1906. Hearst formally secured the Attorney General's right to intervene if he saw fit to do so but decided there was nothing to be gained at the trial stage that might not also be accomplished on appeal. The matter of Ontario's formal participation was therefore left open 'in case it might be thought better to meet the situation by legislation if that should be found necessary.'[56] Thus alternative responses were considered in light of the anticipated dynamics of the litigation process.

The decision at the trial level was generally favourable to the Kenora argument that a Crown grant of lands bordering navigable rivers gave the grantee title only to the water's edge: 'In our rivers which are navigable in fact, because the public rights in them are recognized to have always existed, ex jure naturae, the title to the alveus must be presumed to remain in the Crown unless expressly granted.' This conclusion was founded upon Anglin's willingness to modify or adapt English common law doctrine on waterways in applying it to the rivers and lakes of Ontario. Such an approach was by no means innovative in the province after Justice James Buchanan Macaulay's decision in *R*. v *Meyers*, which dealt explicitly with the need to adapt certain principles of English common law to the different circumstances and geographic conditions of the Canadian frontier.[57]

As appeal proceedings were expected, the exact nature of the provincial interest raised by the Kenora case was re-examined. Hearst warned that if the companies succeeded, 'the grantees of land on navigable waters have obtained greater rights than it was intended to confer upon them.' Similar consequences would follow if the court accepted that the same rights as enjoyed by riparians on non-navigable streams also applied to the non-navigable portions of otherwise navigable waterways. To avoid the possibility of subsequent Crown leases perpetuating a serious problem, Hearst urged that they be reworded, 'making it clear that where lands are granted bordering on navigable waters, that the grant does not extend beyond high water mark.' To protect future water power rights on non-navigable streams he also proposed amending the Water Powers Act to clarify its intended meaning. But all this failed to resolve the practical question of the Crown's best course of action in *Kenora* v *HBC*.

Government files do not reveal a clear explanation for the Attorney General's unwillingness to participate in the litigation directly; but it is probable that the provincial government did not expect the company's legal argument to succeed and the residual response of legislation was always available. It also appears that the provincial government would have preferred a favourable judicial solution to legislative action.[58] Ironically, the Court of Appeal varied the trial decision and affirmed the private parties' claims to the bed of the Winnipeg River. In the view taken by two members of that Court, precedent and statutory interpretation necessitated a conclusion which it was not open to the judiciary to alter or circumvent. Richard Martin Meredith doubted that 'judicial legislation is the proper or is it all a permissable remedy.' Chief Justice Charles Moss was equally plain in stating the widely and forcefully held view that the legislature alone was the proper forum for any necessary changes to be introduced.[59]

There were no further appeals, but three years later in 1911, with important power developments on the St Lawrence in contemplation, the legislature reversed the result of the Kenora case. Henceforth, in the absence of an express grant it should be presumed that the bed of a navigable water was not intended to pass to the grantee of the shoreline lands. Premier Whitney gave assurances that the legislation would not be abused, while Frank Cochrane, the Minister of Lands and Mines, defended the measure as an attempt 'to protect the interests of the people in water powers which were never granted by the Crown and which are claimed by owners of land on each side of the stream, land which in many cases was purchased by speculators for a mere song with the avowed object of securing control of the power.' Thus the legislature ultimately achieved the result it either desired or assumed while exhibiting an apparent preference for privately initiated determination at law. Statutory intervention continued to function as a correcting mechanism where the judicial result was inconsistent with public policy. Thereafter the Bed of Navigable Waters Act was rarely examined in the courts and seems to have been applied chiefly as a reinforcing device where the common law presumption was actually rebutted on the facts.[60]

Within a decade of the Water Powers Act, Ontario embarked on the controversial public power experiment with the creation of the Hydro Electric Power Commission (HEPC). Both private leasing subject to conditions and public ownership were then available as alternative vehicles to implement provincial power development goals. As a means of harmonizing the two systems of water power development, at least to a limited degree, HEPC officials were given some responsibility for investigating the private operations, estimating productive capacity, and advising on appropriate rates. In this regard, the HEPC in the early years of its existence worked closely with the Department of Lands, Forests, and Mines. When first established, the HEPC was also authorized to report to the provincial executive on any private water privileges and lands which should, in its opinion, be acquired by the Commission in connection with its general mandate to provide Ontario municipalities with electrical power. Much of the HEPC's production capacity was thus obtained by acquisition of existing privately owned facilities. Because of the extensive discussion which Ontario's public power movement has already received from historians, the focus here remains on the management and control of water use by private power operations.[61]

Instrument Choice and the Control of Water Power Monopolies

Through direct grants, special legislation, and leases of a particularized nature, or in the general form provided for under the Water Powers Act Regulations, numerous water power sites had passed to private hands by the early twentieth century. Conflicts emerged between competing water power users, and between water power users and other interests concerned with navigation, timber drives, or the public availability of hydroelectricity. It is possible to view most of the conflicts as resulting from the existence of a monopoly position, a tendency to act as though monopoly control existed, or an attempt to secure it. However, the number and nature of affected interests also distinguished the conflicts. Several techniques were used to resolve such conflicts, including informal negotiations conducted through the Department of Lands, Forest, and Mines, anticipatory legislation, litigation and regulatory directives, or ministerial orders. The existence of this variety of techniques and institutions for resolving water management conflicts suggests that the turn of the century was a period of active experimentation with what is now known as choice of instrument. Available solutions differed in regard to the location of initiative, speed, flexibility, and general effectiveness in contributing to the utilization of Ontario's water resources.[62]

Prior to a discussion of comprehensive water management powers conferred on the Minister by legislation, it is instructive to examine a sample water-use conflict and the informal manner in which it was treated. The geographical and industrial character of this conflict is entirely representative of one type of dispute; administrative treatment of it may or may not conform to standard practice within the Department of Lands, Forests, and Mines. Lake Temagami, a large northeastern Ontario lake, from which (at the turn of the century) water flowed northward into the Montreal River-Lake Temiskaming system and southward via the Temagami and Sturgeon rivers to Lake Nipissing, was the source of a major clash between mining interests in the Cobalt area which depended upon the northern outlet and pulp milling operations at Sturgeon Falls. The two industries regarded Lake Temagami as a natural storage reservoir for their industrial water supply. Maximum utilization by either would drastically reduce or even eliminate the flow available through the other outlet. The situation at Sturgeon Falls became particularly difficult in the fall and winter of 1910–11. The Cobalt Hydraulic Power Company then controlled both outlets. The Minister reacted sharply to complaints about water shortages from the Imperial Paper Mills Company at Sturgeon Falls: 'I have been more than surprised at this in view of the fact that we have been most lenient in allowing the company to run on, though practically in default. If these groundless and needless complaints are to continue, it may be necessary to return the compliment by taking up the question of cancelling the concession.' There is no indication at this point that the

Minister had any independent information on water conditions or any means of assessing the validity of the Sturgeon Falls claim or contrary arguments, if any, from the Cobalt-based dam operators. When the water shortage at Sturgeon Falls reportedly became acute in the spring, the deputy minister ordered an examination of the south end dam and notified the legal representative of the Cobalt company of the action he had taken. At that point the Cobalt group reopened part of the southern facility, a step which high spring water levels might in any event have required.[63]

The negotiated settlement process had several advantages including promptness and flexibility to meet seasonally changing conditions. But informal procedures for participation and information gathering appeared increasingly less satisfactory as the number of affected interests and the complexity of the situation increased. One possible response to increased complexity was special legislation concerning private power developments. This technique was not uncommon after 1900 and is illustrated below.[64]

The sensitive and complex problems of protecting public interests in the context of aggressive private claims were evident, if not necessarily resolved, in the Rainy River episode centring on the ambitions of E.W. Backus, a Minnesota lumberman active in the northwestern Ontario forest industry, and his Ontario-Minnesota power export projects. In an effort to eliminate uncertainty resulting from a federal statute concerning the rights of Rainy River water power developers and Canadian electricity consumers in Fort Frances on the Canadian-American boundary, provincial legislation in 1906 recognized the possibility of power exports from the Ontario and Minnesota Power Company facilities. The legislation provided that 'there shall not be less of the said power or electrical energy available for use on the Canadian side of the international boundary line than on the American side, and subject to the provisions of this Act such power or electrical energy shall be delivered on the Canadian side as and when demanded.' However, when there was not a 'reasonable prospect of the utilization within a reasonable time of power or electrical energy, unemployed, though actually available for use on the Canadian side,' the Lieutenant Governor in Council might set terms and conditions for export.[65]

The subsequent export application of the Ontario and Minnesota Power Company provoked a heated controversy in Fort Frances and more generally throughout the province. The municipality argued vigorously against the export before all the water power resources on the United

States side were fully developed and rejected the suggestion that any Canadian power could be regarded as not being in demand for use on the Canadian side of the river at the present time, nor until such time as a fair and reasonable chance has been given to the people of Ontario to promote their own industries and utilize their own power. The mayor of Fort Frances posed the spectre of a 'dead village on the Canadian side of Rainy River, a prosperous City on the Minnesota side, all because our provincial and Federal government have not the backbone to say We Will Retain Our Resources for our own people, which if not required today will be in the near future.' The Fort Frances situation thus raised the still familiar and still unresolved questions of whether the public interest was to be assessed in the short or the longer term and the relative weight to be accorded strong local claims as against potential benefits more widely dispersed across the provincial community.

In the Fort Frances case an export agreement was reached in June 1910 and confirmed by the legislature.[66] The agreement concluded that the export conditions had in fact been satisfied. The export conditions here echoed the principles underlying the Water Powers Act of 1898 and continued in the philosophy of the Hydro Electric Power Commission. Hydro-electricity had a public purpose or public utility function and was intended to support industrial growth and diversification in Ontario. Thus, through the details of the agreement between the company and the Minister, an effort was made to establish a framework that would ensure that the government retained ultimate control. To this end, export authorization was declared to be for a temporary purpose only, and the right to divert could be revoked at any time. Specifically, termination of any power export from the Fort Frances facilities of the Ontario and Minnesota Power Company was to be on a thirty-day written notice from the Minister. By agreement, liquidated damages were settled, and the parties accepted the imposition of an immediate perpetual injunction. Moreover, price regulation powers for electrical energy supplied to Canadian consumers were conferred upon the HEPC, which was empowered to fix conditions of energy delivery and methods of distribution. But in practice the ability of Ontario authorities to reclaim export power production facilities greatly deteriorated.[67] Other Backus enterprises elsewhere in northern Ontario show that judicial responses to tension between private and public interest in water use might be required where disputes arose after the original water power rights had been granted rather than during the allocation process.

In 1913 the Keewatin Power Company sold an important water power property on the Winnipeg River to Backus, who was attracted to the site by its suitability in connection with a large pulp and paper mill he had in contemplation. His concern about the extent of the water power available to him in the light of nearby artificial channels, which were also utilizing Lake of the Woods water, led to court action. In 1916 the Keewatin Power Company began proceedings for an injunction to prevent the Lake of the Woods Milling Company and the Keewatin Flour Mills Company from diverting any further lake water through artificial channels to their mills. But the cases against the two milling companies did not proceed to trial until 1927, by which time a power plant had been completed at the Backus site.[68]

At trial Keewatin Power or Backus claimed all of the hydro-electricity that could be developed from the full volume of water that would ordinarily flow through its natural outlet.[69] The Backus interests further contended that the artificial channels used for flour milling were not accompanied by any grant of water and that the diversion through these mill races was accordingly an infringement of rights granted to the Keewatin Power Company. The defending milling companies asserted limitations of the power company's privileges and claimed that their own grants incorporated full recognition of the water power rights they had been exercising for many years. This contention led the courts into a detailed review of land titles in the old 'disputed territory' of northwestern Ontario and the specific terms of negotiations related to the use of the three Keewatin shoreline properties, which were then in the hands of the Keewatin Power Company, the Lake of the Woods Milling Company, and the Keewatin Flour Mills Company.

Justice David Inglis Grant based his decision on an interpretation of the facts which precluded Backus from restricting the water rights of the defendant flour mills. The milling companies' rights under the original federal grants, concluded the judge, had been recognized by Ontario according to the spirit of a provisional agreement between the two levels of government in 1874, that is, before any grant of a water power was made to the Keewatin Lumbering and Manufacturing Company from whom Keewatin Power later obtained it. The provincial authorities were at all times fully aware of the facts and showed their active approval of the construction and use of the 'mill-races' by the plans prepared by the departmental surveyors, and the references made to such mill races in the descriptions of lands conveyed by Crown grants.

In the Ontario Court of Appeal Keewatin Power again claimed exclusive use of the waters of Lake of the Woods flowing through the natural outlets which were in Backus' hands.[70] Chief Justice Francis P. Latchford highlighted the significance of the appeal by remarking that if it succeeded, the vast area of the Lake of the Woods – over 1500 square miles in extent – would be the personal mill pond of Backus. Latchford confirmed the result of the trial decision, albeit following a somewhat altered process of factual interpretation.

The underlying arguments on both sides were essentially unmodified by their transatlantic passage to the Judicial Committee of the Privy Council in London.[71] Appellant's counsel put forth the view that there was no dominion or provincial legislation which enabled the Crown to make a grant so as to impair the natural rights of lands still ungranted. Otherwise stated, previous grants could not diminish the water power to which riparian owners were entitled. Thus the grantees of the patents upon which the respondents relied were bound to keep the property in the state in which it was when they applied for the grants, so that the Keewatin Power Company as riparian owners of the outlet could use all of the water which naturally flowed through this channel. In giving judgment Viscount Dunedin found Keewatin Power's principal argument 'untenable,' and 'so extravagant as to be scarcely worth repeating.' In the end, then, the positions of the Lake of the Woods Milling Company and the Keewatin Flour Mills Company were protected. The several owners of the neighbouring power sites were each entitled to use the waters of the Lake of the Woods whether their locations were at natural or established artificial outlets.

Dunedin perceptively summarized the nature of the legal battle, finally resolved after fifteen years: 'There is no trace of any real damage being done to the water power of the plaintiffs, unless the taking of any water is a damage, but they conceived the idea of securing a monopoly to themselves of the whole of the water power of this enormous lake – an idea never entertained by the Crown, their author, when the whole arrangements were still to make.' Legislative developments contemporary with the beginning of Backus' campaign in the courts clearly indicate that the Crown was looking to regulation as a more direct and less time-consuming way to manage or supervise water power development elsewhere in the province.

The scope of ministerial authority over river and stream use and private water development was substantially extended between 1913 and 1916. The changes were a response to the intractability of water use conflicts between water power developers and lumbermen and were in part the result of perceived wartime exigencies which greatly concerned the HEPC.

In 1913 a general power to make such regulations as he might deem expedient regarding the use of rivers and their waters, including stored waters, was conferred on the Lieutenant Governor in Council.[72] Two years later, through legislation supplementing the Rivers and Streams Act, the Minister of Lands, Forests, and Mines assumed extensive decisionmaking powers. Thenceforth, on waterways designated by Order in Council as subject to the new legislation, all questions about the construction and use of river improvements, timber drives, and any stream flow alterations were to be determined by the Minister on the application of any party concerned by these activities. Ministerial control was intended to promote the efficient and proper use of designated rivers where competing rights existed. Recourse to the courts regarding any matter over which the Minister had jurisdiction under the legislation was eliminated.[73] Moreover, the legislation provided for delegation of ministerial powers to subordinate officials, since in the event of a conflict or dispute arising between the various interests operating on a designated river, or where it appeared expedient in the public interest, the Minister could delegate the power to regulate the use of the river and any improvements in such a way as 'shall seem best calculated to afford to persons having diverse interests on the river ... a fair and reasonable use of the waters of the river.'[74]

By the Water Powers Regulation Act (1916), the formal authority of the executive in matters connected with the development of Ontario water powers in private hands generally was extended to all such water powers, no matter how they had been acquired. The same legislation furthered a long-established policy by imposing on every owner of a water power in Ontario a statutory duty 'to ensure as far as possible the economical and efficient use of the water used by him.' To achieve this objective the legislation provided for the appointment by Order in Council of an individual or commission to examine water power operations and to make orders concerning their improvement. Subject to reasonable hearing requirements, the inspector could order removal, alteration, or reconstruction of works 'to such an extent as may be necessary to secure the proper degree of efficient and economical use of the water,' when it appeared to him that water was not being used efficiently or could not be so used because of the type or condition of the existing works. Inspectors were also authorized to determine the volume of water to which the owners were entitled, and rather elaborate guidelines were laid down for specifying the extent of a water power operator's entitlement in terms of volume. Presumably these were intended to reduce waste and promote efficiency by encouraging operators to modernize their plants and facilities as industry standards advanced.[75]

The Water Powers Regulation Act embodied the legislative response to difficult legal entanglements which had arisen or were anticipated concerning earlier water power agreements in the Niagara area. The HEPC foresaw increased competition from private power producers for the use of limited productive capacity, while anxiety about export levels and contract commitments increased during the wartime period. The courts could not be relied upon to compel full and efficient water use by private producers where this had not been contemplated in the original leasing agreements. In *Attorney General for Ontario* v *Electrical Development Co. Ltd* (1919), for example, where an agreement entitled the company to use enough water to produce 125,000 hp, the court determined that this volume of water should be related to the machinery the company had installed, maintained in a state of reasonable efficiency, since the agreement did not contemplate any change in the system as the standard of efficiency advanced. Under the judicial view, therefore, the company was entitled to more water than a commission or inspector under the Water Powers Regulation Act might have authorized it to use to produce the same quantity of power.[76]

The scope of potential interference with existing rights entailed by the legislation provoked a bitter and angry response from private power companies. In their eyes, the new legislation further demonstrated that the HEPC and its Chairman Adam Beck would stop at nothing in their efforts to expand the public power movement at the expense of private interests. Calls upon the federal government for disallowance of the provincial measures ultimately failed. But the sensitivity of the issues raised by the Water Powers Regulation Act is the probable explanation for the hearing and appeal procedures which accompanied and followed it. Inspectors' orders for repairs, alterations, or improvements might be appealed to the Lieutenant Governor in Council, who would have regard to 'material public advantage, by reason of the more efficient and economical use of the water.' Where requested, and at the discretion of the executive, reference proceedings were available to determine appropriate compensation for water power owners who had suffered a limitation upon their rights, or who 'will not presently receive a corresponding commercial advantage' from alterations they had been compelled to make. Considerations relevant to a compensation reference included 'the circumstances which render any limitation or restriction of such rights [to water powers] necessary and desirable in the public interest.'[77]

Under procedures later established, where the Inspector determined that a water power owner was exceeding his rights, he would simply report this finding to the executive, which might then establish a commission of inquiry under the Public Inquiries Act, composed of three judges of the Supreme Court of Ontario, with responsibility to report upon the same matters previously reported on by the Inspector. Where power production or capacity exceeding the owner's level of entitlement was confirmed, the commission would report also on the price, the terms, and the conditions under which the excess should be made available to the HEPC. Despite criticism of such judicial commissions, the legislation soon resulted in an order for the Electrical Development Company to provide the HEPC with 25,000 hp of surplus capacity.[78]

Notwithstanding any particular dispute or controversy for which they might have been intended, measures such as the Water Powers Regulations and the wartime Rivers and Streams Act amendments substantially increased direct regulatory authority over water use and management in Ontario. Wartime measures expanded the scope for executive decision-making, although the legislation retained some involvement for the influence of the expert whose role would shortly expand still further.

The extension of regulatory or executive authority over the operation of the hydro-electricity industry was also evident in rate-setting, where the technical issues raised were seen to require precise, prompt, and certain responses. Although many of the intricacies and refinements of rate regulation which are in evidence today were not found in the early records of the province's hydro-electricity industry, it is possible to discern some continuity of themes and objectives for basic rate-setting. When the Keewatin Lumber and Manufacturing Company purchased land and water power rights from the province in 1891, it undertook to spend up to a quarter of a million dollars on the power development, to submit all its plans for approval prior to construction to a government-appointed engineer, and to supply power 'to the extent of the capacity of the works' at rates to be set by 'a competent engineer' appointed for that purpose by the Lieutenant Governor in Council, who would consider the difficulty of the project and the company's expenditure.[79]

The Water Powers Act regulations encouraged price agreements between the lessee of the water power and the consumer, but, in the absence of agreement, remuneration set by Order in Council would be 'final and conclusive and binding.' Guidelines for pricing arrangements involving municipalities emphasized uniformity for 'all takers or users of like quantities delivered or supplied under similar conditions in any one municipality' and where two or more municipalities were associated in the same power production operation, any price differential between them could not be 'a greater amount than is necessary to provide for any additional cost of transmission.' Hearing procedures conducted by the HEPC were available to settle disputed municipal rate levels, while the Power Commission Act described the per horse power rate chargeable by the HEPC itself to municipalities as 'the cost of the power to the Commission at the point of development, or of its delivery to the Commission.'[80] Administrative responses were also resorted to for two further dimensions of water management, environmental protection, and international or interjurisdictional use, which emerged in the early twentieth century.

Environmental Protection and International Water Basin Management

Concern for environmental protection accompanied industrial expansion in Ontario and the objective of full and efficient industrial water power development was not universal. Distinctive characteristics of the environmental issue had significant implications for decisionmaking processes. A clean and uncontaminated environment, though typically regarded as a community asset – if regarded at all – had traditionally been protected – if protected at all – as a private right through nuisance actions or riparian claims. Common law and statute provided compensation for property damage from flooding. Limited safeguards for fish were in place, but there were serious obstacles to enforcement. As concern for the natural environment – especially the public domain of the northern lakes and forests – grew more vocal in the early twentieth century, the problem of protecting a widely diffused public interest against the competing claims of often highly capitalized and concentrated industries was exposed.[81] How would water law accommodate aesthetic and recreational values where traditional property-based protections were unavailable or inadequate?

Competitive uses were concentrated in provincial parks, where landscape appreciation and resource utilization were expected to co-exist. This situation produced some of the earliest expressions of discontent. In Algonquin in 1894 and Quetico in 1914, recreational users complained of the visual impact of flooding from lumbering operations. Comparable concerns arose in response to dam-building to improve water storage for industrial use in the Cross Lake-Temagami-Lady Evelyn Lake district. The sportsman's magazine *Rod and Gun* published an unsigned commentary stating that 'any raising of the level of these lakes which would destroy the trees along their edges and thus render them not only unsightly but exceedingly repellant to any person who had to affect a landing on their shores, should be strongly opposed.' Another correspondent cited the probable destruction of bass spawning grounds and the prospect of an increased insect population on newly created areas of 'comparatively stagnant water' as further grounds for opposition.[82]

The outcome of this particular controversy is of no immediate significance. The incident reveals, though, the existence in water management issues of concerned or affected interests who were without property-based claims and typically unorganized. There were no obvious channels of public participation intended to obtain the views of persons 'indirectly' affected by environmental change. However, in response to environmental criticisms of its water management programs in recreational areas, the provincial administration none the less imposed certain limited conditions on developers. Dam builders were expected to pay for the costs of surveying drowned lands in advance of flooding, to remove and pay for standing timber which would otherwise be destroyed, and to respect water level fluctuation limits. Although the developer now bore these costs of ameliorization, they provided only moderately satisfactory relief for the concerns of Ontario's early environmentalists.[83] The public interest in landscape preservation did gain a further limited measure of respectability in the course of the Riddell-Latchford Timber Commission.[84] But no new legislative action on the environmental issue resulted, and in general the administrative monitoring of landscape change by industry likely remained at a low level of effectiveness, unless other established interests were present, were threatened with injury, and were prepared to press the government for enforcement or control measures.[85]

Pressures over enforcement and control measures to regulate water use were most complicated in the context of international water basins. In response to problems generated by diverse uses and competing claims over water resources around Lake of the Woods, for example, a relatively sophisticated management program was introduced following prolonged discussions and negotiations involving private interests and governments from several jurisdictions.

The task of regulating Lake of the Woods water levels involved complex interjurisdictional questions, which also illuminate the important role of lawyers and legal institutions in the administration of Ontario waters. Lake of the Woods and its adjoining waters are partly situated within Ontario, Manitoba, and the state of Minnesota. Hence, these three governments and the two national governments were each interested to some degree in the selection and consequences of any arrangements for water management. However, the form of the administrative body which ultimately resulted from the hearings and negotiations reflected the fact that most of the water system is physically located in Ontario.

Canada and Ontario at different times had authorized dam construction for water level control in the interests of improved navigation and power production. The longstanding complaints of American residents, who experienced flooding of their properties at the upstream end of Lake of the Woods and then a year of unusually low water which severely interfered with navigation, encouraged the two national governments to refer Lake of the Woods regulation to the International Joint Commission, which had recently been formed to assist in the resolution of Canada-United States boundary water disputes. After a four-year inquiry (1912–16) the IJC produced recommendations which were accepted in principle in 1919 and became the basis of subsequent international agreements. It is sufficient here to indicate that the IJC inquiry accumulated several volumes of transcript testimony from a series of hearings as well as scientific and engineering studies concerning the diverse preferences and objectives of those using the lake and its shoreline for recreational, residential, navigational, agricultural, power, and industrial uses. The IJC offered guidance with regard to an appropriate range of regulated water level fluctuation but did not materially contribute to the resolution of the compensation questions – past and future – which would result from the implementation of a water management system.[86]

The IJC recommendations on the Lake of the Woods Reference, as embodied in the Canada-United States agreement of 1919, were to be implemented under the direction of the Lake of the Woods Control Board (LWCB), a body consisting of four 'duly qualified engineers,' two appointed by the federal government and two by Ontario. In order to secure 'the most dependable flow and the most advantageous and beneficial use' of the waters of the English and Winnipeg rivers, the LWCB had the power to regulate and control the flow of those two rivers and to control water levels in Lac Seul and Lake of the Woods. In addition to a comprehensive grant of 'all the powers necessary for effectively carrying out the control vested in it,' the Board was authorized to take possession of 'any mill, dam, plant, works, machinery, land, waters or premises' necessary to carry out its orders where any person or corporation either neglected or refused to do so, and to use the property for as long as required to accomplish its purposes, free from liability. Moreover, the Board's expenses arising from the operation of works it was necessary to possess 'shall constitute a debt due from such persons or corporations to the Board.' Somewhat like the HEPC, then, the Control Board combined regulatory powers and operational capabilities.[87] Although the problems are not central to this essay, the Lake of the Woods control question was not free from Canadian constitutional wrangling.[88]

To clear the way for the Lake of the Woods Control Board's work, compensation claims also had to be resolved. The grievances of flooded American landowners (the Canadian shoreline was generally steeper, rockier, and less populated), dating from the 1880s, had never been settled. Theoretically, these claims for damage caused by dam-building in Canada might have been brought through diplomatic channels, but on a practical level this was impossible, since the American government itself had consistently favoured navigational (high water) interests over the riparian farmers and had actually urged Canadian authorities to raise the lake level long before the IJC recommendations. When proceedings pursuant to international convention were taken to acquire flowage easements over 850 parcels of land on the United States shore, several owners entered the courts to settle compensation claims. Their argument, ultimately unsuccessful, was that the lands taken were particularly adapted to the purpose for which they were to be put – water storage for hydroelectric power – and should be valued accordingly, rather than as marginal agricultural land, their actual use in the hands of the individual owners. Based on the valuation criteria proposed by the landowners, total compensation claims could have reached $89 million.

Lawyers who represented and advised the Canadian and American governments during the litigation shared certain concerns about the compensation process, as the governments shared some responsibility for the financial outcome. While the test cases were under way, American lawyers contemplated three methods of solution. Commissioners' awards were apparently attractive on the basis of procedural convenience, but entailed the risk of excessive sympathy to the storage reservoir argument. Litigated compensation cases, for reasons not elaborated on, were regarded as generally 'lacking in scientific basis.' The most desirable solution, carrying with it the virtues of economy, consistency, and convenience of administration, was a settlement scheme based on unit values, if a suitable scale of land types and shoreline elevations could be agreed upon. Such a procedure entailed careful initial consideration of an overall valuation policy, on the basis of which it was assumed classification of individual parcels might be made. Compensation was then simply computed.[89]

While the Americans had primary responsibility for the mechanics of compensation to United States landowners, Canada had assumed certain obligations in regard to cost-sharing associated with the water regulation program as a whole. Canada participated directly in the American easement proceedings and the litigation. However, one fundamental consideration affected Ottawa's attitude to the process:

It is thought that a good case can be made out for refusing to pay half of these costs, if the point is ever raised by the United States Government. On the other hand, the desirability of avoiding the raising of the issue, will justify the adoption of a generous attitude by Canada in all proceedings prior to and during the settlement of the international claim. It would certainly pay Canadian interests to avoid minor issues at any cost, in order to prevent, if possible, the raising of this major issue, which might result in a complete transformation for an extremely profitable venture to a bargain of doubtful value.[90]

John Read's candid remark is a useful reminder to students of legal process – particularly where the balancing of multiple interests is involved – that attitudes to any given legal manoeuvre, institutional choice, or procedure are not necessarily best evaluated or understood in light of their immediate or most apparent functions. Purposes and objectives are often combined at several levels so that short-term preferences may be overridden by long-term strategies. Institutional and procedural design, where two or more parties are engaged in this initial phase of decision-making, can itself be a subject for trade-offs and bargaining.

CONCLUSION

Between the 1870s and the 1920s new water-dependent activities including the generation of hydro-electricity and recreation were introduced to Ontario alongside the well-established uses of the mid-nineteenth century such as floating timber, navigation, and the operation of local mills. The diversity, concentration, and interconnectedness of competitive or possibly incompatible water uses gave rise to increasingly complex problems of water use and management. The institutional framework within which conflicts about water use were resolved was substantially altered in response to the new strains and pressures of resource allocation. The overall transition may be briefly described. In the mid-nineteenth century Ontario water law was primarily a judicial system emphasizing settlement by the courts of disputes between individuals according to common law and a few statutes. Arbitration was available for certain conflicts within the lumbering community. By the 1920s a legislative régime increasingly oriented towards intervention and control had emerged to deal with the complex balancing of widely divergent but often interdependent claims on water resources. The legislature's resort to regulatory controls and administrative agencies was an attempt to respond to pressures that were perceived as qualitatively new aspects of water resource use and conflict.

The changed institutional arrangements represented a conscious (if not necessarily comprehensive) response to judicial attitudes and reactions as these appeared from judges' values and in the judicial process. Questions about which individuals or interests had the rights to use specific water resources were still being successfully resolved by the courts and the common law through the application and refinement of general principles and the courts were also effective in determining when rights, once defined, had been exceeded. In addition, they were generally capable of compensating for or preventing damage to property-related interests. Indeed, the courts had a tendency to adopt a strict approach in dealing with injury to established property interests, with the result that economic initiative was not always favourably received.[91] The courts' strength in making determinations between competing claims of a similar nature was matched by a general incapacity and a marked reluctance to apportion rights between different types of uses. In protecting property-based claims the judiciary repeatedly sanctioned partial use or even inactivity. Full and effective use as measured in the light of technological capacity or demand was not a goal which judicial decisions tended to foster. Accordingly, a divergence of view developed between the evolving concern of the legislature for resource utilization and the view generally taken by the courts. One key to understanding this difference is the changing perception of the public interest between the mid-nineteenth and the early twentieth centuries.

At the outset of the period the public interest may well have been perceived as equivalent to the dominant private interest or the reconciliation of the competing claims of separate private interests. The concept, R.C.B. Risk has shown, was rarely considered explicitly or elaborated extensively at mid-century.[92] Yet, by the 1870s, the 'public good' appeared as a statutory criterion for certain types of decisions about the allocation of resources.[93] Determining the public good or public interest was regarded as a legislative function, a process involving broad value judgments apportioning benefits among diverse interests and an exercise which the courts were not well suited to perform. The shortcomings of the courts were exposed as decisions about water use increasingly required some balancing of community needs in navigation, hydro-electric power production, sewage and sanitation, recreation, as well as private concerns about property and economic activity. Thus the components of a public interest were broadening. As an example of the resultant divergence of views between legislature and judiciary, the emphasis on promoting actual use, and indeed 'full' use of water resources may be noted. To the legislators, it no longer appeared adequate to allocate resources to private hands; efforts were required to control or influence the nature and extent of water use. To accomplish this end a statutory duty of 'economical and efficient use' was introduced, together with monitoring and inspection programs reflecting the fact that the public generally suffered the harm, injury, or damage resulting from mismanagement of water resources. The relevant costs and benefits of resource use were recognized as more extensive than the traditionally more direct consequences which often gave rise to litigation. Thus consideration was given to future interests, as in the case of power exports from Fort Frances, and to widely dispersed interests such as environmental concern.[94] This is not to suggest that the responses were always appropriate or desirable, but simply to observe that the complex forces of a modernizing and industrializing society did have consequences for the evolution of legal institutions.

The transformation that saw legislation, administrative regulation, and management displace the judicial process, as the lumber industry's demands on water resources were joined by the pressures resulting from the growth of the hydro-electric power industry, was at least in part a response to what has been described as 'the limits of adjudication.'[95] Early twentieth-century water management issues possessed a polycentric quality: 'Polycentric problems can be solved only by taking account of numerous interdependent and highly variable factors which oblige the decisionmaker to manage a kind of cybernetic process involving tentative probe, feedback, adjustment and reconciliation.'[96] Accordingly, historical assessment of the attitudes and performance of the judiciary faced with social and economic change and industrialization must involve some examination of the quality and characteristics of decisionmaking processes as well as the quality and characteristics of judges and their values.

The factors which can be identified from this essay as considerations favouring a shift away from traditional judicial proceedings do not differ significantly from the standard catalogue of reasons for developing administrative tribunals.[97] As Riddell demonstrated in *Ireson* v *Holt Timber*, the courts were often unwilling and considered themselves poorly equipped to act in cases where the meeting point between those participating in different but legitimate activities was uncertain and where interaction was likely to be continuous.[98] This was especially the case where technical standards and subsequent monitoring were required. In addition to remedial constraints and uncertainty, inconvenience and delay, there was also some reluctance to be involved at all where public rights were in issue. In the Kenora case, for example, Richard M. Meredith recognized that 'the main question [the ownership of the bed of the stream] is one of the very widest range, affecting innumerable titles to land.' But as it arose indirectly through arbitration concerning land values, he believed it should not have been examined at trial unless it had been found to be a real obstacle to the proceedings. Meredith regarded the issue as 'essentially one which ought not to be determined except in litigation between persons having a substantial interest involved in its determination, and having the right to have it considered.'[99] This attitude to judicial involvement corresponds to a typical view of the functions and boundaries of decisionmaking in the courts, and in many circumstances would be entirely appropriate. Where rights associated with public property and community interests are concerned, however, judicial reserve has certain disadvantages. For example, certainty of title was of considerable significance to investment decisions in the developing provincial community, such as those to be made in connection with hydro-electric power production. Where confident development must await the outcome of prolonged judicial settlement of so fundamental a question as the ownership of the beds of navigable waterways, the pace of economic investment might be adversely affected. Interests other than those of the immediate parties to a dispute were often involved, but where those affected included the Crown with its own objectives for management and use of public property, the need for certainty appeared to be more compelling. With these disadvantages to judicial inaction revealed, it becomes important to explain the seemingly passive and certainly cautious stance of judges, which occasional calls from the bench for legislative intervention also reflected.

In some circumstances judicial reluctance to propose solutions to controversial problems derived from the limitations of the process of adjudication in fostering participation of affected interests. The legislative forum simply seemed better suited to reconciling the varied viewpoints of widely dispersed members of the community.

The courts have often been criticized for adopting a relatively non-interventionist position and for an apparent failure of initiative. In stating that certain functions should properly be performed by the legislature, however, the courts were also implicitly asserting that other functions were properly judicial. The concept of the separation or classification of functions was not carefully or extensively developed, but its recognition alone is significant. Judicial deference to legislative authority and reluctance to perform apparently legislative functions may well have helped to protect the integrity of courts and to preserve their distinctive qualities. Such consequences, however, would require more careful assessment and are perhaps more relevant to future research on the judiciary's subsequent response to legislative and administrative decisionmaking. This latter issue is, of course, a central theme in the development of twentieth-century administrative law, a subject that lawyers tend to associate with public decisionmaking generally, but which is probably equated by more people with the field of economic regulation, especially of public utilities.

The association between regulation and the public utilities has generated considerable speculation among historians and others about both the causes and the consequences of regulation, with particular emphasis on the role of industry itself in fostering the regulatory environment as a means of limiting competition and protecting established concerns. The contribution of this essay to that important and ongoing debate is modest, yet certain observations help to link the historical process surveyed here to wider and more controversial issues. The movement towards the regulation of water use in twentieth-century Ontario appears to have had its origins or at least strong parallels in nineteenth-century attitudes to economic progress. Such attitudes were sufficiently widely shared that it is not easy to attribute any resulting pressure for regulation to the enthusiasm of private interests. Indeed, in the field of hydro-electric power production, regulation and public ownership advanced together. Future research may well reveal exceptions such as the Ottawa River legislation, which is strongly similar to the lumbermen's ongoing efforts to control the economic climate of their industry and to reduce its vulnerability to legal disruption and uncertainty. This could well be a case of private interests channelling decisionmaking into a forum where they expected to enjoy a variety of advantages such as access. It appears, though, that those in the private hydro-electric power industry were hostile to government intervention and felt generally more comfortable asserting private rights through the courts. Perhaps our understanding of the consequences of the growth of regulation over water management will be clarified by future studies assessing the influence of various participants in the process of institutional innovation and change described here. The contributions of industry, politicians, the judiciary, an emerging bureaucracy, public opinion, and possibly American precedents where these existed would have to be considered.

NOTES

I would like to thank R.C.B. Risk for his guidance and encouragement in the preparation of this essay.

1 This essay is not about the social and economic history of turn-of-the-century Ontario, nor is it about the industries whose operations provide its background. A concise survey of these matters may be found in Robert Craig Brown and Ramsay Cook *Canada 1896–1921: A Nation Transformed* (Toronto 1974) ch. 5. A chart documenting the transition in forest products exports from lumber to pulp and paper appears in Roy I. Wolfe 'Economic Development' in John Warkentin, ed. *Canada: A Geographical Interpretation* (Toronto 1968) 220–1.

2 A.R.M. Lower *The North American Assault on the Canadian Forest: A History of the Lumber Trade between Canada and the United States* (Toronto 1938) 36

3 Accounts of the hydro-electric power industry's development in Ontario include Merrill Denison *The People's Power: The History of Ontario Hydro* (Toronto 1960); H.V. Nelles *The Politics of Development: Forests, Mines and Hydro-Electric Power in Ontario, 1849–1941* (Toronto 1974); W.R. Plewman *Adam Beck and the Ontario Hydro* (Toronto 1947).

4 These themes are illuminated in Morton J. Horwitz *The Transformation of American Law 1780–1860* (Cambridge, MA 1977); Jennifer Nedelsky 'Judicial Conservatism in an Age of Innovation: Comparative Perspectives on Canadian Nuisance Law 1880–1930' in David H. Flaherty, ed. *Essays in the History of Canadian Law* 2 vols (Toronto 1981–3) I 281–322.

5 *Graham v Burr* (1853), 4 *Grant's Chancery Reports* 1 (hereafter GCR)

6 R.C.B. Risk 'The Last Golden Age: Property and the Allocation of Losses in Ontario in the Nineteenth Century' *University of Toronto Law Journal* XXVII (1977) 199, 222

7 *Globe*, 27 Apr. 1859

8 *Dickson v Burnham* (1868), 14 GCR 594

9 An Act for the Improvement of Water Privileges, 36 Vict. (1873), c. 40 (Ontario), 'Preamble'

10 Ibid. ss. 2, 6; An Act to Amend the Act Respecting the Improvement of Water Privileges, 38 Vict. (1874), c. 27 (Ontario), s. 2 (5)

11 An Act to Amend the Act Respecting the Improvement of Water Privileges, s. 2 (3). The legislature's intent to favour use over inactivity may be inferred from the location of the procedural burden concerning the existence of an 'occupied water privilege.' The applicant was not responsible for proving that the location claimed was unoccupied. Rather, where the mill privilege, water power, or mill was not in actual use or under construction, anyone claim-

ing to be its owner was required to produce 'satisfactory evidence' that it was held bona fide for use. In the absence of satisfactory evidence produced by the claimant, the site would not be considered occupied for purposes of protection under the act.

12 *The Parry Sound Lumbering Co.* v *Ferris et al.* (1882), 18 *Canada Law Journal* 413 at 415–19. At the time of this decision the statute existed as the Water Privileges Act, *Revised Statutes of Ontario* (hereafter RSO) 1877, c. 114.

13 *In Re Burnham et al.* (1895), 22 *Ontario Appeal Reports* (hereafter OAR) 40 at 41–2 per W.R. Meredith, 50 per Maclennan. Justice Featherston Osler at 43 clearly stated that 'compensation should be based upon the value of the rights of property of which the owner is deprived, not depending upon the question whether he had used them in the past or not.' At the time of this decision the statute existed as the Water Privileges Act RSO 1887, c. 119.

14 An Act to Amend an Act Passed in the Parliament of Upper Canada in the Ninth Year of the Reign of His Late Majesty King George the Fourth, entitled, 'An Act to Provide for the Construction of Aprons to Mill Dams over Certain Streams in this Province, and to Make Further Provision in Respect Thereof,' 12 Vict. (1849), c. 87, s. 5. See also An Act to Provide for the Construction of Aprons to Mill Dams over Certain Streams in This Province, 9 Geo. IV (1828), (Upper Canada).

15 *Boale* v *Dickson* (1863), 13 *Upper Canada Common Pleas* (hereafter UCCP) 337 at 349; Risk 'The Last Golden Age' 220

16 Proudfoot, VC did not deliver a written judgment when he granted the injunction.

17 *McLaren* v *Caldwell* (1881), 6 OAR 456 at 469 per Chief Justice John Godfrey Spragge and at 487 per Justice Christopher S. Patterson

18 *McLaren* v *Caldwell* (1882), 8 *Supreme Court Reports* (hereafter SCR) 435 at 440 per Chief Justice William J. Ritchie, and at 467 per Justice John W. Gwynne; (1884) 9 *Appeal Cases* 392

19 An Act for Protecting the Public interest in Rivers, Streams and Creeks, 44 Vict. (1881), c. 11 s. 1; *Globe*, 15 Jan. 1881, 23 Feb. 1881, 1 Mar. 1881, 7 Feb. 1882; 'A History of Crown Timber Regulations' in *Annual Report of the Clerk of Forestry* (1899), *Ontario Sessional Papers* (hereafter OSP) No. 36 at 117

20 Christopher Armstrong *The Politics of Federalism: Ontario's Relations with the Federal Government 1867–1942* (Toronto 1981) 27. See also J.C. Morrison 'Oliver Mowat and the Development of Provincial Rights in Ontario: A Study in Dominion-Provincial Relations, 1867–1896' in *Three History Theses* (Toronto 1961).

21 Above note 9

22 *Globe*, 7 Feb. 1882

23 *In the Matter of the Dam and Slide on the Little Bob River* (1896) 23 OAR 177; *The Hardy Lumber Co.* v *The Pickerel River Improvement Co.* (1898), 29 SCR 211; *Neely* v *Peter* (1902), 4 OLR 293; *Re Beck Manufacturing Company and Ontario Lumber Company* (1904), 3 OWR 333 aff'd (1905), 6 OWR 54 (CA); *Pigeon River Lumber Company* v *Mooring* (1909), 13 OWR 190 aff'd (1910), 14 OWR 639 (DC); *Rainy Lake River Boom Corp.* v *Rainy River Lumber Co.* (1913), 27 OLR 131; *Re Kyro River Improvement Company Ltd* [1929] 4 *Dominion Law Reports* 610 (CA) (hereafter DLR); *Re Arrow River and Tributaries Slide and Boom Company Ltd* [1932] 2 DLR 250

24 *Re Kyro River Improvement Company* [1929] 4 DLR 610 at 615. The two statutory bases on which tolls could be collected after the mid-1880s were An Act for Protecting the Public Interest in Rivers, Streams, and Creeks, RSO 1887, ch. 120 s. 11 and An Act Respecting Joint Stock Companies for the Construction of Works to Facilitate the Transmission of Timber down Rivers and Streams, RSO 1887, ch. 160 s. 39.

25 For an example of practice concerning the tenure provisions, see *Re Arrow River and Tributaries Slide and Boom Co. Ltd* [1932] 2 DLR 250 at 261.

26 Irving Papers, Public Archives of Ontario (hereafter PAO) 'Rainy River Boom Slide and Navigation Company'

27 Rivers and Streams Act, note 24 above, s. 13; Timber Slide Companies Act, note 24 above, s. 41

28 Above note 26

29 Timber Slide Companies Act, note 24 above, s. 39 and subsequently RSO 1914, ch. 181 ss. 30, 33

30 Rivers and Streams Act, RSO 1914, ch. 130 ss. 11, 12. And see *The Hardy Lumber Company* v *The Pickerel River Improvement Company*, *Pigeon River Lumber Company* v *Mooring*, *Re Beck Manufacturing Company and Ontario Lumber Company* above note 23.

31 The Lakes and Rivers Improvement Act, 17 Geo. v (1927), c. 40, s. 53

32 An Act Respecting the Driving of Saw Logs and Other Timber on Lakes, Rivers, Creeks, and Streams, 50 Vict. (1887), c. 17; see also An Act Amending the Saw Logs Driving Act, 1 Edw. VII (1901), c. 17 s. 2, which envisages claims arising between the same parties in successive seasons. Cases on the Saw Logs Driving Act include *Cockburn and Sons* v *The Imperial Lumber Company, Limited* (1898), 30 SCR 80; *Central Contracting Company* v *Russell Timber Co.* (1919), 15 OWN 415; *Pigeon River Lumber Co.* v *Pulpwood Co. and Russell Timber Co.* (1921), 67 DLR 263.

33 An Act Respecting Damage to Lands by Flooding in the New Districts, 52 Vict. (1889), c. 16

34 *Rainy River Navigation Co.* v *Watrous Island Boom Co.* (1914), 26 OWR 456 at 460

35 *Booth* v *Lowery* (1917), 54 SCR 421 at 422 per Chief Justice Charles Fitzpatrick and 432–8 per Justice Francis A. Anglin

36 *Ratte* v *Booth* (1885), 10 OR 351 (1886), 11 OR 491 (1887), 14 OAR 419 (CA), (1890), 15 AC 188 (PC); *Globe*, 24 Mar. 1885; An Act Respecting Saw Mills on the Ottawa River, 48 Vict. (1885), c. 24 (hereafter the Ottawa River Act). References to federal concern with lumber refuse as an interference with navigation may be found in Judith Tulloch *The Rideau Canal: Defence, Transportation, Recreation* (Ottawa 1981) 25.

37 *Cain* v *Pearce* (1910), 2 OWN 887, *Miller* v *Beatty* (1906), 7 OWR 605, *Cardwell* v *Breckenridge* (1913), 4 OWN 1295, *Carter* v *Suddaby* (1926), 31 OWN 337

38 *Cain* v *Pearce*, above note 37 at 888 per Justice William R. Riddell, *Bradley* v *Gananoque Water Power Co.* (1901), 3 OWR 913, *Smith* v *Ontario and Minnesota Power Co. Ltd* (1918), 13 OWN 445

39 *Neeley* v *Peter* (1903), 5 OLR 381 (CA)

40 *Dickson* v *Burnham*, above note 8, and see the appeal decision in *Dickson* v *Burnham* (1870), 17 GCR 261.

41 *Crandell* v *Mooney* (1873), 23 UCCP 212; Rivers and Streams Act (1922), 12–13 Geo. V (1922), c. 55 s. 6

42 *Booth* v *Lowery*, above note 35, at 438

43 *Ireson* v *Holt Timber Company* (1913), 30 OLR 209

44 Above note 38

45 *Report on the Lakes and Rivers, Waters and Water-Powers of the Province of Ontario* quoted in Nelles *Politics of Development* 36

46 T.W. Gibson 'Water Powers in Ontario' in OSP, 1898, No. 33, 251 at 253

47 An Act Respecting Water Powers (hereafter Water Powers Act), 61 Vict. (1898), c. 8

48 'Regulations re Water Powers' in OSP, 1898, No. 33, 254

49 Ibid. s. 11 (b)

50 Water Power Lease Books in Records of the Provincial Secretary, PAO

51 E.H. Bronson Papers, Public Archives of Canada (hereafter the PAC), George Ross to E.H. Bronson 12 Feb. 1900, E.J. Davis to E.H. Bronson 17 June 1901, Aubrey White to E.H. Bronson 8 Feb. 1902

52 OSP, 1913, No. 59 NP in Sessional Papers RG49 PAO. The enforcement of default provisions was often difficult in other areas. See *New Ontario Colonization Co* v *The King* (1925), 29 OWN 58.

53 OSP, 1913, No. 57, NP in Sessional Papers RG49 PAO

54 *Keewatin Power Company and Hudson's Bay Company* v *Town of Kenora* (1906), 13 OLR 237; (1908), 16 OLR 184 (CA)

55 An Act Respecting the Town of Rat Portage, 2 Edw. VI (1902), c. 62

56 Premiers' Papers, Whitney, RG3 Box 9 PAO, 'Water Power Dispute'

57 *Keewatin Power* v *Kenora*, above note 54, at 263; *R.* v *Meyers* (1853), 3 UCCP 305
58 'Return of Correspondence re Kenora Power Case' OSP 1914 No. 70 (NP) in PAO RG8, I-7-B2
59 *Keewatin Power Company and Hudson's Bay Company* v *Town of Kenora* (1908), 16 OLR 184 CA per Moss at 189–90 and per Meredith at 196
60 *Mail and Empire* (Toronto), 17 Mar. 1911, 'Minister's Views on the New Bill'; An Act for the Protection of the Public Interest in the Beds of Navigable Waters, 1 Geo. V (1911), c. 6; *Mail and Empire*, 17 Mar. 1911. The Beds of Navigable Waters Act ss. 3 and 5 provided some protection for those who acquired land in good faith under the common law presumption or other special circumstances, but emphasized that the full use of the power potential was required and that the price of power might be regulated by the Lieutenant Governor in Council. See also *Haggerty* v *Latreille* (1913), 29 OLR 300.
61 For historical discussions of the public power movement and the development of the HEPC, see above note 3.
62 An introductory discussion of some of the factors influencing the process of instrument choice together with contemporary applications may be found in Michael J. Trebilcock et al. *The Choice of Governing Instrument: Some Applications* (Ottawa 1981). For a summary of factors supporting the adoption of statutory responses to legal problems, see Guido Calabresi *A Common Law for the Age of Statutes* (Cambridge, MA 1982).
63 'Return of Correspondence re Water Diversion ... etc.,' Unprinted Sessional Paper 1913 No. 107 in Records of the Provincial Secretary PAO; see also Latchford Papers, PAC, MG27 II F7 Vol. 24 and Robert Bell Papers, PAC, MG29 B5 Vol. 44.
64 Examples of special legislation concerning private power development include An Act to Incorporate the Northern Power Company, 2 Edw. VII (1902), c. 102 (Ont.); An Act to Enable Edward Spencer Jenison to Develop the Water Power of the Kaministiquia River, 4 Edw. VII (1904), c. 106 (Ont.); An Act to Incorporate the Current River Power Company, 7 Edw. VII (1907), c. 114 (Ont.)
65 An Act Respecting 'The Ontario and Minnesota Power Company Limited,' 6 Edw. VII (1906), c. 132 (Ont.). For additional information on the Backus enterprises, see Armstrong *Politics of Federalism* 68–72, 92–3 and Russell Newell Searle *Saving Quetico-Superior: A Land Set Apart* (1977). The federal legislation involved was An Act Respecting the Ontario and Minnesota Power Company (Limited), 4 & 5 Edw. VII (1905), c. 139.
66 An Act Respecting the Ontario and Minnesota Power Company, 1 Geo. V (1911), c. 7 (Ont.), and Whitney Papers PAO, H. Williams to J.P. Whitney 25 May 1910. The agreement recently became the subject of litigation in *Boise*

Cascade Canada Ltd v *The Queen in Right of Ontario et al.* (1981), 34 OR (2d) 18 (CA); leave to appeal granted 7 Dec. 1981 (1981), 34 OR (2d) 576 (SCC).

67 The issues in early power exports, including the problem of reclaiming the resource once costly facilities had been established, are discussed in A.E. Dal Grauer 'The Export of Electricity from Canada' in R.M. Clark, ed. *Canadian Issues: Essays in Honour of Henry F. Angus* (Toronto 1961).

68 The background and development of this episode may be found in the Lake of the Woods Milling Company Papers, PAO.

69 *Keewatin Power Company* v *Keewatin Flour Mills Ltd* [1928] DLR 32

70 *Keewatin Power Company* v *Keewatin Flour Mills Ltd* [1929] 3 DLR 199

71 *Keewatin Power Company* v *Lake of the Woods Milling Co.* [1930] AC 640

72 An Act for Protecting the Public Interest in Rivers, Streams and Creeks, and Respecting Dams and Other Works Thereon, 3–4 Geo. V (1913), c. 26 (Ont.) s. 27

73 An Act for the Better Regulating of the Use of Certain Public Waters, 5 Geo. V (1915), c. 15 (Ont.) s. 3

74 Ibid. s. 8; and see the Statute Law Amendment Act, 8 Geo. V (1918), c. 20 (Ont.) s. 57

75 An Act to Regulate the Use of the Waters of the Province of Ontario for Power Development Purposes (hereafter the Water Powers Regulation Act, 1916), 6 Geo. V (1916), c. 21 (Ont.) ss. 3, 4 (d); and see An Act to Amend the Water Powers Regulation Act, 7 Geo. V (1917), c. 22 (Ont.).

76 *Attorney General for Ontario* v *Electrical Development Co. Ltd* (1919), 45 OLR 186. For discussion of political dimensions of the wartime regulatory statutes and the role of the HEPC, see Armstrong *Politics of Federalism* 76–9.

77 Water Powers Regulation Act, 1916, above note 75, ss. 5, 9–11

78 Armstrong *Politics of Federalism* 79

79 'Agreement re Tunnel Island between the Crown and the Keewatin Lumber and Manufacturing Company' 24 Nov. 1891 in John E. Read Papers, PAC

80 See above note 48. An Act to Provide for the Construction of Municipal Power Works, 3 Edw. VII (1903), c. 25; An Act to Enable Edward Spencer Jenison to Develop the Water Power of the Kaninistiquia River, 4 Edw. VII (1904), c. 106; An Act to Provide for the Transmission of Electrical Power to Municipalities, 6 Edw. VII (1906), c. 15; An Act to Provide for the Transmission of Electrical Power to Municipalities, 7 Edw. VII (1907), c. 19

81 For an analysis of the implications of this competition, see Michael J. Trebilcock, Leonard Waverman, and J. Robert S. Prichard 'Markets for Regulation' in *Government Regulation* (Toronto 1978) 11–66.

82 R.S. Lambert and Paul Pross *Renewing Nature's Wealth* (Toronto 1967) 287; *Rod and Gun in Canada*, Vol. 2, Feb. 1901, 454; Robert Bell Papers, PAC, Archibald M. Campbell to the Commissioner of Crown Lands, 26 Mar. 1900

83 Ontario Department of Lands, Forests and Mines, PAO, 'Memorandum for Mr. Grigg re Lake Timagami,' 9 Aug. 1918

84 Ontario *Royal Commission to Investigate and Report upon the Accuracy or Otherwise of All Returns Made Pursuant to the Crown Timber Act, Section 14, by Any Holder of a Timber License* (1922) 26–7

85 See, for example, Latchford Papers, PAC, T.W. Gibson, Deputy Minister of Mines to Spanish River Pulp and Paper Mills, Ltd, 8 Aug. 1917.

86 This discussion is based upon the Loring Christie Papers and the John E. Read Papers in the PAC, the Lake of the Woods Milling Company Papers at the PAO, and the Hudson's Bay Company Archives at the Provincial Archives of Manitoba.

87 Lake of the Woods Control Board Act, 12 & 13 Geo. V (1922), c. 21 (Ont.)

88 Armstrong *Politics of Federalism* 161–4

89 John E. Read Papers, Donald D. Harries (Special Assistant US Attorney) to the Hon. Seth W. Richardson (Assistant Attorney General) 28 Feb. 1933

90 John E. Read Papers, 'Memorandum on the Present Situation in Relation to the Lake of the Woods Flowage Easements' 31 May 1935

91 See above at notes 11 and 12.

92 Risk 'The Last Golden Age' above note 6

93 See above at note 8.

94 See above at notes 65–7, and 79–83.

95 Lon Fuller 'The Forms and Limits of Adjudication' *Harvard Law Review* XCII (1978) 353

96 Ibid. 394–404

97 Carmen D. Baggaley *The Emergence of the Regulatory State in Canada, 1867–1939* (Toronto 1981) 1–24, provides a convenient summary of rationales for regulation.

98 See above at note 43.

99 *Keewatin Power* v *Kenora* above note 59 at 195

8

'This Nuisance of Litigation': The Origins of Workers' Compensation in Ontario

R.C.B. RISK

When the province of Ontario enacted the Workmen's Compensation Act in 1914, the *Industrial Banner*, a labour paper, proclaimed it to be 'the inauguration of real social legislation' and 'the most far-reaching legislation that has ever been enacted by any government in Canada in the interests of the workers.'[1] This enthusiasm was justified. The act was an important expression of fundamental changes in attitudes about individual and social responsibility and about the functions and structure of government. During the nineteenth and early twentieth centuries a worker had a right to compensation for an injury suffered at work only if it had been caused by someone's fault. Instead, the act gave a right to compensation regardless of fault from a fund created by contributions of employers. Sir William Meredith, who was the chief architect of the act, captured the extent of the change by saying that one of the objectives was 'to get rid of this nuisance of litigation ... It is social legislation ... all the manufacturers ... are simply tax gatherers.'[2]

Many jurisdictions throughout Europe and the United States established workers' compensation in the late nineteenth and early twentieth centuries; the reasons for its eventual appearance and general nature in Ontario were not distinctive. However, the story in Ontario is both interesting and instructive, because it includes a wide range of representative experience, an interesting personality, and some distinctive elements, especially the use of an administrative agency and the fate of private insurance. The story might be told from many different perspectives.[3] The emphasis here will be the ideas about law, especially about the content of law and how to think about it, and about legal institutions.

THE COMMON LAW

In the mid-nineteenth century a worker injured at work had only a very small chance of receiving adequate compensation. Apart from the generosity of an employer or family or compensation from a private insurance fund, the only prospect was a claim for damages in the courts. For all practical purposes the common law governed this action. The claim might be made against a stranger; for example, a railway engineer might make a claim against another railway because its engineer carelessly ignored a signal and caused a collision at an intersection, or a carpenter injured in a fall from a scaffold that collapsed might make a claim against the contractor who built it. However, both the doctrine and the typical accidents and arrangements of work made a worker's employer the most likely defendant. The employer had a duty to take reasonable care to make the conditions of work safe. For example, claims might be made that the machinery, the work place, or the system of doing the work was not safe, or that the other employees were not competent, all because reasonable care had not been taken, but knowledge by the employer of the unsafe conditions was an essential element of each claim. Contributory negligence and assumption of risk were also formidable defences.[4]

The carelessness of fellow workers caused many injuries. For example, a worker in a railway yard trying to couple a car to a train might be injured because a foreman carelessly gave a signal to the engineer to start the train, or a worker cleaning a machine in a factory might be injured because another worker carelessly turned on the power. The fellow workers would be liable but probably would not have enough money to pay compensation. Employers were generally liable for the negligence of their workers but not for negligence that caused injury to fellow workers. This rule, the fellow servant rule, needs extensive discussion because it was the only defence distinctive to the employment context and because it was the major single doctrinal obstacle to recovery.

Priestley v *Fowler* (1837), an English case which is usually cited as the foundation for this rule, is one of the most discussed and debated cases in the common law.[5] Priestley, who was an employee of Fowler, was helping another employee to transport some goods in a van when it broke down. Priestley was injured and brought an action for damages. His claim was based primarily on Fowler's duty to take reasonable care for the conditions of work, and it failed because his declaration did not allege that Fowler knew about the unsafe conditions. No claim was made for vicarious liability, but Lord Stanley Abinger considered the possibility, perhaps because the claim based on the employer's duty seemed so clearly to fail. He gave a series of examples of liability and concluded that the 'inconvenience, not to say the absurdity of these consequences' alone were sufficient to justify denying liability. He continued: 'but in truth, the mere relation of master and servant can never imply an obligation on the part of the master to take more care of the servant than he may reasonably be expected to do of himself.' He argued that workers could decline to do work that seemed to them to be dangerous and were usually just as likely as the employer to know about any dangers. This reasoning implied general propositions that were expressed in many subsequent judgments: liability would not be imposed unless the employer knew (or should reasonably have known) about the dangerous conditions and the employee did not. To perceive 'absurdity' in vicarious liability was merely a manifestation of this general attitude.

Five years later, in Massachusetts, Chief Justice Lemuel Shaw expressed the fellow servant rule precisely and starkly in *Farwell* v *Boston and Worcester Rail Road Corporation* (1842).[6] Farwell was an engineer employed by the railroad. A switchman, who was also employed by the railroad, carelessly left a switch in the wrong position. A train driven by Farwell was derailed and he was injured. He made a claim for damages against the railroad and failed. Shaw began by asserting that the general principle of vicarious liability did not govern claims by workers against employers because the risks of employment might be regulated by contract and, 'in contemplation of law, must be presumed to be thus regulated.' Of course, there was no express term, and therefore the issue was whether there was an implied term that the employer would provide compensation. Shaw denied such a term and asserted that 'considerations as well of justice as of policy' required that workers assume 'the natural and ordinary risks and perils' of work, including the carelessness of fellow workers, and 'in legal presumption, the compensation is adjusted accordingly.' The considerations of justice seem to have been the likely knowledge of the employer and the worker. The carelessness of fellow workers constituted 'perils which the servant is as likely to know, and against which he can as effectually guard, as the master ... and can be as distinctly foreseen and provided for in the rate of compensation as any others.' The considerations of policy were the prevention of accidents. Shaw asserted that accidents were more likely to be reduced by making each worker 'an observer of the conduct of the others' than by giving a claim against the common employer. Farwell's major argument was that these conclusions should govern only situations in which the workers had a reasonable opportunity to 'supervise and control each other' and not situations in which the workers were in different departments or undertakings – an engineer and a switchman. Shaw rejected this limitation, because 'it would be extremely difficult to establish a practical rule.'

In England the fellow servant rule became firmly settled during the 1850s. In 1858 the House of Lords approved Shaw's reasoning in *Bartonshill Coal Company* v *Reid*. Lord Cranworth said: 'When several workmen engage to serve a master in common work, they know, or ought to know, the risks to which they are exposing themselves, including the risks of carelessness, against which their employer cannot secure them, and they must be supposed to contract with reference to such risks.'[7] This faith in contract and individual choice was unrealistic in two ways. Workers doubtless did not usually consider these risks, let alone choose to assume them, and they usually had no power to bargain for an adjustment in wages or to take other, safer jobs. However, contract was a way of expressing basic values about individual responsibility and allocation of losses.

General beliefs about the substance and form of the common law shaped this doctrine.[8] At the centre was a belief that the law should establish and encourage individual autonomy by setting generous spheres for living in which each individual was free from interference from other persons or from the state and conversely by setting limits on the conduct of all individuals and the state. Each person should be responsible for his or her own fate. This responsibility depended upon individual will, and fault was both a moral failing and a condition of liability. The function of the state should be to enforce the rules of responsibility without exercising substantial discretion. These beliefs about responsibility and will depended upon assumptions about conduct and causation. Individuals could choose to work or not to work, and the causes of conduct were relatively few, immediate, and independent. Liability and fault were a product of personal failing which a person could, by taking care, have avoided. This law should govern all individuals equally and indifferently, and also be a set of general rules from which particular conclusions could be deduced without choice or discretion, so that a person could know the permissible limits of conduct. Since the ultimate justification of these rules were age, authority, or moral rightness, empirical testing and counting were irrelevant.

The doctrine made success unlikely, even if a worker could overcome the emotional and financial barriers to litigation. In Ontario sixteen cases involving claims by workers were reported between 1865 and the legislation in the 1880s, and workers failed in almost all.[9] The fellow servant rule barred recovery in eight of the cases.[10] In two of these the plaintiff sought to demonstrate that the accident was caused by inadequate equipment, for example, faulty brakes on a train, but the courts concluded that the cause was a failure by a careless fellow employee to make repairs or adjustments.[11]

Two examples present recurring contexts and issues. In *Deverill* v *Grand Trunk Railway* (1869), the facts were virtually the same as in *Farwell*, except the engineer was killed and his widow brought the action.[12] The fellow servant rule was so well established that she assumed its existence and sought to avoid it. She claimed that the switchman was incompetent and that the employer therefore had not taken reasonable care to make the conditions of work safe. The jury gave a verdict for her; the railway made a motion for a non-suit on the ground that the evidence was not adequate to leave the issue to the jury. This pattern of a jury finding for the plaintiff and a motion for a non-suit on the ground that the evidence was inadequate recurred many times during the next five decades. Justice John Hagarty concluded that the evidence about negligence was not adequate to leave the issue to the jury, and the fellow servant rule barred recovery: 'to leave such a case to the jury is ... simply to direct a verdict for the plaintiff, where a railway company are defendants ... Very great compassion may be felt by the court, as sincerely as by the jury, for the family of the sufferer by this collision. Whatever jurors may feel at liberty to do, we at least must not allow this feeling to sanction what we believe to be a violation of a well settled legal principle ... Each servant in entering the service assumes the risk of his fellow servants' neglect.'

Rudd v *Bell* (1887), was decided more than twenty-one years later.[13] The plaintiff was hired to operate a 'Daniel Planer,' which did not have a guard. He had no experience with machines of this kind; he asked if it was dangerous and was told that workers had been cut. After about an hour and a half, his hand was badly cut. His claim against the employer failed, because the danger was obvious. Justice John Boyd said that 'the maxim volenti non fit injuria applies ['he who consents cannot receive an injury'] ... the risks were open to his observation and his opportunities and means of judging the danger were at least as good as those of his employer. His safety depended very much on himself, as he must have known.'

THE NINETEENTH-CENTURY LEGISLATION

During the second half of the nineteenth century the construction of railroads, the development of mines in the north, and the increasing use of power-driven machinery in the expanding urban centres greatly increased the risk of accidents to workers. Both the federal and provincial governments enacted legislation about accidents and compensation. The provincial legislation was by far more important because allocation of powers by the British North America Act and by the interpretations of the Privy Council gave the provinces much more scope than the federal government for this kind of legislation, and Ontario tended to be more responsive than the federal government to the needs of labour.

Most of this legislation was designed to reduce or eliminate accidents and did not make any express provisions for compensation. The law about railroads was the first to appear and was the only significant federal enactment. Provisions about accidents appeared in 1851 in the first general railway legislation of the Province of Canada and were subsequently expanded in both federal and provincial statutes.[14] Most were designed to protect passengers and the public – and cattle. For example, the 1851 act required bells on locomotives and fencing at level crossings. Requirements about brakes and speeds through populated areas and the beginnings of administrative control of construction were added in 1857.[15] Most of the legislation throughout the remainder of the nineteenth century expanded provisions of this kind and added detail and administrative regulation.[16] Provisions designed to protect workers in particular appeared late in the nineteenth century and were essentially responses to specific and common causes of accidents. In 1879 the federal legislation required clearance of seven feet between the top of boxcars and bridges.[17] In 1881 Ontario imposed the same requirement and added that running boards should be put on the top of boxcars and spaces between converging rails should be packed to prevent workers catching their feet between the rails.[18] The federal statutes added more requirements about equipment in 1888 and 1903, especially about using automatic coupling devices.[19] Ontario adopted the same requirements in 1906.[20]

Labour organizations made demands during the 1870s for legislation about the conditions of work in the factories. Six bills were introduced in parliament between 1879 and 1885, but none was enacted because the government lacked enthusiasm and because the constitutional power seemed at best uncertain and most likely inadequate.[21] In 1884 Ontario enacted a factories act, which was one of its major initiatives in seeking labour support. It governed factories employing more than twenty persons, included requirements about health and safety, especially for children and females, and about fire prevention, and authorized inspections. Several amendments expanded its scope, added details, and increased administrative discretion.[22] Legislation about the mines came last. In 1890 Ontario enacted the Mining Operations Act, which regulated such matters as the storage and use of explosives, support of the walls and roofs of the mine shafts, and the security of lifting devices.[23] Amendments in 1900 and 1912 expanded its scope and added detail.[24]

One Ontario statute, the Workmen's Compensation for Injuries Act, enacted in 1886, dealt particularly with injuries suffered at work and was the most important single piece of legislation in the field before the Workmen's Compensation Act of 1914.[25] The 1886 title was misleading. It was substantially different from the 1914 act and not a compensation statute in the sense that the phrase is now used. It modified the common law about employers' liability, but claims for compensation continued to be made in courts and to depend ultimately upon fault.

The 1886 act was complex, but its major effect was simple: the scope of the fellow servant rule was diminished by excluding the negligence of workers who had responsibility for the condition of machinery or authority over other workers. The damages were limited to three years' wages for a person 'in the same grade employed ... in the like employment ...' and an employer could not contract out of liability unless, in the opinion of the court hearing the worker's claim, the contract was 'just and reasonable' and the consideration given was 'ample and adequate.' Amendments made in 1889 and 1899 expanded its benefits, and in 1899 extensive arrangements for arbitration of claims were added.[26] The 1886 act was virtually a copy of the Employers' Liability Act, 1880, except for the addition of the prohibition against contracting out.[27] The English act was the product of public and political debate, which had continued for four decades and became intense during the mid-1870s. It was a compromise, which contributed to its complexity. Old values about responsibility and fault were fading, even though Baron George Bramwell vehemently expressed them in their classical form during the debate, but the changes fell short of adopting some other proposals, such as entire abolition of the fellow servant rule and compulsory insurance.[28] In Ontario no substantial campaign for this particular change had been made and it created little discussion or controversy, but labour was generally more confident and active during 1886 than it had been for more than a decade.[29]

THE COURTS AFTER 1886

A study of the courts after the enactment of the Workmen's Compensation Act of 1886 is both a large part of the story of the Workmen's Compensation Act of 1914 and a small part of a general study of the courts in the late nineteenth and early twentieth centuries. The study includes two perspectives. The first, simply put, is counting. For example, how many actions were brought, what proportion of trials and appeals were won by workers, and what amounts of damages were given? The second is more impressionistic. It is the form of the reasoning of the courts, and their attitudes about the factual and doctrinal issues and about their functions.

At the outset the kinds of cases and the structure of the courts must be described. Some of the claims made by the workers were not made against their employers, and these comprised a wide range of doctrine and kinds of defendants. The most common defendants were railways and owners of property. For example, claims were made against railways by employees of customers who were injured by trains on spurs and sidings and against the owners of property by the employees of contractors. These were usually based on negligence or occupiers' liability. However, most of the claims, by far, were made against employers, because the doctrine, especially the legislation, made them more likely to be able to pay judgments than fellow servants. This discussion is limited to these claims because they were by far the most important to the workers, best demonstrate the attitudes of the courts, and are the most useful contrast to compensation regardless of fault.

The Judicature Act of 1881 established the basic structure of the courts.[30] The Supreme Court had two branches, the High Court and the Court of Appeal. Judges of the High Court conducted trials and also participated in Divisional Courts (panels of judges of the court), which heard motions for non-suits and new trials. (For convenience, the term 'appeal' will generally be used to include motions to Divisional Courts for new trials or non-suits.) Appeals could be made to the Court of Appeal, although they were constrained by requirements of leave. In 1913 the Divisional Courts of the High Court were abolished and their jursidiction assigned to the Court of Appeal.[31] Claims for compensation could also be brought in the County Courts; the limit was $200 until 1913 and $500 afterwards.[32] Appeals from the County Courts could be made to the Court of Appeal until 1895, to Divisional Courts of the High Court between 1895 and 1913, and to the Court of Appeal again after 1913.[33]

THE RESULTS OF CASES

Counting numbers of cases is difficult and accuracy is impossible to achieve. Many court records have been lost, destroyed, or damaged, and the records that remain are not adequately organized or indexed. The judgments in the law reports are easy to find and read, although they are limited to decisions of the Supreme Court. There are not enough surviving records of the County Courts to enable any useful study of them to be made. The figures for the Supreme Court are based on the reports and court records for one year, 1903, and for one county, Wentworth (which includes the city of Hamilton and the surrounding area) from 1886 to 1914.[34]

Table 1 shows the number of actions begun in Wentworth. At the outset only a few actions were begun each year. After the late 1880s the numbers slowly increased. This growth was much greater than the increase in population or industrial activity and was probably caused by the Workmen's Compensation Act. Numbers jumped sharply in the early 1900s, probably reflecting an expansion in industrial activity, and continued to increase for about five years, but dropped slightly near the end of the period. Throughout, the numbers are only a small fraction of the total number of all actions begun in the county.

For 1903 incomplete records are available for sixteen of forty-five counties. However, they include the five largest counties – Carleton, Elgin, Middlesex, Wentworth, and York, and the largest cities, Hamilton, London, Ottawa, and Toronto, and they include eighty per cent of the total number of actions begun in the province. These records contain 111 actions by workers. The total is doubtless larger, but it is almost certainly not more than 150. All these numbers are small, perhaps surprisingly so, considering both the incidence of injuries and actions of all kinds.[35] Claims were made for only a tiny fraction of the injuries that were suffered, and they never were and never could have reasonably been perceived to be a dangerous strain on the capacities of the courts.[36] The numbers of claims made are much smaller than comparable figures in the United States. Some of the difference may have been caused by the lack of a contingent fee or private means for provision of advice and subsidization of costs. The winning party was generally entitled to recover costs

TABLE 1

Actions begun by workers against employers for injuries suffered at work, Wentworth County

Years	Total	Annual average
1888–92	23	4.6
1893–7	57	11.4
1898–1902	81	16.2
1903–7	152	30.4
1908–12	210	42.0
1913–14	73	36.5
TOTALS	596	22.1

Source: Ontario Archives, RG 22, Wentworth, Supreme Court Actions and Matters Files

from the loser, although this general rule was often not applied to workers. These costs did not cover all the expenses of litigation, and who could know in advance who would be the winner? Only a small proportion of the actions proceeded to trial and judgment. The records from Wentworth suggest that the number was usually between twenty and thirty-five per cent. This figure was not significantly different from the proportions for actions of all kinds.

The results of the cases can be counted in many different ways. The most useful are the results of jury verdicts, the eventual results of trial, the numbers of appeals by plaintiffs and defendants, and the results of the appeals. However, because the records are incomplete, the numbers gathered from what remains can suggest only approximate proportions and general trends. For the purpose of describing change, the results in the text and the tables have been compiled in five-year periods.

Some of the judges and participants in the Meredith Commission, which will be described later, said that juries always found for the plaintiffs. The results from Wentworth County in Table 2 demonstrate a strong tendency, but not an invariable one, and a small drop at the turn of the century that is paralleled by some of the other findings. The number of verdicts that are available is substantially less than the number of actions that went to trial (and even this figure cannot be known precisely) and therefore these figures may be misleading. In the reported cases the jury found for the plaintiff much more often. This difference is not surprising, and the figures from Wentworth County are more likely representative.

TABLE 2

Jury verdicts in trials of actions by workers against employers for injuries suffered at work, Wentworth County

Five-year period	Known verdicts	Verdicts for plaintiffs	Per cent
1888–92	5	5	100
1893–7	19	17	89
1898–1902	15	11	73
1903–7	24	22	92
1908–12	26	21	81
TOTALS	89	76	85

Source: Ontario Archives, RG 22, Wentworth, Supreme Court Actions and Matters Files

Trial judgments do not often appear alone in the reports. Instead, they usually appear as the first stage of appeals or motions for a new trial or non-suit. The odds of upsetting a jury verdict against a worker must have appeared relatively low, and these verdicts were not likely to be challenged and to appear in the reports. Also, to the extent that employers appealed more often than workers, the cases would involve jury findings for workers.

A favourable jury verdict did not entitle a plaintiff to succeed. For example, a trial judge might rule that there was not enough evidence to go to a jury or bar a claim for lack of some statutory requirement but obtain a jury verdict nevertheless, because the ruling might be reversed on appeal. Table 3 shows the eventual results at trial in Wentworth County and in the reported cases. Workers usually succeeded more often than employers, but there is no clear pattern of change, except perhaps for the indication that the rate of success increased after 1900.

The reports are the best source of information about appeals. However, they include only some unknown and changing proportion of the total number of cases. Editors chose to report judgments because of their apparent importance in making or illustrating doctrine and not to reflect the numbers being decided about any particular issue. Also, two new series of reports that appeared early in the 1900s included a far larger proportion of the cases than previously. Although the reports cannot be used as evidence of total volumes, they do give reliable information about the relative tendencies of plaintiffs and defendants to appeal and the patterns of results. Tables 4 and 5 show the number of appeals by workers

TABLE 3

Results in trials of actions by workers against employers for
injuries suffered at work, Wentworth County

	Known results	Judgment for plaintiffs	Per cent
1888–92	5	4	80
1893–7	25	16	64
1898–1902	27	10	37
1903–7	37	22	59
1908–12	30	22	73
TOTALS	124	74	60

Source: Ontario Archives, RG 22, Wentworth, Supreme Court
Actions and Matters Files

and employers to the Divisional Courts and the Court of Appeal, and
the results of these appeals calculated in several different ways.

Descriptions of the relative volume of appeals are simple. Workers
generally appealed to Divisional Courts more often than employers. In
contrast, employers appealed much more often to the Court of Appeal,
probably because they had greater resources. The reason for the larger
proportion of workers' appeals in Divisional Courts is probably that a
non-suit was a common result at trial, and usually the appropriate
challenge to a non-suit was a motion for a new trial, which was made to a
Divisional Court.

Descriptions of the results must be much more complex. Two sets of
calculations can be made even though in some periods there are not
enough cases to be useful. The first is the success rates of workers and
employers in their own appeals, and the differences between these rates.
The second is the overall success rates of workers and employers in all
appeals, for example, the workers' overall success rate during any period
is a total of the appeals they made and won plus the total of the appeals
employers made and lost, divided by the total number of appeals made.

In the Divisional Courts the calculations show the same general trend:
before the 1886 act workers lost almost all appeals. After 1886, they
continued to lose most appeals, but the gap decreased. During the
mid-1890s workers began to win more often than employers, and this
continued during the 1900s, although the results may have been tending
towards a rough equality. In all, both workers and employers won less

TABLE 4

Results of appeals to divisional courts from trial division in actions by workers against employers for injuries suffered at work

	Appeals by workers			Appeals by employers			Workers' overall success		
	Appeals	Allowed	Success rates (%)	Appeals	Allowed	Success rates (%)	Total appeals	Successful workers	Success rates (%)
To 1886	7	1	14	4	3	75	11	2	18
1887–91	9	3	33	4	2	50	13	5	38
1892–6	6	2	33	11	1	9	17	12	71
1897–1901	4	2	50	1	0	0	5	3	60
1902–6	23	14	61	19	8	42	42	25	60
1907–11	19	10	53	16	7	44	35	19	54
1912–14	4	1	25	8	2	25	12	7	58
TOTALS	72	33	46	63	23	37	135	73	54

Source: Ontario Reports, Ontario Appeal Reports, Ontario Law Reports, Ontario Weekly Notes, Ontario Weekly Reporter, Supreme Court Reports

TABLE 5
Results of appeals to the Court of Appeal from trial divisions in actions by workers against employers for injuries suffered at work

	Appeals by workers			Appeals by employers			Workers' overall success		
	Appeals	Allowed	Success rates (%)	Appeals	Allowed	Success rates (%)	Total appeals	Successful workers	Success rates (%)
To 1886	0	0	0	1	1	100	1	0	0
1887–91	1	0	0	1	0	0	2	0	0
1892–6	2	0	0	3	1	33	5	2	40
1897–1901	0	0	0	13	3	23	13	10	77
1902–6	7	4	57	50	12	24	57	42	74
1907–11	4	1	25	41	14	34	45	28	62
1912–14	15	4	27	49	7	14	54	46	85
TOTALS	29	9	31	158	38	24	177	129	73

Source: Ontario Reports, Ontario Appeal Reports, Ontario Law Reports, Ontario Weekly Notes, Ontario Weekly Reporter, Supreme Court Reports

than fifty per cent of their appeals, but the workers won about ten per cent more than the employers and were successful in about fifty-four per cent of all the appeals.

The patterns were more complex in the Court of Appeal. There were not enough cases during the first decade after the 1886 act to support any conclusions. In each period after the late 1890s workers were successful in substantially more than fifty per cent of all appeals. Only fourteen appeals were made to the Supreme Court of Canada, all after 1890: ten by employers and four by workers. The workers were successful in twelve of these fourteen.

The general trend is clear. Workers lost almost all cases before the 1886 act and continued to lose most for a few years afterwards, but during the 1890s the results shifted and, from the late 1890s onwards, workers were successful in significantly more than half of the cases.

The results obviously demonstrate the proportion of workers who recovered compensation in the courts. Whether they also demonstrate attitudes of the courts, and in particular a preference for workers to succeed, is a difficult issue. Analysis can most usefully begin by making a distinction between the general rules and their elaboration and application. This distinction assumes that the general rules existed as working rules for courts and lawyers advising clients, and that these rules required choices to be made, for example, in the interpretation of legislation or in the determination of the adequacy of evidence for a jury. The rules were harsh to workers, considering the likelihood of recovery for the entire universe of accidents. If these results do indicate attitudes, they were demonstrated in application and were substantially different from the attitudes expressed in the rules. This situation can be explained by differences in time and, perhaps, purpose. A half century elapsed between the making of the rules and the deciding of these cases. Changes in attitudes during this time created pressures for change in both the rules and their application, but prevailing beliefs about the function of courts and precedent restricted expression of these changes to the choices made in application. More important, rules and application may have been affected by different purposes. Even in the early twentieth century judges may have continued to believe that the good of the social and economic fabric required the large degree of individual responsibility expressed by the rules, but that the plight of an injured individual invited a favourable exercise of the choice in application.

The possibility must be considered that attitudes towards appeals or juries accounted for the success rate of workers. Because employers appealed so much more often to the Court of Appeal and the Supreme Court, the success of the workers may have been accounted for entirely or in part by a general inclination to dismiss appeals. Contrasts to other appeals suggest that such an attitude existed, but it accounted for only a small part of the success. In three years during this period, 1905, 1908, and 1913, the Court of Appeal dismissed 56, 64, and 63 per cent of all the reported appeals, excluding these cases. During these years the court dismissed 77, 80, and 100 per cent of the employers' appeals. Moreover, the disposition of appeals by workers suggests the same conclusion, although the number of appeals is small and the record is erratic. From 1902 to 1914 workers won 9 of 26 appeals (35 per cent), and employers won 33 of 140 appeals (24 per cent).

Many of the appeals were about juries, either challenges to jury verdicts, usually made by employers, or assertions that issues should have been decided by juries and not by judges, usually made by workers. Courts may have been inclined to respect juries, especially jury verdicts, and because such a large proportion of the verdicts favoured workers, this attitude would have caused a large proportion of the workers to succeed. Testing this possibility is difficult because appeals about juries in other kinds of cases were surprisingly rare, perhaps because the chances of upsetting jury verdicts were small, and therefore comparisons are difficult to make. The largest single group of cases involved claims by individuals against railways and street railways for injuries suffered in collisions. Juries seem likely to have had the same reactions for these claims as for the workers' claims – to favour the plaintiff, especially over a large corporation. (Perhaps these corporations, which were often the employers in the workers' cases, were inclined to appeal for the purpose of discouraging plaintiffs.) In three years – 1905, 1908, and 1913 – these defendants failed in 16 of 24 challenges to jury verdicts (67 per cent). In the same three years employers failed in 18 of 22 challenges (82 per cent). The remainder of the cases were extremely diverse. There was no large group in which the nature of the context or the parties seems to contain anything that would have tempted juries or courts to have some general preference. The only other useful comparison is to a small group of defamation cases between 1905 and 1915 in which defendants failed in 4 of 7 challenges (57 per cent).[37] These figures suggest that respect for juries existed but was not the sole cause of the success of workers. They also suggest that courts had a significant preference for workers.

The issue remains: do the results alone demonstrate an attitude? If each participant in a series of disputes of the same type considers only the prospects of success and the immediate consequences in deciding whether to litigate, if their resources are adequate, and if the court makes decisions in a consistent way, the results will tend towards an equal division, regardless of the nature of the standard for decision.[38] An unequal division of results may be caused by a preference for plaintiffs or defendants, but it may also have other causes, which operate either in addition to or instead of a preference. Attitudes towards appeals and towards juries have already been considered. One other possible explanation is simply chance. The number of cases is small, but it is a large proportion of the entire range of cases, and the difference in the results continued for a long period. A difference in resources is another and more important possibility. The resources were knowledge about the prospects of success and ability to litigate claims effectively, although this separation is largely unrealistic because both were ultimately a product of money. The workers' resources were less than the employers', and doubtless often inadequate, which may have affected decisions about litigation in different ways. It may have made workers' knowledge inadequate, but the cases that were not litigated for this reason would not have included more cases that workers would have lost than cases they would have won. More important, it probably caused workers to decide to give up litigating some claims, and employers doubtless augmented this tendency by offering small but prompt settlements and by appealing decisions to discourage current and prospective plaintiffs. The effect of these decisions on the workers' success rate is difficult to analyse and impossible to measure. An aversion to risk might have tended to make workers litigate only cases that had relatively good chances of success, but this effect assumes knowledge they did not always have, and it would have been opposed by the effect of settlements offered by employers. However, the appeals by employers would have increased workers' success rates, because cases were appealed that should not have been appealed, if the prospects of success according to the standards for decision alone had been considered. Unequal resources may also have affected the conduct of litigation, but this could only have caused workers to lose cases they might otherwise have won.

In short, these results demonstrate that the courts had a small but significant preference for workers to succeed. If this took the form of a minor change in the rules, for example, in the standard for the adequacy of evidence to go to a jury, or a determination of some unsettled issue, for example, an interpretation of the legislation, the results should eventually have tended towards an equal division as knowledge of the change came

TABLE 6

Amounts of damage awards in
trials of actions by workers
against employers for injuries
suffered at work, Wentworth
County

Years	Mean amount
1888–92	$1021
1893–7	$1109
1898–1902	$1278
1903–7	$1389
1908–12	$1783
1913–14	$1992

Source: Ontario Archives, RG
22, Wentworth, Supreme
Court Actions and Matters
Files

to affect the decision to litigate. Some of the figures suggest this tendency. However, the preference may have been a simple and continuing inclination to decide most cases in favour of workers rather than a change in the rules.

Most of the claims that proceeded to trial involved injuries that caused permanent disability or death. The measure of damages for these injuries was rarely mentioned and never discussed thoroughly. However, the few comments that were made and the amounts awarded suggest that pain and suffering were given little consideration, and that the damages were awarded almost entirely for lost income or the loss of support. Table 6 gives averages for Wentworth County. The amounts tended to increase throughout the period, except for a drop at the turn of the century, and to increase more than monetary and real wages, but it is impossible to determine whether the severity of the injuries and the magnitude of the losses changed. The amounts in the reported cases tended to be higher, and it is impossible to determine whether this is a product of a difference between Wentworth and other counties or between reported and unreported cases.

Examples taken from cases in the reports during the ten-year period from 1904 to 1913 suggest that these amounts were not generous contrasted to wages, nor were they niggardly. The restriction to three years' wages in the Workmen's Compensation Act was a severe limitation, especially for claims for death or serious injury. In ten typical cases from the reports involving the death of workers, the dependants recovered an average of $2210; the amount ranged from $1300 to $4000. In seven cases in which the dependents recovered under the common law alone, the average was $5800, and the amount ranged from five to eight years of the worker's wages. For loss of an arm, the average of seven cases was $2160; for loss of an eye, the average of five cases was $2860; for loss of a hand, the average of five cases was $1000. During the same period wages rose. For example, from 1900 to 1914 average wages in manufacturing rose about forty per cent from $370 to $520 per year, but Michael Piva has argued that real earnings declined slightly. The annual expenditure for a family of five rose from approximately $760 in 1904 to $1084 in 1913.[39]

These findings can be used for conclusions about the adequacy of the courts and the common law. If the criterion is replacement of the loss of income caused by injury (because need is not affected by the cause of the injury), they were utterly inadequate. At trial, substantially more than half the claims succeeded, but the amounts recovered were usually not enough to replace income. Only a tiny proportion of injured workers brought actions, and substantially less than half of them proceeded to trial. Of course, settlements and voluntary payments prompted by the probability of liability or a sense of obligation created or supported by the doctrine must also be considered. Doubtless many were made. They cannot be counted, but the relative lack of power of most workers and comments made during the hearings of the Meredith Commission suggest that the voluntary payments were usually pitifully small.

THE JUDGMENTS OF THE COURTS

Numbers and proportions alone are not enough. The judgments of the courts must be assessed, but this process is even more impressionistic than counting, and therefore much more of the evidence must be displayed to support the conclusions. The Workmen's Compensation Act dominated the doctrine. The general effect of the act was simple – to diminish the scope of the fellow servant rule – but its terms were complex. Section 3, which was crucial, provided that if an injury to a worker was caused in one of five specified ways, he or she would have 'the same right of compensation against the employer as if the workman had not been a workman ... of the employer.' These ways were a 'defect in the condition of the ways, works, machinery, or plant ... '; the negligence of any employee, 'who has any superintendence entrusted to him ... '; the negligence of any employee 'to whose orders and directions the workman

... was bound to conform ... '; any 'impropriety or defect' in the 'rules or by-laws of the employer'; and the negligence of any employee, 'who has charge or control of any signal-points, locomotive, engine, or train upon a railway.' The provision that a worker would have 'the same right of compensation ... as if the workman had' not been a workman ... of the employer' removed the fellow servant rule but preserved defences that were not peculiar to the employment relationship, especially contributory negligence and assumption of risk. Also, section 5(3) provided that the worker could not recover if he or she knew of the defect or the negligence that caused the injury and did not give an appropriate warning to the employer. In 1889 this limitation was qualified by adding 'without reasonable excuse.' Section 3(1) was qualified by section 5(1), which provided that the worker could not recover 'unless the defect ... arose from or had not been discovered or remedied owing to the negligence of the employer or of some person in the service of the employer, and entrusted by him ...' with responsibility 'to keep the ways, works, machinery and plant' in proper condition. At common law, the employer was liable for negligence, including anything affecting the 'ways, works, machinery and plant,' but not for the negligence of employees, including those given responsibility for the condition of these matters, so long as they were competent. Therefore, the phrase 'entrusted by him' effected the expansion of liability. This phrase included sub-contractors, unlike the English act, which was limited to the negligence 'of some person in the service of the employer, and entrusted ...'[40]

A good example of the effect of sections 3(1) and 5(1) is *Schwoob* v *Michigan Central Railroad Company* (1906).[41] Schwoob's husband, a railway engineer, was scalded to death in the cab of his engine when a pipe parted from the hot water tank. This pipe was a replacement for the original one and had been installed in the railway's workshop shortly before the accident. At trial the jury found that the job of replacing the pipe had not been done properly, and that the system of having the work done, especially the arrangement for inspection, was inadequate. Therefore the employer was liable at common law for the inadequate system, and the jury gave $9000 damages. On appeal, both a Divisional Court and the Court of Appeal firmly denied the common law liability, simply because the plaintiff had not presented any evidence that the system was inadequate. However, liability under section 3(1) was imposed. The accident was caused by a 'defect in the condition of ... machinery ... ,' and the defect had been caused by the negligence of a worker 'entrusted ... with the duty of seeing that the ... machinery ... [was] in proper condition.'

Because the liability under the act was limited to three years' wages, the plaintiff recovered only $3240.

Section 3(1) presented many problems of interpretation. An early case was one of the very few in which the courts gave an interpretation of any of the legislation that was unfavourable to the workers. In *Hamilton* v *Groesbeck* (1890), Chief Justice John Armour held that a lack of a guard on a saw was not a defect, because it was 'no part of the saw ... nor at all necessary for any proper or reasonable fitness of the saw for the purpose for which it was used.'[42] Section 3 was immediately amended by adding the phrase 'or arrangement.' Afterwards, the question whether a defect existed was usually left to a jury, and the findings were usually favourable to the plaintiff.[43]

Section 3(2) and (3) overlapped greatly, and the nature and extent of the difference between them was never an issue in Ontario. The most common problem was simply whether a foreman had been negligent in giving orders, for example, about starting machinery or shoring an excavation. These problems were usually left to juries, and the findings were, again, usually favourable to the plaintiff.[44]

Section 2(4) about rules of the employer was not considered in any cases in Ontario. In contrast, section 2(5) about 'a locomotive, engine, or train upon a railway' was considered in many cases because railway operations, especially switching, were a common cause of injuries to workers. The most common problem was whether a railway engineer or conductor had been negligent, for example, in starting an engine while the worker was making a coupling.[45] In 1889 the section was amended to include, among other things, a 'machine ... upon a railway,' and in *McLaughlin* v *Ontario Iron and Steel Company* (1910), Chief Justice Meredith held that this phrase included overhead cranes running on tracks, which became common in factories early in the 1900s.[46] Section 5(3) prohibited recovery if the worker knew of the defect or negligence that caused the injury and failed to give notice to the employer, and section 7 barred an action unless notice of the injury was given within twelve weeks.[47] In 1889 this requirement was modified by providing that notice was not necessary if the plaintiff had a 'reasonable excuse.' Almost all the problems of interpretation of these sections were decided in favour of workers. In *Armstrong* v *Canada Atlantic Railway* (1902), Justice Featherstone Osler said, 'the injured workman is evidently the first object of the Legislature's care,' and 'I cannot but think that reasonable excuse for want of notice may be very slight indeed ...'[48]

The Workmen's Compensation Act was the only statute designed primarily to give workers a claim, but general legislation about railways, factories, mines, and construction supported claims in two ways: some of the statutes included express grants of claims, and in the absence of these the courts used the statutory requirements as support for common law claims.

The express grants of rights were all in the legislation about the railways. The 1881 Ontario act gave workers a right to recover from the employer railway 'all damages and loss' for personal injury caused by breach of the requirements. In 1888 a general provision added to the federal Railway Act gave 'any person' right to recover losses caused by breach, and in 1903 an overlapping right was given in a particular section that added more protections for workers. Ontario adopted these provisions in 1906.[49] The argument that 'any person' did not include workers was dismissed without hesitation or doubt by the Court of Appeal.[50] These sections caused no other difficulties for the courts, but some claims presented problems of interpreting other sections that are examples of a general tendency towards interpretations that favoured workers.

In *Smith* v *Grand Trunk Railway* (1914), Smith was a conductor on a Grand Trunk train. He was on the ground and signalled it to start but stayed to check some squealing brakes. He climbed on the train as it was moving, walked along the tops of the cars towards the caboose, and climbed down the ladder on the last one. It gave way and he fell under the wheels. This car, and the ladder in particular, had been damaged in an accident. It was being taken for repairs and the bottom of the ladder had been blocked to prevent use. Smith's claim succeeded. The Railway Act required ladders to be installed on the outside of all cars 'on two of the diagonally opposite ends and sides ...' Justice Roger Clute, for the majority, held that the cause of the injury was the defective ladder, which did not comply with the act. Justice William Riddell dissented, primarily because it seemed to him entirely reasonable for the railroad to take the car, as part of a train, to its shops to be fixed, and his attitude demonstrates the strength of the feeling that liability should be based on fault.[51] *Lamond* v *Grand Trunk Railway* (1908), involved a requirement to give a warning to 'persons standing on, or crossing or about to cross the track ...' Chief Justice Meredith held that this protection included a watchman whose duty was to warn pedestrians at a level crossing and who was killed by a car being shunted at night without warning.[52]

The work of the court in using laws that did not expressly give claims is a large part of the early doctrine about the use of statutes as standards and as causes of action. For this purpose the most important legislation was the Factories Act, especially section 15. The original version required fencing for the 'moving parts' of machinery and safeguards for elevators. In *Hamilton*, Chief Justice Armour interpreted 'moving parts' to be transitive and limited to those parts that supplied power. The act was immediately amended to require fencing for all 'dangerous parts' of machinery.

Shortly after the act was proclaimed, the courts concluded without any significant hesitation that a violation of section 15 was evidence of negligence.[53] However, this conclusion never led to any significant inquiry into the defendant's conduct and reasons or excuses for the violation. The defendant simply was liable if the violation caused injury. For example, in *McCloherty* v *Gale Manufacturing* (1892), McCloherty worked in the laundry department of a factory owned by the defendant.[54] She climbed on a bench to reach some windows near the ceiling, and her hair caught in an unguarded revolving shaft that hung near the ceiling. She asserted that she wanted to open the windows for ventilation; the defendant asserted that she wanted to chatter with some persons on the street and was therefore not within the course of her employment. The findings of the jury favoured her on this issue and her claim succeeded. Her knowledge of the existence of the shaft was an issue that will be considered later. Apart from this issue, Justice Osler seemed to conclude that the claim should succeed under both the Workmen's Compensation Act and the Factories Act. Considering the addition of the term 'arrangement' to section 3(1) of the Workmen's Compensation Act and its purpose, the lack of a guard was a 'defect.' Moreover, violation of the Factories Act in itself could be considered a defect. The violation of the Factories Act was also 'negligence consisting in the omission to comply with a statutory duty.' In these early cases, the language used suggested that the breach was a standard or evidence of negligence, but the effect was that the breach was a cause of action. This reality was suggested in some of the cases in the phrases 'negligence per se' and 'deliberate negligence.' In 1902 the Supreme Court relying on English authority said simply that 'an action will lie' for injury caused by breach of the act.[55] None of these cases contained any discussion of the purpose of the legislation and the role of the courts in using it to support recovery.

The same sort of reasoning and results were used under the Building Trades Protection Act and the Mining Act. In *Hull* v *Seneca Superior Silver Mines* (1915), the courts' lack of a thorough analytical understanding of these issues was combined with an apparent sympathy for a worker.[56] Hull's job was to take cars of ore from a cage at the top of a hoist, empty them, and return them to the cage, once every four minutes. One night the operator of the hoist raised the cage out of the shaft and above the floor. Hull was returning an empty cart and fell down the empty shaft. The Mining Act required that 'the manner of carrying on operations shall always conform to the strictest consideration of safety.' His widow's claim succeeded both at trial and in a Divisional Court. Clearly the operator of the hoist had been negligent, and the fellow servant rule could have been avoided by basing recovery on incompetence, inadequate training, or on an inadequate system of signals. However, the majority based recovery on breach of the statute, which was another way of avoiding the fellow servant rule. The question whether liability should be based on such a general provision was not considered, except by Justice Riddell, who dissented: 'I cannot convince myself that the Legislature, by the very general language employed, intended to render the defendant liable for an accident ...'

In *Siven* v *Temiskaming Mining* (1912), the requirement was much more specific, and the issue was whether it had been performed.[57] The Mining Act required a 'suitable pentice,' which is a covering or canopy, at each level of shafts. The mine constructed a covering with a trap door, which was carelessly left open. A rock rolled through the door and hit the plaintiff working below. A majority of the Court of Appeal held that the structure was inadequate, but Justice William Meredith sensibly pointed out in dissent that some sort of opening was necessary for the operation of the mine.

This willingness of the courts to impose liability for breach of statutes also appears in a series of three cases about the Factories Act and children. Sections 5 and 6 prohibited employment of persons under the age of fourteen in factories. In *Roberts* v *Taylor* (1899), a twelve-year-old boy was injured while operating a circular saw.[58] Justice Boyd held that the employer was not liable: the boy had been properly instructed, the saw was properly guarded, and there was no evidence 'coupling the accident with the illegal employment.' For example, there was no evidence that the work was 'too dangerous for a child, or too exhausting in its demands ...'

Section 7 prohibited boys under fourteen and girls under eighteen from working 'between the fixed and traversing part of any self-acting machine ...' *Fahey* v *Jephcot* (1901) presented the courts with a problem involving this section and the mind-numbing effect of repetitive work on machinery.[59] Fahey, a fifteen-year-old girl, operated a stamping machine. Her job was to place a piece of cardboard on a plate, which swung up against a die, and to remove the cardboard and insert another piece. The machine operated continuously at the rate of twenty times each minute. In removing the cardboard she had to put her hand between the plate and the die and, after several days, she made the mistake that might have been predicted: she left her hand between them as they came together and it was crushed. At trial Justice William Street dismissed her claim, relying on *Roberts* v *Taylor*. Her appeal to the Court of Appeal succeeded. Justices Osler and Charles Moss both asserted that the purpose of this particular prohibition was to protect children from the dangers of working at specified kinds of machinery and based the liability on this purpose. Justice Osler seemed to use the prohibition as a declaration that the machinery was, in relation to children, dangerous for the purpose of common law liability. Justice Moss said 'whether the defendant's conduct is to be classified as negligence or as a breach of a statutory duty resulting in injury, does not seem to me to be very material.' He was much less discriminating about the purpose of the particular prohibition and said simply that the violation was 'in itself evidence of negligence.' He also said that the effect of the decision was to overrule *Roberts* v *Taylor*. The reasoning in *Fahey* and the purposes of sections 5 and 6, contrasted to section 7, hardly justify this conclusion.

In the last case in this series, *McIntosh* v *Firstbrook Box* (1904), analysis of these purposes was undertaken but only in dissent.[60] McIntosh was ten years old. He represented himself to be fourteen and was hired by the company to put glue on boxes. While walking in a roundabout way through some machines to his work place, he was distracted by some other boys and put his hand on top of a planer. Unfortunately, it was operating and he lost a couple of fingers. At trial a non-suit was granted because of his misrepresentation about his age. In a Divisional Court the majority held that the employer must take reasonable precautions to ensure that a youth was as old as he or she represented, and it was a question for a jury whether these precautions were taken. If they were not, the employer would be liable, either at common law for failure to give adequate warning and instructions to a child, or under the Factories Act because 'illegal employment may be, in some circumstances, evidence of negligence.' Justice William Meredith dissented, primarily because there was no suggestion that the employer knew or should have known about the misrepresentation of age, and because the danger from the machines was obvious. About the act, he stated: 'It is said that the prohibition of the employment of persons under 14 years of age is solely for the protection of children from injury by dangerous machinery. I cannot at all agree in that … I would have thought the prohibition is mainly at least in the interest of the state and for the better physical, mental and moral growth and development of its children, and in complete accord with the enactment respecting compulsory school attendance, which requires all children between 8 and 14 years of age to attend school ...' This impressive analysis justifies the result in *Roberts* v *Taylor*, but it was, after all, a dissent. The Court of Appeal affirmed this decision but limited its reasoning to the common law liability.

This series of cases is an example of the tendency for workers to succeed in decisions about the effect of statutes, both interpretations of the Workmen's Compensation Act and the general legislation, and the use of statutes as support for claims. Understanding these decisions depends upon understanding the function of courts. In interpretation, courts must make choices. The terms of statutes do not control outcomes, despite a persistent judicial faith in 'plain meanings.' The established canons and presumptions are vague, and any one of them can usually be opposed by another of equal dignity. For example, the presumption about liberal interpretation of remedial statutes was occasionally invoked in these cases, but another about preservation of common law rights might have been invoked to adorn opposite results. The primary obligation of the courts is to be faithful to the purpose of the statute, but in difficult cases independent values and attitudes influence the results. In using statutes as support for claims, purposes unite with common law doctrine about liability, and again the influence of attitudes and values is inescapable.

Given either of the conditions specified in section 3(1) of the Workmen's Compensation Act, or breach of one of the general requirements about safety and accidents, the most common defences were the established common law ones: the fellow servant rule, assumption of risk, contributory negligence, and a denial that the breach had caused the accident. The fellow servant rule was, of course, partially displaced by the Workmen's Compensation Act, but it governed claims based on the negligence of fellow servants who were not 'foremen,' and in this way it continued to be a formidable obstacle. However, it did not govern claims based on breach of statutes because these claims were not based on negligence.[61] Assumption of risk also did not govern claims based on breach of statutes for elaborate conceptual reasons given in English authority.[62] It did govern claims under the Workmen's Compensation Act, because under the act these were fundamentally common law claims, but the courts did not apply it harshly.[63] In the late 1880s the major problem was the effect of a worker's knowledge of the risk. The English cases were unsettled, but in 1889 an amendment in Ontario declared that 'a workman shall not, by reason only of his continuing in the employment of the employer with knowledge of the defect, negligence, act, or omission, which caused his injury, be deemed to have voluntarily incurred the risk of the injury.' This amendment anticipated *Smith* v *Baker* (1891),[64] in England and was applied sympathetically by the courts. For example, in *McCloherty*, Justice Osler said:

Here beyond the fact that the plaintiff continued in the employment with knowledge, if she had knowledge, of the defect, there is no evidence that she voluntarily ran the risk of injury from the unguarded shaft. The defect was one which could have been remedied by a trifling expenditure, or the danger obviated by the simplest precaution, which the plaintiff, if she thought about it at all, might well suppose that the defendants would have made or taken, and thus there could be nothing to suggest to her that if she remained in the employment, she would be relying on skill or caution to avoid the danger, or taking a risk which it would be unreasonable to expect the master to prevent.

The contributory negligence defence was well established. For example, in *Deyo* v *Kingston and Pembroke Railway* (1904), Deyo was a brakeman who was last seen alive standing on top of a box car.[65] The train went under a bridge that was less than seven feet above the top of the train. Deyo was killed, and his widow claimed damages. The Court of Appeal held that the requirement in the Railway Act for seven feet of clearance governed the bridge, even though it was not owned by the railway and was constructed before the requirement was imposed. This holding was beneficial to railway workers, although it was hardly startling, given the general language of the requirement. However, the court also held that Deyo had been careless. The bridge was clearly visible, and he had often been warned about it. The rules of the railway singled out this particular bridge and prohibited employees from riding on the top of trains under it. The courts never questioned or even articulated the basic premise of contributory negligence, that is, that each individual should be responsible for his or her own fate. However, both contributory negligence and assumption of risk were issues of fact for juries, and their findings were usually sympathetic to the plaintiff and respected.[66]

These defences are the most useful approach to a much more general issue: the dangers created by repetitive operations on machinery, for example, the operation of the press described in *Fahey* v *Japhcot*. Each individual operation considered alone was simple and safe, but mind-numbing repetition could cause inattention and confusion. These operations caused injuries that were expected and predictable but they were not dangerous for the purposes of employers' liability. This machinery was becoming common and seemed to promise great advances in productivity. The workers' need for compensation was not strong enough to make the courts declare that this promise demanded unreasonable dangers or even to imagine this possibility. Therefore if an injury was caused solely by a worker's slip, there was no hope for recovery.[67] For liability, some more particular danger was needed, for example, a malfunction, an unusually fast speed, or lack of a guard. For claims based on dangers of this kind, contributory negligence and assumption of risk were likely defences, because the conditions were likely to be known. The courts tended to prefer the workers in considering these defences.[68]

The Workmen's Compensation Act and the general legislation about safety and accidents greatly expanded the liability of employers, but some claims continued to be based on the common law, either alone or, more often, combined in one action with claims under one or more of the statutes. These common law claims were made either because a claim under the legislation might fail or clearly would fail, or, even if it might succeed, to avoid the limits on recovery in the Workmen's Compensation Act. The disability or the death of a young worker, especially a skilled one, caused losses that were much greater than three years' wages (even though the courts never awarded the full amount of these losses). These common law claims were less common and less likely to succeed than actions under the legislation. Counting is difficult, because many claims could succeed under both common law and legislation, and the judgments often do not clearly distinguish among them. However, recovery was not rare. In at least thirty of the reported cases, workers were successful on common law grounds. For example, workers recovered for injuries caused by defective handles on boxes, lack of brakes on carts, lack of shoring in a trench, failure to instruct and to warn about unusual dangers, and inadequate systems of signalling, inspecting after blasting, controlling flying metal, and filtering gas.[69]

Juries were used in almost all cases and determined a wide range of factual issues, such as whether an individual was a foreman, whether a foreman had been negligent or knew of a defect, whether a defect existed, whether the system was adequate, and whether a plaintiff had been negligent or assumed a risk. The strong tendency of juries to make findings favourable to workers has already been described. In *Deverill* v *Grand Trunk Railway* (1869), Justice Hagarty said that 'To leave such a case to the jury is ... simply to direct a verdict for the plaintiff, where a railway company are defendants.'[70] In *Woolsey* v *Canadian Northern Railways* (1908), Justice Garrow stated: 'Juries are, it is common experience, too apt ... to follow their sympathies rather than the evidence, and to find for the plaintiff whenever possible.'[71] In many cases defendants made motions for non-suits or to set aside judgments, because the evidence was not adequate to support the jury findings. These motions invoked extensive general doctrine about the functions of judge and jury, especially the kind of evidence necessary to permit a decision to be made by a jury, and this doctrine obviously gave much scope for choice. The courts tended to permit these decisions to be made by the jury. Respect for the jury as an institution was a major cause of this tendency, but both the results, which have already been discussed, and the impressions from reading the judgments suggest that the courts also had a preference for workers.

The most difficult problems about the jury findings were presented by findings about causation and, in particular, whether a defect or a breach of a statute had caused an injury to a worker. One of the leading cases, *Canadian Coloured Cotton Mills* v *Kervin* (1899), is a good example.[72] The machinery in the mill was powered by two large wheels in the basement, which were about forty-five feet apart, partly sunk in a trench, and joined by a moving belt. The wheels were not fenced and doubtless should have been. Kervin's job was to oil and maintain them and he had put a couple of planks across the trench to use as a short cut. Because walking across them involved walking between the upper and lower parts of the belt, this arrangement was obviously foolish. He was found dead. There was no doubt that he had died because he fell under the belt, but the issue was why he had fallen. If he had fallen in doing his job, for example, while inspecting or oiling the wheels, the mill was liable because of the lack of a fence. If he had fallen while crossing the planks, the widow's claim would fail because of contributory negligence. At trial, Chief Justice Armour left the issue to the jury and said that 'from the position of the body and the condition and the way in which the belt was moving, there are circumstances to go to them from which they may come to the conclusion that it was at the pulley the accident occurred.'

A Divisional Court affirmed, although Justice Ralph Meredith dissented: 'No man can tell how; any man can guess ... but if right in his surmise he would be right not upon evidence, but purely on chance ... there is no presumption that the man was doing right when the accident happened ...' The Court of Appeal also affirmed, but only because it was equally divided, and without giving reasons. The Supreme Court reversed. In a short judgment for the majority Justice Désiré Girouard said: 'We are left to hypothesis, theories and conjectures ... there was no evidence whatever that the negligence imputed to the appellant was the cause of the accident ...' There were at least a dozen similar cases in which the phrase 'mere conjecture' appeared often.[73] Of course a complete lack of evidence about causation was extremely rare. Usually there was some evidence, albeit perhaps very little, from which implications might be made.

The disposition of costs was a significant part of some of the judgments. The general rule was that the losing party was ordered to pay a large part of the winner's costs, but the courts had a discretion to order some different result, and especially to refuse to make any order at all, which left both the parties to bear their own costs. After about 1904 the courts often exercised this discretion in workers' favour by refusing to make an order for costs against a worker who lost or by discouraging the employer from enforcing a right to costs. From 1904 to 1914 the courts refused to order costs in about thirty per cent of the appeals in which employers were successful, and in about fifteen per cent they ordered 'costs if exacted' or some similar phrase. These dispositions were never explained and there was nothing in any of the cases that might have explained them, except the fact that the plaintiffs were workers. Considering the reported cases as a whole, the courts made these kinds of orders more often than they do now; nevertheless this tendency to favour workers was distinctive.

Taken as a whole, these judgments demonstrate the preference for workers to succeed that the results alone demonstrated. However, its significance for both the doctrine and the workers must not be exaggerated. Again, it was demonstrated in the application of general doctrine that was unfavourable to workers and never questioned.

Last, the ways in which the results changed over time needs explanation, especially the changes in the mid-1890s. The common law doctrine and the nature of the cases coming before the courts did not alter in any significant way. Reading the judgments alone gives no sense of change and only a small suggestion of a preference in the comments about interpretation. The Workmen's Compensation Act was, of course, crucial. Before it was enacted, workers lost almost all the cases, and most of those who lost would have won under its terms. After its enactment, workers continued to lose more than half the cases for a short time, but the total numbers of cases were small, and the eventual change was caused in two ways. First, the narrow holding in *Hamilton* v *Groesbeck* was superseded by the amendments to the Factories Act and the Workmen's Compensation Act, which governed many similar cases afterwards. Second, and more important but less conspicuous, were changing attitudes towards the scope of issues to be determined by juries, especially questions about causation, the negligence of an employer or foreman, and contributory negligence. Single cases cannot be any more than examples, but one is especially useful. In *Plant v Grand Trunk Railway*, decided in 1867, a train approached a group of workers in a narrow cutting without warning.[74] Plant panicked and tried to run ahead along the track instead of jumping to the side. Chief Justice Henry Draper held that a jury finding of no contributory negligence was unsupportable and ordered a non-suit. Thirty years later jury findings that mistakes of judgment and momentary inadvertence were not contributory negligence were usually upheld.[75]

SOME CONCLUSIONS ABOUT COURTS

The reasons for the preference for workers were not suggested in the judgments, because the form of the reasoning denied admission of change let alone an attempt to explain and justify it openly. Any attempt to analyse these reasons must be confined and tentative, until a much wider range of Canadian legal experience has been studied, but doubtless they were complex. Beliefs about the value of individual responsibility and freedom were declining in the late nineteenth century, and the doctrine of fault and the reasoning in cases like *Farwell* seemed less realistic and just. As industrial capitalism matured and the power of employers increased, it became obvious that individual workers usually had no significant opportunity to choose the terms of their work, and interdependence and machinery made the attribution of personal fault more and more unrealistic. (Some assumptions about the responsibility of employers to pay, their ability to pay, or the ultimate imposition of the burden on consumers were involved, although they were not clearly perceived or analysed.) These general changes combined with more specific influences. The slowly growing consciousness and power of workers was apparent. The injuries and suffering were visible and immediate, and the employment relation established familiar doctrinal limits. Recovery by a few workers could satisfy their needs and the impulse of sympathy without challenging the settled doctrine and without making a shift in the balance of power between employers and labour or a threat to the established economic order. It may also be seen as giving the subtle control that can come from being merciful.

Changes in the form of the common law may also have contributed. Arguably the faith in rigorous general rules declined, and the courts became more willing to consider the facts of specific contexts more intensively and to reach results that seemed fair for these facts.[76] But to say this much and no more is not enough, because it does not explain the results. In particular, it does not explain the changing components of the sense of fairness, and this explanation returns the inquiry to changing attitudes. However, the changes in attitudes tended to fragment the scope of the existing rules, and, moreover, the greater willingness to permit issues to be determined by juries can be perceived as a shift away from general rules.

Another probable influence is a perception of encouragement from the legislation, but its nature and effect are much more uncertain. Clearly the courts were usually faithful to the purposes of the legislation; restrictive interpretations were often possible but unusual. This conclusion itself is interesting and important, but it is not an independent reason for the preference for workers. The separate but more speculative possibility is that the courts perceived or felt that the legislation encouraged and authorized the courts to make changes of the same nature or tendency for issues just beyond its terms.

The style of the courts' reasoning and their perception of their function were also distinctive. Important recent writing in England and the United States has explored these topics, and some consensus seems to have been established that change occurred during the second half of the nineteenth century.[77] The term 'formalism' is common and expressive, although it masks uncertainty and lack of consensus about precisely what happened, and when and why. Canadians must not assume that their courts were simply shadows of English or American courts – only duller.

In Ontario the courts seemed to assume that the common law was composed of rules firmly settled by authority, primarily English authority. It was almost never expressly justified, beyond the justification implicit in its mere existence and the internal authority of courts in a hierarchy. For example, it was almost never justified by invoking science, or by its age, fairness, or utility. The process of making decisions seemed usually to be simply finding facts and applying the rules. If the law was obscure or uncertain, the court simply had to look harder to find it. This process of finding almost never included any reasoning, even to deduce implications from the rules. The judgments contain virtually no discussions of the functions of courts, especially their responsibility for the common law or interpreting statutes, but a basic and pervasive article of faith was apparent: their function was only to apply the law in an impartial way. The primary power and responsibility for initiating change was for the legislature, not the courts, but the latter were willing to accept and implement change initiated by the legislature and also may even have been encouraged by legislation to make modest supplementary changes. These thoughts parallel some of the suggestions made by Jennifer Nedelsky in her study of nuisance cases in the first volume of this series.[78]

The courts during this period were different from the Ontario courts in the mid-nineteenth century, especially in the form of their reasoning.[79] This difference is clear, although it may not be large and it is not as considerable as differences between the same periods in England and the United States. The judges in the mid-nineteenth century were more willing to modify and justify the law and the results, and especially more willing to invoke utility for economic development and appropriateness for Canadian conditions. They were more inclined to reason, albeit to reason from given general principles, and more willing to express opinions about the merits of the law and the results. In contrast, the judges in these cases half a century later appear to have been intelligent and conscientious bureaucrats, persevering without question at a timeless routine.

PRIVATE INSURANCE

Workers could obtain insurance against the consequences of accidents, and some, but far from all, did. Many commercial companies offered life, accident, and sickness insurance. More important for workers were insurance plans established by employers, employees and unions, and social or fraternal organizations. The distinction between plans established by employers and by employees and unions was not precise, and individual plans could be a combination of both; for example, management and administration could be shared. Most of the funds for these plans were contributed by workers; employers did not always contribute, and where they did, the contributions were usually small. The largest Canadian plan was the Grand Trunk Insurance and Provident Society, which provided insurance against death, sickness, and accident. Membership in the society and a waiver of any other claims against the company was a condition of employment. Two-thirds of the directors were appointed by the company, and one-third were elected by employees. In 1902, 10,144 employees (or retired employees) were members; 957 were injured in accidents and 2848 were sick. They received a total of $36,734 for lost wages and $20,074 for medical expenses; 128 died and $81,771 was paid to dependants. The employees paid $80,105 for the life insurance and $47,999 for sickness and accident insurance in monthly payments of twenty to fifty cents per month according to the risks of their jobs. (Retired employees paid $899.) The company contributed $12,500. Railway employees were also insured in plans operated by unions, especially those based in the United States.[80]

Most of the other plans provided insurance against sickness (which included accidents) and funeral expenses; a few included insurance against death or unemployment. Two examples are the Massey Harris Toronto Employees' Mutual Benefit Society, which in 1909 included 1450 employees. It paid $300 in funeral benefits for five employees who died and $3876 for lost wages for 331 employees who were sick for a total of 1300 weeks. The Gendron Manufacturing Company's Employees' Mutual Benefit Society included in 1909 sixty-two employees and paid $58 for lost wages and medical expenses to three employees who were sick for a total of six weeks.[81]

Contracting out of common law liability was a major issue in England. In *Griffiths* v *Earl of Dudley* (1882), a strong general faith in freedom of contract was invoked to enforce a waiver of the benefits of the Employers' Liability Act, which was imposed as a condition of employment.[82] Attempts to amend the act to prevent contracting out failed. Some of the workers who were required to waive were provided for at least as well by insurance funds, and others, where unions were weaker, were not.[83] The issue was not thoroughly considered and expressly and firmly settled in Ontario, but in the absence of legislation doubtless the reasoning and result of *Griffiths* would have prevailed.[84] Some of the railway legislation contained prohibitions against contracting out of claims.[85] The Workmen's Compensation Act of 1886 permitted contracting out only if the employer provided some benefit in exchange that was 'ample and adequate' and 'just and reasonable.'[86]

The other source of insurance for workers was the social or fraternal societies, for which providing insurance was usually a major objective. Only a few of these societies were expressly established for workers. The large ones such as the Foresters, the Oddfellows, and the Orange Lodge had tens of thousands of members, and some of the smaller ones had only a handful.

Many questions can be asked about insurance. How many different plans were there? What kinds of employment did they generally cover? How many workers, and what kinds of workers, obtained insurance from them? What were the coverages, the amounts of benefits, the costs, and the procedures for determining entitlement? Comprehensive and precise answers are difficult or impossible to find, but some estimates and generalizations can be made. In 1910, 103 funds were registered under the

Friendly Societies Act, which required registration of all insurance funds (excluding the commercial companies), and about forty-five of these seem to have been established primarily for workers. Doubtless there were more that were not registered. About 80,000 workers obtained life insurance from these forty-five funds, and about 6600 obtained insurance against sickness. The total of workers obtaining insurance was much higher because many would have used other funds or the commercial companies. The totals of insured persons for the registered funds were 265,000 for life insurance and 99,400 for sickness insurance and funeral benefits, but what proportion of these totals were workers cannot be determined. However, whatever number of workers insured themselves was only a small proportion of the total number of workers. The benefits were not large. In 1909 the average payment for life insurance was about $1170, and the average for each week of sickness was about $4.25.[87]

The shift to compensation in 1915 made much of this insurance unnecessary. It was a shift from decentralization to centralization, from private to public, from variety to uniformity, from individual initiative to social responsibility, and from payment of the immediate cost by the workers to payment by the employers.

THE BEGINNINGS OF COMPENSATION

During the late nineteenth and early twentieth centuries a shift to giving compensation regardless of fault occurred throughout Europe and North America. The beginnings were in Germany. In 1881 Kaiser Wilhelm I proposed social insurance to protect workers against loss of income resulting from accidents and old age. In 1884 compensation for accidents was given, which was a proportion of the worker's salary during disability or a pension for dependents. The payments were made by groups or associations of employers and guaranteed by the state. Unlike the schemes established later in England and North America, this compensation was integrated with medical treatment and compensation for sickness, and the associations of employers played a substantial role in efforts to prevent accidents.

In England the change came in 1897 in the Workmen's Compensation Act, which greatly expanded the liability of employers, although only for some kinds of employment, especially railways, factories, and certain types of construction projects.[88] A worker was entitled to compensation from his or her employers for injuries caused by accidents 'arising out of and in the course of the employment.' This compensation was substantially less than the common law gave; the worker was entitled to fifty per cent of salary while unable to work, subject to a maximum of £1 per week and, if the worker was killed by the accident, the dependents were entitled to three years' salary, subject to a maximum of £300. Disputes about entitlement and amount were decided by arbitration, although an appeal on questions of law could be made to the courts. Agreements between employers and employees that the act would not apply were permitted, if the employer had established a private compensation scheme that was 'not less favourable' than the compensation required by the act. The common law and the 1880 Employers' Liability Act continued as an alternative; that is, a worker could claim damages at common law instead of compensation under the act.

In the United States the change began in a substantial way in 1908 and 1909 with a series of conferences and commissions. In 1909 New York enacted a compensation scheme, which was declared unconstitutional in 1910. In 1911 ten other states enacted schemes that avoided the constitutional obstacles in different ways, and by 1920 all but six southern states had followed.[89] In Canada, British Columbia established a compensation scheme based on the English model in 1902, Alberta followed in 1908, Manitoba and Nova Scotia in 1910, and Saskatchewan in 1911. Quebec enacted a blend of the English model and the civil law in 1910.[90]

In Ontario in 1899 Thomas Crawford, a member of the Conservative opposition, introduced a bill that was substantially the same as the English act of 1897. It was opposed by the government, because it had not been demanded or supported by labour groups, because it was opposed by the Canadian Manufacturers' Association and the Board of Trade of Toronto, and because the extended liability might crush small employers. However, the Premier, Arthur S. Hardy, seemed to believe that some change was necessary and suggested a form of compensation based on contributions from workers and employers and administered by a Commission. Ultimately consideration of the bill was deferred until a study of the English system was made. The job was given to Professor James Mavor of the University of Toronto.[91]

The bulk of the Mavor report in March 1900 was an extensive description of developments in Europe and England.[92] The nature of his analysis was suggested by the remark that 'the question must be looked at largely from an actuarial standpoint.' This analysis required an empirical study of the cost of the risk, the ultimate incidence of this cost, and its effect on the markets for capital and labour. This was the first time this kind of economic analysis of the issue had appeared in Canada, and it reflected emerging perceptions of social issues. Considerations of individual morality and fault would no longer dominate debates about liability and compensation. However, Mavor did not undertake such a study and made no suggestions how it might be done. Without these facts, his own predispositions were apparent: compensation threatened to discourage investment. The needs of workers and their dependents and the unreality of the liberal model of the market were not mentioned. He recommended that 'it would appear to be wise to wait for some time in order to ascertain more fully what has been the effect of the change of principle in the English law.' His transition from 'a young reformer of Fabian sympathies in 1885' to 'an orthodox classical economist dedicated to preserving the capitalist status quo' had apparently been completed.[93]

Crawford's bill was not resurrected, and between 1900 and 1907 the issue of workers' compensation substantially disappeared from public affairs. No substantial demand for change was made by labour, and none was considered by the government. Nor were proposals made by the civil service, particularly the factory inspectors, or private reform groups, unlike other jurisdictions such as England, Massachusetts, and Quebec.[94]

The Conservatives under James P. Whitney responded more quickly than the Liberals to the urbanization of Ontario and came to power in 1905.[95] In 1899 Whitney as leader of the opposition had declared himself in favour of Crawford's compensation bill during a debate about some amendments to the existing Workmen's Compensation Act.[96] In 1907 Crawford introduced another compensation bill, which failed to get second reading, although it probably prompted an undertaking from Whitney to act.[97] Labour seems to have rediscovered the issue late in 1909, probably prodded by developments in the United States. In January 1910 a delegation appeared before Whitney and some of his cabinet and asked for the appointment of a commission.[98] The speech from the throne, made shortly afterwards, promised such a commission, and in June Meredith was appointed.[99] In December one of his fellow judges, Justice William Middleton, spoke to the Ontario Bar Association about law reform and made reform of workers' compensation the foremost need.[100]

Meredith is the crucial individual in the story of workers' compensation. He was a lawyer who practised in London and later in Toronto. Elected to the legislature in 1872 as a Conservative, he became leader of the opposition in 1878, but the reign of Oliver Mowat doomed him to remain in opposition throughout his political career. He had sympathetic attitudes towards social legislation and urban workers and had some reputation as a radical. Occasionally he saw his proposals adopted by Mowat. One experience of this kind was in 1885 when he introduced a bill

Sir William R. Meredith, Legislative Assembly of Ontario 1872–94,
Chief Justice of Common Pleas 1894–1912, Chief Justice of Ontario 1913–23
Oil portrait by Sir Edmund Wyly Grier (The Law Society of Upper Canada)

based on the English Employers' Act of 1880, with changes that expanded
the liability. The government opposed it, and introduced its own bill in
the next session – without most of his changes.[101] In 1894 he left politics
and became the Chief Justice of the Court of Common Pleas.[102]

As a judge, Meredith's style was the same as that of his colleagues. His
judgments demonstrated no sense of change or responsibility for change
and virtually no assessment of the law. His perception of his function
appeared to be simply the impersonal and autonomous application of
settled doctrine, and he expressed these beliefs during the hearings of his
commission. A worker speaking about the 'class struggle' asserted that
'when we get into law, we always know who comes out best. We know
the man with the money and the man with the influence comes out on top,
and we know the District judge ... is not a member of the working class,
but a member of the wealthy class himself.' Meredith responded:

I venture to say that as a whole the sympathies, as far as a judge is permitted to
have sympathies, have been with the working man, and where they have had to
determine against him in hard cases it is because they have been compelled by the
law to do so ... you think a court is entitled to do natural justice, but the court has
no such power. The court is confined to administering justice according to the law,
and a judge sitting would have no more right in determining a case contrary to the
law than he would have to go to you and take out of your pocket your money. The
fault is not in the administration of justice; you must change your law. It is the law
that is at fault.[103]

But differences appeared despite the mask of formalism; he was clearly
more sympathetic to workers than most of his colleagues.[104]

THE HEARINGS AND THE RECOMMENDATION

Meredith held twenty-seven public sessions from 23 October 1911 to 20
March 1913.[105] Most were held in Toronto, but he also travelled to
London, Hamilton, Berlin, and Cobalt, where he was upset by some blunt
comments by workers about the class struggle.[106] The major participants,
apart from Meredith himself, were F.W. Wegenast, counsel for the
Canadian Manufacturers' Association (CMA) and Fred Bancroft, representing the Trades and Labour Congress. These two appeared at almost
all the sessions; no one else appeared at more than a few. Representatives
of other labour and employer organizations appeared briefly, usually to
support Bancroft or Wegenast, and a large number of individual em-

ployers and workers also appeared, although it is impossible to tell the extent to which they represented organizations. Railroads, unions of railroad workers, and accident insurance companies appeared relatively late in the sessions. Seven witnesses served as experts to give the Commission some specialized knowledge and expertise. One who described the accident insurance business in Canada seems to have appeared as a result of a request by Meredith himself. The other six were from the United States; three were presented by Wegenast and three by the railroads or the insurance companies.

The procedure at the sessions was informal, especially in contrast to the procedure of most agencies and commissions today. Most sessions began with a statement by a participant or witness, but interruptions were frequent and uncontrolled by any rules about the kinds of questions that could be asked, by any difference between question and argument, and by any settled order in which the participants would proceed. Most of the sessions became discussions, which often wandered erratically among different topics. The witnesses were not simply asked questions by the participant who had arranged their appearance and then cross-examined by the others. Instead they were usually permitted or asked to give their opinions comprehensively and to join in the discussion. They tended, as might have been expected, generally to support the positions of the party which had arranged their appearances but also often gave contrary opinions about particular issues.

Bancroft presented his brief in the fourth session.[107] It was a simple and blunt demand for compensation regardless of fault, but it was vague about some of the important issues. During discussion of the brief Bancroft seemed confused and unsure about the implications of the proposals and the legislation in other jurisdictions.[108] Wegenast did not present his brief until the seventh session because the CMA was slow in preparing its policy, and Meredith, not unreasonably, was openly annoyed at the delay.[109] However, the brief itself was a long and thorough study, which is still impressive and useful.[110] Throughout the hearings other labour and employer organizations presented briefs and made presentations. The only significant ones were from the railroads, the unions of railroad workers, and the insurance companies.

On 27 March 1912 between the eleventh and twelfth sessions Meredith made an interim report in which he said that the existing law was 'entirely inadequate' and that the participants seemed to agree that some compensation scheme should be established.[111] He presented a draft bill on 1 April 1913 and made his final report on 31 October 1913. He recommended that compensation be given for accidents and industrial diseases, paid for by employers, although he assumed that this cost would ultimately be passed on to consumers. Injured workers were entitled to compensation after seven days' absence from work. This compensation was a proportion of salary – fifty-five per cent – to be paid periodically. It continued as long as the worker was disabled, and, if the worker died, the dependants received a pension. The common law claims, including damages for pain and suffering, were barred. The collection and the payment of this compensation were to be administered by a government agency, the Workmen's Compensation Board. For most industries the responsibility to pay was collective, and employers were divided into groups. The Board made the payments from a fund, which was created by assessments upon each of the groups. The result was, in effect, mutual insurance adminis-tered by the state. A few large and stable (and politically powerful) employers, especially the railroads and municipal governments, were excluded from this collective responsibility, and the duty to pay was imposed upon them individually. Meredith recommended that no appeal from the Board be permitted, and that review by the courts be prohib-ited.[112] This compensation scheme was to govern almost all industries in the province. A few, especially agriculture and domestic employment, were excluded, because of political or practical difficulties. Some small changes were made (by Meredith himself); the bill was enacted on 1 May 1914, and the act came into force on 1 January 1915.

THE ACCEPTANCE OF THE GENERAL PRINCIPLE

From the outset all the participants agreed that the existing law was unsatisfactory and that compensation should be established. In the first few moments of the first session Wegenast said that 'compensation in some form should be provided. The discussion ... will be confined probably to the means by which that compensation should be effected.'[113] Bancroft said that 'a Workmen's Compensation Act of the nature of the British Act is in the interests of the workmen of this country.'[114] With only a few trivial exceptions, all participants agreed with Wegenast and Bancroft. Meredith described this consensus in his Interim Report, and it continued throughout the hearings. It was a product of a complex accumulation of reasons. Some were expressed openly and others were implicit. In general, compensation offered advantages for both workers and employers, and no great disadvantages to them or to the public.

The example of other jurisdictions created substantial pressure for change. Both armchair speculation and experience demonstrate that compensation is not necessarily associated with any particular form or stage of economic organization. However, the existence of compensation throughout Europe and English-speaking countries and its reputation as a reform measure made it difficult to oppose its adoption in Ontario.

The courts and the doctrine of fault appeared more and more unsatisfactory as years passed and had fewer and fewer defenders after the late nineteenth century. All the participants joined in condemning them, especially conflict, delay, uncertainty, and inefficiency. Any kind of dispute about liability must create some conflict and tension, which is manifested and often exacerbated by bringing it to court. The employers especially believed that this conflict damaged harmonious relationships between employers and workers and that this damage was increased by the attitudes of insurance companies and lawyers. They complained that insurance companies seemed to care only about avoiding liability, and lawyers created trouble – and did a disservice to the workers by fomenting litigation that made voluntary, fair, and prompt payments impossible. Of course, their perception of harmonious relationships often included not only happiness but subservience, and the payments they wanted to make were usually far smaller than employees would get in court. Some delay was inevitable, but it usually took months to reach a decision even after a writ was issued, and it could take years, although it was usually much less than the delays for personal injury litigation now. This delay could be crushing for a disabled worker who had no savings. Uncertainty was also inevitable, simply because the outcome of litigation could not be predicted, especially if it involved disputed facts and the application of general standards. For workers, this uncertainty brought worry. It also made the decision to bring an action a gamble. Success brought some compensation including costs, but failure brought an obligation to pay a lawyer and the likelihood of paying a large part of the employer's costs.

Workers alleged that employers exploited the delay and uncertainty by appealing cases only to force workers to give up and accept unfair settlements and to discourage others from making claims. The number of cases in which the Grand Trunk alone appealed cases involving small amounts invites some sympathy for this allegation. For employers, uncertainty created the simple and foreboding possibility of suddenly being obligated to pay a large or crushing damage award. It also made prediction of this cost of production impossible and was therefore an obstacle to rational cost allocation and financial planning. Theoretically, insurance could avoid these consequences, but insurance was unattractive not only because it created conflict but because it seemed to be inefficient. Several accounts of the disposition of premiums were given, and although they differed, they demonstrated that the proportion paid to injured workers was remarkably low, and the proportion paid for expenses, especially commissions and lawyers' fees, was remarkably high. Even the lawyers joined in condemning the courts and the role of their profession. Meredith himself spoke about 'the hungry lawyer' and made the comment about 'this nuisance of litigation' quoted in the introduction.[115]

The doctrine of fault itself was being eroded in two ways. First, studies of causes of accidents demonstrated that many of them were not caused by the fault of either the worker or the employer. Most of these studies were done in the United States, although a few crude ones were done in Ontario for the commission. They were not rigorous, and the details and percentages varied, but their essential conclusions were clear and powerful: approximately half the accidents seemed to be inevitable.[116] Second, increasing interdependence and changing perceptions of causation shifted the search for causes and effects from single, immediate, and independent causes such as a momentary act or omission by an individual, to more remote and interdependent causes such as the needs of the industrial system, the effect of piece work, tiredness, monotony, and the consequences of disability for a worker's family.[117]

The employers' defences, especially the fellow servant rule and contributory negligence, also seemed unjustified. The increasing self-awareness and power of labour and the declining faith in individual responsibility contributed to this change in attitude. For the fellow servant rule, the beliefs that the rule influenced the conduct of workers and that they had freedom to bargain about risk became increasingly unrealistic.[118] For contributory negligence, the perceptions of causation contributed to the belief that workers' claims should not be entirely denied for momentary negligence. Meredith's comments demonstrate both the strength of this feeling and his restraint as a judge. His judgments contain almost no assessment of the common law, but during the hearings and in the reports he had no hesitation in condemning it as 'entirely inadequate' and 'unfair and inequitable.' The doctrine of assumption of risk was 'a fallacy resting upon the erroneous assumption that the workman is free to work as he pleases,' and the fellow servant rule was a 'fundamental error' and 'a relic of barbarism.'[119]

The conclusion that the courts and their doctrine were unsatisfactory did not necessarily lead to compensation. For example, compensation avoided the need to determine fault, but it did not necessarily avoid the courts or insurance. However, this conclusion did create a need for some change, and compensation was the most appealing of the existing possibilities.

The reason expressed most frequently by the participants was that compensation would provide relatively efficient and humane provision for disabled workers and replace dependence on litigation, private insurance, family resources, and municipal welfare. It was, in effect, an efficient welfare scheme for workers. Meredith said in his Final Report that 'the true aim of a compensation law is to provide for the injured workman and his dependants, and to prevent their becoming a charge upon their relatives or friends, or upon the community at large.'[120] The phrase 'social legislation' was often used, usually in this context, to express the belief that compensation was a social obligation and would eventually be paid by the consumers – that is, the public generally. Early in the hearings Bancroft said: 'After all, it is a tax upon industry. In the last analysis ... the consumer will pay for it.' Much later, Meredith made the other comment quoted in the introduction: 'It is social legislation ... and all the manufacturers ... are simply tax gatherers.'[121]

This welfare objective was closely related to the wider and vaguer objective of encouraging better relations between employers and workers. An employer's hope for 'no rows or trouble or fighting with people, and no arguments'[122] may have been naïve, but it might have been expressed by any of the participants. From the employers' perspective, security and lack of conflict and uncertainty would tend to make workers more content and therefore more passive and productive. In this way support for compensation shared some of the motives of the industrial betterment schemes of the time, although workers also expressed the same hopes.

Both workers and employers stressed the importance of prevention contrasted to compensation, and employers often spoke of the need to conserve human resources, especially specialized skills.[123] Prevention was associated with compensation in several different ways. For example, Bancroft asserted that compensation would tend to prevent accidents because employers would have an incentive to minimize the cost, although he seems not to have perceived that under individual liability the cost would have been allocated more precisely and the incentive would be limited to avoidable accidents. Wegenast proposed a sophisticated structure for prevention, which he clearly had derived from the German scheme, in which the responsibility for enforcement of safety requirements would be assigned to the Board and administered by groups of employers. Meredith had little or no interest in this proposal or in prevention generally, probably because he preferred to make a simple proposal and because he had some constitutional reservations about assigning public powers to private groups. The entire German system of employer associations was never considered seriously, probably because it was based on associations and traditions that did not exist in Canada.

Compensation offered two advantages peculiar to employers. First, it could make the payments for accidents predictable, regular, and relatively constant. This use of planning, standardization, and routine was emerging in other aspects of economic activity, especially in the organization of work in factories. Compensation could be, in effect, an efficient mutual insurance scheme administered by the state. Morton Horwitz has argued that the fellow servant rule was 'the triumph of contractarian ideology.'[124] Perhaps, with some exaggeration, it can be argued that compensation was the triumph of the actuary. Second, compensation may have seemed to offer a small decrease in competition through standardization of one cost of production. There is no direct evidence of this possibility, but it is consistent with a general tendency of businessmen at the time. In a similar way it may also have seemed attractive to employers who believed, for whatever reason, that workers should be compensated, but who feared competition from employers who did not share their beliefs. Compensation would enable all employers to seem to be humane without fear from competition.[125]

In short, compensation gave workers the assurance of compensation and it replaced the erratic coverage and low benefits of the private schemes and the costs and risks of litigation, although whether the compensation was fair depends upon perceptions of fairness and the terms of the compensation, which will be described later. The employers did not take the initiative in proposing compensation, but they eventually supported it because it promised to solve the problem of injured workers in an efficient, peaceful, and conservative way. They expressed some humanitarian motives, but not often, and did not disguise self-interest. Wegenast said: 'With us it is a matter of business, and is looked at very largely from a business standpoint.'[126] Compensation would increase costs, but not dramatically and probably not as much as some alternatives, especially the common law without the defences of the fellow servant rule, assumption of risk, and contributory negligence. Compensation did not threaten any major elements of the industrial capitalist system and it diminished the appeal of more radical solutions. Meredith was very sensitive about – horrified by might be a better phrase – socialism and any suggestion of fundamental conflict between classes. He concluded his final report by stressing the need to do justice 'in these days of social and industrial unrest' and hoping for 'the blessing of industrial peace and freedom from social unrest.'[127] This perspective on the proposal makes it consistent with much of government policy. In 1909 Whitney asserted that 'it is indeed a ghastly joke to charge the Ontario government with being socialistic etc., when it is the bulwark by means of which such influences will be shattered.'[128]

The principle of compensation and these reasons were not extensively discussed outside the hearings except in a few journals and newspapers sponsored by the participants, and these discussions tended simply to anticipate or to repeat positions expressed in the hearings.[129]

Given the consensus about the general principle of compensation, two limitations of its scope must be considered. First, it was compensation for the consequences of physical injury and not other work-related misfortunes. If the welfare element was the dominant reason, why was compensation not given for unemployment, which could be just as inevitable as accidents and could have the same consequences for dependants? This limitation was not discussed in any significant way, but perhaps unemployment was not considered to be as inevitable and as independent of fault as some accidents were, although compensation was also given for accidents caused by the fault of workers. To the extent that both were considered to be inevitable, perhaps accidents were made distinctive by the impact of visible physical injury and suffering, and the continuity of doctrine. Workers had always (at least since the early nineteenth century) had some right to compensation for work-related accidents, and the change was an expansion of this claim, not the creation of a new one. Second, the compensation was for accidents to workers at work, and not accidents or sickness happening to anyone else or anywhere else, which also could be just as inevitable as accidents at work and have just the same consequences for dependants. The participants in the hearing wondered occasionally how this limitation could be justified, especially as a departure from the general rules of the common law. They could not find any satisfying reasons, but continuity of doctrine and the existence of labour as a group and as a particular problem were probably strong pressures. Whatever power and cohesiveness workers may have had, persons who caught pneumonia or who tripped over a curb during an evening walk had none at all.

THE TERMS AND STRUCTURE FOR COMPENSATION

Given the acceptance of the principle of compensation, the particular scheme had to be chosen from a wide range of terms and structures. This choice was not determined by general pressures nearly as much as the acceptance of the principle itself. It was made primarily by the participants and especially by Meredith.

The question whether the common law claim would be barred was not extensively or carefully discussed. Wegenast asserted that a bar was necessary, and Bancroft conceded the loss at the outset of the hearings. The notion that a bargain had been made and that labour surrendered the claim for some unspecified benefits was mentioned only casually until the last few sessions, when the measure of benefits was debated. The question was important, because the bar prevented some, albeit a very few, workers from recovering much more than the compensation. The common law claim had been preserved in England and in most of the schemes in the United States. The decision and the lack of debate in Ontario is evidence of labour's lack of a coherent and considered program at the outset and the extent of dissatisfaction with the courts and fault.[130]

All the participants assumed that the employers would pay all or most of the compensation. (Whether workers would also contribute was a major issue, which will be discussed later.) This assumption presented two issues about structure: whether the responsibility to pay the compensation should be imposed upon individual employers or on groups of employers, and how the process of collection and payment should be administered, by courts, private associations, or a government agency. These issues were entangled with the issue of insurance for employees against accidents, which might be provided by private companies or the government, and which might be optional or compulsory. All these issues and possibilities could be arranged in many different combinations, which tended to reduce the differences among the primary choices, but the alternatives that were considered were limited and shaped by a comprehensive and persuasive analysis in Wegenast's brief and by the temptation to discuss existing schemes in other jurisdictions.

The English legislation was the pre-eminent example of imposition of responsibility on individual employers. Bancroft favoured the English example at the outset but did not understand it fully and confused it with the Washington legislation, which was substantially different. He revised his preferences later. Despite Bancroft's initial support and the appeal of English law to lawyers, individual liability never seemed to be a feasible possibility. It was alleged to have two peculiar disadvantages. First and most important, an employer liable to pay compensation might be unable to pay or might disappear, leaving the worker with a worthless claim. This disadvantage could be avoided, but only by adding regulations that made the scheme approach group liability. The second disadvantage was stressed by Wegenast and several of the witnesses he presented, and it was more debatable. They argued, in effect, that regulation for prevention of accidents could be more conveniently added to the administrative arrangements for group liability.

More generally, individual liability seemed to require courts, lawyers, and insurance, probably because the English scheme used them, and the English experience seemed to suggest that conflict, delay, inefficiency, and uncertainty had continued. Wegenast's statement that 'the great defect in the individual liability system is that it seeks to operate a socialist doctrine with inadequate individualistic machinery,' is a reminder to subsequent generations that they did not invent 'institutional design.'[131]

Group liability was opposed in principle only by Tecumseh Sherman, a witness from New York presented by the insurance companies, and by the railroads, especially the Canadian Pacific. Sherman seems to have made little impact on Meredith, but the railroads did. The CPR's brief asserted grandly that Canada had been developed by 'individualistic effort' and that its traditions were inconsistent with the 'bureaucratic supervision' grouping would require. It also argued that grouping would not prevent accidents because it would not impose the costs of accidents on the individual employers and would unfairly force employers with relatively good safety records to subsidize employers with poor records.[132] The unions of railroad workers objected that employers who were individually liable might penalize workers who made claims and that this prospect might discourage making claims at all. Meredith compromised. He recommended group liability for most employers and individual liability for a few, including railroads and units of municipal government, that seemed stable enough to ensure payment.

Virtually no room was left for the private insurance companies because most of the employers who were individually liable were self-insurers. The insurance companies made surprisingly little effort during and after the hearings to avoid this result. Their lawyers appeared late in the sessions, and neither their participation nor their briefs were impressive or forceful defences of insurance.[133]

Group liability seemed to need some institutions other than the courts for administration, and experience in other jurisdictions presented two models: associations of employers, which were used in Germany, and a government agency, which was used in several American states, especially Washington. Wegenast recommended a government agency and authorization for creation of associations of employers. Bancroft eventually also came to recommend an agency, and most of the other participants agreed without much apparent hesitation, either expressly or by assuming its existence in their discussions. Meredith recommended that for group liability the Board was to make and collect assessments from employers, to manage the fund, and to decide and pay claims by workers. For individual liability it was only to decide claims and order payment by the employers. The authority and the functions of the Board were centralized. Meredith and some of the employers occasionally wondered about decentralized administration using local boards, perhaps tripartite in composition, to consider claims, but the possibility was never developed, and Meredith did not even mention it in his reports. The use of an agency imposed the cost of administration on the public and deflected the conflict and hostility of making compensation away from employers.

This choice of an agency was an important part of making the compensation scheme and a deliberate decision to be different from England and the overwhelming majority of the states of the United States. It was also part of the beginnings of the growth of administrative agencies, which has continued throughout the century. This choice itself and questions of structure and procedure were not discussed extensively or rigorously, and the general implications were not considered or perceived.

Issues of principle about the use of an agency and appropriate allocation of functions were raised in a significant way only by the insurance companies and the railroads, and especially by the witnesses they brought from the United States. Their objections seemed to be set speeches, which had little effect and were forgotten after they left. Ontario Hydro and the Board of Railway Commissioners were often invoked as examples of efficient and analogous government functions, and the inappropriateness of the analogies demonstrates the lack of experience and insight about the nature of the institutional change. The immediate reasons for the choice were the apparent implications of group liability, and the strong determination to escape courts and lawyers, and these reasons were supported by the Canadian tradition of using the state to encourage private business activity.

There was a simple and widely shared concern that the Board be free from political pressures and control, and the contexts clearly demonstrated that 'political' meant day-to-day temptations and favours. Meredith was more sensitive than any of the participants to the need for the Board to have discretion to determine details and the need for government to have responsibility for policy. For example, he recommended that the Board have discretion to transfer industries from individual to group liability and among the groups but only with the approval of the government, and that it have discretion, without approval, to make sub-classes, to impose penalties on employers who had poor safety records, and to set the rates for each group. Only a few of the participants considered the relation between the courts and the Board. They preferred to follow the examples of England and the United States and to permit an appeal on questions of law. Meredith alone was determined to prevent any judicial supervision at all. He recommended no appeal and drafted one of the original privative clauses to bar review. Problems of procedure, especially the need to deal humanely and efficiently with large numbers of claims and the need for continuing lawmaking about entitlement, were virtually ignored. Late in the twentieth century these problems are still not solved, but they are painfully apparent. The lack of sensitivity to them may have been caused by the strength of the dissatisfaction with insurance and lawyers, who would presumably disappear, an unexamined and misleading faith in efficient business methods, and the prevailing assumptions about adjudication. The *Monetary Times* expressed the assumptions accurately and graphically by saying that lawyers believed cases were decided 'automatically, like the sand in an egg timer.'[134]

This compensation scheme governed most forms of employment in the province. Employees in farming, merchandising, and domestic service were the major groups excepted. During the hearings Meredith asked several times about the attitudes of farmers and was obviously worried about the political and administrative difficulties of including them, even though he was aware that large numbers of accidents happened on farms. Wegenast proposed that employers with fewer than five employees be excluded, because of the administrative difficulties they presented. These problems were real and were discussed, but Meredith ultimately disagreed. He proposed major changes for employment that was governed by the common law: abolition of the fellow servant rule and assumption of risk, and transformation of the role of contributory negligence from a prohibition against recovery to a measure of fault and damages. These changes were not extensively discussed during the sessions and were primarily a product of Meredith's beliefs about the existing law.

In short, the basic structure was made without any substantial or continuing disagreement. Conflict appeared over three secondary issues:

contribution to the fund by the workers, capitalization of pensions, and the amount of payments. The participants assumed without hesitation that employers would pay at least most of the compensation. The question whether workers would contribute appeared as a divisive issue during the first few moments of the first session. Wegenast proposed that the workers contribute and gave three reasons. The first was that the pride and self-respect of the workers required contribution, a reason he expressed in a patronizing and provocative way. The second was that prevention of accidents would be promoted if workers had a pecuniary interest in the fund, because they would be more willing to encourage compliance with safety requirements by fellow workers. Finally, 'justice' and 'natural justice' required that the workers pay whatever proportion of accidents was caused by their fault. At the outset Wegenast presented this proposal diffidently and almost as an empty form, but later he asserted that contributions from workers were a crucial condition of the CMA support.

The contrary arguments were that fault was no longer a measure of liability, that workers already contributed through a waiting period before compensation started and by receiving only a proportion of their salary as compensation, and that the 'irritation' of contribution would prejudice the harmonious relations between workers and employers. All these arguments were made well by Miles Dawson, a witness from New York presented by Wegenast himself. At the outset Meredith seemed noncommittal or even inclined towards contribution, but his attitude began to change when he heard Dawson, and near the end of the sessions he was clearly opposed.[135]

The second major conflict was about the capitalization of pensions. The choice was between two plans: capital cost and current cost. In the capital cost plan the rates for each year would include the capital value of the pensions awarded during the year. In the current cost plan the rates would include only enough for the payments to be made during that year plus a reserve, and the rates would rise slowly until they were equal to the rates for the capital cost. Wegenast proposed the current cost plan. He argued that the capital cost of pensions could not be accurately determined and, even if it could, the high initial rates would depress industry and tie up scarce capital. The current cost plan would avoid these difficulties and encourage prevention of accidents because the slow increase in the rates would be a continuing reminder of the cost of accidents. It became another of a list of allegedly crucial conditions of the support of the CMA. He never gathered much support for this proposal and perhaps not even much understanding, and he was strongly opposed by S.H. Wolfe, another witness from New York. Meredith was sceptical from the outset, primarily about the fairness of making the present pay for the past and the possibility that all of an industry, or a large part of it, might simply disappear, leaving an unfair burden on the remaining employers. The draft bill required the board to make assessments sufficient to pay the compensation in each year and to provide a reserve fund 'as the Board may deem necessary' to pay the claims created during that year. However, this discretion was limited by the requirement that the fund and reserves be sufficient to make all payments and not 'unduly or unfairly' burden employers with payments for accidents in the past. Meredith's proposal seems to have been an attempt to achieve three objectives: to avoid making the choice himself, to give the Board discretion to use its experience and expertise, and to ensure fairness. However, the result was confusing. The context gave no help for interpreting the words 'unduly or unfairly,' except to suggest that some kind of payment for claims from the past was fair and some was not. Wegenast not unreasonably presumed that the current cost plan was prohibited, even though Meredith argued that the Board had substantial discretion.[136]

The third issue was the amount of the payments. There was never any doubt that lump sum awards generally should not be made because the purpose of the compensation was to provide continuing support for workers who were temporarily or permanently unable to work or for the dependants of a worker who was killed. Meredith and Wegenast both often asserted in a patronizing way that workers were likely to squander a lump sum. Nor was there any doubt that the periodic payments would be a percentage of the worker's wages before the accident (except for the pensions for dependants). Bancroft made a proposal that a minimum amount be established, which Meredith abruptly rejected because it was in effect a proposal for a minimum wage. The particular percentage was not determined during the hearings, but it was clearly going to be at least fifty per cent and not much more. A worker who was temporarily disabled would receive the compensation until he or she returned to work, and workers who were permanently disabled and the dependants of workers who were killed at work would receive pensions. To provide a pension for life could be extremely costly, and the issue was whether some maximum limit would be imposed on the amount or the duration of the total payments. The issue was not discussed, and perhaps not even apparent to most of the participants until late in the sessions. Wegenast proposed a basic pension of $20 per month (to be increased to a maximum of $35 for dependant wives and children) or fifty per cent of wages, whichever was less. This was hardly generous, considering that in 1914 the minimum monthly expenditure for a family of five was about $90.00.[137] However, the proposal was more generous than the pensions in almost all other compensation schemes in common law jurisdictions, and it was exceeded by none. Meredith was immediately and firmly opposed to any limit, and the reason he gave was simple: a limit would deny the basic purpose of compensation. 'It just means the whole object of the act would be defeated, or at least one of the main objects ... A man is totally permanently disabled; every day he lives he gets less able probably to support himself ... and you cut him off just at a time that he would be thrown upon the charity of the world ...'[138]

Meredith presented a draft of his proposal at the second last session. The pensions for dependants in this draft were substantially the same as Wegenast's proposals; the amounts were not specified, but the understanding seemed to be that they would be substantially the same. But the pensions for permanently disabled workers had no limit; they were simply a percentage of wages for life. Wegenast protested vehemently that these pensions were extravagant and simply too expensive for manufacturers to pay: 'We have proposed a scale of benefits more generous than any other country in the world, and this is taken as a minimum instead of a maximum. We cannot conceive that it should involve such anomalous and oppressive results ...'[139] He seems to have persuaded Meredith to hesitate and to encourage a compromise, but no change was made.

In the last two sessions Wegenast was thoroughly routed. Meredith's proposal was a rejection of most of Wegenast's ideas, including proposals about prevention, contribution, current cost, and pensions. Wegenast remained uncharacteristically silent until the end of the session, when he said: 'I do not consider myself competent, on behalf of my clients, to go on discussing the proposition that has been brought down. It is so entirely and radically different from anything we had supposed was under consideration that I would like to ask for time to consult my clients with regard to it.'[140]

At the last session Wegenast restated his proposals forcefully, tactlessly, ineffectively, and unsuccessfully. The relationship between Meredith and Wegenast had occasionally seemed strained before. During this session it became far worse. Even more than sixty-five years later, the tension and hostility can be felt from the transcript. Counsel have rarely again, if ever, described a proposal made by a chief justice as 'preposterous,' 'beyond all reason,' and 'unjust and unreasonable.' Meredith replied in kind and occasionally humiliated Wegenast; he described his arguments as 'unreasonable objections,' 'nonsense,' 'purely fanciful,' 'monstrous,' and 'most improper,' and accused him of masking selfishness under complex arguments about structure.[141]

In retrospect, Wegenast deserves some sympathy. He contributed far more effort and imagination to the hearings than any other participant. He raised all the issues in his brief and focused much of the discussion, but he failed on all of the substantial and disputed issues. In contrast, Bancroft contributed little initiative and imagination to the design of the scheme. His function was to be a constant reminder to Meredith of labourers' interests and political power, and he performed it well.

THE ENACTMENT OF THE PROPOSAL

Meredith made some small changes to his draft, chose fifty-five per cent of salary for the level of benefits, and submitted a draft bill to the government on 1 April 1913. The legislature greeted the prospect of legislation with enthusiasm and support.[142] The new leader of the Liberal opposition, Newton Wesley Rowell, had already committed himself strongly to compensation. The platform for the provincial election in 1911 included compensation modelled on the English act.[143] In 1912 Rowell made a major speech on social legislation, which was dominated by an eloquent appeal for compensation. Accidents were an inescapable cost of industrial progress, and the cost should be imposed on industry: 'If modern industry demands this sacrifice, why should not industry bear the cost.' He set out principles for legislation, which avoided the commitment to the English act, and argued that it was humiliating for Ontario to lag behind the major countries of the Empire and Europe and even behind Spain and Russia.[144]

Both the CMA and labour waged campaigns about the bill. The CMA claimed that it wanted a compensation scheme but a fair one and attacked some of the terms of the proposal, especially the benefits. Wegenast wrote articles and submissions, including a detailed critique of Meredith's draft bill, but businessmen did not impose large and sustained pressure on the government.[145] Labour supported the proposal wholeheartedly, and the *Monetary Times* eventually complained that Meredith had become labour's 'particular pet.'[146] The campaign, organized primarily by Bancroft, was composed essentially of speeches to labour groups to encourage demonstrations of support.[147] The insurance business made only a modest effort. The *Monetary Times* editorially supported the proposal, except for the benefits and, of course, the use of an administrative agency.[148] The companies made a submission to the government that asked almost meekly that the employers have the option to be individually liable and therefore have the option to have private insurance. The submission was ignored.[149]

During January and February, Meredith revised the proposal privately for the government. Some of the notes for the revision were made on a copy of the CMA critique, and doubtless he took pleasure abusing his nameless but known critic.[150] He also made a speech to the Ontario Section of the Canadian Bar Association in which he explained his proposal a little more candidly than in the Final Report and said that

the Legislature should be careful to put upon the statute book a fair law, not to be influenced by the pressure of a strong body which wields a powerful influence to temporize with the matter, to give only half justice. There are some who think that the manufacturers of this country are pretty well taken care of, and it seems to me it is bad policy on the part of the manufacturers to antagonize the workmen at a time like this. There are sounds in the air of an attack upon their privileges, and I could not imagine a stronger weapon with which to attack than to say: 'You protect the manufacturers but you will not protect the working man.'[151]

The revised bill was given first reading on 17 March and debated on seven days during March and April. No new issues were introduced and the bill was enacted without any significant changes.[152] There is no doubt in retrospect, and there was none to the participants, that compensation legislation would be enacted and that it would be substantially the proposal made by Meredith. The CMA had openly accepted the principle of compensation for several years; the government owed little to the manufacturers; labour had demonstrated strong and widespread support; and, most important, Meredith's influence was great. He was widely known and respected; the long process of consultation and the extensive report itself gave the proposal an air of authority; and he had considerable informal influence on the government, especially on Whitney.[153]

LAWYERS' FUNCTIONS AND MINDS

The law in Canada changed greatly during the late nineteenth and early twentieth centuries and the coming of workers' compensation was part of this transition. It included changes in lawyers' practice, their beliefs about the proper content of law and the ways to think about it, and the functions of legal institutions.

The most visible alteration was the change in lawyers' practice. Before

1915 virtually all injured workers who sued and virtually all employers who were defendants were represented by lawyers, and doubtless countless others were given advice about the prospects of litigation. After 1915 this work ceased, abruptly and entirely. Only a very few workers claiming compensation from the Board have been represented; only a few of them have been represented by lawyers; and only a few members of the Board and its staff have been lawyers. Meredith in his speech to the Ontario lawyers said that compensation 'would no doubt be detrimental' and made a plea for support, but the record demonstrates lack of interest. Despite this predictable loss of work, lawyers did not participate extensively in the discussions of compensation, either individually or as a profession. The law journals contained relatively little about industrial accidents, and most of what did appear was descriptions of narrow points of doctrine. Beyond doctrine, *The Canada Law Times* published only the addresses by Meredith and Justice Middleton.[154] The *Canadian Law Journal* made strong editorial protests against reform in 1907 and 1908, but in 1912 the same editors accepted Meredith's interim report without adverse comment.[155] Individual lawyers participated in the hearings, but only as representatives, and the profession made no public statement.

There are two possible reasons for this record. First, the lawyers did not have a large and widely shared economic stake in the issue. The amounts to be recovered were relatively low; the plaintiffs were usually relatively poor, and contingent fees were prohibited. Lawyers for large employers or insurance companies generally had better prospects for collecting their fees, and some of these lawyers were among the leaders of the profession, but they did not lack work and most of these cases could not have been especially interesting or rewarding. Second, lawyers may have felt that this change was not part of their interest or competence as lawyers. Their vision of their function and reform seems to have been limited to the traditional practice, the common law, and the structure and procedure of courts. This reason merely transposes the search for explanations, but puts it beyond the scope of this essay.

The changes in beliefs about the content of law and the ways to think about it were much more complex and much more debatable. Workers' compensation abandoned the faith in individual autonomy and responsibility. Instead it gave a claim for compensation to a worker regardless of whether an accident was caused by the employer's fault, no one's fault, or even the worker's own fault, and the liability to pay the compensation became a general social responsibility rather than a product of an individual's fault. The participants in the hearings were well aware of the magnitude of this change and had various degrees of difficulty accepting it. For example, Meredith's problem in deciding that employees should not contribute was, in part at least, caused by his belief in individual responsibility. Contribution would be a symbolic recognition of principle by an individual employee and a collective responsibility of all employees. Meredith had even more difficulty accepting compensation for accidents caused by the fault of employees. During the first half of the hearings, he asked again and again why an employee who had caused an accident wilfully or recklessly or by disobeying rules should receive compensation.

The role of the state changed from the impersonal enforcement of the rules of conduct and liability to the provision of benefits. The adjudication of the individual claims was assumed without much discussion to be a simple and autonomous function, but discretion was considered and given for some other decisions, for example, about classes and reserves. In the background, the consideration of relevant causes and effects of accidents changed. The participants in the hearing considered machinery, working conditions, and tiredness as causes, contrasted to momentary personal failings, and much of the acceptance of the principle was based on perceptions of the effects of accidents on dependants and the community.

Much of this change, and many of the difficulties of thinking about it, are expressed in an exchange between Meredith and Dawson. Meredith suggested that compensation might be postponed and asked whether the employers' three defences should be abolished until it was established. Dawson replied:

Personally I would not ... I regard our present Employers' Liability Law as it stands with very slight modifications, if any, as just between man and man if the payment was finally going to rest on the shoulders of the man who was going to pay the money just now ... The reason why the system itself is wrong is because what we have really been doing is permitting John Jones over there, who in this matter is only an intermediary between the community at large as consumers, to be dealt with and treated precisely as if it was his loss ... I would not be in favour of a workmen's compensation system which held the employer individually liable.[156]

This answer demonstrates in a simple way the basic assumptions and beliefs about the common law, and especially its preoccupation with the conduct of immediate individuals. It also demonstrates the emerging awareness of interdependence and the remote consequences of conduct and liability, and an awareness that new institutions were needed to implement the new policy.

Other elements of the lawyers' beliefs were abandoned. The law about compensation was obviously not general and comprehensive because it governed only workers, and only workers while at work. Moreover, the terms for compensation could not be derived from some general rule about liability. The choice of fifty-five per cent as a level for benefits could not be related in any rational way to the choices about the length of the waiting period, contribution, and capitalization. They were all products of compromise, not rules. Finally, the justification of the law changed. Compensation was justified by efficiency, compromise, and acceptability, and by observation. Throughout, Meredith was openly determined to make a proposal that was politically acceptable and workable, but it would not have occurred to him, let alone to Baron Bramwell, that political acceptability, statistics about causes of accidents, or the ultimate incidence of liability were relevant to considering the rightness of the common law.[157] Some of this alteration in form, reasonings, and justification was probably a change in attitudes towards law generally, but much of it was instead a product of differences in beliefs about the proper function of courts and legislatures. Meredith must have felt more free, to say the least, to consider compromise and acceptability in proposing legislation than to change the common law acting as a judge.

Meredith and Wegenast accommodated these changes and the structure of the rule of law in their minds by making two compartments. One contained law, which included principle, the common law, and its interstitial legislation. The other included politics, expediency, legislation, and the change to compensation. A gulf between law and politics had existed in lawyers' minds for at least two centuries, but it probably became deeper and more apparent at this time, perhaps because the massive changes were usually done by legislation and made the lawyers' need for the gulf more pressing.

But Meredith probably was not thinking about these issues at the end of 1914. At the age of seventy-five he may simply have been pleased that he had accomplished much more for the workers than he had during his long years in the legislature.

NOTES

1 4 Geo. V (1914), c. 25 (Ont.), *Industrial Banner* 1 May 1914
2 Sir William Ralph Meredith CJO *Final Report on Laws Relating to the Liability of Employers to Make Compensation to Their Employees for Injuries Received in the*

Course of Their Employment Which Are in Force in Other Countries (Toronto 1913)
(hereafter *Final Report*) Minutes of Evidence 505–6, 578

3 The story of workers' compensation in Ontario has been already told in D.
Guest *The Emergence of Social Security in Canada* (Vancouver, BC 1980) ch. 4,
D.J. Campbell 'The Balance Wheel of the Industrial System: Maximum Hours,
Minimum Wage, and Workmen's Compensation Legislation in Ontario, 1900–
1939' (PH D thesis, McMaster University 1980), and Michael J. Piva 'The Work-
men's Compensation Movement in Ontario' *Ontario History* LXVII (1975) 39.
The difference between these writings and this essay is in part a product of
differences in perspectives.

4 Description of this law can be found in the multitude of late nineteenth- and
early twentieth-century texts on torts generally and on employers' liability in
particular. One of the most useful is T. Bevan *Principles of the Law of Negligence*
(London 1889) book 1, part 3.

5 (1837), 3 M & W 1, 150 ER 1030 (Exch.). For discussion and references, see
Leonard W. Levy *Law of the Commonwealth and Chief Justice Shaw* (Cambridge,
MA 1957) ch. 10, Morton J. Horowitz *The Transformation of American Law 1780–
1860* (Cambridge, MA 1977) 208–10, Lawrence M. Friedman and Jack Ladinsky
'Social Change and the Law of Industrial Accidents' *Columbia Law Review* LXVII
(1967) 50, and T. Ingman 'The Rise and Fall of the Doctrine of Common Employment' 23 *Juridical Review* (NS) XXIII (1978) 106.

6 (1842) 45 Mass. (4 Met.) 49

7 (1858), 3 Macqueen 266, 31 *Law Times* (OS) 255

8 Robert Gordon 'Review' *Harvard Law Review* XCIV (1981) 903 (hereafter HLR);
Gordon 'Lawyers and Legal Thought in the Age of Enterprise: Notes towards
an *Ideological* Approach' forthcoming in *The Professions in the Modern West*,
ed. Gerald Geison

9 *Torpy v Grand Trunk Railway* (1861), 20 *Upper Canada Queen's Bench Reports*
(hereafter UCQB) 446; *Deverill v Grand Trunk Railway* (1866), 25 UCQB 517; *Plant
v Grand Trunk Railway* (1867), 27 UCQB 78; *Vicary v Keith* (1873), 34 UCQB 212;
Sheerman v Toronto, Grey, and Bruce Railway (1874), 34 UCQB 451; *Macdonald v
Dick* (1874), 34 UCQB 623; *Jarvis v May* (1876), 26 *Upper Canada Common Pleas
Reports* (hereafter UCCP) 523; *O'Sullivan v Victoria Railway* (1879), 44 UCQB 128;
Wilson v Hume (1880), 30 UCCP 542; *Drew v East Whitby* (1881), 46 UCQB 107;
McFarlane v Gilmour (1884), 5 *Ontario Reports* (hereafter OR) 302; *May v Ontario
and Quebec Railway* (1885), 10 OR 70; *Miller v Reid* (1885), 10 OR 419; *Matthews v
Hamilton Powder Company* (1886), 12 OR 58; 14 *Ontario Appeal Reports* (hereafter
OAR) 261; *Rudd v Bell* (1887), 13 OR 47; *Murphy v Ottawa* (1887), 13 OR 334

10 *Deverill v Grand Trunk Railway*, above note 9; *Plant v Grand Trunk Railway*,
above note 9; *O'Sullivan v Victoria Railway*, above note 9; *Wilson v Hume*,

above note 9; *Drew* v *East Whitby*, above note 9; *McFarlane* v *Gilmour*, above note 9; *May* v *Ontario and Quebec Railway*, above note 9; and *Matthews* v *Hamilton Powder Company*, above note 9

11 *Plant* v *Grand Trunk Railway*, above note 9; *McFarlane* v *Gilmour*, above note 9

12 Above note 9

13 Above note 9

14 Railway Clauses Consolidation Act, 14 & 15 Vict. (1851), c. 51 (Can.)

15 Accidents on Railways Act, 1857, 20 Vict., c. 12 (Can.)

16 For example, Railway Act, 22 Vict. (1859), c. 66 (Can.); Railway Act, 1868, 31 Vict. c. 68 (Can.); Consolidated Railway Act, 1879, 42 Vict. c. 9 (Can.); An Act Further to Amend 'The Consolidated Railway Act, 1879,' 47 Vict. (1884), c. 11 (Can.); Railway Act, 51 Vict. (1888), c. 29 (Can.); An Act Further to Amend Railway Act, 55 & 56 Vict. (1892), c. 27 (Can.); Railway Act, 1903, 3 Edw. vii c. 58 (Can.); Railway Act of Ontario, *Revised Statutes of Ontario* (hereafter RSO) 1877 c. 165; Railway Accidents Act, 1881, 44 Vict. c. 22 (Ont.)

17 Consolidated Railway Act, 1879, above note 16, s. 15.5

18 Railway Accidents Act, 1881, above note 16

19 Railway Act, 1888, above note 16, ss. 192.4, 262; Railway Act, 1903, above note 16, ss. 211, 230

20 Ontario Railway Act, 1906, 6 Edw. vii, c. 30, s. 76(3)

21 See Margaret A. Evans 'Oliver Mowat and Ontario 1872–1896: A Study in Political Success' (PH D thesis, University of Toronto 1967); Eugene Forsey 'A Note on the Dominion Factory Bills of the 1880s' *Canadian Journal of Economics and Political Science* XIII (1947) 580 (hereafter CJEPS); Bernard Ostry 'Conservatives, Liberals and Labour in the 1880s' CJEPS XXVIII (1961) 141.

22 Ontario Factories Act, 1884, 47 Vict. c. 39 (Ont.); Ontario Factories Amendment Act, 1889, 52 Vict. c. 43; Factories Amendment Act, 1895, 58 Vict. c. 50 (Ont.); An Act to Further Improve the Factories Act, 1 Edw. vii (1901), c. 35 (Ont.); An Act to Amend the Ontario Factories Act, 2 Edw. vii (1902), c. 36 (Ont.); An Act to Amend the Factories Act, 4 Edw. vii (1904), c. 26 (Ont.)

23 Mining Operations Act, 1890, 53 Vict. c. 10 (Ont.). In 1892 this act was incorporated in the Mines Act, 1892, 55 Vict. c. 9 (Ont.).

24 An Act to Amend the Mines Act, 63 Vict. (1900), c. 13 (Ont.); Mining Amendment Act, 1912, 2 Geo. v c. 8 (Ont.)

25 49 Vict. (1886), c. 28 (Ont.)

26 Workmen's Compensation for Injuries Amendment Act, 1889, 52 Vict., c. 23 (Ont.). Three smaller amendments were made: An Act to Amend the Workmen's Compensation for Injuries Act, 1886, 50 Vict. (1887), c. 22 (Ont.); An Act to Amend the Workmen's Compensation for Injuries Act, 1892, 56 Vict. (1893), c. 26 (Ont.); and An Act to Make Certain Amendments to the Statute

Law, 60 Vict. (1897), c. 14 s. 6 (Ont.). The act was consolidated in 1892 by
the Workmen's Compensation for Injuries Act, 1892, 55 Vict. c. 30 (Ont.).

27 Employer's Liability Act, 1880, 43 & 44 Vict., c. 42 (UK)

28 See D.G. Haines *The First British Workmen's Compensation Act, 1897* (New
Haven, CT 1968) ch. 2, and Peter Bartrip and Sandra Burman *The Wounded
Soldiers of Industry: Industrial Compensation Policy, 1833–1897* (Oxford, forthcoming). For Bramwell's arguments, see, for example, a submission to a select
committee in the form of a letter to its chairman, Sir Henry Jackson, dated
9 June 1880, and reproduced in the *Sessional Papers of Ontario* (hereafter Sessional Papers), Vol. 17 (1885) No. 56.

29 See the references in note 20 above, and Gregory S. Kealey *Toronto Workers
Respond to Industrial Capitalism 1867–1892* (Toronto 1980) ch. 12.

30 Ontario Judicature Act, 44 Vict. (1881), c. 5

31 Law Reform Act, 9 Edw. VII (1909), c. 28, s. 7 (Ont.), which came into effect
on 1 Jan. 1913. Confusion was created for readers decades later by dividing the
Court of Appeal into divisions, which were also called Divisional Courts.
See the essay by Margaret Banks in this volume.

32 County Courts Act, RSO 1887, c. 47, s. 19.1; An Act Respecting the County
Courts ... 10 Edw. VII (1910), c. 30, s. 22 (Ont.)

33 County Courts Act, RSO 1887, c. 47, ss. 41, 42; Law Courts Act, 1895, 58 Vict.,
c. 13, s. 44(1) (Ont.); Law Reform Act, 1909, s. 10(3) above note 31

34 Ontario Archives, RG 22, Wentworth, Supreme Court Actions and Matters
Files. The documents for actions begun in each county are stored together,
roughly chronologically. Despite the availability of some lists and ledgers kept
by the court office, it is difficult to determine whether they are complete for
any year and, if they are not, what is missing. My impression from all the
sources is that they are substantially complete for this county and this period.
I thank Catherine Shepard of the Archives staff for help kindly and generously
given, and Candy Saga, a student at the Faculty of Law of the University of
Toronto for patience and ingenuity in finding the workers' actions among all
the others and doing counting for the tables.

Before 1900 the reports were the *Ontario Reports* and the *Ontario Appeals
Reports*, for which the editors selected only some of the judgments. In 1900
these reports were replaced by the *Ontario Law Reports*, which also included
only some of the judgments. In 1902 another series began: the *Ontario Weekly
Reporter*, which included far more judgments and claimed to report all appeals
decided in Toronto. In 1909 the *Ontario Weekly Notes* began, which also included far more judgments than the *Ontario Law Reports*.

35 Statistics about the total volume of cases can be found in the *Report of the Inspector of Legal Offices*, printed annually in the Sessional Papers.

36 The numbers and kinds of accidents are difficult to determine even very roughly. Some evidence can be gathered from reports of inspectors of factories, mines, and railroads, but these reports have large deficiencies, some of which are apparent simply from reading them. It is tempting to assume that the numbers of accidents and their severity increased more or less continuously with industrialization, but the temptation is dangerous. Much careful research and analysis are needed before any firm conclusions can be made; such work is beyond the scope of this essay. For some of the difficulties and figures for England, see Bartrip and Burman *Wounded Soldiers of Industry*. In 1908 a speaker raised the question during a discussion at the Insurance Institute of Toronto and suggested that guards and factory inspectors may have even reduced the rate of accidents (proceedings of the Insurance Institute of Toronto, 1907–8, 25 Feb. 1908).

37 These figures do not include grants of new trials and variations in the amounts of damages because it is difficult to determine what was really at stake and who succeeded. If they are included and counted as wins for the appellant, the percentages change, but the distinctiveness of the workers' cases does not disappear: railways fail in 53 per cent of challenges, employers fail in 60 per cent, and defendants in defamation cases fail in 50 per cent. Another way of making the comparison is to include cases in which plaintiffs appeal and compare plaintiffs' success rates: a difference is presumably not attributable to the common element, the jury. The figures are 67 per cent in railway cases, 82 per cent in workers' cases, and 57 per cent in defamation cases excluding new trials and variations of damages, and 53 per cent, 63 per cent, and 50 per cent inclusive.

38 Much of this analysis was prompted by an unpublished paper by G.L. Priest and B. Klein 'The Selection of Disputes for Litigation' given in Jan. 1981 at a workshop of the Law and Economics Programme at the Faculty of Law, University of Toronto.

39 Michael J. Piva *The Condition of the Working Class in Toronto – 1900–1921* (Ottawa 1979) 27–59

40 In *Hallett* v *Abraham* (1914), 6 OWN 355 Justice Lennox managed to persuade himself that section 3(1) could be expanded to make a contractor liable to an employee of a sub-contractor for a defect in the absence of a common law duty.

41 (1905), 9 OLR 86; (1905) 10 OLR 647; (1906), 13 OLR 548

42 (1890), 19 OR 76; affirmed on other grounds (1891), 18 OAR 437

43 See, for example, *Wilson* v *Owen Sound Portland Cement* (1900), 27 OAR 328; *Fraser* v *Algoma Central and Hudson Bay Railway* (1904), 3 OWR 104; *Woods* v *Toronto Bolt and Forging* (1905), 11 OLR 216; *McCarthy* v *Kilgour* (1906), 7 OWR 44; *Connell* v *Ontario Lantern and Lamp* (1906), 7 OWR 77; *Lougheed* v *Collingwood*

Shipbuilding (1908), 12 OWR 871; *Kirkby* v *Briggs* (1911), 2 OWN 1511; *Simpson* v *Tallman Brass and Metal* (1911), 3 OWN 398; *Corea* v *McClary Manufacturing* (1912), 3 OWN 1071; *Chadwick* v *Tudhope* (1914), 6 OWN 151, affirmed with reduced damages (1914), 6 OWN 363.

44 See, for example, *Madden* v *Hamilton Iron Forging* (1889), 18 OR 55; *Aillo* v *Fauquier* (1902), 1 OWR 833; *Miller* v *King* (1904), 34 SCR 710, *Mitchell* v *Canada Foundry* (1904), 3 OWR 907; *Parker* v *Lake Erie and Detroit River Railway* (1905), 5 OWR 634; *Bassani* v *Canadian Pacific Railway* (1906), 7 OWR 271; *Higgins* v *Hamilton Electric Light and Cateract Power* (1906), 7 OWR 505; *Frawley* v *Hamilton Steamboat* (1907), 10 OWR 308; *Kitts* v *Phillips* (1907), 10 OWR 986, and *Grand Trunk Pacific Railway* v *Brulott* (1911), 46 *Supreme Court Reports* (hereafter SCR) 629.

45 See, for example, *Snell* v *Toronto Railway* (1900), 27 OAR 151; *Muma* v *Canadian Pacific Railway* (1907), 14 OLR 147; *Darrant* v *Canadian Pacific Railway* (1908), 12 OWR 294; *Smith* v *Grand Trunk Railway* (1912), 3 OWN 659; *Jones* v *Canadian Pacific Railway* (1913), 30 OLR 331; *Allan* v *Grand Trunk Railway* (1912), 4 OWN 325; and *McCauley* v *Grand Trunk Railway* (1914), 7 OWN 336.

46 (1910), 20 OLR 335. See also *Dunlop* v *Canada Foundry* (1913), 28 OLR 141.

47 Also, the action had to be commenced within six months or, if the worker died, within twelve months. The employer had to give notice of intention to rely on lack of notice as a defence.

48 (1902), 4 OLR 560. See also *Cox* v *Hamilton Sewer Pipe* (1887), 14 OR 300; *Cavanagh* v *Park* (1896), 23 OAR 715; *Potter* v *McCann* (1908), 16 OLR 535; *Giovinazzo* v *Canadian Pacific Railway* (1909), 19 OLR 325; *Leitch* v *Pere Marquette Railway* (1911), 2 OWN 617; *Quist* v *Serpent River Logging* (1912), 4 OWN 159; *Gower* v *Glen Woollen Mills* (1913), 28 OLR 193

49 *Railway Accidents Act*, 1881, above note 16, s. 7; *Railway Act*, (1888), above note 16, s. 289 (s. 243 also gave a cause of action, but it was much more re-stricted); *Railway Act*, 1903, above note 16, s. 211; *Ontario Railway Act*, 1906, 6 Edw. VII c. 30, ss. 764, 243 (Ont.)

50 *Le May* v *Canadian Pacific Railway* (1889), 18 OR 314; affirmed (1890), 17 OAR 293. The breach was a failure to pack frogs, and Chief Justice Hagarty said that: 'It must certainly be a matter of very great regret if the court requires us to hold that the certain statutable requirements for the safety apparently of all persons must be held to have excluded from its operation the class almost exclusively affected by the non-observance.'

51 (1914), 32 OLR 380

52 (1908), 16 OLR 365

53 *Dean* v *Ontario Cotton Mills* (1887), 14 OR 119. See also *Finlay* v *Miscampbell* (1890), 20 OR 29; *Thompson* v *Wright* (1892), 22 OR 127; and *Goodwin* v *Newcombe* (1901) 1 OLR 525.

54 (1892) 19 OAR 117

55 *Sault Ste Marie Pulp and Paper* v *Myers* (1902), 33 SCR 23. Subsequent cases are *McBain* v *Waterloo Manufacturing* (1906), 8 OWR 333; *Lennox* v *McAuliffe* (1908), 12 OWR 181; *Doherty* v *MacDonell* (1910), 1 OWN 368; and *Oskey* v *Kingston* (1914), 32 OLR 190.

56 (1915), 33 OLR 557. See also *Hunt* v *Webb* (1913), 28 OLR 589; *Scholfield* v *Blome* (1913), 5 OWN 328; and *Doyle* v *Foley-O'Brien* (1915), 7 OWN 780.

57 (1912), 25 OLR 524

58 (1899), 31 OR 10

59 (1901), 1 OLR 18; reversed (1901), 2 OLR 449

60 (1904), 8 OLR 419; affirmed (1905), 10 OLR 526

61 *Le May* v *Canadian Pacific Railway*, above note 50; *Sault Ste Marie Pulp and Paper* v *Myers*, above note 55

62 *Dean* v *Ontario Cotton Mills*, above note 53; *McClemont* v *Kilgour Manufacturing* (1912), 27 OLR 305

63 In *Dean* v *Ontario Cotton Mills* above note 53, Justice Armour and Chief Justice Sir Adam Wilson divided about the effect of knowledge of the danger but granted recovery under the Workmen's Compensation Act. In *Le May* v *Canadian Pacific Railway*, above note 50, Chancellor Boyd and Justice Thomas Ferguson held that knowledge the worker should reasonably have had, but did not have, was not to be considered. In *Madden* v *Hamilton Iron Forging* (1889), 18 OR 55, Justice Hugh MacMahon held that continuing to work despite a known risk, because of fear of dismissal, was not a voluntary acceptance of the risk; this holding was repeated several times. It was a recognition of dependence and power that the courts had made fifty years before in making the general rules. See also *Haight* v *Wortman and Ward Manufacturing* (1894), 24 OR 618.

64 [1891] *Appeal Cases* (hereafter AC) 325

65 (1904), 8 OLR 588

66 See, for example, *Godwin* v *Newcombe* (above note 53; *Fraser* v *Algoma Central and Hudson Bay Railway* (1904), 3 OWR 104; *McCarthy* v *Kilgour* (1906), 7 OWR 44; *Connell* v *Ontario Lantern and Lamp* (1906), 7 OWR 77; *Fairweather* v *Canadian General Electric* (1913), 28 OLR 300; and *Phillips* v *Canada Cement* (1914), 6 OWN 185. The jury findings were upset in *Reid* v *Paul* (1904), 3 OWR 821; *Smith* v *Royal Canadian Yacht Club* (1911), 3 OWN 19; and *Pressick* v *Cordova Mines* (1913), 4 OWN 1334.

67 See, for example, *McCarthy* v *Kilgour* (1906), 8 OWR 515, reversed 7 OWR 44; *Corea* v *McClary Manufacturing* (1912), 3 OWN 1071.

68 See, for example, *Goodwin* v *Newcombe*, above note 53; *Holman* v *Times Printing* (1902), 1 OWR 756; and *Connell* v *Ontario Lantern and Lamp* (1906), 8 OWR 201. In *Mercantile Trust* v *Canada Steel* (1912), 3 OWN 980, Justice William Riddell

held that 'pure inadvertance ... a mere temporary forgetfulness ... was contributory negligence,' but the context did not involve repetitive actions, and Riddell was conspicuously harsh towards workers. In *McIntosh v Firstbrook Box*, above note 60, Justice John Idington said: 'He laid his hand upon a dangerous machine ... simply in a moment of thoughtlessness or forgetfulness or inattention when passing it.' See also *Moore v J.D. Moore Co.* (1902), 4 OLR 167.

69 See, for example, *Choate v Ontario Rolling Mill* (1900), 27 OAR 155; *Sim v Dominion Fish* (1901), 2 OLR 69; *Cassellman v Barry* (1906), 7 OWR 328; *Dodds v Consumers Gas* (1907), 9 OWR 905; *Dagg v McLaughlin* (1908), 11 OWR 1080; *Fralick v Grand Trunk Railway* (1910), 43 SCR 494; *Magnussen v L'Abbé* (1911), 3 OWN 301; *Stokes v Griffin Curled Hair* (1912), 3 OWN 1414; and *Sturgeon v Canada Iron Corporation* (1913), 4 OWN 1386. The most difficult issue of doctrine about common law liability was whether an employer could satisfy the duty to take reasonable care by assigning the function to a competent employee, for whose negligence the employer would be liable only under the Workmen's Compensation Act. In *Canada Woollen Mills v Traplin* (1904), 35 SCR 424, Justice Davies sought to declare the governing general principles.

70 Above note 9

71 (1908), 11 OWR 1030. In 1909 the Toronto Trades and Labour Council disapproved a rumoured proposal to abolish juries in claims by street railway employees and approved attempts to restrict appeals from jury verdicts to workers under $1000, Minutes, 18 Feb. 1909.

72 (1899), 29 SCR 478, reversing 25 OAR 36, affirming 28 OR 73

73 See, for example, *Badgerow v Grand Trunk Railway* (1890), 19 OR 191; *Farmer v Grand Trunk Railway* (1891), 21 OR 299; *Young v Owen Sound Dredge* (1900), 27 OAR 649; *Armstrong v Canada Atlantic Railway*, above note 48; *Brown v Waterous Engine Works* (1904), 8 OLR 37; *Finch v Northern Navigation* (1906), 8 OWR 412; *Thompson v Ontario Sewer Pipe* (1907), 11 OWR 32; and *Brennan v Grand Trunk Railway* (1910), 1 OWN 365. Examples of cases in which the evidence was sufficient are *Billing v Semmens* (1904), 7 OLR 340; and *Jones v Canadian Pacific Railway* (1912), 30 OLR 331.

74 Above note 9

75 Ibid.

76 See P.S. Atiyah *From Principles to Pragmatism: Changes in the Function of the Judicial Process* (Oxford 1978); O. Kahn-Freund 'Review of Atiyah' *Journal of the Society of the Public Teachers of Law* xv (1980) 81; and J. Stone 'From Principles to Principles' *Law Quarterly Review* xcvii (1981) 224.

77 See, for example, Lawrence M. Friedman *A History of American Law* (New York 1973) 540–1; Horwitz above note 5, ch. 8; Karl Llewellyn *The Common Law*

Tradition: Deciding Appeals (Boston 1960) 38–40; Stevens *Law and Politics: The House of Lords as a Judicial Body, 1800–1976* (Chapel Hill, NC 1978) chs 2, 3, and 4; Grant Gilmore 'Formalism and the Law of Negotiable Instruments' *Creighton Law Review* XIII (1979) 441; Duncan Kennedy 'Form and Substance in Private Law Adjudication' HLR LXXXIX (1976) 1685; William E. Nelson 'The Impact of the Antislavery Movement upon Styles of Judicial Reasoning in Nineteenth-Century America' HLR LXXXVII (1974) 513; and Stephen A. Siegel 'The Aristotelian Basis of English Law' *New York University Law Review* LVI (1981) 18.

78 Jennifer Nedelsky 'Judicial Conservatism in an Age of Innovation: Comparative Perspectives on Canadian Nuisance Law 1880–1930' in David H. Flaherty, ed. *Essays in the History of Canadian Law* 2 vols (Toronto 1981–3) I 281

79 For some observations on the courts in the mid-nineteenth century, see, R.C.B. Risk 'The Law and the Economy in Mid-Nineteenth-Century Ontario: A Perspective' in Flaherty, ed. *Essays in the History of Canadian Law* I 107

80 See the *Labour Gazette* III (1903) 900.

81 *Report of the Inspector of Insurance and Registrar of Friendly Societies, 1909* Sessional Papers Vol. 42 (1910), Number 10, Division C, Comparative Tables Showing ... Sick and Funeral Benefits Table 2

82 (1882), 9 *Queen's Bench Reports* 357

83 See Bartrip and Burman *Wounded Soldiers of Industry.*

84 The issue was raised several times in Quebec. In *The Queen v Grenier* (1899), 30 SCR 42, a release imposed by the International Railway was considered, and Chief Justice Sir Henry Strong said: 'that a workman may so contract with his employer as to exonerate the latter from liability for negligence for which the former would otherwise be entitled to recover damages cannot be disputed. Further that such a renunciation would be a sufficient answer to an action under Lord Campbell's Act is conclusively settled by authority: *Griffiths v Earl of Dudley*, 9 Q.B.D. 357.' In *Ferguson v Grand Trunk Railway* 20 *Quebec Supreme Court Reports* 54, the release of the Grand Trunk was enforced, although several members of the court reserved their opinions about some negligence of an employer personally. In Ontario the issue was considered squarely only in trial judgments. In *Holden v Grand Trunk Railway* (1903), 2 OWR 80, the agreement was enforced at trial but on appeal the decision was affirmed on other grounds. Justice Osler said 'it becomes unnecessary to consider the other ground of defense.' In *Harris v Grand Trunk Railway* (1904), 3 OWR 211, the trial judgment in *Holden* was invoked, but the facts seem to have involved a release given after the accident in return for a payment. Releases of this kind are substantially different from an agreement made before an accident. There could have been no doubt that they were generally enforceable, although the courts were clearly sympathetic to claims such as duress and incapacity.

85 The Railway Act, 1888, above note 16, s. 243, which included some safety provisions for passenger trains, gave a cause of action 'notwithstanding any agreement to the contrary.' In the Railway Act, 1903, above note 16, this section was expanded to include more safety provisions and all trains, but the 'notwithstanding ...' provision was qualified by adding 'unless such agreement is conformable to the law of the province in which it is made and is authorized by a regulation of the Board.' This section was adopted in the Ont. Railway Act, 1906, above note 20, s. 76, except for the qualification. In 1904 the federal government enacted a comprehensive prohibition against contracting out of liability (4 Edw. VII [1904], c. 31), which was aimed primarily at the Grand Trunk fund, but it was not to be effective until a reference was made to the Supreme Court to determine its constitutionality, and, if constitutional, until it was proclaimed by the Governor General in Council. The Privy Council held it was *intra vires* in *Grand Trunk Railway* v *Attorney General of Canada* [1907] AC 65.

86 The courts only considered these requirements a few times. The sole carefully considered judgment involved a plan established by International Harvester. The company made specified payments upon death, loss of limbs or eyesight, or disability. The employees contributed three-quarters of one per cent of their salary and receipt of benefits was a waiver of other claims. Justice Riddell held that this waiver was not a bar of a common law claim, if benefits were not taken and therefore the employee had a choice. Given this interpretation, he concluded that the plan was fair and the plaintiff, having accepted benefits, failed. An appeal by the plaintiff succeeded, but no reasons were given: *Fisher* v *International Harvester* (1908), 12 OWR 1126; reversed (1909) 13 OWR 381.

87 The information in this and the preceding paragraph is taken from the tables in the *Report of the Superintendent of Insurance ... 1910*, above note 81.

88 Workmen's Compensation Act, 1897, 60 & 61 Vict. c. 37 (UK)

89 Some recent discussions of developments in the United States are Roy Lubove *The Struggle for Social Security 1900–1935* (Cambridge, MA 1968) ch. 2; James Weinstein *The Corporate Ideal in the Liberal State 1900–1918* (Boston 1968) ch. 2; Robert Asher 'Business and Workers' Welfare in the Progressive Era: Workmen's Compensation Reform in Massachusetts, 1888–1911' *Business History Review* XLIII (1969) 452; Asher 'The 1911 Wisconsin Workmen's Compensation Law: A Study in Conservative Labor Reform' *Wisconsin Magazine of History* LIX (1973), 123; Asher 'The Origins of Workmen's Compensation in Minnesota' *Minnesota History* XLIV (1974) 142; Asher 'Radicalism and Reform: State Insurance of Workmen's Compensation in Minnesota, 1910–1933' *Labor History* XIV (1973) 19; Friedman and Ladinsky 'Social Change ...' and J. Tripp 'An

Instance of Labour and Business Co-operation: Workmen's Compensation in Washington State (1911)' *Labor History* XVII (1976) 530.

90 Workmen's Compensation Act, 1902, 2 Edw. VII, c. 74 (BC); Workmen's Compensation Act 1908, 8 Edw. VII c. 12 (Alta.); Workmen's Compensation Act, 1910, 10 Edw. VII, c. 81 (Man.); Nova Scotia Workmen's Compensation Act, 10 Edw. VII (1910), c. 3, (NS); Workmen's Compensation Act, 1910–11, c. 9 (Sask.); An Act Respecting the Responsibility for Accidents Suffered by Workmen ... , 9 Edw. VII (1909), c. 66 (Que.); The background of the Quebec Act is discussed in J.T. Copp *The Anatomy of Poverty: The Condition of the Working Class in Montreal 1897–1929* (Toronto 1974) 123–6. The reports of the Royal Commission on the Relations of Labour and Capital (1889) made recommendations about compensation. The commissioners seemed to assume that the fellow servant rule was the only obstacle to recovery and had been removed in Ontario by the 1886 act. This mistake made the recommendations confusing, but the general objective was to permit recovery even though the employer had not been negligent, unless the worker had been negligent. The recommendations had no effect. See Gregory S. Kealey *Canada Investigates Industrialism* (Toronto 1973) 17, 33.

91 *Journals of the Legislative Assembly, 1898*, 72, 175. The bill was opposed by several petitions, ibid. 124, 137. See *Globe* 16 Mar. 1899. The *Bulletin*, an insurance journal, reported predictions of a 'large increase in employers' liability and accident insurance' if the bill were enacted, VIII (1899), 53.

92 *Workmen's Compensation for Injuries* Sessional Papers, Vol. 32 (1900) Number 40. A letter from Premier George Ross to Mavor on 10 Jan. 1900, urged Mavor to report before 1 Feb. to enable the government to consider legislation before the legislature met. (Mavor Papers, Thomas Fisher Rare Book Room, University of Toronto)

93 S.E.D. Shortt *The Search for an Ideal: Six Canadian Intellectuals and Their Convictions in an Age of Transition 1890–1930* (Toronto 1976) 123

94 Inspectors appointed under the Factories Act made annual reports, which were reprinted in the Sessional Papers and which are primarily lists and descriptions of accidents. Comments about the need for guards or machinery and proposals to compel manufacturers to install them were common. Compensation and claims by workers were rarely mentioned, and an early proposal for a compensation scheme stood alone (Sessional Papers, XXII [1890] Number 35, 14). For discussions of the role of private reform groups, see Asher 'Business and Workers' Welfare in the Progressive Era'; Copp *Anatomy of Poverty*, and Bartrip and Burman *Wounded Soldiers of Industry*.

95 See Margaret Prang *N.W. Rowell: Ontario Nationalist* (Toronto 1975) 91–134; Charles Humphries 'The Political Career of Sir James P. Whitney' (PH D thesis,

University of Toronto 1966); and Humphries 'The Sources of Ontario "Progressive" Conservatism, 1900–1914' *Canadian Historical Association Papers*, 1967, 118.

96 *Globe* 9 Mar. 1899, 9

97 *Journals*, 1907, 51, 305. Assertions about an undertaking are made in *Industrial Canada* IX (1908) 219, in a speech by N.W. Rowell, the leader of the Liberal opposition, in Woodstock on 29 Aug. 1912 (Ontario Archives, Pamphlet), and in the *Industrial Banner* 23 Jan. 1914.

98 Trades and Labour Congress of Canada, Proceedings, 1910, Report of the Executive Committee for the Province of Ontario (10 Aug. 1910): 'The most important legislation for consideration of your Committee this year has been the contemplated alteration, revision or substitution of a new Act by the Ontario Government for the present obsolete Workmen's Compensation Act. It came first to our knowledge during the American Federation of Labour Convention held in Toronto last November ... it was thought advisable to present our views this year to the Cabinet before the session opened and consequently before legislation was shaped for the Legislature ... The Premier assured us that a Commission would be appointed and lately it has been announced that Sir W. Meredith was the Commissioner and organized labour is now preparing evidence, as the present Act in Ontario is, in the opinion of many, the worst on the North American Continent.'

99 *Journals*, 1910, 7. On 27 Jan. 1910 Whitney stressed the need for uniformity among the provinces, *Globe* 27 Jan. 1910, and in Mar., William Proudfoot, a Liberal member, introduced a compensation bill, which failed to get second reading, *Journals*, 1910, 182, 220. On 2 Mar. 1911 Proudfoot asked what the government was doing about the compensation issue, and Whitney simply said that Meredith was considering it.

100 Middleton 'Legal Reform' *Canadian Law Times* XXXI (1911) 138

101 *Globe* 2 Mar. 1885. The major differences from the English act were: an exclusion of the fellow servant rule in claims for the negligence of any fellow servant in a 'separate and distinct' part of the employer's business; an expansion of section 3(5) to include 'or any other engine, boiler, or other machinery'; an increase in the limitation on recovery to five years' wages; a prohibition against contracting out; and an expansion of the scope to include domestic employees.

102 What has been written about Meredith emphasizes his role as a politician. See Peter Dembski 'William Ralph Meredith: Leader of the Conservative Opposition in Ontario' (PH D thesis, University of Guelph 1977); and Sherree Mahood 'William Ralph Meredith and the Ontario Progressive Party: Social Policy and the Politics of Failure, 1879–1894' (Master's thesis, Queen's University 1980).

103 Sir William Ralph Meredith CJO *Interim Report on Laws Relating to the Liability*

of Employers to Make Compensation to their Employees for Injuries Received in the Course of Their Employment Which Are in Force in Other Countries (Toronto 1912) (hereafter Interim Report), Minutes of Evidence 187–8

104 In *Markle* v *Donaldson* (1904), 7 OLR 376 he made one of the few comments in the cases on the purposes of the Workmen's Compensation Act: 'The object of the legislation was to mitigate the rigour of the common law doctrine of common employment ... and to have made the employer liable only [under a proposed narrow interpretation] would have been to retain the rigour of the common law doctrine in its most obnoxious form.' He seems to have been inclined to find adequate evidence to go to the jury, for example, *Brown* v *Waterous Engine Works* (1904), 8 OLR 37; and *Billing* v *Semmens* (1904), 7 OLR 340; and he made several generous interpretations of legislation, for example, *Markle* v *Donaldson*, *McLaughlin* v *Ontario Iron and Steel* (1910), 20 OLR 335; and *Lamond* v *Grand Trunk Railway*, above note 52.

105 The first session was held just before a provincial election and after a long delay – a small piece of evidence that Meredith had not entirely abandoned politics.

106 Interim Report, Minutes of Evidence, 171–96

107 Interim Report, Schedule 1, and Minutes of Evidence, 197–225

108 Interim Report, Minutes of Evidence, 198–200, 203, 204

109 The Parliamentary Committee of the CMA recognized a need for change in the report in 1908 and again in 1910, after Meredith was appointed, and the Montreal branch supported the Quebec legislation. However, nothing more was done until mid-1911, when Wegenast, who had been hired as secretary of the newly-created legal department, recommended creation of a special committee. It was appointed at the annual convention in October, at about the same time as Meredith's first meeting, and in December the committee was given permission by the Executive Council to present a brief for the Association without approval. At the annual convention in 1912 there seems to have been some feeling that the committee had gone too far in its presentation. Wegenast was the secretary of the committee, and he seems to have pressed his own ideas strongly. During the hearings the railroads sought to persuade Meredith that Wegenast was not accurately representing the beliefs of CMA members, especially about the issue of individual liability, but Meredith properly ruled that this relation was none of their business. The *Montreal Times* made the same accusation, and the CMA replied firmly that it was wrong. See *Industrial Canada* IX (1908–9) 219–20, XI (1910–11) 296, 1287–9, XII (1911–12) 594, XIII (1912–13) 398–400, and XIV (1913–14) 1009–10; and Final Report, Minutes of Evidence, 443–4.

110 Interim Report, 54–132, Minutes of Evidence, 277–307

111 Interim Report, 5

112 Appeal and review are the two ways in which courts supervise administrative agencies. A right to appeal exists only if given by statute; review is part of the general jurisdiction of the courts and a right to review exists unless it is barred by statute. See generally J.M. Evans, H.N. Janisch, D.J. Mullan, and R.C.B. Risk *Administrative Law* (Toronto 1980) 19–26. For the purposes of this essay, the implications of the distinction need not be thoroughly described and analysed.

113 Interim Report, Minutes of Evidence 140

114 Interim Report, Minutes of Evidence, 143–4

115 Interim Report, Minutes of Evidence, 195, Final Report, Minutes of Evidence, 511–12

116 See, for example, the evidence given in the fifteenth session by James Boyd, an expert from Ohio presented by Wegenast and G.W. Watts, manager of the Canadian General Electric plant at Petedrborough. Interim Report, Minutes of Evidence, 311–62

117 See Thomas L. Haskell *The Emergence of Professional Social Science* (Urbana, IL 1977) chs 2, 11. These perceptions appear in the reports of the Factory Inspectors, particularly in 1889, 1892, 1896, 1898, and 1906.

118 For an example during the hearings, see Final Report, Minutes of Evidence, 41–2. Meredith said: 'When it is compulsory for a man to do work he has no choice.' Interim Report, Minutes of Evidence, 424

119 Interim Report, Minutes of Evidence, 424, Final report, xi, xii. In his address to the Ontario Bar Association, above note 99, Justice Middleton expressed the same attitudes, although with more restraint.

120 Final Report, vii

121 Interim Report, Minutes of Evidence, 167, Final Report, Minutes of Evidence, 578

122 Interim Report, Minutes of Evidence, 359

123 See, for example, comments made during the twelfth session, Final Report, Minutes of Evidence, 5–32, especially: 'I think it is becoming a recognized principle that manufactured goods should bear the cost of not only what it takes to make them, and the wear and tear upon the machinery that is making these goods, but to a certain extent the wear and tear upon the employee who is engaged in making these goods' (8), and 'It is a small matter to scrap machinery, but it is a very expensive matter to scrap your employees. There is a very large investment in employees by every factory and by every manufacturer in the world, and that must be preserved' (10).

124 Horwitz *Transformation of American Law* 210

125 See Michael Bliss *A Living Profit* (Toronto 1974) ch. 2, for attitudes of businessmen towards competition.

126 Interim Report, Minutes of Evidence, 295. In 1911 Louis Brandeis wrote that

'Possibilities of lengthening lives and of avoiding sickness and invalidity, like the possibilities of preventing accidents, will be availed of *when business as well as humanity demands that this be done.*' L. Brandeis 'The Road to Social Efficiency' *New York Outlook*, 10 June 1911, as quoted in the CMA brief, Interim Report, 54, Appendix III.

127 Final Report, xix

128 Whitney Papers, Ontario Archives, Whitney to A.J. Dawson, 7 July 1909, as quoted in Humphries, above note 95, at 128

129 See especially, *Industrial Canada*, the publication of the CMA, and the *Industrial Banner*, the labour paper that gave compensation the most enthusiastic coverage.

130 In the United States, labour was often much more sensitive to the loss of the common law claim. See the references in note 89. In this context, in setting the amounts of the payments, and in considering whether to permit appeals, Meredith stressed the need for general rules and efficiency, even though a few cases of injustice might result. For example: 'We are dealing with the mass, we want to deal with the whole body; individual cases must be sacrificed for the whole,' and 'even if injustice is done in a few cases, it is better to have it done and have swift justice meted out to the great body of men.' Final Report, Minutes of Evidence, 503, 512

131 Interim Report, Brief of the CMA, 87

132 Final Report, Appendix IX

133 The brief is Final Report, Appendix X. One possible explanation for the lack of struggle is that the business was not especially profitable. Papers and journals contain complaints of losses and harmful competition, for example, the *Monetary Times* 16, 23 Aug. 1913, although businessmen may have been especially prone to complain about competition at this time: Bliss *A Living Profit*.

134 *Monetary Times* 23 Jan. 1914

135 See, for example, Interim Report, Minutes of Evidence, 142, 297, 317, 331–3, 374–5, 437–44, Final Report, Minutes of Evidence, 70–7, 448, 520.

136 See, for example, Interim Report, Minutes of Evidence, 291–3, 399–410, 452–8, Final Report, Minutes of Evidence, 84, 145–53, 411–43, 565–70, Final Report, viii–ix.

137 Piva *The Condition of the Working Class* ch. 2

138 Final Report, Minutes of Evidence, 501; see also 538–41, 545–50, 573–84, 595–619.

139 Final Report, Minutes of Evidence, 549

140 Final Report, Minutes of Evidence, 537

141 Final Report, Minutes of Evidence, 541–72

142 *Globe* 3, 15 Apr. 1913. The legislature adjourned soon afterwards. Rowell protested, and referred again to Whitney's undertaking made in 1907.

143 See Prang N.W. *Rowell: Ontario Nationalist,* above note 95.

144 Above, note 97

145 The detailed criticism was a pamphlet composed of section by section comments, 'Workmen's Compensation, Draft Bill of Sir William R. Meredith ...'
CMA, Ontario Archives. Wegenast's articles (and editorials apparently written
by him) are in *Industrial Canada* XVI (1914), 894, 900, 919, 1009–10, 1032, 1035,
1138, 1389, 1505. The series concluded with a sad survey of the entire story,
1551. The submissions and a few letters from businessmen are in the Whitney
Papers, Ontario Archives.

146 23 Jan. 1914

147 Bancroft's speeches were reported in the *Industrial Banner,* which acted as the
cheer-leader for the campaign. Some examples of the headlines and editorial
comments are 'Sir James Whitney Fails to Make Good ... Shameful Surrender
to the Interests' 18 Apr. 1913, '... the great struggle will be on the floor of the
Ontario Legislature next session ...' 19 Sept. 1913, '... it is plainly apparent
that [the CMA] is prepared to put up a strenuous struggle ... Throughout the
length and breadth of the Province the organized workers must exert themselves as never before ...' 19 Sept. 1913, 'The time has come for united demonstration, united effort and united determination' 5 Dec. 1913, 'Ontario's
Workers Are Fully Aroused' 16 Jan. 1914, 'Manufacturers are clearly out of
touch with public sentiment' 27 Feb. 1914, 'Government Standing Firm ...'
3 Apr. 1914, 'Workmen's Compensation Opponents Out Generalled,' 8 May
1914. Throughout, the *Banner* exaggerated the strength of the CMA opposition. Letters and telegrams are in the Whitney Papers, Ontario Archives.

148 *Monetary Times* 20 Dec. 1913

149 The submission is printed in the *Monetary Times* 20 Feb. 1914. See the *Monetary
Times* 23 Jan. 1914, for a lament about the way that the submission of the
insurance companies was ignored at the Jan. meeting.

150 Meredith made his notes in an interleaved copy of the pamphlet cited in note
145 above, Ontario Archives, RG 6 Series 1-2, Box 35, Treasury Department –
Workmen's Compensation, 1913–34. Opposite the criticism of s. 101, which
need not be described to appreciate his comments, he wrote: 'This is very
learned, but not of much practical use except to show how very learned the
critic is ... any school boy could give the answer to the questions the critic
puts ... The critic has shown his want of confidence in (1) the Board, (2)
the Lieutenant Governor in council, and now this the jury ... and there is
probably no one left in whom he has any confidence, except perhaps the
Canadian Manufacturers Association, and from what is said that even is
doubtful, and the critic himself.'

151 CLT XXXIV (1914) 109. In Mar. 1914 the Social Service Congress met in Ottawa,
and its Council included workers' compensation in the short list of needed

reforms it presented to the federal government at the conclusion of the meeting. Richard Allen *The Social Passion: Religion and Social Reform in Canada 1914–28* (Toronto 1973) ch. 2

152 A motion by Proudfoot to include payments for medical treatment failed. *Journals* 1914, 123–4, 125, 127, 134, 157, 266, 283, 326, 366–7

153 See Humphries 'The Sources of Ontario "Progressive" Conservatism, 1900–1914' above note 95, 128–9.

154 Above notes 100 and 151

155 'To throw the expense of insuring one particular class of the community upon another class is class legislation of a most indefensible kind.' 'The time has come to make a stand against the insane pandering to the unjust demands of so-called "labour" leaders who for their own selfish purposes claim and obtain class legislation which disorganizes the social fabric and works injustice, and which in the end is hurtful to those whom they pretend to help.' *Canada Law Journal* LXIII (1907) 185. 'Legislation of this kind is nothing less than a pandering to a class which is supposed to be powerful in votes, regardless of justice to the rest of the community.' CLJ LXIV (1908) 716. The acceptance is in CLJ LXVIII (1912) 602. Note, however, that it was qualified by the thought that 'equality seems to demand ... universal insurance against accidents,' and 'any scheme of general insurance against accidents cannot be fairly limited to any one or more classes of the community.' This qualification is a demonstration of the continuing power of the belief that law should govern all individuals equally and indifferently. The protest against legislating for one class failed to acknowledge the substantive injustice caused by formal equality, but the belief was not simply a cynical form. It pushed these editors and some of the participants in the hearings to the apparently logical conclusion of universal accident insurance. See also misgivings about the prohibition of common law claims in CLJ L (1914) 201.

156 Interim Report, Minutes of Evidence, 421–3

157 For example, one participant argued that accidents on farms should be included, and Meredith replied: 'Logically that is so, but logic does not always prevail in this world. There is a great deal of opportunism instead. We have to propose a measure that will pass.' Interim Report, Minutes of Evidence, 274. Closely associated with this attitude was his realization that compromise and experiment were necessary. For example, Wegenast protested against excluding the railways 'on the ground of principle,' and Meredith said: 'Principle is nothing; it is all expediency.' Later, Wegenast protested against experiment, and Meredith replied 'My dear Sir, it is all experiment. It is all empirical legislation.' Final Report, Minutes of Evidence, 263, 551

9

The Evolution of the Ontario Courts
1788–1981

MARGARET A. BANKS

Figure 1 shows, in outline, the structure of the Ontario court system today. Some of its components are relatively new; for instance, the Divisional Court of the High Court of Justice was established in 1972 and the Provincial Offences Courts as recently as 1980.[1] Others are much older, going back to the early days of Upper Canada and having their origins in still earlier English practice. The Small Claims Courts, at the foot of the civil hierarchy, have been called by this name since 1971, but that was not the beginning of their history. They are the successors of the Division Courts (1841–1970), which in still earlier days were called Courts of Requests (1792–1841).[2]

County Courts, originally with only civil jurisdiction, were established in 1849, taking the place of the older District Courts (1794–1849) which, along with the districts of Upper Canada, were abolished that year. Ontario today has both County and District Courts though, for brevity, the term 'County Courts' is sometimes applied to both. In areas of the province, mainly in the north, which are organized into districts rather than counties, the correct name is District Courts.[3] The province's Surrogate Courts, which deal with wills and intestate estates, have a long history going back to 1793.[4]

The Provincial Courts, Criminal and Family Divisions, established in 1968, perform functions which were formerly the responsibility of Magistrates' Courts and Juvenile and Family Courts, though duties in relation to

Figure 1
The Courts of Ontario 1981

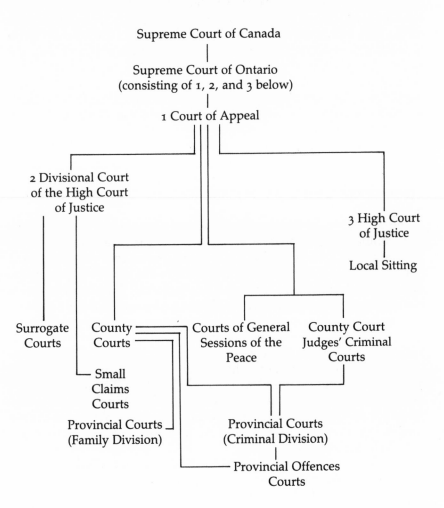

family matters have expanded greatly as a result of recent widespread statutory changes in relation to this area of the law.[5]

The Courts of General Sessions of the Peace and the County Court Judges' Criminal Courts are courts of criminal jurisdiction presided over by a judge of a County or District Court.[6] The General Sessions (originally called General Quarter Sessions) have had a longer history than any other court in the province, though the District judges did not preside over them *ex officio* until 1841. County Court Judges' Criminal Courts (originally called County Judges' Criminal Courts) began to sit in 1869 for the speedy trial of criminal matters out of session and without a jury.[7] Thus, although County and District Courts originally had only civil jurisdiction, their judges, constituting other courts, acquired criminal jurisdiction as well. The practice of having the same judges sitting in different courts or in different divisions of the same court is one of the most confusing aspects of court structure and composition. It will emerge again and again in the pages which follow. In addition, County and District Courts themselves now have some criminal jurisdiction; they are named in the Criminal Code to act as appeal courts in relation to summary conviction offences.[8]

The purely theoretical Supreme Court of Ontario exercises both civil and criminal jurisdiction through its two branches, the Court of Appeal and the High Court of Justice. It was established in 1881 under the name Supreme Court of Judicature for Ontario, in imitation of the system adopted in England a few years earlier.[9] A long history of the administration of law and equity in separate courts forms the background for this important change.

At the top of the hierarchy in Ontario today is the Supreme Court of Canada, a general court of appeal for the whole country, established by statute in 1875 under the authority of s. 101 of the British North America Act, recently renamed the Constitution Act.[10] When hearing an Ontario case, this federal court is regarded as part of the Ontario court system. There are no longer appeals from the Supreme Court of Canada or from superior courts in the provinces to the Judicial Committee of the Privy Council in England.[11]

As an aid to understanding the jurisdiction of the various courts, it is useful to remember on the civil side that monetary actions in the High Court, County and District Courts, and Small Claims Courts are similar, but the amount involved generally determines the court in which the action is commenced. The Small Claims Courts have jurisdiction where the amount claimed does not exceed $1000. The County and District

Courts have jurisdiction in most civil matters where the amount involved does not exceed $15,000. If a larger sum is claimed, the High Court has jurisdiction, though should such an action be commenced in a county court and the defendant does not then question the court's jurisdiction, the matter cannot be raised later unless otherwise ordered by a court or a judge. It should be emphasized that this summary oversimplifies the civil jurisdiction of the various courts. For instance, the High Court, as a superior court of law, has extensive inherent jurisdiction, whereas the County, District, and Small Claims Courts have only those powers expressly conferred on them by statute. However, the ten specific categories set out by the County Courts Act are quite broad. The result is that most civil cases within the specified monetary limit fall within the statutory jurisdiction of the County Courts. Contract, tort, easements, and recovery of property are among the categories included within their jurisdiction; libel, however, is an example of a subject with respect to which the County Courts have no jurisdiction.[12]

In criminal matters summary conviction offences are tried in the Provincial Courts (Criminal Division) with an appeal either to a County Court or to the High Court, where a judge sits without a jury. The bulk of indictable offences are tried either by a Provincial Court judge or by a County Court judge with or without a jury. Such offences may also be tried by a High Court judge and jury, but the number of such trials is relatively small.[13]

Ontario's present court structure is really more complex than Figure 1 suggests. To put the whole story in chart form would create such a complex picture that the lay reader would probably be frightened off before reading the first page. For instance, the administration of family law in the courts of Ontario is now in a state of experimentation and change. Family law comprises a variety of subjects, some criminal, others civil, such as juvenile delinquency, criminal and quasi-criminal charges arising from family disputes, custody, guardianship, adoption, support obligations, divorce, and division of matrimonial property. It is administered in several courts – the Supreme Court of Ontario, the County and District Courts, the Surrogate Courts, and the Provincial Courts (Family Division).[14] Since the mid-1970s, in response to a recommendation of the Law Reform Commission of Canada for a Unified Family Court, there has been a trend towards greater consolidation of the administration of family law. In 1976 a Family Law Division of the High Court came into existence.[15] Since there is no statutory basis for this change comparable to the legislative provisions for the Family Division of the High Court of Justice in England, it is not included on Figure 1.[16] It is simply an informal arrangement whereby a variety of matrimonial and related matters are assigned to a division which deals only with such subjects. In 1976 the Ontario legislature also passed an act to establish a Unified Family Court in the Judicial District of Hamilton-Wentworth. This was designed as an experiment, and the act was to be repealed three years after it came into force. A 1977 amendment set the date of repeal as 1 July 1980, and a further amendment in 1979 extended the operation of the act to 1 July 1982.[17]

Anyone who has read the opening pages of this essay must be aware that there is nothing static about Ontario's court system. In a continuing state of evolution, it responds, though not always quickly enough, to such variables as population growth and social development and change. Some developments, such as the establishment of the courts of Upper Canada in 1792–4, the addition of a Court of Chancery in 1837, and the merging of the administration of law and equity in 1881 were modelled on the English system. Others are more complex and less easily explained. Indeed, as one studies the history of the courts, it is difficult to understand why some changes were made, especially when close together in time and seemingly in conflict with each other. For instance, in 1903 a fourth division was added to the High Court of Justice, but six years later provision was made for abolishing all the divisions of the High Court. Another example of conflicting changes occurred in 1923–4. Amendments affecting the composition of the High Court and Appellate Divisions of the Supreme Court of Ontario were adopted in 1923. Quite different provisions made the following year never came into effect. If one looks at the changes only in the context of the history of the courts, there seems to be no sensible explanation for them. The reasons were at least partly political, since there was change of government in 1905, as well as between the 1923 and 1924 amendments to the Judicature Act. Political factors were not, of course, the only ones. Changes in the structure and composition of the courts were sometimes part of a more general program of law reform and cannot be understood in isolation from it. Other developments, such as increases in the number of judges, are more easily explained; growth of population and litigation added to the workload of the courts.

In addition to the figure showing the structure of the Ontario courts in 1981, figures dated 1800, 1860, and 1910 have been prepared. The choice of these dates rather than others that might seem more obvious requires some explanation. Figures bearing these dates were already in existence, though they required some revision, and the reasons given by the compiler for choosing them seem valid.[18] The choice of 1800 has no special significance; it is a convenient date, showing the courts at the beginning of the nineteenth century; any date from 1794 to 1836 could equally well have been used. Major changes in court structure came into effect on 1 January 1850, but 1860 was chosen so that the effect of the abolition of the Court of Probate in 1858 could be shown. The acquisition of equity jurisdiction by County Courts in 1853 and appeals from them in equitable matters to the Court of Chancery are also indicated. The 1910 figure shows the structure of the courts before the divisions of the High Court were abolished.

Because of the complexity of the system, none of the figures gives a complete picture of court structure. Sometimes a line from one court to another indicates an avenue of appeal; at other times it shows the position of the courts in the judicial hierarchy. For instance, the line from 'Requests' to 'District' on Figure 2 indicates court hierarchy, but not an avenue of appeal, since there was no appeal from the judgment of a Court of Requests. The emphasis in Figure 1 is on avenues of appeal; thus there is a line from Small Claims Courts to the Divisional Court of the High Court rather than to County Courts.

BEFORE AND AFTER THE CONSTITUTIONAL ACT 1791

The name 'Ontario' was not adopted until 1867, but the history of its courts predates even the formation of the province of Upper Canada in 1791. Before that time, according to the boundaries established by the Quebec Act, 1774, the territory which became Upper Canada was part of the old province of Quebec.[19] Until the early 1780s there was little permanent settlement in the area, but the conclusion of the American War of Independence in 1783 and the consequent northern migration of United Empire Loyalists, who wished to remain within the British Empire, brought about a change. Most of the Loyalists who chose Quebec came to its western regions rather than to the older parts already settled by the French.

The area in which the Loyalists settled was within the boundaries of Quebec's western district, Montreal, but remote from its courts. Additional justices of the peace were appointed for the new localities, but their jurisdiction in judicial matters was at this time solely criminal. In all matters which could not be lawfully disposed of in a summary manner by one or more magistrates, there had to be recourse to the courts at Montreal.[20] Justice in civil affairs was virtually non-existent; in practice only those suits from the fur-trading area around Detroit (at that time still part of the province) were of sufficient importance to repay the expense of taking them to Montreal.[21]

Under an ordinance of 1764 establishing civil courts in the province of Quebec, justices of the peace had been given limited civil jurisdiction One of them could hear and finally determine matters of property not exceeding £5 current money of Quebec; two justices of the peace were required if the amount in dispute was between £5 and £10. Any three justices of the peace were empowered to hold quarter sessions in their respective districts every three months and to hear and determine matters of property between £10 and £30; in such cases an appeal lay to the provincial Court of King's Bench.[22] An ordinance of 1770 annulled this civil jurisdiction of justices of the peace; henceforth they could act in such matters only under a special commission.[23] In response to petitions from Loyalists in the newer parts of the province showing the impossibility of protecting their civil rights under existing conditions, the council at Quebec in 1785 decided to confer on justices of the peace in the newer areas, but not throughout the province, some of the civil powers they had had between 1764 and 1770. They were to hear and determine without appeal suits involving personal rights, and for the recovery of debts of not more than £5; for any case involving more than £2, two justices of the peace were necessary. This measure was intended only as a temporary one, for it was clear that some permanent courts were needed in the new area.[24]

In 1788 four new districts were established in the territory that was later to become Upper Canada; from east to west in what is now southern Ontario, they were called Luneburg, Mecklenburg, Nassau, and Hesse.[25] In each of these districts the Governor commissioned justices to constitute a Court of Common Pleas.[26] These new courts, like those of the same name in the older districts of the province, had unlimited civil but no criminal jurisdiction. The courts in Luneburg, Mecklenburg, and Nassau had three judges each, all laymen, but Hesse, a commercial rather than an agricultural district, had only one judge, a lawyer. In cases involving £10 and over, appeals lay from the Courts of Common Pleas to Quebec's Court of Appeals, which was composed of the Governor, Lieutenant Governor, or Chief Justice as presiding officer and any five members of the Council. In cases over £500 there could be a further appeal to the King in Council.[27]

The judges of the Courts of Common Pleas in the new districts, unlike their counterparts in Quebec and Montreal, were not appointed surrogates to the Governor and could not, therefore, grant letters of probate or administration. They had, however, the power of holding family councils, called Prerogative Courts, to appoint a tutor (guardian) for minor children of a deceased or absconded father or a curator of an intestate estate.[28] These procedures were of French origin; it seems curious that provisions for granting probate, which was an English practice, were made in the older French districts of the province and not in the newer ones, which were predominantly British.

The Quebec Act's requirement that Canadian (that is, French Canadian) law should apply in matters of controversy relating to property and civil rights caused problems in the new districts.[29] In 1789 the judges of Mecklenburg sent a memorial to the Council at Quebec asking whether Canadian law, of which they declared themselves ignorant, must be introduced in a district inhabited entirely by the English. Although the Council approved in theory of the introduction of English law in the new districts, it did not feel called upon to take any action and its reply to the judges was non-committal.[30] A remedy would not be found until the four new districts became a separate province.

Quebec's Court of King's Bench had originally had both civil and criminal jurisdiction, but since 1777 it had been solely a criminal court.[31] Probably it was easier to administer civil and criminal justice in separate courts, since under the Quebec Act the former was Canadian and the latter, English.[32] Each year the Court of King's Bench held two sessions in Quebec and two in Montreal. In addition, criminal offences could be tried in the districts by Courts of General Sessions of the Peace presided over by justices of the peace, and more serious crimes, mainly capital felonies, by Courts of Oyer and Terminer and General Gaol Delivery created by commissions issued by the Governor and presided over by a judge of the Court of King's Bench.[33] These courts were of particular importance in the newer districts of the province because of their distance from Montreal and Quebec, where the King's Bench sessions were held.

The Constitutional Act of 1791, which made provision for the government of the two new provinces which were to be created out of the old province of Quebec, declared that all laws in force at the commencement of the act should continue in force as though the province of Quebec had not been divided, except in so far as they were repealed or varied by the Constitutional Act or would be by provincial legislation in the future. Thus Upper Canada began its separate provincial existence with the courts described in the foregoing paragraphs, except that it was the Governor or the Lieutenant Governor and the Executive Council of Upper Canada which constituted a Court of Appeal in civil cases.[34] It was up to the legislature of the new province, subject to review by the British government, to decide what changes were needed.

THE COURTS OF UPPER CANADA 1792–1800

In 1792 the first act of the first legislature of Upper Canada repealed the provision in the Quebec Act which stated 'That in all matters of controversy relative to property and civil rights, resort shall be had to the Laws of Canada as the rule for the decision of the same' and provided that in all such cases in future resort was to be had to the laws of England.[35] The second act of the same session provided that from 1 December 1792 every issue of fact in every court of justice should be tried by a jury.[36] Because this was recognized as altering the constitutions of the Courts of Common Pleas in relation to actions under £10, a further act abolished summary proceedings in such cases and directed that all actions above 40s. be tried in the same way as those above £10.[37] For 'the more Easy and Speedy Recovery of Small Debts' – that is, those not exceeding 40s. – Courts of Requests were established. The justices of the peace of a district, meeting in their General Quarter Sessions, were to divide the district into divisions, each with a Court of Requests. Two or more justices of the peace were necessary to constitute such a court. They had full power to give judgment and award execution against goods and chattels.[38] Thus the civil power of justices of the peace was continued.

Another act of the first legislature of Upper Canada changed the names of the districts of Upper Canada and consequently of their courts. Luneburg, Mecklenburg, Nassau, and Hesse became respectively the Eastern, Midland, Home, and Western districts.[39]

The reception of English law in Upper Canada in matters relating to property and civil rights had the effect of automatically abolishing the Prerogative Courts, which were unknown to that system. It also meant that some method had to be provided for granting letters of administration instead of curatorships in intestate estates. In addition, letters probate were necessary to give effect to wills concerning personal property, which had not been the case under the French Canadian system. To meet these needs, an act in 1793 established 'a Court of Probate in this Province, and also a Surrogate Court in every District thereof.' The Governor, Lieutenant Governor, or person administering the government of the province in theory presided over these courts but in fact appointed an Official Principal to act as judge of the Court of Probate and surrogates to preside in the Surrogate Courts. In each district the Surrogate Court had authority to grant letters of probate and administration in relation to the estates of persons who died there. However, if the estate included personal property valued at £5 or more elsewhere in the province, the Court of Probate alone had jurisdiction. In cases involving more than £50 in which a Surrogate Court had jurisdiction, an appeal lay to the Court of Probate.[40]

Though the court legislation of the first two sessions of the legislature of Upper Canada was impressive, that of the third session, held in 1794, was of even greater significance. Short titles of acts had not then been introduced, but Riddell referred to the statute entitled 'An Act to Establish a Superior Court of Civil and Criminal Jurisdiction' as the Judicature Act of 1794.[41]

The practice of having a Court of Common Pleas in each district with unlimited civil, but no criminal, jurisdiction was comparable to the system which had been in force in the old province of Quebec and in most of the American colonies, but it was quite different from the system in England, where the superior courts had civil jurisdiction throughout the country and the Court of King's Bench had unlimited criminal jurisdiction as well.[42]

John Graves Simcoe, the first Lieutenant Governor of Upper Canada, was determined to make its institutions as similar as possible to those of the mother country. At his request the Chief Justice of the province, William Osgoode, drew up a bill to establish a Supreme Court of Judicature to be called 'His Majesty's Court of King's Bench for the Province of Upper Canada.'[43] The bill that Osgoode drafted provided that the Court of King's Bench would be 'a court of record of original jurisdiction, and shall possess all such powers and authorities as by the law of England are incident to a superior court of civil and criminal jurisdiction.'[44] There were, however, important limits to its jurisdiction; it was a court of law, not of equity. Although this was similar to the Court of King's Bench in England, the mother country had a Court of Chancery with equitable jurisdiction. At this time no such court existed in Upper Canada. The result was that equitable remedies, available in England, were unavailable to residents of Upper Canada. This became increasingly inconvenient as the business life of the community developed. For instance, an equitable jurisdiction was needed to provide for foreclosure of mortgages and to enforce specific performance of contracts for the sale of real property.[45]

The Chief Justice of Upper Canada was to preside in the Court of King's Bench along with two puisne justices.[46] Although the court was to sit 'in a place certain,' this did not mean that residents of the province had to travel to the capital for the administration of justice. The Court of King's Bench did not usually try cases; when the record was complete, it was sent to be tried at the assizes. Following the English practice, Commissions of Assize and Nisi Prius were issued periodically by the Lieutenant Governor to the judges of the Court of King's Bench, empowering them to try civil causes at the district towns. These commissions were in practice combined with Commissions of Oyer and Terminer and General Gaol Delivery so that both civil and criminal cases could be tried at the assizes. Following trial of a case with a jury at the assizes, the record was brought back to the Court of King's Bench, with judgment being entered and process awarded.[47]

The Constitutional Act had provided that the Governor and Executive Council should be a court of appeal.[48] In addition to establishing a Court of King's Bench, the Judicature Act of 1794 regulated the Court of Appeal by providing that it should consist of 'the governor, lieutenant-governor, or person administering the government of this Province, or the chief justice of the Province, together with any two or more members of the executive council.' Should it happen that a judge of the court below sat in the Court of Appeal on the same case, he was permitted to give his reasons for judgment, but not to vote. An appeal lay from the Court of King's Bench to the Court of the Governor and the Executive Council (the Court of Appeal was sometimes referred to by this name), if the matter in controversy exceeded £100. There was a further appeal to 'His Majesty, in his privy council,' if the amount exceeded £500.[49]

Along with the establishment of the Court of King's Bench went the abolition of the Courts of Common Pleas in the four districts. Actions pending there were transferred to King's Bench.[50] It was thought, however, that local courts would still be needed to deal with small debts. The Courts of Requests had jurisdiction up to 40s., provincial currency. The new District Courts, established by an act of 1794, were given jurisdiction in actions of contract for sums above 40s. and not exceeding £15. They were presided over by one or more judges appointed by commission under the great seal of the province and sat four times a year.[51] In 1797 the jurisdiction of the District Courts was enlarged in contract to £40 if the amount was already liquidated. A jurisdiction in tort up to £15 was added, although there were certain limitations; for instance, the District Courts had no jurisdiction in actions of assault and battery or false imprisonment.[52]

Figure 2
The Courts of Upper Canada 1800

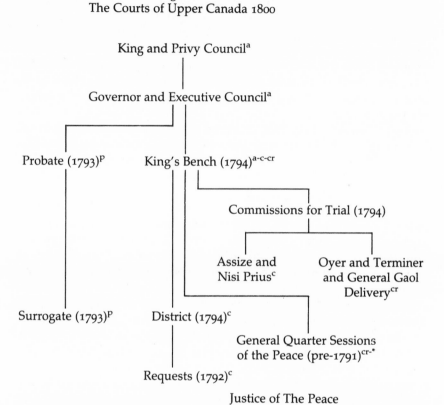

King and Privy Council[a]

Governor and Executive Council[a]

Probate (1793)[p]   King's Bench (1794)[a-c-cr]

Commissions for Trial (1794)

Assize and   Oyer and Terminer
Nisi Prius[c]   and General Gaol
                     Delivery[cr]

Surrogate (1793)[p]   District (1794)[c]

General Quarter Sessions
of the Peace (pre-1791)[cr-*]

Requests (1792)[c]

Justice of The Peace
(pre-1791)[c-cr]

a APPEAL
c CIVIL/COMMON
cr CRIMINAL
p PROBATE
* IN THE EARLY YEARS
   IT ALSO HAD SOME
   CIVIL JURISDICTION

THE NEED FOR A COURT OF CHANCERY

The administration of law and equity in separate courts had its roots in medieval England. When the common law courts were established, the Crown as the fountain of all justice delegated its ordinary jurisdiction to the judges of these courts but retained an extraordinary or residuary jurisdiction to be used if the regular courts failed to do justice. The King received so many petitions for extraordinary relief that he could not deal personally with all of them. He therefore began to refer them to the Council. Dealing with these petitions eventually became the responsibility of the Chancellor, a leading member of the Council, who acquired both administrative and judicial duties. As head of the Chancery, a royal secretariat, which took its name from the latticed screen or chancel behind which the clerks worked, he had custody of the great seal of England, which was used to authenticate writs, charters, and letters-patent, drawn by the clerks of Chancery. The work of this department had little connection with the judicial functions of the Chancellor and what came to be called the Court of Chancery. Most of the medieval Chancellors were bishops or archbishops; the practice of appointing a lawyer to the position came later. Though lawyers tend to think of the Chancellor as the head of a court which administered equity, this never was in England his only or even his principal function. Today the Lord Chancellor continues to hold a position of major importance, being the only officer of state who serves in all three branches of the government. He is a minister of the Crown, Speaker of the House of Lords, and the head of the judiciary in England and Wales. The office never attained this degree of importance in Upper Canada or Ontario and indeed it has ceased to exist.[53]

Since Lieutenant Governor Simcoe was so anxious to establish English institutions in Upper Canada, it is surprising that a Court of Chancery was not established at the same time as the Court of King's Bench. Chief Justice Osgoode, who drafted the 1794 statute, was an experienced Chancery practitioner; Riddell expressed the view that it might have been Osgoode's removal to Lower Canada the same year that prevented the full assimilation of the courts of the colony to those of England.[54]

There were, however, differences of opinion in both England and Upper Canada as to the need for a Court of Chancery in the province. An English statute of 1562 gave the keeper of the great seal the power of Chancellor; from this fact evolved the theory that the Lieutenant Governor of Upper Canada, as keeper of the great seal of the province, was automatically its Chancellor.[55] At the beginning of the nineteenth century

Lieutenant Governor Peter Hunter asked Henry Allcock, a Justice of Upper Canada's Court of King's Bench, to draft a bill establishing a court of equity. He did so, but it appears never to have been introduced in the legislature. Apparently it was submitted for an opinion to the British government which in 1802 disapproved it on the ground that the Lieutenant Governor was already Chancellor and could 'call for the assistance of any of His Majesty's Judges or law officers of the Province.' Riddell's view was that the real objection was financial, since payment of colonial judges' salaries was then the responsibility of the mother country.[56]

Within the next few years the attitude of the British government changed and it appeared anxious to see a Court of Chancery established. However, the War of 1812 intervened, followed by other problems more pressing than the judicial one. When the matter was taken up again in 1827, and it was suggested that no legislation was required to appoint an equity judge, the imperial law officers were asked for an opinion. They reported that they were 'in considerable doubt whether His Majesty can by Letters Patent under the Great Seal or in any other manner without the intervention of Parliament or of the local legislature create any new Judge in Equity by whatsoever name he may be called in Upper Canada.' In the light of this opinion, they recommended that if an equity judge was to be appointed as Vice Chancellor (the Lieutenant Governor being Chancellor), it be done with the aid of parliament or the local legislature. Fearing that there might be a clash of jurisdictions between King's Bench and Chancery, they put forward for consideration an alternative proposal that an equity lawyer be appointed a puisne judge of the existing Court of King's Bench and that that court be given some equitable jurisdiction.[57]

In Upper Canada the opinion of the judges and legislators was divided as to whether a separate Court of Chancery should be erected or equitable jurisdiction conferred on the Court of King's Bench. In 1832–3 a Select Committee of the Legislative Assembly considered the matter and recommended a separate court. However, the draft bill prepared by the committee failed to secure passage.[58]

At last in 1837 the attempt to erect a Court of Chancery met with success. The act passed that year provided for the establishment of such a court with 'the Governor, Lieutenant-Governor or Person Administering the Government of this Province' as Chancellor. The judicial powers, however, were to be exercised by 'a Judge to be known as the Vice Chancellor of Upper Canada.' Appointed by the Crown under the great seal of the province, the Vice Chancellor was to hold office during good behaviour.[59] This provision, helping to ensure the independence of the judiciary, had already been applied to the judges of the Court of King's Bench in 1834.[60] The Court of Chancery was given jurisdiction in specified equitable matters such as fraud, trusts, executors and administrators, mortgages, dower, infants and mentally-incompetent persons ('Ideots and Lunatics' was the terminology of the day) and their estates, and specific performance of contracts.[61] Appeals were to be allowed from the Court of Chancery to the Governor and Council (that is, the Executive Council) of Upper Canada with a further appeal to the King in Council in the same manner as in judgments of the Court of King's Bench. The Vice Chancellor was to be a member of the Court of Appeal; so were the puisne judges of the Court of King's Bench in all cases of appeal from the judgments and decrees of the Vice Chancellor.[62]

Other Developments to 1848

The fact that there was no Court of Chancery for the first forty-five years of Upper Canada's history had the effect of conferring on the Chief Justice functions and honours which in England belonged to the Chancellor. From the beginning, it was normal practice for the Chief Justice to be a member of the Executive Council and Speaker of the Legislative Council.[63] The last Chief Justice to hold all three positions was John Beverley Robinson, who was appointed to the highest judicial office in the province in 1829 and to the Executive Council the same year. He became Speaker of the Legislative Council in 1830. But already in 1826 the House of Assembly had passed a resolution expressing its opposition to the Chief Justice serving on the Executive Council.[64] This and another resolution emphasizing the need for the judges of the Court of King's Bench to be independent of the Crown and of the people were incorporated into an address to the King. The British government took no action on this address or on another sent in 1828. Eventually, however, the views expressed in these addresses found acceptance, and Robinson resigned from the Executive Council in 1831 on being told that such an action would be agreeable to the imperial authorities. He continued as Speaker of the Legislative Council until 1838 and was a member until the union of the Canadas in 1841, but did not sit after the former date.[65]

Robinson's relinquishment of the speakership of the Legislative Council did not end judicial appointments to its speakership. From 1838 until the legislative union of Upper and Lower Canada in 1841, Jonas Jones, a puisne justice of the Court of King's [Queen's] Bench, served as Speaker of the Legislative Council of Upper Canada.[66] After the union, Robert

Sympson Jameson, who had been Vice Chancellor of Upper Canada since the establishment of the Court of Chancery in 1837, was appointed Speaker of the Legislative Council of the Province of Canada, an interesting development in the light of the Lord Chancellor of England's position as Speaker of the House of Lords. However, Vice Chancellor Jameson resigned as Speaker of the Legislative Council in 1843.[67] Statutory provisions of 1841, 1843, and 1857 made judges ineligible for membership in the Legislative Assembly; the 1857 act also applied to elected membership in the Legislative Council.[68]

The movement to exclude judges from the legislature and the Executive Council was part of the broader movement for the attainment of responsible government. In the Canadas there was some confusion between responsible government, in which the executive sits in the legislature and is responsible to it, and the American congressional system, where there is a greater separation of powers between legislature, executive, and judiciary. Perhaps this is why the Province of Canada in one sense went a step further than the mother country where, then as now, the Lord Chancellor is a prominent member of all three branches of government and judges sit in the House of Lords, which is a court of appeal as well as the upper house of the legislature.

The establishment of a Court of Chancery was not the only important development in the history of the courts of Upper Canada in 1837. In the same year an act authorized the addition of two new puisne judges to the Court of King's Bench. The increase in the population of the province and the creation of new districts had added greatly to the workload of the court, making these appointments necessary. Henceforth, the membership of the Court was to consist of the Chief Justice of the province and four puisne judges. Once the new appointments were made, the puisne judges were to sit in rotation in each term or otherwise as they should agree among themselves. No more than three were to sit at the same time unless the Chief Justice was absent. Any one of the judges, while the others were sitting 'in Banc,' might sit apart for the business of justifying special bail, discharging insolvent debtors, administering oaths, and dealing with various procedural matters; such actions were to have the same force and validity as those of the court sitting 'in Banc.'[69] This sitting of one judge, which was important in relieving pressure on the court during term, became known as the Bail Court. It was described by Riddell, writing in 1928, as 'the beginning of our present weekly (or Single) Court and Chambers practice.'[70] The distinction between court and chambers has now been abolished.[71]

Although Queen Victoria ascended the throne in June 1837, the name of the Court of King's Bench was not changed to Court of Queen's Bench until May 1839. The act of 1794, by which the court was established, had made no provision for such a change in the event of having a female monarch. The 1839 act provided that the court should be known as 'His Majesty's Court of King's Bench' during the reign of a male sovereign and as 'Her Majesty's Court of Queen's Bench' during the reign of a female sovereign.[72]

There had been several amendments to the legislation concerning the Courts of Requests; in 1833 a new act thoroughly reorganized them. Because the flexible rule concerning divisions in the original act had caused some problems (the boundaries were not always satisfactory), the first quarter sessions to be held in each district after 1 April 1833 was required to declare the divisions for the district. Two or more commissioners for each division were to be appointed not by quarter sessions, as in the past, but by the Lieutenant Governor. The jurisdiction of the courts was increased to £10.[73] The 1833 act left in doubt the power of the quarter sessions to vary the divisions. An amending act in 1837 provided that the magistrates in quarter sessions might vary the divisions 'as to them from time to time may seem necessary.'[74] Since under the 1833 act commissioners no longer had to be justices of the peace, some areas that did not before have Courts of Requests now attained them. By 1840 the fifteen districts of the province had a total of 187 divisions and 1143 commissioners.[75]

In 1827 the Court of Probate and the Surrogate Courts were given jurisdiction in the guardianship of infants.[76] There was a further addition to the jurisdiction of the Surrogate Courts in 1831, when their judges were given authority to examine married women as to their free and voluntary execution of deeds of their property; the powers of the Surrogate Court judges in this area were shared with the judges of the Court of King's Bench and the District Courts.[77]

The legislative union of Upper and Lower Canada to form the Province of Canada in 1841 was not accompanied by a union of their courts. Because of differences between the legal systems of the constituent parts of the new province, each retained its own courts. The one exception was the Court of Appeal, since there was now only one Governor and Executive Council to constitute such a court. The Act of Union, 1840, provided that the powers exercised by the Governor and Executive Council of each province would now be vested in the Governor of the Province of Canada and his Executive Council; thus following what was said to be the composition of the pre-union court, the Governor of the Province of Canada or the Chief Justice of Upper Canada and any two or more members of the Executive Council of the Province of Canada constituted the post-union Court of Appeal for Upper Canada.[78] The Act of Union's statement of the composition of the pre-union court is misleading because an 1837 statute had added certain judges to it. They continued to be members after the union.

In addition, some other changes took place in the courts of Upper Canada soon after the legislative union. Lack of legally trained persons in a new and thinly populated colony had led to many of Upper Canada's judicial positions being held by laymen. The availability of lawyers and the need for their services on the bench became greater as the complexity of society and its legal disputes increased. In 1841 the legislature of the new Province of Canada enacted that in future only 'a Barrister at law of this Province' should be appointed a judge of any District Court in Upper Canada; it also provided that a District Court judge was to reside in the district of which he was the judge.[79] Another enactment of the same session abolished the Courts of Requests, replacing them with Division Courts, in which the District Court judge was to preside. There were to be no more than six Division Courts in a district; the Home District had had twenty-three Courts of Requests in 1840 and some other districts almost as many.[80] The desire to replace the lay judges of the old Courts of Requests made it necessary to reduce the number of courts. There had been complaints that the old divisions were too small; now there were complaints that the new ones were too large. In 1845 the number was changed from six to not fewer than three and not more than nine; five years later 'nine' was changed to 'twelve.'[81] The monetary jurisdiction of the Division Courts, like that of the Courts of Requests since 1833, was set at £10. However, if the sum claimed exceeded £2 10 s., either the plaintiff or the defendant had the right to require the summoning of a jury. As had been the case with the Courts of Requests, there was no appeal from the judgment of a Division Court.[82]

The 1841 act relating to Division Courts also provided that in case of illness or other unavoidable absence, the District Court judge might 'appoint some other person who would be otherwise qualified to be appointed a Judge of such District Court, to act as his Deputy ...'[83] Thus even in the case of a temporary appointment, a Division Court was to be presided over by a legally trained person. Since the act dealt with Division

Courts, presumably the intent was for deputy judges to preside only in them; however, the wording is not really clear and certainly later deputy judges served in other courts. It seems curious too, in view of the subject-matter of the act, that it also provided that a District Court judge, while holding this office, was to be ineligible for election to the Legislative Assembly of the Province of Canada.[84]

The provision that legally trained persons preside over courts was applied to the criminal side as well as the civil. The act which required District Court judges to be barristers-at-law also declared that the judge of the District Court, being also a justice of the peace therein, was to preside as Chairman at the General Quarter Sessions of the Peace for the District.[85] There was, however, no requirement that justices of the peace participating in quarter sessions, other than the chairman, be legally trained.

With the District Court judge being assigned so many new duties, it was not surprising that some District Courts soon required more than one judge. The deputy judgeship was a temporary appointment which, if continued, had to be renewed from month to month; the office of junior judge, which was soon to appear, would be a permanent one.[86]

In 1845 An Act to Amend, Consolidate and Reduce into One Act the Various Laws Concerning the District Courts further clarified the status of these courts and their judges. It was not simply a consolidating act; it made some amendments. Every district in Upper Canada was to have a Court of Law and Record known as the 'District Court' over which one or more judges appointed under the great seal of the province and holding office during good behaviour would preside. Not only must a District Court judge be a resident of the district and a barrister-at-law, but, if appointed under this act, he was to have been a barrister for at least five years. It was now specified that 'the first or Senior Judge of the District Court ... being also a Justice of the Peace therein' should preside as Chairman at the General Quarter Sessions of the Peace; in his absence, the justices of the peace present would elect a chairman *pro tempore*. The jurisdiction of the District Courts was somewhat extended by this act. In all suits relating to debt, convenant, or contract, the limit was £25, but in cases of contract or debt, if the amount was ascertained by the signature of the defendant, the amount was £50. In matters of tort, relating to personal chattels, where titles to land were not brought into question, the limit was £20. Under certain conditions, there was now to be for the first time an appeal from the decision of a District judge on a point of law to the Court of Queen's Bench.[87]

The Annus Mirabilis, 1849

Writing of the history of the courts in Ontario, Riddell called 1837 the *annus mirabilis*.[88] Unquestionably it was an important year, but 1849 is even more deserving of the name. One of the problems of writing a concise history of the courts is the difficulty of relating developments in this field to the broader political and social events of the times. Riddell's *annus mirabilis* was important not only because of changes in the courts; it was also a period of political unrest, culminating in the short-lived and unsuccessful Rebellion of 1837. The year 1849 was also one of important political developments, notably Lord Elgin's signing of the controversial Rebellion Losses Bill, an event of major significance in the struggle for responsible government.[89] The statute which laid the foundation for municipal government in Upper Canada and later Ontario was also passed in 1849.[90] Yet another event was the abolition of the districts of Upper Canada. The original four districts of 1788 had, with increase in population and wider settlement, grown by then to twenty.[91] The act which abolished 'The Territorial Division of Upper Canada into Districts' cited as the reason for this step the fact that 'the boundaries thereof have, in many cases, become identical with the boundaries of Counties.' Up to this point, the counties had served primarily as the electoral limits for general elections. It was now decided to follow the English practice of retaining only the name, county, as a territorial division for judicial as well as all other purposes. Henceforth the District Courts were called County Courts. To prevent the need for an immediate increase in the number of such courts and other institutions in areas where districts had included more than one county, provision was made for temporary unions of counties for judicial and other purposes.[92] The abolition of the districts is a good example of a change not primarily judicial in nature which nevertheless had an effect on the courts.

Two other statutes passed in 1849 dealt exclusively with the courts, making changes of major importance. These changes did not come about suddenly or without thought; they had their origin earlier in the decade. The establishment of a Court of Chancery in 1837 had not ended the dispute as to whether such a court was necessary. There was jealousy between it and the Court of Queen's Bench. Some wanted to strengthen the Court of Chancery by giving it two additional judges; others wanted to abolish it and transfer its jurisdiction to the Court of Queen's Bench. The choice of Robert Sympson Jameson as Vice Chancellor was not popular; his extreme caution and intrinsic conservatism led to long delays in settling suits. In fairness to Jameson it should be added that the task of hearing the whole Upper Canadian caseload in Chancery was an enormous one.[93] A Chancery Commission appointed in 1843 reported in January 1845 in favour of retaining a separate court of equitable jurisdiction; its main recommendation was to curtail proceedings and reduce costs.[94] The Chancery Commission Report reflected the views of senior members of the legal profession, whereas moderate reformers in the profession and in the legislature thought the report did not go far enough and that changes in the composition of the Court were needed. Indeed in their view it was not only the Court of Chancery that required reform; other changes including the establishment of an appeal court separate from the executive were needed. The essential elements of the judicial reforms of 1849 were first presented in a petition to the House of Assembly early in 1845; its principal author was Robert Easton Burns.[95] William Hume Blake assisted him in drafting it and later presented the proposals to Robert Baldwin, the leader of the moderate reformers in Upper Canada, and to the public in a pamphlet. Though cautious at first, Baldwin eventually accepted the proposals. A fact revealed by the Blake pamphlet and the Burns petition appended to it is that although in theory there was an appeal from the Court of Queen's Bench to the Court of Appeal (the Court of the Governor and the Executive Council), in practice this did not take place. The 1837 statute creating the Court of Chancery had made the Vice Chancellor a member of the Court of Appeal; it had also made the puisne judges of the Court of King's Bench members in all cases of appeal from the judgments and decrees of the Vice Chancellor. (The Chief Justice, though no longer a member of the Executive Council, presided in the Court of Appeal under a provision of the Judicature Act of 1794.) It appears, however, from the Blake and Burns documents that the Court of Appeal heard only appeals from the Court of Chancery. This is confirmed by the few reported cases of the pre-1850 Court of Appeal which are published in the first volume of *Error and Appeal Reports*, all being appeals from the Court of Chancery.[96]

The success of the moderate reformers at the polls in 1847, Blake's personal victory in the East Riding of York, and his appointment as Solicitor General for Upper Canada in the Baldwin-Lafontaine ministry in 1848, combined to provide the opportunity to carry out the moderate reformers' proposals for judicial reform. It was Blake who drafted the Judicature Bills of 1849 and guided them through the House of Assembly.[97]

One of the 1849 statutes established 'an additional Superior Court of Common Law and also a Court of Error and Appeal'; the other reorganized the Court of Chancery.[98] What these acts together did was to establish a judicial system consisting of two superior courts of common law, each with three judges, and a Court of Chancery, also with three judges; these nine judges constituted a Court of Error and Appeal, replacing the old appeal court. This was an important change, for it removed judicial functions from the executive and ended a practice whereby laymen could sit on an appeal court. However, the result was not entirely satisfactory, because no provision was made to prevent a judge from sitting on an appeal from his own judgment and this, in fact, was quite common.[99]

The other changes were in part brought about by transferring two of the four puisne judges of the Court of Queen's Bench to the new Court of Common Pleas. Instead of having a Vice Chancellor, as in the act of 1837, the Court of Chancery was now presided over by a 'Chief Judge, to be called the Chancellor of Upper Canada' and two Vice Chancellors.[100] The Chancellor of Upper Canada ranked immediately below the Chief Justice of the Court of Queen's Bench, a reversal of the situation in England. The Chief Justice of the Court of Common Pleas ranked immediately below the Chancellor. The new Court of Common Pleas was to have equal and concurrent jurisdiction with the Court of Queen's Bench in both civil and criminal matters. The 'Bail Court' or 'Practice Court' established by the act of 1837 was abolished, but the judges were authorized to transact in Chambers or elsewhere such business as might lawfully be handled by a single judge. Chancery was given jurisdiction to try the validity of last wills and testaments. Where an appeal from a District or County Court might be taken to the Court of Queen's Bench, it might now as an alternative, at the option of the appellant, be heard in the Court of Common Pleas.[101] In the Court of Error and Appeal, which was to have appellate civil and criminal jurisdiction throughout Upper Canada, the Chief Justice of the Court of Queen's Bench would preside or, in his absence, the highest ranking judge present. Judgments of the court were to be final where the amount in dispute did not exceed £1000; in larger disputes and in other instances specifically provided for, an appeal lay to 'Her Majesty, in Her Privy Council.'[102]

From 1850 to Confederation

With some modifications, the judicial system established in Upper Canada by the statutes of 1849 was the one with which Ontario entered Confederation in 1867. The acts passed in 1849 establishing a Court of Common Pleas and a Court of Error and Appeal and altering the composition of the Court of Queen's Bench and the Court of Chancery came into force on 1 January 1850.[103] Since Queen's Bench and Common Pleas now had equal and concurrent jurisdiction, it was expected that each would deal with approximately the same number of cases, but this did not happen. For several reasons, chiefly, said Riddell, 'the preeminence in public and professional estimation of the Chief-Justice,' it was found that Queen's Bench had a much heavier workload than Common Pleas.[104] John Beverley Robinson had been Chief Justice of the Court of Queen's Bench since 1829. Canadian history books deal mainly with his political views, describing him as an ultraconservative opposed to the attainment of responsible government. As a judge, however, he was unquestionably conscientious and efficient, dispensed speedy justice, and was held in high regard by his Upper Canadian contemporaries.[105] To equalize the work of the two courts, an act of 1853 provided that all writs of summons and other writs should be issued by one office and in alternate twelves, twelve in the Common Pleas and twelve in the Queen's Bench.[106]

Legislation passed in the 1850s regarding criminal trials was of some significance in the history of the courts. At common law there was no appeal in felony; the same was true in misdemeanour, except in certain quasi-civil cases. An 1851 act allowed the trial judge, in the event of conviction, to reserve the case for either common law court, but it was held that this did not enable the court to grant a new trial.[107] A further act of 1857 provided that any person 'convicted before any Court of Oyer and Terminer or Gaol Delivery or Quarter Sessions of any treason, felony or misdemeanour' might apply for a new trial to either Queen's Bench or Common Pleas, if the conviction had taken place before a judge of either court, or to a Court of Quarter Sessions if the conviction had taken place there. If the conviction was affirmed, an appeal was allowed to the Court of Error and Appeal.[108]

Another change worthy of note was the provision in 1855 that in order to hold Courts of Assize and Nisi Prius and of Oyer and Terminer and General Gaol Delivery, anywhere in Upper Canada, it would no longer be necessary for the Governor to issue commissions. This was part of an effort to relax 'the technical strictness of criminal proceedings' which was said to have caused offenders to escape conviction.[109] The change was confirmed by the Common Law Procedure Act, 1856, which provided for the holding of such courts 'with or without commissions as to the Governor of this Province shall seem best.'[110]

Even after the reorganization of the Court of Chancery in 1849, attempts were made to abolish it and transfer its jurisdiction to the common law courts. There was criticism of the appointment of William Hume Blake as Chancellor; since he had sponsored the bill reorganizing the court, it was said that he had created the position for himself.[111] In spite of the criticism, all attempts to abolish the court were unsuccessful and indeed its jurisdiction was extended. In 1857, with the object of 'increasing the efficiency and simplifying the proceedings of the Court of Chancery,' it was given 'the like power, authority and jurisdiction as the Court of Chancery in England possesses, as a Court of Equity, to administer justice in all cases in which there may be no adequate remedy at law.' The same act provided for Chancery judges to go on circuit to hold sittings for the taking of evidence and hearing causes.[112] In 1865 the Court of Chancery was granted the same jurisdiction as the Court of Chancery in England with regard to leases and sales of settled estates and enabling minors to make binding marriage settlements. At the same time it received 'the same equitable jurisdiction in matters of revenue as the Court of Exchequer in England possesses.'[113]

Some changes in the composition of the Court of Error and Appeal were made before Confederation. In 1857 retired judges of the superior courts of law and equity were made eligible for appointment to this court; the first to be named was James Buchanan Macaulay, who had resigned as Chief Justice of the Court of Common Pleas in 1856, thereby losing his seat on the Court of Error and Appeal. Under the new legislation he was appointed to the Court of Error and Appeal on 23 July 1857.[114]

In 1861 an act authorized 'the Governor ... by Commission under the Great Seal' to appoint any retired judge of any of the superior courts of Upper Canada to be the Presiding Judge of the Court of Error and Appeal.[115] It was known that Sir John Beverley Robinson intended to resign as Chief Justice of the Court of Queen's Bench (and consequently as Chief Justice of Upper Canada); the act was passed to allow him to continue to preside in the Court of Error and Appeal. On his resignation, he was appointed on 18 March 1862 to the new position.[116] In June 1862 the Presiding Judge of Error and Appeal, whenever one was in office under the provisions of the 1861 act, was given precedence over all other judges in Upper Canada.[117]

Since doubts had arisen 'as to the power of the Junior Judges of County Courts in Upper Canada,' an act was passed in 1852 to clarify their status. If a county court had more than one judge, the judge first appointed would be known as its Judge and any other judge of the same Court as its Junior Judge. The junior judge was declared to have full power and authority to preside over any of the Division Courts in the county; he was also in the absence of the County Court Judge to hold the County Court. He was not to preside as Chairman of the Quarter Sessions of the Peace.[118] Presumably this was because under the 1845 act authorizing the appointment of junior judges, in the absence of the County Court judge, the justices of the peace present were to elect a chairman *pro tempore*.[119]

In 1853 County Courts were given equity jurisdiction in certain enumerated matters. The monetary jurisdiction varied, depending on the subject, from £50 to £200. Claims entered in a County Court under the provisions of the Equity Jurisdiction Act might, on the application of either party, be removed to the Court of Chancery, if the latter considered such action proper. An appeal lay to the Court of Chancery against any order or decree made by a county court under the provisions of the Equity Jurisdiction Act.[120]

The County Courts received other extensions of jurisdiction during this period. The monetary limits were increased in 1850 and in 1856, and jurisdiction in ejectment was given in certain cases by an act of 1860.[121] Riddell also emphasized an 1857 change – the right given to a defendant to set up a 'defence on equitable grounds'; he described it as 'an anticipation of Mowat's celebrated Administration of Justice Act of 1873.'[122]

Tenure during good behaviour rather than pleasure, which District Court judges had enjoyed briefly in 1845–6, was restored to their successors, the County Court judges, by the County Court Amendment Act, 1857. The Governor could now remove a County Court judge only for inability or misbehaviour established to the satisfaction of a new Court of Impeachment constituted by this act.[123] Apart from some changes in the composition of the Court of Impeachment in 1866, this was the position at Confederation; soon afterwards the issue arose again.[124]

The districts of Upper Canada had been abolished in 1849, but an act of 1853 established a new type of district. The object of the act was to make better provision for the administration of justice in the unorganized tracts of country in Upper Canada – newer areas of settlement associated with farming, mining, and lumbering, which were not yet organized into counties.[125] The act authorized the Governor to declare by proclamation that certain parts of the unorganized tracts would form a provisional judicial district. Judges with the same qualifications and powers as County Judges were to be appointed for these districts; they would be called District Court Judges.[126] Thus there were now both County and District Judges in Upper Canada, a situation which continues to the present day.

The principal changes in the Division Courts during this period were in

Figure 3
The Courts of Upper Canada 1860

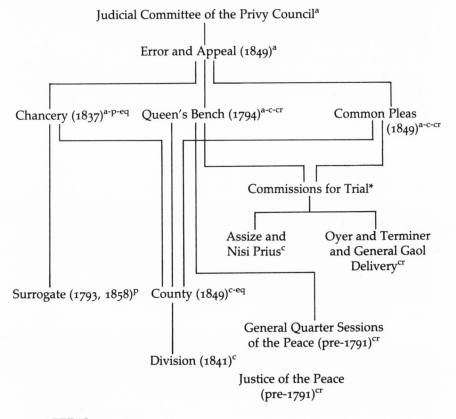

Judicial Committee of the Privy Council[a]

Error and Appeal (1849)[a]

Chancery (1837)[a-p-eq]   Queen's Bench (1794)[a-c-cr]   Common Pleas
                                                                    (1849)[a-c-cr]

Commissions for Trial*

Assize and   Oyer and Terminer
Nisi Prius[c]   and General Gaol
                        Delivery[cr]

Surrogate (1793, 1858)[p]   County (1849)[c-eq]

General Quarter Sessions
of the Peace (pre-1791)[cr]

Division (1841)[c]

Justice of the Peace
(pre-1791)[cr]

a   APPEAL
c   CIVIL/COMMON
cr CRIMINAL
p   PROBATE
eq EQUITY
*   optional from 1855

the extension of their jurisdiction. By Confederation they had jurisdiction in contract and debt up to $100, in tort up to $40, and in replevin if the value in goods did not exceed $40.[127]

In an effort to simplify and expedite proceedings, the Court of Probate was abolished in 1858 and its jurisdiction in both probate and guardianship transferred to the Surrogate Courts of each county.[128] If an estate exceeded £500, the matter might be transferred to the Court of Chancery. In guardianship and in points of law in other matters, an appeal lay to the Court of Chancery.[129] The judge of the County Court was declared to be *ex officio* judge of the Surrogate Court for the county; in his absence, the junior judge, if there was one, or the deputy judge should act.[130] Figure 3 outlines the structure of the court system of Upper Canada in 1860 after the abolition of the Court of Probate.

From Confederation to 1880

In 1867 the legislative union of Upper and Lower Canada gave way to a wider federal one in which the constituent parts of the Province of Canada were renamed Ontario and Quebec. Some of the provisions of the British North America Act, which brought the federation into being, are relevant to the history of the Ontario courts. Among the matters subject to exclusive provincial legislative jurisdiction was 'the administration of justice in the Province, including the constitution, maintenance, and organization of provincial courts, both of civil and criminal jurisdiction, and including procedure in civil matters in those courts.'[131] On the other hand, 'the criminal law, except the constitution of courts of criminal jurisdiction, but including the procedure in criminal matters' was assigned to the Parliament of Canada.[132] Thus in the area of crime provincial courts became responsible for administering federal law according to federally-established procedure. Provincial courts also administer federal law in several other areas, including some aspects of family law, since power to legislate on marriage and divorce is assigned to the Parliament of Canada.[133] Judges of the superior, district, and county courts of each province, except those of the courts of probate in Nova Scotia and New Brunswick, were to be federally appointed and their salaries fixed and provided by the Parliament of Canada. In addition, Parliament might 'provide for the Constitution, Maintenance, and Organization of a General Court of Appeal for Canada, and for the Establishment of any additional Courts for the better Administration of the Laws of Canada.' Finally, 'except as otherwise provided by this Act, all Laws in force in

Canada, Nova Scotia, or New Brunswick at the Union, and all Courts of Civil and Criminal Jurisdiction ...' were to continue in 'Ontario, Quebec, Nova Scotia, or New Brunswick,' until altered by the legislative authority competent to make the change.[134]

Although 1881 was the year of greatest significance in the early post-Confederation history of the Ontario courts, some of the changes before that date were important steps towards the Ontario Judicature Act of that year.[135] Others were relatively minor amendments, some of them resulting from the change in the name of the province. In 1869 the 'Court of Error and Appeal in Upper Canada' became the 'Court of Error and Appeal in Ontario' and henceforth its presiding judge was to be 'styled and addressed as Chief Justice of Appeal.'[136] The change from 'Upper Canada' to 'Ontario' in the names of the Courts of Queen's Bench, Chancery, and Common Pleas did not take place until 1871.[137] In the same year the Chief Justice of Appeal was authorized to sit in the Courts of Queen's Bench, Chancery, or Common Pleas, and any of the judges of the three courts might sit in either of the others if invited to do so.[138] The one-section statute which brought this about is likely to be overlooked; yet it was an important first step towards the merging of the administration of law and equity in the same courts.[139]

Another step in the same direction was taken in 1873 by the Administration of Justice Act, which declared that 'the courts of law and equity shall be, as far as possible, auxiliary to one another ... for the more speedy, convenient and inexpensive administration of justice ...' To bring this about the act provided, among other things, that a purely money demand, even though equitable only, could be recovered in a court of law, and that equitable pleas could be set up in an action at law.[140]

In 1874 a significant change occurred in the composition of the Court of Error and Appeal. Provision was made for the appointment of 'three additional judges ... appointed in the manner prescribed by the British North America Act, 1867' to be called 'justices of the Court of Error and Appeal.' When a vacancy occurred in the office of Chief Justice of Appeal, it was to be filled in the same way; the person appointed need not be a retired judge of any court. No more than four judges were to sit at a time except for the purpose of giving judgments. The judges appointed under this act were to have a variety of duties in addition to hearing appeals. They were to preside over Courts of Assize and Nisi Prius and of Oyer and Terminer and General Gaol Delivery and to hold Chancery sittings for the examination of witnesses and the hearing of causes. They were also authorized to sit in Queen's Bench, Chancery, and Common Pleas, if invited to do so. The Court was also to provide a judge or judges for the trial of controverted elections.[141]

Although the judges of the superior courts continued to be ex officio judges of the Court of Error and Appeal, they were not expected to sit unless one or more of the appellate judges were not available. The intent of the act was to establish an appeal court, the personnel of which was different from that of the superior courts. The act made the very sensible provision that no judge who took part in the hearing of a case in the court below should sit on appeal.[142]

In 1876 the name of the Court of Error and Appeal was changed to the Court of Appeal.[143] The next year an act provided that when a vacancy occurred in the office of Chief Justice of the Court of Queen's Bench (the office still carried the title of Chief Justice of Ontario, although the Chief Justice of Appeal was of higher rank), the Chief Justice of Appeal should be called Chief Justice of Ontario, and the Chief Justice of Queen's Bench, Chief Justice of that court.[144] This provision came into effect in 1878.[145]

The Law Reform Act of 1868 made several changes relating to the inferior courts. It took away from the county courts the equity jurisdiction with which they had been entrusted in 1853. It changed the name of the Courts of General Quarter Sessions of the Peace to Courts of General Sessions of the Peace; they were now to be held semi-annually instead of quarterly. It also made various provisions for the union of cities to counties for judicial purposes; the larger cities in the province had for a few years been treated to some extent separately from the counties in which they were situated.[146]

In 1869 the question of whether County Court judges should hold office during good behaviour or pleasure was raised again. Unlike superior court judges, County Court judges were not assured tenure during good behaviour by the BNA Act, and an 1869 Ontario statute repealed the 1857 Province of Canada provision conferring on County Court judges tenure during good behaviour; another act of the same year abolished the Court of Impeachment, which heard charges of inability or misbehaviour.[147] County Court judges were now to hold office during pleasure; they could be removed 'by the Lieutenant Governor for inability, incapacity, or misbehaviour, established to the satisfaction of the Lieutenant Governor in Council.'[148] Since it was now the Governor General in Council, not the Lieutenant Governor in Council, who appointed County Court judges, it was doubtful if the Ontario legislature had any right to pass such legislation. Eventually, the federal government notified the government of Ontario that the provision relating to tenure would be disallowed, if not repealed; no objection was raised to the act abolishing the Court of Impeachment.[149] In the next session and before the end of the year 1869, the objectionable section was repealed and tenure during good behaviour restored to County Court judges. However, the new section contained the same statement regarding removal by the Lieutenant Governor.[150] Curiously, the federal government allowed it to stand, and it remained on the statute books until 1955, although no attempt was ever made to act on it.[151]

The 1869 act which attempted to take away security of tenure from County Court judges also provided that no more junior judges should be appointed for any county or union of counties in Ontario. Those already appointed were allowed to continue in office.[152] The provision for no further appointments was repealed in 1872; instead, no junior judge was to be appointed except in a county or union of counties where the population exceeded 40,000.[153]

Further clarification of the status of junior judge was made in this act and in the Administration of Justice Act, 1873. In 1852 a junior judge had been given authority to preside over any Division Court in the county and, in the absence of the County Court Judge, to hold the County Court. Now he was authorized, in the absence of the judge, to transact business in chambers.[154] The 1852 act specifically excluded the junior judge from being Chairman of the Court of Quarter Sessions in his county. The 1873 act made it clear that he was authorized to act in this capacity. In fact, it provided that if the county court judge, junior judge, or deputy judge was presiding in a Court of General Sessions of the Peace, it was unnecessary that any associate or other justice of the peace be present.[155]

Until 1872 a county court judge had had no jurisdiction outside his own county. Now it was made lawful for him to sit for a judge of another County Court if requested to do so; while acting in this capacity, he would have all the powers of the judge within whose county or union of counties he was sitting.[156]

Anyone reading sections 57 and 58 of the Administration of Justice Act, 1873, is likely to infer that the County Judges' Criminal Courts were established by this act. In fact, however, a federal act of 1869 had provided for the trial with the consent of the accused, out of session and without a jury, of persons committed to jail for offences triable at quarter sessions. The judge trying such a case was constituted a court of record, and in Ontario (the act applied to Ontario and Quebec) 'any County Judge, junior or Deputy Judge, authorized to act as Chairman of the General Sessions of the Peace' was eligible to preside in this new court.[157] The act dealt in part with criminal procedure, a federal matter, but in establishing new criminal courts, it appeared to encroach on provincial jurisdiction, though it might be argued that Parliament had such power under section 101 of the BNA Act. The name 'County Judge's Criminal Court' was not used in the 1869 federal act, but the courts established under its authority adopted that name. The provisions in Ontario's Administration of Justice Act, 1873, which appeared to establish these courts, seem really to have recognized an existing situation. The name 'County Judge's Criminal Court' was used in the act.[158]

In 1876 the County Court Judges Act provided that the province might be divided into districts or groups of counties by proclamation of the Lieutenant Governor; the districts so erected might be 'dissolved, re-established, altered or re-arranged' in the same manner. All such proclamations were to be published in the *Ontario Gazette*. After the erection of a district, the several County Courts, Courts of General Sessions, Division Courts, and other courts which a county judge was authorized to hold were to be held by the judge and junior judges in the district in rotation, as far as might be 'just, convenient and practicable' taking into account such matters as the age, length of service, and strength of the various judges. The judges of a district were to meet at least once a year to make these arrangements.[159]

In an essay covering many courts and the time span that this one does, it is impossible to deal with every court that has existed and all the duties of the county judges. For instance, in listing some of the courts over which they then presided, the 1876 act mentioned Courts of Appeal under the Assessment Act and Courts for the Revision of Voters' Lists.[160] Judge Helen Kinnear, writing in 1954 about the County Judge in Ontario, devoted one section to 'The Judge as Persona Designata,' describing some of the special powers and duties conferred on the office by various statutes.[161]

An important change relating to Division Courts occurred in 1880. For the first time an appeal was allowed from some of their judgments. Where their jurisdiction had been limited to $100, it was increased to $200; where $40, to $60. There was an appeal to the Court of Appeal, if the sum in dispute on appeal exceeded $100.[162]

A federal statute of 1875 established the Supreme Court of Canada with appellate civil and criminal jurisdiction throughout Canada. Subject to limitations specified in the act, appeals lay from the court of last resort in each province to the Supreme Court of Canada.[163] However, decisions of the new court were not final; they could be appealed to the Judicial

Committee of the Privy Council in England.[164] Indeed, the Supreme Court of Canada could be by-passed, appeals being taken directly from the court of last resort in a province to the Judicial Committee.[165] This procedure was quite common; for instance, until appeals to the Judicial Committee were abolished in 1949, about half its decisions on Canadian constitutional questions were given on appeals that had come directly from a provincial court of appeal.[166] Nevertheless, from the time of its establishment the Supreme Court of Canada, although a federal court, has a place on any chart illustrating the Ontario court system.

THE ONTARIO JUDICATURE ACT 1881

The Ontario Judicature Act, 1881, was modelled on England's Supreme Court of Judicature Act, 1873.[167] It was a landmark in the history of the Ontario courts, but it cannot be regarded as a sudden or unexpected development. The administration of law and equity in separate courts was expensive and time-consuming; the change was made to remedy these evils.

The act brought about a union of the Courts of Appeal, Queen's Bench, Chancery, and Common Pleas to form 'one Supreme Court of Judicature for Ontario.' However, there was not a complete merging of the courts because it was provided that the Supreme Court should consist of two permanent divisions – the 'High Court of Justice for Ontario' and the 'Court of Appeal for Ontario.' The use of the word 'divisions' in this context is confusing because there were also to be divisions of the High Court, the Courts of Queen's Bench, Chancery, and Common Pleas becoming the Queen's Bench, Chancery, and Common Pleas Divisions of the High Court.[168] To minimize confusion, this essay will adopt the terminology of the Judicature Act currently in force, calling the High Court and the Court of Appeal branches, rather than divisions of the Supreme Court.

There was no change in the number of judges. Indeed, the act did not state the number in each division of the High Court; it was simply implied that each would have three, as did the court it replaced. The Chief Justice of the Queen's Bench, the Chancellor of Ontario, and the Chief Justice of the Common Pleas were to be President of their respective divisions. They were to rank in order of seniority of appointment, the senior one being also President of the High Court. The other branch of the Supreme Court, the Court of Appeal, was as before to consist of the Chief Justice of Ontario and three Justices of Appeal. The Justices of the High Court were to be ex officio Judges of the Court of Appeal, just as they had been as judges of the former courts.[169]

The High Court of Justice was declared to be a superior court of record and to have the jurisdiction not only of the former superior courts, but also of the Courts of Assize and of Oyer and Terminer and Gaol Delivery, whether created by commission or otherwise.[170] Riddell has explained that this provision made a radical change in the constitution of trial courts. Before the passage of the Ontario Judicature Act, 1881, the trial court in civil cases was generally the Court of Assize and Nisi Prius; in criminal cases it was the Court of Oyer and Terminer and Gaol Delivery. By the 1881 act, commissions of assize and other commissions might still issue to try civil and criminal cases, but the commissioner sitting under such a commission was deemed to constitute a Court of the High Court of Justice. This made the High Court the trial court.[171] These local sittings were to be held at every county town.[172] The Court of Appeal was also declared to be a superior court of record and to continue to have all the jurisdiction it had before the passage of the act.[173]

Though the branches of the Supreme Court and divisions of the High Court seem to be much the same as the old courts, the important change was that law and equity were to be concurrently administered in all of them according to rules set out in the act. In matters not specifically mentioned in which there was conflict between the rules of law and equity, the rules of equity would prevail.[174]

A confusing provision of the Ontario Judicature Act, 1881, concerns the establishment of Divisional Courts of the High Court. These Divisional Courts were not the same as the Divisions of the High Court; on any given Divisional Court, the judges could be members of any of the three divisions.[175] Any number of Divisional Courts might sit at the same time; each was constituted by two or three judges, preferably three.[176] The jurisdiction of the Divisional Courts was appellate; they heard appeals from orders of a judge in Chambers and dealt with other specified matters. In some cases there was a choice between appealing to a Divisional Court of the High Court or to the Court of Appeal and, with certain exceptions, an appeal lay from a Divisional Court to the Court of Appeal.[177]

To confuse the matter further, the Court of Appeal might, if the Lieutenant Governor in Council or the judges of the Supreme Court should decide, sit in two Divisions. The judges were to decide among themselves the necessary number of judges to form these two Divisions or Divisional Courts. Judges of the High Court, being ex officio justices of the Court of Appeal, could be members. However, two of the ordinary judges of the Court of Appeal were if practicable to sit in each Divisional Court.[178]

An appeal lay from the Court of Appeal to the Supreme Court of Canada if the matter in controversy on appeal exceeded $1000 and by special leave in other cases.[179] There was no mention of appeals to the Judicial Committee of the Privy Council, but they were still permissible under section 129 of the BNA Act.[180]

The Ontario Judicature Act, 1881, also made important provisions relating to County Courts. Equitable jurisdiction, which had been extended to them in 1853 and withdrawn in 1868, was now restored. Division Courts were also declared to have both equitable and legal jurisdiction. Judges of the County Courts were to be 'Judges of the High Court for the purposes of their jurisdiction in actions in the High Court' and were to be styled 'Local Judges of the High Court.'[181] This jurisdiction was not completely new; it has been described by Loukidelis as 'the codification of powers that had gradually been given to the County Court in interlocutory and other matters beginning in 1849.'[182]

The Judicature Act came into force on 22 August 1881, but questions soon arose as to the validity of some of its provisions.[183] By declaring in effect that the judges of the previously existing courts should be judges of the new one, the act appeared to encroach on the federal power to appoint superior court judges. To remedy this situation and place the authority of the judges beyond question, new commissions under the great seal of Canada were issued to them. County Court judges were also federally appointed, and the right of the Ontario legislature to name them local judges of the High Court was questioned not only by the government in Ottawa, but also by some of the judges who refused to act in this capacity without federal sanction. This problem was solved in the same way, commissions being issued to the County Court judges appointing them local judges of the High Court for purposes of the Judicature Act.[184] In an interesting and controversial three to two decision, the Supreme Court of Canada in 1883 declared that the Divisions of the High Court were the former courts existing under new names.[185]

The Supreme Court of Ontario: Its First Hundred Years

A great many changes have taken place in the structure and composition of the Supreme Court of Judicature for Ontario (now the Supreme Court of Ontario) during the first hundred years of its history. A summary of them follows.

It was found that the workload of the Chancery Division was greater than that of the other divisions of the High Court.[186] A somewhat indirect way of remedying this situation was adopted. An 1883 act provided for the appointment of an additional judge not to the Chancery Division, but to the Court of Appeal, making its total membership five. One of the judges was to assist in the transaction of the business of the High Court and especially of the Chancery Division when his duties as a Justice of Appeal permitted; while so assisting, he would have 'the rights, powers and privileges of a Judge of the High Court.'[187] Two years later, however, it was decided that when a vacancy occurred on the Court of Appeal, no new judge would be appointed, 'it being intended that the permanent number of Judges of the Court of Appeal shall not exceed four, including therein the Chief Justice of Ontario.' The act which contained this provision also stipulated that when the number of judges on the Court of Appeal was reduced to four, an additional judge would be appointed to the High Court and attached to the Chancery Division.[188] Thus the total number of judges on the High Court would be ten, four of them being members of the Chancery Division, with Queen's Bench and Common Pleas each having three. The death of one of the Justices of Appeal late in 1885 reduced the membership of the Court of Appeal to four; in 1887 a tenth judge was appointed to the High Court and attached to the Chancery Division.[189]

An 1890 act made a significant addition to the jurisdiction of Ontario's Supreme Court. The Lieutenant Governor in Council might refer to the High Court, to a Divisional Court of the High Court, or to the Court of Appeal, for hearing and consideration, any matter which he thought fit to refer.[190] Some interesting references, especially on constitutional questions, have been dealt with under the authority of this act and its 1909 successor, including one which will be mentioned later in this essay concerning the validity of legislation relating to the composition of the Supreme Court.[191] Changes in the source to which reference is made have resulted mainly from alterations in the structure of the Supreme Court. Reference today is 'to the Court of Appeal or to a judge of the Supreme Court.'[192]

In 1891 a somewhat peculiar provision was made 'for detaching from the Chancery Division of the High Court one of the Judges thereof.' The act stipulated that one of the four judges of the Chancery Division might, 'with his consent, be detached from the said Division without being appointed to any other Division ... or ceasing to be a judge of the High Court.' If a vacancy occurred in the Chancery Division before a judge had been detached, the judge appointed to the High Court in consequence of the vacancy was not to be attached to any particular Division. The judge so detached or appointed was to continue a judge of the High Court and to 'exercise his judicial functions in any of the Divisions ... according as he may appear to be ... most needed for the convenient and expeditious despatch of business ...'[193] Not only did no judge of the Chancery Division consent to be detached, but it happened that all of them remained in office until the provision was repealed in 1903. With no vacancy occurring, an opportunity never arose for the 'floating judge' provision to come into effect.[194] At the time of its repeal, a writer in *The Canadian Law Times* referred to it as 'an absurd provision' whereby the detached judge would have 'become a kind of Judex in partibus, belonging to no particular division.'[195]

In 1894 An Act to Facilitate the Local Administration of Justice in Certain Cases provided that, beginning on 1 January 1895, sittings of the High Court would be held in Ottawa and London at least one day in each week except during the long and Christmas vacations.[196] These sittings are not to be confused with the local sittings of the High Court held in every county town and generally presided over by the county judge as a local judge of the High Court. The weekly sittings in Ottawa and London were for the hearing of matters disposable by a single judge in court or in chambers; not included, however, were such proceedings as might 'in the first instance be heard and disposed of by the Master in Chambers or Local Judge.'[197] A note in the *Canada Law Journal* protested against the new system, which would take two judges away from Toronto for part of each week 'for the sake of keeping a few dollars in the pockets of counsel in Ottawa and London.' It also expressed fear of a trend towards further decentralization with High Court judges having 'to rush wildly about the country with their judicial robes flying in the wind, in a vain effort to bring justice to every man's door.'[198]

The Ontario Judicature Act, 1881, as amended, had been incorporated into *The Revised Statutes of Ontario, 1887*, its short title being changed to 'The Judicature Act.'[199] A new Judicature Act, which repealed the version in RSO 1887 and subsequent amending acts, was passed in 1895. It was mainly a consolidating act and was so described in its long title, but it did include a new provision that no appeal should lie from a Divisional Court of the High Court except in specified cases. If a party in a case in which an appeal lay to the Court of Appeal appealed to a Divisional Court of the High Court, he could not then appeal from its decision to the Court of Appeal, though other parties to the action might do so.[200] The matter of appeals was dealt with in another statute of the same year, the Law Courts Act, which aimed to diminish them; with certain exceptions, there was to be no 'more than one appeal in this Province from any judgment or order made in any action or matter.'[201]

In 1897 there was another change in the composition of the Court of

Appeal. After consisting of four justices, then five, then four again, it was now once more to have five. Appeals from decisions of Divisional Courts and under the Controverted Elections Act were to be heard by the full Court; other appeals could be disposed of by three judges. The same act made it obligatory, when the Court of Appeal sat in two divisions, for at least two of the Justices of Appeal to sit in each.[202] Riddell said that the practice of having the court sit in two divisions had not been satisfactory and that with this new requirement the scheme was doomed.[203]

In 1903 a fourth division called the Exchequer Division was added to the High Court; it was to consist of a Chief Justice as President and two other judges. Each of the four divisions would now have three judges; it was at this time that the 'floating judge' provision of 1891, which had been unsuccessful in reducing the size of the Chancery Division to three, was repealed. The purpose of the 1903 act seems to have been to enlarge the High Court and make it easier for the Court of Appeal to sit in two divisions, though it was still required that two Justices of Appeal sit in each division.[204] The choice of the name 'Exchequer Division' for the new division of the High Court had no significance; indeed, the name was added as an afterthought in committee shortly before the bill received third reading.[205] Since in England the Common Pleas and Exchequer Divisions of the High Court had merged with the Queen's Bench Division in 1881, there was criticism of the creation of a new division in Ontario as a backward step.[206] One critic feared that it would 'accentuate and stereotype distinctions between the divisions of the High Court, which it was supposed from past legislation were to be minimized and, if possible, obliterated.'[207]

An act of 1904 clarified and amended the jurisdiction of the Court of Appeal and the Divisional Courts of the High Court.[208] Mr Justice Horace Krever of the High Court of Justice for Ontario has summarized the effect of this legislation by saying that 'general appellate jurisdiction of the Court of Appeal was confined to appeals from Divisional Courts only, although in some cases, appeals might be taken from the decision of a Judge at trial by its leave or by consent of the parties; also motions for new trials might be made in the same way.'[209]

The Law Reform Act of 1909 was another landmark in the history of the Ontario courts. Since the merging of the administration of law and equity in 1881, it was natural to question the need for the various divisions of the High Court which seemed to differ little from the courts that they replaced. The above criticism of adding a fourth division in 1903 expressed the view of those who wished to simplify court structure and make the merging of law and equity complete. The Liberal government of George (later Sir George) W. Ross was replaced in 1905 by a Conservative administration under James (later Sir James) Whitney. It was this government which sponsored the 1909 measure. By this act the Supreme Court of Judicature for Ontario became the Supreme Court of Ontario; its two branches, instead of being called the Court of Appeal and the High Court of Justice, were to be known as the Appellate Division and the High Court Division of the Supreme Court (see Figure 4). More important than the name changes was the fact that the Divisions and the Divisional Courts of the High Court were abolished.[210] The current Chief Justices of King's Bench, Common Pleas, and Exchequer and the Chancellor of Ontario were to retain their existing rank and title, but when vacancies occurred, their office would be abolished.[211] No reduction in the number of judges was intended, but there would be only one Chief Justice in the High Court Division; he would be styled Chief Justice of the High Court and would rank immediately below the Chief Justice of Ontario.[212]

The jurisdiction of the Court of Appeal and the Divisional Courts of the High Court (being appellate in nature) was vested in the Appellate Division of the Supreme Court. Judges of the High Court had always been ex officio members of the Court of Appeal; it was now made clear that the reverse was also true. Every judge of the Supreme Court was declared to be 'ex officio a Judge of the Division to which he is not appointed or does not belong.'[213] There were to be as many Divisional Courts of the Appellate Division as were necessary for the proper dispatch of business. At all times there would be at least two; they were to be numbered consecutively, the first two being regarded as permanent Divisional Courts, any additional ones as temporary. Each Divisional Court was to consist of five judges, the quorum being four, except when considering cases under the Criminal Code or the Ontario Controverted Elections Act, when a full court of five judges was required. The Chief Justice of Ontario and the four other regular members of the Appellate Division were to constitute the First Divisional Court. The members of the Second Divisional Court were to be chosen annually from the judges of the High Court Division by the judges of the Supreme Court. If additional Divisional Courts were needed, their members were to be chosen in the same way. A member of one Divisional Court might sit in another if necessary.[214]

Although the Law Reform Act received royal assent on 13 April 1909, it was not brought into force until 1 January 1913.[215] No doubt time was needed to implement its sweeping changes. In abolishing the Divisions of the High Court, Ontario went further than England, where the High Court still consists of three Divisions.[216]

An amendment affecting the old High Court, as it still existed, was

Figure 4
The Courts of Ontario 1910

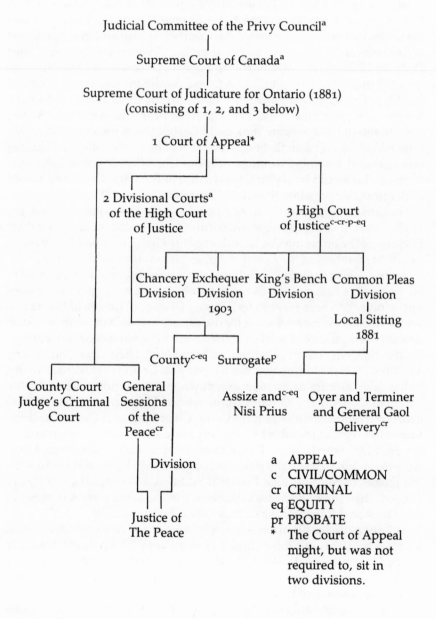

Judicial Committee of the Privy Council[a]

Supreme Court of Canada[a]

Supreme Court of Judicature for Ontario (1881)
(consisting of 1, 2, and 3 below)

1 Court of Appeal*

2 Divisional Courts[a]
of the High Court
of Justice

3 High Court
of Justice[c-cr-p-eq]

Chancery   Exchequer   King's Bench   Common Pleas
Division   Division   Division   Division
                1903   Local Sitting
                                             1881

County[c-eq]   Surrogate[p]

County Court   General   Assize and[c-eq]   Oyer and Terminer
Judge's Criminal Sessions   Nisi Prius   and General Gaol
Court   of the   Delivery[cr]
                  Peace[cr]

Division   a   APPEAL
                c   CIVIL/COMMON
                cr CRIMINAL
                eq EQUITY
Justice of   pr PROBATE
The Peace   *   The Court of Appeal
                    might, but was not
                    required to, sit in
                    two divisions.

made in 1910. It was to consist of four divisions with three judges each and two additional judges not attached to any division.[217] This was reminiscent of the 'floating judge' provision of 1891. The intent, however, seems to have been simply to increase the membership of the High Court to fourteen before the Law Reform Act came into effect. Two new appointments were made before 1 January 1913.[218]

Under the system which came into force in 1913, the principal duty of five of the fourteen judges of the High Court Division was to serve on the Second Divisional Court of the Appellate Division. However, the membership of the Second Divisional Court changed from year to year. In 1923 an amending act in effect transferred five of the judges of the High Court Division to the Appellate Division to make possible the establishment of a permanent Second Divisional Court. The provision for additional temporary Divisional Courts, which had never been put into effect, was repealed; there were now to be only the two permanent Divisional Courts of the Appellate Division. The High Court Division was now to consist of nine judges and the Appellate Division of ten. The Chief Justice of Ontario was to continue to be President of the First Divisional Court. Next to him in rank would be the Chief Justice of the Second Divisional Court, a new position created by this amending act. Each Divisional Court of the Appellate Division would now consist of a Chief Justice and four Justices of Appeal.[219]

Some of the provisions of the 1923 act came into force on the date of royal assent (8 May 1923), the remainder on 1 January 1924.[220] The act was scarcely in effect when another act was passed repealing it and making radical changes in the composition of the Supreme Court. Perhaps 'radical' is the wrong word because the new act was sponsored by the Conservative government of George Howard Ferguson, which had assumed office in July 1923 following the defeat of the United Farmers of Ontario in a general election. This act received royal assent on 17 April 1924, but the date of its coming into force was to be fixed by proclamation.[221] In fact, it never was proclaimed, so the provisions of 1923 which it repealed remained in effect.

The 1924 act provided that the Supreme Court of Ontario should consist of nineteen judges to be appointed as provided by the British North America Act, that is, by the Governor General (in effect the federal government). The judges so appointed would then be assigned to either the Appellate or the High Court Division by the Lieutenant Governor in Council. The Divisional Courts of the Appellate Division were to be abolished, their jurisdiction being vested in the Appellate Division.

Judges in office when the act came into force would be assigned to the Division of which they were already members, but eventually the Appellate Division was to consist of eight judges, one of whom would' be designated by the Lieutenant Governor in Council to be President of the Appellate Division and Chief Justice of Ontario. Similarly, the Lieutenant Governor in Council would designate a judge of the High Court Division to be its President with the title, Chief Justice of the High Court Division. The Chief Justices in office when the act came into force would, however, retain their offices until their retirement or death.[222]

When doubts arose as to the constitutionality of the 1924 act, the Lieutenant Governor in Council referred to the First Divisional Court of the Appellate Division of the Supreme Court the question of whether its provisions were within the legislative competence of the legislature of Ontario. In a four to one decision, the Court declared that they were not.[223] The Attorney General for Ontario appealed the decision to the Judicial Committee of the Privy Council, which upheld it.[224] The reasoning of both the First Divisional Court and the Judicial Committee was that in giving the Lieutenant Governor in Council power to 'assign' judges to a Division and to 'designate' the Chief Justices, the act entrenched on the federal power to appoint superior court judges, there being no difference between 'assigning' or 'designating' and 'appointing.'[225] The major provisions of the Judicature Act, 1924, having been held ultra vires the Ontario legislature, the Supreme Court of Ontario continued as constituted on 1 January 1924.

The next major change relating to the Supreme Court of Ontario occurred in 1931. The names of its two branches were changed back from the Appellate Division and the High Court Division to the 'Court of Appeal for Ontario' and the 'High Court of Justice for Ontario.' The two Divisional Courts of the Court of Appeal were to be merged into the Court of Appeal, which was to consist of the Chief Justice of Ontario, the Chief Justice in Appeal (formerly the Chief Justice of the Second Divisional Court), and eight Justices of Appeal. As vacancies occurred, the number of Justices of Appeal was to be reduced from eight to six. The office of Chief Justice in Appeal was also to be abolished when a vacancy occurred, but if the total number of judges on the Court had before that time been reduced to eight, there was to be no further reduction. Although the Divisional Courts of the Appellate Division were abolished, the Court of Appeal was authorized to sit in two divisions in alternate weeks or at the same time. Every appeal to the Court of Appeal was to be heard by not less than three Justices of the Court sitting together and always before an uneven number. As vacancies occurred in the Court of Appeal and it was reduced in number, the High Court was to be increased in number until it consisted of the Chief Justice and ten other judges.[226]

The reasoning behind some of these changes was described in a statement by William H. Price, the Attorney General:

It has been felt that there were not enough Judges taking trial work throughout Ontario to enable the business in the various county towns to be handled expeditiously, and that it would be wise to have additional Judges for that work. 'Justice delayed is often justice denied,' and it is very important that the trial work be proceeded with as rapidly as possible, and that these trials take place within the county jurisdiction.

The Appellate work has been carried on by ten Judges. Many have thought that this was a little top heavy, considering that only nine Judges were provided for trial work. It has, accordingly, been decided to cut down the number of Judges in Appeal to eight, and as vacancies occur, to appoint two more Judges for trial work.[227]

Mr Justice Krever has said that the structure of the Supreme Court of Ontario remained pretty much the same from 1931 until April 1972.[228] For this the legal historian must be grateful, since the changes during the first fifty years of its history are almost too much to keep straight either in one's mind or on paper. The reduction in the size of the Court of Appeal and the corresponding increase in the High Court contemplated by the Judicature Act, 1931, were accomplished within a short time, since two Justices of Appeal died in 1932 and two additional High Court judges were appointed the same year.[229] A vacancy in the office of Chief Justice in Appeal did not occur until 1938; it was then abolished as provided by the 1931 act, as re-enacted and updated in 1936.[230] The most notable change in the composition of the Supreme Court in the years which followed was the rapid increase in the number of judges on the High Court; less frequent additions were made to the Court of Appeal. The number of High Court judges, in addition to its Chief Justice, had been increased from ten to twelve in 1936. Provisions were made for further increases (two each time) in 1946, 1949, 1951, 1958, and 1962, bringing the total, excluding the Chief Justice, to twenty-two. In 1967 there was a further increase to twenty-six and in 1970, to thirty-one. Two increases occurred in 1976, the first to thirty-six, the second to thirty-seven.[231] During the same forty years, 1936–76, there were only two increases in the size of the Court of Appeal. Its membership, in addition to the Chief Justice of Ontario, was increased from six to nine in 1949 and from nine to thirteen in 1974.[232] In 1977 the new offices of Associate Chief Justice of Ontario and Associate Chief Justice of the High Court were created. At the same time provision was made for adding three more judges to the High Court.[233] Thus the Court of Appeal was to consist of the Chief Justice of Ontario, the Associate Chief Justice of Ontario, and thirteen Justices of Appeal; the High Court, of the Chief Justice of the High Court, the Associate Chief Justice of the High Court, and forty other judges. This was the composition of the Supreme Court of Ontario (except for the addition of supernumerary judges) until 1981, when a fourteenth Justice of Appeal was added to the Court of Appeal making its total membership sixteen, and provision was made for the number of judges on the High Court, apart from its Chief Justice and Associate Chief Justice, to be fixed by regulation.[234] The reason for the latter amendment was to 'enable the government to respond more quickly to changes in the court's requirements.'[235] The first regulation under the new provision fixed the number of judges at forty-one, making the total membership of the High Court forty-three.[236]

Until 1961 judges of the Supreme Court of Ontario held office during good behaviour under section 99 of the British North America Act.[237] In 1960 the addition of a provision requiring retirement at the age of seventy-five amended this section.[238] A 1971 amendment to the Judges Act, a federal statute, made it possible, if the legislature of a province passed legislation to this effect, for a superior court judge, on completing at least ten years of continuous judicial service and attaining the age of seventy, to elect to hold only the office of supernumerary judge.[239] A provision was added in 1973 allowing such election at the age of sixty-five, if fifteen years of continuous judicial service had been completed.[240] A supernumerary judge was to perform special duties assigned to him by the chief justice or the associate chief justice of the court to which he belonged.[241] In 1972 the Ontario legislature passed an act to provide for supernumerary judges.[242] If a judge of the Court of Appeal or the High Court eligible to become a supernumerary judge elects to do so, another judge is appointed in his place, though he remains a member of the court at his full salary and performs special judicial duties until the mandatory retirement age of seventy-five.[243] At the time of writing in 1981, there were three supernumerary judges on the High Court and two on the Court of Appeal.[244]

The decade of the 1970s saw the first appointment of women to the Supreme Court of Ontario – Madam Justice Mabel Margaret Van Camp to the High Court in 1971 and the Honourable Bertha Wilson a Justice of Appeal in the Court of Appeal in 1976; Madam Justice Janet Boland was also appointed to the High Court in 1976.[245]

Of historical interest is the fact that in 1943, at the same time as Ontario's Collective Bargaining Act, which required the creation of a Labour Court, was passed, an amendment to the Judicature Act provided for the establishment of 'a branch of the High Court of Justice for Ontario to be known as The Labour Court of Ontario.'[246] This court has been described as constituting 'the first administrative machinery in Canada for the operation of a general collective bargaining law.'[247] However, soon after the federal Wartime Labour Relations Regulations were proclaimed in February 1944, Ontario, like several other provinces, suspended its legislation on the subject and made the order applicable to its jurisdiction.[248] The Labour Court of Ontario was replaced by the Ontario Labour Relations Board.[249]

Apart from the addition in membership already noted, the most important statutory change in the Supreme Court of Ontario in recent years was the establishment in 1972 of the Divisional Court of the High Court. One of the reports of the Royal Commission Inquiry into Civil Rights, chaired by the Honourable J.C. McRuer, former Chief Justice of the High Court, had recommended in 1968 the establishment of 'a court to exercise an appellate jurisdiction inferior to that of the Court of Appeal'; specifically it had suggested 'an Appellate Division of the High Court of Justice.'[250] An act to implement this recommendation was passed in 1970.[251] However, it did not become effective at that time; it was incorporated into the Judicature Act in RSO 1970, with a statement that it would come into force by proclamation.[252] The section concerning its jurisdiction was re-enacted in amended form in 1971 before the provisions establishing the Divisional Court were proclaimed in force on 17 April 1972.[253] The Divisional Court consists entirely of judges of the High Court, all of whom are also judges of the Divisional Court. The Chief Justice of the High Court is President of the Divisional Court and from time to time designates the judges to serve on it. The Divisional Court has jurisdiction to hear and determine applications and appeals referred to it under any act.[254] In effect this means that it hears appeals from courts other than the High Court and County and District courts, since there is statutory provision for appeals from their judgments to be heard by the Court of Appeal.[255] The Divisional Court also has jurisdiction to hear appeals from interlocutory judgments or orders of a judge of the High Court and from final judgments or orders of the master, local judge, local master, or other officer of the Supreme Court, except final judgments made by a local judge under the Divorce Act (Canada).[256] On any question of law, unless otherwise provided by statute, an appeal lies, with leave as provided in the rules, from the Divisional Court to the Court of Appeal. The Divisional Court has no jurisdiction in criminal appeals; the Criminal Code of Canada provides, as it has since 1900, that such appeals lie to the Court of Appeal.[257]

When the Supreme Court of Ontario completed its first hundred years on 22 August 1981, it differed considerably from the Supreme Court of Judicature for Ontario, established in 1881. The most obvious change was in its size. In 1881 the Supreme Court had thirteen judges, four on the Court of Appeal and nine on the High Court. Today its total membership (excluding supernumerary judges) is fifty-nine, sixteen of whom serve on the Court of Appeal and forty-three on the High Court. Experiments with changes in numbers began early in its history with continuing differences of opinion as to whether the trial or appeal side was more in need of strengthening. Sometimes the numbers on one branch of the Supreme Court were increased at the expense of the other. In recent years there have been increases in both, though the High Court has grown more rapidly than the Court of Appeal. The 1931 statement of the Attorney General expressing the need for more judges to do trial work has been borne out by events of the ensuing fifty years. Looked at in percentages the increase does not seem quite so startling. In 1881 30.8 per cent of the judges of the Supreme Court served on the Court of Appeal and 69.2 per cent on the High Court. Today the corresponding percentages are 27.1 and 72.9. Before the passage of the Judicature Amendment Act of 1931, 52.6 per cent of the Supreme Court judges were members of the Appellate Division and only 47.4 per cent of the High Court Division. Considering the relative strength of the two branches at other periods of its history, the Attorney General's statement that many had thought this a little top-heavy seems justified.

Another major change was the abolition of the divisions of the High Court. In one sense this was a natural step, making more effective the merging of the administration of law and equity. However, there now seems to be a trend towards the development of another type of division. The informal establishment of a Family Law Division of the High Court, mentioned in the opening pages of this essay, is a significant development of the recent past, which invites research into the relationship between social and legal change.

Other Ontario Courts and Judges 1881–1981

The County Judge – One of the most notable developments in the history of the Ontario courts has been the evolution of the office of county judge. Serving as judge of the County Court is only one of many functions of the office. The Local Courts Act in RSO 1887, the first consolidation of provincial statutes after the passage of the Ontario Judicature Act, 1881, gives some facts about county judges, their juniors and deputies. Both judge and junior judge were to be barristers of at least five years standing at the bar of Ontario. The provision that no junior judge was to be appointed in any county or union of counties unless the population exceeded 40,000 continued in force. A deputy judge was to be a barrister of at least three years' standing; he held office during pleasure. A judge or junior judge was not to practise law during the continuance of his appointment; no such prohibition attached to the office of deputy judge. The distinction between junior judge and deputy judge was clear. The junior judge's position was permanent; he had the same power and authority as the county judge subject to the latter's general regulation and supervision. A deputy judge, on the other hand, acted in place of a county judge in the event of the latter's illness, other absence, or death.[258]

Some amendments had been made by the time RSO 1897 was published. A county judge or junior judge now had to be a barrister of at least ten years standing at the bar of Ontario.[259] A junior judge was to be appointed only if the population of a county or union of counties exceeded 80,000; moreover, if a vacancy in the office of junior judge occurred, it was not to be filled unless the population exceeded 80,000.[260] However, there were certain specified exceptions to these rules.[261] The principal change between 1897 and 1914, the date of the next consolidation of statutes, was that judges and junior judges of the County and District courts needed to be barristers of only seven years' standing at the bar of Ontario.[262]

A study of the office of county judge reveals much confusion as to the distribution of federal and provincial legislative powers over it. The constitution, maintenance, and organization of provincial courts are a provincial responsibility, but county court judges are federally appointed. The provision that the Lieutenant Governor might remove such a judge for inability, incapacity, or misbehaviour was carried forward from one revision of Ontario statutes to another, in spite of the fact that a federal act of 1882 assigned to the Governor General in Council the right to remove a county court judge 'for inability from old age, ill health, or any other cause or for incapacity or misbehaviour, established to the satisfaction of the Governor General in Council.'[263] Federal legislation also provided for compulsory retirement of county judges; the age was set at eighty in 1903 and lowered to seventy-five in 1913.[264] When compared with the situation relating to superior court judges, the extent of the confusion is obvious. Superior court judges are ensured tenure during good behaviour by the BNA Act; since attaining the age of seventy-five can hardly be considered misbehaviour, an amendment to the act was necessary in 1960, when it was desired to provide for compulsory retirement at that age.[265] But in the case of county court judges, although those in Ontario were said by provincial statute to hold office during good behaviour, and tenure on the same terms was extended to county court judges throughout the country by federal statute in 1882, both the Lieutenant Governor in Council and the Governor General in Council had statutory authority to remove a county court judge for cause; moreover, there was federal statutory provision for compulsory retirement. The provisions for removal for cause and compulsory retirement in the federal act were valid, since county court judges were said to hold office during good behaviour 'subject to the provisions of this act.'[266] However, there is little doubt that the removal powers in the provincial act were ultra vires the Ontario legislature, even before they were superseded by federal legislation on the subject, because they encroached on the federal appointing power.[267]

A still more obvious conflict in federal and provincial law occurred in relation to the qualifications of county court judges. In 1912 the Parliament of Canada added a provision to the Judges Act (which dealt mainly with salaries of federally appointed and paid judges) requiring that a superior, circuit, or county court judge be a barrister or advocate of at least ten years standing at the bar of any province.[268] The Ontario provision, adopted in 1909, that a county court judge need be a barrister of only seven years' standing at the Ontario bar was clearly in conflict with this new federal requirement. Unlike the provincial removal of judges provision, which was almost certainly ultra vires even in the absence of federal legislation on the subject, the seven-year requirement was probably within provincial legislative competence until parliament entered the field. The constitutional position seems to be that qualifications of county court judges relate to both the constitution of the courts (a provincial responsibility) and the appointing power (a federal one); thus legislative authority with respect to such qualifications not being assigned exclusively to the provinces, a federal provision, once in force, automatically supersedes any provincial ones. Yet the Ontario provision that a county judge be a barrister of at least seven years' standing was carried forward from one statutory revision to another, remaining on the books as long as the one relating to the Lieutenant Governor's power of removal.[269]

It is difficult to understand why the situation was not corrected until 1955. Strictly speaking, repeal of the provincial provisions was not necessary; they could have been omitted from a revision of the statutes as being no longer in force. When at last it was decided to repeal the sections of the County Judges Act in RSO 1950 which conflicted with federal legislation, Dana Porter, the Attorney General (later Chief Justice of Ontario), explained to the legislature that the subject-matter of the sections to be repealed was 'now dealt with by the Judges' Act of Canada so that these sections in the provincial Act are obsolete.' When the Leader of the Opposition, F.R. Oliver, asked how long these matters had been dealt with by federal legislation, the Attorney General replied that he 'had not a note here,' but that he could find out; on further questioning as to whether it was ten years, he expressed the opinion that 'it would go back before that.'[270] The bill passed through its remaining stages and received royal assent on 31 March 1955, but no further discussion of it is included in the debates.[271] In fact, at the time of the repeal of the provincial provisions, the removal of county court judges had been dealt with by federal legislation for seventy-three years; the qualifications of county court judges, for forty-three. The 1955 act also repealed all the provisions in the County Judges Act relating to deputy judges; they too had apparently become obsolete.[272]

Most other provincial legislation after 1914 relating to county judges concerned the appointment of additional judges or junior judges. In 1919 the provision that no junior judge should be appointed until the population exceeded 80,000 was repealed, though the repeal did not affect any appointments already made.[273] Thereafter the counties and districts that were allowed a junior judge or more than one junior judge were named.[274] An act of 1958 made a further change. It continued to name counties and districts entitled to junior judges, but it also provided that in addition to these judges, 'one or more judges or junior judges, not exceeding six in number, may be appointed (a) for the county or district court of any county or district that the Lieutenant-Governor in Council may designate; or (b) for the county and district courts of the counties and districts of Ontario.'[275] The provision in (a) made it possible for an additional judge or judges to be appointed in a specified county or district without resort to the legislature; that in (b) was another attempt to appoint 'floating judges,' or judges at large as they came to be known.

The changes since then seem very similar to those in the Supreme Court of Ontario – a rapid increase in the number of judges, corresponding with an increasing burden of court business. Between 1961 and 1971 the number authorized by the new section of 1958 was increased from six to twenty.[276] The need for further amendments was dispensed with in 1972 by striking out 'one or more judges or junior judges, not exceeding twenty in number' and inserting 'such judges or junior judges as are considered necessary.'[277] By 1981 there were forty-three judges at large; the name, however, is misleading since all but one were attached to specific counties or districts.[278] A 1971 amendment to the federal Judges Act lowered to seventy the compulsory retirement age for county court judges appointed in future; for those in office on 6 October 1971 it remained at seventy-five.[279] In 1975 a further amendment to the same act allowed the legislature of a province to provide for supernumerary judges in county courts. If it did so, a county court judge appointed since enactment of the provision for retirement at seventy might elect to hold office as a supernumerary judge on attaining the age of sixty-five years, if he had 'continued in judicial office for at least fifteen years.' A judge who had held office on 6 October 1971 and who was permitted to remain in office until the age of seventy-five might elect to become a supernumerary judge at age seventy, if he had completed at least ten years of continuous judicial service.[280] A 1976 amendment to the County Judges Act applied the above provisions for supernumerary judges to County and District Courts in Ontario.[281] Since 1962 there has been a Chief Judge of the County and District Courts with general supervisory powers over arranging sittings; in 1977 provision was made for appointing an Associate Chief Judge of the County and District Courts.[282] A very recent development is the abolition of the title of junior judge. If more than one judge is appointed to a County or District Court, the one first appointed is now designated the senior judge.[283]

County and District Courts – The short title of the act dealing with County and District Courts has long been the County Courts Act, it being understood that in using the term 'County Courts,' District Courts are included.[284] The principal changes in the years following 1881 related to extensions in their jurisdiction. There were substantial extensions in subsequent years.[285]

Since 1876 the Court of Appeal had heard appeals from County Courts, but an 1895 act provided that a divisional court of the High Court was to hear such appeals.[286] Further changes became necessary when divisional courts of the High Court were abolished by the Law Reform Act, 1909 (in force 1 January 1913), and their jurisdiction was vested in the Appellate Division of the Supreme Court of Ontario. Since then appeals from judgments of county courts have lain to the Appellate Division, to the Court of Appeal, or to a divisional court of the Court of Appeal (depending on the date).

Although the jurisdiction of the county courts is, for the most part, civil, their judges also preside in criminal courts – the Courts of General Sessions of the Peace and the County Court Judges' Criminal Courts. The county courts themselves also have some criminal jurisdiction; since 1933 they have been named in the Criminal Code of Canada as the courts in Ontario to which lie appeals from convictions for summary conviction offences.[287] However, an Ontario statutory provision, adopted in 1934 and still in force, states that where the Criminal Code or the Summary Convictions Act (an Ontario statute now replaced by the Provincial Offences Act) provides for an appeal to a county court, the appeal may be heard by the county judge in the County Court Judge's Criminal Court.[288]

The organization of parts of Ontario into regional municipalities for purposes of local government, a development of the 1970s, has had an effect on the county courts in these areas. For instance, there is no longer a County of York; on 1 January 1971 it was replaced by the Regional Municipality of York and the Municipality of Metropolitan Toronto. For judicial purposes, from 1 January 1971 to 11 June 1980, both these areas formed the Judicial District of York. Now, however, there are two judicial districts, York (its boundaries coinciding with those of the Municipality of Metropolitan Toronto) and York Region (its boundaries coinciding with those of the Regional Municipality of York). Other judicial districts formed to coincide with regional municipalities are Durham, Haldimand-Norfolk, Halton, Hamilton-Wentworth, Niagara North and Niagara South (the regional municipality is Niagara), Ottawa-Carleton, Peel, and Waterloo. Some of these regional municipalities and judicial districts constitute only one county; for instance, the Regional Municipality of Hamilton-Wentworth was formerly the County of Wentworth. In others the reorganization was more complex; Durham Regional Municipality was formed out of the counties of Durham and Ontario, but the town of Port Hope was not included, it being transferred to Northumberland County. The courts and judges of the judicial districts continue to be called county, rather than district, courts and judges. The form used is 'The County Court of the Judicial District of _____.'[289]

Division Courts (now Small Claims Courts) – Changes in the Division Courts were, for the most part, similar to those in the County Courts. There were extensions in their jurisdiction in 1920, 1937, 1949, 1965, and 1977.[290]

Subject to certain restrictions, the justices of the peace in General Sessions retained until 1886 the power to vary division boundaries. A statutory amendment that year transferred the power to 'the County

Judge, the Sheriff, the Warden of the County, and the Division Court Inspector.'[291] Since 1935 the Lieutenant Governor in Council has had authority to make such changes.[292]

Up to 1935 the provision that there should be not less than three or more than twelve Division Courts in a county continued in effect; in that year the minimum requirement was dropped, but it was still stated that there should not be more than twelve.[293] A new Division Courts Act passed in 1950 did not contain this provision.[294]

One thinks of the Division Courts as courts of civil jurisdiction, but from 1905 to 1933 they had limited criminal jurisdiction as well. During that period the Criminal Code of Canada named them as one of the courts to which an appeal lay from convictions for summary conviction offences. The relevant subsection read as follows: 'in the province of Ontario, when the conviction adjudges imprisonment only, to the Court of General Sessions of the Peace; and in all other cases to the Division Court of the division of the county in which the cause of the information or complaint arose'.[295] A section added to the Division Courts Act in the 1961–2 session of the Ontario legislature stated that the Lieutenant Governor in Council might appoint division court judges. This did not mean that county court judges would no longer preside in Division Courts, since 'judge' was now defined as '(i) a division court judge appointed under this act, (ii) the judge or a junior judge of a county court.'[296] The intent was rather to provide additional division court judges where they were needed. Since there is no requirement that division court judges be federally appointed, it was perfectly proper to assign the task of appointing these additional judges to the Lieutenant Governor in Council.[297]

By a statute passed in 1970, which came into force on 1 January 1971, the name of the Division Courts was changed to Small Claims Courts.[298] Under the 1962 amendment, as incorporated into the Small Claims Courts Act, ten judges have been appointed by the Lieutenent Governor in Council. Their powers extend throughout the province, but all serve mainly in the new judicial districts – seven in the Judicial District of York, one each in the Judicial Districts of Ottawa-Carleton and Hamilton-Wentworth, and one in the two Judicial Districts of Niagara North and South.[299] It is also still permissible for a judge of a Small Claims Court to appoint a barrister to act as his deputy, and this practice is not uncommon.[300]

In the Municipality of Metropolitan Toronto (that is, the Judicial District of York) the Small Claims Courts were replaced on an experimental basis in 1979 by the Provincial Court (Civil Division). The Lieutenant Governor in Council, on the recommendation of the Attorney General, appoints the judges of this court (as many as are considered necessary), including a senior judge who has general supervision over arranging sittings and assigning judges. The divisions established under the Small Claims Courts Act for the municipality became local divisions of the Provincial Court. Whereas the monetary jurisdiction of Small Claims Courts in the rest of the province is limited to $1000, that of the Provincial Court (Civil Division) of the Municipality of Metropolitan Toronto is $3000. With simplified procedures the intent is to make civil remedies more accessible and to reduce delays.[301] With its increased monetary jurisdiction, the Provincial Court (Civil Division) should relieve pressure on the County Court of the Judicial District of York, thereby extending any beneficial effects to that court. The experiment is scheduled to end on 1 January 1983, but if successful it seems likely to be continued and perhaps extended to other parts of the province.[302]

Surrogate Courts – In the years after Confederation there was considerable doubt as to whether the federal or the provincial government had the power to appoint Ontario's Surrogate Court judges. The BNA Act excepted the Courts of Probate in Nova Scotia and New Brunswick from the provision that judges of the superior, district, and county courts were to be federally appointed.[303] Ontario no longer had a Court of Probate, but it was at first thought its Surrogate Courts were comparable and that, not being excepted, their judges were to be federally appointed. As long as the county court judge was ex officio judge of the Surrogate Court, as provided by provincial legislation, the question was not of major significance, since the county court judge was federally appointed, and the government at Ottawa evidently did not object to his also being judge of the Surrogate Court. In 1896 a change in the legislation relating to Surrogate Courts determined that only county court judges then in office were to be ex officio judges of such courts.[304] Although the 1896 act made no express assertion of the right of the province to appoint judges of the Surrogate Courts, this was its underlying intent. However, the fact that Sir Oliver Mowat, who as Premier of Ontario had sponsored the legislation, was Minister of Justice in Ottawa by the time it was being reviewed there, helped to prevent its disallowance. At last in 1910 came a statutory assertion of the right of the province to appoint surrogate court judges, together with a validation of appointments already made.[305] As the provisions were neither disallowed nor challenged in the courts, they successfully established the right of the Ontario government to appoint Surrogate Court judges. Having established its right, the province has for the most part followed the practice formerly required by statute of appointing county court judges to the Surrogate Courts as well.[306]

Courts of General Sessions of the Peace – An act of 1890 clarified the jurisdiction of Courts of General Sessions of the Peace and other inferior criminal courts. Only the High Court of Justice or Courts of Assize, Nisi Prius, Oyer and Terminer, and General Gaol Delivery had power to try treason, felony punishable by death, homicide, or libel.[307] This legislation was not new; for the most part the act simply explained the application to Ontario of federal statutory provisions contained in the Criminal Procedure Act.[308] Although federal statutes relating to criminal law were consolidated into a Criminal Code in 1892, it was not until 1909 that an Ontario act referred to it in defining the jurisdiction of the Courts of General Sessions of the Peace. It stated that they had 'jurisdiction to try all criminal offences except homicide, and the offences mentioned in section 583 of the Criminal Code of Canada.'[309] In the Criminal Code of 1892 appeals from convictions for summary conviction offences were to be heard by the Court of General Sessions of the Peace.[310] From 1905 to 1933 this court's jurisdiction was limited to appeals 'when the conviction adjudges imprisonment only,' other cases being heard by a Division Court. In 1933 jurisdiction in both situations was transferred to the County and District Courts.[311] The judge of the county or district court or an acting judge continues to be chairman of the Court of General Sessions of the Peace.[312]

County Court Judges' Criminal Courts – When established in 1869, these courts were called County Judges' Criminal Courts. The change to their present name, County Court Judges' Criminal Courts, occurred in 1909.[313] As mentioned when discussing the criminal jurisdiction of the County Courts, a provision added to the County Court Judges' Criminal Courts Act in 1934 gave these courts authority to hear appeals assigned to the County and District Courts by the Criminal Code or the Summary Convictions Act.[314] Under the statute currently in force, a judge of a County or District Court authorized to preside at the sittings of the Court of General Sessions of the Peace is constituted the County Court or District Court Judges' Criminal Court.[315]

Juvenile and Family Courts – Juvenile and family courts are a development of the twentieth century. Until an act for the protection of children passed in 1893, Ontario had no legislation for the special treatment of children who had broken the law. The Children's Protection Act dealt only with cases where children were convicted of offences under provincial statutes.[316] The passage of the federal Juvenile Delinquents Act in 1908 led to the establishment of Juvenile Courts in Ontario. However, the act was not of general application; it was brought into force on a local option basis. Juvenile courts were established only in those areas where they were authorized by the local authorities. Thus whether a child was treated as an adult or as a juvenile offender depended on the area in which the offence was committed. Not until 1963 was the federal act proclaimed for all counties, districts, cities, and towns in Ontario.[317]

A 1910 Ontario act constituted 'every County or District Court Judges' Criminal Court and every Police Magistrate ... a Juvenile Court within the meaning of *The Juvenile Delinquents Act, 1908.'*[318] Thus, in areas where the latter act had been proclaimed, such court or magistrate acted as well as a juvenile court. The 1910 act, as incorporated into RSO 1914, was repealed in 1916 by an act which provided for the establishment of juvenile courts in cities, towns, and counties where the Juvenile Delinquents Act had been or would be proclaimed. The judge of a juvenile court was to be appointed by the Lieutenant Governor in Council and to hold office during good behaviour and residence in the county for which he was appointed. Provision was also made for 'any Justice of the Peace,' on the written request of the Attorney General, to act as a juvenile court judge for the trial of any case specified in the request.[319] These provisions remained much the same in a new Juvenile Courts Act of 1927, but an important change was made in 1934. The name of the act (not the courts) was then changed to the Juvenile and Family Courts Act, and provision was made for a change in the name of a court from 'Juvenile Court' to 'Family Court,' if jurisdiction was conferred by provincial legislation, general or special, on its judge or deputy judge to conduct inquiries or to try matters 'in addition to those in respect of which jurisdiction is conferred by this Act.'[320]

In 1954 all juvenile courts and family courts in Ontario were renamed juvenile and family courts. In addition, more flexible rules were made regarding the organization of such courts. There might be one for a county, two or more counties, a local municipality separated from the county for municipal purposes, two or more local municipalities, various combinations of the above, or one or more provisional judicial districts or parts of them.[321] As well as jurisdiction relative to the enforcement of criminal law, juvenile and family court judges exercised powers under several Ontario statutes, such as the Training Schools Act, Deserted Wives and Children's Maintenance Act, and Child Welfare Act.[322] Other changes in the 1950s and 1960s related to the appointment of additional judges, compulsory retirement, and allowing judges to sit in juvenile and family courts elsewhere in the province. In 1968 the Provincial Courts (Family Division) replaced the juvenile and family courts.[323]

Magistrates' Courts – In 1968 a report of Ontario's Royal Commission Inquiry into Civil Rights (the McRuer Report) called the magistrate's court 'the most important and most neglected court in Ontario,' adding that in 1965 ninety-five per cent of those charged with indictable offences in the province were tried by magistrates.[324] The term 'magistrate's court' does not seem to have been adopted until 1934, but the police magistrate who constituted the court had been exercising judicial functions in the province for many years. The office goes back at least to 1849, when the Municipal Corporations Act established a Police Office in each town listed in a schedule to the act and directed the police magistrate of that town 'to attend daily, or at such times and for such period as shall be necessary for the disposal of the business to be brought before him as a Justice of the Peace ...'[325] Later legislation provided that there should be a police magistrate in each city and town where the population exceeded 5000; there might also under certain conditions be a police magistrate in smaller towns and in counties. There are also references in the legislation to police magistrates sitting in police courts.[326] The 1934 act declared that in future every police magistrate and deputy police magistrate was to be styled as a magistrate or deputy magistrate and 'his court shall hereafter be known as the magistrate's court.' Though the intent seems to have been to dispense with the word 'police' in the names of both the official and the court, it was provided that where jurisdiction was conferred on a police magistrate by the Criminal Code, a magistrate or deputy magistrate would continue to be a police magistrate.[327] This was necessary because in the Criminal Code of the day, the terms 'magistrate' and 'police magistrate' were not used interchangeably.[328]

The 1934 act amended the legislation already in force concerning police magistrates.[329] In 1936 a new Magistrates Act was passed. Some of its provisions simply re-enacted earlier legislation; others were new. As in the past, magistrates and deputy magistrates were to be appointed by the Lieutenant Governor in Council and were to hold office during pleasure. In a city having a population of 100,000 or over, a woman magistrate or deputy magistrate might be appointed if the council considered it desirable; if the city had more than one magistrate, such an appointment might be in addition to any magistrate then in office or to fill an existing vacancy.[330] This provision, which was probably regarded as progressive at the time but would now be considered discriminatory, remained on the statute books until 1952; it was not included in the new Magistrates Act of that year.[331] The 1934 act contained a new provision for the establishment of magisterial districts and for the designation of a senior magistrate for a magisterial district. Every magistrate was declared to have jurisdiction to act anywhere in Ontario though, on appointment, he might be assigned to a specified magisterial district or part thereof; this might be varied from time to time. As in the past, every magistrate was to be a justice of the peace and to have power to do alone whatever was authorized to be done by two or more justices of the peace. Every judge and deputy judge of a juvenile court was declared to be ex officio a magistrate, but was to act as such only when directed to do so by the Attorney General.[332]

In 1941 a change was made regarding a magistrate's tenure of office. During the first two years of his appointment he would hold office during pleasure, but thereafter he could be removed by the Lieutenant Governor in Council only for 'misbehaviour, or for incapacity or inability to perform his duties properly on account of old age, ill health, or any other cause.' A deputy magistrate continued to hold office during pleasure. The 1941 amending act also provided for compulsory retirement of magistrates and deputy magistrates to be appointed in the future at the age of seventy; those already in office were to retire at seventy-five.[333] There were modifications and changes in this rule in the years which followed; for a time magistrates who retired at seventy might be reappointed to hold office during pleasure but not past the age of seventy-five.[334]

The provision that every judge and junior judge of a juvenile court was ex officio a magistrate was updated and carried forward from one Magistrates Act to another. In RSO 1960, it read: 'Every judge and deputy judge of a juvenile and family court is *ex officio* a magistrate in and for the area served by his court.'[335] If one looks only at the Magistrates Act, it appears that this provision was repealed in 1961; in fact it was transferred, in amended form, to the Juvenile and Family Courts Act, the words 'area served by his court' being replaced by 'Province of Ontario.'[336]

In 1964 provision was made for the appointment of a chief magistrate, whose position in relation to magistrates' courts was similar to that of the Chief Judge of the county and district courts. The chief magistrate was declared to have 'general supervisory powers over arranging the sittings of magistrates and assigning magistrates for hearings, as circumstances require.' He was also to serve as 'the senior magistrate for The Municipality of Metropolitan Toronto.'[337] In 1968 the Magistrates' Courts were replaced by the Provincial Courts (Criminal Division).[338]

Provincial Courts – In 1968 the McRuer Report made several criticisms of juvenile and family courts and of magistrates' courts. One was that there were no stated qualifications for appointment to either office and that some appointees lacked legal training. Another was that some served only on a part-time basis and that too many judges of other courts served as well in the juvenile and family courts. Some of the statistics given in the report help to explain the situation. Of the 114 magistrates in the province, ninety were qualified lawyers and seven of these served on a part-time basis. Fifty-two of the seventy-three juvenile and family court judges in Ontario served part-time, whereas twenty-one were engaged on a full-time basis; seventeen of the total were without legal training. Thirty-nine of the seventy-three were magistrates performing their duties as such; eight were county court judges. The 1968 report recommended that all magistrates should be qualified lawyers and should serve on a full-time basis, that there should be a special course for prospective juvenile and family court judges, that the jurisdiction of magistrates should not be conferred on juvenile and family court judges, and that the latter should be appointed to that office alone.[339]

The bill which sought to replace the magistrates' courts and the juvenile and family courts with provincial courts was prepared before the McRuer Report became available. However, it was modified after receipt of the report and, on introducing the bill in the Legislative Assembly on 29 March 1968, the Attorney General, A.A. Wishart, said that it now represented 'the practical application of the relevant recommendations of the McRuer report ...'[340] Following passage through the legislature the bill received royal assent on 30 May and was proclaimed in force on 2 December 1968.[341]

As many provincial judges as considered necessary were to be appointed by the Lieutenant Governor in Council on the advice of the Minister of Justice and Attorney General. They could be removed before retiring age only for misbehaviour or inability to perform their duties. The normal retirement age was to be sixty-five (as it already had been for juvenile and family court judges), but the provision for magistrates already in office to retire at seventy-five or seventy depending on the date of their appointment was continued. So too was the provision for reappointment of a judge to hold office during pleasure, if retirement took place before seventy-five.[342]

A Judicial Council for Provincial Judges was to be established; it would consist of the Chief Justice of Ontario, the Chief Justice of the High Court, the Chief Judge of the Provincial Courts (Criminal Division), the Chief Judge of the Provincial Courts (Family Division), the Treasurer of the Law Society of Upper Canada, and not more than two other persons appointed by the Lieutenant Governor in Council. The function of the Judicial Council would be to consider and report on the proposed appointment of provincial judges and to receive and inquire into complaints respecting the misbehaviour of judges or their neglect of duty.[343]

Although no specific qualifications for appointment as a provincial judge were included in the act, there was a provision that a judge was not to exercise the powers conferred on a magistrate under Part xvi of the Criminal Code (Indictable Offences – Trial without Jury), unless he had been a member of the bar of a Canadian province for at least five years, had acted as a provincial judge for at least five years, or had been a full-time magistrate or judge of a juvenile and family court at the time the Provincial Courts Act came into force.[344]

Every provincial judge was declared to have jurisdiction throughout Ontario, as well as all the power then vested by provincial statute in a magistrate, two justices of the peace sitting together, or a juvenile and family court or judge. Similarly, subject to the exception relating to Part xvi of the Criminal Code, he had all powers and duties conferred by federal statute on a magistrate, provincial magistrate, or one or more justices of the peace. Some of these provisions seem contrary to the recommendations of the McRuer Report. In each county and district of Ontario there was to be a Provincial Court (Criminal Division) and a Provincial Court (Family Division).[345]

Provision was made later in the act for the offices of Chief Judge of the Provincial Courts (Criminal Division) and Chief Judge of the Provincial Courts (Family Division), which were already mentioned in relation to the composition of the Judicial Council for Provincial Judges. The Chief Judges were to have general supervision and direction over arranging the sittings of their courts and assigning judges for hearings.[346] A 1977 amendment to the Provincial Courts Act, as incorporated into rso 1970, provided for the appointment of an Associate Chief Judge of each of the divisions.[347] This coincided with similar developments in other Ontario courts.

An important amendment in 1979, which came into force on 31 March 1980, provided for the establishment in each county and district of a provincial offences court with jurisdiction in relation to offences included in the Provincial Offences Act, 1979, and in other matters assigned to it by statute. The purpose of the Provincial Offences Act was to replace the summary conviction procedure for the prosecution of provincial offences with a new procedure reflecting the distinction between provincial and criminal offences. A provincial offences court was to be presided over by a provincial court judge or by a justice of the peace. Under some circumstances, there was to be an appeal from a judgment of a provincial offences court to the provincial court (criminal division) of the same county or district, in others to the county or district court.[348]

The Provincial Courts (Criminal Division), the Provincial Courts (Family Division), and the Provincial Offences Courts continue today to be constituted as described above.[349] Some of the experiments now under way could lead to new developments. Because of the establishment of a Unified Family Court in the Judicial District of Hamilton-Wentworth, there is no Provincial Court (Family Division) in that judicial district.[350] One wonders if the work of the Provincial Courts (Family Division) throughout the province will eventually be taken over by a Unified Family Court with much more extensive jurisdiction in family matters. On the other hand, will Ontario's Small Claims Courts be replaced by Provincial Courts (Civil Division) comparable to the experimental court of that name in the Municipality of Metropolitan Toronto?

THE COURTS TODAY – CONCLUSION

Looking back over nearly 200 years, the chief characteristics which emerge in relation to the history of the courts in Ontario are complexity and change. In this essay, not every court that ever existed in the province has been described. For instance, until now there has been no mention of the Mining Court of Ontario, established by statute in 1924 and replaced in 1956 by a Mining Commissioner.[351] Nor has there been a discussion of judges' salaries, a subject which could be a study in itself.[352] Very little has been said about individual judges. Instead, the changing structure and composition, together with the jurisdiction, of the various courts have been emphasized in order to provide basic information that will encourage others to make more detailed studies of specific courts, judges, time periods, and topics.

In 1981 the Ontario courts are in a state of experimentation and change. This is nothing new; it seems always to have been the case. The most notable current experiments are with the Unified Family Court in the Judicial District of Hamilton-Wentworth and the Provincial Court (Civil Division) in the Municipality of Metropolitan Toronto. Another proposal in recent years was for a merger of the High Court of Justice with the County and District Courts; the Ontario Law Reform Commission considered it in 1973 but, with one dissenting vote, rejected it.[353]

This study of the courts leads to at least two conclusions. The first is that the Constitution (formerly BNA) Act's distribution of legislative powers relating to the administration of justice is unsatisfactory and has led to much conflict and confusion. Many examples of the trouble it has caused have been dealt with in this essay. Some of the conflicts have been resolved, but the basic problem remains. The situation with regard to criminal law is especially unsatisfactory. An important distinction between crimes and civil wrongs is said to be that one is prosecuted for a crime and sued for a civil wrong. In English law a crime may also be called an offence.[354] In Ontario, however, there are now provincial offences courts, where one is tried for offences under provincial statutes. Such offences, of course, are not new, but only the method of dealing with them. Presumably they are not crimes, since the making of criminal law is under federal jurisdiction, but neither do they seem to be civil wrongs, since there is no suit between plaintiff and defendant but rather a prosecution in the name of the Queen. Undoubtedly, there are advantages to having criminal law uniform throughout the country; on the other hand there may be merit in proposals for transferring criminal law and procedure to provincial jurisdiction. In a proposed constitutional charter for Canada, Albert Abel suggested that the power of a provincial legislature should extend to 'civil and criminal law and procedure without prejudice to the power of parliament to provide for carrying out measures enacted in the exercise of powers given it by this constitution.'[355] At least the whole matter of federal and provincial responsibilities for the administration of justice should be reviewed with the object of establishing a more satisfactory distribution of legislative powers.

The other conclusion is that something should be done to simplify Ontario's court system. Is it necessary to have so many different courts presided over by the same judge? The Ontario Law Reform Commission asked this question in 1973 and answered it in the negative. One of its recommendations was that the County Courts, District Courts, County Court Judges' Criminal Courts, District Court Judges' Criminal Courts, and Courts of General Sessions of the Peace be reconstituted as a single court of record with only one name.[356] A simplified court system would not only be better understood by lay members of the public; it would also be more efficient and less costly to maintain. Writing of the high cost of court proceedings, especially on the civil side, the Ontario Law Reform Commission placed the largest share of the blame on 'the nature of the organization and the inefficiency of the system.' Specifically it complained of 'inefficient or uncertain scheduling of cases and unnecessarily complicated procedures' as 'by far the largest contributor to cost.'[357] The Provincial Court (Civil Division) project in Metropolitan Toronto is one attempt to correct such faults. Similarly the experiment with a Unified Family Court in Hamilton-Wentworth aims to bring greater efficiency to the administration of family law.

It would also be less confusing if different terminology were adopted to distinguish the three types of districts in Ontario – the districts mainly in northern Ontario which have District instead of County Courts, the districts, now eight in number, into which the province is divided for judicial purposes, and the judicial districts which correspond to regional municipalities. If the Ontario Law Reform Commission's proposal for reconstituting County, District, and certain other courts into a single court with one name were adopted, this might remove one use of the word 'district.' Even if this does not happen and the District Courts remain, the other two uses could easily be changed. The Ontario Law Reform Commission recommended that the districts into which the province is divided for judicial purposes be renamed 'circuits.'[358] With regard to the judicial districts which correspond to regional municipalities, it is noteworthy that the experimental Provincial Court (Civil Division) is described as being in the Municipality of Metropolitan Toronto, not the Judicial District of York. Perhaps this is a step towards using the names 'Municipality' or 'Regional Municipality' for judicial as well as municipal purposes, just as the name 'county' has been used since 1849.

NOTES

I am grateful to The Osgoode Society for a generous research grant and to Curtis Cole, my research assistant, without whose help this essay could not have been completed in the limited time available. Also appreciated is the work of Linda Aitkins, who typed the essay, and Robert Turner, who drew the figures.

1 Judicature Amendment Act, 1970 (No. 4), c. 97, s. 3 (Ont.). The provisions were incorporated into the Judicature Act, *Revised Statutes of Ontario* (hereafter RSO) 1970, c. 228, ss. 6, 7, and 17 and amended by 1971, c. 57, before being proclaimed in force, 17 Apr. 1972. The Provincial Offences Courts were established by the Provincial Courts Amendment Act, 1979, c. 5, s. 4 (Ont.), proclaimed in force 31 Mar. 1980. Note that in this essay Ontario sessional or annual statutes will be cited only by calendar year from 1949, the year the regnal year was dropped from the pages of the sessional volumes.

2 4 & 5 Vict. (1841), c. 3 (P. of Can.); 32 Geo. III (1792), c. 6 (UC); 1970, c. 120 (Ont.)

3 12 Vict. (1849), c. 78 (P. of Can.); 34 Geo. III (1794), c. 3 (UC); County Courts Act, RSO 1980, c. 100; Ontario Law Reform Commission Report on Administration of Ontario Courts (hereafter OLRC *Report*) Part I (Toronto 1973) 157

4 33 Geo. III (1793), c. 8 (UC)

5 Provincial Courts Act, 1968, c. 103 (Ont.); Magistrates Act, 24 Geo. V (1934), c. 28 (Ont.); An Act Respecting Juvenile Courts, 10 Edw. VII (1910), c. 96 (Ont.)

6 General Sessions Act, RSO 1980, c. 187; County Court Judges' Criminal Courts Act, RSO 1980, c. 99

7 There is some confusion as to whether these courts were established in 1869 or 1873, but court records in the Ontario Archives confirm that sittings began in most counties at the earlier date or at least before the later one. For the cause of the confusion see below pages 521–2.

8 Criminal Code, *Revised Statutes of Canada* (hereafter RSC) 1970, c. C-34, as amended (hereafter Criminal Code), s. 747. However, by provincial statute, the County Court Judges' Criminal Courts are authorized to exercise this jurisdiction.

9 Ontario Judicature Act, 44 Vict. (1881), c. 5, s. 3 (Ont.); Supreme Court of Judicature Act, 36 & 37 Vict. (1873), c. 66, ss. 3, 4 (UK)

10 38 Vict. (1875), c. 11, s. 1 (Can.); 30 & 31 Vict. (1867), c. 3, s. 101 (UK); Canada Act 1982, c. 11 (UK), incorporating Schedule to the Constitution Act, 1982, Item 1

11 Such appeals were abolished by An Act to Amend the Supreme Court Act, 13 Geo. VI (1949, 2nd Sess.), c. 37, s. 3 (Can.). Criminal appeals had been abolished in 1933. See 23–4 Geo. V (1932–3), c. 53, s. 17 (Can.).

12 Small Claims Courts Act, RSO 1980, c. 476, s. 55; County Courts Act, RSO 1980, c. 100, s. 14, as am. by 1981, c. 24, s. 1 (Ont.); OLRC *Report* I 159

13 Criminal Code, Part XXIV; OLRC *Report* I 110. However, specified serious offences, noted in s. 427 (a) of the Criminal Code, must be tried in the High Court. Examples are high treason, murder, and acts intended to alarm Her Majesty or intimidate parliament.

14 A.H. Lieff 'Pre-Trial of Family Law in the Supreme Court of Ontario: Simplify and Expedite' *Law Society of Upper Canada Gazette* X (1976) 300–1

15 Law Reform Commission of Canada *The Family Court* Working Paper No. 1 (Ottawa 1974) 7; 'Court Reform' *Chitty's Law Journal* 24 (1976) 299; Ian F.G. Baxter 'Family Litigation in Ontario' *University of Toronto Law Journal* XXIX (1979) 200

16 Administration of Justice Act, 1970, c. 31, s. 1 (UK)

17 Unified Family Court Act, 1976 (2nd sess.), c. 85 (Ont.); 1977, c. 4, s. 5 (Ont.); 1979, c. 108, s. 1 (Ont.)

18 The three figures with the heading 'The Historical Evolution of the Court Systems in the Southwestern Ontario Region 1800–1910' were compiled in 1977 by Richard S. Alcorn for the Landon Project, the University of Western Ontario.

19 14 Geo. III (1774), c. 83, s. 1 (GB)

20 Adam Shortt 'Early Records of Ontario. Extracts from the Record of the Court of Quarter Sessions for the District of Mecklenburgh, (afterwards The Midland District). With Introduction and Notes' *Queen's Quarterly* 7 (1899) 52. The terms 'Justice of the Peace' and 'magistrate' are often used interchangeably. However, 'Justice of the Peace' is sometimes defined as 'a lay magistrate' (that is, without legal training). J.A. Clarence Smith and Jean Kerby make a distinction based on whether the official is paid. 'When the time came to replace him [the unremunerated "Justice of the Peace"] by a paid judge with the same jurisdiction ... this judge was called "Magistrate".' J.A. Clarence Smith and Jean Kerby *Private Law in Canada: A Comparative Study I General Introduction* (Ottawa 1975) 31

21 Hilda M. Neatby *The Administration of Justice under the Quebec Act* (Minneapolis, MN 1937) 283

22 'Ordinance Establishing Civil Courts' in Adam Shortt and Arthur G. Doughty, eds *Documents Relating to the Constitutional History of Canada, 1759–1791* (Ottawa 1918) 207

23 'An Ordinance for the Most Effectual Administration of Justice and for Regulating the Courts of Law in the Province' ibid. 401–2

24 Neatby *Administration of Justice under the Quebec Act* 283–4, 287. Neatby noted that the civil authority of Justices of the Peace did not extend even to all the newer areas of the province. It ended at the Bay of Quinte, so it had no effect in what became the districts of Nassau and Hesse.

25 'Patent creating new districts' 24 July 1788 in Shortt and Doughty, eds *Constitutional History of Canada* 953–4

26 William Renwick Riddell *The Courts of the Province of Upper Canada or Ontario* (Toronto 1928) 49. This book was bound with *The Bar of the Province of Upper Canada or Ontario* by the same author but is paged separately. Riddell explained that there was no express legislation creating courts in the new districts. The commissioning of judges of a court was considered to create it.

27 Riddell *Courts of Upper Canada* 59, 61. The jurisdiction of the Courts of Common Pleas in the new districts was the same as in the courts of the same name in the older districts of Quebec and Montreal. Their powers were outlined in 'An Ordinance for Establishing Courts of Civil Jurisdiction in the Province of

Quebec' 25 Feb. 1777 in Shortt and Doughty, eds *Constitutional History of Canada* 679–82.

28 Riddell *Courts of Upper Canada* 59–61. The appointment and duties of tutors and curators are dealt with in greater detail by Neatby in *Administration of Justice under the Quebec Act* 320–32.

29 14 Geo. III (1774), c. 83, s. 8 (GB)

30 Neatby *Administration of Justice under the Quebec Act* 289–90. Neatby noted that English usage in evidence was permitted in the new districts. Except where real property was concerned, no evidence acceptable under either English law or the laws of the province was to be rejected.

31 'An Ordinance for Establishing Courts of Criminal Jurisdiction in the Province of Quebec' in Shortt and Doughty, eds *Constitutional History of Canada* 690; Riddell *Courts of Upper Canada* 61–2

32 14 Geo. III (1774), c. 83, ss. 8, 11 (GB)

33 Riddell *Courts of Upper Canada* 62–4

34 31 Geo. III (1791), c. 31, ss. 33–4 (GB). There was at this time no appeal in criminal cases.

35 32 Geo. III (1792), c. 1, s. 1 (UC)

36 Ibid. c. 2, s. 1. Although it appears that this latter provision continued in force until shortly after Confederation, in fact suits for small claims in the Courts of Requests were generally heard and determined without a jury. See Spyros D. Loukidelis 'Some Aspects of the Development of the County Courts of Ontario and the Evolution of the Office of County Court Judge, 1792–1881' (Master's essay, Laurentian University, Sudbury 1978) 18, 61 (hereafter 'County Courts of Ontario'). Writing of the period shortly before Confederation, Judge Loukidelis states that small civil cases in the county courts were heard 'with or, as was increasingly more often the case, without a jury.' In 1868 (32 Vict. c. 6, s. 18) the Ontario legislature enacted that all issues of fact and every assessment of damages in either of the Superior Courts of common law or in any of the County Courts should be tried by a judge unless either party served notice requiring a jury. See Riddell *Courts of Upper Canada* 217.

37 32 Geo. III (1792), c. 4 (UC)

38 Riddell *Courts of Upper Canada* 78. The act authorizing the establishment of Courts of Requests was 32 Geo. III (1792), c. 6 (UC). For a study of these courts, see J.H. Aitchison 'The Courts of Requests in Upper Canada' *Ontario History* XLI (1949) 125–32.

39 32 Geo. III (1792), c. 8, ss. 2–5 (UC)

40 Riddell *Courts of Upper Canada* 79–80; 33 Geo. III (1793), c. 8, ss. 2, 3, 16 (UC)

41 Riddell *Courts of Upper Canada* 86–9

42 Ibid. 86

43 For the story of the passage of the Judicature Bill through the Legislative Council and Assembly, see ibid. 86–9.

44 34 Geo. III (1794), c. 2, s. 1 (UC)

45 John D. Blackwell 'William Hume Blake and the Judicature Acts of 1849: The Process of Legal Reform at Mid-Century in Upper Canada' in David H. Flaherty, ed. *Essays in the History of Canadian Law* 2 vols (Toronto 1981–3) I 134 (hereafter 'Blake and the Judicature Acts of 1849')

46 34 Geo. III (1794), c. 2, s. 1 (UC). 'Puisne' is from the French 'puisné,' later-born, hence junior or lower in rank. See *Jowitt's Dictionary of English Law*, 2nd ed. (London 1977) 1466.

47 The procedure is outlined in Riddell *Courts of Upper Canada* 92.

48 31 Geo. III (1791), c. 31, s. 24 (GB)

49 34 Geo. III (1794), c. 2, ss. 33–6 (UC)

50 Ibid. s. 31

51 Ibid. c. 3, ss. 1–2 (UC)

52 37 Geo. III (1797), c. 6, ss. 1–2 (UC). Legislation relating to District Courts was consolidated into one act by 2 Geo. IV (1822), c 2.

53 There has been no Chancellor of Ontario since 1916. See below page 529 and note 211. For further information on the history of the office of Chancellor in England see John H. Baker *An Introduction to English Legal History* 2nd ed. (London 1979) 83–100.

54 Riddell *Courts of Upper Canada* 161. Riddell 'Early Proposals for a Court of Chancery in Upper Canada' *Canadian Law Times* (hereafter CLT) XLI (1921) 740

55 The English statute was 4 Eliz. I (1562), c. 18. See Riddell *Courts of Upper Canada* 161.

56 Riddell *Courts of Upper Canada* 161

57 Ibid. 163–4

58 Ibid. 164–6. See also *Journal of the House of Assembly of Upper Canada* (hereafter JHAUC) 1832–3 (York 1833) 11, 66, 77, 119, 127 and Appendix 79–80.

59 7 Wm IV (1836–7), c. 2, s. 1 (UC)

60 4 Wm IV (1834), c. 2, s. 1 (UC)

61 7 Wm IV (1836–7), c. 2, s. 2 (UC). An 1846 act (9 Vict. c. 10 – P. of Can.) clarified the Court's jurisdiction relating to mentally incompetent persons.

62 7 Wm. IV (1836–7) ss. 13, 16, 17. The name of the appeal court was not consistent in the statutes of Upper Canada. Court of Appeal, Court of Appeals, and Court of the Governor and the Executive Council were all used.

63 Riddell *Courts of Upper Canada* 149. For lists of Chief Justices, members of the Executive Council, and Speakers of the Legislative Council, see Frederick

H. Armstrong *Handbook of Upper Canadian Chronology and Territorial Legislation* (London, Ont. 1967) 109, 11–15, 36.

64 JHAUC 1826 72 (13 Jan.); Riddell *Courts of Upper Canada* 149

65 Riddell *Courts of Upper Canada* 149–50. Riddell gives the date of Robinson's resignation from the Executive Council as 1832, but Armstrong lists it as 25 Jan. 1831. See Armstrong *Handbook of Upper Canadian Chronology* 14.

66 Riddell *Courts of Upper Canada* 150. Armstrong lists Jonas Jones as Speaker *pro tem* (*Handbook of Upper Canadian Chronology* 36).

67 Riddell *Courts of Upper Canada* 150. Vice Chancellor Jameson's appointment as Speaker of the Legislative Council led to the Court of Chancery's being moved to Kingston, then the seat of government of the Province of Canada, although the Court of Queen's Bench remained in Toronto. There was much opposition to the move. The Court of Chancery returned to Toronto when Jameson resigned the speakership. For further details, see ibid. 188–9.

68 4 & 5 Vict. (1841), c. 3, s. 5 (P. of Can.); 7 Vict. (1843), c. 65 (P. of Can.); 20 Vict. (1857), c. 22 (P. of Can.). The 1841 provision applied only to District Court judges in Upper Canada. The 1843 act applied to judges of the Court of Queen's Bench, the Vice Chancellor, District Judges, the Official Principal of the Court of Probate, Surrogate Court Judges, and a long list of other officials. The 1857 act repealed the 1843 one but re-enacted it in updated form; for instance, it extended the disqualification to the Chancellor and Vice Chancellors of Upper Canada and the Judges of the Court of Common Pleas. The 1843 and 1857 acts applied as well to specified judges and other officials in Lower Canada.

69 7 Wm IV (1836–7), c. 1, ss. 1, 5 (UC). These reasons for adding judges were given in the preamble to the act. 'In banc' referred to sittings of a superior court of common law as a full court as distinguished from the sitting of a single judge. See *Jowitt's Dictionary of English Law* 179 and *Black's Law Dictionary* 5th ed. (St Paul, MN 1979) 131.

70 Riddell *Courts of Upper Canada* 153. When noting its abolition in 1849, he called it the Practice Court. Riddell ibid. 187

71 In 1973 the Ontario Law Reform Commission recommended the abolition of the distinction between court and chambers practice. See OLRC *Report* I 195–215. It was achieved in 1978 by Ontario Regulation 520/78 which amended *Revised Regulations of Ontario 1970*, Regulation 545 (Rules of Practice and Procedure of the Supreme Court of Ontario made by the Rules Committee). The section mainly affected was that dealing with motions in court and chambers, beginning at Rule 207, but amendments were also necessary to strike out references to chambers elsewhere in the rules.

72 2 Vict. (1839), c. 1, s. 1 (UC)

73 3 Wm IV (1833), c. 1 (UC); Aitchison 'Courts of Requests' 128

74 7 Wm IV (1836–7), c. 12, s. 9 (UC). Aitchison cites this act incorrectly as c. 11.

75 Aitchison 'Courts of Requests' 131

76 8 Geo. IV (1827), c. 6, ss. 1, 4, 5 (UC)

77 1 Wm IV (1831), c. 3 (UC)

78 3 & 4 Vict. (1840), c. 35, ss. 44, 45 (UK)

79 4 & 5 Vict. (1841), c. 8, ss. 2, 3 (P. of Can.). In the early years of the Province of Canada's existence, there was no uniform way of referring to the constituent parts of the province. This statute referred to 'that part of this Province formerly Upper Canada' as 'Canada West.' The use of this terminology in the statute books was common only in the early 1840s and ceased altogether after 1849 when the use in statutes of the names 'Upper Canada' and 'Lower Canada' for the constituent parts of the province was officially adopted. See Interpretation Act, 12 Vict. (1849), c. 10, s. 5 (4) and (5) (P. of Can.). For a study of this question, see Margaret A. Banks 'Upper and Lower Canada or Canada West and East, 1841–67?' *Canadian Historical Review* 54 (1973) 473–80. I am here following the advice I gave in that article by continuing to refer to 'Upper Canada' throughout the period of the union.

80 4 & 5 Vict. (1841), c. 3, ss. 1, 2, 5 (P. of Can.). As with the Courts of Requests, the Justices of the Peace in General Quarter Sessions were to declare the divisions. They were not required to follow county or township boundary lines, and there was no uniformity in the matter. Sometimes the county was used as a basis for division. A single township might contain two divisions and contiguous parts of two or more adjacent townships might constitute a single division. Divisions could be adapted to the actual state of settlement. Aitchison 'Courts of Requests' 127. The number of Courts of Requests in the Home District is noted in Aitchison ibid. 132.

81 8 Vict. (1844–5), c. 37, s. 3 (P. of Can.); 13 & 14 Vict. (1850), c. 53, s. 3, (P. of Can.); Aitchison 'Courts of Requests' 131–2

82 4 & 5 Vict. (1841), c. 3, ss. 20, 28–9, 44 (P. of Can.). Regarding the use of juries, see above note 36.

83 4 & 5 Vict. (1841), c. 3, s. 6. Judge Helen Kinnear said that this provision was made in 1850, but the 1850 act consolidated the earlier provision. See Helen Kinnear 'The County Judge in Ontario' *Canadian Bar Review* 32 (1954) 132. The first instalment of this two-part article appeared earlier in the same volume, beginning at page 21.

84 4 & 5 Vict. (1841), c. 3, s. 5 (P. of Can.)

85 Ibid. c. 8, s. 18

86 The provision for renewal of a deputy judge's appointment was contained in ibid. c. 3, s. 6.

87 8 Vict. (1844–5), c. 13, ss. 2, 3, 5, 57 (P. of Can.). The provisions of the 1845 act and their significance are effectively summarized in Loukidelis 'County Courts of Ontario' 53–6. The security of tenure granted to the District Court judge by s. 2 of the act did not last long. An 1846 act provided for a return to the earlier practice of holding office during pleasure. See 9 Vict. (1846), c. 36, ss. 1–2 (P. of Can.).

88 Riddell *Courts of Upper Canada* 154

89 12 Vict. (1849), c. 58 (P. of Can.)

90 Ibid. c. 81 (P. of Can.). Concerning this act's provisions for courts, see Paul Craven 'Law and Ideology: The Toronto Police Court 1850–1880' in Flaherty, ed. *Essays in the History of Canadian Law* II 260–2.

91 For an account of the growth of the districts, see George W. Spragge 'The Districts of Upper Canada; 1788–1849' *Ontario History* XXXIX (1947) 91–100 reprinted in Ontario Historical Society *Profiles of a Province Studies in the History of Ontario* (Toronto 1967) 34–42.

92 12 Vict. (1849), c. 78, ss. 1, 3, 5–8 and Schedule A (P. of Can.)

93 Blackwell 'Blake and the Judicature Acts of 1849' 136

94 *Journals of the Legislative Council of the Province of Canada* 1844–5 Appendix JJ

95 *Journals of the Legislative Assembly of the Province of Canada* 1844–5, 188. Burns, who had been a judge of the Niagara District, returned to the practice of law in 1838. In 1844 he was appointed Judge of the Home District and from 1850 until his death in 1863 he was a puisne judge of the Court of Queen's Bench. See *Dictionary of Canadian Biography* IX (Toronto 1976) 108–9.

96 W.H. Blake *A Letter to the Hon. Robert Baldwin upon the Administration of Justice in Western Canada* (Toronto 1845); Alexander Grant *Reports of Cases Adjudged in the Court of Error and Appeal* 3 vols (Toronto 1865) I 9–264. The pre-1850 cases are headed 'In the Executive Council.'

97 For further details regarding the background of the judicial reforms of 1849, see Blackwell 'Blake and the Judicature Acts of 1849' 132–55.

98 12 Vict. (1849), cc. 63, 64 (P. of Can.)

99 This can be seen from a study of Alexander Grant *Reports of Cases Adjudged in the Court of Error and Appeal* 3 vols (Toronto 1865–6). The reports cover the years 1846–66. Thus some of the cases in volume I were decided by the pre-1849 Court of Appeal.

100 The Governor was no longer Chancellor. According to Riddell (*Courts of Upper Canada* 196) there had theoretically been no Chancellor since the union of the provinces in 1841 because there was no longer a keeper of the great seal of

Upper Canada. I question this reasoning since the act of 1837 had named the Governor, Lieutenant Governor, or person administering the government of Upper Canada as Chancellor (without any reference to his being keeper of the great seal of the province), and the Act of Union had vested the power of the Governor or Lieutenant Governors of the individual provinces in the Governor of the Province of Canada. 7 Wm IV (1836–7), c. 2, s. 1 (UC); 3 & 4 Vict. (1840), c. 35, s. 45 (UK)

101 The act containing this provision and the act abolishing the districts of Upper Canada received royal assent the same day, 30 May 1849. The term 'District or County Court' was presumably used to cover both past and future practice.

102 12 Vict. (1849), c. 63, ss. 2–3, 8–10, 39–40, 46–7; c. 64, ss. 1–2, 10 (P. of Can.)

103 12 Vict. (1849), c. 63, s. 50; c. 64, s. 16 (P. of Can.)

104 Riddell *Courts of Upper Canada* 198

105 See the comments on Robinson as a judge in David H. Flaherty 'Writing Canadian Legal History: An Introduction' in Flaherty, ed. *Essays in the History of Canadian Law* I 28–33.

106 16 Vict. (1852–3), c. 175, s. 2 (P. of Can.)

107 14 & 15 Vict. (1851), c. 13 (P. of Can.). It was similar to an English act of 1848–11 & 12 Vict. (1847–8), c. 78 (UK) – which also was held not to justify an order for a new trial. On this subject see W.R. Riddell 'New Trial at the Common Law' *Yale Law Journal* 26 (1916–17) 49–60 and Riddell 'New Trial in Present Practice' *Yale Law Journal* 27 (1917–18) 353–61.

108 20 Vict. (1857), c. 61 (P. of Can.)

109 18 Vict. (1854–5), c. 92, preamble and s. 43 (P. of Can.)

110 19 & 20 Vict. (1856), c. 43, s. 52 (P. of Can.)

111 Riddell *Courts of Upper Canada* 200; Blackwell 'Blake and the Judicature Acts of 1849' 161–4

112 20 Vict. (1857), c. 56, preamble, ss. 1, 6 (P. of Can.); Riddell *Courts of Upper Canada* 203

113 28 Vict. (1865), c. 17, ss. 1–2 (P. of Can.)

114 Riddell *Courts of Upper Canada* 204. Riddell noted that Macaulay was knighted at the same time.

115 24 Vict. (1861), c. 36, s. 1 (P. of Can.)

116 Riddell *Courts of Upper Canada* 204. Robinson died in 1863 and was succeeded as Presiding Judge of the Court of Error and Appeal by Archibald McLean.

117 25 Vict. (1862), c. 18, s. 1 (P. of Can.)

118 16 Vict. (1852–3), c. 20, ss. 1–2 (P. of Can.)

119 8 Vict. (1844–5), c. 13, s. 3 (P. of Can.)

120 16 Vict. (1852–3), c. 119, ss. 2, 17–18 (P. of Can.). Regarding the acquisition of equity jurisdiction by the county courts, see Loukidelis 'County Courts of Ontario' 57.

121 13 & 14 Vict. (1850), c. 52, s. 1 (P. of Can.); 19 & 20 Vict. (1856), c. 90, s. 20 (P. of Can.); 23 Vict. (1860), c. 43, s. 1 (P. of Can.)

122 Riddell *Courts of Upper Canada* 114; 20 Vict. (1857), c. 58, s. 2 (P. of Can.)

123 20 Vict. (1857), c. 58, s. 11. The Court of Impeachment was composed of the Chief Justice of Upper Canada, the Chancellor of Upper Canada, and the Chief Justice of the Court of Common Pleas. For the situation in 1845–6 see above note 87.

124 29 & 30 Vict. (1866), c. 38, s. 1. This allowed one or more of the puisne judges of the superior courts of common law to sit in the Court of Impeachment in the absence of one or more of the regular members. The question of the tenure of District and County Court judges is dealt with at length and very effectively in Loukidelis 'County Courts of Ontario' 70–7.

125 Loukidelis 'County Courts of Ontario' 58

126 16 Vict. (1852–3), c. 176, ss. 1, 3, 5 (P. of Can.)

127 Loukidelis 'County Courts of Ontario' 32; Division Courts Act, *Consolidated Statutes of Upper Canada* 1859, c. 19, s. 55

128 22 Vict. (1858), c. 93, s. 1 (P. of Can.). The Surrogate Courts of the districts had become Surrogate Courts of the counties in 1849. The 1858 act provided for a Surrogate Court in each county (s. 2), but they were not deemed to be new courts (s. 59).

129 22 Vict. (1858), c. 93, ss. 22, 57 (P. of Can.)

130 Ibid. s. 60 (P. of Can.). Riddell called this a 'marked change' (*Courts of Upper Canada* 134). It appears that up to then it was common for a County Court judge to be appointed Surrogate Court judge, but there was no statutory provision requiring it.

131 30 & 31 Vict. (1867), c. 3, s. 92 (14) (UK)

132 Ibid. s. 91 (27)

133 Ibid. s. 91 (26). However, legislation dealing with 'the solemnization of marriage in the Province' is the responsibility of the provinces, s. 92 (12).

134 30 & 31 Vict. (1867), c. 3, ss. 96, 100, 101, 129

135 44 Vict. (1881), c. 5 (Ont.)

136 32 Vict. (1868–9), c. 24, s. 1 (Ont.). But it appears also to have been correct to call him 'Chief-Justice of the Court of Error and Appeal in Ontario.' See Riddell *Courts of Upper Canada* 216. He is so referred to in later Ontario acts.

137 34 Vict. (1870–1), c. 8, ss. 1–3 (Ont.)

138 Ibid. c. 9, s. 1 (Ont.)

139 In dealing with the Court of Error and Appeal, Riddell mentioned the pro-

vision relating to the Chief Justice of Appeal (*Courts of Upper Canada* 216), but there appears to be no mention in his book of the provision relating to the judges of the other courts.

140 36 Vict. (1873), c. 8, ss. 1–3 (Ont.)

141 37 Vict. (1874), c. 7, ss. 1–4, 14 (Ont.)

142 Ibid. ss. 8–9; Riddell *Courts of Upper Canada* 216. An 1869 act had provided that no more than two such judges should sit on an appeal. 32 Vict. (1868–9), c. 24, s. 6 (Ont.)

143 39 Vict. (1875–6), c. 7, s. 22 (Ont.)

144 40 Vict. (1877), c. 8, s. 2 (Ont.)

145 Riddell *Courts of Upper Canada* 217

146 32 Vict. (1868–9), c. 6, ss. 4, 7, 10–16, 22–6 (Ont.)

147 The provision granting tenure during good behaviour to superior court judges is contained in s. 99 of the BNA Act. The act depriving county court judges of such tenure was 32 Vict. (1868–9), c. 22, s. 2. The Court of Impeachment was abolished by c. 26.

148 32 Vict. (1868–9), c. 22, s. 2

149 Riddell *Courts of Upper Canada* 223, also note 4 on 227

150 33 Vict. (1869), c. 12, s. 1 (Ont.)

151 Riddell *Courts of Upper Canada* 223; see below pages 537–9.

152 32 Vict. (1868–9), c. 22, ss. 3–5 (Ont.)

153 35 Vict. (1871–2), c. 9, s. 1 (Ont.)

154 Ibid. s. 2

155 36 Vict. (1873), c. 8, s. 56 (Ont.)

156 35 Vict. (1871–2), c. 9, s. 3 (Ont.)

157 32 & 33 Vict. (1869), c. 35, s. 8 (Can.). See also ss. 1, 5.

158 36 Vict. (1873), c. 8, s. 58 (Ont.). I am grateful to Catherine Shepard of the Ontario Archives for drawing my attention to early minute-books of the County Judges' Criminal Courts which confirm the existence of these courts before the passage of Ontario's Administration of Justice Act, 1873.

159 39 Vict. (1875–6), c. 14, ss. 1–3 (Ont.)

160 Ibid. s. 2

161 Kinnear 'County Judge in Ontario' 28–34. See also Loukidelis 'County Courts of Ontario' 79–83.

162 43 Vict. (1880), c. 8, ss. 2–3, 17 (Ont.)

163 38 Vict. (1875), c. 11, ss. 1, 11 (Can.)

164 Ibid. s. 47. The wording of this section might be thought to indicate that the judgment of the Supreme Court of Canada was final, but the clause 'saving any right which Her Majesty may be graciously pleased to exercise by virtue of

Her Royal Prerogative' allowed appeals to the Judicial Committee of the Privy Council.

165 The pre-Confederation rules allowing such appeals continued in force until 1949 by virtue of s. 129 of the BNA Act except for the fact that criminal appeals were abolished in 1933 (note 11 above). See J.D. Whyte and W.R. Lederman *Canadian Constitutional Law* 2nd ed. (Toronto 1977) 3–10 (ie, chapter 3, page 10; each chapter in this edition of the book is paged separately).

166 Ibid.

167 36 & 37 Vict. (1873), c. 66 (UK); 44 Vict. (1881), c. 5 (Ont.). The Ontario act was cited 'The Ontario Judicature Act, 1881' until the publication and proclamation of RSO 1887; the act in that revision changed the short title to 'The Judicature Act.' See 44 Vict. (1881), c. 5, s. 1 (Ont.) and RSO 1887, c. 44, s. 1. For a recent summary of the events leading up to the passage of the English act, see Anthony H. Manchester *A Modern Legal History of England and Wales 1750– 1950* (London 1980) 144–7.

168 44 Vict. (1881), c. 5, s. 3 (Ont.)

169 Ibid. ss. 3–4

170 Ibid. s. 9

171 Riddell *Courts of Upper Canada* 232–3. If Riddell is correct, the change does not seem to have been fully understood at the time. The act dealing with the issue of Commissions of Assize and Nisi Prius and of Oyer and Terminer and General Gaol Delivery continued to refer to courts of those names. This act was included as c. 45 of RSO 1887 and as c. 53 of RSO 1897. However, the table showing the disposal of acts in RSO 1914 states that it had been superseded by 3 & 4 Geo. V (1913), c. 19, ss. 44–9. This was the Judicature Act of 1913. The cited sections deal with local sittings of the High Court Division (as the High Court was called between 1913 and 1931); there is no mention of Courts or Commissions of Assize and Nisi Prius or of Oyer and Terminer and General Gaol Delivery.

172 44 Vict. (1881), c. 5, s. 46 (Ont.); Riddell *Courts of Upper Canada* 233

173 44 Vict. (1881), c. 5, s. 13 (Ont.)

174 Ibid. ss. 16, 17 (10)

175 Ibid. s. 29; Horace Krever 'Historical Sketch of the Supreme Court of Ontario' 1. This unpublished paper, written by Mr Justice Krever, now of the High Court of Justice for Ontario, for the use of his students when he was Professor of Law at the University of Western Ontario, gives a helpful explanation of the Divisional Courts of the High Court, established by the Ontario Judicature Act, 1881.

176 44 Vict. (1881), c. 5, s. 29 (2)–(3) (Ont.). The Law Courts Act, 58 Vict. (1895),

c. 13, s. 15, made three obligatory, but an amending act of 1896 (59 Vict. c. 18, s. 10) again allowed two in the unavoidable absence of a third judge.

177 44 Vict. (1881), c. 5, ss. 32–6 (Ont.); Krever 'Supreme Court of Ontario' 1

178 44 Vict. (1881), c. 5, s. 42 (Ont.)

179 Ibid. s. 43

180 This section provided that all laws in force in Canada, Nova Scotia, and New Brunswick at the time of the union, all courts, powers, etc. would remain in force until altered. As the act establishing the Supreme Court of Canada did not prohibit appeals from the court of last resort in a province to the Judicial Committee of the Privy Council, they were still permissible under this section. Appeals from the Supreme Court of Canada to the Judicial Committee of the Privy Council were also permissible under s. 47 of the act establishing the Supreme Court. See above notes 164 and 165.

181 44 Vict. (1881), c. 5, ss. 76–7 (Ont.)

182 Loukidelis 'County Courts of Ontario' 92

183 The in-force date is contained in s. 2 of this act.

184 For further details regarding the attitude of the federal government to the Ontario Judicature Act, 1881, see 'Report of the Minister of Justice to His Excellency the Governor General in Council, 30 Jan. 1882' in W.E. Hodgins *Correspondence, Reports of the Ministers of Justice and Orders in Council upon the Subject of Dominion and Provincial Legislation, 1867–1895, Compiled under the Direction of the Honourable the Minister of Justice* (Ottawa 1896) 185–6.

185 *Mitchell* v *Cameron* (1883), 8 *Supreme Court Reports*, 126 at 132 and 136. See also Riddell *Courts of Upper Canada* 233.

186 Riddell *Courts of Upper Canada* 233

187 46 Vict. (1883), c. 6, ss. 2–3 (Ont.)

188 48 Vict. (1885), c. 13, ss. 2–3 (Ont.)

189 Riddell *Courts of Upper Canada* 233–4

190 53 Vict. (1890), c. 13, s. 1 (Ont.)

191 See below pages 531–2. References were not restricted to constitutional questions. The original title of the act was 'An Act for Expediting the Decision of Constitutional and Other Questions.' The 1890 act, as incorporated into RSO 1897, was repealed in 1909, but re-enacted in much the same form. See 9 Edw. VII (1909), c. 52. It adopted the short title 'The Constitutional Questions Act,' but 'any matter that he [the Lieutenant Governor in Council] thinks fit' can be referred. The 1909 act has ben carried forward from one revision to another since that time. A study of four cases dealing with constitutional questions referred to the Court of Appeal under the authority of this act was made in 1978 by Maurice Jones, a graduate student in history at the University

of Western Ontario. His essay is called 'Some Ontario Court of Appeal Decisions under the Constitutional Questions Act.'

192 RSO 1980, c. 86, s. 1

193 54 Vict. (1891), c. 13, ss. 1–2 (Ont.)

194 Perhaps because of this Riddell made no mention of the 1891 act in his book on the courts. The provision as incorporated into the Judicature Act, RSO 1897, c. 51, s. 4, was repealed by 3 Edw. VII (1903), c. 8, s. 2. The members of the Chancery Division during the years 1891 to 1903 were the Chancellor, John (later Sir John) Alexander Boyd, and Thomas Ferguson, Thomas Robertson, and Richard (later Sir Richard) Martin Meredith. See the lists at the front of the relevant volumes of *Ontario Reports* [1st Series] (hereafter OR) and *Ontario Law Reports* (hereafter OLR).

195 N.W. Hoyles 'The Statutes of Ontario, 1903, 3 Edw. VII' CLT XXIII (1903) 410

196 57 Vict. (1894), c. 20, s. 1 (Ont.)

197 G.S. Homested and T. Langton *The Judicature Act of Ontario and the Consolidated Rules of Practice and Procedure of the Supreme Court of Judicature* 3rd ed. (Toronto 1905) Rule 104, 249

198 *Canada Law Journal* xxx (1894) 332

199 RSO 1887, c. 44, s. 1

200 58 Vict. (1895), c. 12, s. 73 (Ont.). This was slightly changed by an 1899 amendment which provided that the party who appealed to the Divisional Court might appeal from its decision to the Court of Appeal if special leave was obtained; 62 Vict. 2nd Sess. (1899), c. 11, s. 27 (Ont.). See also Krever 'Supreme Court of Ontario' 1

201 58 Vict. (1895), c. 13, s. 2 (Ont.)

202 60 Vict. (1897), c. 13, ss. 1, 2, 4 (Ont.)

203 Riddell *Courts of Upper Canada* 234

204 3 Edw. VII (1903), c. 8, ss. 1, 2, 5 (Ont.)

205 Toronto *Globe* 12 June 1903, Summary of Legislative Debates, 9

206 The merging had taken place, under authority of s. 32 of the Supreme Court of Judicature Act, 1873, by order in council dated 16 Dec. 1880, in force 26 Feb. 1881. See William S. Holdsworth *A History of English Law* 7th ed. (London 1956) I 640n

207 Hoyles 'Statutes of Ontario, 1903' CLT 409

208 4 Edw. VII (1904), c. 11 (Ont.)

209 Krever 'Supreme Court of Ontario' 1

210 9 Edw. VII (1909), c. 28, ss. 3–7 (Ont.)

211 Ibid. s. 8. The offices were abolished as follows: Chancellor in 1916, Chief Justices: King's Bench, 1920; Exchequer, 1923; Common Pleas, 1930.

212 9 Edw. VII (1909), c. 28, ss. 8(2), 9(2) (Ont.)

213 Ibid. ss. 10–11. Previous legislation came close to implying that this was the case, but this was the first direct statement of it.

214 9 Edw. VII (1909), c. 28, ss. 12–14, 16 (Ont.)

215 Section 43 (1) of the Law Reform Act, 1909, provided for the act's coming into force by proclamation. A few months after it came into force on 1 Jan. 1913, its provisions were incorporated into a new Judicature Act, which repealed the Law Reform Act. See 3 & 4 Geo. V (1913), c. 19 (Ont.), which became c. 56 of RSO 1914.

216 Queen's Bench, Chancery, and Family; the Family Division is the successor to the Probate, Divorce, and Admiralty Division. See above note 16.

217 10 Edw. VII (1910), c. 28, s. 1 (Ont.)

218 Anyone looking today at the OLR (1901–31) might wonder why at the front of volume 26 one of the judges of the High Court is listed as unattached and in volume 27 two are so listed. The explanation lies in the 1910 amendment to the Judicature Act. The unattached judges were Haughton Lennox and James Leitch.

219 13 & 14 Geo. V (1923), c. 21, ss. 2–6 (Ont.); Riddell *Courts of Upper Canada* 235

220 13 & 14 Geo. V (1923), c. 21, s. 6 (Ont.)

221 14 Geo. V (1924), c. 30, s. 9 (Ont.)

222 Ibid. ss. 2 and 4

223 *Re Judicature Act, 1924* (1924), 56 OLR 1

224 *Attorney General for Ontario* v *Attorney General for Canada*, [1925] *Appeal Cases*, 750

225 The reasoning of the judges is dealt with at some length in Jones 'Some Ontario Court of Appeal Decisions under the Constitutional Questions Act' 10–14. See above note 191.

226 21 Geo. V (1931), c. 24, ss. 2–4, 6 (Ont.)

227 *Globe* 28 Mar. 1931

228 Krever 'Supreme Court of Ontario' 2

229 For details, see the list of Judges of the Supreme Court of Ontario and the notes of changes at the front of the 1932 volume of OR.

230 1 Edw. VIII (1936), c. 31, s. 2 (Ont.). See also list of judges at the front of the 1938 and 1939 volumes of OR

231 1 Edw. VIII (1936), c. 31, s. 3 (Ont.); 10 Geo. VI (1946), c. 43, s. 1 (Ont.); 1949, c. 46, s. 1 (Ont.); 1951, c. 40, s. 1 (Ont.); 1958, c. 46, s. 1 (Ont.); 1961–2, c. 65, s. 1 (Ont.); 1967, c. 41, s. 1 (Ont.); 1970, c. 92, s. 1 (Ont.); 1976 (2nd sess.), c. 16, s. 1 (Ont.); 1976 (2nd sess.), c. 86, s. 1 (Ont.)

232 1949, c. 46, s. 1 (Ont.); 1974, c. 81, s. 1 (Ont.)

233 1977, c. 45, ss. 1 and 2 (Ont.)

234 1981, c. 23, ss. 1–2 (Ont.)

235 *Legislature of Ontario Debates* (hereafter LOD) 1981 p 1506 (11 June)

236 Ontario Regulation 494/81 in *Ontario Gazette* 8 Aug. 1981

237 30 & 31 Vict. (1867), c. 3, s. 99 (UK)

238 9 Eliz. II (1960), c. 2 (UK). The amendment came into force on 1 Mar. 1961.

239 RSC 1970, c. 16 (2nd supp.), s. 5. The amendment was passed in 1971–19–20–21 Eliz. II (1970–1–2), c. 55, s. 6 (Can.) – and incorporated into the second supplement of RSC 1970, which was published in 1972.

240 21–3 Eliz. II (1973–4), c. 17, s. 6 (Can.)

241 RSC 1970, c. 16 (2nd supp.), s. 5

242 1972, c. 159, s. 2 (Ont.)

243 Judges Act, 23–4–5 Eliz. II (1974–5–6), c. 48, s. 7 (Can.). This provision relates to the salary of supernumerary judges.

244 See list of Judges of the Supreme Court of Ontario at the front of (1981) 29 OR (2d).

245 Ibid. Dates of appointment are given in the list.

246 7 Geo. VI (1943), c. 11, s. 2 (Ont.). The Collective Bargaining Act was c. 4 of the same session.

247 Alfred W.R. Carrothers *Collective Bargaining Law in Canada* (Toronto 1965) 50

248 Ibid. 55

249 8 Geo. VI (1944), c. 29, s. 4 (Ont.)

250 Ontario *Royal Commission Inquiry into Civil Rights* Report No. 1 Vol. 2 (Toronto 1968) 669–70

251 1970, c. 97, ss. 1–4 (Ont.)

252 RSO 1970, c. 228, ss. 6, 7, 17

253 1971, c. 57 (Ont.)

254 RSO 1980, c. 223, ss. 7, 17

255 Formerly the Divisional Court was said to have jurisdiction to hear and determine 'all appeals to the Supreme Court under any Act other than this Act [ie, the Judicature Act] and the County Courts Act.' RSO 1970, c. 228, s. 17 (a). The practice then was for provision to be made by statute for appeals to the Supreme Court, without specifying which branch would hear them. However, in RSO 1980 appeals are to the Divisional Court or the Court of Appeal. See Judicature Act, RSO 1980, c. 223, s. 28; County Courts Act, RSO 1980, c. 100, s. 34; Small Claims Courts Act, RSO 1980, c. 476, s. 108; Surrogate Courts Act, RSO 1980, c. 491, s. 33.

256 RSO 1980, c. 223, ss. 17 and 28

257 Criminal Code, s. 2. Until 1900, the court of appeal in Ontario had been defined in the Criminal Code as 'any division of the High Court of Justice.' See Criminal Code, 55 & 56 Vict. (1892), c. 29, s. 3 (e) (Can.).

258 RSO 1887, c. 46, ss. 2–4, 6–9, 12

259 RSO 1897, c. 54, s. 3. The amendment had been made by 58 Vict. (1895), c. 13, s. 27 (Ont.).

260 RSO 1897, c. 54, s. 5 (1)–(4). These amendments had been made by 60 Vict. (1897), c. 14, s. 62 (Ont.).

261 RSO 1897, c. 54, s. 5 (5)

262 RSO 1914, c. 58, s. 3. The change had been made by 9 Edw. VII (1909), c. 29, s. 3 (Ont.).

263 45 Vict. (1882), c. 12, s. 3 (Can.). See above pages 516, 520–1.

264 3 Edw. VII (1903), c. 29, s. 2 (Can.), incorporated into Judges Act, RSC 1906, c. 138, s. 25; amended by 3 & 4 Geo. V (1913), c. 28, s. 9 (Can.)

265 See above page 534.

266 The federal tenure during good behaviour provision was enacted by 45 Vict. (1882), c. 12, s. 2 (Can.).

267 See above pages 520–1; Riddell *Courts of Upper Canada* 222–4

268 2 Geo. V (1912), c. 29, s. 9 (Can.)

269 County Judges Act, RSO 1914, c. 58, s. 3; RSO 1927, c. 90, s. 2; RSO 1937, c. 102, s. 2; RSO 1950, c. 76, s. 2

270 LOD 1955 58 (14 Feb.)

271 The discussion noted was on introduction of the bill. Its passage through second reading, report following committee stage, and third reading and the granting of royal assent are noted in LOD 1955 pp 377, 563, 590, and 1502. The act is 1955, c. 12 (Ont.).

272 1955, c. 12, s. 1 (Ont.)

273 9 Geo. V (1919), c. 26, ss. 2, 3 (Ont.)

274 9 Geo. V (1919), c. 26, s. 2 (Ont.); RSO 1927, c. 90, ss. 4, 5; RSO 1937, c. 102, ss. 4, 5; RSO 1950, c. 76, ss. 4, 5

275 1958, c. 18, s. 2 (Ont.)

276 1960–1, c. 15, s. 1 (Ont.); 1961–2, c. 25, s. 2 (Ont.); 1964, c. 13, s. 1 (Ont.); 1966, c. 32, s. 1 (Ont.); 1971, c. 4, s. 2 (Ont.)

277 1972, c. 86, s. 1 (Ont.)

278 *Canadian Law List 1981* (hereafter CLL) (Toronto 1981) 763–4. It is not clear from published sources that judges at large are attached to specific counties or districts. For this information I am indebted to Judge Loukidelis.

279 RSC 1970, c. 16 (2nd Supp.), s. 8. The amendment was passed in 1971–19–20–21 Eliz. II (1970–1–2), c. 55, s. 9 – and incorporated into the second supplement of RSC 1970, which was published in 1972. The date '6 Oct. 1971' was not included in the 1971 amendment; it read 'on the coming into force of this section.' The in-force date was inserted when the provision was incorporated into RSC 1970.

280 23–4–5 Eliz. II (1974–5–6), c. 48, s. 8 (Can.)
281 1976, c. 15, s. 1 (Ont.)
282 1961–2, c. 25, s. 1 (Ont.); 1977, c. 44, s. 1 (Ont.)
283 1979, c. 66, ss. 1, 2 (Ont.); proclaimed in force 6 Apr. 1981
284 RSO 1980, c. 100
285 59 Vict. (1896), c. 19, s. 2 (Ont.); 9 Edw. VII (1909), c. 28, s. 21 (Oct.); 1 Geo. VI
     (1937), c. 14, s. 3 (Ont.); 1949, c. 19, s. 1 (Ont.); 1961–2, c. 24, s. 5 (Ont.); 1970,
     c. 98, s. 3 (Ont.); 1981, c. 24, s. 1 (Ont.)
286 39 Vict. (1875–6), c. 7, s. 6 (Ont.); 58 Vict. (1895), c. 13, s. 44 (Ont.)
287 23 & 24 Geo. V (1932–3), c. 53, s. 6 (Can.) amending s. 497 of the Criminal
     Code, RSC 1927, c. 36
288 24 Geo. V (1934), c. 54, s. 9 (Ont.); RSO 1980, c. 99, s. 2
289 I am grateful to Wendy Hearder-Moan, Librarian/Executive Secretary,
     Hamilton Law Association, for helping to clarify the terminology used in
     these judicial districts, something that was not clear from published sources.
290 10 & 11 Geo. V (1920), c. 34, s. 1 (Ont.); 1 Geo. VI (1937), c. 20, s. 4 (Ont.); 1949,
     c. 29, s. 1 (Ont.); 1965, c. 32, s. 2 (Ont.); 1977, c. 52, s. 4 (Ont.)
291 49 Vict. (1886), c. 15, s. 1 (Ont.). A new Division Courts Act of 1910 provided
     that these officials 'shall be a board who may appoint and alter the number
     and limits of the divisions.' In a provisional judicial district 'the Judge of the
     District Court, the Sheriff and the Inspector' constituted the board. See 10
     Edw. VII (1910), c. 32, s. 15 (1) (Ont.).
292 25 Geo. V (1935), c. 20, s. 4 (Ont.)
293 RSO 1927, c. 95, s. 4, as amended by 25 Geo. V (1935), c. 20, s. 2 (Ont.)
294 1950, c. 16 (Ont.). The Small Claims Courts of the present day retain the
     numbers of the Old Division Courts. The trend seems to be towards a smaller
     number of courts, many of the numbers not being in use. Thus, a county may
     have four Small Claims Courts numbered 1, 3, 6, and 10. See lists of Small
     Claims Courts in the annual CLL.
295 Criminal Code, RSC 1906, s. 749. The amendment had been made by 4 & 5
     Edw. VII (1905), c. 10, s. 1 (Can.).
296 1961–2, c. 35, ss. 1–2 (Ont.)
297 For a discussion of the right of the province to appoint division court judges,
     see Kinnear 'County Judge in Ontario' 133–4
298 1970, c. 120, s. 2 (Ont.)
299 CLL 1981 778; CLD 1981 61. At the time the latter was published, only nine
     judges had been appointed. The seven judges in the Judicial District of York
     now serve mainly in the Provincial Court (Civil Division) of the Municipality
     of Metropolitan Toronto and its local divisions. See below next paragraph
     and notes 301 and 302.

300 Small Claims Courts Act, RSO 1980, c. 476, s. 15
301 Provincial Court (Civil Division) Project Act, RSO 1980, c. 397, ss. 2–6. The original act was 1979, c. 67.
302 The last section of the act provides for its repeal on 1 Jan. 1983. See RSO 1980, c. 397, s. 10.
303 30 & 31 Vict. (1867), c. 3, s. 96 (UK). See above page 518.
304 59 Vict. (1896), c. 20, s. 6 (Ont.)
305 10 Edw. VII (1910), c. 31, s. 6 (Ont.)
306 Riddell *Courts of Upper Canada* 134–5 and 240–1; CLL 1981 764–72
307 53 Vict. (1890), c. 18, s. 1 (Ont.). In effect this meant that only the High Court had jurisdiction in these cases. See above page 524. It seems strange to talk of Courts of Assize and Nisi Prius as if they were criminal courts, but both civil and criminal cases were said to be tried at the assizes.
308 RSC 1886, c. 174, s. 4. However, homicide was not mentioned in the federal statute.
309 9 Edw. VII (1909), c. 30, s. 3 (Ont.). Following a major revision of the Criminal Code in 1953–4, the reference to section 583 was changed in the General Sessions Act to 'subsection 2 of section 413.' See RSO 1960, c. 163, s. 2.
310 55 & 56 Vict. (1892), c. 29, s. 879 (Can.). Note that the terms 'felony' and 'misdemeanour' have been dropped. The distinction was then as it continues to date between 'indictable offences' and 'summary conviction offences.'
311 See above page 542.
312 General Sessions Act, RSO 1980, c. 187, s. 7. 'Deputy' was replaced by 'acting' in 1957 following the repeal in 1955 of the provisions for deputy judges in the County Judges Act, 1957, c. 42, s. 2 (Ont.). See above page 539.
313 9 Edw. VII (1909), c. 31, s. 1 (2) (Ont.). See above pages 494, 521–2.
314 24 Geo. V (1934), c. 54, s. 9 (Ont.). See above page 541.
315 The County Court Judges' Criminal Courts Act, RSO 1980, c. 99, s. 1. The reference to a deputy judge was dropped from RSO 1960, c. 75, s. 1 (1). The change may be seen by comparing it with RSO 1950, c. 74, s. 1 (1).
316 56 Vict. (1893), c. 45 (Ont.)
317 The federal act was 7–8 Edw. VII (1908), c. 40. The foregoing summary is based on *Ontario Royal Commission Inquiry into Civil Rights* Report 1 Vol. 2 pp. 547–8.
318 10 Edw. VII (1910), c. 96, s. 1 (Ont.)
319 6 Geo. V (1916), c. 54, ss. 2–3 (Ont.)
320 24 Geo. V (1934), c. 25, s. 3 (Ont.). The 1927 act was 17 Geo. V, c. 33 (Ont.), incorporated into RSO 1927 as c. 281.
321 1954, c. 41, ss. 1–2 (Ont.)
322 Ontario *Royal Commission Inquiry into Civil Rights* Report 1 Vol. 2 p. 551. Additional acts are listed there and on p. 552.

323 1959, c. 49, s. 4 (4) (Ont.); 1960, c. 53, s. 1 (Ont.); 1964, c. 51, s. 1 (Ont.); 1968, c. 103, s. 17 (Ont.)

324 Ontario *Royal Commission Inquiry into Civil Rights* Report I Vol. 2 p. 526

325 12 Vict. (1849), c. 81, s. 69 (P. of Can.)

326 RSO 1877, c. 72, ss. 1–2; RSO 1887, c. 72, ss. 2, 3, 8, 21

327 24 Geo. v (1934), c. 28, s. 2 (1) and (3) (Ont.)

328 For instance, the definition of 'justice' included police magistrate, but made no reference to magistrate. See Criminal Code, RSC 1927, c. 36, s. 2 (19).

329 RSO 1927, c. 119. Although the short title of the act was 'The Magistrates Act,' references in the act are to 'police magistrates.'

330 1 Edw. VIII (1936), c. 35, s. 3 (1) and (2) (Ont.)

331 RSO 1937, c. 133, s. 2 (2); RSO 1950, c. 219, s. 2 (2); 1952, c. 53 (Ont.)

332 1 Edw. VIII (1936), c. 35, ss. 4–7, 9, 12 (Ont.)

333 5 Geo. VI (1941), c. 28, s. 2 (Ont.)

334 1950, c. 41, s. 2 (Ont.); 1952, c. 53, s. 5 (Ont.)

335 RSO 1960, c. 226, s. 11

336 1960–1, c. 51, s. 1 (Ont.); 1960–1, c. 42, s. 3 (Ont.). See also *Legislative Assembly of Ontario Debates* 1961 pp. 977–8.

337 1964, c. 57, ss. 2–4 (Ont.)

338 1968, c. 103, s. 14 (Ont.)

339 Ontario *Royal Commission Inquiry into Civil Rights* Report I Vol. 2 pp. 527, 529–30, 543–4, 558–9, and 570

340 LOD 1968 1402 (29 Mar.)

341 Ibid. 3646; *Ontario Gazette* 1968, 2882

342 Provincial Courts Act, 1968, c. 103, ss. 2, 4, and 5 (Ont.)

343 Ibid. ss. 7 (1) and 8 (1)

344 1968, c. 103, s. 9 (2) (Ont.)

345 Ibid. ss. 9 (1), 14, and 17

346 Ibid. ss. 7 and 10

347 1977, c. 46, s. 1 (Ont.)

348 1979, c. 4, ss. 2, 93, and 118 (Ont.); 1979, c. 5, s. 4 (Ont.)

349 Provincial Courts Act, RSO 1980, c. 398, ss. 14, 18, 23

350 Ibid. s. 23 (1), but see also s. 23 (3).

351 14 Geo. v (1924), c. 21 (Ont.); 1956, c. 47 (Ont.)

352 For comments on salaries of county judges, see Kinnear 'County Judge in Ontario' 146–9.

353 Ontario Law Reform Commission *Report* I 45–102

354 For a brief explanation of the distinction between crimes and civil wrongs, see Glanville Williams *Learning the Law* 10th ed. (London 1978) 1–4.

355 Albert S. Abel *Towards a Constitutional Charter for Canada* (Toronto 1980) 5

356 OLRC *Report* I 16 and 185

357 Ibid. 14–15

358 Ibid. 185. For the composition of each of the eight districts now established under s. 15 of the County Judges Act, RSO 1980, c. 101, see *1981 Canadian Almanac and Directory* (Toronto 1981) 634.

Table of Cases

Index